CENTRAL AND CARIBBEAN AMERICA

W9-CEZ-730

MILES

0   500

Base Map Copyright A. K. Lobeck. By permission of Geographical Press
(C. S. Hammond Co.).

32

28

24

20

Bahama

(Br.)   Is.

DOMINICAN REP.

HAITI

CUBA

16

72

Jamaica
(Br.)

C A R I B B E A N   S E A

12

BR.
HONDURAS

HONDURAS

COLOMBIA

NICARAGUA

EL SALVADOR

PANAMA

UATEMALA

COSTA RICA

PACIFIC 90   O C E A N   84   8   78

THE GROWTH AND CULTURE OF *Latin America*

THE GROWTH AND CULTURE

OF LATIN AMERICA

DONALD E. WORCESTER and

WENDELL G. SCHAEFFER

ILLUSTRATED BY *Paul Sagsoorian*

NEW YORK · *Oxford University Press* · 1956

© Oxford University Press, Inc., 1956

Library of Congress Catalogue Card Number: 56-6556

Preface

TO cover the more than four-and-a-half centuries of Latin American history in a single, manageable volume is a difficult task, and no two historians will agree on what must be sacrificed in the interest of brevity. A synthesis of Latin American history is difficult also because of the unevenness of research and writing in the field, for on some phases or epochs of Latin American life information is far from adequate. This volume, nevertheless, represents an effort to present Latin American history in broad terms suitable for beginning students. By concentrating first on the fundamental forces rather than on detailed accounts of individual countries, the student is better prepared to understand Latin America at any period. For this reason we have aimed at broad coverage rather than at a chronological treatment of events in detail.

In many textbooks the colonial period suffers from overemphasis of the conquest and the late eighteenth century, to the neglect of the less spectacular interim period. Yet the seventeenth century was a time of emerging social, political, and economic institutions in the characteristic forms they were to maintain even into the twentieth century. It was also an era of gradual expansion, from the early footholds, into the lands of hostile tribes, led by missionaries as well as by soldiers. At the same time, the challenge of the Dutch, English, and French was being repulsed. The relatively small amount of research on the seventeenth century leaves much vital information lacking. However, we have attempted to give this period its proper place and share in the survey of Latin American history.

The winning of political independence from Spain and Portugal appears in many textbooks as a sharp break or abrupt change in Latin American life. Undue stress on independence suggests to the student that Latin America changed drastically in a few years. The new nations, however, retained the anachronistic institutions and attitudes of the colonial regime despite the high-sounding constitutions which served as ornate symbols of independent existence. Even the *alcabala* or sales tax, long considered a detriment to commerce, generally persisted for half a century.

The period since independence is the most difficult to present with any apparent unity. The conventional treatment of one country at a time, from 1810 to the present, makes it difficult for the student to perceive universal currents of the various epochs of the national period. By the time he has studied separately each country from Argentina to Venezuela, the possibility of his recognizing common trends or problems is greatly diminished. Yet despite time lags and differences of degree, there are many parallels among countries whose independent histories may appear at first glance to have little in common.

There is no perfect panacea for this problem, and any attempt at solution must be arbitrary. We have chosen to divide Latin American history into chronological periods based upon internal developments rather than on external forces. The chronological sections are introduced by essay chapters covering Latin America for the period in general terms. The latter are followed by chapters on various regions or groupings of countries on a basis of similarities in development for the period. As a result, the groupings of countries in the national era are not fixed, but change with emphasis on internal problems. This treatment brings to the student's attention the over-all and regional characteristics more emphatically than is possible by considering each country separately for the entire period. With the general pattern in mind, the student is prepared to take up the study of individual countries in proper perspective.

W. G. S.

D. E. W.

February 1956

Acknowledgments

THE AUTHORS wish to acknowledge their very considerable debt to numerous colleagues who have provided stimulating advice and many helpful suggestions during the several years this text was in preparation. In particular they owe thanks to Dr. James F. King and Dr. Lawrence Kinnaird of the University of California, Dr. Irving A. Leonard of the University of Michigan, Dr. Richard Morse of Columbia University, Dr. George Boehrer of Georgetown University, Dr. Lyle N. McAlister of the University of Florida, Dr. John P. Harrison of the National Archives, and the late Oscar Gil and Victor C. Barriere of El Salvador. They are deeply indebted to Mr. Allen K. Philbrick for his prompt and excellent preparation of the maps. Certainly not the least amount of thanks is due the Oxford University Press, whose personnel has been co-operative, understanding, and most patient. Errors of fact or interpretation are of course the sole responsibility of the authors.

Contents

VII.   *The Contest for Hegemony and the Rise*
       of Indigenous Nationalism

Maps

Glossary

Adelantado. Governor of frontier province, usually with both political and military authority. Similar to *capitão mór* of Brazil.

Afrancesado. 'Frenchified' Spaniard, one affecting French ways or ideas. Term of contempt.

Alcabala. Sales tax, usually 10 per cent.

Alcalde. Town mayor.

Alcalde mayor. Governor of a district, similar to corregidor and gobernador.

Aldea. Brazilian Indian village under missionaries.

Alguacil. Constable.

Arriero. Conductor of a mule train.

Asiento. Contract—best known as contract for introducing Negro slaves.

Audiencia. Highest court; also took on certain administrative functions.

Auto de fé. Ceremony in which sentences of Inquisition were announced.

Avería. Convoy tax.

Aviso. Dispatch ship.

Ayuntamiento. Municipal government.

Bandeirante. Paulista slave-raiding expedition.

Cabildo. Municipal council.

Cacique. Indian chief.

Capitania. Large grant of land to individual Portuguese in Brazil.

Capitão mór. Administrative and military official of captaincies and municipalities, Brazil.

Capitulación. Contract with the crown.

Casa grande. The 'big house' of the fazenda owner, Brazil.

Caudillo. Military chief.

Chacra. Farm, Upper Peru.

Cofradía, confraria (Port.). Confraternity—semi-religious brother-hood.

Colegio. Academy, seminary.

Común. The community, from which comunero, one of the group.

Consulado. Guild merchant and commercial tribunal.

Contador. Comptroller or accountant.

Corregidor. Royal official appointed to govern a province.

Cortes. Spanish and Portuguese parliamentary bodies.

Cruzada. Ecclesiastical tax on sale of indulgences. Originally to pro-vide funds for crusades.

Degredado. Exile (Portuguese).

Donatário. Receiver of grant of a captaincy, Brazil.

Ejido. Land reserved for communal use of Indian village, Mexico.

Encomienda. Grant of authority over Indians; carried obligation to Christianize and protect them as well as right to collect tribute.

Engenho. Sugar mill, Brazil.

Fazenda. Plantation, Brazil. Counterpart of hacienda, estancia, finca.

Feitoria. Trading post, Brazil.

Fiscal. Attorney.

Flota. Annual convoyed fleet of merchant vessels to and from Spain.

Gobernador. Governor of a district; similar to alcalde mayor and corregidor.

Gremio. Craft guild, Spanish America.

Guaca. Grave of Indian chieftain, New Granada.

Guano. Seabird deposits, offshore islands, Peru.

Hacienda. Plantation or large ranch, Mexico.

Inquilino. Chilean tenant farmer.

Intendente. Intendant, Spanish American official concerned with fi-nance, contraband trade, and military affairs, eighteenth cen-tury.

Justicia mayor. Presiding officer of the cabildo.

Latifundia. Great landed estate.

Ley fuga. 'Law of flight.' Pretext for shooting prisoners 'while attempt-ing to escape,' Mexico.

Mita. Inca practice of serving a 'turn' on public works. Adopted by Spaniards.

Mameluco. Portuguese mixed breed of São Paulo.

Mesada. Payment to crown of one month's salary by newly appointed officials.

Media anata. Payment of half a year's salary by newly appointed officials.

Mineiro. Resident of Minas Gerais, Brazil.

Obraje. Textile factory.

Oidor, ouvidor (Port.). Judge of audiencia in Spanish America.

Patrón. The 'boss.'

Patronato, padroado (Port.). Right of nominating men to fill ecclesiastical offices.

Paulista. Resident of São Paulo, Brazil.

Peninsular. Spaniard born in Spain.

Porteño. Resident of the port city of Buenos Aires.

Presidencia. Audiencia not in capital of viceroyalty or captaincy-general.

Procurador. Attorney.

Provedor mór. Treasurer, Brazil.

Pulpería. Country store.

Pulque. Fermented drink made of sap of maguey plant, Mexico.

Quilombo. Settlement of runaway slaves, Brazil.

Quinto. Royal fifth on products of mines.

Real hacienda. Royal treasury.

Recua. Mule train.

Regidor. Councilman, Spanish America.

Registro. Ship licensed to sail independently of flota.

Reino. Portuguese born in the kingdom.

Repartimiento. A 'division' of Indian laborers for a particular project.

Residencia. Trial of civil official at conclusion of term of office.

Roça. Small farm, Brazil.

Santa Hermandad. Holy Brotherhood; rural police force.

Senado da câmara. Town council, Brazil. Similar to cabildo.

Sertão. Back country, Brazil.

Tumulto. Riot.

Visita. Inspection.

Visitador. Inspector.

Yanacona. Landless laborer, Upper Peru.

I

GENESIS OF EMPIRE

The Sea Route to India

To the most serene prince our very dear friend, Fernando
and Isabel, King and Queen of Castile, Aragon, Leon, etc.,
greetings and increase of good fortune. We have learned with
joy of your esteem and high regard for us and our nation
and of your great eagerness to receive information concerning our successes. Wherefore we have resolved to dispatch our
noble captain, Christopherus Colon to you, with letters, from
which you may learn of our good health and prosperity . . .

I THE KING   I THE QUEEN
Letter to the Grand Khan *

THE aromatic spices and costly silks of the distant East were the attractions which led to the
accidental discovery of the New World by Christopher Columbus.
In retrospect it is easy to imagine that Columbus dreamed of finding unknown continents and creating new nations when in fact
he would have been gratified to reach a very ancient land —
Cipangu, or Japan. On his memorable first voyage he carried a
letter from Fernando to the Grand Khan, and on the delivery of
this royal epistle his hope of wealth and fame depended. When
suspicion arose that his worldly discoveries were far from the lands
once praised by Marco Polo, royal disappointment dimmed the
luster of his exploit. He was granted other opportunities to make
good his boast, but the half-naked aborigines who timidly stepped
forth from his ships onto Spanish soil little resembled the silken-

* Samuel Eliot Morison. *Admiral of the Ocean Sea.* Little, Brown and Company. Boston, 1942, 107.

3

robed emissaries of an oriental potentate. For all his great efforts and sacrifices, in so far as his real goal was concerned, Columbus was a failure.

The discovery of the New World, while in historical perspective a magnificent feat, disappointed the expectations of Columbus. In vain did he protest that he had actually reached the Orient. Though he was able to give the natives the enduring but improper designation of 'Indians,' the letter to the Grand Khan had to be returned to the sender. While these seemingly unrewarding events were occurring, Portuguese caravels moved relentlessly southward along the coast of Africa, nearer and nearer to the continent's end and the all-water route to the fabulous East.

Why was it that fortune-seeking adventurers opening new avenues of commerce sailed forth under the standards of Portugal and Castile? Many of them, like Columbus, applied for favor and support to various sovereigns of Western Europe. It was rarely in response to the urgings of far-sighted monarchs that they drove their fragile ships and superstitious crews to distant shores unlighted by the pale glow of Christianity. The initiative was largely theirs; they needed, however, the backing of powerful patrons, and this was to be found in the courts of Portugal and Spain. English and French kings only occasionally and reluctantly encouraged these adventurers, for they were generally more concerned with matters of dynasty or state, or aggressions against their immediate neighbors.

Spain and Portugal, although certainly not more prosperous than other kingdoms, were better prepared to embark upon costly undertakings beyond the limited horizons of Europe. The decline of feudalism had been attended by a remarkable increase in commerce and the use of coined money, a shift in the axis of social life from the manor to the town, a revival of Roman law with its stress on the role of princes as law-givers, and the establishment of hereditary monarchies and national states. The transition from numerous feudal principalities to powerful national monarchies had many parallels in Spain, Portugal, France, and England, but the final results were vastly different. Feudalism had been but lightly rooted in the Iberian peninsula, and feudal institutions were less obstructive to the rise of national states than in France and England. The Iberian kingdoms were, furthermore, little involved in European affairs and freer to turn their attention in other directions.

By the fifteenth century Portugal and Castile were emerging as modern nations, but with long histories of foreign invasion and occupation. Geographically the Iberian peninsula had served as a connecting link between Africa and Europe, and its cultural development had been shaped and molded by many currents of Asiatic or African origin which were scarcely felt in the lands north of the Pyrenees. The adage 'Africa begins at the Pyrenees' is not without merit.

While these high mountains tended to insulate the peninsula from European influences, other mountain ranges divided the land into a number of markedly differing regions. Regional differentiation has been so pronounced that at no time in the historical period has there been a single 'Spanish' or 'Portuguese' race or type. In Spain there has not even been uniformity of language. Modern Spain and Portugal are the products of numerous influences introduced by invaders, but vestiges of the distinctive characteristics of the early Iberians noted by ancient writers have not entirely disappeared. Among these are remarkable physical stamina, courage, and a high degree of loyalty.

Since the Iberian peninsula has been accessible both to Europeans and Africans despite the Pyrenees and the Strait of Gibraltar, it is not surprising that a large portion of its early history is involved with invasions and epochs of foreign domination. The populations of Spain and Portugal have been exceedingly mixed between the Iberians and Celts, who were present at the dawn of history, and intruders from Europe and Africa. Among the periods of foreign rule over the peninsula, those of the Romans and Moslems stand out. Rome's contributions lay in the field of legal institutions, governmental concepts, and language, whereas to the Islamic civilization the Iberian peoples are indebted for substantial artistic and scientific development.

To the Romans civilization meant city life, and Iberian cities were the centers of diffusion of Roman culture. Municipal organization in the Roman fashion was established. In the rural districts Roman customs were adopted more slowly, yet after six centuries of Roman rule Hispania became, outside of Italy, the most Romanized province in the empire. The Roman tendency of the rural populations to congregate in towns and villages was carried to the New World, and was one of the peculiarities of Spanish colonization in America.

One of the most important Roman innovations in Hispania was a measure of unification under a central authority. The powerful tendency toward purely local or tribal development was checked. Greater unity under the Romans was accomplished by the widespread use of the Latin language, the adherence to Roman law, the use of Roman coins, and the building of roads to foster commerce. The demands in Rome for precious metals and agricultural products prompted economic activity. At the same time the *latifundia*, or great landed estates of the Romans, were introduced. In the field of learning and the arts, particularly law and architecture, the influence of Rome was also great.

The gradual spread of Christianity in Hispania also began in the Roman period, and Christian communities appeared during the second century. Hispania provided her share of Christian martyrs until the fourth century, when Christians were given legal standing and protection from persecution. The church in Hispania developed along lines suggested by Roman law and administrative divisions, and the Bishop of Rome was its acknowledged head. The clergy was not confined to purely spiritual activities; at an early date it assumed secular responsibilities, and upon occasion priests served as public officials.

The Visigothic period, between the fall of Rome and the advent of the Moslems, was an era of slow decline and cultural stagnation. Roman ideals continued to prevail, and with the conversion of King Reccared and his court to Roman Catholicism in 587, the invaders adopted the religion of the conquered. Their language and even their identity were also disappearing by the time Islamic Arab tribes began pushing across North Africa. While the Gothic invasions of

the Roman Empire cast the remainder of Western Europe into
cultural decline and social chaos from which it did not recover for
many centuries, below the Pyrenees the dark period of Visigothic
domination was brief. Into the peninsula from the south, borne
on the crest of the Moslem invasion, poured the cultural tide of
Greece, Byzantium, and Egypt. Little resistance was offered the
Moslem raiders, who easily swept across most of what is today
Spain and Portugal.

Of the Moslem conquerors, the Arabs left the most indelible
imprint on the peninsular civilizations. The Arab tribes were bitterly disunited; internecine strife began even before the conquest
was complete, and it saved the rest of Western Europe from the
scimitar more surely than did the Frankish knights of Charles
Martel on the field of Tours.

In the mountainous north, Christian nobles initiated the struggle
to recover their lands, and for the next eight centuries the Moslem-
Christian frontiers were crossed and recrossed by innumerable forces
'going to live off their enemies.' Most frequently the conflicts
were for the immediate fruits of battle, and the combatants were
not rigidly aligned behind the Cross or the Crescent. Most of the
campaigns were on a small scale; not infrequently Christian and
Moslem were in the same camp. Eventually the reported discovery
of the remains and sepulcher of the Apostle James in Christian
Spain gave the struggle the nature of a crusade. The animosities
which kept the various Moslem groups disunited and contentious
were to have counterparts among the natives of the New World,
and the reconquest was in many ways an excellent training ground
for the future conquerors of the Aztecs and Incas.

Moslem influence in Hispanic civilization extended far beyond
the field of battle, and was the source of remarkable changes.
Very few of the cultural accomplishments which the Arabs introduced, however, can be correctly classed as Arabic; the major part
of them came through the transplantation of the more ancient
cultures of the eastern Mediterranean. Yet it was the Arabs by
their taste who determined the nature of the Arab-Hispanic civilization. Their appreciation rather than their skill was the decisive

factor, for few of the artisans or scholars who gave Córdoba and other centers their brilliance and renown were Arabs.

Much of the learning of ancient Greece was brought to the peninsula, and through Spain translations of Plato and Aristotle reached other parts of Europe. Arabic numerals and words, the use of the compass, oriental medical knowledge, light, ornate architecture, literature and art, the development of agriculture, the use of irrigation, and the introduction of many Asiatic or African plants are among the tangible material results of the Moslem occupation.

During the reconquest a number of tiny principalities appeared in the lands wrested from the Moslems. By the fifteenth century these had merged into the kingdoms of Portugal, Castile, Aragon, and Navarre, while the Moslems were confined to Granada in southern Spain. Portugal, because of her geographical position, secured the aid of Crusaders who stopped at her ports on their way to the Holy Land. Partly by means of their assistance she overthrew Moslem rule in the thirteenth century. By the beginning of the age of discovery Portugal, a kingdom of not more than one million inhabitants, less plagued than the Spanish dominions by conflicts between kings and nobles, had achieved greater unity than any other monarchy in Europe.

A by-product of the reconquest was the rise of frontier towns to a privileged position, since it was necessary for kings to grant townspeople unusual concessions in order to keep the frontiers secure. In the fourteenth century municipal administration was flourishing, and town councils exercised considerable authority without excessive interference by kings or nobles. Towns which had been granted special privileges or *fueros* in time of danger did not voluntarily surrender them when the threat had vanished. Many towns were walled and fortified and protected by their own troops. While this condition had been satisfactory when the Moslems were an ever present threat, with the gradual emergence of the national monarchy the virtual independence of many towns came to be regarded as injurious to royal interest.

The Crusades, the travels of the Polos and other Europeans who visited the East, the Italian city-state predominance in eastern Mediterranean trade, and the extension of commercial activity to the Atlantic are matters which are at least indirectly concerned with the age of discovery. The first three resulted in a European traffic in oriental commodities and an interest in the coast of Africa. The preponderance of the Italian city-states in the Mediterranean made it desirable for the merchants of the rising maritime communities of the rest of Europe to discover new routes and marts which they themselves could dominate. The first European country to make a serious effort to find other paths of trade with the East was Portugal.

Portugal had a long history of commercial activity, but the most famed promoter of her maritime expansion was Prince Henrique, known to history as 'Henry the Navigator.' In 1415 Henry and his brothers turned their attentions abroad in the hope of winning knightly honors against the Moslems of North Africa. In that year a Portuguese expedition captured the thriving commercial city of Ceuta, the port from which the Moslem invasions had been launched almost exactly seven centuries before. Prince Henry — impelled by a desire to trade for gold and to seek alliance with Prester John, a legendary Christian monarch somewhere in Africa or Asia, if he could be found — could now indulge his interest in voyages along the African Coast.

At the beginning of the voyages made under the sponsorship of Prince Henry, the coast of Africa was known only as far south as Cape Bojador. Owing to the difficulties of long voyages at that period, it was not until 1434 that Cape Bojador was passed. To facilitate the enterprises to which he devoted his life, Henry established an astronomical observatory and center for navigators at Sagres in southern Portugal. In 1441 another important economic motive for the voyages was found when one of his captains returned with a cargo of African tribesmen to be sold into slavery. Navigational instruments, such as the compass and astrolabe, a forerunner of the sextant, came into general use at this period. Long voyages had to be broken at 'scurvy ports' where the debilitated crews could be revived from time to time. The Portuguese made great progress in maritime skill during the lifetime of Prince Henry, and at the outset of the race for empire Portugal was favored by the number and skill of her navigators.

After the death of Prince Henry in 1460, maritime expeditions southward along the African coast were continued because of royal interest and for the profits to be gained in trade for gold and ivory, and in the enslavement of Africans. Prester John was forgotten as hopes began to mount for the discovery of a sea passage to India. It was not lack of wisdom on their part that induced the counselors of João II to recommend rejecting the proposals of Columbus for a westward voyage less than three decades after the death of Prince Henry. No better mariners were to be found than those of Portugal, and these seemed on the verge of finding the much-desired sea route to India. Subsequent events justified this decision. Receiving no encouragement in Portugal, Columbus reluctantly departed for Castile, where he tried to enlist the aid of Fernando and Isabel.

In 1485, when Columbus arrived in Spain, Castile was engaged in the conquest of Granada, the last Moslem-held territory on the peninsula. Although Fernando and Isabel listened attentively to his overtures, they were not prepared at the moment to undertake other projects than the one at hand. The conquest of Granada was an important part of their program for unifying Spain, and until it was completed they were content to let less pressing problems wait. Even if they had not belatedly sponsored the voyages of Columbus and acquired a remarkable empire, their accomplishments still would have been impressive, for during their reign the independent kingdoms of Spain except Portugal were joined under their rule. The project of unifying Spain did not, however, begin and end with Fernando and Isabel.

The marriage of Fernando of Aragon and Isabel of Castile in 1469 was of immense importance for Spain. It marked a significant step toward uniting Spain under a single monarch, although much remained to chance and to Fernando's astuteness. The royal union established the basis of a powerful Spanish monarchy and prepared the way for the extraordinary reigns of Carlos I and Felipe II in the century following.

In the endeavors to extend royal authority where little had existed before, one of the first tasks of the new monarchs was to establish law and order and to curb the turbulent nobles. To these ends they employed the *Santa Hermandad* or Holy Brotherhood, a police force of the towns which was then brought under royal control and improved, and which quickly and sternly enforced the king's peace. Banditry was suppressed, and recalcitrant nobles were constrained from warring. The nobles were induced to abandon their castles and become courtiers, making them dependent for political favor on the pleasure of the monarch. To support the Santa Hermandad a universal tax was levied for the first time, no class being exempt. The Holy Office of the Inquisition seems also to have served royal ends other than the extirpation of heresy. It was unfortunate, but perhaps not illogical, that Spanish kings felt that since they helped fight the battles of the church it was only reasonable to expect the assistance to be reciprocated.

By increasing the authority of the Royal Council Fernando and Isabel further enhanced their power; and by annexing to the crown the grandmasterships of the three most important military orders in Spain, Fernando acquired greater importance and prestige than any of his predecessors had enjoyed. Many lesser devices and institutions were employed for improving and strengthening royal administration, some of which were later transferred to the Spanish colonies. Among these were the *audiencia*, a high court, and the *residencia*, a practice of requiring officials to stand trial for their conduct in office at the conclusion of their administrations. An attempt to undermine the power of the cities was made by the appointment of *corregidores*, royal officials who were the crown's first representatives in the municipal councils, and who brought about the subordination of the councils to the royal government. But royal victory over the towns did not come until 1520, when the league of cities was defeated in battle by the forces of Carlos I.

While the war against Granada continued, Fernando and Isabel were not prepared to support the unique plan of Columbus and enter the race for a sea route to the legendary East. Already far behind Portugal in maritime activity, Castile had begun to acquire

overseas possessions earlier in the century with the conquest of
the Canary Islands. As Ceuta was for Portugal the first stop on
the road to India, the Canary Islands provided Spain with a similar
stepping-stone to the New World.

Even before Castile tardily entered upon the search for a sea
route to the Orient, Portugal's efforts seemed rewarded. In the
summer of 1487 Bartolomeu Dias sailed southward along the
African coast far beyond all previous discoveries. While Dias was
away on this voyage, Columbus returned to Portugal to try a
second time to enlist the king's aid. He was in Lisbon in December,
1488, when Dias triumphantly returned with the stirring news that
the cape had been doubled and the road to India lay open. Once
again Columbus departed to seek better fortune in Castile.

Early in 1492, shortly after the fall of Granada, Columbus de-
spaired of receiving support in Spain, and set out for France. A
recently found advocate of his plan convinced the queen that
royal interest demanded his recall, and she sent a messenger to
overtake him. European and domestic affairs were still urgent, but
little wealth was risked by backing Columbus. In April he signed
a contract with the crown, and on August 3 his famous adventure
began. A large part of the money to finance the project was borrowed from the treasury of the Santa Hermandad, while Columbus
and his friends supplied about a fourth of the cost.

On March 15, 1493, Columbus returned from the first of his
four voyages and announced that the islands he had discovered
were not far from Japan and the Asiatic mainland. His efforts to
begin a slave trade in the natives of the islands met with prompt
rebuke by Isabel, who demanded to know why he presumed to
enslave her subjects! Columbus' request for settlements in the
new lands was granted, and on his subsequent expeditions he
brought plants, animals, and colonists.

The news of Columbus' apparent success was received by Portugal with little satisfaction, for Spain's belated efforts seemed to be
defeating the purpose of a century of Portuguese endeavor. The
king hastily sent agents to Rome to seek papal support in determining the rights of the claimants in newly discovered, non-

Christian lands. Fernando and Isabel likewise were not slow to request papal sanction for their pretensions, and as a result of the petitions, Pope Alexander VI issued four bulls dividing the areas of future discoveries between the two nations and stating their legal right of conquest. Not satisfied with the result of this arbitration, which the king of Portugal suspected was more favorable to his competitors than to himself, he suggested a modification of the line by direct negotiation. Fernando and Isabel, whose maritime forces were no match for those of their rival, discreetly agreed. Their reasonable attitude led to the signing of the Treaty of Tordesillas on June 6, 1494; the Line of Demarcation was moved from 100 to 370 leagues west of the Cape Verde Islands for lands yet to be discovered, and 200 leagues for those already known. The treaty neglected to specify which of the various islands was to serve as the base, thus leaving the way open for future discord. West of the line all discoveries were to belong to Castile; east of it any newly found lands should fall to Portugal. This division was to prevail regardless of the nationality of the discovering expedition. Under the new arrangement a part of Brazil, then still unknown to both Spain and Portugal, lay in the sphere consigned to the latter. A foothold in the New World was gained at the expense of valuable islands in the Far East.

It was expedient for Spain and Portugal to accept the Pope's statement of the legality of their claims to the new lands. Spanish jurists and theologians of the age, however, did not consider the matter satisfactorily settled. In the thoughts of many Spaniards the papal grant was by itself insufficient to justify the subjugation of the New World natives. But the conquerors rolled inexorably onward, little hindered by the doubts and indecision of lawyers and priests at home. Early in the sixteenth century François I also expressed some doubt as to the legality of the papal bulls, demanding to see 'the clause in father Adam's will' which excluded France.

On his second voyage Columbus, after establishing the settlement of Isabela on the island of Española, set out to explore Cuba, which he believed to be a peninsula of Asia. Isabela soon became the first American 'ghost town,' and Cuba was found to be an island. But even to the time of his death Columbus refused to admit that the lands he had discovered were not a part of the Orient. His convictions were not widely accepted, and soon other navigators in the Spanish service were continuing the search he had begun for a route to Asia.

Neither Columbus nor any of his contemporaries foresaw or could have anticipated what his discoveries might mean for Spain in the future, despite his failure to bring within reach the riches of the Orient. In his lifetime only dim outlines of the New World were known; the silver mines of Zacatecas and Potosí awaited other adventurers not less imaginative and daring than he. Within half a century after his death European cartographers placed on their maps of the Western Hemisphere continents not the name of Christopher Columbus but that of Amerigo Vespucci, because of his account of voyages to South America. The name 'America' was given at first to a part of the southern continent, but gradually was applied to the whole of both continents.

Portugal, at the time of Columbus' third voyage, reached her long sought goal. After the discovery of the Cape of Good Hope, João II ordered the construction of new vessels to complete the unfinished project. Not until 1497, however, was the fleet finally ready to sail; neither the monarch nor the admiral who began work on it lived to see its conclusion. It was to Vasco da Gama that the honor fell of accomplishing the dream of countless navigators. Rounding the Cape of Good Hope, he sailed along the eastern coast of Africa and ultimately reached Calicut, where the already established Tunisian Arabs, who saw their trade threatened, greeted him with hostility. The prolonged voyage and the inroads of scurvy reduced his crew by half before he arrived back in Portugal, in September of 1499, but the cargoes of his ships sold for a fabulous sum. Nearly a century of Portuguese endeavor was at last adequately rewarded, and João's rejection of the proposals of Columbus vindicated.

Excited by the success of Vasco da Gama, Spanish explorers made the quest for a transit through or around the American continental barrier a primary motive for their voyages. This was

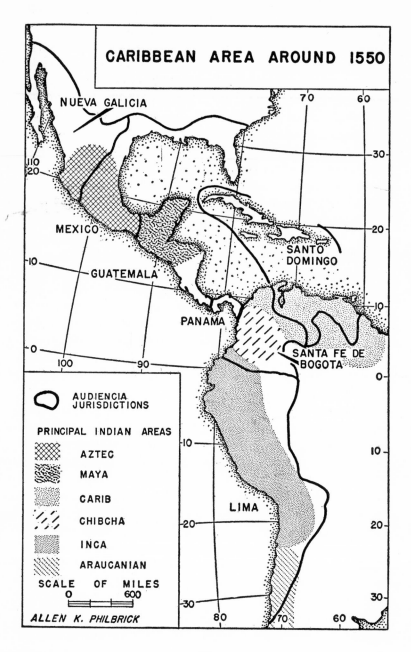

CARIBBEAN AREA AROUND 1550

NUEVA GALICIA

MEXICO

GUATEMALA

PANAMA

SANTO DOMINGO

SANTA FE DE BOGOTA

AUDIENCIA JURISDICTIONS

PRINCIPAL INDIAN AREAS

AZTEC

MAYA

CARIB

CHIBCHA

INCA

ARAUCANIAN

SCALE OF MILES
0   600

ALLEN K. PHILBRICK

LIMA

especially true of the expeditions sent out before 1521, but interest in the mythical Strait of Anián and the Northwest Passage endured for centuries. More and more ships were sent probing into the bays and rivers of the lands bordering the Caribbean Sea. In 1499 Ojeda examined the Pearl Coast beyond the discoveries of Columbus, and in the next year Bastidas continued the exploration to Panamá. In 1506 the peninsula of Yucatán was skirted. By these and other voyages the Gulf Coast was soon known. The Atlantic coast north of Florida and the coast of South America beyond the mouth of the Orinoco River were visited and examined; still no passage was found. All efforts to find a strait through the vast, mysterious continents were unsuccessful. As a consequence of these failures Vasco da Gama died a hero of Portugal, while Christopher Columbus spent his last days in near-oblivion.

The fruitless search for a strait led to an ever-widening knowledge of the continental coastlines. In 1509 Ocampo proved conclusively that Cuba was an island, while other Spanish mariners sailed farther afield. After Cabral's brief sojourn on the Brazilian coast in 1500, Spanish ships were sent farther south to see what lay beyond the Portuguese discoveries. In 1513 Balboa crossed the Isthmus of Panamá and reported the South Sea. On the alert for a passage through the continent, Solís found the Plata estuary promising, although a lengthy examination disappointed his expectations, and a skirmish with the Indians cost him his life.

Still on the search for a sea route to the Indies, Fernão de Magalhães or Ferdinand Magellan, a Portuguese navigator in the Spanish service, ventured beyond the coasts explored by Solís. In 1519 he left Spain with five ships; by November of the next year he had passed the strait which today bears his name, and entered the Pacific. In 1521 he was killed by natives in the Philippines. Only one of his vessels survived the entire voyage to complete the first circumnavigation of the world, one of the most remarkable achievements in the age of discovery. The cargo of spices carried to Spain in the *Victoria*, the ship which Sebastián del Cano brought home, more than paid for the cost of the entire enterprise. But news of Magellan's feat, and that of Cano, was overshadowed by other intelligence even more inspiring to Spanish imagination. Before the *Victoria* dropped anchor in a Spanish port in September, 1522, news of the conquest of Mexico by Hernán Cortés had already reached Spain. Consequently, even though Spain had finally found the much-desired western route to the Orient, oriental trade was handicapped by lack of a convenient return route, and half a century was to pass before the founding of Manila.

In the same year that Magellan was killed in the Philippines, having succeeded at last in completing Columbus' project, Spanish interest was forcibly diverted to the unexpected treasures of the New World. No longer did the Western continent appear a barrier and a land of puny aborigines and meager wealth; the Aztecs were energetic, skillful people whose conquest promised riches far beyond the prospects of the primitive Arawaks or the man-eating Caribs of the Antilles. In the hectic period that followed, Spanish explorers pursued fable and myth from Patagonia to the plains of Kansas in search of Amazon ladies in golden girdles, the Seven Cities, El Dorado, and 'otro México.' These turbulent expeditions made known to Spain all the regions that were worth acquiring. The continents which had frustrated the hopes of Columbus now revealed their treasures of peoples and minerals, and after the conquest of Mexico Spanish energies were absorbed in building an American empire, to the neglect of the land of silk and nutmeg.

II

The Indians of the Conquest

In America, man appears under the rudest form in which we can conceive him to subsist. We behold communities just beginning to unite, and may examine the sentiments and actions of human beings in the infancy of social life . . . The greater part of its inhabitants were strangers to industry and labour, ignorant of arts, imperfectly acquainted with the nature of property . . . There were only two nations in this vast continent which had emerged from this rude state . . .

WILLIAM ROBERTSON *

BY FAR the richest prize won by the conquerors of the New World was human beings. There were too few Spaniards or Portuguese to perform the tasks necessary to create flourishing colonies even if their attitude toward manual labor had been more appropriate to such an undertaking. It was the American Indian who supplied the bone and sinew that went into the building of Iberian empires in the Americas. Wherever mountains were opened by mines, the ore was laboriously carried to the surface in baskets on the backs of Indians; plantations flourished by their patient toil; a thousand tasks they performed which otherwise would have been left undone. It did not matter if the earth of any region was the most fertile in the world or that mountains harbored tons of silver and gold. Where there were no docile Indians accustomed to climate, altitude, and hard physical labor, the riches of the earth remained uncaptured. Negro slaves,

* The History of America, 3 vols., London, 1840 (16 ed.).

it is true, modified this situation in certain of the tropical lowlands. Their proportion of the total number of laborers in the sixteenth century, however, was small.

The regions populated by highly civilized Indians were quickly seized and zealously held by the Spaniards. The sedentary tribes were skilled in agriculture and crafts such as weaving; some of them mined gold and silver, which they fashioned into ornaments. The native abilities were soon put to the service of the conquerors. Native and European crops were grown for export, and Indian weavers were herded together into *obrajes* or textile workshops, where they wove cotton and woolen cloth for their new masters.

The Spanish advance did not stop with the conquest of the Aztecs and Incas, but pushed gradually beyond their lands into the hunting grounds of wild, unconquerable nomads. There was a vast difference in cultural levels between the Incas, Aztecs, and Mayas on the one hand, and the multitude of barbarous, warlike tribes such as the Puelche, Tehuelche, and Araucanians of southern South America, and the so-called Chichimecos and Apaches of northern New Spain. Although Spaniards entered the lands of the nomads and managed to establish various frontier settlements, the subjugation of many of the less sedentary groups was not achieved during the colonial period, but had to await the day of the six-shooter and repeating rifle. Tenuous military advantage was occasionally achieved by alliances with frontier tribes against their traditional enemies, as was true in Brazil, but the absence of a stable labor force and the continuous distractions of Indian warfare were constant obstacles to the security and prosperity of isolated settlements in the primitive wilderness. Most of the lands inhabited only by warlike nomads remained untouched by the conquest, and the inhabitants continued to live as always, disturbed only occasionally by Spanish war parties or particularly zealous missionaries.

The New World of the Spanish and Portuguese conquerors was not a region quickly seen nor easily described. Perhaps its most striking characteristic was diversity — diversity of land, vegetation, resources, altitude, temperature, rainfall, and humidity. Much of the land lay within the moist tropics; the bulk of South America lay north of the Tropic of Capricorn. Even along the Equator, however, climate was not uniform, altitude rather than latitude being the determining factor. Cooling trade winds and seasonal rainfall, furthermore, greatly ameliorated living conditions in many of the tropical regions. Vegetation, too, was immensely varied; some areas were covered by dense rainforests, while others barely supported cactus and mesquite. Extremely fertile lands supporting large populations contrasted sharply with territory suitable only for hunting grounds.

One of the most noteworthy features of both North and South America was the series of great mountain chains. The Andean cordillera, one of the most remarkable mountain systems in the world, stretched from the Strait of Magellan in the south to the Caribbean Sea on the north. Fairly narrow but exceedingly high, the Andes proved a serious obstacle to east-west communications in South America for many centuries. In Central America and Mexico as well, high mountains were the predominant features of the landscape. Along the great chains volcanoes added their fertile ashes to the fruitfulness of the soil. In these mountainous areas of both North and South America lay a vast storehouse of precious metals, a fact of which the preconquest Indians were scarcely aware, although they had engaged in limited exploitation of precious ores.

Hardly less remarkable than the mountains were the majestic rivers of the New World. The Magdalena, Orinoco, Amazon, La Plata, and Mississippi systems all rose in the centers of large continental regions and discharged their enormous streams into the Atlantic. The Amazon, although one of the most extensive river systems in the world, traversed a tropical valley which, despite its potentialities, has never supported a large population. The Magdalena and La Plata, being more favorably located, were utilized to greater human advantage.

The peoples occupying the New World before the arrival of the Europeans had tested the fertility and productiveness of both continents for many centuries, and where they had established large populations the intruders founded their most successful early colonies. It should be emphasized that it was not climate which marked out the lines of early Spanish and Portuguese settlement but the availability of native labor and foodstuffs. The existing Indian civilizations formed the foundation upon which the great structure of Latin American colonial civilization was erected.

The American Indian tribes were as different from one another in language, physique, and cultural accomplishments as were the great continental regions in climate and resources. From archaeological and ethnological evidence it appears most likely that the so-called Indians of the Western Hemisphere came from northeast Asia, crossing to the North American continent in the vicinity of the Bering Strait in successive waves of migration possibly centuries apart. Their gradual advance southward to the most remote lands of South America was a process which must have taken thousands of years, since it was necessary for the Indians to adapt themselves to life in one area before proceeding to another. The exact time of their coming has not been established, yet there are a number of factors which may be considered as indicative. The ancestors of the American Indians apparently brought domesticated dogs, a knowledge of coiled pottery, and the bow-drill for making fire, but not the wheel. It is likely that a rudimentary knowledge of weaving may have been brought, for a number of tribes developed it to a high degree of excellence. Various indications of migrations from Polynesia and Australia also have been noted, but this field of investigation is still too embryonic for certain knowledge.

With a few outstanding exceptions the native peoples were totally lacking in political systems beyond simple tribal organization. Disunity among the American Indians was accentuated by ancient enmities and internecine strife. The struggle for land, and especially for hunting grounds, prevailed in America long before Europeans arrived on the scene, and certain tribes made a practice of enslaving the young captives taken in war. The Spanish and Portuguese added little that was new in the American struggle for land. They simply turned inter-tribal animosities to their own advantage, as when Cortés conquered the Aztecs with the invaluable aid of the Tlaxcalans and other allies, and when the Portuguese relied upon the military aid of various tribes. Owing to the bitterness of inter-tribal strife it was usually possible for Europeans to win allies among the Indians for almost any conflict. A large share of the burden of inter-colonial warfare and of the later wars of independence was borne by Indians on both sides.

The basic crops raised by American Indians were corn, beans, and squash. Planting practices, however, differed considerably between the two continents. The planters of North America relied almost exclusively upon seed crops, while the natives of South America showed a marked predilection for root crops such as manioc, a starchy tuber and the modern source of tapioca, yams, and many varieties of potatoes. The growing of tobacco was widespread; coca, from which cocaine is derived, was limited to the Andean area and northern South America. A multitude of other plants and agricultural products were known to the Indians, cotton, cacao, the pineapple, the avocado, vanilla, the peanut, the tomato, and the green pepper being among the more important ones.

The role of domesticated animals among the Indians was insignificant. For the Andean peoples, however, the llama and alpaca, camel ruminants, were important for burden, meat, and wool, and in the same region the guinea pig was grown. The dog was universal, and in some tribes was raised for food, especially in the tropics. Among the plains Indians of North America it also served as a beast of burden. It was primarily in the regions where dogs were used as pack animals that the Spanish horse was to become most thoroughly exploited by the natives. Most of the Indians, however, were totally without beasts of burden of any sort before the Spaniards and Portuguese introduced horses, mules, and cattle. In the sixteenth and early seventeenth centuries strays from ranch herds roamed into the trackless wilderness, and their progeny soon numbered hundreds of thousands. The food supply of the nomadic hunting tribes was greatly increased by the wild herds.

The fertile and temperate Valley of Mexico was the birthplace of a number of ancient Indian civilizations, among which the Nahua-speaking groups were outstanding. The most important of the early peoples were the Toltecs, whose cultural traits were greatly influenced by the Mayas, and who in turn exerted a similar influence on the last of the Nahua tribes to become prominent, the Aztecs. Highly developed calendrical systems, huge pyramids and temples, and human sacrifice were common to all three civilizations.

The Aztecs, a poor, wandering people, migrated southward into Anáhuac, later known as the Valley of Mexico, where they arrived about two centuries before Cortés. Their genius lay in warfare, and after forming a military confederacy with two of their more prosperous neighbors, they began extending their authority over the other tribes of the valley and forcing them to pay tribute to their chieftains at Tenochtitlán, the Aztec capital. Soon the Aztecs dominated even their former allies. Their control extended north to the lands of the bellicose tribes known as 'Chichimecos,' and south to the Isthmus of Tehuantepec. They made no effort to assimilate and incorporate the vanquished, and their tenuous control was maintained solely by the club.

The Aztec ruling and priestly classes enjoyed great luxury and prestige, and the mass of people were docile and obedient to their accustomed officials. Once their native rulers had been replaced by Spaniards, it was relatively easy to maintain order among them. This docility and obedience made possible the rule of relatively few Spaniards over a vast population.

Aztec artisans were highly skilled in the making of pottery, in weaving, stone-cutting, and in the use of gold and silver in ornamentation. The fact that the Aztecs were accustomed to paying tribute to their officials gave the Spaniards a profitable source of saleable articles almost as soon as the battle for Tenochtitlán or Mexico City was over. Commerce was an important part of the Aztec economy, and the merchant class ranked after the military in the social order.

The Mayas of Yucatán, Chiapas, and Guatemala were a people whose civilization had reached its zenith hundreds of years before the conquest, and whose origins extended back into the obscurity of antiquity, possibly being as old as the cultures of Egypt and Mesopotamia. Maya civilization was the most extraordinary in the New World, yet centuries before the first Spaniards set foot on American soil it had already passed into obsolescence and decay. Little is known of the life of this ancient people, but that which is known justifies ranking them far above the New World contemporaries of Atahualpa and Montezuma. They are most noted for their art, architecture, hieroglyphic writing, and for their mathematical and astronomical achievements made possible by the invention of a symbol for zero. They alone of the New World peoples had developed a fairly advanced written language. Their calendar, which was created to assist in the punctual observance of religious ceremonies concerned with the fertility of crops, was one of the most unique features of their civilization. Owing to the destruction of most of the Maya chronicles and to the fact that the existing hieroglyph have not been deciphered, little is known of their ancient history.

The archaeological remains of Maya cities are numerous and extensive, and they indicate the existence of huge populations as well as unexplained changes in location. Like the other highly civilized peoples of the New World, the Mayas had hereditary ruling classes and powerful priestly groups. At the time of the conquest the whole Maya civilization was in a state of decline which greatly facilitated its subjugation by the Spaniards.

Also among the most advanced peoples of the New World were the Quechua-speaking Indians of the central Andes, known as 'Incas' after the title of their ruling class. While many of the handicrafts by which civilizations are often measured were learned by the Incas from the peoples they conquered, the greatest development of their own civilization was in military, political, and social organization. The imperial system of the Incas was one of the most effective ever known. Recently conquered tribes were divided into small groups and dispersed among more trustworthy peoples until they became thoroughly 'Incaized.' Recalcitrants were sent to labor on the coca plantations of the eastern slopes of the Andes. A system of roads, bridges, and messenger service enabled the rulers in Cuzco to maintain rapid communications with the remote provinces. Traditionally it was the duty of each ruler to increase the territory of the empire. Pizarro arrived on the scene at a critical time, for he found the Inca rulers divided in one of their occasional conflicts for power.

Inca society was rigidly disciplined under a hierarchy of hereditary officials. Individuals paid tribute to the state in products of the soil, in products of their various skills, or by labor on public roads and buildings. Many features of the Inca social and political systems were found suitable for modification and adoption by the Spaniards, and the society of colonial Peru emerged as a blending of Spanish and native custom as well as race. The Spaniards employed Inca governmental institutions and the custom of assigning workers to public and private projects. This last, the *mita*, which to the Incas meant a 'turn' on public works, came to be an instrument of oppression and involuntary servitude.

The social organization of the Incas was the most interesting accomplishment of this remarkable people. Society was divided into three groups, the hereditary ruling class, the priestly hierarchy, and the rest of the people. All of the land was divided among these three estates; the third group, however, performed all of the labor. The products of the soil as well as the wool of llamas and alpacas went into government storehouses and were apportioned according to need. Certain plants or products were reserved solely for the ruling family or for the priests of the sun. Families were annually assigned plots of land sufficient to support the number of members. There was a vast difference in the living standards of the bulk of the people and those of the ruling and priestly classes, but among the mass of people there was neither affluence nor extreme poverty.

The center of the Inca empire was the city of Cuzco, 'the navel.' From this capital a series of ambitious rulers extended Inca control northward through the central Andes, northwest along the coast of Peru, southward into Chile, and east into modern Bolivia and northwestern Argentina. Huayna Capac, who came to power about 1493, pushed the Inca frontier north of Quito, and established posts near the modern boundary between Ecuador and Colombia. His sudden death in Quito left control of his veteran army in the hands of an illegitimate son, Atahualpa, who attempted to take precedence over his half-brother. The revolt of Atahualpa against Huáscar, the legitimate heir, was not the first insurrection in Inca history, but the fact that the usurper controlled a powerful army made his uprising unique. He was able to defeat Huáscar. For nearly a year after the death of Huayna Capac the Inca state was torn by strife between the contenders for the succession. At first Atahualpa apparently sought only to establish separate rule in Quito, but his early success led to more grandiose plans. Had Pizarro arrived a few years later instead of in the crucial year 1532, he might have found Atahualpa securely in power and Huáscar forgotten. The conquest would have been much more difficult without the two factions to pit against one another. As it was, just at the moment Atahualpa learned of his army's triumph at Cuzco, Pizarro and his tiny force were struggling through the rarefied air of the high passes over the Andes on their way to Cajamarca.

The Chibcha civilization of modern Colombia was less remarkable than those of the Incas, Aztecs, and Mayas, and Chibcha customs did not carry over so strongly into colonial society. There is little archaeological evidence of great antiquity for Chibcha culture, yet its advance was sufficient to merit mention. At the time of the conquest the Chibchas were in the process of organizing their territory under a single ruler. There were two principal chiefs, but each local *cacique* still retained considerable authority over his village. There was no immediate and uniform attempt to resist the Spaniards, and the conquest of the Chibchas was relatively easy.

The Chibchas made use of gold for ornamentation, and practised intensive agriculture. A custom of these Indians as well as neighboring tribes was to place golden ornaments in the graves or *guacas* of their chieftains, and it led to an early interest in their territory on the part of the Spaniards, and to an important 'extractive' industry. Grave-robbing expeditions found thousands of dollars worth of gold. Heredia's search of the Sinú region probably brought him more immediate wealth than either Cortés or Pizarro acquired in their more noteworthy exploits.

In addition to the more advanced civilizations just described there were other sedentary peoples who planted crops and who had developed modest skills in such crafts as weaving and pottery-making. The Pueblo tribes of New Mexico are the best examples of this intermediate group. All of the sedentary peoples were less warlike and more inclined toward obedience than the nomads, and they alone of the New World natives promised to make useful subjects for European conquerors.

It would be useless to catalogue all the wild Indian tribes, as their influence on colonial development was usually transitory. A few, however, are worth mentioning. The so-called Araucanians of Southern Chile and Argentina remained an important force for more than three centuries. The northern division of this tribe had been conquered by the Incas and much influenced by them. The southern portion so bitterly resisted all encroachments into its territory that it became a symbol of patriotic independence to Chileans. Soon after the conquest the Araucanians acquired horses and, like the Apaches of New Mexico and the Puelche and Tehuelche of the Plata region, became devastating foes in mounted combat. The Araucanians and their neighbors prevented the southward expansion of Spanish rule from Chile and Río de la Plata. The Apaches and Comanches placed similar limitations on Spanish colonization north of the Río Grande.

The Indians of Brazil compared unfavorably with those of the more important Spanish colonies. Their relatively low state of cultural development was one reason for their gradual disappearance along the coast, although racial mixture also played a part. The Brazilian Indians were physically unequal to the demands of plantation labor, and work on the sugar *fazendas* in the sixteenth century killed off large numbers of them. Their crops, and manioc in particular, their labor, and their military assistance, however, were primarily responsible for the success of the few Portuguese settlements which managed to survive.

The effect of European domination upon the sedentary or insular tribes, despite the paternalistic policies of Spanish monarchs, was generally unfortunate. In most instances once their accustomed masters had been replaced, the Indians readily submitted. The

earliest Spanish and Portuguese plantations were begun by employing Indian labor obtained by barter or force, and the food
provided by the natives sustained the conquerors for many years.
The Indians of the Caribbean islands were not prepared by diet or
custom to engage in the hard physical labor of plantation and mine.
They were unaccustomed to many common European diseases.
When they were congregated into villages for the purpose of
making their labor available where needed, malnutrition and sick-
ness were extraordinarily devastating. In little more than a quarter
of a century after the discovery, most of the native population of
the West Indies had literally disappeared. The sedentary peoples
of the continental areas were more inured to labor and less directly
exposed to brutal exploitation, and they survived in large numbers.

Wherever warlike nomadic tribes were found the problems of
the European colonists were similarly difficult. Far from being
able to employ these Indians for useful purposes, their mere existence was an obstacle and threat to colonial development unless
effective alliances could be made. Successful settlements in such
areas depended upon the removal or extermination of hostile tribes.
In the Plata region, in southern Chile, in New Mexico, and in the
English colonies of North America warfare against wild Indians
was chronic throughout the colonial period and in some instances
long after. The absence of many survivors of the warlike tribes
today is concrete evidence of the long-standing policy which was
pursued in all of the European colonies. Although it is impossible
to speak in other than general terms regarding Spanish treatment
of the Indians, which treatment usually suited the situation, a
generalization may be made for all of the European colonies.
Wherever the Indians were an asset to the settlements the Indians
survived; wherever they were an obstacle or of little aid they
disappeared.

Spanish and Portuguese Indian policies revolved around two
poles: on the one hand was the meritorious desire to see the Indians
raised to a position of equality with other subjects, while on the
other was the need for an abundant and cheap labor supply. The
Indians found themselves torn between the opposing currents,

but powerless to direct their own destiny. Between the proponents of the 'dirty dog' and the 'noble savage' schools of thought in the sixteenth century there were numerous compromises. The kings insisted that the Indians were free persons and royal subjects; the Spanish and Portuguese landowners maintained that they were beasts of the field and should labor gratuitously like other animals. In the final analysis it was the will of the colonists which prevailed, for although numerous edicts were issued by the monarchs for the protection of the Indians, few were effective, and most were repealed if the economic condition of the colonies was felt to be jeopardized. Thus the Spanish orders of 1503 legalized forced Indian labor, but with reservations aimed at preventing uncontrolled exploitation. The work was to be moderate and for reasonable wages, and the Indians were to be assembled in villages for their better protection. They were to be treated with consideration and their spiritual education promoted. Nevertheless secret instructions to the governor recommended locating the villages reasonably close to the mines.

Royal policy toward the Indians and the actual manner in which the colonists dealt with them were always different and distinct matters. Already mentioned was Isabel's rebuke of Columbus for enslaving the natives of Española. Her wish, although often supported by the clergy, that the Indians should become Spanish subjects of equal standing with the colonists was stoutly resisted by the conquerors and their descendants. The question of the status of the Indians was argued in theological terms — whether Indians were rational human beings and possessed souls or whether they were beasts of the field and lacked such metaphysical manifestations. As far as basic policy was concerned the opinions of the clergy prevailed; in order to save the Indians from the labor which was hastening their extinction certain priests urged the introduction of Negro slaves from Africa. In the Caribbean area and a few other tropical lands under Spanish control, Negro slavery gradually replaced that of the Indians. In Brazil also, the same change took place, especially after the potential supply of Indian labor had declined drastically. In the Andean region, in Paraguay, and in the

Valley of Mexico, however, Indian laborers continued to be the most numerous.

Although Indian labor ordinarily was involuntary, outright slavery was not widely prevalent after the middle of the century. Probably no colonizing nation has ever devised a more humane theoretical system of controlling subject peoples and preparing them for a position of equality with their masters than did Spain in the early years of the conquest. It was the great misfortune of the Indians that the altruistic policies of Spanish and Portuguese monarchs met with neither the social desires nor economic interests of the colonists.

In Brazil the efforts of the Jesuits to improve the condition of the Indians were vigorously resisted by the half-breed slave-raiders, the *paulistas* or *mamelucos* of São Paulo, and the priests had to be content with the recommendation that Negroes be introduced. The indifference of the Portuguese to considerations of race and color alleviated the situation of the Indians somewhat, and wholesale intermingling of blood occurred. The result was the gradual disappearance of pure Indians in coastal Brazil and the emergence of a mixed race part of which later combined with the Negro.

The Spanish method of protecting the Indians was the *encomienda* system, under which groups of Indians were entrusted or 'commended' to the care of individual Spaniards who were expected to observe the royal wishes. But distance from authority encouraged license, and in actual practice the encomienda often became a means of virtually enslaving the Indians. Spanish encomenderos believed that the success of the colonies depended upon their forcing the Indians to work. Even if the conquerors themselves had possessed a greater esteem for humble toil their numbers were insufficient to meet the demand for cheap, unskilled labor. They had no desire, furthermore, to see the Indians become their equals in any way. Their prejudices triumphed, and the Indians were kept in a state of subservience, royal edicts prohibiting Indian slavery, abolishing the encomiendas, or forbidding the use of Indians as personal servants notwithstanding.

Obviously such a contradictory system depended entirely, from the Indians' standpoint, upon the character of the individuals chosen to administer it. The need of revenue from the royal mines was pressing, and as a result the king was reluctant to take action which would seriously hinder mining. The encomienda system seemed an appropriate solution to the problem of treating the Indians with consideration and providing the colonists with the necessary labor force. In 1509 Fernando legalized the practice of permitting the governor of a newly conquered region to divide the natives into encomiendas among his followers. An encomienda did not, as often assumed, include a grant of land, although both were frequently given to the same person.

Other methods of allocating Indian labor to individual Spaniards were employed, some of which were borrowed from the natives themselves, for example the mita in Peru. The *repartimiento de indios* was a system of allocating Indian laborers without the corresponding obligations of encomenderos to see to their physical and spiritual well-being. Methods might vary, but for the Indians the end result was usually the same — involuntary servitude. The Portuguese, less secure in the possession of their territory in Brazil, were not in a position to force many Indians to labor until late in the sixteenth century, but rather had to depend upon barter.

The Laws of Burgos, promulgated by the king of Spain in 1512, established basic principles for regulating intercourse between Spaniards and Indians which were never completely effective. They established detailed rules for the treatment of the Indians, and decreed that those capable of governing themselves and eager to become Christians should be set free. A third of all the Indians were to be kept at work in the mines, however, and all Indians were obliged to devote nine months of each year to serving the Spaniards.

One of the priests who was foremost in shaping royal policies concerning the Indians in the sixteenth century was Father Bartolomé de Las Casas, the 'Apostle of the Indians.' His vigorous denunciations of Spanish mistreatment of the natives led to the issuance by Carlos I of various decrees intended to check the evils. In order to impress the king with the unhappy fate of the Indians Las Casas wrote a number of books and pamphlets, the most famous of which was his *Brevíssima relación de la destrucción de las indias*, the *Very brief relation of the destruction of the Indies*. One of the most curious results of his efforts was that his writings became extraordinarily popular among the enemies of Spain, for those who missed out in the acquisition of valuable colonies could find some measure of consolation in self-righteous horror at the successes of the more fortunate.

The unceasing efforts of Las Casas and other priests convinced Carlos I that the encomienda system was the chief evil, and he decided upon its abolition soon after the conquest of Mexico. By this time the question was an academic one for the islands, as the native population there was near the vanishing point. It had more serious consequences for New Spain, as Cortés had been persuaded by the importunings of his followers to grant a number of encomiendas immediately after the fall of Tenochtitlán. Cortés followed a prudent policy on this occasion, and one which was to serve well many later viceroys; he withheld announcement of the order revoking grants already made, and petitioned the king so earnestly that the decree was withdrawn as detrimental to the colony's welfare.

In the beginning encomiendas were granted for one life only, but need for stability and the clamor of the encomenderos induced the king to make them hereditary in 1535. Even before this time, however, certain encomiendas already had passed from father to son in Española. Again torn between the needs of the colonists and the desire to prevent the destruction of the Indians, Carlos issued secret instructions to the audiencia to bring about the gradual abolition of the encomienda system. The result of this vacillating policy was unfortunate for both colonists and Indians, for the uncertainty discouraged enterprise on the one hand and made solicitude for the Indians unprofitable on the other. If an encomendero was threatened with the loss of his laborers at an undetermined date, his desire to preserve them for future use might easily yield to his anxiety to increase his wealth before the unwelcome day arrived. Once again it was necessary for the crown to reverse its policy in the face of threatened ruin of the colonies.

These problems were concerned only with the so-called 'free' Indians. From 1500 onward Indian slavery was forbidden, with the exception of cannibals and captives taken in 'just' wars against the royal authority. In 1526 and frequently thereafter, indicating that abuses were still being reported, royal edicts forbade the enslavement of Indians for any reason, under pain of confiscation of the property of the transgressors. In the matter of Indian slavery, however, crown policy alternated as it did with regard to the encomienda, and from time to time enslavement was legalized in certain areas. For all practical purposes Indian slavery was illegal for most of the colonial period, but it was to be found under various guises all during that time.

In 1542, owing largely to the strenuous efforts of Las Casas, Carlos I issued the famous New Laws for the government, good treatment, and preservation of the Indians. In these laws the functions of the Council of the Indies and the colonial audiencias were set forth. The Indians were declared to be free persons who might not be employed against their will. Enslavement again was prohibited under any pretext, and no further encomiendas were to be granted. Those in existence could not be transmitted by inheritance. Compulsory personal service, one of the most serious abuses reported, was also abolished. If put completely into effect, the New Laws meant the eventual end of the encomienda and of the use of Indians as a source of cheap labor.

Resistance to the New Laws was immediate and insurmountable. Nowhere could they be completely enforced, and civil war threatened in New Spain until the viceroy prudently suspended the orders until he could inform the king of the hazardous situation. In Peru, where less caution was observed, a bitter revolt of the encomenderos seriously disrupted the colony. For a short time Peru, under Gonzalo Pizarro, was in fact independent, and similar resistance was to appear from time to time in other colonies when conditions of rule were unsatisfactory. By 1545 Carlos was convinced of his error, and he compromised by retaining only the decrees prohibiting slavery and personal service. A few years later the audiencias were instructed to appoint attorneys to conduct the legal processes necessary to secure the freedom of Indian slaves. Some audiencias freed all illegally held natives within their jurisdictions, while others were restrained from similar action by the evident ruin which such a course would bring to the mining industry.

Indian affairs continued in much the same condition throughout the sixteenth century. The king and his ministers persisted in the view that the natives were free persons and vassals of the crown, while in practice many of them were far from free. One reason for the king's attitude in this matter may have been that free Indians paid tribute, while slaves did not. There were many Indians in towns who worked at various trades who contributed substantial revenues to the royal treasury in the form of tribute. Royal interest in the welfare of the Indians was a mitigating factor, especially after the sixteenth century, but the factors which motivated that interest were not always clear.

Regardless of the institutions employed or the regulations issued by the respective governments, the Spanish and Portuguese colonists made use of the natives wherever possible. It would be difficult to discover a colonial regime in any epoch of history in which the conquered peoples did not suffer. The charge of special cruelty on the part of the Spaniards is, however, greatly exaggerated. The Portuguese, happily lacking a Las Casas to make known to the world the plight of Indian slaves on the sugar plantations, have escaped a similar stigma, while the later Anglo-Saxon maxim: 'A good Indian is a dead one,' indicates the English frontier philosophy.

III

Spanish and Portuguese Colonial Administration in the Sixteenth Century

> Spain in America reflected the indissoluble union of the altar and the throne.
>
> C. H. HARING *

T HE crimson and gold flag which Columbus planted in the sands of Watling Island was the royal standard of Isabel of Castile. It was not the emblem of the Spanish monarchy, for no such unified kingdom as yet existed. Under Fernando and Isabel, Spanish unification had greatly advanced, but Aragon and Castile still remained distinct realms united only tenuously by the royal marriage. Both monarchs followed a policy of centralization in their respective domains, but most of their efforts were concentrated upon chaotic Castile. They pursued the strategy of increasing their authority over the towns by appointing corregidores and other royal agents, and by subjecting local officials to the residencia. The New World settlements were from their foundation the property of the crown of Castile, and consequently the practices and institutions transferred to the Spanish colonies were primarily Castilian. The fact that unification of the two kingdoms had not progressed very far is evident from the fact that Fernando was ousted as regent of Castile in favor of his son-in-law, Philip, until the latter's death, and from the advice of

---

* *The Spanish Empire in America*, Oxford University Press, New York, 1947, p. 179.

35

Fernando to his grandson and successor, Carlos I, to preserve the separation of the two realms and to govern them through their own officials.

In their struggle against the turbulent nobility the Castilian kings had created a royal bureaucracy, the basis of which was the *Consejo Real* or Royal Council. Establishment of regional audiencias and other reforms in the administration of justice were elements of the same program, for the judiciary was to be one of the primary agencies for establishing royal control. With the increased cost of government, new forms of revenue were needed, and the modern treasury department appeared in this period. It was only natural that these changes which strengthened royal authority in Castile should be reflected in the administration of Spanish colonies beyond the seas. In the New World, moreover, there were none of the traditional institutions or privileges to hinder the flowering of royal power. The lands conquered by Spain were direct possessions of the crown of Castile. All concessions in any field came from the king and from no other source. Even the right to conquer a new region had to be acknowledged in a *capitulación* or contract with the crown.

Upon his death in 1516, Fernando was succeeded by his grandson, Carlos I, heir to an extensive empire. From his deceased father, Philip the Handsome, Carlos received valuable feudal holdings in the Low Countries and Burgundy; his Hapsburg connections facilitated his election as Holy Roman Emperor in 1519. Carlos' Spanish heritage included the kingdoms of Castile, Aragon, and Navarre, as well as their possessions in Italy, Africa, and the New World. As Charles V, head of the Holy Roman Empire, he had, in addition, certain rights and responsibilities in the Germanic kingdoms and principalities. Although the title of Emperor did not carry with it a treasury or genuine imperial authority, no western ruler since the fall of Rome had presided over so vast a domain.

The Emperor's heritage involved Spain continuously in Central European affairs, and drained her energies and resources in countless European wars to the detriment of internal development. The activities of Martin Luther in Germany and the events of the

Protestant Reformation encouraged separation among the German princes of the Holy Roman Empire and involved Carlos in a costly struggle on behalf of the church. Spain's most bitter enemy, however, was François I of France, ruler of Europe's other great Catholic kingdom. Throughout the lifetime of Carlos and François these monarchs waged almost continuous warfare, and this bitter rivalry was partly responsible for the failure of early efforts to stamp out Lutheranism.

In the midst of his troubles with France, his imperial responsibility forced Carlos to take up arms in defense of Western Christendom against the Moslem Turks who had penetrated the Balkan region to the gates of Vienna. While German and Austrian troops bore the brunt of the Turkish attacks, diversionary campaigns were launched by the Spaniards in North Africa. Victories of the moment proved indecisive, but the enormous realm of Carlos was held intact throughout these conflicts. The effect upon Spain was unfortunate, for to maintain the imperial prestige on so many fronts revenues were pledged years in advance and Spanish manpower was dissipated in prolonged and fruitless strife.

The reign of Carlos' son, Felipe II, 1556–98, was even more exhausting for Spain. Added to the conflicts carried over from his father's rule were others — the revolt of the Netherlands and the maritime incursions of the English. The rise of Holland was the more immediate hazard for Spain, as Dutch sea power placed Spanish commerce and overseas possessions in jeopardy; but the failure of the Great Armada to subdue England in 1588 encouraged the Elizabethan 'Sea Dogs' to make an honored profession of 'singeing the beard of the King of Spain.' In 1580 Felipe acquired the Portuguese crown and assumed the burden of administering an additional far-flung overseas empire whose subjects accepted the change with little grace. Unlike his father, who spent much time in his non-Spanish dominions and neglected the Iberian kingdoms, Felipe was truly a Spanish monarch who remained at home and who ruled in a very personal sense. His reluctance to delegate responsibilities to subordinates led to administrative stagnation and a general decline in the effectiveness of his government. Such great responsibilities were not to be successfully discharged by the techniques of direct personal management.

In Portugal, meanwhile, internal decline had set in. The flood of riches from the Orient had increased royal prestige and enabled the kings to rule and meet their financial obligations without summoning the old popular assemblies, with the result that the representative *cortes* lost its former power. In the hastily acquired wealth were the seeds of decay, for the vast capital that poured into Portugal did not find its way into the channels of industrial development. Domestic industries languished while the opulent court patronized the luxury marts of neighboring states, particularly those of France, Holland, and England. At the same time pirates of many nationalities eagerly awaited the arrival of spice-laden caravels homeward bound from the Indies, and the puny efforts of the Portuguese monarchs to check these depredations by diplomacy and force were unavailing.

The 'Spanish Captivity,' as the period of rule by Spanish kings has been called, led to the loss of the major part of the Portuguese eastern empire. The enemies of Spain became those of Portugal, and the remote Portuguese holdings in the East as well as in Brazil began to fall as prizes of war, especially to the Dutch. Felipe's rule was wise and tactful, and he employed only Portuguese officials in the administration of the kingdom, but the alienation of those powers who formerly traded peacefully with Portugal and who looked upon her empire with benign neutrality spelled ultimate ruin.

It is obvious that neither Spain nor Portugal gave her undivided attention to the settlement and development of overseas territory. The cost of Old World wars remained a steady drain on the national treasuries, and was reflected in the colonies by a constant search for new sources of revenue, and by frequent triumph of material consideration over humanitarian principle. Against such a background must be viewed the institutions and policies which governed the New World possessions in the sixteenth century.

The new lands discovered by Columbus and his successors were not absorbed into established imperial systems. The colonial adminstrations of Spain and Portugal evolved fully as spectacularly as did the conquest and settlement. Within half a century after the first voyage of Columbus the most valuable and desirable areas had been conquered and settled, and an administrative pattern for those regions had been developed and put into operation so successfully that it defied major modifications for the remainder of the colonial period.

At the apex of the Spanish and Portuguese political systems were the kings of those lands, whose paternal interests embraced all subjects, Iberian or Indian. The administration of their New World possessions, however, differed considerably, especially in the sixteenth century. At first the Portuguese had carried on colonial affairs through the councils already established in the peninsula, while the Spanish created the independent Council of the Indies for the governance of New World lands.

In considering Iberian colonial administrations it is necessary to emphasize a highly significant aspect — the dual nature of royal control. The kings had, in fact, two branches of their imperial organizations, each with special fields of endeavor, but with some overlapping duties. On the one hand was the secular branch, which was charged with managing the political, military, and economic affairs of the colonies. On the other was the religious establishment, which was responsible for the spiritual instruction of colonist and native, the education and indoctrination necessary for the various levels of society, and the physical welfare of the sick and needy.

The secular church in Spanish and Portuguese America was under the direct and immediate control of the kings in all matters except doctrine and religious discipline. It was, because of the union of cross and scepter in the New World, genuinely a branch of royal administration and must be considered as such. Because of the inability of the Holy See to keep pace with the need for religious establishments in the newly discovered heathen lands, the kings of Portugal and Spain were granted rights, collectively known as the *patronato real* or royal patronage, to compensate for the responsibilities they assumed in the propagation of the faith wherever their conquests carried. In the New World possessions of the

Iberian kings, church and crown mutually supported one another; the church, because of royal favor, became the most potent force for maintaining royal control over remote and turbulent colonists and hordes of semi-barbarous natives. The church was regarded and employed by the monarchs in Lisbon and Madrid as a means of political control. It was not unusual for members of the clergy to be called upon to serve in the secular administration as well; eleven of the sixty-two viceroys of New Spain were from the clerical hierarchy.

Spanish administration of the New World in the time of Carlos I centered in the Council of the Indies, a committee which grew out of the earlier personal management of colonial affairs by Juan Rodríguez de Fonseca, Isabel's chaplain. Shortly after the return of Columbus from his first voyage Fonseca was assigned the conduct of all business concerning the newly discovered lands. The task was relatively simple at first, but it soon became more than one man could perform satisfactorily, and he received the aid of crown secretaries and members of the Council of Castile. In 1503 Fonseca's labors were considerably lightened by the creation of the *Casa de Contratación*, or House of Trade, which relieved him of problems relating to commerce and navigation. The Casa was the first institution created specifically for the management of New World affairs. Fonseca continued in his role of colonial administrator until his death in 1524, although by that time a coterie of assistants had developed.

Even before the edict of Carlos I in 1524, which officially established the *Real y Supremo Consejo de las Indias*, the Royal and Supreme Council of the Indies, the group composed of Fonseca and his aides was already known by that name. With the rapid expansion of the conquest after the success of Cortés, the Council was given judicial as well as administrative functions, and it came to constitute, with respect to the colonies, the central governmental body, similar in virtually all respects to the corresponding council used by the king for the governance of Castile. Its jurisdiction in the New World was not shared by other councils or officials, and it prepared, in the king's name and subject to his pleasure, the bulk of colonial legislation. Its authority and its duties were extensive in the appointment and surveillance of civil and ecclesiastical officials and in the supervision of clerical affairs; it also served as a court of final appeal from the colonial audiencias, and it was charged with the over-all responsibility of protecting the interests of the Indians. In the sixteenth century it audited the accounts of colonial treasurers and other officials of the royal treasury. The legislation which it enacted was detailed and voluminous. The 'Laws of the Indies,' of which the most complete compilation was made in 1680, constituted the most comprehensive code of colonial regulations ever devised.

The membership of the Council of the Indies increased during the sixteenth century along with its responsibilities. Upon occasion the Council sent *visitadores* or inspectors to the various colonies to investigate and report upon general conditions or particular matters. At the conclusion of an official's term as viceroy or governor, the Council arranged for judicial review of his conduct in office, the process known as the residencia. In addition to these functions the Council had other important duties relating to the Spanish possessions, such as the defense of the empire and the protection of commerce between the colonies and the homeland. Special committees within the Council were assigned specific matters to consider, such as patronage. The principal defect in the system was the absence of individual responsibility and the growth of a spirit of routine.

In 1580, when Felipe II became king of Portugal, the Portuguese still had not developed a special administrative body for handling colonial affairs. The subsequent creation of special colonial institutions and laws was a direct result of Spanish influence. In 1591 the Portuguese Council of Finance was organized and divided so that separate units functioned for Portugal on the one hand and her various possessions on the other. After 1604 the *Conselho da India* governed the colonies, but it never played as important a role as its Spanish counterpart. In general the Brazilian communities were allowed to develop with little royal interference.

In Spain the Casa de Contratación was concerned with the

matters of commerce and navigation. Its location at Seville gave
that city an overwhelming advantage in colonial trade, a superiority which it vigorously maintained despite bitter opposition, well
into the eighteenth century. The duties of the Casa, in addition
to preserving the Spanish monopoly of colonial commerce, included
the licensing of ships, merchants, and emigrants, and the enforcement of laws pertaining to these matters. It collected various
duties and taxes and received royal revenues sent by officials in
the colonies. An interesting activity of the Casa concerned actual
details of navigation. It supervised the collection and correction
of navigational charts and conducted a school for navigators to
train pilots for service overseas.

The Casa also functioned as a judicial body to hear civil suits
growing out of colonial trade as well as cases of shipwreck involving
negligence on the part of ship's officers. Admirals in command of
fleets sailing to America were required to furnish bonds for their
conduct, and severe penalties were enforced against captains who
willfully took their ships out of convoys. In 1539 Carlos I reserved
to the Casa complete authority over local civil suits concerned with
crown revenues, but the establishment of *consulados* or commercial
courts in Seville and later in the New World subsequently relieved the Casa of jurisdiction over civil suits between merchants.

In 1514 one of the officials of the Casa was named postmaster of
the Indies, and he had charge of the dispatches sent by colonial
officials and persons trading with the colonies. He maintained
couriers to carry messages to court and to the various ports, but no
regular mail service between Spain and America was established
at this time. When speed in communications was urgent, the Casa
sent *avisos* or special dispatch ships with messages.

In the first half-century the king's share of New World wealth
was comparatively small, and it was not until 1550 that Carlos I
received from the colonies annually an amount equal to that
which came from his ancestral holdings in the Netherlands. By
this time placer mining in the West Indies was negligible, and the
disappearance of the natives in the islands precluded the possibility
of Indian tribute or head tax from that region. Only New Spain

and Peru, where the silver mines of Zacatecas and Potosí were just beginning to produce, were able to contribute substantial sums to the royal treasury. But after the creation of the viceregal governments in North and South America, the expenses of administering these unwieldy jurisdictions gradually consumed up to half of the royal revenues. Much of the money legally due the king, however, was diverted into the pockets of his numerous officials.

The more important sources of royal revenues in Spanish America were the *quinto* or royal fifth, the king's share of precious metals, the tribute paid by all male Indians, and the tithe or tenth part of agricultural and pastoral production. In addition to these were a number of royal monopolies such as those of quicksilver, salt, stamped paper for legal documents, gunpowder, and playing cards. Other sources of royal revenues were taxes and customs duties, some of which were allocated for special purposes. Among these was the *avería*, a variable tax on imports and exports levied to pay the cost of providing convoys for the merchant fleets.

The *almojarifazgo* was a duty paid on the value of goods from Europe, later extended to include those from the colonies. The *alcabala*, a tax on all sales and exchanges, was introduced into the Spanish viceroyalties before the end of the sixteenth century, where it constituted a serious obstacle to trade. The sale of public offices was another method of raising revenues; in the seventeenth century it was followed by the *mesada* and the *media anata*, exactions of one month's and half a year's salary from royal appointees to offices of both church and state. Occasionally *indultos* or heavy fines were levied on all of the merchants involved in colonial trade; like some other temporary measures the practice was repeated so regularly that it became virtually a form of taxation.

The king's ecclesiastical taxes were the tithe and the *cruzada*. The former was used primarily to support the ecclesiastical establishment, and only one-ninth of it was set apart for the royal treasury. The cruzada was originally a means of raising funds for carrying on crusades against the infidels by the sale of indulgences, but it became in effect a progressive tax, for the fee was based on the wealth of the purchasers. Although it was always held to be an ecclesiastical levy, the proceeds from it went into the royal exchequer.

In addition to these and other tax measures of lesser importance the kings in time of emergency called upon their American subjects for 'voluntary' gifts, loans, and other levies. Large sums were raised in this fashion by the viceroys of New Spain and Peru, while officials of less-favored districts usually sent little more than regrets.

The commercial system adopted by Spain and Portugal at the outset of their imperial careers was in accord with prevailing mercantilist theories. Colonies and mercantile enterprises existed for the enhancement of national power — the maintenance of suitable military and naval forces for defense, the control of an adequate supply of gold within the nation, and the promotion of self-sufficiency in the production and distribution of essential materials. Under this policy colonies were regarded as plantations or mines operated for the benefit of the mother country. The profits of commerce, too, were to accrue to the advantage of national merchants and shipowners. The colonies themselves were treated as closed markets which were expected to supply necessary commodities exclusively to the mother country, and at the same time to purchase only from merchants of the homeland. Spain's attempt to adhere strictly to this system was the source of endless dispute and eventually produced economic decline.

Unfortunately for the successful operation of a restrictive commercial system Spain did not measure up to her task industrially, and leaks in her commercial dikes were apparent from the outset. It has never been entirely clear why the demand for manufactured products failed to serve as a stimulus to Spanish industry as a similar demand fostered the great industrial development of Holland and England. It is only possible to note a variety of factors bearing on the problem. In the first place, Spain lacked an adequate system of internal transport and communication, and the configuration of the land made the rapid development of such a system costly and difficult. Related to this lack was the absence of dependable water power, a major item in the later industrialization of England. Furthermore, the Spanish cultural tradition placed a low value on efforts in skilled labor and commerce and a high value on the ownership of land whether productive or not. Those with surplus capital avoided investments in productive assets the ownership of which did not carry social prestige, but on the contrary placed one in the same class with non-Christians. In a society predominantly agricultural and paternalistic there was little incentive to demonstrate initiative in industrial enterprise. Of major importance was the fact that Spanish imperial commitments in Europe drained off considerable resources in non-productive military and political expenditures both for current operations and for repayment of debts incurred in past adventures. Finally, Spanish tax structure and policy placed enormous burdens on commerce in all its forms, discouraged its development, and put domestic goods at a disadvantage in competition with foreign products even in Spanish ports. No one of these factors was wholly responsible for Spain's industrial failure, yet each had its effect and helped to make of Spain not the industrial center of a vast colonial empire, but a mere hourglass through which the sands of commerce flowed to and fro between America and the expanding industrial nations of northern Europe.

By means of commercial regulations and restrictions, an inflexible and complicated system evolved for the purpose of draining off the wealth of America exclusively for the Iberian kingdoms. The policy of Portugal was in practice less exclusive than that of Spain, for the merchants of friendly European countries frequently traded with Brazil in the sixteenth century apparently without subterfuge. Such was not the case in Spanish America, where commerce with foreigners was, in the early years, punishable by death. To many poorly supplied colonists in Spanish America the punishment was unreasonably severe, and they found means of evading the law without losing their heads.

Portugal's industrial accomplishments were even less spectacular than those of Spain, and for similar reasons. Spain's domination of Portugal in what was perhaps a most critical moment for laying the foundation of a modest industry served only to impress upon the Lusitanian kingdom the same mark of impotence that characterized the industrial and commercial activities of her larger neighbor.

Since it was impossible for Spain and Portugal to supply even domestic needs for manufactured goods, they could not provide for their growing colonial populations. Inescapable dependence on foreign merchants resulted, and although an effort was made to control the flow of goods through Spain to America, many foreign merchants discovered obvious shortcuts. The demands of the colonists were not met by Spanish commerce, and alien smugglers rushed to supply them, appearing on the scene with goods at less cost than those coming legally from Spain. Such traffic could not be carried on safely in the open, but unguarded parts of the coast were always available when bribery of royal officials did not suffice. The participation of foreigners in Spanish trade, directly and indirectly, increased steadily, so that one Spaniard was moved to complain that all the wealth which his countrymen acquired at great sacrifice in America was carried off by the merchants of other nations.

Carlos I, whose position as Holy Roman Emperor made him unique among Spanish monarchs during the colonial period, for a time permitted all of his subjects to trade with his possessions, and Germans in particular became active in various enterprises. Under Felipe II, however, although many Portuguese participated in Spanish American commerce, trade with the Spanish colonies became increasingly the legal monopoly of the wealthier merchants of Cádiz and Seville. These merchants exerted tremendous power in preserving their prerogatives, and the argument that rigidly enforced monopoly was the best method of controlling traffic and excluding smugglers prevailed until the middle of the eighteenth century despite its manifest shortcomings.

In Spanish America Seville and Cádiz had their counterparts in Veracruz, Cartagena, and Portobelo. Upon occasion trading was carried on between other ports in both Spain and the colonies, but most of it was barred through the efforts of the merchants of Seville. The policy of so strictly limiting the colonial trade was a serious obstacle to the easy flow of goods which would have given greater prosperity to Spain and more comfort to her colonists.

Early experiences in attempting to enforce the exclusion policy and to protect commerce from attack by enemy vessels led to the adoption of a convoy system. After 1526 merchant ships were not permitted to sail alone between Spain and America, and warships escorted the merchant fleets and guarded the homeward-bound treasure. By mid-century the convoy or *flota* system was the common practice. In the time of Felipe II it became customary to dispatch two fleets annually, one to Veracruz and another to Cartagena and the Isthmus. In the early spring the ships assembled at Habana and returned to Spain in company. European wars occasionally caused an interruption of the schedule, and the sailings became increasingly irregular.

Royal authority reached farther in the government of the Spanish colonies than it did in Brazil. The more important officials were appointed by the king and the Council, and were allowed to correspond directly with them. This fact, together with the detailed legislation on matters of even routine administration, limited the control of the major officials over their subordinates. Their administrative activity was further curtailed by the necessity of securing prior approval from the Council for all projects other than those of ordinary government. The slowness of communications and the unhurried deliberations of the councilors in Madrid often delayed the inception of desired projects for many years. Unusual eagerness or initiative on the part of a colonial official, furthermore, was likely to win him only suspicion in Spain.

This aspect of Spanish policy was for the purpose of preventing the rise of rivals to royal authority in the New World, a danger which loomed large to the monarchs in Madrid. By dividing responsibility and authority between officials and institutions and by maintaining a distrustful attitude toward the colonists and those who governed them, the king and his councilors prevented the concentration of power in ambitious officials overseas. The system of checks and balances by which the king upheld his supremacy in the empire was a division of powers not among the governmental branches but among individuals or agencies exercising the same powers. The overlapping of authority was by no means accidental, for when disputes arose, both contestants appealed to the king, and with him lay the final decision. The result was that effective administration in the colonies was difficult to achieve.

In the New World the principal agents of the king were the viceroys, the captains-general, and the audiencias, as instruments of the secular state, and the archbishops, bishops, and regular orders of the ecclesiastical branch. The first two were officials who, as direct representatives of the king, were the chief civil and military administrators within their territories and the supervisors of the activities of the church. Their duties and responsibilities were similar, although captaincies-general were usually frontier areas requiring of the incumbent greater emphasis on military control.

The duties of viceroys were defined by Carlos I and modified by later kings. Both viceroys and captains-general supervised the administration of justice and both were required to devote their attention to the welfare of the Indians. Military defense was one of the most important duties of each, and as commanders of all military forces in their jurisdictions they enjoyed considerable power. In matters of finance they had general supervision of treasury affairs, and they were expected to sustain and augment royal revenues, a responsibility frequently difficult to fulfill. When encomiendas fell vacant they re-alloted them, and they nominated most of the minor officials, lay and clerical. They were permitted to enact ordinances of local application without prior approval from Madrid. The title of captain-general was commonly given to viceroys and other officials who had military responsibilities, and it was not until after 1550 that the captaincy-general as an administrative concept clearly emerged.

In Brazil the sixteenth-century counterpart of the Spanish viceregal system was the captaincy-general established in 1549 under a governor and captain-general who replaced the decentralized government of individual and nearly independent proprietors. The duties of the governor-general were to centralize the administration for purposes of defense, to check arbitrary acts against the colonists, and to serve as royal fiscal agent. In these tasks he was aided by an *ouvidor* or justice, a *provedor mór* or treasurer, and lesser military officers. The authority of the treasurer superseded some of the financial powers of the colonial proprietors, and he was in effect independent of the governor-general. He controlled the customs houses, collected taxes, and supervised fiscal administration. Like the officials of the Spanish *real hacienda*, he also exercised judicial powers in cases pertaining to his sphere of activity.

Ecclesiastical authority was vested first in the bishops, who were under the jurisdiction of the archbishops of Seville and Lisbon. After 1545 three independent archbishoprics were created in Spanish America, in Santo Domingo, Mexico City, and Lima. By mid-century there were twenty-two bishoprics. Five more were added during the next half-century, and two more archbishoprics were created in the same period. Bishops presided over ecclesiastical courts in each diocese. These courts were generally concerned with cases involving marriages, tithes, matters of religious discipline, and disputes within the clergy.

The clerical establishment was divided into two not always harmonious groups, the regular clergy — those living by the rules of the orders and withdrawn from worldly affairs — and the secular clergy, which comprised the ecclesiastical hierarchy from archbishop to parish priest. The long and acrimonious conflict over ecclesiastical jurisdiction between regulars and seculars stemmed from the early years of the conquest, when there were too few members of the latter available to perform the rites of the church in the widening empire. Dominicans and Franciscans, along with smaller orders and the later Jesuits, were permitted to administer the sacraments and to assume other responsibilities of parish priests. The Council of Trent, however, had repeated the principle laid down earlier that no clergyman might have jurisdiction over the laity unless he was subject to a bishop's authority, and the friars were subordinate to the heads of their own orders. When attempts were made to replace friars by parish priests, the conflict became heated. Practice varied in different parts of the Spanish empire, but in general the friars continued to hold Indian parishes only where no secular priests were available.

Below the viceroys and captains-general, the archbishops and bishops, but co-equal with them in certain matters, were the *oficiales reales de hacienda*, royal officials of the treasury. At first there were only a few in each colony, but as the conquest spread their ranks enlarged. There was invariably a *contador* or comptroller in the capital of each province; deputies were assigned at seaports and other important towns. In the time of Felipe II the 'royal officials' were given judicial authority over all fiscal cases involving royal revenues.

Despite the difficulties inherent in the administrative organization of the Spanish empire, the results were not entirely unsatisfactory to the king. The principal complaint which Spanish kings might have made was that distance, remissness on the part of colonial officials, and other circumstances which could not be foreseen nor prevented hindered their wishes being carried out with the exactness they desired. Distance and the time necessary for communication between the colonies and Madrid alone were factors of considerable importance in hampering effective administration. In order to avoid causing serious damage to a region or inconvenience to a viceroy, however, it was permissible for the official to withhold publication of orders thought to be improper, and to refer them back to the Council with suggestions for more appropriate legislation. Since it might take two or three years to receive an answer, the viceroys and other agents often enjoyed considerable latitude that was perhaps not intended.

The audiencia, which was introduced at first as a court of appeals in order to avoid the need of numerous petitions to the king, gradually assumed or was assigned other functions and became one of the most powerful instruments of royal control in the New World. As a consultative council it was similar in its association with viceroy or captain-general to the relationship between the Council of the Indies and the king. The audiencias also exercised legislative power to a limited degree, especially with regard to the government of the Indians. The *Relação da Bahia*, a high court with judicial powers similar to those of the audiencia of Spanish America, was established in Brazil in 1608, along with the *Casa de Suplicação* and the *Desembargo do Paço*, two lesser courts with special functions.

In the sixteenth century Spain established only two viceroyalties, those of New Spain and Peru. After 1549 all Brazil was under the jurisdiction of the governor-general, except for a brief interlude after 1572, when the country was divided into two jurisdictions. Audiencias were organized in the principal cities of each important Spanish American province. In the capitals of the viceroyalties and captaincies-general the viceroy or captain-general presided over them, while provincial audiencias came to have presidents of their own, and their jurisdictions were known as *presidencias*. The number of officials assigned to the audiencias differed according to their locations; the first audiencias created were composed of from three to five *oidores* or judges, and one or two *fiscales* or attorneys.

The duties which ordinarily occupied the audiencia were hearing appeals from local officials and administrative courts, and protecting the interests of the Indians. In criminal cases the audiencia's decision was final, but important civil suits might be appealed to the Council of the Indies. The Indians were relieved of the costs of lawsuits, and lawyers were appointed to defend them. In the late sixteenth century special courts, *juzgados de indios*, were established in New Spain and Peru to relieve the audiencias of the many cases involving appeals of the Indians. All the audiencias were of equal authority as judicial tribunals, and there was no appeal from one to another. Many special courts existed below the audiencia, and administration of justice in the colonies eventually became dispersed to an unusual degree, although in the sixteenth century this development had not reached its peak.

In addition to the judicial duties described briefly above, the audiencia served as a council of state in the consideration of matters of political administration. It was through this function that it came to have legislative and administrative powers. These powers were shared with the viceroy or captain-general who served as president, and in cases where there was no executive, owing to death or other reason, the audiencia frequently governed until a replacement had been appointed. The audiencia and the executive were expected to work together harmoniously, and in many cases they did. On the other hand there frequently arose serious differences between them, and the struggles were long and bitter, with the outcome depending upon the force and character of the participants and the favor which they enjoyed in Madrid. The authority granted to the audiencia as well as to its president, in his capacity of captain-general or viceroy, to communicate directly with the royal agents in Madrid, served the king's purpose well. It did not, however, promote harmonious relationships in the colonies, for much time and energy was spent in writing letters of complaint.

The most unique feature of the audiencia was its combination of judicial, legislative, and administrative powers. In the sixteenth century audiencias were frequently assigned the responsibility of governing enormous territories, as was the case in New Spain in the decade after the fall of Cortés from favor and before the appointment of the first viceroy, in Peru on several occasions before 1550, and in New Granada before the captaincy-general was established in 1563. Government by audiencias was generally unsatisfactory, because the division of executive authority among unco-operative officials led to much friction. The establishment of audiencias in most of the important regions of colonial activity, however, helped to give these areas a further measure of unity and cohesion which carried over into the national period.

The viceroys, captains-general, presidents, and oidores, and to a lesser degree the members of the upper clerical hierarchy, ordinarily were chosen from among the *peninsulares*, Spaniards born in Spain. The creoles, persons technically of unmixed European descent born in the New World, were usually limited to positions of inferior rank, for the most part in local administration and the lower clergy. The same was generally true for Brazil, where the *reinois* — those born in the kingdom — monopolized the preferred positions.

During the reign of Felipe II the audiencias which were not located at the residence of a viceroy or captain-general were as-

signed presidents of their own. The districts over which these outlying audiencias had jurisdiction were still nominally under the
government of a viceroy, although it gradually became the practice to appoint relatively autonomous governors to the presidency
of the tribunals in these provinces. Matters of general policy remained the prerogative of the viceroy, but in actual practice virtually
all phases of local administration were treated as the domain of
the presidents.

The municipal districts into which the larger political jurisdictions were divided were governed by officials of the principal town.
The functionaries in these cases, depending upon the size and importance of the region or upon mere chance, were called *gobernadores, corregidores,* or *alcaldes mayores.* Usually the district administered by a gobernador was larger than those of the other two
and was either an area formerly conquered by an *adelantado,* or
was a sparsely settled frontier where the preservation of peace required firm control. Each of these officials possessed political and
judicial authority within his jurisdiction; the gobernador sometimes had military duties as well when the title of captain-general
was added. With this exception, the responsibilities of the three
officials were essentially the same. No systematic plan was followed
in designating these local administrative units, and it was not unusual for all three to appear in the same viceroyalty or even the
same captaincy-general or presidency. In the jurisdictions of Lima,
Quito, and Charcas, however, only corregimientos were designated.

Administrative officials from the provincial level upward were
generally appointed for fixed terms, although a strict adherence
to such terms was infrequent. In order to prevent malpractice
officials were required to present a list of their possessions and to
deposit a bond to insure payment of fines which might be levied
during the residencia. They were obligated by law to make a tour
of their districts and to report the findings of their inspections to
the audiencia. They were prohibited from entering into private
business while in office, and they were forbidden to marry within
their districts without special permission from the king. Other
restrictions aimed at preventing the abuse of their authority over

the Indians forbade the acceptance of gifts or personal service from the natives.

The provincial officials were often too remote from royal or vice-regal authority for effective control. As a result they enjoyed considerable independence, and since local justice and police powers were in their hands, the temptation to despotic rule was little restrained. These officials as political leaders, legislators, military chiefs, and judicial heads of their often isolated provinces are the colonial ancestors of the provincial *caudillos* so famous in the chaotic years after independence.

In Brazil the office of *capitão mór*, like that of captain-general in Spanish America, came to have administrative as well as military functions. At first the colonial proprietor was given the military title of capitão mór in his 'captaincy,' as the grant came to be known. Later in the century, when Rio de Janeiro and other areas were conquered and colonized by the king at his own expense, he named capitães mores to govern some of them. In this case a capitão mór corresponded in position and authority to a governor and captain-general of a Spanish American province, and the capitão mór also earned a reputation for tyrannical abuse of power.

The *corregidores de indios* of the Spanish colonies were officials similar in authority to ordinary corregidores, but assigned to Indian districts or communities with special responsibility for protecting the interests of aboriginal peoples. Unfortunately protection was often misplaced by conscienceless exploitation, particularly in remote districts, where corregidores were able to rule in despotic autonomy. Their infamous practices precipitated numerous riots and rebellions on the part of their wards for two and a half centuries, and the slow-moving Spanish government failed to take adequate steps to remove the cause until the very end of the colonial period.

The *cabildo* or town council was the local unit of government in Spanish America, while the *senado da câmara* filled a similar position in Brazil. Cabildos customarily were set up immediately after a new region had been entered, and since there often was a delay before the area might be brought under the close supervision of high-ranking royal officials, the cabildo frequently served as an interim administrative agency for the surrounding territory. This early assertion of municipal autonomy was gradually curtailed by royal edicts before the end of the sixteenth century. Even the town plan became a matter of regulation, and the size and shape of the central plaza and the width of the streets were explicitly stated in royal ordinances. It was not by accident that virtually all Spanish American towns were laid out in similar fashion, even to the location of the public buildings around the *plaza mayor*. Legislation for the founding of towns in Brazil, on the other hand, was neither so detailed nor so strictly observed.

The officials who composed the cabildos were known as *regidores* or councilors, and *alcaldes ordinarios* or magistrates. The number of the former varied from four to eight and the latter from one to two, depending upon the size of the town. Other officials might be appointed to the cabildos when there was some special need. In the early years of the conquest the alcaldes and regidores were named by the conqueror of the region, or elected annually by the property owners. The sale of these offices, begun in 1559, became standard practice before the end of the sixteenth century, and made them virtually private property, transmissible from father to son. The prebendal practice probably cost the king more in lost revenue than he gained by the sale, but the custom persisted for the remainder of the colonial regime.

The functions of the cabildos included the distribution of land, the imposition of local taxes, the provision of police and military protection, the regulation of market prices, and other duties of a similar nature. The officials were not prohibited from engaging in private business, and in the frequent absence of fixed salaries, private income was often essential.

The principal duties of the alcaldes concerned civil and criminal jurisdiction. In most of the towns they presided over the regidores in the cabildo. A law of 1573 excluded them from the cabildo unless custom prescribed otherwise, but since it was customary for them to attend, the law was ineffective. Appeals from their judgments went to the governor and ultimately to the audiencia.

When faced by serious problems the governor or the cabildo

itself might summon an assembly of the more important citizens to meet and deliberate with them. Such an informal assembly was called a *cabildo abierto* or open council. A cabildo abierto was by no means completely representative of the citizenry of the community, but it did serve as a forum where property owners might express their desires and grievances. Cabildos abiertos were particularly effective in frontier towns where emergencies were frequent.

In the sixteenth century there were a number of meetings of representatives or *procuradores* of the towns of an area or province, usually for the purpose of petitioning the king or solving a pressing common problem. These assemblies were important only in the early decades of the century of conquest; thereafter they were infrequent, for the existence of a hierarchy of royal officials made them unnecessary as well as unwanted. Thus what under more favorable circumstances might have developed into a colonial assembly was effectively relegated to the role of submitting unwelcome petitions to kings who regarded such gatherings with suspicion and disfavor.

The role of the cabildo in Spanish America changed considerably after its early importance declined, and there remained a great difference between the councils of metropolitan communities such as Mexico City, and those of remote frontiers such as Asunción. Some writers have seen in the cabildo the antecedent of democratic institutions and the basis for later federalism. For sparsely populated and isolated towns like those of the Plata region, these arguments have some validity; elsewhere the functions of the cabildo were overshadowed by those of the more powerful organizations and officials. The senado da câmara seems to have preserved its powers for a much longer time, largely owing to royal indifference and to frontier conditions.

The ecclesiastical branch of royal administration played an equally important role in colonial life. It administered to the spiritual and educational needs of European and Indian, and to the physical wants of the poor, the oppressed, and the feeble. The religious organization conducted its program through its monastic orders, parish priests, schools, missions, hospitals, and other ameliorative institutions. The social and charitable contributions of the church to colonial society were not less important than its purely spiritual activities.

In many colonial cities the church established and operated, in conjunction with semi-religious civic organizations, numerous hospitals and asylums. As early as 1503 Governor Ovando was ordered to build in Santo Domingo 'hospitals to care for the poor, both Spanish and Indians.' The hospitals were, in fact, refuges of those who were homeless, or whose dwellings were not fit places for invalids. Persons with even modest means and social standing made no more use of the hospitals than they would have of any other kind of charity. Colleges or universities were established in most of the more important cities, beginning with those of Mexico City and Lima shortly after 1550. *Colegios* or academies were more widespread, so that in almost every settled region the trusted class of colonial society — the sons of the great landowners — had some educational opportunities, beginning usually with family tutors. The only genuinely popular instruction was religious, and was designed to maintain purity of the faith and submission to the king.

Purity of the faith was protected in other ways. Until the introduction of the Inquisition into the New World during the reign of Felipe II, bishops exercised inquisitorial powers. In 1570 and the following year Holy Tribunals were established in Lima and Mexico City. The spiritually immature Indians were not subject to the jurisdiction of the Inquisition, but to the bishops. Suppression of heresy was the most publicized activity of the Inquisition in the sixteenth century although its main function was as a police court and as guardian of good morals; later the king called upon it to exorcise political doctrines regarded as dangerous. No separate tribunal was set up in Brazil; bishops exercised inquisitorial powers, and the accused generally were sent to Portugal for trial.

The most impressive contributions of the orders were their educational institutions of all levels and their missions among the wild tribes on the periphery of civilization. In their missionary activities the padres served both the secular and spiritual arms of royal administration. For the one they worked to save souls and to increase the number of the faithful. For the other they acted as royal Indian agents and persuaded the Indians to live in villages, to learn useful trades, and to obey constituted authority. From a military standpoint as well, the mission was a vital imperial institution, for defense of thinly populated frontier provinces of Spanish America and Brazil was often left to the priests and their wards, with only a token force of professional soldiery to assist them. The *aldéias* or Indian villages under the missionaries of Brazil were far less numerous or successful than the missions of Spanish America, but the Jesuits nevertheless played an important role in controlling warlike tribes.

In the settlement of Brazil the Portuguese employed a much simpler system of colonial administration, as indicated. Shortly after 1530 a method of frontier government reminiscent of feudal practices was inaugurated. This was the captaincy system, whereby all Brazil was divided into fifteen *capitanias* assigned to individual *donatários* or proprietors. The donatary method was adopted because Portuguese efforts were concentrated principally on the more lucrative trade with the East, and occupation of Brazil was important primarily to substantiate Portuguese claims and to discourage the French from settling there. The responsibilities and the expense of settlement were thrust upon private shoulders, and the crown's territorial claim was upheld with a minimum of expenditure.

The Spanish counterpart of the donatário was the adelantado. During the reconquest this title had been given to governors of large districts on the Moslem frontier. The adelantado was also a direct representative of the king, and like the donatário, was granted unusual military, judicial, and political powers commensurate with the risks to which his life and property were exposed. At the time of the conquest the office was revived, for Castile once more had frontiers on non-Christian lands. The device, like that of the donatário, was employed as the cheapest and most effective means of bringing under royal control vast, unconquered areas. In both cases the recourse was only temporary, and the extensive powers and privileges were revoked as soon as it was convenient and safe to do so. The proprietary system disappeared more slowly in thinly populated Brazil than in Spanish America, and traces of it lasted well into the eighteenth century.

The donatário was expected to bring settlers at his own expense. He was given sweeping powers to administer his domain in a fashion calculated to make it self-sufficient, and he was empowered to enslave Indians. He was permitted to found and charter towns, and to appoint officials. He had many other powers, including jurisdiction over criminal cases, and he enjoyed considerable freedom from royal authority. The lack of a central government, however, was an obstacle to the defense and development of the colonies.

In 1549 João III issued a decree limiting the power of the donatários and establishing the office of governor-general of Brazil. The lack of cohesion in the system of virtually independent captaincies necessitated some such step, although the problem of establishing unity in so vast and empty a territory was too great for any method to win immediate success. Bahia was chosen for the capital, and the first governor-general brought with him priests from the newly organized Society of Jesus. The clerical and secular authorities co-operated in the task of giving justice and peace to the colony, and Brazilian administration gradually assumed a more regular and orderly form.

IV

The Settlement of the Caribbean Area

Many who made a fortune returned to Spain; and others went to settle in other islands or on the mainland, for most of the Indies have been discovered, settled, and supplied from here, this island [Española] being the head and mother and nurse of all the other parts of this empire.

OVIEDO *

THE four voyages of Columbus gave the Spaniards only a partial outline of the West Indies and the northern coast of South America. On his first expedition Columbus saw little more than the Bahamas and Española, but on his second visit, in 1493, he passed among the Windward Islands and skirted Jamaica and Cuba, which he thought was a peninsula. On his third visit in 1498 he discovered the island of Trinidad and the nearby coast of South America. In the meantime Spanish navigators were infringing on his exclusive rights, and making voyages to other parts of the Caribbean. Complaints against the government of Columbus in Española led to his loss of authority, and his efforts to recover his former power were in vain. The basic difficulty was that Columbus was not a Spaniard, but those who opposed him used their imaginations freely in devising reasons for his removal.

Early in 1499 the king and queen appointed Francisco de

* Gonzalo Fernández de Oviedo y Valdés, *Historia general y natural de las Indias, islas y Tierra Firme del mar Océano*, 4 vols., Madrid, 1851–5, Sevilla, 1535.

Bobadilla chief justice and royal commissioner and sent him to Española to resolve the difficulties among the settlers. In a moment of overzealousness, Bobadilla ordered Columbus and his brother Diego sent to Spain in chains. The complaints against Columbus and his brothers had been violent; Bobadilla did not take time to determine the justice of the accusations, and his treatment of Columbus was severe and unwarranted. Columbus had proved a poor governor of Spaniards, but it is doubtful that any ordinary man could have done better, for the adventurers of Española had tasted the joy of wealth without labor and pleasure without restraint, and they were little inclined to worry about the consequences of misdeeds.

Columbus was soon restored to royal favor, but not to his former prerogatives. The reports coming in from other voyagers indicated that the New World was more extensive than a group of islands, and Fernando did not intend to permit the hereditary monopoly promised to Columbus on his first voyage to embrace so vast a territory. In 1501, Nicolás de Ovando was appointed governor and supreme justice in all the new lands except where jurisdiction already had been granted to Vincente Yáñez Pinzón and Alonso de Ojeda. A year later Ovando sailed for Española with 2500 men and women, and Columbus' last hope of recovering his exclusive privileges vanished. The great discoverer decided to make one final expedition to the Caribbean, to vindicate his assertions of having reached the Orient, and to recoup his fortune.

In May of 1502 Columbus set out on what he expected to be the crowning voyage of his career. As on his first expedition he carried a letter of introduction to a high official of the East; on this occasion, however, it was not the Grand Khan that he sought but his Portuguese rival, Vasco da Gama, who had become governor of the Lusitanian king's Asiatic dominions. The letter to da Gama, like its predecessor, was not delivered, and Columbus once more suffered humiliating defeat.

When Columbus' fleet reached Santo Domingo, a hurricane was approaching. His request to enter the port and ride out the storm was haughtily denied by Ovando, and his advice that the homeward-bound fleet be delayed until the wind had subsided was ridiculed. Columbus removed his ships to a safe harbor and weathered the storm, but the twenty-one vessels bound for Spain were caught by the hurricane in Mona Passage, and only one survived, the caravel containing gold belonging to Columbus. It was not without reason that the admiral's opponents accused him of exercising magic.

Columbus sailed on to Jamaica, and from there to the coast of Honduras. The voyage eastward along the Central American coast was difficult and disappointing, for the winds were contrary and no sign of India nor a strait was to be found. In Veragua, Panamá, he did find some trace of gold, for Indians were using the metal in ornamentation. A suitable port site was located, which Columbus named Portobelo, little realizing that it was to become the terminus of a great transisthmian traffic.

His ships becoming rotten and unsafe, Columbus was forced to abandon the coast and sail for Española. He barely reached Jamaica before the last two vessels gave out. The castaways were saved after a year on the island only by the hardiness of Diego Méndez, who set out in a canoe with a few Indians to solicit help from Española. Columbus, his health ruined by the many hardships he had endured, arrived in Spain in November, 1504. He had not found a strait to the land of Vasco da Gama, but in his discovery of the isthmus, he had found a region richer in gold than any thus far seen in the New World.

By 1505 Columbus abandoned his efforts to have his rule restored in the West Indies, and instead sought to confer his rights and titles on his son, Diego. In this he was more successful, and in 1506 Diego assumed the title of Admiral at the death of his father. In 1509 Diego was appointed governor of Española, and his rule in the once-turbulent island was far more orderly than his father's had been. Most of his life, however, was spent in Spain petitioning the king for restoration of his hereditary rights as Viceroy of all the Indies. After his death in 1526, his wife, Doña María de Colón y Toledo, surrendered his grand but worthless titles in exchange for a more substantial grant — the Duchy of Veragua in Panamá — which in turn was traded for a small family pension in 1556.

The principal activity in Española during the years immediately following the conquest was that of exploiting the gold-bearing streams and acquiring what golden ornaments and nuggets the Indians possessed. Once both the Indians and the streams had been relieved of their precious metals, a feverish search for mines was initiated. Some success attended these efforts, but the yield was limited, and it soon became evident that the Spaniards would have to turn farther afield in their search for treasure.

Nicolás de Ovando, who replaced Bobadilla in 1502, ruled the island until 1509 when Diego Columbus succeeded him. By this time the conquest was beginning to spread beyond Española, as the search for mines and Indian slaves led men to seek more fruitful regions. Expeditions to other islands were sent out by Ovando, and Juan Ponce de León occupied Boriquén, modern Puerto Rico, in 1508. In the same year Ocampo circumnavigated Cuba, disproving at last Columbus' contention that it was a peninsula. It was Diego Columbus, however, who gave the greatest impetus to the extension of Spanish control in the islands. In 1509 he ordered Juan de Esquivel to begin the settlement of Jamaica. Towns and shipyards were established, and livestock introduced. In 1511 the town of Villa Rica de Puerto Rico, now San Juan, was founded in Boriquén, and Diego de Velázquez began the conquest of Cuba. Santiago was laid out the same year, and Habana was founded in 1514, but Velázquez secured the island for himself by defrauding Diego Columbus of his rights. One of the men instrumental in winning the case for Velázquez was Hernán Cortés.

The accessible wealth of the islands was quickly exhausted, and restless adventurers dreaming of great riches were loath to settle down as planters. Agriculture and cattle raising were introduced in all of the islands, nevertheless, even before the shallow mines played out. The inability of the Indians to endure the conditions of life and work under Spanish rule was a perplexing obstacle, making necessary a constant search for new sources of slaves. Slave-raiding expeditions led to important continental discoveries, which in turn drew off the population of the islands. The era of prosperity in the islands lasted only a few decades, after which many of them, bereft of their once numerous Indians, were virtually deserted.

Complaints against Diego Columbus led to the establishment of a high court of appeals in Santo Domingo to avoid the costly and difficult process of carrying petitions to the crown. In 1524 the tribunal became the Audiencia of Santo Domingo, and was composed of a president, four judges, and a fiscal. The territorial jurisdiction of the audiencia was extended as the conquest spread to other islands and to the mainland.

The conquerors of Cuba established their own rule, unhampered by outside interference, royal or otherwise. At the request of Velázquez's agent, Pánfilo de Narváez, *regidores perpetuos* — permanent councilmen — were appointed in the seven Cuban towns. The purpose of this move was simply to strengthen the ruling clique. Velázquez and his friends became so strongly entrenched that Diego Columbus failed in his attempt to oust his nominally subordinate governor. Usurpation of authority and general insubordination became common among the conquistadores as they moved beyond the immediate control of their constituted superiors. Velázquez himself was soon to sample the bitter fruit flung at him from Mexico by a disloyal emissary.

One of the most unusual features of early Cuban political development was the attempt to establish representative government. As rapidly as appointive town councils achieved importance in local affairs, the use of popularly elected district *procuradores* — advocates — appeared to check these bodies. The right of townspeople to this type of representation was a part of Spain's Roman heritage, and had been recognized in royal decrees. The procuradores were the champions of the townspeople against the cabildos and even the governor. They assembled annually in Santiago, and drew up petitions to the crown in the interest of their municipalities. The elections of procuradores became scenes of violent acts, for the governor and his friends in the cabildos tended to interfere in their own interest.

In 1528 the Cuban procuradores presented the king a series of proposals expressing public resentment against the growing tyranny of the cabildos. They asked that the king appoint governors for three-year terms from among the settlers of the island, that the office of regidor be made elective, and that it be for a short term rather than for life. They also requested that their own authority be enlarged, and that they be authorized to meet regularly. These proposals, coming less than a decade after the king's victory over the league of cities in Spain, must have caused him misgivings. Carlos I, nevertheless, adopted a part of the proposals. He increased the authority of the procuradores and permitted them to institute suits and to appeal them to the Council of the Indies, and he empowered them to deliver protests against the cabildos, the governor, and other royal officials.

The meetings of the procuradores seemed well on the way to evolving into a genuinely representative assembly of considerable importance when they received a severe setback. In 1531 one of the judges of the Audiencia of Santo Domingo arrived in Cuba to hold the residencia of Governor Gonzalo de Guzmán. This judge, Juan de Vadillo, reflected the audiencia's prejudice against popular elections, which were not allowed in the choosing of procuradores in Española. Vadillo regarded the elections as against the king's interests and injurious to local tranquility. His authority was sufficient to bring an end to the practice, and thereafter the procuradores were chosen by the cabildos. Vadillo's opinion undoubtedly was strengthened by the fact that the procuradores who met in 1528 were adherents of the governor.

The difficulties involved in carrying out the residencia of a governor in a conscientious fashion were apparent in the case of Vadillo. The governor's friends went to extreme lengths to hinder the judge and to prevent him from inflicting penalties on Guzmán. Bishop Miguel Ramírez, who illegally held an encomienda through Guzmán's connivance, excommunicated witnesses against the governor, and even Vadillo himself was excommunicated, 'to ruin him by way of the inquisition.'

After 1518 new discoveries and conquests constantly drained

Cuba of her most enterprising men. The lure of Mexico, Peru, and Florida was irresistible, so that by mid-century the total population of the island was approximately 300 Spanish families, 1000 Indians, and a smaller number of Negro and Indian slaves. Among the 'Spanish' residents were a few Germans, Italians, and Portuguese.

While the occupation of the greater Antilles was being accomplished, the Spaniards made numerous expeditions to the northern coast of South America. Columbus had discovered pearls there on his third voyage, and these, together with such Indians as could be captured for labor on the plantations or in the mines of Española, provided ample incentive to adventurers. Many of the visits made were unauthorized, but in 1499 Alonso de Ojeda was given permission to explore. He sailed from the Gulf of Paria, where Columbus had turned away from the coast, and continued westward to the Gulf of Maracaibo. The native dwellings built on piles in Lake Maracaibo inspired in the explorer a thought of Venice, and he named the place *Venezuela* — 'Little Venice' — as a result. And although later visitors failed to perceive or appreciate the connection, the name persisted.

In 1500 Pinzón and de Lepe examined the Pearl Coast, and Bastidas continued the explorations from Maracaibo to Nombre de Dios in Panamá. In 1504 La Cosa and Vespucci made a trading voyage to the Gulf of Urabá and ascended the Atrato river. Other voyages to the Pearl Coast were made, and interest in the region quickened.

The search for a strait continued after Columbus abandoned it, and in 1508 Pinzón and Juan de Solís explored the Gulf of Honduras and the eastern shore of Yucatán. No passage was found, but the golden ornaments of the Indians and the pearl fisheries inspired attempts to plant colonies on the mainland.

The first serious colonial ventures on the mainland, or *Tierra Firme*, as it was called, were far from encouraging. The organizers of these attempts to plant colonies were Alonso de Ojeda and Diego de Nicuesa, who received the grants of Urabá and Castilla del Oro east and west of the Gulf of Darién. In 1509 Ojeda built a temporary fort at San Sebastián, and it was appropriately named for a saint usually portrayed pierced by arrows. Not only were the Indians of the region extremely warlike, but their use of poisoned arrows caused unusually high casualties among the Spanish soldiery. Ojeda was gravely wounded, and returned to Santo Domingo, leaving Francisco Pizarro in charge until reinforcements arrived under Ojeda's alcalde mayor, Martín Fernández de Enciso.

Nicuesa's colony, although located beyond the lands of Indians using poisoned arrows, was no more successful, and the 700 men who accompanied him were reduced to a pitiful few by 1511, when they abandoned the colony and sailed along the coast. Nicuesa and his survivors came upon the remnants of Ojeda's men, who had moved west into Nicuesa's territory to escape the Indians.

Among the remaining settlers of Ojeda's force were two men whose careers demonstrated to varying degrees that the New World was indeed a land of opportunity. Francisco Pizarro, hampered by illegitimacy as well as illiteracy, rose from a career of common soldier to organize the American adventures which made his name the symbol of success. The other was Vasco Núñez de Balboa, who, according to the chroniclers of the conquest, was smuggled aboard Enciso's ship in a barrel to escape his creditors in Española. From inglorious beginnings such as these, the two men soared to prominence through their talents as leaders.

The methods by which Balboa and Pizarro attained power in Tierra Firme, simple though they were, are worth brief consideration at this point, since they represent the devices employed by scores of Spaniards to circumvent their superiors and defraud them of their legal rights. By persuading Enciso to remove Ojeda's men to Nicuesa's grant and then by expelling Enciso, Pizarro and Balboa were able to argue that Ojeda's authority had expired. Had Nicuesa been in a co-operative frame of mind when he arrived at Santa María la Antigua del Darién, he might have shared their future fortunes, and made unnecessary further steps to insure their power. But Nicuesa, though in desperate straits, nevertheless demanded their unqualified acknowledgment of his rights. His impractical demands cost him his life, for he was in no position to support his threats. With little more than a dozen men who refused to be enticed away from him, he was cast adrift in a sinking ship. None of them was heard from again, which cannot have surprised Balboa and Pizarro.

With Nicuesa removed Balboa rose to a pre-eminent position in the colony, and quickly proved adept at extending his authority over the tribes of the region. His expeditions brought not only welcome treasure in the form of gold and pearls, but persistent rumors of a great sea to the south. In 1513, with the aid of a multitude of Indians who performed the arduous labor of clearing a path through the jungle, he made the difficult journey southward across the Isthmus to secure immortal fame by setting up the crimson and gold standard of Spain on the shores of the Pacific. Of more immediate interest, however, was the immense loot which the expedition collected.

Word of this exploit was carried to Spain by trusted agents bearing also the king's share of gold and pearls. For his celebrated discovery Balboa was named Adelantado of the South Sea. But the grand-sounding title had a hollow ring, for Enciso had already convinced the king of Balboa's insubordination, and one of the most unattractive figures of the conquest — Pedrarias Dávila — had already been appointed governor of Castilla del Oro. In 1514, the year Pedrarias arrived at Darién, Castilla del Oro was made independent of Española. The 'Mother of Spanish Colonies,' as Española has been called, soon became an unimportant part of the Spanish American empire.

With Pedrarias came 1500 fame-hungry young men unprepared for the hardships thrust upon them. Nearly half of them died within a few months, but a few were destined to win renown and fortune in later conquests. Diego de Almagro, a soldier of humble birth, was to participate with Pizarro in the overthrow of the Incas. Hernando de Soto, one of the most ubiquitous of the conquerors, was to take part in the plundering of Central America and the capture of Atahualpa in Peru before his body finally was laid to rest in the Mississippi River. Francisco Vásquez de Coronado was to explore the Great Plains of North America as far as present-day Kansas. Bernal Díaz del Castillo, who fought beside Cortés in the conquest of Mexico, was to write a delightful chronicle in later years to correct the impression that Cortés alone was responsible for the triumph.

Relations between Balboa and Pedrarias were cool from the outset, for the former's enemies had exploited the governor's natural susceptibility to suspicion of his subordinate's loyalty. A basis of operation was agreed on, however, and Balboa was permitted to continue his explorations on the Pacific side of the Isthmus. Balboa's success as well as his reputation so irritated Pedrarias that he decided to rid himself of his rival. The discoverer of the Pacific was seized, accused of treason, and delivered to the executioner with unseemly haste and highly questionable justice.

The Indian policies of Balboa, aimed at maintaining control over the natives by keeping them friendly, were abandoned in an orgy of raids. Roused to desperation, the Indians fought back and the retaliatory measures of the Spaniards quickly reduced their numbers drastically.

After the elimination of Balboa, Pedrarias sent Gaspar de Espinosa to carry on explorations in the Pacific. The prosperity of Castilla del Oro was diminishing rapidly and the more ambitious men sought new avenues to wealth. Raiding parties pushed rapidly westward by land and sea, and the better to promote these activities Pedrarias moved his capital to the city of Panamá which he founded on the Pacific side of the Isthmus. Nicuesa's town of Nombre de Dios was refounded, and a transisthmian trail connected the two ports.

The conquest of Central America became a virtual civil war among opportunistic Spaniards, between the lieutenants of Pedrarias Dávila and those of Hernán Cortés, and between renegades from the authority of these two leaders who sought to usurp power for themselves. In these contests the Indians and their wealth were the ultimate prizes, but the subjugation of the Indians was long delayed by the strife among the would-be conquerors. The bewildering struggles in Central America demonstrated vividly to the king and his councilors the enormous difficulties involved in administering remote, unknown lands and controlling ungovernable men.

While Spanish adventurers fought among themselves for the isthmian region, others established profitable pearl fisheries farther east in Nueva Andalucía. Slave-raiding had attracted attention to this region earlier, and the employment of Indian slaves in gathering pearls gave an added incentive to the traffic. The pearl fishers established themselves on islands near the coast of Venezuela, while the slavers carried on their operations over a wide expanse of the coast.

Two attempts of Dominican and Franciscan friars to establish monasteries in Cumaná without military protection ended in martyrdom for those involved. The first was begun in 1510 by the Dominicans Pedro de Córdoba and Juan Garcés, and was successful until slave-raiders appeared. In 1518 Dominicans and Franciscans established themselves at the same place and labored peacefully among the Indians for two years before they were killed. In 1521 a punitive expedition under Gonzalo de Ocampo was sent against the rebels, as the Indians were regarded, and large numbers were enslaved. On the same expedition Ocampo founded the town of Nuevo Toledo near the Cumaná river.

In the wake of Ocampo's devastating visitation, the priest Bartolomé de Las Casas arrived with a small group of idealistic colonists determined to undertake a daring social experiment. More adverse circumstances could not have been found, for the Indians were still smarting from the cruel treatment inflicted by Ocampo. Las Casas and his followers hoped to prove that unavaricious, law-abiding Spaniards could live peacefully among the Indians, and that the excesses so common throughout the Indies were not only unnecessary but ill-advised. Slave-raiding in the vicinity continued, however, and while Las Casas was in Santo Domingo seeking the assistance of the audiencia, the Indians destroyed his settlement and killed most of his colonists. Nueva Córdoba was founded near by.

The lower Orinoco region and the Gulf of Paria soon drew attention away from the Cumaná area, and in 1530 Pedro de Acosta founded a settlement near the mouth of this great river. Carib

Indians ended its brief career, and a similar attempt by Antonio Sedeño to found a town on the island of Trinidad failed. Only the arrival of Diego de Ordaz as governor, adelantado, and captain-general of Nueva Andalucía saved the twenty-five survivors of Sedeño's force from probable destruction. On an expedition which cost the lives of many of his men, Ordaz explored the Orinoco as far as the mouth of the Meta. On his return to Paria a dispute with Sedeño resulted in Ordaz being sent in irons to Santo Domingo. Further explorations of the Orinoco failed to divulge any treasure, and the slave trade was made unattractive by the skill with which the Indians employed poisoned arrows. For the remainder of the century there were fruitless attempts to open mines and found colonies in Nueva Andalucía. Cumaná managed to survive, but its existence was neither happy nor prosperous.

West of Nueva Andalucía the coastal region was settled with greater success. In 1525 Rodrigo de Bastidas, who had made earlier voyages of exploration, founded the town of Santa Marta in New Granada.

With the appointment of García de Lerma as governor of Santa Marta the audiencia made another attempt to enforce more humane treatment of the Indians. García de Lerma was required to prevent the enslavement of Indians and to try to locate and return those who previously had been carried off to other regions. To execute his orders the new governor would have needed the co-operation of the Spanish colonists and unusual wisdom. Since slave owners were steadfastly opposed to surrendering their Indian slaves and to abandoning Indian slavery, he was far from successful. In an attempt to provide a broader economic basis for the colony than that provided by slave-raiding, García de Lerma sought to promote agriculture by introducing seeds from Spain, and he sent expeditions to explore the Magdalena river as far as its confluence with the Cauca. But the enslavement of Indians continued.

West of Santa Marta a more important city, Cartagena, was founded in 1533 by Pedro de Heredia, who had served earlier in Santa Marta. Heredia became well versed in the ways of the Indians, and his qualities of leadership fitted him for enterprises of his own. He went to Spain to secure a concession for himself, and was given the right to conquer the unoccupied coast from the mouth of the Magdalena to the Gulf of Darién. In Spain he recruited a small force, and on the voyage to South America stopped at Puerto Rico and Santo Domingo to enlist additional soldiers. With this force Heredia established Cartagena, one of the major strongholds of Spanish settlement in South America.

Heredia's plan to establish friendly commercial relations with some of the tribes in his domain proved no simple matter. Since the time of Ojeda the region had been shunned by Spaniards because of the ferocity of the natives and their skill in using poisoned arrows. By tactful treatment of the Indians and an iron control of his own men, Heredia was able to conduct some of the most profitable expeditions of the conquest, and virtually all of these were managed peacefully with minimum expenditure in lives and resources.

News of Heredia's excellent fortune spread rapidly through the Indies and made Cartagena famous. Gold-seekers flocked there from many directions, and it quickly became a major port city and the base for expeditions. In 1534 a new and larger force was sent to exploit the gold of the Sinú region, gold in the form of ornaments found in the graves of the chieftains. Like many another successful man of his time, Heredia had many enemies, who complained bitterly to the audiencia. After a visitador who was sent from Spain to conduct his residencia died on the way, Juan de Vadillo was appointed to the task, and he promptly found Heredia guilty of defrauding the public treasury in the distribution of gold taken from the Sinú, and of a universally available charge when others were lacking, maltreatment of the Indians.

A more unusual effort to establish settlements on the northern coast was made in the same epoch. In 1528 Carlos I granted the Alfingers and other Germans the right to explore and establish settlements on the coast of Venezuela. The Alfingers and the Welsers, to whom Carlos was in debt, prepared to exploit the grant. They agreed to found two towns within two years, and to build three forts. For a period of eight years the colonists introduced by them were to be free of taxes, and the king's share of minerals was reduced from one-fifth to one-tenth. The colonists were allowed to enslave Indians who resisted their authority.

Among the three hundred colonists the company brought to Coro in 1529 were Spaniards and Portuguese as well as Germans. The primary purpose of the German enterprise was commercial, and Indian slaves proved to be the most available commodity, for rumored treasures were not found.

Because of the obvious abuses in the slave trade of the Germans, Indian slavery in Venezuela was abolished in 1530. The Germans protested that their investments had been heavy, and that the slave trade was the only promising source of revenue. Carlos revoked his decree, but ordered that slaves not be sold outside the province. This ruling also met with protest, and it was impossible to enforce.

The period of German activity in Venezuela offers little contrast to the general story of the conquest and settlement of Tierra Firme. Only the fact that non-Latins were permitted briefly in the great undertaking and that a few important discoveries were made by them is of interest. After the death of Governor Ambrosius Alfinger, the Audiencia of Santo Domingo appointed the official Protector of the Indians, Bishop Rodrigo de Bastidas, provisional governor of the province. Once again the interests of the company were jeopardized, and the audiencia's appointee was disregarded in favor of George Hohermut von Speier, while Nikolaus Federmann, a strong candidate for the same office, received the title of captain-general. Thus the highest military and political ranks were separated. Caught by the universal fever for immediate gain, von Speier ignored the king's order to distribute and colonize the lands already explored. Both he and the captain-general made long and costly treks through the wilderness in search of mines. Federmann's expedition was noteworthy only for the number of Indians who perished as a result of it and for his arrival on the savanna of Bogotá in 1538, where he met Spanish forces from Santa Marta and Quito.

In 1535 Fernández de Lugo was appointed governor of Santa

Marta, which province was separated from that of Cartagena by the Magdalena river. His instructions were similar to those issued to other governors of the time: to grant lands to new settlers; to introduce 100 slaves, a third of whom should be women; and to prevent the enslavement of Indians except those who refused to receive priests. Lugo appointed Gonzalo Jiménez de Quesada as his *justicia mayor*. Reports of the colony's wealth enabled Lugo to recruit more than 1000 men, who hastened to Santa Marta to live in ease. Great was their astonishment when they beheld the tiny straw-thatched village and its jaundiced inhabitants. Almost at once Lugo sent an expedition into the interior under the command of his son, Luis. On the return of this force Luis left secretly for Spain, carrying with him all of the gold that had been collected.

Left with the choice of idleness and starvation or further raids on the Indians the remaining Spaniards prepared another expedition by way of the Magdalena river. Quesada was given command of the force and led it on a strenuous march through the almost impenetrable jungles of the interior. In six months half of the original 600 men had perished, and the survivors vainly begged Quesada to return to Santa Marta. When the army reached the highlands, the men were quickly restored to health and courage, but their number had been reduced to less than 200. On the plateau the army found the Chibchas, whose conquest is not a part of the settlement of the Caribbean. The expedition of Quesada met two others near modern Bogotá, that of Federmann and that of Sebastián Benalcázar, who had marched north from Quito. All three were searching for *El Dorado*, the Gilded Man, a Chibcha priest who was said to dust his body with gold. In 1538 Quesada founded the city of Santa Fé de Bogotá. Benalcázar had already established Cali and Popayán. For many years disputes between the conquerors and their partisans disturbed the region.

The Welser grant was rescinded in 1546. Its only lasting accomplishment was the founding of Tocuyo, in 1545. Coro remained little better than a starting point for expeditions and a slave market for those which returned. Most of the coastal area had been depopulated of Indians, for those who had escaped slavery had sought more remote refuges. When title to Venezuela returned to the Spanish crown, Governor Juan de Villegas was appointed and charged with dividing the remaining Indians in encomiendas, and with bringing in permanent settlers. Under his regime land was distributed and put to use, and the resulting need for Indians to labor on the plantations made it less profitable to export them as slaves. Venezuela now enjoyed a more orderly existence, but the havoc that had been wrought among the Indians precluded a rapid pacification of the country, and the ravages of foreign pirates in the second half of the sixteenth century brought additional troubles.

The succeeding governors gradually extended the conquest and founded new towns, the most important of which were Valencia, Trujillo, and Caracas. Several attempts were necessary before a permanent settlement could be made at Caracas, for the Indians were numerous and determined to maintain their freedom. It was not until 1567 that the city was finally laid out, and for years it was so constantly beset by Indians that on a number of occasions the settlers considered abandoning the region. Warfare with the Indians was the chief factor in discouraging and impeding Venezuelan settlement throughout the sixteenth century.

In 1567 the governor and captain-general, Juan de Pimental, chose Caracas as his place of residence, and the city replaced Coro as the unofficial capital of the province. Most of the municipalities had been under the rule of their own cabildos with little outside interference, and they bitterly resented the attempts to extend the governor's power over them. In 1586, for example, Governor Luis de Rojas appointed the alcaldes of Caraballeda, port of Caracas, instead of permitting them to be selected according to custom. When their protests were unavailing, the townspeople forcibly ejected the governor's alcaldes and installed those of their own choosing. The governor retaliated by arresting the four regidores of the town, whereupon most of the townspeople abandoned their homes and went elsewhere to live. As a result of the affair Rojas was removed from office in 1587. Caraballeda was not re-established, but the new governor founded the port city of La Guaira to serve the inland capital.

Some of the problems of Spanish colonial administration are illustrated by the events described above and those which followed. During the residencia of Rojas many complaints were made, with the result that he was imprisoned and deprived of his property despite the fact that his action was in accordance with the king's wishes. So great was the feeling against him and so articulate were his enemies that the audiencia was moved to send a special investigator authorized to try such persons as he saw fit. Part of the fines and penalties accrued to the magistrate, and it appeared that he regarded the entire population as guilty. The prospect of everyone's suffering severe losses for their customary actions caused resentment to rise. The cabildo of Caracas feared that the town would be ruined, and warned the audiencia in Santo Domingo. The latter body, undoubtedly considerably confused by the unexpected events, replaced its agent and relieved him of his loot.

One of the difficulties apparent to the governor, Diego Osorio, was that the office of governor embodied too little authority. Osorio did not choose to follow the ill-fated course of Rojas in extending his power, but instead sent Simón de Bolívar to Spain in 1589 to obtain royal acquiescence and assistance. One of the changes instituted after the return of Bolívar to Caracas in 1592 was the introduction of the sale of municipal offices.

In 1595 Caracas received a severe setback. English pirates raided the coast and marched inland, seizing the capital during the governor's absence in Maracaibo. After burning the town the invaders withdrew, for the prospects of obtaining ransom were poor. Had Caracas been a city of more substantial construction than the ordinary thatched huts, the damage undoubtedly would have been more costly.

The second half of the sixteenth century was a time of consolidation and slow growth for Venezuela. Farms and plantations absorbed the energies which earlier had been spent in seeking El Dorado. Wheat, sugar cane, indigo, and tobacco were the principal crops. The numerous cattle produced all that their lean breed permitted: hides and a small amount of beef and tallow. Manufacturing was limited to the production of flour, sugar, and soap.

Caracas as a tropical, provincial capital presented little external grandeur. At the close of the century it contained some 1500 inhabitants among whom there was no great variation in wealth. Socially, however, two distinct classes were acknowledged. An aristocracy had been created by the king's practice of ennobling daughters of Indian chiefs in order to encourage intermarriage with the Indians. Europeans who married these fortunate women acquired the privileges of nobility. Those Spaniards whose titles originated in Spain, however, regarded themselves as superior to the 'breechclout nobility,' and animosity between the two groups was strong, corresponding to the peninsular-creole antagonism of other Spanish colonies.

The opening of gold-bearing lands on the continent greatly diminished the attraction of the islands, and the populations of Española, Cuba, Jamaica, and Boriquén fell off rapidly. By mid-century, when the major explorations had been made and the conquest of Mexico and Peru completed, the regions lacking in precious metals and sedentary natives to mine them were already relegated to obscurity unless considerations of defense dictated otherwise.

As the focal point of Spanish defenses in the New World, Habana began to acquire attention which its resources had not merited earlier. The capture of Spanish treasure ships off the Azores by French pirates had excited French interest in the West Indies. The French smugglers not only found themselves treated as pirates — not a few died dancing from the end of a rope on Spanish warships — but discovered that the profits offered by piracy were far greater than those of trade. Attacks on Spanish shipping and colonial towns followed, and soon English seamen joined in the sport. To prevent the depredations of pirates on their shipping, the Spaniards resorted to annual fleets convoyed by warships.

Until audiencias were created in New Spain and Panamá, the Audiencia of Santo Domingo exerted some authority as far as

Honduras. The New Laws of 1542 replaced the Audiencia of Panamá by a separate audiencia for Central America located at Gracias a Diós, in modern Honduras. The *Audiencia de los Confines,* as the new tribunal was called because of its location on the boundary of Nicaragua and Guatemala, did not acquire a permanent seat immediately, and its jurisdiction also was fluid. In 1550 Panamá was placed under the Audiencia of Lima; later it was returned to the Central American court, but finally was reunited with the Viceroyalty of Peru in 1567 with an audiencia of its own.

Until mid-century there was no audiencia in the interior of northern South America. Santa Marta remained under the jurisdiction of the audiencia in Santo Domingo. In 1550 the Audiencia of New Granada was established at Santa Fé de Bogotá with authority over the interior and over some of the coastal towns of modern Colombia.

Ecclesiastical governments were established in the various Spanish settlements in the Caribbean region contemporaneously with political jurisdictions. The bishoprics created for the West Indies and the continental colonies were on an equal footing with those of Spain. Before 1545 all of them were subject to the archbishop of Seville, but after that date Santo Domingo, Mexico City, and Lima became the centers of ecclesiastical provinces independent of those of Spain.

Before 1560 French and English maritime smugglers' activity in the Caribbean was merely annoying, and Spain relied upon naval power to defend her unfortified settlements. In 1540 an inadequate wooden fort was constructed in Habana, but visiting corsairs seem not to have been intimidated or injured by its guns.

As French raiders escaped unpunished and frequently won prizes they considered well worth the risk, their activities became extremely costly to Spain. Ports in Boriquén, Cuba, and Tierra Firme were ruined, but the crowning blow was the burning of Habana, in 1555. Spanish patience and perseverance, which Sir Walter Raleigh later found reason to applaud, was sorely taxed. Felipe II patiently negotiated a treaty with France which stipulated that French subjects were not to sail to the Indies without license from Spain, but French raids continued. Spain thereupon abandoned diplomacy and resumed her reliance on force to protect her commercial monopoly.

By 1570 French activity began to decline, but the Elizabethan 'Sea Dogs' and the Dutch 'Beggars of the Sea' more than replaced it. By the 1580's the depredations of corsairs in the Caribbean endangered the flota as well as all settlements. Typical action was that of Sir Francis Drake, who in 1586 captured Santo Domingo, terrified the residents of Cuba, and destroyed St. Augustine, Spain's outpost on the eastern coast of Florida.

The king of Spain's beard had been singed too often for comfort, and the year 1586 marked the end of an era in Spanish policy. Previously the Spaniards had relied on their naval preponderance and ineffective diplomacy to protect commerce and colonies. Felipe now resolved to fortify and garrison the port towns in the Indies that they might defend themselves. The wisdom of this policy may be deduced from the fact that in the years that followed Spain's important colonies successfully resisted the invasions of European enemies, often with little but moral support from Madrid. Felipe dispatched engineers to the Indies to make an inspection and determine what needed to be done. Their answer is to be found in the mighty stone bulwarks which tower above the entrances to Habana, San Juan, and Cartagena.

Foreign intrusions made it necessary for Spain to protect the flanks of her trade routes with an increasing number of fortified harbors, and the occupation of strategic areas which had nothing to commend them in the form of wealth became unavoidable. Such an area was Florida. In 1513, Ponce de León, conqueror of Boriquén, sighted the Florida peninsula, and began to plan for its conquest. He secured royal permission for this adventure, but did not return to the task until 1521. His attempt was a complete failure, and he was mortally wounded in combat with the Indians. Since Ponce had not proceeded far enough to confirm or deny Florida's alleged wealth, in 1526 Lucas Vásquez de Ayllón sailed from Española with 500 men to establish a colony on the Carolina coast. Ayllón died, and the survivors of his force returned to Española.

The next adventurer to seek fortune in Florida was Pánfilo de Narváez, who was rewarded for his loyalty to the king by the gift of the vacant grant. Narváez landed near Tampa bay with 600 men, and made a laborious and costly peregrination in search of rich cities. In attempting to escape from Florida, Narváez and a few hundred men sailed westward along the Gulf coast in crude rafts which were wrecked on the coast of Texas. Only Cabeza de Vaca and three others survived the eight-year ordeal and eventually reached Mexico City bearing rumors of the Seven Cities of Cíbola.

In 1539 Hernando de Soto, a veteran of the conquests of Central America and Peru, landed in Florida near where Narváez had begun his ill-fated expedition. De Soto led his force on a far more extensive search for rich cities than any of his predecessors, but the final result was no less disappointing. His discoveries, like those of his contemporary Francisco Vásquez de Coronado in New Mexico, merely indicated to the Spaniards that in the northern wonderland they could not hope to find another Mexico or Peru. Interest in Florida and the continental region to the north declined. Consequently when the viceroy of New Spain offered Luis de Moscoso, de Soto's successor, the chance to establish settlements in Florida, Moscoso refused.

In 1549 the pacification of Florida was attempted by Fray Luis Cancer and other friars who abjured the use of force. The courageous priests waded ashore with no more protection than a wooden cross held over their heads. Indians were awaiting them on shore, and they won martyrdom even before they had dried their feet.

Control of the Bahama passage was necessary to protect the treasure fleets during the wars with France, and for years after the unfortunate Cancer episode unsuccessful attempts were made to establish a colony. Finally Felipe II, concluding that if Spaniards could not colonize Florida no other people could, instructed the viceroy of New Spain to cease trying.

Scarcely had Felipe decided to leave Florida without settlement when someone else did establish a colony. René Goulain de Laudonnière, the leader of a group of French Protestants, built a settlement on the St. John's river. Spain was faced with the un-pleasant alternative of expelling the French and securing Florida or seeing enemy mariners molesting the treasure ships in the Bahama channel.

Felipe was not to be outdone by any French heretic. He en-trusted the task of dislodging the intruders to one of the ablest officers ever to serve a Spanish king, Pedro Menéndez de Avilés. Menéndez founded St. Augustine, and all available heretics were put to the sword. In carrying out his orders Menéndez won the gratitude of his king and universal notoriety for his cold-blooded killing of the French Huguenots who had surrendered to him under a promise of being sent to Spain. Florida was destined to be little more than a strategic outpost for the time being and it was necessary to provide it with financial support from Mexico. As a missionary field the region offered countless opportunities for martyrdom, and Jesuits who came to work among the Indians gained few converts.

By the close of the sixteenth century Spain held securely the Greater Antilles as well as a number of important centers in northern South America, Central America, and New Spain. The desirable regions had been discovered and secured, while European enemies had been discouraged from occupying near-by positions which might pose a threat to the vital Caribbean area. The turbulence and excitement of the age of conquest had died down, but much of the more mundane and less glamorous work of empire-building still lay ahead.

V

The Conquest of the Aztecs

When we beheld the number of populous towns on the water and firm ground, and that broad causeway, running straight and level to the city, we could compare it to nothing but the enchanted scenes we had read of in Amadis of Gaul . . . To many of us it appeared doubtful whether we were asleep or awake . . . for . . . never yet did man see, hear, or dream of anything equal to the spectacle which appeared to our eyes on this day . . . I thought within myself that this was the garden of the world! This place was, at the time of which I am speaking, with one half of the houses in the water, and the other half on dry land; but all is destroyed, and that which was a lake is now a tract of fields of Indian corn, and so entirely altered that the natives themselves could hardly know it.

BERNAL DÍAZ DEL CASTILLO *

THE occupation of the West Indies was a rather prosaic and unprofitable effort in comparison to the subjugation and assimilation of the empire of the Aztecs. Balboa's epic march through the isthmian jungles to sight the Western Sea, Ponce de León's luckless search for rich kingdoms in the north, and the plunder of the graves of the Sinú chieftains in New Granada were less momentous, less portentous, and less sanguinary than the conquest of Anáhuac — the land of the Aztecs. These adventures, it is true, were not without tangible rewards or momentary notoriety; what was lacking was the element of permanent ascendancy in a vast new social milieu. The new society was exemplified

* The True History of the Conquest of Mexico, 1632, various editions.

in the case of Mexico by numerous people advanced in handicraft and military skills and complex social and political organization. It was only with the occupation of Mexico that Spain was presented with an opportunity to do more than experiment in the administration of ignorant savages. New political and social institutions here had an opportunity to emerge. The Mexicans or Aztecs did not disappear as did the unhappy natives of other regions; they remained to provide the artisans and laborers of a new culture.

There was little promise in the early career of Hernán Cortés to mark him as a future conqueror. In 1502 he was prevented from accompanying the Ovando expedition to Española by injuries sustained in one of his typical nocturnal adventures owing to the slipping of a ladder, the crumbling of a wall, and the blows of a jealous husband. In 1504, his wounds healed, he finally took passage to Española, where he became a planter and a notary public in the village of Azúa near Santo Domingo. Another illness, also attributed to his sportive life, prevented him from accompanying Ojeda to Darién.

In 1511 Cortés set out with Diego de Velázquez for the relatively easy conquest of Cuba, along with red-bearded, hollow-voiced Pánfilo de Narváez from Jamaica and pious Bartolomé de Las Casas, the future 'Apostle of the Indians.' Cortés took part in the Cuban enterprise as secretary of Velázquez, while Narváez served as captain-general. Cortés and the governor fell out, and for a time the jolly Velázquez considered hanging his upstart secretary. Friendly relations were at length restored, and Cortés aided Velázquez in casting off the authority of Diego Columbus. The lessons of this intrigue were not lost on Cortés, as Velázquez was to discover to his profound chagrin.

The 'madness of Mexico' infected Cuba after Hernández de Córdoba returned from Yucatán in 1517 bringing persistent rumors of great cities and wealth to the west. Two Yucatán natives, captured for training as interpreters, also told fantastic stories of rich cities beyond the coast. Córdoba died of wounds soon after reaching Cuba, but Velázquez hastily prepared another expedition commanded by his nephew, Juan de Grijalva.

Grijalva departed in January and returned in October of the same year with tales which excited the Spaniards of Cuba to the point of frenzy, especially since Grijalva brought enough gold to give his stories credence. On the coast of Mexico he had interviewed agents of the Aztec emperor, Montezuma. Since his commission did not permit founding a settlement, the cautious, unimaginative Grijalva sent Alvarado back to Cuba for instructions, but then returned himself without waiting for reply. Velázquez was deeply mortified at his nephew's banal naïveté, for he feared that bolder adventurers would win the prize. Another expedition was nearly ready when Grijalva returned, and Velázquez gave the command of it not to his own kinsman, but to Hernán Cortés.

The energetic measures of Cortés to obtain supplies and recruits and the whisperings of rival candidates awakened some doubts in the mind of the governor about his fidelity. The new commander momentarily allayed Velázquez's fears and hastened his preparations. Forewarned that the governor had decided to replace him, Cortés ordered his men aboard ship the night of November 17, 1518, and when Velázquez arrived next morning he could only stand helplessly on the shore while the ships sailed from the harbor. Inasmuch as the departure was premature, Cortés was obliged to enter other Cuban ports to complete the provisioning of his ships and the recruitment of his men. It was not until February, 1519, therefore, that the fleet left Cuba and crossed to the island of Cozumel, off the coast of Yucatán.

The good fortune which attended Cortés for the next three years served him well on this occasion, for he freed a Spaniard named Aguilar who had been living among the Indians of Yucatán for eight years, and who knew their language well. After a short stay, the fleet sailed on to Tabasco. Using Aguilar as an interpreter, Cortés demanded that the natives permit his men to land and take on provisions and water. The answer was a flight of arrows.

The army landed and marched inland to do battle with an immense force of Indians. The tumultuous conflict was turning in the favor of the Indians until the Spanish cavalry, little more than a dozen men and horses, could be brought up. The sight of the horses, which none of these Indians had seen before, as well as their effective use in battle turned the tide, and the field was left to the Spaniards. Cortés released some prisoners to open negotiations, and a delegation of chieftains or *caciques* arrived. Impressive entertainment had been prepared for them. A small cannon was fired over their heads without warning, and the ball crashed through the trees in a terrifying fashion. The climax was the appearance of a restive stallion, which pawed the earth and neighed. When the caciques were on the verge of flight, Cortés had the horse led away, but by this time the Indians were extremely anxious to please one who possessed such powerful gods.

The meeting ended, the natives hastened to their villages and sent presents of gold, food, and twenty attractive young women. One of these was the daughter of an Aztec cacique, and was fluent in both the Mayan and Aztec languages. Because of her father's rank, she was entitled to be called *Doña* Marina. After baptism and christening Doña Marina was to prove a most invaluable aid to Cortés long before he reached Tenochtitlán, the Aztec capital, and although messages must have lost some meaning in the process of being translated by Aguilar into Mayan and by Doña Marina into Aztec, Cortés was extremely fortunate in having these interpreters.

The fleet sailed on to San Juan de Ulúa, where the envoys of Montezuma appeared with presents and ceremonial clothing for Cortés on the possibility that he might prove to be the long-awaited Toltec god, Quetzalcoatl, who had vowed to return and claim his patrimony from the Aztecs. The emissaries of Montezuma had little difficulty in deciding that Cortés was not the feathered serpent deity, but the fatalistic Montezuma was far from relieved by their assurance. He sent his priests to exorcise the strangers by magic, but for good measure added a few gifts to bribe the Spaniards to depart should other means fail. One of these presents, a huge golden disc, had just the opposite effect. Cortés resolved to conquer Tenochtitlán.

This undertaking was no simple affair as had been the subjugation of Cuba. With only 500 men and sixteen horses, cut off from any base from which reinforcements might arrive, Cortés proposed to conquer a martial people who might muster a huge army against him. There could be no halfway measures; he must succeed completely or die in the attempt. Furthermore, his only chance to justify his insubordination to Velázquez lay in an astounding triumph.

By astutely playing off the Velázquez faction of his army against the soldiers who were eager for conquest and spoils, Cortés permitted himself to be pushed along the course he had chosen. He founded the town of Villa Rica de la Veracruz, and appointed regidores. Legal forms were followed implicitly, for Cortés was building his case for presentation at court. He administered the oath of office to the cabildo in the king's name, and then resigned his commission from Velázquez. After founding a municipality Cortés was legally able to appeal directly to the king, without having to obtain the approval of his superior, the governor of Cuba. To justify his actions he wrote five letters to the king, the *Cartas de Relación*, which are justly famed among the early literary works of the conquest. The newly appointed cabildo met and chose Cortés as its captain-general and justicia mayor, and quickly invested him with the authority of these offices.

The Velázquez faction was far from satisfied with his course and it took swift and severe action on the part of Cortés, magistrate of a town yet to be built, to convince them that affairs had genuinely changed. Once the ringleaders were seized Cortés won over most of the others with little difficulty, for he could not afford to sacrifice many men even in the interest of discipline.

A delegation of Totonac Indians visited Cortés, and from them he learned of the dissatisfaction among the tribes subjugated by the Aztecs. He paid a visit to the cacique, for he was in great need of allies. His arrival was timely, for it coincided with that of Montezuma's haughty tax-gatherers. At his suggestion the Totonacs imprisoned the Aztec agents, an act which assured him of their assistance, inasmuch as an irreparable breach had been made. Cortés then secretly released the astonished Aztecs, and sent them on their way with words of friendship, the better to spread confusion in the ranks of the enemy.

Before setting out on the perilous journey to Tenochtitlán, Cortés took additional shrewd steps to secure his position for the present and the future. He sent a ship to Spain with trusted men and all the treasure so far collected to be used in liberal gifts to the king and to powerful officials at court. The envoys were given strict orders to avoid stopping at Cuba, but one of them could not resist the temptation to enter an out-of-the-way port and display some of the gold. By the time news of this visit reached Velázquez, the story was magnified to the point of suggesting that the entire ship was ballasted with precious metals! Portly Velázquez was visibly moved.

Learning of a plan on the part of a few men to seize a ship and return to Cuba, Cortés arrested the leaders, and executed them summarily. Lest such a plot be repeated, the commander literally burned his bridges by ordering the ships dismantled and run aground. This bold stroke left the entire force with the alternative of triumphing over the dangers ahead or perishing at the hands of the Indians.

In August, 1519, Cortés began his memorable march to Anáhuac with an army of 400 men, leaving a small garrison to continue the construction of Veracruz. The road to Mexico led through the lands of the redoubtable Tlaxcalans, who were almost continuously at war with the Aztecs. Cortés realized that he could go no farther without an alliance with the Tlaxcalans. The price of this treaty was a costly conflict in which the Spaniards lost many men and came perilously close to defeat. Indeed, the victory over the Tlaxcalans was one of the most critical moments of the entire campaign, for defeat would have been fatal.

From Tlaxcala Cortés proceeded by way of the Aztec-dominated city of Cholula, 'so as not to show weakness,' as he put it. He was at first accompanied by a tremendous force of Tlaxcalans, which he estimated at 100,000 men. When he learned that his new-found allies planned to destroy Cholula, he sent back all but a few thousand, for he contemplated the use of craft as well as force.

In Cholula, Doña Marina discovered a plan to massacre the Spaniards with the help of an Aztec army camped not far away. Cortés employed this opportunity to teach the foe an impressive lesson. He accused the surprised Cholulans of treachery, and in a wild battle his men killed several thousand of them. The Tlaxcalans eagerly entered the fray, and finally had to be restrained by Cortés. Before leaving Cholula the Spanish commander had gained new allies, established peace between that city and Tlaxcala, and won tremendous prestige throughout the land. The stage was now set for the triumphal entry into Tenochtitlán.

The Aztec capital had been erected on an island in Lake Texcoco, and access was possible only by boat or by crossing one of the several causeways that connected the mainland with the island. On November 8, 1519, Cortés selected one of the causeways and proceeded across the lake. Montezuma met him in person and, still fearful that Cortés might be Quetzalcoatl, welcomed him and offered him the city. Great indeed was the astonishment of the Spanish soldiers on entering the magnificent city, but the presence of multitudes of obviously well-disciplined Aztecs made them feel more like captives than captors.

Soon after arriving in the city Cortés made one of the boldest moves of his intrepid career. He had learned earlier of an attack by Aztecs on the men left near the coast, but had remained silent on the matter until he saw an opportunity to use the information to advantage. One day he and a few trusted soldiers surrounded Montezuma and demanded an accounting for the death of the soldiers at Veracruz. Montezuma promised immediate satisfaction, but Cortés insisted that the emperor reside with him as hostage until the guilty had been punished. The weeping emperor became the virtual prisoner of Cortés. Only the immense religious and temporal authority exercised by Montezuma over his people now prevented the Aztecs from rising against the Spaniards.

When the Aztec officials from the coast had been surrendered,

Cortés decided upon a punishment which not only would create a terrifying impression in a land where human sacrifice was common, but would weaken the Aztecs militarily as well. The culprits were burned at the stake in the plaza in front of Montezuma's palace, and the fuel used for the pyre was composed of weapons from the Aztec arsenal.

In spite of his revenge Cortés continued to retain Montezuma as a prisoner, and thus made himself ruler of Anáhuac. The Aztecs, however, were not so easily resigned to such a fate as was their fatalistic emperor, and plots were made to release him. The precautions of Cortés caused the failure of these plots, and Montezuma's prestige began to diminish. At the same time Cortés persuaded Montezuma and the principal Aztec officials to acknowledge their subordination to the faraway king of Spain.

The first news of the arrival of Pánfilo de Narváez on the coast was in the form of pictorial messages brought by Aztec runners to Montezuma. The force which Velázquez had sent to subdue his rebellious agent was double that of Cortés, and happily provided with eighty horses. Cortés left impetuous Pedro de Alvarado in command of Mexico in May, 1520, and hastened to the coast to meet the new threat in person. On arriving in Tlaxcala he requested his allies to provide him with 5000 men, which they politely declined, for they preferred to fight Aztecs.

The road to victory over Narváez was paved by sending messengers to his camp with gold to be distributed liberally and secretly among his soldiers. This device worked so well that Narváez soon found many of his men and officers unduly sympathetic toward Cortés. He failed to take any decisive action, however, and waited indolently in Cempoala for Cortés to surrender. With 250 men against 800, Cortés attacked the camp at night after a heavy rain. One detachment was sent to seize the artillery, while another captured a greater prize — Narváez himself. At daybreak the army of Narváez filed past to swear allegiance to Cortés.

Scarcely was this ceremony over when Tlaxcalan messengers dashed up with dire news from Alvarado — the Aztecs had risen in rebellion. The exchange of messages between Narváez and

Montezuma had raised Aztec hopes of deliverance, for the Spaniards had become tiresome guests. But the revolt was owing to the
rashness of Alvarado, who had attacked a group of unarmed young
men peacefully performing religious ceremonies. Soon the Spaniards were besieged in their quarters.

Cortés returned to Mexico in June, and attempted to salvage his
former authority, but even his greatly augmented army was insufficient. He made the error of trying to appease the Aztecs by re-
leasing Montezuma's brother, Cuitláhuac, who assembled the
council and deposed the imprisoned emperor. Cuitláhuac was
appointed to the vacant office, and warfare began in deadly earnest.

Montezuma, shorn of his power, soon fulfilled the ancient adage,
'For a deposed prince the distance is not long between the throne
and the grave.' While the fighting was at its height he appeared
before his countrymen and begged them to cease waging war. Their
answer was a shower of stones and arrows, a sufficient demonstration that his authority was no longer respected, for previously the
Aztecs cast their eyes downward the moment Montezuma appeared
in public. Three days later the wounded Montezuma, surrounded
by weeping Spaniards, perished. The Spaniards had ample reason
for their tears.

After the death of Montezuma, retreat from Tenochtitlán was
the only course open to the Spaniards, and their hopes of escape
were jeopardized by three breaches which the Aztecs had opened
in the causeway. Cortés ordered his men to construct a portable
bridge. At midnight of June 30, 1520, the *Noche Triste* or sorrowful night, the retreat began. The Spanish army marched quietly
through the deserted streets to the water. As they placed their
bridge across the first opening in the causeway, Aztec sentinels
aroused the city.

Before the army could cross the bridge it was assailed on all sides
by Aztecs, who showered stones and arrows into its ranks with
deadly effect. The bridge meanwhile became wedged fast in place,
and could not be removed. Panic infected the soldiery, and the
orderly retreat became a disorganized flight, those at the rear
forcing the van into the water ahead, while Aztec canoes swarmed

on all sides. Many a Spaniard was carried off in the canoes to serve the bloodthirsty Aztec gods as a human sacrifice, while others were dragged to the bottom of the lake by the weight of the treasure they carried.

By morning the battered remnant of the Spanish and Tlaxcalan army reached the shore of the lake. Lost in the flight were most of the firearms and the artillery, half or more of the men, and most of the horses. The Noche Triste was a terrible disaster, and the career of Cortés seemed ruined. The remainder of his force was saved merely because the Aztecs failed to follow up their advantage, and he led his men to Tlaxcala, where he found a safe refuge among his powerful allies.

Cortés immediately began reorganizing his army to attack the Aztec cities on the road to Mexico, for he was determined to return to the capital, and his army's morale was badly in need of repair. With the help of Tlaxcalans he drove the Aztecs from their frontier posts, and his tarnished prestige resumed some of its former brilliance. Ships arrived from time to time with reinforcements and supplies for Narváez, and others came from Garay in Jamaica to be used in his grant of Pánuco near modern Tampico. Men, horses, and arms were quickly appropriated by Cortés.

While Cortés was preparing to return to Mexico a devastating smallpox epidemic spread through the land slaying enemy and ally alike. While his expeditions gradually extended his authority in the direction of Mexico, his carpenters were building thirteen brigantines to be transported in pieces and launched on Lake Texcoco. In the six months after the calamity of Noche Triste, Cortés had regained a remarkably strong position.

The Aztecs, now ruled by Cuauhtémoc, 'The Fallen Eagle,' prepared themselves for a desperate defense. By the end of the year 1520, Cortés was again on the march, this time with a tremendous force of Tlaxcalans organized and trained by his own officers. The conquest of the Aztecs was an extremely bitter campaign in which probably more than 100,000 perished from warfare and starvation. A large part of the city was systematically destroyed, because the Aztecs heroically chose to defend it house by house.

As soon as the Aztecs were defeated Cortés settled down to re-building the city and exploring the conquered territory. His lieu-tenants fanned out to seek mines in distant provinces. Towns were established and town councils appointed. Land was distributed among the conquerors and to some of the more prominent native caciques. But land without laborers was a hollow luxury, and a solu-tion to the labor problem had to be found despite Cortés' declared aversion to forced labor. He finally yielded to the clamor of the conquerors and granted them Indians in encomienda, but he en-deavored to make the system more than a cloak for slavery as it had been in Española and Cuba.

Once more Cortés collected a treasure to send to the king, for he had not heard from his earlier agents, and the towns he had created sent procuradores to Spain to uphold his cause. The ship bearing the treasure, however, was captured by a French corsair in European waters, and the golden ornaments of the Aztecs were appropriated by the astonished François I of France. Cortés did not lose in fame by this episode, and Carlos I had already acknowl-edged him as governor and captain-general of New Spain in October, 1522.

Along with his instructions to Cortés Carlos sent a group of royal officials to watch over the collection of the royal fifth and to help in the administration of justice. With regard to the king's instruc-tions, Cortés followed a policy which was to be used by many a viceroy in later years. He acknowledged the orders but did not en-force those he regarded inappropriate, especially the one which declared Indians to be free. He justified his action by informing the king that the natives had known even less freedom under their former native masters.

Late in December, 1523, Cortés sent Pedro de Alvarado to Guatemala, and a month later Cristóbal de Olid was dispatched to Las Hibueras or Honduras, both ostensibly to discover the elusive strait to the Pacific, but attracted more by stories of gold. By summer Cortés had a fleet ready at Zacatula on the Pacific coast, for he was determined to discover a better passage than Magellan had recently found. This fleet discovered the pearl fisheries of Lower California, but no strait.

In 1524 Cortés issued his own ordinances for the conduct of Spaniards in New Spain. Each man who received Indians in encomienda was obliged to maintain arms and horses for defense of the land, and was responsible for converting the Indians to Christianity. Spaniards were not free to come and go at their pleasure; those who came from Spain were obliged to agree to remain eight years. Married men were required to bring their wives to New Spain within eighteen months; single men were commanded to acquire wives during the same period. They were required to plant and cultivate certain Spanish crops which Cortés wished grown. These regulations applied equally to native caciques who were given land and Indians in trust.

In May, 1524, the first large group of Franciscan friars arrived in New Spain; three had preceded them in 1522, and were already engaged in studying the native languages. Cortés had requested the king to send only priests of pure life and morals, and he welcomed the priests with a show of deference which made a lasting impression on the Indians, and the earnest, barefoot friars entered the city of Mexico scarcely less triumphant than Cortés before them. The natives were astonished at the attentions shown the priests by the all-powerful Cortés, and his conduct greatly aided the missionaries in superseding the native priests. Admittedly the work of making Christianity a powerful force for good conduct among the natives was necessarily slow, a fact which the missionaries understood better than Cortés. The Franciscans, and a few years later the Dominicans, set about the task with immense faith, energy, and good will, and although many of the early baptisms probably meant little to the natives, the fact that human sacrifice was soon abolished was a distinct improvement. Later a reaction set in, and some of the friars became motivated by a spirit of emulation and competition not directly concerned with propagation of the faith.

Late in 1524 Cortés learned that Olid had rebelled against his authority in Honduras. He sent an expedition to punish the rebel, and then decided to follow up in person. His decision to go by land to chastise his insubordinate officer was one of the most unfortunate errors of his career, for he abandoned his post of authority at a time when a firm hand was needed, and he left New Spain to the free machinations of his enemies. To discourage a possible native uprising in his absence, he took Cuauhtémoc and other high Aztec officials with him. The army plunged into the maze of unknown swamps and jungles which made the march one of the most arduous in the annals of the conquest.

By the time the exhausting journey was over Cortés learned that Olid already had been executed and that his own efforts had been unnecessary. Discouraging news came from New Spain, for during his prolonged absence anarchy had triumphed. When he finally returned, after twenty months' absence, he had been given up for lost and his enemies were in control.

In 1526 Cortés received an order to send a squadron to rescue the expedition of Jofre de Loaisa which had sailed to the Orient by way of the Strait of Magellan in the previous year, and he sent Alvaro de Saavedra to fulfill this command. News of the chaotic state of New Spain meanwhile had reached Spain, which news the enemies of the conqueror used to arouse the fears of the suspicious king. The calumnies against Cortés were fantastic, and it is not surprising that the king was moved to have a residencia held to determine the truth. In the quarrels which ensued Cortés lost authority rapidly, so that in 1528 he decided to visit Spain and take his case directly to the king. In his absence anarchy once more became widespread.

The first audiencia of Mexico, presided over by Nuño de Guzmán, seemed bent on gaining wealth quickly even at the cost of undoing all that had been accomplished. Exorbitant charges were leveled against Cortés, and his friends suffered loss of their property. Guzmán led costly expeditions through northern Mexico in a hasty but futile search for treasure.

The protests against the highhanded acts of the first audiencia led to the appointing of a second one in 1530. Cortés retained the title of captain-general, but his responsibilities and those of the tribunal were not clearly defined, with the result that the Spaniards split into two hostile groups. The second audiencia, nevertheless, won a reputation far different from that of the first. One of the most popular acts of these judges was punishing the crimes of their predecessors, with the exception of Guzmán, who wisely avoided their jurisdiction. They also organized Indian towns with native alcaldes and regidores elected according to the Spanish custom.

The many difficulties involved in establishing order and harmony in New Spain led the emperor to appoint a viceroy with sufficient power to cope with the contending and turbulent factions, and to uphold the royal interests. New Spain was made a kingdom, presumably on an equal footing with the kingdoms of the peninsula. The first viceroy to be named was Don Antonio de Mendoza, a member of one of the most powerful noble families of Spain, and an experienced diplomat and administrator. In 1535 Mendoza arrived to assume the duties of his difficult assignment. He was a fortunate choice for the task of governing the newly conquered kingdom, as he was a match for the conquistadores, and his loyalty to the king was above dispute.

The problems of the new viceroy were many and complex. In the first place, he had to discourage by tactful means the making of additional conquests by Cortés and other ambitious men who might flaunt royal authority. Quarrels between the conquerors were numerous and violent, and these had to be quelled by the weight of viceregal power. In extending the conquest and enlarging the scope of exploration, the viceroy had to take into account the warlike tribes beyond the region once dominated by the Aztecs. The Mixton War, which broke out soon after Francisco Vásquez de Coronado left Compostela in 1540 for his famous peregrinations in New Mexico and the Great Plains, seriously threatened the land for several years and was not ended until Mendoza took command of the troops in person. In this same war one source of possible trouble was removed when Alvarado was killed by the Indians. The Spanish victory opened the way to the rich silver lodes, and a series of silver 'strikes' pushed the frontier northward rapidly for the remainder of the century. During Mendoza's rule many expeditions were sent out by land and sea, and Spanish geographical knowledge grew enormously.

Another result of the Mixton War was that Mendoza fell heir to the naval expedition which Alvarado had been preparing for voyages of discovery in the Pacific. The ships were sent on two long cruises, that of Ruy Gómez de Villalobos to the Orient, and that of Juan Rodríguez Cabrillo to the coast of California. Neither expedition accomplished anything concrete in adding rich lands to the empire, but knowledge of the Pacific region was measurably expanded.

The question of the status of the Indians was aggravated by the promulgation in 1542 of the famous New Laws. The purpose of these laws was to make the Indians free in fact and to end their involuntary servitude. News of their promulgation in Spain preceded the arrival of Francisco Tello de Sandoval, who came in 1544 with the title of *visitador-general* and with sweeping powers to effect the change in the rights of the Indians inherent in the laws. The encomenderos were violently opposed, and they were supported in their opposition to the laws by the higher clergy. Mendoza was fully aware of the strife which would inevitably follow the abolition of the encomiendas, and he prevailed on Sandoval to delay putting some of the more obnoxious edicts into effect until an appeal had been made to the king. As a result of his strong plea the unpopular portions of the laws were postponed until the regime of his successor. That there was great danger to the welfare of the colony in the strict enforcement of the New Laws was evident from the fact that business stopped almost completely in anticipation of their execution, and the population was in a state near panic. Although the astuteness and moderation of Mendoza prevented serious rioting, on the first fleet returning to Spain 600 persons abandoned the colony.

The New Laws, which were now re-examined and modified to remove their most objectionable features, combined two useful purposes from the point of view of the king of Spain. They complied with the legal interpretation of Spanish jurists like Francisco de Vitoria, who argued that the Spaniards had no right to the land or

labor of the Indians despite their duty to convert the heathen
natives to Catholicism. They were also a part of the general movement to break the dangerous power of the conquistadores and to
reinforce royal authority.

One of Mendoza's many recommendations to the king was that
a university be established in Mexico. The proposal was put into
effect in 1553, after Mendoza had been transferred to Lima as
viceroy of Peru. The university was patterned after the famous
University of Salamanca in Spain, as was the one created at Lima
in the same period. The traditional fields of learning were offered:
canon law, civil law, the arts, rhetoric, and grammar. In 1580
courses in medicine were introduced.

In the fifteen years of Mendoza's rule in New Spain peace and
order were established, and respect for royal authority firmly im-
planted. Part of his success was due to his sagacious handling of
the Indians, in which he owed much to the earlier example of
Cortés. One of his most effective devices was to devote one day
each week to listening to the complaints and protests of native
delegations. Even though he did not immediately grant their requests or remove the cause of their grievances, the hearings were
eminently popular, and the number of Indians who took advantage
of the opportunity continued to grow in the time of later viceroys,
who wisely continued the practice.

An unusual feature of Spanish rule in New Spain was the use
of the more highly civilized natives in extending the conquest. The
Tlaxcalans, because of their invaluable aid to Cortés, enjoyed a
favored position. They and the Aztecs were called upon to furnish
colonists for towns founded on the embattled northern frontier. As
civilizing agents of Spain the Aztecs carried the conquest far beyond the limits of their former domain. Both tribes rendered
valuable service in desolate outposts where life was a daily battle
with the desert as well as with warlike nomads.

Under the sixteenth-century viceroys New Spain became an exceedingly valuable kingdom. The silver mines of Zacatecas and
other regions produced great quantities of silver, especially after
1559, when the patio process of extracting the metal by means of

quicksilver amalgamation was introduced. The silver production
of New Spain was extraordinary, and the fortunes made in mining
permitted the growth of a 'silver nobility' who purchased titles
from the king. Agriculture was improved by the addition of European crops and animals, but methods remained primitive and crop
failures were frequent. The textile crafts of the Aztecs were appropriated to Spanish uses, and the weavers were congregated in
obrajes or workshops, where living and working conditions were
deplorable despite repeated laws forbidding the more injurious
practices. The obraje has been aptly described as one of the most
obnoxious of colonial institutions.

The social life of Spaniard and Indian in New Spain as elsewhere in Spanish America was largely under the control of the
clergy. Not only were the priests influential in matters of daily life
and conduct, but their supervision of education helped to perpetuate
their influence, while their special courts gave them a privileged
position with respect to their own actions. In the time of the early
zealots who embraced the strenuous life of missionaries, this was
not particularly significant. But as the church acquired more and
more property owing to the generous gifts of the wealthy, its missionary zeal suffered an unfortunate decline. On the frontiers
proselytizing activity continued with success, while in the more
civilized regions the role of the priests became vastly different. The
wealth of some of the orders attracted to them men who were not
motivated by piety or desire to sacrifice for the sake of improving the
spiritual life of others. Rivalries were strong among the religious
and the conflicts between secular and regular clergy were long and
bitter, with unfortunate consequences in the conduct of the laity.

The orders, especially the Franciscans, became the principal
protectors of the Indians almost immediately after their arrival.
Indian towns were placed under their authority in co-operation
with native officials. One of the most effective devices of the friars
was to organize the villagers into *cofradías* or brotherhoods, each
dedicated to a certain religious celebration. Participation in these
functions was eagerly sought, and membership in the cofradía was

on the basis of proper behavior. But the work of the missionaries was not without criticism and opposition.

One of the principal causes of unrest in the sixteenth century and later was the secularization of the missions, over which a struggle began about 1559. The difficulty arose because of the fact that the orders were expected to surrender their charges to secular priests after a reasonable time for indoctrination, which eventually was set at ten years. When the time for secularization came the friars resisted. In some cases the Indians rioted, probably inspired by the friars, and the feud between the regular and secular clergy occasionally threatened the land with civil war. The citizenry usually sided with the secular clergy, for they often complained that the orders planned to keep the natives in perpetual tutelage and to continue to employ their labor wastefully, when other and more profitable uses could be made of it. The power of the orders was diminished gradually, for the king usually decided against them in their quarrels with the secular clergy. And although the friars had a supportable point that ten years was not enough time to prepare Indians for 'useful' lives, the persistence of this argument for centuries weakened it considerably and ultimately raised doubts as to the friars' intentions.

Strife between civil and clerical officials was also pronounced, and these disputes anticipated the later struggle between church and state for temporal power after independence from Spain had been won. Some cabildos requested the king not to authorize the construction of additional religious houses, but without avail, for the building of ornate churches proceeded beyond a reasonable degree. The church was the principal patron of the arts and architecture of the period, and the skills of Indian craftsmen were employed in architecture, art, and music pleasing to clerical officials.

The society in New Spain was stratified almost from the outset. At the peak were the peninsulares, creoles, and a few important native caciques. Among the mixed peoples the amount of Spanish ancestry helped to determine the relative status of an individual, for the lower classes were also sharply divided. The fact that the mestizos and mulattoes and various other combinations regarded themselves as distinct groups rather than as one homogeneous mass fitted conveniently into the Spanish scheme of 'divide and rule.' When, as often happened after the unrest of the conquest period diminished, Spanish immigrants of humble birth acquired wealth by industry and married into aristocratic families, dissension increased. The creoles, while resenting their position of political inferiority, imitated the peninsulares and accepted lesser posts in the cabildos and the clergy. The City of Mexico became the haven of the wealthier creoles, who formed a part of the viceroy's court, and whose carriages and dress often exceeded in richness those of persons of high rank in Madrid.

The mestizos, who were to become the basis of a new Mexican race, were in the sixteenth century an intermediate group between creoles and Indians. They did not suffer the forced labor and payment of tribute of the latter, nor did they enjoy the social and political advantages of the former. In many ways they were little better off than the Indians, although they were freer in their movements and were able to enter certain crafts. Their influence upon the Indians was restrained by prohibiting them from living in Indian villages. Resentment against their lot increased during the colonial period as the new race gradually emerged from the early mixtures. It should be borne in mind, however, that many prominent 'creoles' were in fact mestizos. Martín Cortés, the son of the conqueror and Doña Marina, is the first of countless examples.

For the majority of the sedentary town Indians, after the modified New Laws had been put into effect, conditions of life differed little under the Spanish regime from Aztec rule, although in one respect there was considerable improvement. No longer were they faced with the threat of being 'elected' to satisfy some bloodthirsty god by having their palpitating hearts cut out with obsidian knives. The town Indians worked in textile factories or similar industries, or produced articles for trade with their own people, while peonage on the great *haciendas* or the more arduous labor in the mines was the lot of many of the rural peoples. Conditions in New Spain were more attractive than life in the motherland, and a stream of Spaniards continued to flow to the colony.

Beyond the agricultural and mining frontiers the wild tribes preyed on Spanish settlements and herds, but they were steadily pushed back into the more arid and mountainous region by a series of wars. In some cases missionaries were able to bridge the gulf between these Indians and civilization by reducing them to village life and instructing them in trades, although many natives continued living in isolated groups beyond Spanish authority.

Postponing execution of the New Laws in the time of Mendoza by no means settled the question of relationship between Spaniards and Indians in New Spain. The code was modified under the aegis of Prince Felipe, to make the laws more practical and enforceable. The Indians were declared free subjects of the king, although their freedom remained largely theoretical. Abolition of the encomienda was abandoned as too risky, but Spaniards were prohibited from using Indian labor without recompense, and Indian slavery was again outlawed. When the second viceroy, Luis de Velasco, attempted to free the Indian slaves he was met with an outcry as loud as that which had been raised by the encomenderos. Despite the fact that many of the slaves were employed in the mines, and their freedom would jeopardize that vital industry, the Council of the Indies turned a deaf ear to the delegations sent to plead for retention of their slaves. The freeing of the Indian slaves was one of those ostensibly humanitarian acts which also had powerful economic incentives — free Indians paid tribute to the king. The incorruptible Velasco emancipated an estimated 60,000 or more Indian slaves and abolished personal services in lieu of tribute.

Although the revised New Laws made the Indians technically free, 'necessary' work still had to be done. The result was the adoption of the *repartimiento* or 'division' as a means for coercing 'free' Indians into working for wages. The basic idea was that the state could require its citizenry to contribute their labor toward ends deemed necessary, and these included all of the major occupations. This labor, however, was to be paid for in cash and according to standard rates for different types of work. A part of the population of Indian communities was to be available each week for work in agriculture or in the mines. Spaniards needing laborers applied to the local corregidor or *juez de repartimiento*, who assigned the required number of men. In the sixteenth century the wages were one *real* a day for agricultural work, and twice that modest sum for mining and construction. If the Indians had depended upon wages for subsistence, their life would have been far more austere, but fortunately they raised their own foodstuffs, and they were in general better off than the European peasantry of the same era. Abuses in the system were constantly exposed by the Franciscans, who in 1594 protested so violently that the Council of the Indies began the complete codification of the labor laws, resulting in the Ordinances of 1609.

The repartimiento proved less at variance with native customs than other systems. Before the advent of the Spaniards the humbler Indians had been required to perform labors for the state and to pay tribute, so the principle was not foreign to them. The labor shortage which became chronic as the Indian population was diminished by disease and famine caused competition for laborers, especially in the mines and towns, and it was necessary to increase wages. The repartimiento proved unsuitable for the mining industry, where it was gradually replaced by free, voluntary labor. The effective enforcement of the laws by the General Indian Court, established in 1573, was another reason why the repartimiento was more acceptable to the Indians. The argument that the system prepared Indians for a status of free wage-earners, however, was unsupportable, for the growth of such a class came about in spite of, not because of, the wishes of Spanish employers.

Uneasiness as to the future intentions of the king toward the encomienda kept the encomenderos on their guard. After the death of Velasco in 1564, persistent rumors that the encomiendas were to be abolished led to plans of armed resistance and to the so-called conspiracy of the Dávila brothers and Martín Cortés. Effective leadership was lacking, and the plot was stamped out with severity. The harsh treatment of these leaders of the encomenderos signaled the triumph of the crown over the turbulent descendants of the conquerors. The humane intentions of Spanish kings remained embodied in the Laws of the Indies along with their more practical purposes, but thereafter attempts at enforcement were not serious enough to produce similar turmoils, for there was no need to weaken the encomenderos further. Although legal enslavement of the Indians declined, debt peonage began to appear even before the end of the sixteenth century. Far from being incorporated into Spanish life after the wishes of Isabel, the Indians were kept strictly apart by peninsular and creole alike.

As long as many of the Indians of New Spain lived in scattered hamlets and isolated locations, Spanish administration could not be satisfactorily imposed on them. It was difficult to win these peoples to Christianity and to collect the tribute from them. One of the obligations of encomenderos was to induce the Indians to live in towns, but since this task could not be accomplished without severe hardships and dislocations, progress was extremely slow. By the middle of the century the Council of the Indies had determined to see that the program was carried out completely. In 1584 Viceroy Moya de Contreras was ordered to concentrate the scattered native population in towns, but his reluctance to inflict additional hardships on the Indians caused him to evade the responsibility. In 1590 Luis de Velasco II, son of the former viceroy, received similar orders. He attempted to comply with them without the requisite information, and the result was chaos and confusion. Finally in 1598 the able viceroy, Count of Monterrey, assumed the task and gave it his earnest attention. Investigators were sent out to various regions to study the problem for a full year before he undertook what for the Indians was a genuine political, social, and economic upheaval.

Detailed instructions were provided for carrying out the removal. Each village was to be located where sufficient arable land, wood, and water were available, and the village was to be given at least six and one-half square miles of inalienable land. Part of it was set aside as a public pasture, like the *ejidos* of ancient Spanish towns. The administrative organization was also clearly marked out. Attendance at Mass was compulsory, as the church was the central civilizing institution. Native alcaldes and regidores were to be elected, and they were empowered to punish minor offenders. Spaniards, mestizos, mulattoes, and Negroes were prohibited from living in the Indian villages, and the villagers were forbidden to abandon the town. To protect the crops of the Indians, cattle and sheep ranches were to be kept at a safe distance.

When the plans were completed Monterrey spent the next five years carrying them out, and with reasonable success. The project had few supporters, however, for it was opposed on various grounds by the Indians, the encomenderos, and the regular clergy, who saw in it a long advance toward secularization. But the plan was realistic and practical from the point of view of Spanish administration, and the basic organization has endured for centuries where it was established.

Interest in the sea route to the Indies had never completely died out in Spain nor Europe; circumstances had merely delayed its pursuit. The expeditions sent to the East after Magellan had not accomplished the most essential task — discovering a return route. One of the survivors of the Loaisa expedition, which had sailed in 1525, was a hardy Basque named Andrés de Urdaneta. Urdaneta had remained in the East Indies engaged in trade, and he did not return to Spain until 1536. He went to New Spain and became an Augustinian friar. In 1564 Velasco urged him to take command of an expedition, but could persuade the old man to go only in an advisory capacity. Miguel López de Legazpi was given command of the fleet which sailed in the same year to conquer the Philippine islands. Legazpi remained at this task, but Urdaneta accompanied others in search of a return passage. The route he chose led them far to the north, where favorable winds carried the ship across to the coast of California. The inroads of scurvy among the crew were so severe that when they reached Acapulco hardly a man had strength enough to stand on his feet.

The way to oriental trade was at last open, and soon galleons made the incredibly long voyage between Manila and Acapulco, laden with the silks of China in exchange for the silver of New

Spain. Although the Philippine islands were thousands of miles away from New Spain, they were placed under the jurisdiction of the viceroy. An audiencia was established in Manila in 1583, and it too, for a time, remained subordinate to the viceroy of New Spain. The Manila galleon trade grew and became the source of considerable complaint by the merchants of Seville. By 1592 raw silk was brought from the Orient to New Spain, and thousands of Indians in Oaxaca, Puebla, and Mexico City were employed in silk weaving.

As the sixteenth century closed, the frontier of New Spain was pushed northward to New Mexico by Juan de Oñate, nephew of one of the great adelantados. The region had been explored by Coronado, 1540–42, after Cabeza de Vaca and three other survivors of the Narváez expedition to Florida had wandered back to New Spain with rumors of seven great cities to the north. Oñate hoped to find mines, and the sedentary Pueblo Indians promised a source of labor. But Oñate's hopes were vain, and New Mexico remained a tiny impoverished outpost, surrounded by warlike Apaches and others. In some ways the history of New Mexico and Paraguay were similar. Both were lands occupied by Indians of an intermediate culture, who were worth exploiting as a labor force despite the absence of mines. Both regions were scenes of remarkable missionary activity, and from the ranches of both stray horses and cattle gradually grew into herds of thousands, wandering over the pampas and the Great Plains. From apostate Pueblo herders the wild tribes of New Mexico learned the use of horses, a knowledge which made them almost invincible. Navahos, Apaches, and Comanches successfully marked off the limits of Spanish expansion to the north by land.

By the close of the sixteenth century Spain's hold on New Spain was firmly established. The towns founded during and after the conquest had, with few exceptions, prospered and grown. The turbulence of the period of colony-planting had subsided under the rule of capable viceroys. The desirable regions had been occupied; Indian labor made mine and plantation profitable, although the sharp decline in Indian population lessened the food supply and caused a labor shortage. In the more prosperous areas a caste system prevailed, but on the frontiers the lack of wealth was an equalizing factor. Church and state had co-operated in the task of making useful, Christian subjects of the sedentary Indians, although their relations were marred by conflicts over the exercise of temporal power. Individualism and personal interest remained strong in the Spaniards and their creole descendants, and these characteristics were too deep-rooted to be banished by the disapproving frown of a distant king.

VI

Fall of the Inca Empire

Let every one of you take heart and go forward like a good soldier, nothing daunted by the smallness of your numbers. For in the greatest extremity God ever fights for his own; and doubt not he will humble the pride of the heathen, and bring him to the knowledge of the true faith, the great end and object of the Conquest.

FRANCISCO PIZARRO TO HIS MEN, 1532 *

I will be no man's tributary. I am greater than any prince upon earth. Your emperor may be a great prince; I do not doubt it, when I see that he has sent his subjects so far across the waters; and I am willing to hold him as a brother. As for the Pope of whom you speak, he must be crazy to talk of giving away countries which do not belong to him . . .

ATAHUALPA TO PIZARRO, 1532 *

THE conquest of Peru followed the triumph in Mexico by about a decade, and the pattern set by Cortés in the rapid subjugation of the Aztecs inspired Pizarro in establishing Spanish rule over the Quechua-speaking rulers of the central Andes. Pizarro was fortunate in that the Incas, by a gradual process of conquest and 'Incaization,' had subdued and disciplined the Andean peoples. Spanish soldiers toiling through the steaming jungles of Panamá heard tantalizing tales of wondrous cities to the south. Far off in another direction stories of Inca silverwork

* Prescott, *Conquest of Peru*, various editions.

were heard by Juan Díaz de Solís and his men as they ascended the river later known as the Río de la Plata, 'River of Silver,' in hope of discovering a passage through the continent. Before Solís could reach the lands of the 'White King,' who undoubtedly was the Inca, he was killed by the Indians, and his force broke up. A few years later on his way south Magellan passed by the region without stopping, and it was not until the coming of Sebastián Cabot in 1526 that the survivors of the Solís expedition were able to relate what they had heard of Peru. By this time the movement to Peru from Panamá was already underway. Disregarding his instructions to make further explorations in the Orient, Cabot ascended the Paraguay river and founded a post at Sancti Spíritu in the same year that Pizarro was marooned on Gallo Island, near the coast of modern Ecuador, in his effort to reach Peru from Panamá. Cabot learned enough to convince him that a conquest of the White King would be rewarding, but on his return to Spain he was not given the desired authority. No one else succeeded at the project, and the opportunity to begin the conquest of Peru from the Plata region was lost.

The conquest of the Inca empire was delayed by the intense rivalry over Central America between Spaniards from Panamá and the lieutenants of Cortés from Mexico. Despite the concentration of interest upon the northwesterly regions, Pascual de Andagoya sought his fortune to the south, sailing in 1522 for a short distance down the Pacific coast. Dense mangrove forests concealed the shore, making it impossible to discover from the sea what might lie inland. Much of the delay in reaching the lands of the Incas was owing to time lost in useless landings along the northern coast. Andagoya soon abandoned the project and it was taken up by others: Francisco Pizarro, a survivor of Ojeda's colony in Darién; Diego de Almagro, another soldier of fortune; and Hernando de Luque, a priest and vicar of Panamá. They agreed that Pizarro could command the expedition, while Almagro would take charge of equipping and provisioning the ships. Luque, who obtained most of the necessary funds, had the additional and unpleasant task of keeping Pedrarias and later governors agreeable.

Although Pizarro consulted Andagoya about the regions he had visited, he, too, lost valuable time among the mangroves. The terrible hardships endured by the soldiers caused many to forsake the project, yet Pizarro's determination remained firm. Little reason was found for optimism on the first voyage, but expectations remained high, and the three men drew up a contract in which they agreed to divide equally the whole of any territory which might be conquered.

On the second voyage, which proceeded as far as Gallo Island, one of the captains sighted an Inca *balsa* or raft, on which the Indians were making a long trading voyage. The excellence of the cloth and the skillful workmanship in golden ornaments found in the cargo of this craft gave the Spaniards a strong desire to learn more of Inca civilization. But impatient though he was to see Peru, the need for provisions and reinforcements forced Pizarro to wait on Gallo Island while Almagro sought the necessary supplies and recruits in Panamá. Pizarro did not allow his starving and despondent soldiers to return to Panamá for fear that they would desert, but one smuggled a terse message to the governor indicating their plight: 'Look out, Señor Governor, For the drover while he's near, Since he goes home to get the sheep, For the butcher who stays here.'

The governor refused to permit Almagro to recruit soldiers in Panamá, for they were needed for the campaigns in Central America; instead he dispatched two ships to rescue the men remaining with Pizarro. It was on this occasion that Pizarro passed the greatest crisis in his career. Messages from Luque and Almagro promised help as soon as they could manage it. While most of his men joyfully abandoned the discouraging project Pizarro steadfastly refused to return. Drawing his sword he dramatically drew a line in the sand and declared: 'On that side are toil, hunger, nakedness, the drenching storm, desertion, and death; and on this side ease and pleasure. There lies Peru with its riches; here, Panamá and its poverty. Choose, each man, what best becomes a brave Castilian. For my part, I go to the south!' With that Pizarro stepped across the line.

Twelve men remained with Pizarro. Always on the verge of

starvation, they managed to survive for seven months until a rescue vessel finally arrived with ample provisions but no reinforcements. Following information received from the Indians who had been met on the raft, Pizarro continued directly south beyond the Bay of Guayaquil to Túmbez, an Inca town of large stone buildings surrounded by fertile, irrigated fields. Since his force was far too weak to undertake a conquest, Pizarro wisely refrained from any unfriendly act and learned as much of the Incas as possible.

When he had acquired enough information to satisfy him, Pizarro returned to Panamá. Although news of the discovery aroused excitement, he could not persuade the governor to aid in organizing an expedition for conquest. The only solution was for one of the three promoters to visit Spain and win royal support. With some obvious and justifiable misgivings on their part Luque and Almagro entrusted the task to Pizarro, who left with Luque's parting prayer that no partner should ever defraud the others! Pizarro arrived in Seville in the summer of 1528. Cortés was in Spain at the same time, and the two men talked long and earnestly about the problems of conquest, much to the advantage of Pizarro.

Affairs in Spain proceeded slowly, and it was not until early in 1530 that Pizarro departed for Panamá. He had returned to Estremadura and assembled his various half-brothers from both sides of the family, if such it may be called. His cause had been well favored by the king and his agents, and his brothers accompanied him to Panamá to share in the rewards he might reap. In the contracts made with Pizarro all of the high positions in the lands to be conquered were reserved for him, in spite of his agreement to share equally with his partners. Harsh words were spoken by Almagro, but the quarrel was smoothed over by Luque, and preparations were made for the third and final expedition. With only one hundred eighty men and twenty-seven horses, Pizarro boldly set out to conquer Peru, a land which extended from modern Colombia to the Maule river in Chile.

The Inca town of Túmbez, so prosperous a few years earlier, lay in ruins and almost deserted on Pizarro's return. The causes of its decline were the civil war raging between Atahualpa and Huáscar, rival claimants to the succession, and an epidemic that had swept away most of the coastal population. Pizarro eagerly received reports of the civil war, for it seemed likely that it would serve his purpose well. The rift had been caused by the sudden death of Huayna Capac, last of the great Inca rulers, who left the bulk of his army in the control of his favorite son, Atahualpa. The latter secured control of the province of Quito, while the remainder of the Inca realm went to Huáscar, the legitimate heir. The origin of the war between them is not clear, although it is probable that it was inspired by Atahualpa's ambitions. For Pizarro the most significant news was that shortly before his arrival Atahualpa had captured Huáscar and the ancient Inca capital of Cuzco. Atahualpa was beyond the sierra in Cajamarca when Spanish sails reappeared on the coast of Túmbez. With the advice of Cortés in mind, Pizarro decided to make the hazardous journey across the Andes without delay.

Before he could undertake a campaign into the interior it was necessary to establish a base to receive the reinforcements expected from Panamá. When San Miguel had been founded to serve this purpose, Pizarro was ready to begin the venturesome march into the forbidding Andes with a force of less than 200 men. While crossing the mountains Pizarro was visited by an emissary of Atahualpa, ostensibly to invite him to Cajamarca, but actually to determine the strength of his force. The apparent weakness of the Spanish troops allayed Atahualpa's fears, and Pizarro was permitted to advance over the difficult mountain trails unmolested. On his arrival in Cajamarca he found the campfires of the Inca army at night a terrifying sight, for the country seemed covered with enemy troops.

Because the smallness of the Spanish army gave him undue confidence Atahualpa incautiously accepted Pizarro's invitation to meet with him in Cajamarca, where he boldly went with an unarmed guard. Atahualpa, after all, had had no opportunity to talk with Montezuma. At a pre-arranged signal the Spaniards surrounded him, killed his guard, and made him prisoner.

Events moved swiftly after this coup; for his ransom Atahualpa agreed to fill one room with gold and another with silver. His offer was accepted, but by the time that the immense amount of treasure had been collected Pizarro had begun to reflect upon the likely fate of the Spaniards if Atahualpa were released. The Inca's freedom would mean the loss of Peru to Spain, and Pizarro had not come so far merely to lose his prize. Since Huáscar had been executed by agents of Atahualpa, Pizarro found it convenient to try his captive for fratricide and a score of other crimes such as polygamy. Instead of winning his release according to the agreement, Atahualpa was executed despite the protests of Hernando de Soto and other Spaniards.

To replace Atahualpa, Pizarro established as Inca Manco Capac, a son of Huáscar, and prepared to govern the natives through him. Pizarro's government was centered in Cuzco the next year, but in 1535 he founded a new capital, the City of Kings, or Lima as it was soon known, near the coast. Unlike Cuzco and the City of Mexico, Lima was not built on the site of a large native city nor in the center of a vast Indian population, with the result that it was less influenced by native culture than the other two. Other towns were founded and municipal governments established. Churches and missions were opened, and the real task of making Peru an integral part of the empire began. Spaniards were invited to settle there, and liberal grants of land and Indians in encomienda were made. Needless to say, the highly colored reports of the inexhaustible treasure attracted to Peru a multitude of adventurers who were to become a greater source of conflict and bloodshed than the docile natives.

The occupation of other parts of South America followed rapidly the settlement of Peru. Even before the founding of Lima, Pedro de Alvarado, who will be remembered as one of the most famous of the lieutenants of Cortés, was attracted by the stories coming out of Peru and organized an expedition to Quito, which he chose to regard as beyond the grant of Pizarro. Early in 1534 he landed at the Bay of Caraques with some 500 adventurers and made a laborious and costly march across the Andes to Quito. On his arrival he found that Pizarro's agent, Sebastián Benalcázar, had preceded him. Finding the rumored riches disappointing Alvarado sold his equipment and returned to his own grant in Guatemala to prepare an expedition to the Spice Islands. Benalcázar advanced the conquest northward to Popayán in modern Colombia a few years later, and pursued the quest of El Dorado to the region of Santa Fé de Bogotá in 1538.

Hernando Pizarro, who had been sent to Spain in 1534, returned with new grants from the king to his brother and to Almagro. Pizarro's grant extended 270 leagues starting far south of the San Juan river, while Almagro's territory extended for an equal distance beyond Pizarro's. In 1535 Almagro led a force through the Andes to Chile to inspect his lands. His men suffered intensely from the altitude and extreme cold, and when they found little in Chile to compensate for their sacrifices they were enraged at Pizarro. The return trip was little more endurable, for in crossing the Atacama desert, the hardships were hardly less than in the mountains. At Arequipa Almagro learned of the revolt of the puppet Inca, Manco Capac, at Cuzco. That city lay close to the dividing line of the two grants, and Almagro was persuaded to believe that it actually was within his own. On this assumption he seized the ancient capital of the Incas and claimed it for himself.

Pizarro, while pretending to negotiate in good faith with Almagro, prepared to wage war against him. By convincing the latter of his pacific intentions, he gained the needed time. The climax to the feud came in April of 1538, when Almagro was defeated on the plains of Las Salinas. The old soldier was executed and his son and followers despoiled of their lands. Though the war between the two factions was at an end, the breach between the Almagristas and Pizarros was irreparable.

While Almagro was conducting his ill-fated expedition to Chile, a Basque noble named Pedro de Mendoza began settlement of the Plata region. Late in 1535 Mendoza arrived at the mouth of the Plata with a large force of soldiers and colonists. The town which he established at Buenos Aires suffered from constant attacks by the warlike plains tribes, and was maintained only at great cost. Hoping to win a share of the silver mines of Peru, Mendoza sent a force there under Juan de Ayolas, and soon followed himself. The towns which his men founded, Corpus Christi and Señora de Buena Esperanza, were soon abandoned. Ayolas continued his march to Upper Peru while Mendoza, seriously ill, returned to Buenos Aires and embarked for Spain. Before his departure he appointed Ayolas as captain-general in his place, leaving Ruiz Galán in charge until Ayolas returned from Peru. On the way to Spain, Mendoza died.

In 1537 the men sent to inform Ayolas of Mendoza's decision built a fort at Asunción, in the country of the Guaraní Indians. Unlike most of the tribes of the Plata country, the Guaranís were relatively docile and suitable for use as a labor force. Their presence helps account for the success of the settlement of Asunción, while the absence of Indians of a similar level of culture at Buenos Aires was largely responsible for the early failure of the colony there. The Guaranís were a valuable asset to the colonists of the Plata region, and in later years they composed an effective military barrier to invasions from Brazil.

When Ayolas had begun the final stage of his journey to Peru, Domingo de Irala remained at a post named Candelaria. On his return Ayolas found the place deserted, for Irala had transferred the camp to the fort at Asunción. Ruiz Galán came from Buenos Aires at the time, and the two men fell into dispute as to which of them was properly in authority, Irala basing his claim as the representative of Ayolas and Ruiz depending upon his interim appointment from Mendoza. While they disputed Ayolas was killed by the Indians. By the time a royal official had arrived from Spain with instructions from the king for the colonists to elect their own representative if Mendoza had not named one, Irala, one of the most capable colonial officials in the service of Spain, already had taken charge of the colony. He now concentrated the remnants of Mendoza's forces in Asunción. By 1541 the settlement of Buenos Aires was abandoned. Other posts were established, such as Ontiveras near the frontier of Brazil, and Santa Cruz de la Sierra in the lower mountain regions of Upper Peru.

A remarkable feature of the colonization of the Plata region was that it became the meeting place of Spaniards from various directions as well as Portuguese from Brazil. The men brought by Mendoza, disappointed adventurers from Peru, and colonists sent across the Andes from Chile gave the region local rivalries and the towns a spirit of provincialism and competition which endured into the modern period. Rivalry with the Portuguese and Brazilians was also a common theme in the Plata region. Another aspect of the area was the turbulent, independent spirit displayed by the townspeople on various occasions. The deposition of governors and election of their successors was not unusual in the sixteenth century. The king was little concerned with an area which produced only cowhides, while the viceroy in Lima regarded it as a convenient place to dispose of incorrigible trouble-makers who had flocked to Peru. In the century of the conquest Asunción had little to recommend it to Spaniards except Indians available for labor.

Except for the Guaraní revolt of 1547 Irala's relations with the Indians were pacific and successful. Realizing the need for an increase in the number of Spaniards in the colony and at the same time its limited attractions for colonists, he legalized polygamy, setting an example himself by marrying numerous Indian women. The offspring of these unions were regarded as creoles, although the colonial population was characterized as much by Indian cultural traits as by those of Spain. Irala's laws for obtaining the submission of the Indians were wise, and during his administration the encomienda system was more nearly consonant with the wishes of Carlos I than was usual. Irala was, furthermore, as the first popularly elected governor of the area, a maker of traditions.

Since Asunción seemed likely to be the only colonial center in the area it was made the seat of a bishopric, the first bishop taking office in 1555. Making Asunción a center of ecclesiastical authority helped to give the region even greater independence from the remote viceroy of Peru and the Audiencia of Charcas in Upper Peru.

After Almagro's misadventure in Chile and his subsequent fatal revolt, Pizarro dispatched Pedro de Valdivia, a veteran of the conquests of Venezuela and Peru, to found a settlement in Almagro's grant. In 1540 he founded the town of Santiago in the central Chilean valley, where the Indians were agricultural, but his efforts to subdue the Araucanians in the south were fruitless. Their resistance had prevented the Incas from advancing beyond the Río Maule. Valdivia, however, struck boldly across the Maule and Bío Bío and founded a number of towns. Concepción lay near the mouth of the Bío Bío, but Imperial, Valdivia, Angol, and Villarica were south of that river. These towns were abandoned and re-occupied several times during the chronic Indian wars of the sixteenth and seventeenth centuries. After his death at the hands of the Indians in 1553, Valdivia's successors temporarily recrossed the Bío Bío and advanced as far south as the archipelago of Chiloé. They crossed the Andes and founded the towns of San Juan and Mendoza in the foothills of Argentina, as this region lay within Valdivia's grant.

While the conquest of Chile was under way, turbulence and violence in Peru increased. The Almagrista faction, led by Almagro's son, smarting from frequent affronts by Pizarro and his followers, attacked the old man in his home and assassinated him. Vaca de Castro, a royal official sent from Spain to help Pizarro establish order in Peru, refused to negotiate with young Almagro, and in the battle which ensued Almagro was taken prisoner, and later executed.

Vaca de Castro's next problem was to appease the encomenderos, who resented any serious attempt to restrict their control of the Indians. Their agitation increased when news of the promulgation of the New Laws reached Peru. The encomenderos rallied about Gonzalo Pizarro, a brother of the conqueror, who reluctantly accepted the leadership of the movement, although his greatest concern at the moment was in developing the silver mines.

Carlos I, perceiving ominous signs of the gathering storm in Peru, sent as his first viceroy to that region Blasco Núñez Vela, whose lack of tact and moderation proved unfortunate. Before arriving in Peru he aroused serious opposition by the humane but ill-considered act of freeing some 300 Indian slaves brought by their owners to Panamá. By acting in this peremptory fashion, without becoming better informed about the conditions and prejudices of the people he was to govern, he jeopardized his chances of accomplishing his mission. His uncompromising manner solidified the encomenderos against him, and they were in consternation over his coming.

After his arrival in Peru, Blasco Núñez stirred the encomenderos to violence by his severe policy. Gonzalo Pizarro led the offensive against him, but before the opposing forces clashed in battle the Audiencia of Lima had deposed the viceroy. In October of 1544 Gonzalo Pizarro entered Lima to be proclaimed governor of Peru. By his actions he had become a rebel against royal authority. He sent Vaca de Castro and Blasco Núñez to Spain under guard with the hope that the king could be persuaded to show compassion to the encomenderos. Pizarro's expectations in this regard suffered a grave disappointment when Vaca de Castro escaped from custody and Blasco Núñez was released by the official of the audiencia conducting him to Spain. The viceroy, greatly incensed at the indignities he had suffered in Peru, invoked the aid of other colonies and went to Quito to prepare an onslaught against Pizarro and the encomenderos.

After being proclaimed governor Pizarro quickly established his authority in Peru and made preparations for its defense. Almost without opposition he absorbed the powers of the Audiencia of Lima. The return of Blasco Núñez was a bitter disappointment to him, for it precluded a peaceful settlement of the issue, and Pizarro was loath to regard himself as actually in rebellion against the king. In Quito the viceroy was assured of the support of Benalcázar, who was now governor of Popayán, after which he felt safe in marching to the coast and setting up his standard at San Miguel, where Francisco Pizarro had begun his epochal march to Cajamarca. By this time Blasco Núñez had assembled a force of about 500 men, and felt ready to commence hostilities. Finding the enemy already close at hand, however, he discreetly recrossed the mountains to Quito, hotly pursued by Pizarro, until he found safety with Benalcázar in Popayán. In January of 1546 the two armies met in battle at Añaquito. Pizarro won a complete victory, his opponent falling on the battlefield.

The triumph at Añaquito left Pizarro unchallenged in his authority from Panamá to Chile. His followers, who seem to have been satisfied with his government, pointed out to him that he had already gone too far to turn back, and urged him to take the next logical step of renouncing his allegiance to the king. He considered marrying an Inca princess and establishing an independent monarchy, but the idea of avowed rebellion was still abhorrent to him, and he continued to pursue the futile hope of winning royal approval of his course. His wish in this respect was vain, for the breach was irreparable.

The problem of restoring order in Peru was a perplexing one for Carlos I and his ministers, for Spain was greatly concerned at the moment with more immediate dangers, and could ill afford to detach military forces for use in South America. Pizarro, an early precursor of Latin American 'caudillismo,' was also reminiscent of the insubordinate nobles of Castile, whose subjugation had been a crucial problem for Isabel, and who were still a menace to royal authority. The king summoned a council of eminent and experienced men to discuss suitable methods for dealing with the encomenderos. They agreed that Pizarro's actions called for retribution of the kind that distance and other conditions made impracticable. Conciliatory methods offered the greatest possibility of success, humiliating as this procedure might be. Such a course depended upon the skill and tact of the official sent to carry it out, for if he could not persuade most of the Spaniards in Peru to rally to the royal standard, restoration of authority would be accomplished only by the unpleasant recourse of yielding to rebels. The question was particularly delicate because any show of force might induce the encomenderos to abandon their pretended loyalty to Spain and carry their movement to its logical conclusion.

The choice of the priest Pedro de la Gasca for the critical mission proved wise. As a member of the Council of the Inquisition Gasca had demonstrated remarkable skill and impartiality which had won him widespread recognition and missions of trust. For the hazardous project he was asked to undertake in Peru he sought no reward, but wisely demanded that he be given full authority not only in making decisions but in putting them into execution. Carlos I assented, and Gasca departed clothed with extraordinary powers which could be revealed if occasion demanded. As president of the audiencia he had legal charge of the civil, judicial, and military departments of

the colony. In addition he was given sweeping powers with regard to the appointment or removal of officials and the granting of
repartimientos. Of utmost importance were the instructions he carried to announce the cancellation of the most onerous parts of the
New Laws. The most unusual powers given him, however, were in
the form of blank letters bearing the king's signature which could be
filled in according to need.

Gasca's preparations for his enormous and perilous task were surprisingly simple, for he avoided any show of authority which might
arouse fears in Peru. Not long after landing at Santa Marta in
July, 1546, he learned of Pizarro's victory at Añaquito and of the
death of Blasco Núñez. The absence of the unpopular viceroy was
fortunate for Gasca, for he was spared from having to link his
interests with one so much distrusted in Peru. Gasca's modest demeanor and concealment of his immense authority disarmed his
opponents, for in him they could perceive no serious peril. In
Panamá Gasca delayed, for Pizarro's fleets dominated the waters
between that land and Peru. He set about winning over Pizarro's
officers with whom he came in contact by calming their fears of
royal vengeance. While he was involved in the gradual process of
inducing them to support him in reward for amnesty, Gasca planted
the seeds of disunion in Peru by secretly introducing proclamations
which reminded the adherents of Pizarro of the perilous course they
were taking. These papers served their purpose well, and Pizarro
too late discovered the disaffection thus caused in the ranks of his
followers. Carbajal, his most astute aide, called the broadsides 'more
to be dreaded than the lances of Castile,' and endeavored to steel
Pizarro for the ordeal which faced him. The defections of his
officers disturbed Pizarro profoundly, but he refused to turn back
and seek royal grace.

When Pizarro's admirals had been completely won over, Gasca
prepared for the most crucial part of his undertaking, the voyage
to Peru. In June, 1547, he arrived at Túmbez. Gonzalo Pizarro,
attempting to abandon Peru for Chile, met one of Gasca's forces
barring the way. The battle fought on the high plains of Huarina,
near Lake Titicaca, ended in a victory for Pizarro only because of

the skillful leadership of the veteran Carbajal. Much encouraged
by the triumph, Pizarro returned to Cuzco. Despite this failure on
the part of royal forces, reinforcements continued to join Gasca.
From the north came Benalcázar, while Valdivia, conqueror of
Chile, arrived from the south. The latter's support was vital, for
he was regarded as the ablest soldier in Peru.

Early in 1548 Gasca marched on Cuzco. In the brief encounter
which took place near the city Pizarro's forces deserted and left
him with no recourse but to surrender. Carbajal and Pizarro were
executed for their rashness, and others were punished severely. Victorious Gasca was as much troubled by the problem of rewarding
his supporters, who considered him ungenerous, as in chastising
his opponents. His interest in the welfare of the Indians — he dispatched inspectors to various regions to report upon the treatment
of the natives — was regarded as ungracious conduct on his part
and a poor reward for the efforts of his supporters. He decided upon
a uniform system of taxation for the Indians lighter than formerly
imposed by their own chiefs, but although the idea of personal
service on the part of the Indians was abhorrent to him, Gasca
prudently did not forbid it. That he was able to place limitations
upon the amount and nature of the service, however, was an important step in the preservation of the natives. Outright enslavement was prohibited.

The mission of Pedro de la Gasca had been accomplished skillfully and tactfully. Rebellion was severely punished at little cost
to the royal treasury, and the country was fairly tranquil for the
first time under Spanish rule. His task concluded, Gasca lost little
time in surrendering his authority to the audiencia pending the
appointment of a successor. He was generally applauded for his
invaluable services to the king. Indeed, in an age of universal violence, his pacification of Peru was an amazing feat, in some ways
overshadowing the more dramatic exploits of Cortés and Pizarro.

In 1551 Antonio de Mendoza ended his long career in New Spain
to become viceroy of Peru. Seriously handicapped by ill health, he
nevertheless continued the wise policies he had followed in New
Spain. He set about learning the condition of the natives employed

in the mines, and endeavored to give them some relief from the harsh and devastating labor. His brief rule was not without grave problems. Against his judgment the audiencia rashly put into execution an order prohibiting personal service on the part of the natives. In the midst of the resulting turmoil Mendoza died, and Peru fell again into costly disorders. There were about 8000 Spaniards in Peru, but less than 500 of them possessed grants of land and Indians. The bulk of the remainder were landless adventurers and a constant source of trouble.

After a troubled interval of two years, the country was placed under the charge of another able viceroy, Andrés Hurtado de Mendoza, whose activities were concerned largely with restoration of domestic order and further exploration and settlement. His rule was severe but effective, and lawlessness sharply declined. Diego Hurtado de Mendoza, the viceroy's son, was appointed governor of Chile in 1557, and his attention was concentrated upon the wars with the Araucanians. Although both father and son seem to have been successful administrators, complaints of partisan opponents reached the ear of Felipe II, whose suspicious nature made him reluctant to permit such concentration of power in a single family. In 1560 both were recalled, and an audiencia temporarily governed Chile. The viceroy was replaced by a governor, Lope García de Castro, who divided the country into districts under corregidores. In Chile the warfare with the Araucanians went against the Spaniards, and by 1598 all posts south of the Bío Bío were abandoned.

During the second half of the sixteenth century the Huancavelica mercury mines were discovered, a fact which greatly stimulated silver production, for the use of mercury in the extraction of silver had already been introduced. Another event was the coming of English seamen to the Pacific, led by Sir Francis Drake and Thomas Cavendish, whose raids on coastal towns on the Pacific caused an attempt by Spain to occupy and fortify the Strait of Magellan. Expeditions under Alvaro de Mendaña from Peru led to the discovery of the Solomon Islands and an unsuccessful attempt to establish a colony there shortly before the close of the century.

By far the most famous of the sixteenth-century viceroys of Peru was Francisco de Toledo, whose penchant for lawmaking earned him the title 'Solon of Peru.' A man of unusual energy and remarkable devotion to duty, he concerned himself especially with the problem of controlling the Indians. Believing that Spanish rule must remain insecure as long as the natives were permitted to retain their veneration for ancient practices, he had their laws and customs studied with a view to eliminating those which seemed unsuitable. During his long rule the Incas rebelled under a young chief named Tupac Amaru, who was captured and executed.

In attempting to bridge the gap between Spanish rule and Indian custom Toledo left local administration in the hands of native chieftains, who collected the tribute and provided men for labor in the mines under the mita system. The Spaniards adopted the arrangement from the natives, but extended it to include private enterprises as well as public works. Toledo planned to settle the Indians in small villages according to their special skills, such as villages of carpenters and silversmiths. Each was to have a priest, a church, and a hospital, and Indian caciques were given commissions as justices. These officials were free from arrest by the corregidores except for serious crimes. The plan was not fully carried out, but Spanish authority over the Quechuas increased through Toledo's measures. They were, in fact, reduced to complete subservience. Toledo's success in destroying the social order of the Incas and his elimination of native princes who might serve as tools for rebellious Spaniards moved the half-Spanish Inca Garcilaso de la Vega to write his celebrated *Royal Commentaries* on the life and history of his mother's people.

While Toledo eliminated the sources of possible native opposition in Peru by severe methods, he built up the Plata region by sending there the troublesome element of the Spanish population. The potential trouble-makers were sent to battle the Indians of northwestern Argentina, and in the decade after 1582 Salta, La Rioja, La Madrid, and Jujuy were founded. The establishment of the last-named town consolidated the conquest of the warlike Indians in this region.

After the abandonment of Buenos Aires in the time of Irala several attempts were made to found a port settlement. Expeditions were sent in the 1560's and 1570's but none succeeded. In 1573 Santa Fé was founded by a small force from Asunción led by Juan de Garay. The people of the northwest were also engaged in building a line of towns to the sea, but they arrived on the scene too late. A delegation from Córdoba unsuccessfully claimed Santa Fé in the name of Gerónimo Luis Cabrera, whose grant from Toledo included the region. In 1580 Garay refounded Buenos Aires, and for a time commerce came legally into the Plata from the Atlantic. The merchants of Seville, Lima, and Nombre de Dios protested the use of Buenos Aires as a port, and succeeded in persuading the king to restrict its use to occasional licensed ships.

By the end of the sixteenth century strays from the ranches of Paraguay had already produced herds of wild horses and cattle which moved slowly across the plains to the south. Killing these animals for their hides and tallow became one of the principal activities of the area, although the cabildo of Buenos Aires solemnly announced that the wild herds belonged exclusively to the descendants of the conquerors.

The towns of the viceroyalty of Peru were well on their way to stability by the close of the century, although those of Chile and Argentina were small and frequently under attack by Indians. The commercial restrictions which prevented Buenos Aires from becoming the principal entry point for commerce in the Plata region retarded economic development and encouraged illegal enterprises. Buenos Aires, nevertheless, already had surpassed Asunción in political and economic importance by 1600. Commerce among Tucumán, Santiago, and Potosí had been going on since the 1560's, and it gave the interior cities relatively greater importance than they would have had if Buenos Aires had been an open port.

Jujuy, which was supported by its mule and cattle ranches and its soap factories, had only about 100 Spaniards, most of whom were concerned in trade with Potosí. Tucumán was somewhat larger, a number of near-by Indian villages supplying labor. Santiago del Estero was larger still, some 400 Spaniards and mestizos as well as Indians and Negroes in greater number making up its population.

The weaving of coarse cloth and blankets for trade with Potosí and the usual cattle and mule ranches occupied the residents. In Córdoba, the commercial center of the interior, the principal business was providing mules and cloth for the mining regions to the north.

Asunción still had more than 600 Spanish residents, 250 of whom were encomenderos, in whose service were thousands of Indians. The town was well supplied with religious institutions, for in addition to a cathedral it had houses of Dominicans, Franciscans, Mercedarians, and Jesuits. The Jesuits maintained instruction for the inhabitants in a seminary and a *colegio* or academy. The town also had a hospital and a home for orphan girls. Many Indian villages supplied the labor needed for the sugar plantations, wheat farms, citrus groves, and vineyards.

In Chile, too, the Spanish residents were notably few in number. Concepción, which was the usual residence of the governors, due to their preoccupation with carrying on warfare against the Araucanians, had only 200 Spaniards.

None of the towns of Argentina and Chile had large Spanish populations in 1600, and their location on the extreme frontier gave them a measure of political independence, or more properly, neglect, which permitted the emergence of political practices different from those of Peru. For example, the idea that the inhabitants had the right to select or depose their governors was persistent in the Plata region.

Cuzco, the former 'Rome' of the Inca empire, was much more impressive than the small towns of the Plata region and Chile. Its Spanish population probably reached nearly 3000 while the number of mestizos was even larger. More than 14,000 Indians resided in the city, still more living in the environs. Numerous religious houses had been established in Cuzco, and the Indian General Hospital founded in 1555 was considered one of the finest in Spanish America.

In Upper Peru the great estates were known as *chacras,* and the Indians attached to them were called *yanaconas.* Viceroy Toledo had ordered these Indians to live permanently on the chacras to which they were assigned. The owners of the land were required to

provide them with garden plots and instruction in Christian doctrines, and to pay their tribute to the crown. Life on the chacras
was preferable to labor in the mines, and Indians frequently chose
attachment to the former to escape the latter. By royal decree the
yanaconas were classed as free laborers, but in actual practice they
were bound to the soil and restricted in other ways.

The most spectacular city in the viceroyalty of Peru was its
capital, Lima, the 'City of Kings' of Pizarro. Blessed by an equable
climate and endowed with fruitful soil, the city and region supported a sizable population. As the residence of the viceroy, the
audiencia, the archbishop, and the Holy Office, it was the political
and social center of the kingdom. The political domain of the
viceroy was enormous, for the viceroyalty of Peru included all of
Spanish South America except part of the Caribbean coast. By
1600 upwards of 9000 Spaniards resided in Lima, in addition to the
constant stream of travelers which passed through. There were
nearly 50,000 Negroes, mulattoes, and other castes of the service
class and thousands of Indians. The chief sources of revenue of the
viceregal government were import and export duties, the alcabala,
and tribute paid by the Indians.

A multitude of religious institutions were supported, including
seminaries, colegios, and schools of other types providing education
for the more fortunate sons of the conquering class. The members
of the religious orders supplied what charitable institutions there
were, among them one for the relief of poor persons in prisons, who
were provided with food and defended in court by lawyers. The
hospital for the Indians boasted a thousand beds. Other hospitals
were dedicated for specific purposes, like the one for sick sailors
which was supported by a share of the profits and freight charges
of ships entering the port of Callao.

The famed University of San Marcos, founded in the time of
Carlos I, provided the training customary in that day, but in
addition it taught Indian languages to students preparing to become parish priests. The granting of doctor's degrees was one of
the most imposing celebrations of any year. The city's nobility
provided an escort for the candidate; banners were hung, while

trumpets, flageolets, and bugles blared, and processions marched for several days. A number of royal schools provided secondary education for Lima's young men of good family. Less impressive than these and located on the outskirts of the city was a Jesuit school for Indian boys, sons of chiefs and others of high standing, who were instructed in 'good manners, Christian doctrine, reading, writing, and music.'

At the close of the century of conquest, solid gains in colony building had been made in each of the regions of the viceroyalty. Vast differences which existed among the various Indian civilizations were carried over into the Hispanic epoch, so that colonial society was far from uniform. Rivalry between regions was intensified by Spanish individualism, tribal antagonisms, and geographic obstacles. Regional distinctions appeared early and became more pronounced as one generation succeeded another. The viceroyalty of Peru was more a geographical than political expression, for the viceroys in Lima could not have exercised much authority over their far-flung subjects in the hinterlands even if they had tried. Most were content to have their own and the king's rule acknowledged, and to leave well enough alone. The result was that the office of viceroy of Peru appeared much more potent than it was in fact.

VII

The Battle for Brazil

We are obliged to conquer by inches the lands your Majesty
granted us by leagues.

DUARTE COELHO *

THE existence of South America was not even
known to Spain and Portugal when the treaty
of Tordesillas unintentionally gave the latter nation grounds for
a claim to Brazil. By this treaty the Line of Demarcation was moved
so that it accidentally crossed Brazil. Probably more than one Spanish expedition had sighted the Brazilian coast before the arrival
of Pedro Alvares Cabral; at least Pinzón, a veteran of Columbus'
first voyage, visited the region of modern Pernambuco three months
earlier. But the Spaniards were preoccupied with reaching the
Orient, and saw little in Brazil to detain them.

The Portuguese discovery occurred after the return of Vasco da
Gama from India, when a much larger expedition was prepared and
placed under Cabral's command. His course around Africa was
purposely far wider than that of da Gama in the hope of enjoying
more favorable winds. Storms swept his ships farther west than
he had planned, and late in April, 1500, a landfall was made which
the Portuguese admiral assumed was a large island. The accidental
discovery of Brazil by Portuguese navigators on their way to the
Orient by the African route suggests that the Americas would

* From Bailey W. Diffie, *Latin American Civilization*, The Stackpole Company, Harrisburg, 1947, p. 646.

not have remained unknown for long even if Spain had not employed Columbus to seek a westward passage to the Indies.

After exploring the coast until a safe harbor was found, Cabral dispatched a ship to Portugal to inform the king of his discovery. He put two *degredados* or exiles ashore to learn the customs of the natives, and continued his voyage to India. The degredados learned little from the Indians of that region except their attachment to the loathsome custom of cannibalism. On receiving Cabral's report the king sent other ships piloted by Amerigo Vespucci to explore the country further and to determine its value. Nothing of unusual interest was seen, especially in comparison to the Spice Islands of the East. Vespucci sailed south nearly to the Strait of Magellan before returning to Portugal. He visited Brazil again the following year, and after no better fortune in finding economic attractions, he left some men among the Indians and carried away a cargo of brazilwood. Despite the difficulties in cutting dyewoods, the demand for dyes in the European textile industries made dyewood a valuable commodity. The king granted Fernão de Noronha, a Portuguese noble of Jewish extraction, a concession to exploit the brazilwood. French adventurers learned from the cargoes of Portuguese ships they captured the new source of dyewood, and soon sailed to collect it directly in Brazil.

At the time of Brazil's discovery Portugal had a long experience in overseas enterprises, depite her small size and limited resources. In 1500 her oriental undertakings promised far greater reward than did the exploitation of Brazil. Portuguese attention corresponded to the relative promise of the areas under consideration, making it appear that she completely lacked interest in South America. Portuguese neglect, however, has been exaggerated. For more than a century after the discovery Brazil was the prize in a costly struggle between Portuguese on the one hand and Indians, French, and Dutch on the other. Had Brazil been so completely neglected as is sometimes stated, its modern language probably would have been French or Dutch rather than Portuguese. That tiny Portugal was able by gradual steps to conquer and maintain so vast a land against Indian, French, and Dutch opposition was a tribute to her ability and tenacity, although good fortune aided her against her competitors.

In the years from the discovery of Brazil until the colonial proprietorships were granted, the foundation for settlement was established by Portuguese adventurers, degredados, and brazilwood cutters who occupied scattered points along the extensive coast. The French, encouraged by their monarch's refusal to acknowledge the papal division of newly discovered lands between Spain and Portugal, took an active interest not only in the spice-laden caravels from India, but in Brazil as well. They were content at first with trading and collecting dyewood, but their increasing numbers and their influence with the Indians posed a serious threat. Noronha's concession for exploiting brazilwood carried an obligation to defend 300 leagues of coast, a task for which his resources were insufficient. When it was found that coastal defense was beyond the ability of private individuals, the king assumed it, and sent a coast guard to eradicate the French threat. As this danger increased later in the century other steps were taken to counteract it.

The greatest immediate danger was from the numerous Indians. Compared to the natives of Mexico, Central America, and Peru, those of Brazil were exceedingly primitive. Hunting, fishing, and a little planting provided for their simple wants. Cannibalism was common among them, and the taste for human flesh lingered. The principal coastal tribes were all of the Tupí-Guaraní linguistic family, but a common language did not incline them toward peace. The fact that inter-tribal wars were as chronic in Brazil as in other regions of the New World benefited the Portuguese as it did Cortés in New Spain, for it enabled the conquerors to win essential allies in the struggle for Brazil. By a system of barter the Portuguese obtained native food and labor, but dependence upon Indian allies for protection made it unwise to enslave them. For this reason extensive enslavement of Indians was delayed until the establishment of sizable colonies and the introduction of industries requiring large and inexpensive labor forces.

The problems of colonization in Brazil were enormous, for while much of the land promised little hope of immediate reward, thousands of hostile Indians inspired by equally belligerent Frenchmen made military defense of paramount importance. The rival attractions of the Orient were far superior to those of Brazil, and early hopes of discovering mines were in vain. The French activities posed a continuous threat; neither protests to the French court nor severe treatment of Frenchmen caught in Brazilian waters discouraged their coming. By 1530 Portuguese officials realized that concerted action was necessary to avoid the loss of Brazil by default to France. Happily for Portugal the French were concerned only with holding small posts for trade with the Indians and collecting brazilwood. Only their Indian allies made them militarily formidable, but attacks led by Frenchmen on Portuguese *feitorias*, trading posts, emphasized the need for more effective occupation of the land.

Dom João III initiated action to prevent the loss of Brazil to France. He dispatched a squadron commanded by Martim Afonso de Sousa to expel the French, make a survey of the coast, and prepare recommendations on appropriate methods of colonization. Before sailing south to establish his own settlement of São Vicente, Martim Afonso de Sousa built a small fort at the site of the future Rio de Janeiro and established a temporary post at Bahia. In the meantime Dom João relied on earlier experience in the Azores and Madeiras and resolved to introduce into Brazil the policy of dividing the land into captaincies. These captaincies were granted to *donatários*, individuals who were expected to carry on the colonization at their own expense.

The donataries who engaged in the occupation of their grants in the 1530's profited from the experiences and knowledge of numerous Portuguese who had settled among the Indians and who had escaped an unpleasant fate at the hands of cannibals. Two of the early 'squawmen' were especially noteworthy. They were Diogo Alvares, known to the Indians as 'Caramurú,' who had lived among them near the later site of Bahia since about 1510, and João Ramalho, who was met at the site of São Vicente by Martim Afonso de Sousa. These men and others like them played an important role in persuading the Indians to assist the newcomers, while their numerous progeny provided half-caste wives for the colonists. The half-breed men proved a turbulent group in later years, for they scorned the authority of both state and church.

One great advantage to the king in the captaincy system was its slight expense yet considerable promise of success. The land was divided into fifteen captaincies, most of which extended fifty leagues along the coast and penetrated the interior to the Line of Demarcation.

The donataries, in return for sweeping political powers comparable to those of medieval barons, were obliged to found settlements on their own initiative and by their own resources. During the 1530's some of them sent colonists to their extensive domains only to find that the fulfillment of their obligations was extremely difficult and costly. Many donataries ignored the grants, refusing to risk their wealth in such hazardous and unpromising ventures.

In addition to the political powers the donataries received as their personal property ten leagues of tax-free land along the coast. They enjoyed a monopoly of all mills, and their exclusive manorial privileges provided further economic incentives. The donatary system has been aptly called a combination of medieval political power and an element of the rising sixteenth-century capitalism.

The first task of the colonists was construction of a fort, for even though the Indians might welcome them in the beginning, their mercurial nature made a fortification a vital safeguard. Next a wall was built to enclose the homes of the settlers. After these initial steps it was possible to proceed with the construction of warehouses near the waterfront, a church, a customs house, and a jail. The donatary granted land to his colonists in exchange for payment of the tithe. The agricultural activities engaged in were of two types: *roças*, small farms for raising foodstuffs for local consumption, and *fazendas* for raising exportable plantation crops. In the sixteenth century manioc, an easily grown starchy tuber widely used by the natives, was the common product of the roças, while sugar and cotton were grown on the fazendas.

Competition between fazendeiros and brazilwood cutters for Indian workmen soon became keen. As the natives began to demand more costly items, including firearms and swords, the system grew less satisfactory. Distributing weapons among the uncontrollable Indians threatened the safety of the settlements. Since the practice of enslaving prisoners was known to the natives, the fazendeiros began purchasing Indian captives as an answer to their labor problem. At first these were limited to enemy tribes, but famine and smallpox weakened the friendly tribes and permitted the extension of slavery among those on whom the Portuguese had once relied for defense.

Martim Afonso de Sousa's settlement at São Vicente was one of the first to show promise of success, for earlier Portuguese and Spanish adventurers had already established satisfactory relations with the Indians. In spite of the difficulties he faced, Duarte Coelho also founded a successful colony at Pernambuco. By 1548 only two other settlements were firmly established, Ilhéos and Espírito Santo. All of the Portuguese remained within a short distance of the coast, for there was little incentive to penetrate the interior, and it was necessary to keep open lines of communication with Portugal.

Portuguese commercial regulations for Brazil differed from those of Spain. Except for certain articles which were a royal monopoly, Brazilians could send their products to Portuguese or foreign ports by permission of the donataries. Foreign vessels paid higher duties than those of Portugal, but the fact that freer commerce was permitted gave Brazilians an advantage over their Spanish American contemporaries.

Though the captaincy system failed to accomplish a miracle in peopling Brazil, it did preserve the land for Portugal. The Indian problem differed in each captaincy; in some the natives were fairly peaceful and tractable, while elsewhere they were warlike and troublesome. During the half-century after the discovery of Brazil, the colony was recognized as worth retaining, but the system of captaincies afforded little opportunity for unity in defense or in promoting colonial development. The settlements were virtually islands, with little communication among them. By 1548 the king resolved to abolish the political powers of the donataries without depriving them of their lands and to establish direct royal control by means of a governor-general.

The creation of a captaincy-general in 1549 did not immediately solve all problems which disturbed Brazil under the regime of the donataries. The enormous extent of territory and the limited means of communication continued to hinder the colony's progress. The introduction of the governor-general, however, was an important step in forming a single nation instead of a group of independent ones. In 1549 as in 1530 the king was still faced with the choice of making greater efforts to occupy Brazil and exclude the French or loss of the country. The principal duty of the governor-general was to co-ordinate and unify the defense. Complaints against the arbitrariness of the donataries also accounted for the establishment of the captaincy-general.

During the captaincy period a variety of crops were introduced into Brazil, but none were profitably grown. The planting of sugar cane was tried on a small scale earlier, but many years of experimentation were necessary before it became important. In 1549 under Tomé de Sousa, the first royal governor and captain-general, sugar growers were granted a ten-year tax exemption. Within a short time sugar was the basis of Brazilian prosperity, and the colony became the first large-scale producer of sugar in the world.

The interior remained largely unknown. A few expeditions in search of minerals were fruitless, and there was no other incentive for conquest of the hinterland. Even in the coastal area Indian raids on settlements and fazendas continued, and any attempt to move inland was certain to involve constant resistance.

Tomé de Sousa's military force was wholly inadequate for unifying Portuguese authority and defending the land. The vastness of the country alone was a major obstacle, and conquering the multitude of hostile tribes was impossible. The enslavement of friendly Indians jeopardized the alliances upon which the Portuguese relied, and Sousa was ordered to prohibit it in the future. The governor's position on Indian slavery was complicated by yet another order of the king to extend Portuguese authority and make Brazil a paying enterprise. Since the two demands seemed incompatible, Sousa

was forced to temporize and to compromise between them. The
need for friendly allies around the settlements remained, and
Sousa limited enslavement of Indians to captives taken in 'just'
wars, a restriction often difficult to uphold.

Sousa brought 1000 colonists, and his capital at Bahia was soon
a prosperous center. It proved a fortunate choice for a colony,
since it had long been the home of Caramurú, and the multitude
of half-breed children sired by this Portuguese castaway as well as
his influence in tribal councils assisted the colonists in establishing
themselves quickly. Fleets from Portugal brought reinforcements
of troops, additional colonists, and Negro slaves. Orphaned girls
of noble families were sent to Bahia to be given in marriage to
officials of the colony. Livestock was introduced and soon became
plentiful. Native crops such as manioc, tobacco, cotton, and corn
were grown, and cane planting on a large scale begun. The Dutch
were soon interested in the sugar trade and occasionally furnished
vessels for Portuguese commerce with Brazil.

Priests of the recently founded Society of Jesus, including Manuel
da Nóbrega and José de Anchieta, accompanied Sousa. The role
of Jesuits in sixteenth-century Brazil was important despite the
smallness of their number. Since their influence upon scattered
and wandering groups could not be great, they proposed the
reduction of the Indians to village life, which proposal was compatible with the governor's plan to surround the Portuguese settlements with a barrier of friendly peoples. The Jesuits immediately
began the humane works among the Indians for which they have
been justly famous, although their success was undermined by the
Portuguese themselves.

The most grievous shortcomings of the natives in the eyes of the
priests were polygamy and cannibalism, both of which the Indians
were reluctant to abandon. Cannibalism was celebrated with elaborate ritual and associated with warfare. While seeking assistance of
the Indians in defense of the settlements, the Portuguese were
forced to ignore undesirable customs, just as Cortés felt obliged
to overlook the practice of human sacrifice among the Tlaxcalans.
Polygamy was also a venerable custom, and the informal arrange-

ments of the Portuguese with native women weakened the arguments of the priests in favor of monogamy. Under Tomé de Sousa
and some later governors the Jesuits were given official support in
their program, but at other times they faced recrimination and
complaint. Owing to their influence over the Indians, however,
the Jesuits became valuable agents of the governors. Their services
in winning over previously hostile tribes were often decisive.

The rise of the sugar industry gave Brazil an aristocratic society
centered around the fazendas. Cane planting required great tracts of
land and a supply of cheap labor. Small farmers continued producing foodstuffs, but their role was less important. Although some
of the labor on fazendas was still voluntary, Indian slavery was beginning to take its place. The prosperity of plantations worked
by Indian slaves demonstrated the possibility of a successful agricultural economy in Brazil. The increase in enslavement in turn
led to growing hostility of the Indians and to a series of destructive
wars that brought several captaincies near to ruin. For their opposition to Indian slavery the Jesuits faced furious retaliation by
both fazendeiros and slave-raiders.

The growth of the sugar industry greatly increased the demand
for slaves. Despite prohibitions against enslavement of peaceful
and friendly tribes, slave-raiders hastened to supply the demand
wherever Indians were available. Providing slaves for the fazendas
became a lucrative occupation for the half-breed inhabitants of
São Paulo. These paulistas invaded the Guaraní country on the
Paraná in the 1550's, but were defeated and turned back by Irala,
who set up outposts to check their advance.

French interest in Brazil continued strong, and soon after the
captaincy-general had been created French Huguenots established
a colony on an island near modern Rio de Janeiro. 'Antarctic
France,' as the colony was known, was intended as a place where
Catholics and Protestants could live together without strife. In
1555 some 600 Frenchmen arrived under Nicolas Durand de
Villegaignon. The location of the settlement was well chosen, for
the Indians of the region were hostile to the Portuguese and welcomed allies. The anticipated religious harmony failed to material-

ize, however, and the colony was weakened by factional animosities based on religious beliefs even before the Portuguese attacked it. Portuguese officials were slow to awaken to the threat, but at length Father Nóbrega aroused the court, and Mem de Sá was sent as governor-general in 1558 with the task of expelling the French his primary duty.

With the Portuguese and Indian forces he was able to muster Mem de Sá attacked the French and drove them from their island bastion to the mainland, where they were supported by Indian allies. The Portuguese sailed away and the French remained. Rumors that Villegaignon planned to bring 10,000 Huguenots from France and drive the Portuguese from all of Brazil emphasized the danger of permitting the colony to remain. A new campaign was prepared in which the Jesuits took an active part. Nóbrega and Anchieta won allies among the previously hostile Tamóios, and the Portuguese attacked with greater determination. In 1567 the French settlement was destroyed and the Portuguese founded in its place São Sebastião do Rio de Janeiro. The French survivors fled north and sought to re-establish themselves with the capture of Pernambuco. Although they were soon driven from this prize, Frenchmen continued to visit the coast of Brazil and trade with the Indians well into the following century. The religious wars in France distracted that nation from following up its colonial projects, or the French might easily have established themselves permanently in Brazil.

English interest in Brazil also developed early in the sixteenth century, for William Hawkins and other Englishmen arrived on trading ventures during the captaincy period. Because of the cordial relations between Portugal and England, this trade was carried on peacefully. After 1580, however, when Felipe II succeeded to the Portuguese throne, Englishmen were treated as enemies.

In the second half of the century the Indian problem in Brazil became more acute. The number of free Indians around the settlements was drastically reduced by a series of smallpox epidemics beginning in 1562, and by resistance to slave-raiders. The barter system broke down; the barrier tribes disappeared; and the settlements were exposed to attacks by warlike tribes from the interior. Ilhéos and Pôrto Seguro were furiously assaulted in 1560 by the Aimorés. Although Mem de Sá hurried to the defense of these towns, Ilhéos was almost completely destroyed.

In spite of the spreading warfare some progress was made in pacifying the Indians. During the rule of Mem de Sá the Jesuits settled some 34,000 in eleven parishes. These Indians were taught the catechism and helped to organize simple municipal governments based on Portuguese forms. They were made accustomed to daily toil in the fields for the support of the parishes, and trained in other useful occupations. These Indians, unfortunately, could not always be protected against the slave-raiders, and they often ended their lives in slavery.

The rapid expansion of the fazendas after 1550 made a source of cheap labor imperative. The number of captives taken in 'just' wars was insufficient. Fazendeiros began illegally seizing the trained and docile Indians in the Jesuit parishes. Smallpox epidemics, by decimating the laborers, intensified the problem, for in 1562 nearly a third of the natives around Bahia died. Agricultural activity declined abruptly and a severe famine ensued. By the end of 1563 only five of the Jesuit parishes were left, and the ruin was completed by further ravages of disease.

During the epidemics and the hunger that followed, the condition of free Indians became so desperate that many offered themselves as slaves to escape starvation. Others provided captives from among their own tribesmen in exchange for food, and the free Indian population fell off sharply.

The condition of friendly tribes differed from one captaincy to another. In northeastern Brazil the fazendas depended upon Indian labor, and enslavement was customary. In the south, however, the planting of cane was less important, and conditions generally favored the independence of friendly tribes.

As the Portuguese and half-breed population of Brazil increased, dependence upon Indians for defense declined, although at no time in the sixteenth century were the Europeans without some need of native allies. In Pernambuco, one of the most prosperous captaincies, the disappearance of free Indians undermined the defense, and although Bahia was more fortunate in preserving neighboring tribes, neither settlement was strong enough to rely upon the Portuguese population alone. In 1570, the year in which Nóbrega secured the prohibition of slavery in Bahia, there were little more than 1000 Portuguese households in that locality. The population grew fairly rapidly during the next two decades, and the number of *engenhos* or sugar mills increased from eighteen to thirty-five. The churches, monasteries, and houses of wealthy fazendeiros already displayed signs of prosperity and luxury. The tile roofs, the cobbled streets, and the extensive gardens on the bluffs overlooking the sea presented a pleasing sight.

After 1570 immigration from Portugal increased the population and accelerated the economic development of Brazil. Within twenty years the number of engenhos doubled; at the same time the local authority of the remaining donataries yielded to that of royal governors. The Brazilian settlements began to mature, and to assume the form and character they preserved throughout the colonial period. They were not numerous nor strong enough as yet to discourage latecomers who might covet tropical lands in the New World.

Rio de Janeiro prospered immediately, but it did not rival Bahia or Pernambuco for more than a century. The French returned but failed to recover their former post, and thereafter concentrated their efforts in Maranhão and the Amazon valley. In 1572 Rio de Janeiro gained temporary political prominence when it became capital of the southern captaincies, but in 1578 authority was restored to the governor-general at Bahia.

Because of the disturbed conditions in Portugal arising from the question of the Portuguese succession immediately after 1578, the French took advantage of another opportunity to encroach. They established themselves at Paraíba, and soon were involved in Indian attacks on Pernambuco and Itamaracá. Their successes inspired greater efforts on the part of the Portuguese and their Spanish king, and they were driven from their posts.

Even after the expulsion of the French Brazil was not securely won for Portugal. The long expanse of unoccupied coast and the profits of dyewood and sugar traffic attracted other latecomers. With Spanish kings ruling Portugal the latter kingdom's imperial defenses were of secondary importance to those of Spain. The total white population of Brazil in 1580 was estimated at little more than 30,000, and it was divided into widely scattered groups exposed to attack and difficult to defend. The ever-present threat of Indian hostility alone restrained the movements of troops from one region to another.

Pernambuco, unlike most other captaincies, was abundantly supplied with Indian slaves, and able to export them. A drought and subsequent famine in 1583 reduced the free Indians of the captaincy to an inconsequential number, and African Negroes began to replace Indian slaves. The Negroes proved a more economical labor force because of their greater physical strength and their ability to survive hard work under tropical conditions. Their fear of the Indians was a deterrent to flight. After 1580 their numbers increased rapidly, the sugar industry providing the wealth needed for their importation.

The 'Spanish captivity' from 1580 to 1640 was an unfortunate era for the Lusitanian kingdom. Despite some basic changes in colonial administration, such as the creation of a Portuguese royal council similar to the Council of the Indies, Spanish domination brought on imperial retrogression to Portugal. Spain already had many enemies, owing in part to her lofty position in Europe and in part to her role as defender of the faith. Spain's enemies now regarded Portugal as a part of the larger country, and Portuguese overseas possessions were cast into jeopardy the moment Felipe II assumed the Portuguese crown. The revolt of the Netherlands against Spain and the rise of Holland as an independent power led to a Dutch offensive against the Portuguese empire in the Orient and America. The achievements of the Dutch East India Company in seizing Portuguese holdings in the Spice Islands inspired the formation of another privately financed project to seek similar profit at the expense of Spain and Portugal in the New World. Although the major triumphs of the West India Company were won in the seventeenth century, Dutch aggression against Brazil and Caribbean islands commenced before 1600.

While Dutch trade with Brazil was not immediately interrupted by Spain, English vessels were made unwelcome at Brazilian ports shortly after Felipe II began to rule Portugal. In 1582 an English merchant fleet was attacked by Spanish warships at São Vicente, and a few years later Englishmen retaliated by assaulting Bahia. In the 1590's Cavendish and other English raiders attacked Santos, São Vicente, and Pernambuco. In some instances they were joined by Dutch and French ships in Brazilian waters. These events inspired by Spanish rule over Portugal seriously damaged Brazilian trade without Brazil's receiving compensation in other quarters.

Despite Felipe's tact in exercising his authority over Portugal and his slight interference with Portuguese colonial administration, Brazil was seriously affected as a result of his rule. In addition to the rupture with previously friendly nations such as Holland, the Brazilians no longer felt restrained in their westward expeditions by the antiquated agreement concerning the Line of Demarcation. The forays of paulista *bandeirantes* in search of slaves were to bend the Line greatly to the advantage of Portugal. Profitable commerce with the Spanish colonies was another result of the Spanish connection. Trade with Buenos Aires became important for Brazil, and Portuguese interest in the Plata region grew strong. This traffic was largely in merchandise and Negro slaves in exchange for cowhides and for silver brought illegally from Upper Peru. Gradually the Portuguese were attracted to the center of silver production, and many Portuguese merchants established themselves in Spanish American communities.

By the end of the sixteenth century the Brazilian fazenda society was well established and of a distinctive character. Pernambuco was the center of the sugar industry and residence of some of the wealthiest planters, who maintained homes in the city as well as the *casas grandes* or big houses of the fazendas. Their wealth enabled them to affect rich clothing and ostentatious adornments for their homes. Silks and satins were worn by them, and their table services were of silver and gold. Bahia was similarly prosperous.

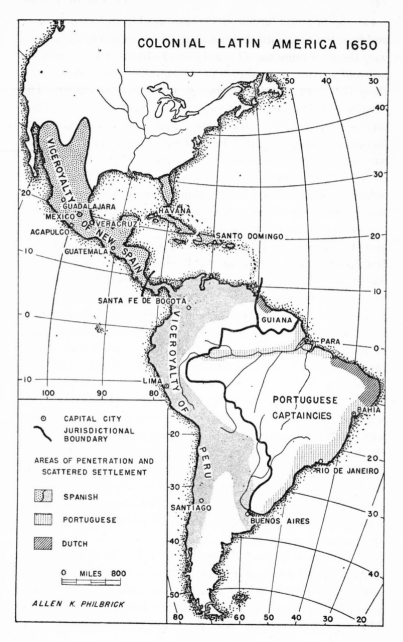

COLONIAL LATIN AMERICA 1650

CAPITAL CITY
JURISDICTIONAL
BOUNDARY

AREAS OF PENETRATION AND
SCATTERED SETTLEMENT

SPANISH

PORTUGUESE

DUTCH

0   MILES   800

ALLEN K. PHILBRICK

VICEROYALTY

GUADALAJARA
MEXICO   VERACRUZ
ACAPULCO
GUATEMALA   NEW SPAIN

HAVANA

SANTO DOMINGO

SANTA FE DE BOGOTA

GUIANA

PARA

VICEROYALTY OF

LIMA

PORTUGUESE
CAPTAINCIES

BAHIA

PERU

RIO DE JANEIRO

SANTIAGO

BUENOS AIRES

On the fazendas Negro slaves were steadily replacing Indians, and from this time until abolition of the slave trade in 1850, Negroes were the most numerous of immigrants to Brazil. They came from different regions and cultures of Africa, and some brought with them skills and energies superior to those of their masters. The African contributions to Brazilian development were great. Plantations depended upon their labor, and many handicrafts were based on the knowledge they brought with them from Africa. Some were acquainted with mining and smelting. These skills were essential to the expansion of the economy of colonial Brazil.

Slavery in Brazil was greatly influenced by Moslem attitudes and practices introduced earlier into Portugal, with the result that a milder form prevailed in comparison to that later in Anglo-America and the French West Indies. Lacking in Brazil was the fear of free Negroes characteristic of the English colonies; manumission was common and slaves customarily were allowed certain days to work for their own interest. Despite the manifest disadvantages arising from their inferior status in society, Brazilian slaves possessed legal rights. They could own property, marry without fear of being separated from members of their families, and defend themselves.

The skills brought by the Africans were for the most part unknown to Brazilian Indians. Negro slavery made possible economic activities and greater self-sufficiency than would have been possible without it. Fazendeiros came to rely more and more upon trusted slaves or freedmen as managers of engenhos.

In the development of the Brazilian race Negroes, because of their superior numbers and their intimate relationships with Portuguese families, played a more influential role than Indians. Racial mixture was wholesale, and the exchange of cultural traits was a two-way process. African words and an occasional doubling of tonic syllables became part of the language of Brazil. African music, dances, and folklore won a place in Brazilian culture. The mixed race and civilization which emerged was regarded by Brazilians as better adapted to the land and climate than the pure originals. The coming of Negroes made possible the flowering of a slave-based, aristocratic fazenda society destined to dominate Brazilian life for centuries.

By the close of the century of conquest the Brazilian settlements were beginning to show signs of solid growth. The land was still by no means populated heavily enough to discourage foreign aggression. While Portugal was ruled by a Spanish monarch imperial defense was a matter of momentary convenience. Spain was still deeply embroiled in costly and exhausting European undertakings which often distracted her from the remote problems of Brazil, although grave threats to Portuguese possession of the land were impending. Even though both Spain and Portugal made gestures toward defending the colony, the future of Brazil rested in large degree with the Brazilians themselves. With occasional aid from Portugal and Spain they had occupied the land and held it against the French. But the greatest challenge yet to be faced appeared when the round hulls and square sails of Dutch 'Beggars of the Sea' arrived in Brazilian waters.

VICEROYS OF NEW SPAIN, SIXTEENTH CENTURY

1535–50   Antonio de Mendoza, Count of Tendilla
1550–64   Luis de Velasco
1564–6   Audiencia
1566–68   Gastón de Peralta, Marquis of Falces
1568–80   Martín Enríquez de Almansa
1580–83   Lorenzo Suárez de Mendoza, Count of Coruña
1583–4   Audiencia
1584–5   Pedro Moya de Contreras, Archbishop of Mexico
1585–90   Alvaro Manrique de Zúñiga, Marquis of Villamanrique
1590–95   Luis de Velasco (the younger), Marquis of Salinas
1595–1603   Gaspar de Zúñiga y Acevedo, Count of Monterrey

VICEROYS OF PERU, SIXTEENTH CENTURY

1544–6   Blasco Núñez Vela
1546–51   Pedro de la Gasca (president of the audiencia)
1551–2   *Antonio de Mendoza
1552–5   Audiencia
1555–61   Andrés Hurtado de Mendoza, Marquis of Cañete
1561–4   Diego de Acevedo y Zúñiga, Count of Nieva
1564–9   Lope García de Castro (governor and captain-general)

* Former viceroy of New Spain.

1569–81 Francisco de Toledo y Figueroa
1581–3   *Martín Enríquez
1583–5   Audiencia
1585–90 Fernando de Torres y Portugal, Count of Villardompardo
1590–6   García Hurtado de Mendoza, Marquis of Cañete
1596–1604 *Luis de Velasco

  * Former viceroy of New Spain.

KINGS OF SPAIN AND PORTUGAL

Spain	Portugal
Fernando, 1479–1516 and	Afonso V, 1443–81
Isabel, 1479–1504	João II, 1481–95
Carlos I (Holy Roman Emperor Charles V), 1517–56	Manoel I, 1495–1521
	João III, 1521–57
Felipe II, 1556–98	Sebastião I, 1557–78
Felipe III, 1598–1621	Henrique, 1578–80
Felipe IV, 1621–65	1581 to 1640, rule by the kings of Spain
Carlos II, 1665–1700	
Felipe V, 1700–46	João IV, 1641–56
Fernando VI, 1746–59	Afonso VI, 1656–83
Carlos III, 1759–88	Pedro II, 1683–1706
Carlos IV, 1788–1808	João V, 1706–50
	José I, 1750–77
	Maria I and Pedro III, 1777–86
	Maria I, 1786–1816
	João VI, 1816–26

SUGGESTED READING

A. S. Aiton, *Antonio de Mendoza, First Viceroy of New Spain*, Durham, 1927.

R. Altamira, *A History of Spain*, New York, 1949.

C. B. G. Anderson, *Life and Letters of Vasco Núñez de Balboa*, New York, 1941.

G. Arciniegas, *Germans in the Conquest of America*, New York, 1943.
——— *The Knight of El Dorado*, New York, 1942.

C. R. Beazley, *Prince Henry the Navigator*, New York, 1897.

H. Bingham, *Lost City of the Incas*, New York, 1948.

H. Birney, *Brothers of Doom: the Story of the Pizarros in Peru*, New York, 1942.

M. Bishop, *The Odyssey of Cabeza de Vaca*, New York, 1933.

H. E. Bolton, *Coronado, Knight of Pueblos and Plains*, New York and Albuquerque, 1949.

E. G. Bourne, ed., *Narrative of the Career of Hernando de Soto in the Conquest of Florida*, 2 vols., New York, 1904.

———— *Spain in America, 1450–1580*, New York, 1904.

C. S. Braden, *Religious Aspects of the Conquest of Mexico*, Durham, 1930.

A. Castro, *The Structure of Spanish History*, Princeton, 1954.

R. S. Chamberlain, *The Conquest and Colonization of Honduras* (1502–50), Washington, 1953.

E. P. Cheyney, *Dawn of a New Era, 1250–1453*, New York, 1936.

B. Chuboda, *Spain and the Empire, 1519–1643*, Chicago, 1952.

S. Clissold, *Conquistador: The Life of Don Pedro Sarmiento de Gamboa*, London, 1954.

B. Díaz del Castillo, *True History of the Conquest of New Spain*, Various editions.

G. Freyre, *The Masters and the Slaves*, New York, 1946.

C. Gibson, *Tlaxcala in the Sixteenth Century*, New Haven, 1952.

R. B. C. Graham, *The Conquest of New Granada*, New York, 1922.

———— *The Conquest of the River Plate*, London, 1924.

E. J. Hamilton, *American Treasure and the Price Revolution in Spain, 1501–1650*, Cambridge, Mass., 1934.

———— *American Treasure and the Rise of Capitalism, 1500–1700*, London, 1929.

G. P. Hammond, *Don Juan de Oñate and the Founding of New Mexico*, Sante Fe, 1927.

L. Hanke, *Bartolomé de las Casas, an Interpretation of His Life and Writings*, The Hague, 1951.

———— *The Spanish Struggle for Justice in the Conquest of America*, Philadelphia, 1949.

———— *The First Social Experiments in America*, Cambridge, Mass., 1935.

C. H. Haring, *Trade and Navigation between Spain and the Indies in the Time of the Hapsburgs*, Cambridge, Mass., 1918.

A. Helps, *The Spanish Conquest in America*, 4 vols., new ed., New York, 1900–1904.

E. L. Hewett, *Ancient Life in the American Southwest*, Indianapolis, 1930.

L. F. Hill, *José de Escandón and the Founding of Nuevo Santander*, Columbus, 1926.

J. V. Jacobsen, *Educational Foundations of the Jesuits in Sixteenth-Century New Spain*, Berkeley, 1938.

J. E. Kelly, *Pedro de Alvarado, Conquistador*, Princeton, 1932.

F. A. Kirkpatrick, *The Spanish Conquistadores*, London, 1934.

I. A. Leonard, *Books of the Brave*, Cambridge, Mass., 1949.

H. V. Livermore, A History of Portugal, Cambridge, 1947.

T. H. Lewis, The Spanish Explorers in the Southern United States, 1528–43, New York, 1907.

W. Lowry, Spanish Settlements in the Present Limits of the United States, 1562–1574, New York, 1905.

F. A. MacNutt, The Letters of Cortés, 2 vols., New York, 1908.

S. de Madariaga, Hernán Cortés, Conqueror of Mexico, New York, 1941.

——— The Rise of the Spanish American Empire, New York, 1949.

A. Marchant, From Barter to Slavery, Baltimore, 1942.

P. A. Means, Ancient Civilizations of the Andes, New York, 1931.

——— The Fall of the Inca Empire and Spanish Rule in Peru, 1530–1780, New York, 1932.

J. L. Mecham, Francisco de Ibarra and Nueva Vizcaya, Durham, 1927.

R. B. Merriman, The Rise of the Spanish Empire in the Old World and the New, 4 vols., New York, 1918–34.

S. E. Morison, Admiral of the Ocean Sea; A Life of Christopher Columbus, Boston, 1942.

——— Portuguese Voyages to America in the Fifteenth Century, Cambridge, Mass., 1940.

S. G. Morley, The Ancient Maya, Stanford, 1946.

B. Moses, The Establishment of Spanish Rule in America, New York, 1898.

C. E. Nowell, A History of Portugal, New York, 1952.

C. M. Parr, So Noble a Captain: the Life and Times of Ferdinand Magellan, New York, 1953.

J. H. Parry, The Audiencia of New Galicia in the Sixteenth Century, Cambridge, 1948.

E. Prestage, The Portuguese Pioneers, London, 1933.

W. H. Prescott, The Conquest of Mexico, Various editions.

——— The Conquest of Peru, Various editions.

H. I. Priestley, The Coming of the White Man, New York, 1927.

K. Romoli, Balboa of Darién, New York, 1953.

O. Schoenrich, The Legacy of Christopher Columbus, 2 vols., Glendale, 1949.

W. L. Schurz, The Manila Galleon, New York, 1939.

L. B. Simpson, The Encomienda in New Spain, Rev. ed., Berkeley, 1950.

——— Exploitation of Land in Central Mexico in the Sixteenth Century, Berkeley, 1952.

——— Studies in the Administration of the Indians in New Spain, 4 vols., Berkeley, 1934–40.

M. Taylor, Impetuous Alvarado, Dallas, 1936.

J. E. S. Thompson, *The Rise and Fall of Maya Civilization*, Norman, 1954.

G. C. Vaillant, *The Aztecs of Mexico*, New York, 1941.

I. S. Weldon, *Pedro de Valdivia, Conquistador of Chile*, Austin, 1946.

S. Zavala, *New Viewpoints on the Spanish Colonization of America*, Philadelphia, 1943

A. F. Zimmerman, *Francisco de Toledo: Fifth Viceroy of Peru, 1569–1581*, Caldwell, Idaho, 1938.

GENERAL

G. Arciniegas, *The Caribbean: Sea of the New World*, New York, 1946.

R. K. Barber, *Indian Labor in the Spanish Colonies*, Albuquerque, 1932.

P. J. Barth, *Franciscan Education and the Social Order in Spanish North America (1502–1821)*, Chicago, 1945.

F. W. Blackmar, *Spanish Institutions of the Southwest*, Baltimore, 1891.

H. E. Bolton, *The Spanish Borderlands: A Chronicle of Old Florida and the Southwest*, New Haven, 1921.

—— *Wider Horizons of American History*, New York, 1934.

C. E. Chapman, *Colonial Hispanic America: A History*, New York, 1933.

—— *The Founding of Spanish California*, New York, 1923.

C. H. Cunningham, *The Audiencia in the Spanish Colonies as Illustrated by the Audiencia of Manila 1583–1800*, Berkeley, 1919.

B. W. Diffie, *Latin American Civilization: The Colonial Period*, Harrisburg, 1945.

J. Esquemeling, *The Buccaneers of America*, Various editions.

L. E. Fisher, *Viceregal Administration in the Spanish Colonies*, Berkeley, 1927.

H. Folmer, *Franco-Spanish Rivalry in North America, 1524–1763*, Glendale, 1953.

V. W. von Hagen, *South America. The Green World of the Naturalists*, London, 1951.

C. H. Haring, *The Spanish Empire in America*, New York, 1947.

B. Keen, ed., *Readings in Latin American Civilization, 1492 to the present*, New York, 1955.

J. T. Lanning, *Academic Culture in the Spanish Colonies*, New York, 1940.

H. C. Lea, *The Inquisition in the Spanish Dependencies*, New York, 1922.

P. A. Means, *The Spanish Main, Focus of Envy, 1492–1700*, New York, 1935.

B. Moses, *Spanish Colonial Literature*, New York, 1922.

M. de Oliveira Lima, *The Evolution of Brazil Compared with Spanish and Anglo-Saxon America*, Palo Alto, 1914.

D. E. Smith, *The Viceroy of New Spain*, Berkeley, 1913.

R. S. Smith, *The Spanish Guild Merchant*, Durham, 1940.

R. Southey, *History of Brazil*, 3 vols., London, 1810–19.

F. Tannenbaum, *Slave and Citizen, the Negro in the Americas*, New York, 1947.

A. P. Whitaker, *The Western Hemisphere Idea: Its Rise and Decline*, Ithaca, 1954.

A. C. Wilgus, ed., *Colonial Hispanic America*, Washington, 1936.

II

CONSOLIDATION OF EMPIRE

VIII

The Contest for Colonies

Here I cannot forbear to commend the patient virtue of the
Spaniards. We seldom or never find any nation hath endured
so many misadventures and miseries as the Spaniards have done
in their Indian discoveries. Yet persisting in their enterprises,
with invincible constancy, they have annexed to their kingdom so many goodly provinces, as bury the remembrance of
all dangers past. Tempests and shipwrecks, famine, overthrows,
mutinies, heat and cold, pestilence, and all manner of diseases,
both old and new, together with extreme poverty, and want
of things needful, have been the enemies, wherewith every one
of their most noble discoveries, at one time or other, hath encountered . . . Surely, they are worthily rewarded with those
treasures and paradises, which they enjoy, and well deserve to
hold them quietly, if they hinder not the like virtue in others . . .

SIR WALTER RALEIGH *

SPAIN'S position in Europe was frequently challenged during the sixteenth century, but with the
exception of the French inroads in Brazil and Florida, the Iberian
empires in America had not been seriously threatened. Raleigh's attempted settlements in Virginia and those of the French in Canada
proved abortive. The Huguenot colonies in Brazil and Florida were
destroyed before they could establish firm footholds, and the religious struggle which broke out in France soon afterward jeopardized
new efforts for the remainder of the century.

The colonial wealth of Spain and Portugal and the growth of

* *Historie of the World*, 5 vols., London, 1628.

151

maritime commerce inspired imperial ambitions among their less fortunate rivals, and the seventeenth century was not long under way before these yearnings began to be satisfied. Since it was still unsafe ·to settle in the proximity of already established colonies, the late-comers began to concentrate their efforts on the more remote and less desirable lands of North America. But as Spain's naval power began to disintegrate before the repeated assaults of the Dutch, English and French adventurers boldly established themselves on neglected islands in the Caribbean. These island settlements gave France and England much-desired tropical plantations, and served as convenient operating bases for smugglers and pirates. French and English appetites for empire were sharpened, and the Spanish colonies were hungrily viewed as fair game.

Throughout the sixteenth century Spain and, with a few exceptions, Portugal had been under capable and energetic monarchs who vigorously resisted attempted encroachments upon their overseas dominions. In that golden era, moreover, Spanish self-confidence had been boundless and Spanish arms invincible. But because of her European entanglements, Spain's energies were too often spent on matters unrelated to either the peninsula or America. The riches of Mexico and Peru, which might have been employed toward more fruitful ends, provided the means for continuing these struggles beyond the bounds of all prudence. The constant wars with France, the complicated efforts to check the spread of Protestantism, and the backbreaking task of repulsing the westward-moving empire of Turkey taxed Spain beyond her human resources, and contributed largely to her decay. The revolt of the Netherlands was especially injurious, for the vast maritime power of the Dutch was turned with enthusiasm and success against the Spanish and Portuguese empires. To meet the Dutch challenge extraordinary measures and astute, inspiring leadership were needed, for England and France were quick to profit by Spanish and Portuguese preoccupation with Holland. Unfortunately for Spain in the seventeenth century, she produced no monarchs the equal of Fernando and Isabel, Carlos I, and Felipe II. The traditional devotion of Spanish rulers to affairs of state did not survive them, and the rule of royal favorites in Spain benefited only her enemies. From 1580 to 1640, it should be recalled, the Spanish and Portuguese crowns were united, and Portugal's fortunes rose or fell with those of her neighbor.

For Spain the seventeenth century was a time of disillusionment and decline not only economically and morally, but militarily as well. Lack of leadership and self-confidence plunged the nation deeper into the abyss to which overextension in European affairs had led her. The failure to contain Holland and chastise England encouraged greater impertinences by these upstart nations. In 1636 a Dutch squadron under von Tromp destroyed a Spanish fleet in the English channel, a defeat which weakened Spanish sea power more effectively than the celebrated loss of the Armada in 1588. Participation in the Thirty Years War, 1618–48, contributed further to Spain's decline, for in 1643 the hitherto invincible Spanish infantry suffered at Rocroi its first defeat in centuries in a battle fought on fairly equal terms. Loss of prestige in international affairs accelerated demoralization and decay within Spain, and in the two decades after 1640 the country was in great danger of breaking up once more into a number of independent kingdoms. In 1640 Portugal became independent; Catalonia launched a revolt for independence which was not crushed until 1652; Andalucía conspired toward the same end, and French-inspired uprisings in Naples and Sicily added to Spanish pessimism.

In 1640, when the Duke of Bragança was proclaimed king of Portugal, he hastily sought alliances with England, France, and Holland to brace his shaky throne against the expected avalanche of retribution from Spain. Spain was in no position to wage war immediately or effectively even against Portugal, however, and in 1668, after a feeble campaign that seems to have been conducted on the basis of preordained failure, she acknowledged Portugal's independence. The need for allies after 1640 placed Portugal in a humiliating position with regard to Holland, for the Dutch West India Company still maintained some of its conquests in Brazil, and most of the former Portuguese colonies in the Orient were firmly held by the Dutch East India Company. A Brazilian campaign against the Dutch was in progress, but Portugal was reluctant to assist her most valuable remaining colony for fear of antagonizing Holland. Instead of assistance and encouragement she sent plaintive pleas to the Brazilians to abandon the struggle.

Under Carlos II, 1665–1700, last of the Spanish Hapsburgs, the ruin of Spain was completed. His wretched rule was characterized by widespread moral depression, and seemed the worse by comparison to the flamboyant regime of his contemporary, Louis XIV of France, under whom the French monarchy was the envy of all Europe. France under *le Roi Soleil* became the dominant power on the continent, and exhausted Spain staggered under the weight of French pressure. She was fortunate that England and Holland ultimately put aside their own maritime contest to oppose French aggrandizement on the continent, although neither of these nations could be considered a friend of once-powerful Spain.

Early in the rule of Carlos II it was clear that he would die without an heir, and thus bring to an inglorious end the Spanish Hapsburg dynasty. The question of the Spanish succession became a lively issue in European diplomacy, for England and Holland were unequivocally opposed to the Spanish throne's passing to a member of the French ruling house of Bourbon. So great was the danger of war simply in anticipation of such a possibility that Louis XIV agreed not to permit a member of his family to accept the Spanish crown should it be offered. In this matter the Austrian Hapsburgs were also greatly concerned, for they were in hopes of the succession passing to one of their number. News that his enemies were virtually writing his will for him agitated the weak Carlos II profoundly, and succumbing to the intrigues of the French party in Madrid, he willed his throne and empire to Philip of Anjou, grandson of Louis XIV.

By this act the Bourbons became rulers of Spain as well as France, and the balance of power in Europe was thrown dangerously out of balance. The worst fears of England, Holland, and Austria were immediately justified by Louis' undisguised intentions, amply demonstrated in announcing his grandson's acceptance of the Spanish throne with the grandiloquent remark: 'The Pyrenees no longer exist!' The seventeenth century ended with Europe on the verge of war over the Spanish succession. There followed more than a decade of bloodshed and impressive French defeats at the hands of the Duke of Marlborough and Prince Eugene of Savoy before the French were convinced that Louis' greatest gift was not prophecy.

The European events described above had various effects upon the Spanish and Portuguese colonies in the Americas. The seventeenth century began with the founding of English, French, and Dutch settlements on the remote and unattractive coast of North America, followed by a more hazardous penetration of the Lesser Antilles and Brazil. A sordid struggle began for the control of warlike Indian hordes to help fight their battles. The fur trade was another reason for Europeans to seek alliances with the hunting Indians of North America, for it became a highly profitable traffic that was contested for avidly by the latecomers among themselves and with neighboring Spanish colonies such as Florida and New Mexico.

The colonizing efforts of England, France, and Holland occurred almost simultaneously after 1600, although the last two nations were more interested in acquiring trading posts than in large-scale colonial enterprise. The buccaneers, corsairs, or, as the Spanish regarded them, pirates of all three countries were active in the Caribbean long before official attempts were made to seize lands. In 1600 Dutch vessels attacked Bahia, and similar assaults occurred over a wide area and with increasing intensity for half a century. In the same year a Dutch fleet under van Noort passed through the Strait of Magellan into the Pacific and held for a short time the archipelago of Chiloé. This expedition continued along the Pacific coast to Upper California, crossed the Pacific to Manila Bay, and sailed around India and Africa to complete the fourth circumnavigation of the world.

In 1609, although the independence of Holland still was not acknowledged by Spain, a twelve-year truce was signed between the two countries. Spain won little advantage by the interlude, while Holland prepared to launch a tremendous assault on the Spanish and Portuguese empires when the truce ended. Beyond the seas aggressions continued, and in 1615 a Dutch fleet under Spillbergen defeated the Spanish Pacific squadron off the coast of South America in one of the major naval conflicts of the Pacific in the colonial period. In the following year another Dutch admiral, Le Maire, discovered the route around Cape Horn, which he named after his native town of Hoorne in the Netherlands.

Since Holland was the major naval power of Europe in 1600, the Dutch offensive was by far the most menacing to Spain and Portugal, and the one which received the greatest attention from them. Less potent England and France perceived their opportunity, and profited by Spanish preoccupation with Dutch aggression by occupying and claiming Virginia, New England, and Canada. When the truce between Holland and Spain ended in 1621 England possessed only a few posts in Guiana and the hunger-ridden settlements of Jamestown and Plymouth. The French had established themselves at Cayenne in Guiana, and Port Royal, Acadia, and Quebec in Canada. The Dutch had founded Fort Orange in the Hudson Valley, Essequibo, in modern British Guiana, and several trading posts along the Amazon river. Despite their interest in tropical colonies, England and France did not acquire any important plantations until after the Dutch offensive was resumed.

Plans for a joint offensive by the Dutch East and West India companies against Spanish South America were abandoned in favor of individual projects on the part of those organizations. In 1624 they attacked the Spanish and Portuguese colonies on both coasts of South America. The East India Company failed in its attempt to seize Lima; the West India Company was temporarily more fortunate in capturing Bahia, but reinforcements arrived only after the city had been recovered by a combined Spanish and Portuguese fleet. At the same time a relentless privateering offensive was sweeping Spanish merchant ships from Caribbean waters. The Iberian empires staggered under the repeated onslaughts of the Dutch, but yielded possession of American soil only in northern Brazil. Some of the highlights of the whirlwind Dutch offensive were the attack on Puerto Rico and capture of a treasure galleon from Honduras in 1626, the seizure of twenty-two loaded vessels in Bahia by Piet Heyn in the following year, and the taking of the entire Mexican treasure fleet in Matanzas Bay, Cuba, by the same admiral in 1628. From a financial standpoint the last event was most remarkable, for the value of the plunder was fabulous. The wealth thus acquired enabled the company to undertake greater assaults against Brazil.

Because of their interest in the sugar trade and the company's desire for a steady flow of profits, the Dutch in 1630 began the occupation of Brazil on a more grandiose scale. The capture of Pernambuco ushered in a brief era of conquest during which the Dutch quickly extended their authority along the coastal plain toward the mouth of the Amazon. Dutch rule in Brazil was generally fairly tolerant for the age of the Thirty Years War, although opposition to the interlopers did not die out. The confiscation of plantations alienated the fazendeiros and made them irreconcilable enemies, while the Jesuits were alarmed at the proximity of Protestants, and called for their expulsion.

While the Dutch were extending their holdings in Brazil they occupied a few of the remaining Lesser Antilles as bases for trade or conquest. Curaçao, Aruba, Bonaire, and a few others were seized in the 1630's. None of these arid islands was attractive to colonists interested in agriculture, but their location off the northern coast of South America made them suitable for illicit trade.

England and France, too, began to acquire bases in the Caribbean. In 1604 James I had restored peaceful relations between England and Spain; this 'peace' lasted for twenty years, during which time Jamestown and Plymouth were established. But when the Dutch offensive came England and France joined the scramble for neglected islands. St. Christopher they occupied jointly if not peacefully, while England claimed Barbados, Nevis, Montserrat, and Antigua.

Domestic strife in England interrupted her activities in acquiring new lands but caused an exodus of Englishmen to some of her overseas settlements. With the rise of Oliver Cromwell as Lord Protector, the English merchants had a champion once more who was not loath to risk war in order to fulfill his desires. Cromwell contemplated a division of colonial spheres between England and Holland, with the former concentrating on America and the latter upon Asia. This project failed to materialize, and he promoted in-

stead a more modest undertaking — the conquest of Spanish possessions in the Caribbean. The ambitious project began inauspiciously
against Santo Domingo, but in 1655 Jamaica was taken — the first
American territory actually occupied by Spain which was lost to
European enemies by conquest. Jamaica fell far short of satisfying
Cromwell's imperial ambitions, but the island became the most important English colony in the Caribbean, and an important smuggling center. Because of the aggressions of Louis XIV on the continent of Europe, Spain, England, and Holland were allied against
France from 1688 to 1697. The Spanish empire was not drastically
molested during this interlude, for the fear of France was great. But
in the interim the ministers of Carlos II failed to put his house in
order.

During England's civil war her colonial commerce had been interrupted to the extent that the Dutch were able to usurp most of it.
Relations between the two nations became severely strained, and
following the promulgation of the English Navigation Acts of 1650
and the following year, the first of a series of Anglo-Dutch naval wars
began. Being more vulnerable through having greater commerce exposed to attack, Holland suffered heavier losses than England from
these wars. The Dutch began relaxing their grip on the less important colonies, as they found their widely dispersed holdings expensive to maintain. Little by little the Brazilian conquests were
surrendered to avoid making the sacrifices necessary to preserve
them. In 1654 Pernambuco, the last important Dutch-held territory
in Brazil, fell to the Brazilians, and ten years later the English easily
seized New Amsterdam in North America, leaving the Dutch only
their Caribbean islands and a few scattered trading posts. By their
expulsion from Brazil the Dutch did not lose pre-eminence in the
sugar trade, and the territorial losses did little injury to the wealth
of the empire. Curaçao was a thriving center for trade with Spanish
America, but like Jamaica after 1655, most of its traffic was illegal.

French efforts to establish themselves in the Caribbean islands
early in the seventeenth century were unsuccessful, and the attempt
to settle in the Guianas in 1602 also failed. After retreating from
Rio de Janeiro and Pernambuco in the sixteenth century, the French

established posts in Maranhão. Driven from their town of Saint Louis, modern São Luís, they founded other posts on the Amazon, where Dutch and English traders were also active. Toward the middle of the seventeenth century Frenchmen moved into uninhabited parts of Haiti, the western end of the island of Española. The introduction of sugar cane planting in the same period brought the French planters considerable wealth, and led to the influx of Negro slaves in large numbers. Frenchmen had moved onto St. Christopher in 1625, and in the next few decades they occupied others of the Lesser Antilles. Finally in the 1660's they successfully established trading posts and plantations in the region now known as French Guiana.

At the Peace of Westphalia in 1648 Spain belatedly acknowledged Dutch independence and at the same time recognized Dutch conquests. Both Spain and Portugal yielded ground only after stubborn resistance, or procrastination, as their rivals regarded it, and it was not until 1670 that the former nation conceded England's claim to the territories she held in North America. The concession was clearly an act of capitulation on the part of Spain, for previously she had claimed all of the lands entered by the late arrivals, both in North America and the Caribbean. And in 1697 Spain was forced to acknowledge French claims to Haiti.

Despite the many injuries which Spain and her colonies suffered during the seventeenth century, and in contrast to the Spanish decline, the colonies themselves grew and expanded. Much of the drama of the age of conquest was lacking, but the results were no less important. Agricultural and mining frontiers were pushed into the wilderness, bringing under control valuable regions, and the protective barriers around Spain's most treasured possessions — New Spain and Peru — were enlarged. Some expansion was purely defensive in motivation, for the purpose of preventing the intrusion of enemy powers into regions adjacent to one of these viceroyalties, such as the temporary move into Texas in the 1690's and the occupation of Pensacola.

The remarkable growth of the fur trade in the seventeenth century animated rivalry between France and England, and the French took advantage of the extensive system of waterways from the mouth of the St. Lawrence river to the Mississippi valley. By making a few portages it was possible for French *voyageurs* to penetrate to the heart of the continent, and to attract valuable allies among the warlike tribes of the interior by providing them with firearms and firewater in exchange for furs. In the 1670's French pioneers began a movement from Canada to the mouth of the Mississippi that brought them into contact with the Indians of Texas and the southern plains. These Indians began appearing in New Mexico with French muskets and swords, and aroused anxiety in northern New Spain. La Salle's projected colony near the mouth of the Mississippi finally came to ruin on the coast of Texas, but the threat which it posed for New Mexico impelled Spanish officials to launch a countermovement. Texas was occupied briefly by Spanish forces and missionaries until it was learned that the French intruders had been killed by the Indians and the immediate danger had passed.

In 1698 La Salle's project for a Gulf coast colony was revived by the French, and plans were laid for a settlement at Pensacola Bay. The Spanish were forewarned, however, and sent an expedition to occupy Pensacola in time to frustrate the French scheme. A French post was established instead at Biloxi, and in 1700 another was founded at Mobile. As the westward progress of the French from Biloxi converged with the movement southward from Canada, the gateway to the rich silver mines of New Spain was imperiled. All that stood between the French and northern New Spain were the warlike tribes of Texas, for the tiny Spanish settlement at Santa Fe had been overthrown by the Pueblo Indians in 1680, and the reconquest was barely concluded by 1700. For Spain, already overextended and exhausted, the only way to meet this new threat was by occupying the lands between her valued possessions and the posts of her enemies, and then to win the wild tribes to alliance. Anglo-French wars were later to diminish the danger and relieve the pressure, although England became more strongly entrenched in North America and the Caribbean as her conflict with France progressed. But Virginia and Carolina were cut off from the Mississippi valley by mountains, and the English colonies did not present any immediate threat to New Spain.

For Portugal, too, the seventeenth century was a period of pushing back the frontiers of Brazil. In the vanguard of the forces which rolled back and penetrated the living wall of Indian resistance were the slave-raiders, the mine-seekers, and the cattlemen. By the end of the century their relentless probings had carried them far into the interior and to the gold deposits of Minas Gerais. The advance of the hardy, independent paulistas was not hindered in the slightest degree by the ancient Treaty of Tordesillas, of which they probably were happily ignorant. The push into Minas Gerais did not bring them into contact with other Europeans, but movement in a southerly direction brought them to the margins of the Plata, where their intrusions were protested by Spain.

Before the close of the seventeenth century international rivalry had come in earnest to the Plata region. After the independence of Portugal had been achieved the Portuguese of Brazil were loath to cease their profitable commerce with the residents of Buenos Aires and Upper Peru. To the terrifying forays of the paulista bandeirantes was now added the open violation of the ancient Treaty of Tordesillas by occupation of lands clearly beyond the Line. Santa Catarina was settled after 1650, and in 1680 the Portuguese boldly moved into the Plata by founding the town of Colônia do Sacramento across the estuary from Buenos Aires. The governor of the latter place called on the Jesuits for Guaraní troops, and soon ejected the intruders. Spanish diplomacy was less effective than colonial action, however, and Colônia was returned to Portugal to become a thriving smuggling center. Colônia remained a bone of contention between Spain and Portugal until 1777; each time Spain won out on the field of battle she forfeited her gain at the council table, where Portugal's interests were ably upheld by England.

In 1695 one of the most unique attempts to encroach on Spanish American territory was begun by a group of imaginative Scots under the lead of William Paterson. From the Scottish parliament they received a generous authorization for planting colonies in parts of

Asia, Africa, or America not held by European nations. Paterson knew the Caribbean area, and chose Darién as the ideal setting for controlling transisthmian commerce. By dominating the isthmian commerce Paterson felt that his company could control most of the traffic of the New World and the Pacific. The bold, fantastic scheme appealed to credulous investors in Scotland, England, and Holland, and an enormous sum was subscribed. The plan met with such universal approval, in fact, that merchants of France and England began to fear the loss of trade to the Scots!

In 1698 the expedition sailed for Aclá in Darién. A fort was built at New St. Andrew, and messages of friendship were sent to the governors of Spanish provinces. In the meantime powerful forces were at work to defeat the project. The British East India Company persuaded the king to order his governors in Jamaica, Barbados, and New York not to furnish settlers and supplies for the Scots' company. In June, 1699, less than eight months after their arrival, the survivors abandoned the colony, not as the result of direct action against them, but because of the ravages of disease. Soon after their departure two ships arrived with a small body of recruits who were sent on to Jamaica.

The Spanish court did not stir from its lethargy to protest until after the colony had been abandoned. Then the Spanish ambassador presented a memorial to William III stating that Carlos II looked on the affair as a rupture of alliance and a hostile act. In the meantime more Scots were sent to Darién, but few remained after seeing the colony deserted. In February, 1700, Captain Campbell arrived with 300 veterans of the Flanders campaign; he soon learned that 1600 Spaniards had been sent against him and were camped at Santa Marta. Campbell surprised this force at night and dispersed it, but a blockade by sea cut off hope of relief. The siege was sustained for six weeks; Campbell finally escaped, and the survivors were permitted by the Spanish commander to leave in their own ship. Their debilitation was so great that the Spaniards had to help them weigh anchor! Thus ended the grandiose scheme, in which more than 2000 men lost their lives and many more their wealth.

At the close of the seventeenth century Spain was hard-pressed to maintain her empire intact while Portugal, owing in part to her English connection, held Brazil more securely than she had in 1600. The Dutch challenge had been repulsed through the efforts of the Brazilians, and the Anglo-Dutch naval wars discouraged a renewal of the conflict by Holland. When Carlos II died in 1700 the horizon was especially gloomy for Spain; lacking was the boundless enthusiasm which had made possible the dramatic adventures of discovery and conquest. Awaiting her was the unpleasant prospect of French domination and endless strife to preserve her imperiled empire. But while Spain and Portugal had pursued their descending spirals down from the dizzying heights of pre-eminence to near-oblivion, their New World offspring were coming of age. The sturdy skeletons constructed by the unruly conquerors and docile Indians had put on flesh, soft and weak at first as befitting tender age, but growing ever more resilient and powerful with the passing years. The imperial infants still lacked the mental maturity to make them wish to leave their parents' care, even though their physical strength might have been equal to the task. By 1700 the Iberian colonies had taken long strides toward manhood, but they had not yet begun to think of leaving the little shelter and comfort still afforded by the parental roofs. Had they wished to forsake the empires, the War of the Spanish Succession, which inaugurated the turbulent eighteenth century, offered them an opportunity only slightly less favorable than that which they seized a century later. But the idea of independence did not emerge.

IX

Life in the Latin American Colonies

America was 'the refuge and haven of all the poor devils of
Spain, the sanctuary of the bankrupt, the safeguard of mur-
derers, the way out for gamblers, the promised land for ladies
of easy virtue, a lure and disillusionment for the many, and an
incomparable remedy for the few.'

CERVANTES *

BEFORE the century of the conquest had ended the
Indian populations of the Spanish and Portuguese
colonies had decreased drastically. In some regions where civilized
Indians had been most numerous, such as the valley of Mexico, the
downward trend continued until the middle of the seventeenth century, when the Indian population began a slow increase. The decline
of the Indians meant a sharp curtailment of the labor supply. Negro
slaves were too expensive to replace the Indians completely, and the
mestizos were not yet numerous enough nor under sufficient com-
pulsion. The shortage of Indian laborers was one of the most striking
features of the seventeenth century, and it necessitated changes in
the type of projects undertaken and in methods of recruiting workmen.

In the seventeenth century there were far fewer of the great building programs so typical of the previous expansive era. The remaining Indians were pushed more and more into agriculture, mining,
and weaving rather than into construction work. Since most of the

* *El Celoso extremeño.*

larger cities had depended almost entirely upon Indians to provide most of the necessary foodstuffs, these cities faced critical food shortages until the large plantations began to help meet the demands.

With the decrease in the number of sedentary Indians the encomienda also declined in importance, and its place was gradually taken by a less idealistic system of debt peonage. Under this system the labor supply of the agricultural estates became far more stable than it had been under the practice of weekly allotments of men from the Indian villages. The gradual increase in the number of Indians after this change took place suggests that it was in some ways, at least, an improvement.

The seventeenth century was not a period of dramatic expansion but rather a time of contraction, readjustment, and consolidation. There were many episodes and currents which affected the Latin American colonies, internally and externally. The decline of Spain, which continued well into the following century, could not help but influence the Spanish colonies. Portugal's independence was reestablished in 1640, but her economy remained so unhealthy that she had to rely on the Brazilians for a large part of the indemnity paid to Holland. Brazil suffered a serious depression after the expulsion of the Dutch, and it did not end until the discovery of gold in the last decade of the century. The recovery of the Latin American colonies from the economic stagnation into which the Iberian empires had fallen, however, was generally more rapid than that of Spain and Portugal.

The inability of the Iberian nations to maintain strong demands for the chief colonial agricultural and pastoral products undoubtedly proved detrimental to colonial production. The failure of Spain and Portugal to provide the manufactured items needed in the colonies in amounts sufficient to meet the requirements and at reasonable prices added to the problems of the colonists, while the fact that food was generally more abundant in the colonies than in the peninsula led to a revival of immigration. The newcomers did not, however, provide a badly needed addition to the labor supply, for social attitudes precluded their performing tasks usually relegated to Indians and Negroes. Spanish viceroys frequently expressed their bewilderment over what to do about so many men seeking official preferment because no occupation except commerce was open to them. At the same time the immigrants complicated the food problem, for they represented more mouths to feed.

The severe economic straits of the Iberian monarchies resulted in increased demands upon the colonists in the form of additional taxes and other exactions in the sale of offices, land grants, and a variety of official favors. This added drain on the colonies at an inopportune time retarded their economic revival.

The colonial towns survived this prolonged period of shrinking economic activity better than those of the peninsula. Gradually they surmounted their principal obstacles and began again to grow. Their success was due in part to the adjustments made and measures devised to meet some of the most critical problems. One solution was the modification of the system of large estates to include production of essential food crops previously raised by Indians and the development of debt peonage to provide a stable labor supply. The seventeenth century was a time of rapid growth of haciendas.

Mining also suffered during the first half of the seventeenth century. The decline was especially marked in Peru, and before the century was over the silver output of New Spain was greater than that of the South American viceroyalty. By the end of the epoch mining was once more expanding, but even in New Spain the annual yields of the 1580's had not yet been surpassed. The continued difficulty in obtaining miners and the exhaustion of the easily worked surface veins made silver production more expensive.

In 1600 the Spanish and Portuguese colonies were characterized by heterogeneous populations, sharply divided into distinct classes and castes, each with its own aspirations and interests. For Europe the seventeenth century was the era of the Thirty Years War and of the divine right of kings. It would be vain to search on the rim of Christendom for what was lacking at its center, and colonial life was occasionally violent and cruel. Yet it should be remembered that conditions in some of the Spanish colonies were more favorable than those in the peninsula and other parts of Europe.

The social and political gulf between the peninsulares and the creoles produced endless strife and resentment. The exclusion of the latter from high political and clerical offices was common in all of the Latin American colonies, for suspicion of the colonists and of those who governed them was a constant feature of the policies emanating from Madrid and Lisbon. It is true that American-born sons of high officials occasionally were appointed to important offices, but these were not typical creoles, for most returned to the homelands at an early age. One of the reasons for the exclusion of the creoles was that they lacked influential friends in Madrid and Lisbon, where importunate candidates for royal favors were legion. Appointments to colonial offices were used as a form of royal patronage; scions of loyal but extravagant houses could be rewarded with opportunities to restore their fortunes without loosening royal purse-strings. Voices occasionally were raised in warning against this practice, but they were drowned out by the clamor of favor-seekers at court.

Until the middle of the seventeenth century Spanish prestige and armed might were impressive. But after 1640, when weak but once more independent Portugal pleaded with Brazilians to yield to the Dutch, and after the defeat of the once-invincible Spanish infantry at Rocroi three years later, the Iberian kingdoms were no longer awe-inspiring. The rule of Carlos II for the final quarter of the century carried Spain to the nadir, even as her colonies were emerging from the long depression.

Although the creoles aspired to a position of equality with the peninsulares and reinois, their feelings toward the mestizos and other castes reflected none of Isabel's pious hope that the natives and their descendants could be raised to a rank of equality with the conquerors. Even among the humbler elements of the population sharp cleavages existed, cleavages based upon the degree of European ancestry, and in the case of Indians and Negroes, upon legal status. The disunity of these classes which composed the bulk of the populations made their continued domination by a small but aggressive white minority fairly easy. Riots were frequent, but it would be difficult to read into them more than discontent with local conditions.

The problems of the mestizos were similar to those of the poorer creoles. Although many of them were talented and energetic, their opportunities for advancement were extremely limited, and they were forced into occupations for which the creoles had little appetite. Some were able to fill the lesser civil and ecclesiastical offices along with creoles, and others served in the ranks of the army. The mestizos were in general a separate group, for although their ambitions led them in the direction of the creoles, their Indian ancestry raised an almost insurmountable barrier to success as a class. Those who succeeded, and many of the so-called creoles were in fact mestizos, were absorbed.

The social and political condition of the civilized Indians continued to be that of exploitable wards of the state. Some of the so-called free Indians lived as small farmers or as artisans in the cities, but those near the mines, in the obrajes, or on plantations were often not far removed from outright slavery. The fact that many Indians still lived in villages under the immediate rule of their own officials did little to mitigate their plight, for few can be more tyrannical than one raised arbitrarily to the status of governor of his own group in behalf of outsiders. Indians were still prohibited from riding horses, carrying arms, or dressing like Spaniards unless specifically authorized to do so. The Christian converts among the Pueblo Indians of New Mexico were allowed to ride horses so they could serve as herders, and to bear arms in defense of the province against its Apache enemies. The Guaranís of Paraguay were armed and organized into military forces by the Jesuits to resist the destructive incursions of slave-raiders from Brazil, but these were exceptional cases.

At the bottom of the social scale were the Negroes, free and slave, who were most numerous in the tropical regions. Negroes were superior in physique and in cultural achievement to the Indians of the torrid zones, but their legal status as slaves determined their low rank in the social scale. In the West Indies and among the coastal plantations of the Caribbean mainland and Brazil they replaced the Indians almost completely. The color line was not sharply drawn, and intermixture led to the formation of a large mulatto class. Manumission was also common, so that free Negroes became a sizable element of tropical populations. Negroes and mulattoes were able to work at certain trades and to enter the lower levels of the guilds, but in general they were relegated to domestic service, agricultural labor, or the army. Because of the presence of a substantial number of free Negroes and mulattoes, and because their contributions to the development of colonial tropical plantations were not in supplying labor alone, the role of the Negro in the Iberian colonies should properly be considered from the standpoint of immigrant rather than slave. Cultural assimilation was a two-way process.

One constant source of difficulty in the colonies was the failure of colonial officials to reflect the good intentions of the kings and their counselors in the peninsula. The administration of justice was corrupted by the venality of the judges, and even viceroys were involved in illegal transactions. The disharmony prevailing between viceroys and audiencias, moreover, made the enforcement of the edicts of the one and the decisions of the other haphazard at best.

Conflicts between officials of church and state were also chronic, but were more pronounced in Spanish America than in Brazil. Royal policy embraced two sometimes conflicting aims: support of the religious establishment in the extension of Catholicism, and the upholding of the patronato. In view of this situation it is not surprising that rivalry prevailed among the ardent and individualistic officials of church and state.

Many of the disputes between civil and clerical officials were over seemingly trivial matters, but occasionally they assumed serious proportions. A saying was current in New Spain that preserving order among the friars and the Indians was a full time job for a viceroy. In 1624 a quarrel between the viceroy and the archbishop over sanctuary led to the violent expulsion of the former by a priest-led mob; the viceregal palace was burned and a part of the city was given up to looting. In Lima a dispute as to whether the viceroy could reserve the use of six mules to his own carriage, or whether the archbishop also merited the use of that number, led to widespread irritation and unrest. Conflicts of a similar nature occurred between provincial governors and bishops, and on down the scale of officialdom. It should be remembered that this friction between lay and civil officials was not concerned with dogma or doctrine.

In every large city there was a horde of riff-raff, beggars by day and bandits by night, who took advantage of any serious disturbance between high officials. When discord or violence prevailed, the mob added to the destruction by wantonly burning public buildings and looting the homes of the wealthy. The ever-present danger of rioting was a brake on impetuous officials, for an ill-considered act might open the floodgates to a torrent of devastation. Fear of *tumultos* was one reason why colonial officials were not more tyrannical in upholding the law and asserting their authority. This was especially true with regard to attempts to dominate the clergy, for clerical influence was powerful over all ranks of society, and especially over the humbler elements.

In New Spain and Peru the church had acquired considerable property, in spite of early laws forbidding the practice. Wealth permitted the friars of some orders to enjoy material comforts not in keeping with their vows. The number of religious houses grew, and as their landholdings increased they began to compete seriously with private enterprise and to constitute a financial burden on the colonial economy. Civil officials occasionally pointed out to the king the dangers and disadvantages inherent in this situation. In 1620 the viceroy of Peru declared that the religious houses of Lima owned more land than the lay population, and in 1644 the cabildo of Mexico repeated its earlier request to the king to prohibit the establishment of additional monasteries. These and similar manifestations of discontent were of little avail, however, even when the king heeded them. In some areas a will which left no legacy to one of the religious orders was regarded as an act against religion. The wealth of the various orders continued to grow, and the number of religious houses more than doubled during the first half of the century. The income derived from church property was not a part of the general wealth. The religious establishments enjoyed tax exemptions, and the lay population paid tithes for the support of the church. Despite the church's support of educational and charitable institutions, the laity resented its favored position.

On the frontiers the role of missionaries became vitally important during the seventeenth century, as the line of settlement advanced into the lands of warlike nomads not easily converted into docile field hands and miners. There was little economic incentive for men to wage war against the wild tribes at their own expense, and the religious orders were therefore given an opportunity to employ peaceful persuasion as the advance agents of civilization. They were expected to reduce the Indians to an orderly life and then to turn them over to the secular clergy. Often they were accompanied by a squad of soldiers to help preserve order and to bring back runaways, but the presence of troops was not always conducive to the rapid adoption of desirable behavior on the part of the neophytes. The task which the missionaries assumed was as difficult as it was enormous, and martyrdom was the reward of many. It was no simple task to persuade free, wandering tribes to settle in permanent villages, to adopt a strange and distasteful way of life, and to accept the doctrines of the church and obedience to royal authority. It is not surprising that when they saw their efforts proving fruitful the missionaries were reluctant to surrender the missions to the secular arm of the church and depart once more for heathen lands. The secularization of the missions was rarely accomplished peaceably.

The widespread efforts and successes of the missionaries made the mission a vital frontier institution serving church and state alike. In the seventeenth century missionaries were active among warlike tribes from southern Chile to Florida and New Mexico. Wherever the padres were able to win the confidence of the natives the natives usually survived in fairly large numbers. The Indians who resisted the blandishments of the missionaries, and who therefore could be of little value to colonial society, were pushed deeper into the wilderness.

In many regions the missionaries won notable triumphs, although the Indians' progress in comprehending and appreciating Christian doctrine was understandably slow. Frequently missions were established among previously destructive raiders, who were transformed into defenders of the frontiers against European interlopers, thus sparing the royal treasury the cost of numerous garrisons. The Pueblo Indians of New Mexico anchored the northern defenses, while the Guaranís of Paraguay were called out like regular militia when danger from the Portuguese threatened. The Jesuits of Brazil rallied powerful tribes to combat the French and Dutch, and Indian aid was a significant factor in both Brazilian triumphs.

In the seventeenth century, despite the usual local *tumultos*, society had become fairly stable; the most important areas were held almost without military forces except for garrisons on the frontiers and in the principal ports. The generations of immigrants who came after the turbulence of the conquest abated had little reason for harshness toward the Indians. The viceroys maintained only token guard forces at their immediate command, and relied upon the principal citizens to preserve or restore order when called upon to do so. In neither Spanish nor Portuguese America did large numbers of Indians desert to join English, French, or Dutch expeditions. Although the threat of force was ever present, it was not the sole means by which the Indians were kept under control. The clergy, by enjoining humility and obedience, played a vital role in preserving order and in maintaining the *status quo*.

Even on the remote frontiers military garrisons were small, inadequately armed, and poorly trained, considering the vastness of the empire and the number and resourcefulness of its enemies. With as little force as was available to Spanish and Portuguese officials in America during the seventeenth century, the preservation of the colonies was a remarkable achievement. The wild tribes became especially troublesome on the frontiers, for the spread of horses gave them an advantage in warfare they were quick to exploit, and the advent of English and other European traders provided an incentive to take to the warpath. In Florida and New Mexico and in southern Chile and the Plata region the Spaniards suffered severe setbacks; yet most of the lands were gradually reoccupied without the employment of sizable armies.

The laws against foreigners residing in the Spanish colonies were not rigidly enforced, and many non-Spaniards were active in commerce and various crafts. After Portugal became independent of Spain in 1640, Spanish officials were greatly concerned over the large number of Portuguese living in Spanish colonies. On several occasions orders were issued for their expulsion, but these were rescinded after local officials protested. In Lima, for example, there were 6000 Portuguese engaged in useful enterprises, and their sudden departure would have disturbed life in the city. In all Spanish colonies where Portuguese were residing, however, steps were taken to prevent sedition.

Foreigners occasionally appeared among the clergy of Spanish America. The English Dominican, Thomas Gage, who abandoned his companions on their way to the Philippine islands for a more comfortable and less heroic life in New Spain, and the German Jesuit, Eusebio Kino (Kühn), who performed noteworthy services among the Indians of Sonora and Arizona, are two well-known examples.

Education in the Iberian colonies continued to be the prerogative of young men from the upper classes. Most of the major cities of Spanish America were granted universities, while not a single institution for advanced study was permitted in Brazil, where sons of the wealthy were obliged to visit Europe for higher degrees. Education remained the domain of the church, and instruction continued to follow the pattern of the University of Salamanca, based primarily on scholasticism.

Scholasticism was the intellectual triumph of the thirteenth century, a system of theological and philosophic thought perfected by St. Thomas Aquinas and based on the precepts of Aristotle and the doctrines of the church. The Aristotelian classification of knowledge, including the various sciences dealing with man, served as the foundation stone, while the upper structure was composed of ecclesiastical dogma. Thus were sacred and profane thought brought into harmony within a single system. Scholasticism influenced learning in sixteenth- and seventeenth-century Latin America as in Europe, and its influence lasted long after its retreat began.

The scholars produced by the colonial universities were lawyers, men of letters, and priests. Occasionally these scholars attained excellence and prominence rivaling that of European contemporaries. The educational development of Latin America lagged behind Europe for the most part, however, although the systems were similar. The weaknesses of education in Latin America were in general the weaknesses of education in Europe.

Because of the fairly large number of educational institutions of various levels in the colonies it may appear that opportunities for education were available for all ranks of society. These were mostly religious seminaries with little purely secular learning, or academies largely limited to the study of Latin, the language of the universities. Even this education remained the privilege of the few at the apex of society who, because of wealth and position, were regarded as safe risks. Those who were thus qualified differed considerably between the metropolitan centers and the fringes of the empire. In the frontier missions the Indians were given as much instruction as was required to weld them to church and sovereign. In the cities Indians and mestizos, except for the sons of caciques, were specifically excluded from the schools by law. The few permitted to learn to read were carefully conditioned so that a little learning would not cause them to disturb the established order.

In the systems of education in Brazil and Spanish America can be found much of the cement which bound these colonies to the mother countries, or which at least restrained the colonists from making overt acts for so many centuries. The church, secular and regular clergy alike, was a powerful force for preserving the authority of the king.

One aspect of Jesuit instruction, however, was disturbing to the monarchs in Lisbon and Madrid. This was *probabilismo*, the doctrine of probable opinions. Not all probabilist conclusions were obnoxious to the kings, but the probable justification of tyrannicide and regicide cannot have appeared safe and reasonable to the imitators of Louis XIV. In 1665 Pope Alexander VII condemned forty-five of the probabilist propositions, and in 1680 Innocent XI ordered the General of the Society to prohibit the propagation of the system. Probabilism did not disappear, however, and it remained a cause of royal concern in the eighteenth century.

Two classic Spanish writers born in the New World, El Inca Garcilaso de la Vega and Juan Ruíz de Alarcón, deserve special mention despite the fact that their works do not properly belong with those of Spanish Americans. Garcilaso was the son of a Spanish soldier and a cousin of Atahualpa. His Inca ancestry and his father's role in the civil wars of Peru hindered his receiving official preferment, and as a young man he went to Spain, never to return to Peru. Toward the close of the sixteenth century he began writing, turning out a readable account of the de Soto expedition and his famous *Royal Commentaries* on the history of the Incas and their conquest by Spaniards, which are among the best early historical works of the New World.

Alarcón also left his homeland, New Spain, to study law at Salamanca. Failing to obtain a chair in the law school of the University of Mexico on his return, he departed once more for Spain, where he ultimately received an appointment to serve the Council of the Indies. It was in Spain that he won a high place among the playwrights of his age.

In the New World the centers of literary and artistic activity were the viceregal courts of Mexico and Lima, and the ecclesiastical seats. Among the many writers whose works merit attention was Bernardo de Valbuena who, though born in Spain, has been called 'the first genuinely American poet.' He was educated in New Spain, but lived in Spain, Jamaica, and Santo Domingo before becoming bishop of Puerto Rico. His most important surviving works were a poem, *The Greatness of Mexico*, a pastoral novel, *A Golden Age in the Forests of Eriphyle*, and the epic of chivalry, *Bernardo*.

Antônio Vieira, a Jesuit priest who spent much of his life in Brazil, is noted for his eloquence as orator and writer. His sermons fill many volumes, and contain articulate arguments against slavery, oppression of the Indians, and exploitation of Brazil by Portugal. He served brilliantly in the diplomatic maneuvers designed to keep Portugal independent in the decade after 1640, and he devoted his later years to protecting the Indians of Brazil.

Two seventeenth-century Spanish Americans, Carlos Sigüenza y Góngora of New Spain and Pedro de Peralta Barnuevo of Peru, were outstanding for their intellectual accomplishments in many fields. Both men devoted attention to mathematics, engineering, astronomy, and natural sciences, and each tried his hand at poetry.

They were the forerunners of a score of eighteenth-century scientists who were to lead the revolt against scholasticism, and who were to make valuable contributions to descriptive sciences.

Several women among the many who wrote deserve to be classed with the great writers of the epoch. First in order of accomplishment was Sor Juana Inés de la Cruz of Mexico, whose intellectual curiosity led her into many branches of knowledge. For women the path to learning was beset with many pitfalls, and Sor Juana's secular studies were not generally appreciated.

Talent and aptitude were found among colonial scholars at widely separated places, despite the many obstacles to intellectual development imposed by the degeneration of education, the limited opportunities for publication, and the slowness of communication which hampered interchange of ideas. It must be remembered, also, that the segment of the colonial population in a position to produce scholars and writers was extremely small, no more than a tenth of the total. Despite the limited size of this group and the fact that it was widely scattered, despite the other handicaps mentioned, Latin American scientists were not far behind those of the peninsula.

In architecture the severely classical style replaced the fortress-like structures of the previous century. This was in its turn abandoned in favor of the highly ornate Spanish American baroque, which was characteristic of most of the seventeenth and eighteenth centuries. The work of colonial architects was among the finest creative achievements of the period. In painting, too, the seventeenth century produced some of the best work of the entire colonial period.

The development of the colonial theater followed that of Spain, and Spanish actors organized a theatrical group in Lima shortly before 1600. The viceroys, universities, and religious houses sponsored dramatic groups, and theaters appeared also in provincial capitals. Especially popular were the comedies of Lope de Vega; more dramatic works were shipped to the colonies in the seventeenth century than other types of non-religious literature. The great popularity of the theater occasionally aroused the opposition of the clergy, and plays were subjected to careful scrutiny by officials of the Inquisition in their role as guardians of public morals.

The church was the principal patron of painting and music. Indians were trained for the choir, with pleasing results. They were also employed as painters by the clergy, and it was they who built, under the direction of the priests, the richly ornamented churches of the seventeenth century.

The general state of health of the colonists was not such as to make for great activity. Scourges of fatal diseases, native and European, were common. In the tropical colonies yellow fever was endemic, and it gave to certain ports the aspect of graveyards. Smallpox appeared with fatal results in most of the settlements, and took a heavy toll of Europeans as well as Indians and Negroes. The poverty and malnutrition of the poorer classes made them easy prey to the pestilence which attended the recurrent famines.

Although chairs of medicine were established in the universities, the study of medicine in Europe had not yet been freed of the vestiges of medieval superstition, and colonial inspiration was derived from the peninsula. It was not until the eighteenth century that noteworthy advances were made during the revolt against scholasticism, and even then provincial drug stores and hospitals continued to rely upon the curative effects of such time-honored remedies as wild boar's teeth, spirits of earthworms, and lizard oil. Colonial physicians decided upon treatments with relation to the position of the stars.

The prevalence of diseases in the Caribbean islands and mainland was not always wholly disadvantageous to Spain, for yellow fever, malaria, and dysentery were important bulwarks against invasion in this region. The defeat of Oliver Cromwell's attempt to seize the Caribbean area, the failure of the Scots' colony at Darién, and many another attempted incursion came to grief because of disease even before Spanish troops appeared.

Agriculture remained the principal livelihood for most Latin American colonists. European and African plants introduced in the century of the conquest had become well acclimated, and many New World plants were cultivated for exportable products such as chocolate and tobacco. Horses, cattle, sheep, and swine were raised wherever there were settlements. The cattle, beyond those needed to supply meat locally, were raised chiefly for their hides. Because of the vast herds in some localities, nothing was done to improve the breeds of livestock. In the Plata region a cowhide was worth more than a live cow.

A constant search for mines was a feature of seventeenth-century activity, and new mines were frequently opened. Their discovery was followed by the usual rush of miners and adventurers to the scene, the hasty erection of mining camps, and the establishment of the industries needed to support the new community. Antiquated mining methods were wasteful of both labor and ore, and as the rich veins were exhausted, the output of the mines declined.

Textiles were the most important products of handicraft in the Spanish colonies; cloth of wool, cotton, and silk was produced. The obrajes, although the target of numerous edicts, continued to be among the most inhumane exploiters of native laborers. Work in the obraje began as soon as it was light enough to see, and continued until it was dark. The owner or overseer distributed the work to be done, and then locked the door. At nightfall the work was gathered up and punishments meted out to those who had failed to accomplish as much as was expected. Severe whippings were the most common punishments. The whole organization was operated like a prison workhouse, and it was unusual for an inmate to escape. Some Indian families spent their entire lives within the obrajes.

In all of the settlements the production of foodstuffs for local consumption was a necessary activity, although some of the mining communities had to rely on commerce for virtually all necessities. Soap-making, tanning, woodworking, and pottery-making were among the common local industries.

Shipbuilding continued to be an important occupation in the Caribbean, in Central America, and in some parts of South America. The production of cordage, sails, and other naval stores provided livelihoods for many, especially in Central America.

The extremely poor state of communications and transportation was a difficult obstacle for colonial merchants to overcome, for little could be transported inland which could not survive a journey on muleback. Despite handicaps and restrictions, however, colonial commerce expanded as the population increased and new lands were opened to settlement. The coining of money and the raising of mules were two vital aids to commerce. Brazil was without a mint until 1694, but before the gold discoveries in Minas Gerais a mint would have had little to do. In Spanish America part of the bullion was minted and put into circulation locally.

For many of the pastoral regions the raising of mules to be used in commerce and mining was a large-scale enterprise, and every year enormous herds were driven to the mining centers from all directions. Cowhides and tallow were the principal exportable items from lands like Argentina. Among the poor people of this area beef and *yerba maté* or Paraguayan tea were the staples of life. The slaughtering methods gave to the towns an unattractive atmosphere, for animals were driven close to where their flesh was needed, slaughtered, and the parts not wanted left on the ground for dogs, rats, flies, and carrion crows. Acres of bleaching bones were a common sight around many provincial towns.

Life in the metropolitan centers probably was not vastly different from that of Iberian cities of the same era. A few families enjoyed all of the available ostentatious luxuries, and the remainder lived in varying degrees of poverty. Among the wealthy personal comfort was little valued in the acquisition of luxuries. An item which suggested wealth beyond need was preferable to one which might make it unnecessary to wear an overcoat indoors in cold weather.

In all of the Latin American settlements amusements were scarce and likely to be crude or violent. Probably the mildest form of entertainment was the afternoon *paseo*, in which men and women circled about the park or plaza in opposite directions. Religious processions were common, not only in celebration of religious holidays but in response to various calamities, such as epidemics of smallpox. Whenever some unusual event occurred, such as the birth of an heir to the throne or the arrival of a new viceroy, large-scale celebrations were held, often lasting for several days. In these there might be bull-fighting, bear-baiting, feats of horsemanship, singing, dancing, poetical contests, and gambling. All segments of society, including slaves, participated in these fiestas.

Brazilian life remained centered in the rural fazendas rather than in cities or towns as in Spanish America. The Brazilian cities did not yet have a prosperous commercial class, and the principal possessors of wealth were still the lords of the plantations. The most stable and influential part of Brazilian society was that of the fazenda, centered around the big house of the fazendeiro, the family chapel, the engenho, and the slave quarters. These well-knit, self-sufficient communities were typical only of the plantation area of the northeast, yet their influence was widely felt.

Life in the mining towns of Spanish America, especially those inaccessible and turbulent ones like Potosí, was unlike anything elsewhere in the Americas. Of the few seventeenth-century women who left their mark, most gained their fame or notoriety in the boisterous frontier mining centers, where the appreciation of charm and talent was sharp, and where the social rules of more stable communities were scorned. Acts of passion and of bloody vengeance were not unusual, and in this tempestuous milieu wealth and fame were ephemeral.

In the seventeenth century the Inquisition was especially active in South America, because of the large number of Portuguese Jews and 'New Christians' who entered Spanish colonies. Clerical officials were greatly aroused over what they regarded as a serious menace to purity of the faith. At the same time the Holy Office was employed occasionally as a means of disposing of especially troublesome colonial officials, though its principal occupation was the preservation of public morals.

By the end of the seventeenth century the colonies of Spain and Portugal had passed through the violent and expansive era of the conquest, and into a period of dwindling Indian populations and shrinking economic activity. In meeting these situations the colonial societies developed the practices and forms which they were to preserve throughout the remainder of the colonial epoch. In most areas the way of life had become fairly well set and the relationships between classes fixed. Among the most far-reaching developments was the gradual incorporation of the growing mestizo population into a system of controlled labor along with the Indians. Debt peonage was to have important consequences in the formation of the new, mixed races which were emerging, for it weakened the tribal, village life of the Indians, and opened the way to a more rapid assimilation of Spanish cultural traits and language.

X

The Caribbean Area, 1600–1700

> What most I wondered at was to see the *requas* of mules which came thither from Panama, laden with wedges of silver . . . which were unladen in the public market-place . . . It was a wonder then to see the multitude of people in those streets which the week before had been empty.
>
> Then began the price of all things to rise . . . whilst the galleons were lading with wedges of silver and nothing else; so that for those fifteen days . . . in the world there is no greater fair than that of Portobello . . .
>
> THOMAS GAGE *

AFTER the initial conquest of the West Indies had given the Spaniards a springboard to the continent, little attention was given to the islands. The hasty exodus of adventurers to more promising lands had left only a small number of planters and merchants. Once the riches of New Spain and Peru were known, Española, Cuba, San Juan, and Jamaica lost what little attraction they possessed earlier. But even though not a single Spaniard had chosen to seek his living in the islands, strategy required Spain's continued control.

Although the islands were virtually depopulated of Spaniards as the conquest swept south and west to the continental areas, a new type of immigration began once more to people the islands. This was the ever-increasing stream of African Negro slaves who were brought in as plantation hands and household servants. Through

* A New Survey of the West Indies, London, 1648, various editions.

this influx of Negroes, tropical America became, ethnically, at least, a colony of Africa. Negroes became the most numerous and productive part of the population and the backbone of the tropical plantation economy. By 1600 they greatly outnumbered the Spaniards in the islands and some of the coastal settlements of the Caribbean mainland. The fact that Negroes could be legally enslaved did not set them far apart from many of the technically free Indians, mestizos, and poor whites. Manumission was common, and a class of freedmen soon appeared. The free Negroes and mulattoes in the tropics corresponded to the free Indians and mestizos of the temperate zones. It is misleading to consider the contributions of the Negro solely as a slave.

At the outset of the seventeenth century Santo Domingo, once the seat of Spanish rule in the New World, was a village of only some 600 Spaniards. More than 4000 Negro slaves labored on the nearby plantations and ranches, while free mulattoes were becoming numerous. Few traces of the aboriginal inhabitants were to be found.

Santo Domingo was still the seat of the audiencia which had been established there in 1511. Under its jurisdiction were San Juan, Jamaica, Margarita, Venezuela, Guiana, and Florida. The archdiocese of Santo Domingo embraced the same area with bishoprics centered in Santiago de Cuba, Villa Rica de Puerto Rico, and Caracas. In the city were several religious houses, a college, and a hospital. A small garrison maintained a precarious and often ineffective defense of the port. The lack of adequate naval protection in the Caribbean Sea made commerce with the island extremely hazardous, for enemy freebooters lay in wait at inlets along unoccupied stretches of the coast and plundered luckless ships which ventured within their reach, to the ruin of merchants and shipowners. Dutch corsairs were especially active in the early decades of the seventeenth century, but those of other nations also frequented the Caribbean, for Spanish commerce was a prize made the more tempting by the marked decline of Spanish sea power. The depredations of the corsairs almost ruined the islands economically, and the convoy system was insufficient protection against

their attacks. In 1628 the Dutch, as already mentioned, captured
an entire convoy on the coast of Cuba. Squadrons were sent against
the intruders, but with their lighter vessels they withdrew to shallow waters where the large warships could not follow. Tortuga, one
of the pirate headquarters of this period, was captured by Spain in
1638, but piracy was checked only momentarily, for other suitable
bases were legion in the Windward Islands, Curaçao, Jamaica after
1655, and unoccupied parts of Española.

Owing to similar conditions Cuba, San Juan, and Jamaica were
in a like state. The few mines which had not been exhausted were
largely unworked because of a lack of miners, although vast plantations and extensive cattle ranches were common. Some copper was
extracted in Cuba and shipped to Spain, but its value was not great.
Habana's importance was determined primarily by its strategic location and use as an assembly point for fleets returning to Spain. The
city had a population of about 1200 Spaniards and many more
Negroes and mulattoes. Shipbuilding was one of its most profitable
enterprises, and many galleons were constructed in the port.

San Juan, which was even more sparsely populated, concentrated
upon the production of sugar and cowhides, and the raising of
horses. As in the other islands, the Indians had long since become
scarce, and most labor was performed by Negroes and mulattoes.
The diocese of San Juan included Cumaná, Guiana, and Margarita;
the official visits required of the bishop to these outlying regions
under his authority were made at considerable risk not only from
pirates but from the hazards of the sea, with the result that his administrative efforts were confined for the most part to San Juan.

St. Augustine, Florida, was a military outpost made necessary by
the unwelcome attentions of English and French vessels to the
Spanish merchantmen plying the difficult waters of the Bahama
Channel, and in the seventeenth century by the need for a bulwark
against the English of Virginia. Franciscan missions north of Florida
replaced those formerly conducted by the Jesuits, and these attempted to offset the machinations of English agents among the
southern tribes. The advent of the English to Virginia marked the
beginning of a lengthy contest for the control and assistance of the

warring Indians, who were to fight a large share of the inter-colonial wars of the future. In this prolonged struggle the Spanish missionaries played a vital role; to have accomplished the same end by the simple expediency of establishing garrisons of sufficient strength would have cost Spain an enormous outlay of money and soldiers, neither of which could be spared.

On the mainland of northern South America were the provinces of Guiana, Venezuela, and New Granada. The first of these had only a minute population and little commercial importance. Venezuela, on the other hand, had a fairly prosperous agricultural district. Caracas, a short distance inland, was a city of some 300 Spaniards, and thousands of Indians, Negroes, and mulattoes, free and slave. A lively commerce was carried on in corn, wheat, and cacao, a crop introduced by the Spanish from Central America. Large ranches supplied hides for shipment to Spain, and mules which were driven to Peru by way of New Granada.

Cartagena, one of the most active trading centers in the Caribbean area, was the chief outlet for goods from the interior of Tierra Firme. Its harbor was the anchorage of the silver fleets and galleons. Through this port flowed the commerce of Spain and much of Spanish South America; Cartagena was surpassed in commercial importance only by Mexico City and Lima. In 1600 it had a Spanish population of approximately 1500 and a much larger service class of Negroes, mulattoes, and mestizos, all of whom increased steadily throughout the century. Because of its importance commercially and its exposed situation, the city was walled and protected to seaward by fortifications. Its prestige was enhanced by the presence of the governor and bishop.

Defense against foreign pirates and Indians was the principal concern of the governor. In this task he had recourse to several companies of cavalry and infantry, a more numerous body of local militiamen selected from among the civilians, and a company of free, native-born Negroes. A well-stocked arsenal provided arms for these troops, and the forts contained fifty pieces of artillery. All of these defenses were tested frequently by foreign expeditions, and fortunately for the city were seldom found to be insufficient.

Since Cartagena was one of the chief commercial centers, royal officials, a customshouse, and warehouses for storing merchandise until the departure of the fleets were to be found there. The sources of the traffic which passed through Cartagena were Peru, the mainland, New Spain, the Windward Islands, Angola and the Guinea river in Africa, and the Cape Verde Islands, from which came twenty or thirty shiploads of slaves each year. Gold and silver, cacao, indigo, cochineal and a multitude of tropical products were shipped from the port to Spain.

Some idea of the city may be gained from a brief account of its non-military activities. It contained a renowned cathedral, Dominican, Franciscan, Augustinian, and Jesuit houses, a nunnery of the Discalced Carmelites, and another of the order of Santa Clara. There were hospitals with wards for maternity cases and for syphilitics as well as for ordinary maladies. Many of the houses were of the same simple construction as those built in the early years, walls of cane plastered with clay and roofs of palm leaves. During the growth and commercial prosperity of the city in the early seventeenth century these dwellings were gradually replaced by more costly and attractive abodes.

The governor appointed a lieutenant-general to take command of the troops, and supervised matters of government, warfare, and the preservation of the Indians. Ships were cleared on his authority. The city council had two regular alcaldes and two belonging to the Hermandad, an *alguacil mayor* (head constable), 12 regidores, a receiver-general, and an attorney-general. Appeals from their decisions were made to the Audiencia of Santa Fé de Bogotá, which was at a considerable distance and difficult to reach. The same was true for appeals from the decisions of judges and royal officials who handled cases dealing with maritime affairs. A galley chief had jurisdiction over cases pertaining to the galleys and their guards. Appeals from his jurisdiction usually went to the Council of the Indies. In Cartagena there was also a tribunal of the Holy Office with its customary inquisitors, attorney, and secretaries.

Because of the great distance separating Cartagena from the Audiencia of Santa Fé de Bogotá it was extremely difficult and expensive to appeal most cases at law. Many complaints were made because of this inconvenience, and suggestions were frequent that the audiencia be removed to Cartagena, or that justices from that court and from the one in Santo Domingo take up residence in the city. Other towns in New Granada suffered from the same difficulty. Santa Marta was under the Santa Fé audiencia while Río de la Hacha, almost an equal distance from Cartagena, was in the jurisdiction of the court at Santo Domingo.

Communications with the interior were by means of the Magdalena river, one of the four principal waterways of South America. Near the coast were farms which harvested abundant crops of corn, manioc, and many varieties of Spanish and native fruits and vegetables. Cattle ranches provided beef for the city, while poultry was obtained through trade with the Indians of Urabá. Fisheries were operated at various places along the coast. Indian villages under the charge of encomenderos produced immense quantities of corn, swine, and poultry, which brought incomes annually to their masters.

Santa Marta was much less prosperous than formerly, most of its residents having departed owing partly to vexations caused by the governors. In the early years of the seventeenth century its population was some sixty Spaniards. Río de la Hacha was somewhat more fortunate, for in addition to the usual products for trade, hides, dyewoods, and other tropical goods, it had control of extensive and profitable pearl fisheries. In pearl fishing Negro slaves gradually replaced Indians.

Many of the natives of the region were still not under Spanish control, and their raids frequently interrupted commerce and communications between the various cities of the interior. Those who were held in encomienda still continued to dress and adorn themselves in their accustomed finery, painted cotton blankets, gold earhoops, and bracelets.

Santa Fé de Bogotá, the largest city in New Granada, contained about 2000 Spanish residents in addition to a multitude of Indians, free and slave. The farms and ranches of the vicinity kept the city bountifully supplied with meat, fruits, and vegetables. Cotton grown locally was woven into coarse cloth for sale to the Indians. Sugar and henequen also were produced. Numerous mines were worked for gold, silver, and emeralds, although the lack of miners was a persistent problem.

Santa Fé was the capital of the presidency of New Granada, which had jurisdiction over a vast, much-dissected country, from Cartagena to Popayán, and from Mérida to Buenaventura on the Pacific coast. The city also was the residence of the archbishop, whose suffragan bishops were those of Cartagena, Santa Marta, and Popayán. The Indians of the capital region were the capable and docile Chibchas, who performed most of the labor. The various cities of the district were active in agriculture and mining. Gold mines especially were productive, and gangs of Indian and Negro miners washed gold from the stream beds. In the Pamplona district were raised great numbers of mules which were driven to Peru for sale. There also were seventeen sugar mills in the area.

Zaragoza and the Cauca valley also were regions of activity in the production of gold. In the former area nearly 4000 Negro slaves were employed under the direction of some 300 Spanish miners. The ratio of slaves to masters was so great that uprisings occurred from time to time; in 1598 a slave revolt did considerable damage before the rebels were subdued in the following year. Other mining regions were discovered in the course of the seventeenth century, but their exploitation had to await the conquest of the tribes in whose lands they lay, and the introduction of slaves to work them.

Plantations in Timaná, New Granada, provided coca leaves which served to dull the pains of hunger and fatigue of Indian laborers. Before the conquest this plant had been reserved to the upper native hierarchy for ceremonial purposes. Its widespread use among the lower classes came about only during the Spanish colonial period, when it was seen to be a profitable item of trade.

The city of Panamá on the Pacific side of the Isthmus was the point of trans-shipment for commerce to and from the viceroyalty of Peru. The city had about 500 residents in addition to the many transients awaiting passage, and large numbers of free Negroes and mulattoes. In 1610, however, Panamá was only a third the size it had been in 1585.

After Portugal won her independence from Spain in 1640, many Portuguese merchants remained in Panamá and other Spanish colonies, where they were regarded with suspicion. When two serious fires broke out in Panamá in 1644 the Portuguese were forced to take up residence twenty leagues in the interior from Panamá City and Portobelo, even though it was not established that they were responsible.

The Audiencia of Panamá was the oldest on the mainland; its jurisdiction extended to Darién on the east and to Costa Rica on the west. During the sixteenth century it was abolished when Panamá was placed under the jurisdiction of the Audiencia of Lima. Toward the end of the century it was re-established. The bishop who resided in Panamá City was suffragan to the archbishop of Lima, and in other ways Panamá was more closely linked to Peru than to other Spanish dependencies.

Panamá enjoyed a profitable trade not only with Peru but with Nicaragua and Guatemala. So much traffic went through its ports that most of its inhabitants were involved in trade or shipbuilding, and many ships were built in Panamá for commerce in the Pacific.

Portobelo, on the Caribbean side of the Isthmus, replaced Nombre de Dios as the port of entry only after the latter harbor had begun to fill with silt. Compared to Panamá City, Portobelo was far smaller, and its climate and location less attractive to settlers. It had a bad reputation among Spaniards as an unhealthful city. Most of its provisions, with the exception of rice, native fruits, and citrus, had to be carried from a distance.

One of the busiest commercial routes in the New World was the trail from Panamá to Portobelo, over which hundreds of mules carried the merchandise bound for Peru or Spain. Some of the owners of *arrieros* — mule trains — amassed substantial wealth. When the galleons were in port, trading was brisk.

As the time for the Portobelo fair approached, *recuas* of mules laden with silver arrived from Panamá on the south shore of the Isthmus. The bars of silver were piled in the public market place, awaiting the arrival of the fleet. When the sails of the approaching galleons were sighted in the distance, prices immediately began to rise. For the next two or three weeks hundreds of merchants from Panamá, Peru, and other regions to the south and west traded with those from Spain, while the silver was loaded for the homeward passage. The visitors, who were unaccustomed to the tropical maladies which infested the region, were invariably beset by fevers, and the friars who conducted the hospital of Portobelo were constantly occupied with caring for the ill and burying the dead.

West of Panamá lay the province of Veragua, where the largest sawmill on the Pacific coast was located. More than 4000 Negroes were employed in the mills and in the famous shipyards of Veragua. In the capital city of Santa Fé there were only thirty Spaniards, and the northern part of the province remained in the possession of hostile Indians.

The Audiencia of Guatemala, which had jurisdiction over Chiapas, Honduras, Nicaragua, Salvador, and Costa Rica, was centered in the city of Antigua, Guatemala. Most of the provinces of Central America produced immense quantities of cacao, indigo, and cochineal for export. Traders came annually with mule trains from Mexico, and commerce was carried on by way of the sea with the Caribbean islands, Spain, and Peru. Cattle and mule ranches in some regions produced great numbers of cowhides for export to Spain, and pack mules which were driven to Panamá to be used in the transisthmian commerce.

In Central America the Franciscans, Dominicans, Mercedarians, and Jesuits had numerous houses, and all except the last named operated sugar and indigo mills for their support. Instruction in the arts and theology was given, and a small college was maintained by the Dominicans. Early in the century a petition was sent the king asking permission to establish a university, since it was inconvenient to send students to Mexico City. The city of Guatemala offered to provide an adequate income for the university. The request finally was approved, and in 1675 the University of San Carlos was founded.

The Spanish population of the Central American provinces was not large in the early seventeenth century, but the entire region was heavily peopled by Indians who were capable of learning trades and whose docility and obedience made a large force of Spaniards unnecessary. Immigration to the area was exceedingly small after the initial conquest, because by then the lands and Indians were in the possession of the conquerors and their descendants, and competition with a servile class of laborers was an unattractive prospect for the newcomers. Commerce was the only occupation which permitted new arrivals a respectable opportunity to earn a livelihood.

Within five leagues (about fifteen miles) of Guatemala City were sixty Indian villages for the service of the city and its some 1000 Spanish residents. Since these natives were skillful workmen and usually obedient to their masters, the region was abundantly supplied with labor. In one district there was a separate village of free Negroes and mulattoes, for the Spaniards ordinarily endeavored to keep them apart from the Indians. In all of the Indian villages the inhabitants took an active part in church services, serving as cantors and choirmasters, many becoming accomplished as musicians and singers.

The city of Granada in Nicaragua was a prosperous commercial center by 1600. The Spanish population was small, less than 300 persons, but Indians, Negroes, and mulattoes were numerous. Sugar mills, cattle and mule ranches, cacao gathering, and tobacco raising were among the most profitable activities. Dyewoods, indigo, and cochineal also were prepared for export. Some of this commerce was sent north by way of Lake Nicaragua and shipped to Cartagena and Portobelo for trans-shipment to Spain. Pine pitch and canvas from cotton grown in the province were shipped to Peru by way of the Pacific port of Realejo. The pitch, which was used in the preparation of wine casks, was especially profitable and in great demand. From the Peruvian trade silver and merchandise were obtained. Realejo, an important commercial port, was also noted for its shipbuilding. The vessels built at Realejo were especially desirable for service in the tropical waters of the Pacific coast of Central America as the native hardwoods were not infested by worms.

Near Realejo was a large Indian village called El Viejo which also enjoyed profitable commerce. Spaniards who traveled through the province were well treated by the Indians and housed and fed at no expense to themselves. Most of the natives of this region spoke Castilian and dressed like Spaniards, in cotton clothing dyed black. They were extremely skillful artisans, and many of their handicrafts flourished. Near by was another district similarly situated, where rope and henequen cordage were made for export. Many other Indian villages were profitably employed in similar enterprises, and a considerable amount of rope and cotton sailcloth was shipped to Peru from Nicaragua.

Costa Rica's commercial activity was largely owing to the fact that the settlement lay along the overland route from New Spain to Panamá. Every year traders from Honduras and Nicaragua crossed Costa Rica on their way to Panamá with herds of mules for the isthmian carrying trade. Gold was extracted and worked into ornaments by the Indians, and henequen, tobacco, and various tropical fruits also were produced for trade.

The province of Chiapas was noted for its cattle and horses as well as for the cotton cloth which the Indians wove. There were more than twenty-five Indian settlements in the province. Chiapa de los Indios was probably the largest in America, for it contained some 10,000 inhabitants. These Indians, like most others already subjugated in Central America, were obedient and intelligent and quick to learn trades. Because of their obedience to Spanish authorities they were permitted the use of horses, and were famous for their feats of horsemanship. Every day markets were held in the towns, fruits and foodstuffs being brought by the Indian farmers of the vicinity. The Indians maintained a successful administration over the other tribal towns, and they were especially famous for their charity and hospitality to indigent travelers.

In the early years of the seventeenth century most of the provinces of the Caribbean area enjoyed a prosperity based upon agriculture and mining. St. Augustine cannot be included in this favorable condition, for it was only a poor outpost maintained by funds from New Spain. The rise of Holland and the founding of the Dutch West India Company, however, greatly increased the inroads of

foreign pirates, for under the assault of the Hollanders the English
and French corsairs became bolder. The seventeenth century was
the period of most active buccaneering, and Spanish colonial commerce, especially that of the Caribbean area, suffered heavy losses.
Despite this fact, none of Spain's enemies was powerful enough to
wrest from her grasp areas which she had considered worth colonizing in the sixteenth century, with the single exception of the island
of Jamaica. The piratical attacks, however, forced Spain to spend
large sums on fortifications and naval protection. These outlays became greater and greater as the century progressed and as Spain's
rivals established bases among the Lesser Antilles. From these island
headquarters they launched numerous raids on the Spanish island
towns as well as those of the mainland. Venezuela, New Granada,
and Panamá were especially hard hit, but even the remote Pacific
towns of Central America were not spared.

The greatest attraction to the buccaneers was the profitable commerce which flowed between the colonies and Spain. Inter-colonial
traffic, too, was disrupted, for coastal ports were frequently attacked.
It is greatly to the credit of Spain and her colonies, however, that
the worst her enemies could do during the seventeenth century was
to make piratical attacks on her commerce, occupy remote stretches
of North America, and encroach on the Lesser Antilles, despite the
fact that some like Oliver Cromwell contemplated conquest of
Spanish territories in the Caribbean region.

Another region of conflict between Spain and her enemies lay
between the English colony of Virginia and Spanish Florida. The
Franciscans had been driven from their Virginia missions in 1597.
In 1612 a new group of missionaries resumed the struggle, reoccupied the former sites, and pushed into the interior. By the middle
of the seventeenth century a line of missions extended northward
to the Savannah river and westward among the Apalachees. The
uprisings of the Apalachees and other tribes forced the missionaries
to withdraw from some of their posts. English fur traders began to
appear among the southern tribes. In the 1680's the Yamassees
joined the English, and the Spanish missions in Georgia were put in
jeopardy. In western Georgia and in Alabama the Creeks became

friendly to the English, and Spanish expeditions failed to subdue them. Inter-colonial warfare began, the southern tribes in alliance with the contending nations doing much of the fighting.

The activities of Spain's enemies in the Antilles, however, were the most costly to her. The isolated settlements of buccaneers, whose name came from the *boucan* used in smoking beef for sale to passing ships, came to be the forerunners of French colonies. In 1625 one of these settlements was established on Tortuga, off the northwest coast of Española. From Tortuga the intruders penetrated into the uninhabited western end of the larger island. Although both English and French adventurers were involved, the former were soon driven out, and the territory came to be regarded by the French as a colony. Before the end of the century Spanish efforts to expel the French failed, and in 1697 French rights to the area they occupied were acknowledged. In the colony a rapid process of racial mixture between the French and Negroes was begun despite the strong disapproval of Louis XIV. By decreeing that freedom should be granted not only to the half-breed offspring but to their mothers as well, he hoped to halt the mingling of races. The *code noir* (Black Code) of 1685, which was ostensibly for securing better treatment of slaves, provided for the religious instruction of those in bondage and relief from their labors on Sundays and religious holidays. The free mulatto class which continued to grow despite the objections of Louis, had the same legal rights as the whites, but discrimination against them remained, and the Black Code worked more against the interests of the slaves than in their favor.

The forays of the English, French, and Dutch in the Caribbean brought new and grave problems to Venezuela and New Granada. The raids soon extended beyond the islands and posed serious problems for the defense not only of the coastal towns but those of the interior as well. Maracaibo, Cartagena, Puerto Cabello, and even Caracas were attacked with more destructive results during the seventeenth century than at any time previously. Although these raids were but a small part of Spain's foreign difficulties, they were costly, and contributed to her decline. Fleets were sent to check the pirates with only moderate success. The enormous profits to be obtained by pillage and the countenancing of such activities by the governments of Spain's rivals made the evil a difficult one to eradicate, and buccaneering remained to plague imperial officials throughout the century.

The English pirate, Henry Morgan, later knighted for his services to England, caused especial havoc in many parts of the Caribbean. In 1668 he sacked Portobelo and in 1671 he destroyed Panamá City so completely that it was not rebuilt on the same site. During the 1680's French and English pirates crossed to the Pacific and raided the coastal towns of South America, Central America, and New Spain. Fleets were sent from Peru, but the intruders were not apprehended. A small number of them survived the rigors of the campaign and returned to the French West Indies with enormously rich booty.

The most devastating attacks upon Spanish commerce in the first half of the seventeenth century were those of the Dutch. With the founding of the Dutch West India Company great fleets under some of the most capable admirals of the epoch were sent to the Caribbean area. Interested in immediate profit rather than long-range colony building, the Dutch pursued the treasure fleets with a tenacity and success previously not shown by any of Spain's other enemies. In the meantime they seized bases for their operations in some of the Lesser Antilles neglected not only by the Spaniards but the French and English as well. Curaçao and Aruba especially were useful way-stations and depositories for merchandise and slaves to be smuggled into Spanish colonies.

Despite the annoyances of the multitude of pirates infesting Caribbean waters, the only major attempt of any European power to seize Spanish territory — Cromwell's 'Grand Design' — ended in almost complete failure. Although Jamaica was conquered and held by England in 1655, it had figured only slightly in Cromwell's plans. Its conquest, however, gave England a convenient base for smuggling and piracy. The Scottish Darién venture at the close of the century was less threatening, and caused no loss of Spanish territory.

Trouble with militant frontier tribes of the mainland, Central America, and Florida was another colonial problem in the Caribbean area during the seventeenth century. Missionary endeavor was prominent among the frontier tribes whose civilization was of a low order and who were therefore not promising as laborers. With relatively little expense to the royal treasury the missionaries in many instances succeeded in pacifying tribes formerly very destructive.

In New Granada and Venezuela Indian attacks often made it necessary, in the early decades of the century, to assemble large forces simply for the defense of the towns. Whenever expeditions marched against the Indians and inflicted salutary defeat on them, however, new regions usually were opened for settlement in districts previously unsafe. Thus Barcelona was founded after the Indians had been subdued in a series of battles, as was Quibdó.

One of the most warlike tribes of New Granada, the Pijaos, was still unconquered when the century began, and it went on the warpath with devastating success. For a number of years pillage continued despite the fact that troops from Santa Fé assaulted the Indians from the north in conjunction with others from Timaná and Popayán from the south. Cali, Cartago, and other towns were threatened with complete destruction, and their plight was rendered more grave because the Indians cut off communications between Popayán and Santa Fé. In 1605 Juan de Borja was put in command of the troops in the war. His astute leadership combined with the invaluable alliance with two tribes inimical to the Pijaos enabled him to triumph over them after four years of fighting.

Toward the end of the century Spanish pressure on the unconquered Indians induced a number of the tribes to ask for peace. Those of the region between Yucatán and Guatemala remained adamant, until they were finally subdued by force in 1697, when Petén became a Spanish outpost. The Indians of the Tegucigalpa district, between Honduras and Nicaragua, were not yet converted at the beginning of the seventeenth century, and Franciscans went among them in 1622. The nomadic habits of the natives handicapped the priests, for the Indians moved suddenly and without warning. By the 1660's raids of the Lencas had become especially injurious, and missionaries once more went among them, this time with gradual success. By 1679 they had established seven villages in which converts were residing. In Honduras, too, unconverted Indians still maintained themselves in isolated areas, although the efforts of Franciscan missionaries slowly reduced them to settled life. By 1700 serious trouble from the wild tribes of these regions was largely ended.

The founding of new towns was another important aspect of seventeenth-century life in the Caribbean area. In 1629 Barranquilla was established as a port town for the Magdalena river traffic, but it remained little more than a fishing village until the nineteenth century. The founding of Barcelona in 1637 already has been noted, and that of Quibdó on the Atrato river. The opening of new roads was one of the contributing factors in the establishment of these towns, although in most cases the first requirement was subduing hostile tribes. The linking of Antioquía with other towns and the Magdalena river by road was an important aid to commerce.

Medellín, a town relatively unimportant during the colonial period, was founded in the middle of the century. In 1640 some farmers settled on the fertile lands along the trail between Antioquía and Popayán. Soon a chapel was erected, in 1649 an alcalde mayor appointed, and in 1675 Medellín was officially recognized as a village.

Other attempts to foster commerce in New Granada in the early seventeenth century were the establishment of a mint at Santa Fé de Bogotá in 1622, which provided gold and silver coins similar to those of Spain, the building of bridges, and the conquest of Indians who lived near the trade routes and who interrupted the traffic.

Violent earthquakes in New Granada caused frequent setbacks. In 1644 Pamplona was almost completely destroyed, hundreds were left homeless, and it was necessary for the audiencia to grant relief to the victims by exempting them from payment of taxes for four years. Another especially famous tremor was that of 1687, which was felt along the entire Andean cordillera. In New Granada it was accompanied by terrifying noises believed to be of supernatural origin and which earned for it the name *El Ruido*.

In addition to the new towns founded on a permanent basis many temporary mining camps sprang up quickly when new gold-bearing streams were discovered. Since placer mining was more common than vein mining in New Granada, the deposits were usually exhausted in a fairly short time, and the miners were forced to be constantly on the alert for new fields. Wherever strikes were made farms and plantations quickly appeared for the purpose of providing food for the miners. When the mining activities ceased many of the farms were abandoned at the same time, and the farmers joined the migration of the miners.

Mining gold in New Granada was an easier undertaking than the production of silver in New Spain and Peru. Placer mining did not require the extensive tunneling along veins such as at Potosí. Little machinery was needed, therefore, and since the gold obtained was usually in the form of nuggets or dust, smelting was not a problem. The metal could be carried out easily by men, so trails sufficed as a means of communication. Toward the end of the century mining became increasingly important, and its profits stimulated commerce. Better roads were required, and road and bridge building became matters of considerable concern to the presidents. The upsurge of commerce changed the condition of many of the towns; those in locations ill-suited for trade, such as Antioquía, declined, while new ones located at the crossroads of trade routes, such as Honda and Mariquita, became flourishing centers.

One effect of the large-scale introduction of Negro slaves was that leprosy appeared in the country, and it was necessary to establish a leper hospital at Cartagena soon after 1600. Between 1615 and 1654 at least 300,000 Negro slaves passed through this port. The Jesuit, Pedro Claver, who devoted his life to serving in the leper hospital and to charitable work among the newly arrived Negroes, performed such noteworthy humanitarian labors that he ultimately received canonization.

Other diseases also infested New Granada to a serious degree. Smallpox epidemics had been especially destructive to the Indians in the previous century. In 1633 a violent epidemic of typhus or typhoid fever called the *tabardillo* raged in Santa Fé de Bogotá and other towns, wiping out entire families. In this disaster the efforts of the Jesuits were especially valuable, for they not only were familiar with current European medical practices but also possessed a store of drugs in Santa Fé.

Physicians were almost totally lacking in the entire region, but in 1639 Diego Henríques arrived with a commission to examine medical students, to grant licenses for the practice of medicine, and to inspect pharmacies. He was also appointed professor of medicine at the University of Santo Tomás, but appears to have done little lecturing there.

Education in New Granada as elsewhere in Spanish America was the domain of the religious orders. The former college seminary of San Luis was reopened in 1605 and placed under the control of the Jesuits, who changed its name to San Bartolomé. In addition to San Bartolomé the Jesuits maintained smaller academies in various towns, and they were especially concerned with instructing the Indians. The Dominicans also were engaged in educational pursuits, and one of their projects was founding the University of Santo Tomás, for which they received royal approval. In 1653 they established the important Colegio Mayor de Nuestra Señora del Rosario, which was provided with fifteen scholarships. San Bartolomé and Rosario produced many of the best educated men of New Granada. The Franciscans, besides their many elementary schools, conducted the academy of San Buenaventura in Santa Fé.

The instruction in all of these institutions was comparable to that of other regions of Spanish America. The humanities, the arts, and theology were taught in all of the colleges. The Jesuit José Dadey lectured on physics, and courses in medicine were taught at Santo Tomás, but neither of these subjects enjoyed large followings.

Some chroniclers were produced in New Granada during the seventeenth century, a few of them graduates of the colleges already mentioned. Noteworthy works were the *Noticias Historiales* of the Franciscan Pedro Simón, who wrote in the early decades of the century, and who furnished modern historians with much information on the campaigns of Borja against the Pijaos. Lucas Fernández de Piedrahita, a native of Santa Fé, was another important historian of the period. He studied at San Bartolomé and later earned a doctorate of philosophy from the University of Santo Tomás. He is best remembered for his *Historia General del Nuevo Reino de Granada*. The Jesuit Manuel Rodríguez, a native fo Cali, wrote a valuable account of the interior called *Marañón y Amazonas.*

In Central America there was similar town-building, commercial development, and erection of educational institutions. In 1610 the old city of León in Nicaragua was abandoned, owing to a series of disasters which befell it, and the population moved to a new site halfway between the coast and Lake Managua. The new location was in a populous Indian district, and the reborn city soon enjoyed prosperity. Granada was even more fortunate, for it carried on extensive commerce with Cartagena, Guatemala, San Salvador, and Comayagua in indigo, cochineal, and cowhides. Its flourishing condition drew to it the unwelcome attention of the freebooters so that in 1665 it was captured, plundered, and burned, and had to be almost entirely rebuilt. In 1671 the king ordered stronger fortifications erected for its protection.

In 1616 the Jesuits of Guatemala established themselves in Nicaragua and attempted to found a college. Little aid was forthcoming from the inhabitants in general, but an ex-captain-general of the province named Vicente Saldívar y Mendoza presented a sum of 27,000 pesos. When the Jesuit priests were withdrawn by their society in 1621, there were many popular demonstrations for the purpose of inducing them to remain. The people of Realejo, meanwhile, had successfully petitioned the king for the establishment of a Jesuit college.

The seventeenth century was for the Caribbean mainland a period of growth and consolidation enhanced by the pacification of enemy tribes, the opening of new mining and agricultural regions, and the enjoyment of commercial prosperity. The progress of colonial society was stimulated by the fostering of educational institutions and attempts to curb the ravages of epidemics. Progress was interrupted occasionally by natural phenomena such as earthquakes, and by the encroachments of foreign pirates, but in the long run growth was steady and genuine. Not all of the injuries to Spanish commerce, it should be added, were at the hands of non-

Spaniards. The colonists themselves frequently were guilty of evading customs duties, although these were not particularly heavy for that period and not all foreign ships in the Caribbean were regarded by them as enemy. Illicit commerce was carried on in collusion with English, Dutch, or French merchants, and Spaniards availed themselves of foreign ships to carry bullion into Europe without giving royal officials an opportunity to collect the king's due. There were in addition many devices employed to evade Spanish commercial restrictions without involving other than the various officials whose duty it was to prevent violations, for venality was widespread among colonial officialdom.

XI

The Rise of New Spain

All things considered, it is remarkable that the viceroys of New Spain during the century of the last three Hapsburgs were not altogether bad. Although they certainly did not measure up to the standard set by the excellent civil servants of Philip II, yet most of them were far from being the conscienceless graft- ers we read about. In any case, the Spanish crown was in such a state of prostration that they would have been helpless to cope with the intricate hierarchy of linked privilege that bound to- gether the magistracy, the clergy, and the landed and mining interests of New Spain. Those who attempted to do so, like the Marqués de Gelves and Bishop Palafox, were broken by the combination. The result was that *New Spain was virtually independent at the end of the seventeenth century.*

LESLEY BYRD SIMPSON *

THE political divisions of New Spain in 1600 were still the two audiencias, Mexico in the east and Nueva Galicia in the west, which were unsystematically subdivided into provinces, captaincies-general, alcaldías mayores, and corregi- mientos. At the outset of the period New Spain was consolidating advances into regions far removed from the seat of the viceroyalty. The most remote of these provinces was New Mexico, which had been conquered as the new century began. In all of the northern regions were numerous tribes of hostile, nomadic Indians, whose tenacious resistance to the invaders of their lands made Spanish

* *Many Mexicos*, University of California Press, Berkeley, copyright 1941, 1946, 1952, pp. 174-5.

control difficult to establish and tenuous at best. Warfare with the frontier tribes was one of the most consistent themes of the century, and it did not end during the colonial period. Some of the northern regions brought under control at this time contained extremely valuable mineral deposits. The value of New Mexico, however, was its strategic position as the northern outpost guarding the silver mines. Affairs of empire required its permanent occupation whatever the difficulties involved, and the petitions of the early colonists to abandon the province were refused. Even as Santa Fe, the capital of New Mexico, was being founded, English and French colonists secured footholds on the Atlantic coast of North America, and New Mexico's imperial role was determined.

Missionary activity was an essential concomitant of frontier life in seventeenth-century New Spain, for the useful, sedentary Indians worthy of private conquest already had been brought under Spanish domination. Most successful of the missionaries were the Jesuits and Franciscans, whose zeal for the arduous life on the frontiers compared favorably to that of the missionaries of the century of the conquest. The west coast of New Spain and later Lower California were the fields allocated to the Jesuits. The still-energetic Franciscans were granted missionary rights in the central area, which brought New Mexico into their domain, while the Dominicans were for a time employed in pacifying and converting the tribes of the eastern part of the kingdom. The efforts of the missionaries cost the royal exchequer less than a military conquest. Their devotion to the difficult and often thankless task of 'reducing' and converting the primitive tribes of the deserts and mountains of Chihuahua, Sonora, Sinaloa, and New Mexico made them invaluable agents of the crown. It is not surprising that Spanish kings were enthusiastic in their support of missionary endeavor, for the priests not only helped to advance the frontiers but also to maintain them by winning over the Indians.

While the northern provinces were disturbed by the ravages of wild tribes, towns of the Valley of Mexico suffered occasional damage at the hands of rioting mobs of more highly civilized natives. For the latter Indians the outward aspects of life were much the

same as they had been before Cortés beached his ships near Veracruz. In many ways the conquest meant only a change of masters,
human and spiritual. Although now there was a distant monarch
who sought to combine humanitarianism with imperialism, the
Indians could bear testimony to the shortcomings of his policies in
practice. It was unfortunately true that the Spanish viceroys and
other officials too often were less concerned with the welfare of the
Indians than with filling the empty treasury of New Spain.

Although it is generally conceded that the kings and viceroys of
the seventeenth century were less energetic than their predecessors
in protecting the Indians, they continued to attempt improving the
condition of native laborers. In 1602 a system of public hiring was
introduced to replace the repartimiento. It now became the practice for Indians to assemble on Sundays at the principal plazas
under supervision of a magistrate, and to deal directly with their
employers. For a time the new plan was beneficial, but speculators
found it profitable to engage the Indians in advance and to hire
them out to others. A few years later it was decreed that food and
clothing be sold to the Indians at reasonable prices. Many other
laws were passed and earlier ones repeated, but officials who were
strict in upholding these regulations were under great pressure
from those who employed Indian labor, and the laws were generally
ineffective.

The mestizo class continued to grow in size and importance, and
it was no longer regarded as completely apart from the less affluent
creoles, while the stigma of illegitimacy was also disappearing. The
growth and progress of the mestizos represents the building of a
new Mexican race and civilization neither Spanish nor Indian, but
a genuine fusion of both. Indian customs and characteristics modified those of the less numerous Spaniards; at the same time the
natives were forced to adopt, outwardly at least, certain of the mores
and traits of their conquerors.

The 'creole' descendants of the conquerors, many of whom
actually were mestizos, though not a large group, included some
who were extremely wealthy. Their magnificent estates, rural and
urban, displayed a grandeur and ostentation unsurpassed even in

Spain. Their very wealth was largely responsible for their being regarded as degenerate, although the climate received the blame. Unwilling to demean themselves by performing tasks considered ordinary, and excluded from the more rewarding careers in church, state, and commerce, they preferred lives of idle debauchery to useful enterprise. Later immigrants from Spain, ambitious and energetic for the most part, were able to monopolize the important positions, to amass considerable wealth in the more prosaic pursuits such as commerce, and to rise rapidly in the social scale.

The principal cities of New Spain — the land was one of towns rather than scattered rural populations — were Mexico, Guadalajara, and Puebla. Acapulco and Veracruz were the important ports for maritime commerce, but both lay in the *Tierra Caliente*, and Spaniards found other regions more healthful. Mexico City, the capital of the kingdom, was the metropolis of the North American continent. It was the official residence of the viceroy, the archbishop, and the Holy Office of the Inquisition. The Audiencia of Mexico, of which the viceroy was president, had jurisdiction over the same region as the archdiocese, roughly from Yucatán to Michoacán. The western limit was Guadalajara, which lay in the presidency of Nueva Galicia. Mexico City was considered one of the most splendid cities of the world at this time, with its wide, straight streets and attractive buildings of pink and white stone.

Every day provisions were brought to the city by more than 1000 boats on Lake Texcoco and by land on some 3000 mules. The population of the city and its suburbs in the early decades of the seventeenth century was composed of perhaps ten or fifteen thousand Spaniards, nearly 80,000 Indians and mestizos, and about 50,000 Negroes and mulattoes, free and slave. Commerce was carried on with Spain, Manila, the provinces of Guatemala, and Peru. In the city domestic commerce took place in four markets which were held daily. In addition there were many stores and shops in which Spanish and native craftsmen manufactured jewelry and articles of clothing.

In Mexico City were numerous richly adorned religious houses in which schools of theology and the arts were conducted. Those of the Jesuits, Franciscans, Dominicans, Augustinians, and Carmelites were most numerous, but other orders were represented. The city contained nine hospitals: the Royal Hospital, which was supported by the king, by private contributions, and by the income derived from a theater; the Hospital of the Destitute for foundling children, 'children of the church door' as they were called; that of Concepción for the indigent sick; the Insane Asylum; the Hospital of the Love of God for syphilitics; others were for Indians, incurable cases, and other specific purposes. All of these hospitals were charitable institutions and were utilized only by the poor.

Mexico's famous university, with its many doctors, masters, and students, was still in successful operation. Degrees were granted in all recognized fields of learning, and the university enjoyed the same privileges and exemptions as its famous parent, the University of Salamanca in Spain. Near the university were various academies, among them that of Santos, whose students were chosen from among the poor, virtuous, and of good family. A number of notable scholars in the humanities and even natural sciences were produced in Mexico during the seventeenth century.

The silver coins produced by the mint of Mexico had a wide distribution, and were well known not only in the Philippine Islands and the Caribbean colonies, but in Spain and other parts of Europe. In New Spain cacao beans were still used for small change, since they had the advantage of being difficult to counterfeit. Counterfeiting was an illicit occupation which attracted a large following among Indians as well as Spaniards. The crime, which struck the royal interest in a vulnerable spot, was severely punished. Those found guilty were hanged, drawn and quartered, and various parts of their anatomies exhibited in public places as a deterrent to others. The extra chastisement of counterfeiters, however, failed to halt the practice.

The city of Puebla was noted especially for its woolen mills, which produced great quantities of fine cloth for export, and for its pottery. In the diocese were 200 towns and villages, numerous ranches, and many farms; and more than 250,000 tribute-paying Indians lived within the same area. The town of Tlaxcala, owing to the assistance given Cortés in the conquest of the Aztecs, enjoyed privileges not accorded others. It was known for its woolen mills and for a fine cochineal dye produced there.

Acapulco, the terminus of the Manila galleon route, contained only some seventy Spaniards and a small garrison. Negroes and mulattoes, who bore the discomforts of its tropical climate with fewer casualties than the Spaniards, made up the bulk of the population. Once a year Acapulco enjoyed a lively traffic in silks and other oriental goods when the galleon arrived. Despite frequent edicts to the contrary, ships from Peru came for a share of the galleon's cargo. If they did not appear, a part of the cargo usually was taken to Callao, for the clandestine trade was too profitable to be curtailed by the disapproval of the monopolists of Seville.

The Audiencia of Nueva Galicia, located in Guadalajara, had wide jurisdiction in the sparsely populated, outlying provinces even as far away as New Mexico. Probably the most important of the numerous mining towns was Zacatecas, which had been productive since the middle of the previous century, although San Luis Potosí kept one hundred smelting ovens in operation. Nueva Vizcaya and some of the towns of other provinces, such as Saltillo and Monterrey, were administered by a governor who also held the title of captain-general, and was subordinate to the viceroy.

Conflicts between civil and ecclesiastical officials marred the administration of New Spain throughout the seventeenth century. Matters of precedence in all things contributed directly or indirectly to most of these disturbances. In many instances the episodes which precipitated the quarrels were far from worthy of the heat which they engendered, and they occurred at all levels of officialdom. The occasional appointment of the archbishop instead of the audiencia as viceroy *ad interim* when vacancies occurred in the viceregal office increased the strife. The priesthood had become unduly numerous in Mexico City as in other large cities, and in 1644 the *ayuntamiento* or municipal government complained about the vast number of idle clerics. Thomas Gage, an English Dominican who traveled in New Spain during the first half of the seventeenth century, left an unflattering account of life in the religious houses. Although Gage's veracity is not above challenge, other accounts lend credence to his remarks. He stated that houses with capacity for twenty priests had only ten, that they might live in greater ease. Gluttony and gambling were vices which he found common in the monasteries. The growing wealth of the church undoubtedly was a corrupting factor, for some individuals were attracted to the priesthood by other than spiritual motives. On the many frontiers where wealth was scarce and hardships and dangers plentiful, true zealots were to be found.

Because of the widespread criticism of the conduct of the friars, in 1658 the Duke of Albuquerque summoned all of the officials of the various orders to a conference for special instructions. His principal charge was that priests should not appear on the streets late at night. As a consequence of his intercession, the officials of the orders issued stricter rules foɪ the conduct of their members. They were forbidden to go out on the streets after ten o'clock at night or to enter gambling houses.

Strife between civil and ecclesiastic officials was not the whole picture. Clashes between regulars and seculars, between different orders, and between the creole and peninsular priests of the same order reached unfortunate proportions. In 1627 the visitador of the Dominicans decreed that no more habits were to be given to creoles in the order. The king overruled this injudicious command, but the trouble did not end there. The feuding which went on among the representatives of church and state undoubtedly was a detriment to the progress of Christianity among the natives.

The religion which the subjugated Indians of New Spain had acquired was a blend of their own paganism and the ritualistic aspects of Catholicism. A sincere appreciation of the principles of Christianity was not easily theirs, and the social conditions of the period were not conducive to Christian behavior. Exhortations of sincere priests often were nullified by the unchristian actions of the citizenry and even by a segment of the priesthood itself. The association of one of the Indian deities with the Virgin of Guadalupe, patroness of the Indians, helped to bridge the gulf between the religions of the conquerors and vanquished.

The progress of agriculture during the seventeenth century was limited by the system of great estates and wasteful methods on the one hand, and by defrauding the Indians of the fruits of their labor on the other. The native farmers were forced by unscrupulous officials to sell their crops at ruinous prices, and corn and wheat crops frequently were monopolized. When the scarcity became acute, prices soared, and the monopolists made tremendous profits. This practice not only helped to push the native farmers into a subsistence economy, for there was little profit in producing a surplus, but also contributed to the restiveness of the populace of the capital. The system of great landholdings and involuntary labor was ill-suited to change and improvement, especially when coupled with absentee ownership. Despite the great Indian population of the Valley of Mexico at the time of the conquest, the inroads of warfare and disease in the sixteenth century had left Mexico with a heritage of chronic labor shortage which has prevailed ever since. Curtailment of certain crops also contributed to the misfortunes of agriculturists. The silk industry, which had been introduced in the earlier century, was terminated by a decree of 1679 in order to protect the silk producers of Andalucía, and the mulberry trees and silkworms necessary to the industry were ordered destroyed.

Despite these various disadvantages Mexico's wealth lay more in agriculture than in minerals, although mining furnished an important incentive to planting in certain regions. The exploitation of the mines of New Spain was far from approaching its potential, although in the seventeenth century the output of silver surpassed that of Peru. Quicksilver necessary to the amalgamation process of extracting silver was available in New Spain, and in 1609 rewards were offered to the discoverers of new deposits. The crown, however, did not permit the operation of the quicksilver mines of New Spain. Quicksilver was brought from the Almadén mines of Spain, and when the produce of these was insufficient, additional quantities were purchased from Austria in preference to Peru, although Huancavelica was owned by the crown. One of the principal reasons for this policy, in addition to the fact that quicksilver was a royal monopoly, was that by keeping an account of the amount of quicksilver purchased by each miner it was possible to discover some who would defraud the king of his share of the silver.

The conditions of prison life were generally melancholy, as was typical of the age. Prison staffs were supported by the fees of prisoners, and since imprisonment for debt was customary, the unfortunate debtors were dependent upon the mercy of charitable organizations, and these were insufficient to meet the demand. Wealthy prisoners were permitted to live in luxury, and they could expect rapid action and leniency on the part of the justices. Poor prisoners were likely to perish in confinement before being brought to trial. Punishments for various crimes were often more severe than for similar offenses in Spain, the fines usually being double. In many cases the punishment of criminals was service in one of the frontier garrisons, a fact which helps explain the low morale and inadequacy these troops often displayed in warfare against Indians. Other prisoners were sent to the Philippines or expiated their crimes pulling an oar in the galleys.

The most common means of execution was by *el garrote*, an ancient form of strangulation. Highway robbers, however, were punished by hanging and quartering. Burning at the stake, which was a form of punishment inflicted by civil authorities, was not reserved solely for the few heretics condemned by the Inquisition. Counterfeiters, whose crime was particularly obnoxious to impecunious monarchs, sometimes shared a like fate, as did a few other types of malefactor.

Sentencing to death by the courts was an awesome spectacle intended to give pause to potential law-breakers. The condemned, after a formal and ceremonious trial, was expected to kiss the paper containing his sentence after it had been read. The priests then took charge of him, dressed him in a white robe, placed him on a hide, and marched with him through the streets as he was dragged to the central plaza. He was proceeded by a crier who proclaimed his crime in a loud voice. In the plaza a prayer was said, the execution performed, and a sermon preached to the assembled multitude to impress upon them the bitter fruits of crime. Afterward the brothers of mercy took charge of the remains, and the ceremony was over.

One of the most significant developments of the seventeenth century was the advance of settlement through the wilds of the northern provinces lying between Mexico City and the Río Grande. The wild, nomadic tribes of these regions resisted the invaders with greater tenacity and success than had the sedentary peoples of the Valley of Mexico. Conquering and controlling these Indians was costly in military endeavor, and made desirable only by the silver deposits in their lands. The warlike natives themselves made a poor labor supply in most cases. The opening of these regions was greatly facilitated by the efforts of missionary priests who took charge of the conquered tribes and who even gained successes among tribes which had not yielded to force of arms. Abandoning the comforts of Mexico City, the missionaries accepted the rude life of the Indians until they were able to reduce them to village ways and a more orderly existence. The Indians among whom they went had no real understanding of discipline and obedience to constituted authority. It remained for the patient labors of the missionaries to instill in their minds these basic concepts. The task was long and arduous, for the Indians were of mercurial temperament.

In the semi-arid country of the north, where most of the wild tribes were daily on the verge of starvation, reducing them to village life frequently entailed severe hardships. Desperate flight and even suicide were not uncommon in such reductions. In 1605 the king heard stories of the tragedies occurring among some of the 'reduced' tribes, and permitted them to return to their former lands.

The medieval type craft guilds (*gremios de artes y oficios*) which were introduced into Spanish America in the sixteenth century continued to increase in number. In addition to controlling various professions such as those of silversmiths and saddlemakers, the gremios were organized as cofradías for religious and charitable purposes, and occasionally they furnished militia companies for local defense.

The organization and activities of the gremios were regulated by the cabildos and confirmed by viceroy and king. The intent of the regulations was to maintain a satisfactory balance between the workmen and consumers, and to safeguard the financial interests of the royal treasury. Membership in the gremios was rigidly limited, and the system of advancement from apprentice to journeyman to master was carefully restricted so that few Negroes, mulattoes, Indians, and even mestizos had the opportunity to rise above the rank of journeyman. The gremios continued to function throughout the colonial period and well into the nineteenth century with little change in attitude or structure, so that they became outmoded and unable to adjust to changing conditions of economic life.

Under mild viceroys corruption spread throughout the official hierarchy, and on occasion the king's chief minister himself was deeply involved. Minor officials committed a variety of excesses with impunity, confident that their misdeeds would not be punished. Those in power maintained a strong interest in the wishes of the wealthy and powerful, and together they forced the poor into greater subjection and subordination. Even the annual grain subsidy from the crown to the needy was looted by public officials who withheld the grain and sold it in their own interest.

The arrival of a visitador was equally unwelcome to the audiencia and the viceroy, since neither was certain of the reasons for his coming. Enemies now had a happy opportunity to air their grievances, fancied or real, and frequently they chose irrelevant grounds for their protests. In 1607 Viceroy Montesclaros compared a visitation to a whirlwind in the plaza, which accomplished nothing more than scattering dirt and trash on the heads of people. The only effect, he maintained, was that evildoers became more cautious and secretive in their illegal acts. Matters were worse when the visitador was especially highhanded or a partisan of the faction opposing the viceroy or audiencia.

In 1602, because of the still-pressing needs of the Manila galleons for a port in California to obtain fresh food to relieve the scurvy-stricken crews and passengers, an expedition was dispatched from Acapulco in search of a suitable harbor. Its commander, Sebastián Vizcaíno, was instructed to reopen the search for the ubiquitous and mythical Strait of Anián. Vizcaíno learned little that was not known to his predecessors along the coast of California, and interest in the region soon subsided. The entry of Franciscan missionaries into Japan in the meantime attracted attention in that direction, and

Vizcaíno was sent to Japan to open commercial relations. This mission failed to prosper, owing to the machinations of Dutch agents as well as to the suspicions of the Japanese.

Politically New Spain was much more stable than in the time of Cortés and Mendoza, yet not beyond danger of riot and rebellion. The conflict between creoles and peninsulares was at times acute, and it divided the ruling class into bitter factions. The prevailing corruption in public life, the squalid condition of a segment of the lower classes, and the widespread ignorance of the masses in general made control weak on the one hand and violence a quick resort on the other. The lack of a standing army in the capital highlighted the weakness of the viceroy, and was in itself an invitation to disorder. The influence of the ecclesiastics over the masses, coupled with frequent rifts between civil and clerical officials, led to grave disorders in at least one important instance.

Riots and revolts caused considerable destruction of property during the seventeenth century. The usual incitements to crime were amply represented, and in addition there were a number of extraordinary ones such as racial antipathies, antagonisms between castes and classes, slavery, and the bitterness of a vanquished race. In 1609 the Negro slaves of the Veracruz region rebelled and established themselves in the hills along the road to Mexico City. Their depredations made travel so hazardous that it was necessary to assemble a force of citizens to combat them. The expedition routed the rebels; the free Negroes who surrendered were permitted to establish a village in the area, while the others were returned to their masters. Elsewhere in New Spain Indian troubles were more common, with the rioting of the sedentary natives in the cities and the forays of the wild nomads on the frontiers. The prevalence of highway robbers was also a constant problem. The establishment of the Santa Hermandad, a police force similar to that of Spain, though it executed many bandits, could not make travel entirely safe.

Hunger was the underlying cause of unrest in Mexico City, and was more feared than foreign pirates. The two most destructive riots, as well as a score of lesser ones, occurred at times of widespread famine and unusually high prices. Although harvest failures were the most frequent cause of food shortages, there were artificial causes of a maldistribution of foodstuffs, such as the machinations of speculators. Preventing the cornering of the food supply was one of the tasks constantly facing the viceroys of New Spain.

Occasionally unwise restrictions were responsible for general hardship. In 1677, for example, an edict was passed prohibiting the planting of white wheat, a variety which produced more heavily than others, because it was regarded as injurious to health. Its suppression helped to bring about the food shortages of the 1690's, and in 1692 the viceroy raised the ban against planting it.

The appointment of the Marquis of Gelves as viceroy of New Spain in 1621 resulted from his excellent reputation as an able administrator in Aragon for many years. In upholding the law his known inflexibility was a reason for his choice, for Felipe IV was resolved to settle the disorders prevailing among the officials of New Spain. As viceroy, Gelves lived up to his reputation, and malefactors were punished according to the law regardless of their wealth or station in society. As might be expected opposition to him mounted in intensity among his subordinates as well as the upper class in general, while the masses remained indifferent. Among the accomplishments of Gelves were the zealous punishment of dishonest officials, the destruction of many of the bandit hordes which infested the highways, the interruption of contraband trade, and a marked increase in badly needed royal revenue. In the course of these achievements, which should have endeared him to the king as well as to the poor of Mexico City, he earned the hatred of the most influential persons, including the archbishop, the clerical orders, and the audiencia. So widespread was the opposition that when the first serious challenge to his authority arose Gelves fell from power.

His downfall came about because of the arrest of an alcalde mayor, Pérez de Varáez, who was denounced for monopolizing the grain supply of Metepec and requiring the Indians of his jurisdiction to purchase maize from him at an exorbitant price. The accused official was arrested but fled and sought sanctuary in the convent of Santo Domingo. Apparently fearing that he intended to escape, Gelves had guards stationed about the convent. The archbishop regarded this action as an infringement of sanctuary, and the viceroy and other officials were excommunicated. After much unseemly recrimination on both sides the archbishop was banished from the kingdom. Before he was conducted to Veracruz, however, a mob rose against the viceroy, his palace was stormed and fired, and he was forced to flee for his life. The officials who should have endeavored to preserve the peace contemplated the attack with indifference if not satisfaction, and some of them were even guilty of inciting the opposition to greater violence. The disgruntled audiencia seized power, and before a new viceroy could arrive from Spain most of the unpopular reforms of Gelves had been annulled. The alcalde mayor who had been the cause of the affair easily recovered his liberty, and once more bandits plied their trade on New Spain's highways. Gelves' successor, by exercising prudence as well as firmness, succeeded in restoring viceregal authority and punishing the leaders of the uprising, several of whom were executed. The event emphasized not only the weak position of a strict viceroy, but the influence of the priests on the mass of people, especially the Indians and mestizos, for it was they who had been inflamed against one of their principal benefactors. The incident reflects the eternal struggle between church and state, and the evils arising from competition between the two institutions.

The lack of a standing army or efficient police force was one of the reasons that the viceroy was so readily unseated by a mob. The only troops of New Spain were stationed at frontier garrisons and at the principal ports to guard against sea raiders. In most instances the local citizenry were relied upon as a militia force against either Indians or foreigners, and to preserve order when called forth by government officials. Except for temporary annoyances caused by the Dutch and English this arrangement proved fairly satisfactory, for no part of New Spain was lost to European enemies. Against the Indians in the far-flung borderlands, however, this policy succeeded only when powerful tribes were won as allies. And against mobs such as those which rose in Mexico City, its success depended largely upon the interests of the wealthy citizens.

In 1629 Mexico City suffered great damage from a flood which inundated the entire city. The project of removing the capital to higher ground was revived, and a new site was selected in case the king granted the petition. The property-holders, who had energetically opposed earlier attempts, protested strenuously, and although many families migrated to Puebla and other towns, the majority continued to occupy their homes, many of which were flooded for more than four years. Relief finally came in 1634 when a series of earthquakes opened chasms in the valley floor and permitted the excess water to escape. The creoles and Indians attributed their deliverance from the nuisance to their patroness, the Virgin of Guadalupe, while the Spaniards gave credit to the Virgin of los Remedios. This was not to be the last competition between the two patronesses, for two centuries later forces of the Indians were contending with those of the viceroy under the banners of the two virgins.

Attempts at reform and improvement in the treatment of the Indians were not limited to the viceroys. Bishop Juan de Palafox y Mendoza, who was appointed to the see of Puebla in 1640, and who served later as *visitador-general*, rectified a number of abuses in the administration of the *doctrinas*, or Indian parishes, which had prevailed since the conquest. Upon meeting with resistance from the less conscientious friars, he deprived their orders of missions, and established thirty-six new curacies. The Franciscans, Augustinians, and Dominicans protested his action to the Council of the Indies, but the bishop, however extreme he had been in some instances, was upheld by that body.

The Duke of Escalona, who served as viceroy from 1640 to 1642, began his rule favorably by supporting Palafox in his program of reforming the doctrinas. At the same time, however, the viceroy maintained a compelling interest in self-enrichment not in keeping with his office. His adherents were placed in charge of lucrative posts such as the public granary and water works, the inspection of the *pulquerías*, which dispensed *pulque*, the favorite drink of Mexicans, and similar agencies which offered an opportunity for illegal gain. The sale of cacao also was illegally monopolized. The maladministration of the viceroy contributed even to the loss of the treasure fleet, for the vessels which he procured were scarcely seaworthy. The convoy was unnecessarily delayed past the time for safe sailing, and was lost in a storm. Escalona, who was a partisan of the Jesuits, became embroiled in a dispute with Palafox because of differences over the payment of tithes between the bishop of Puebla and members of the order in the diocese.

The long-standing resistance to the payment of tithes by the Jesuits became more critical as their possessions increased. The possessors of valuable sugar mills, factories, and commercial enterprises, they had become envied by the members of other orders as well as by the secular clergy and civilians who were at a disadvantage in competition with them. The Jesuits maintained that the papacy had exempted them from paying tithes, and litigation over the issue was carried on for years. Palafox supported the bishops in their demands, thus earning the animosity of the order. The issue was not settled during the seventeenth century, so skillful were the Jesuits in defending their point of view and in delaying final action. Since it was basically a question of the pope's right to take such action with regard to the Spanish colonies, the king eventually decided that the Jesuits should pay the tithe.

In 1641 news of the uprisings in Portugal and Catalonia arrived in New Spain causing general alarm because of the many Portuguese living in the kingdom, and Escalona's relationship to the rebel house of Bragança. The viceroy's apparent predilection for the Portuguese in New Spain, many of whom held public office or military command, increased the apprehensions as to his possible conduct. The king's confidence in Escalona was undermined, and Palafox was ordered to replace him. Despite an energetic effort to brand him as seditious in his residencia, Escalona survived without serious difficulty. Palafox served briefly but ably as viceroy before returning to his see in Puebla. In 1647 Palafox prohibited the Jesuits from preaching until they complied with the law requiring licenses to preach and confess.

Later viceroys and high clerical officials were no less contentious. These chronic differences hindered the administration of New Spain not only in the capital but in all towns and settlements as far away as

New Mexico. Insufficiency of funds, however, was a more acute problem and it limited the success of the most altruistic administrations.

That New Spain was a highly productive and profitable colony cannot be denied; its legendary wealth, however, was much greater than its actual riches. And although strict and efficient officials were able to accumulate royal revenues sufficient to cover the cost of government and still send large sums to Spain, such officials, as has been observed, were not likely to enjoy power for long. Thus it was that despite the numerous and increasing sources of royal revenues, government expenditures from 1644 to 1673 were annually on the average 100,000 pesos in excess of receipts. In 1646 customs-houses were established in Veracruz and Acapulco, and royal officials who previously had been responsible for the collections of duties were relieved of the task. The most immediate consequence was an increase in smuggling activities caused by a more systematic method of collecting duties.

Many viceroys of this period complained that they were in the position of managing a bankrupt concern — only the most pressing obligations could be met. The Marquis of Mancera, viceroy from 1664 to 1673, momentarily alleviated the financial difficulties by reforming the collection of taxes in such a way as to prevent undue leakage. Negligence in the collection of the hated alcabala caused him to transfer this task to the consulado. His similar success in the handling of royal revenues in general made an enormous change in the financial condition of New Spain. Not only was he able to pay off the public debts of many of his predecessors but also he was able to bolster the defenses of other colonies by much-needed annual subsidies. In 1665 he was asked to raise additional funds because of the death of the king, and he succeeded in sending to Spain more than 100,000 pesos.

With reference to the rule that three candidates be proposed by the bishops for each ecclesiastical vacancy Mancera complained that it was not done owing to the lack of suitable men. As a result of the laxness in this regard, unsatisfactory ecclesiastics were appointed. The conflict between Europeans and creoles flared anew among the

Augustinians, who attempted to exclude the former from admission to the order in New Spain. In 1667 Mancera commanded them to receive Europeans. The Carmelites, on the other hand, sought to exclude creoles. In order to eliminate this bitter hostility, which upon occasion led to scandalous street brawls, a policy of alternating between the two groups in elections of priors of the orders was adopted. The new system did not remove the rivalry, and few creoles were able to advance to high positions within the clerical hierarchy.

Literary activity in seventeenth-century New Spain was highlighted by the achievements of the nun Sor Juana Inés de la Cruz and the eminent scholar Carlos Sigüenza y Góngora. Sor Juana spent her entire short life in New Spain. At the age of nine she was taken to the capital from the country town of her birth. A child prodigy, her thirst for learning made her an avid reader at a time when there was little opportunity for young ladies to obtain instruction. So notable was her genius that the Marquis of Mancera caused her to be examined by forty of the outstanding professors, theologians, and humanists of Mexico. In the examination Sor Juana satisfied all by her answers. Her greatest fame, however, was won by her lyric poetry. After entering a convent she continued to satisfy her literary passion despite occasional protests against what was regarded unseemly conduct for one of her sex and profession. In 1695, at the age of forty-four, she fell victim to the plague which was scourging the capital in a year of famine. Though her poetry is the most universally appreciated of her writings, she produced several plays and other prose works.

Probably the greatest scholar of New Spain, not only in the seventeenth century but for the entire colonial period, was Carlos Sigüenza y Góngora. A student of the natural sciences as well as literature, he was well known in Europe. He wrote the *Mercurio volante* which related the reconquest of New Mexico after the Pueblo revolt. Sigüenza was a precursor of eighteenth-century rationalism and the revolt against scholasticism. In addition to these writers there were others of lesser fame, many in the priesthood.

The coasts of New Spain, like those of Central America, were visited by numerous flotillas of Dutch, English, and French pirates and privateers during the seventeenth century. Many merchant vessels fell prey to their assaults in American waters and off the coast of Spain, and coastal populations of New Spain learned to fear their sudden appearance. Defending the ports against the buccaneers was made the more difficult by their attacks being so widespread and unpredictable. In the same year or even month different bands might assail various seaports from Tampico in the north to Tierra Firme, while all unconvoyed ships in the Caribbean and Gulf were in constant danger. In 1683 Veracruz, hitherto considered safe from attack, was captured at night by subterfuge. In the few days the town was held by the enemy, it was completely sacked. It was necessary for the viceroy, on being informed of the invasion, to send forces of citizens from the capital, for the small garrison at San Juan de Ulúa was outnumbered by the enemy and awaited reinforcements before venturing to retake the town.

As a result of the piratical forays in the Caribbean and Gulf of Mexico, a patrol squadron, the *Barlovento* or Windward fleet, was formed, composed of twelve galleons and a few smaller vessels. Its purpose was not only the protection of merchant ships and ports, but the prevention of smuggling, which deprived the king of considerable revenue. The expenses of maintaining the fleet were paid by voluntary subscriptions on the part of the principal ports in need of protection.

The renewal of warfare between Spain and France in 1689 required action on the part of the viceroy not only because of the numerous French subjects in New Spain but because of those on the island of Española. He was authorized to confiscate the property of Frenchmen living in the viceroyalty, and in 1690 a large expedition was sent to destroy the French settlements of Española. It failed, however, and the French were left in control. In 1695 a joint Spanish-English force laid waste two more of the French towns, but the island was not recovered for Spain. The French threat was not confined to the Caribbean islands, for La Salle had departed earlier with a company of colonists for the Mississippi area. His attempted colony, which through error was located in Texas rather than near the mouth of the Mississippi, was destroyed by the Indians. The prospect of future French enterprise in the Gulf region and Mississippi valley remained alarming, and Viceroy Galve dispatched several expeditions into eastern Texas to found missions and win the tribes to the Spanish dependency, and to explore Pensacola Bay.

While coping with these external problems Galve did not escape the usual domestic ones. A sudden flood did immense damage to the city of Mexico and forced new efforts at improving the drainage system. A total eclipse of the sun caused consternation among the superstitious inhabitants, and when the promising wheat crop was lost to the ravages of insects, their fears seemed justified. Prices rose excessively. The public granary was placed under the control of municipal officials, and other prudent measures were taken to relieve the critical situation.

Since the famine was not easily alleviated, popular discontent continued to grow, and was intensified by rumors that the viceroy was speculating in grain supplies. Little precaution was taken against possible uprisings, despite their occurrence under similar conditions in the past. Only one company of infantry, the palace guard, was available in the capital to preserve order. For several days in succession the daily allowance of grain was exhausted before all were satisfied, and feeling against the viceroy ran high among the Indians. A mob assembled in the streets and began to hurl stones at public officials and government buildings. As in the time of Gelves the viceregal palace was fired. Before the mob had been dispersed the viceroy's residence and other buildings had been seriously damaged. Although the ringleaders of the uprising were criminals at large, who saw an opportunity for plunder during the excitement, the chief culprits to suffer were Indians. A similar affair occurred at Tlaxcala for much the same reasons.

Maintenance of order within the capital was insured by the organization of two regiments of militia, and the two cavalry companies formed during the upheaval were maintained until 1696. In that year the shortage of grain was again so acute that a similar riot was prevented only by extraordinary precautions.

Toward the end of the century the viceroys faced another grave problem, on the northern frontier far from the capital. In 1680 the

Pueblo Indians of New Mexico revolted and drove the Spaniards from the province. The refugees settled at the ford of the Río Grande, where the town of El Paso was founded. Not until 1692 was Spanish rule restored over the rebellious Pueblo tribes, and the constant fears of French intrusions from Canada and the Mississippi valley made it appear precarious. After the failure of La Salle's colony, the presence of French weapons and other trade items among the southwestern tribes verified the presence of French agents. Missions were temporarily established in eastern Texas, but they achieved little success in counteracting French influence built on trade in firearms. Frequent expeditions were sent along the Gulf coast to search for evidence of intrusions. Before the end of the century the French under Iberville and Bienville had won footholds at Biloxi and Mobile.

In the closing years of the century Mexico City was again torn by insurrection and conspiracy. Certain Indians planned an uprising after the departure of the fleet in 1696, but the viceroy was forewarned of their plans and mustered the militia. The ships, which were unusually richly laden this year, were fortunately delayed in their departure, for a French squadron had been cruising for some months off Habana awaiting their arrival. The French abandoned the search about the time the fleet left for Habana.

In 1697 the Count of Montezuma, whose wife was a lineal descendant of the last Aztec monarch, arrived as viceroy. His beginning was made inauspicious by a destructive eruption of Popocatépetl, a series of earthquakes, and unusually heavy rains which caused the capital to be flooded once more. Viceroy Montezuma was active in the suppression of banditry, which again had assumed serious proportions, by the organization of an efficient police force. The fortifications of the capital were improved, but the earlier riots convinced him that the most effective means of preserving the peace was in more generous treatment of the Indians. During his rule a successful harvest diminished the food shortage and removed the most immediate source of anxiety in the capital.

The pacification and settlement of Lower California was begun at this time by the Jesuits, after various attempts at military occupation failed. Under the guidance of fathers Kino and Salvatierra, the first permanent settlements were established in the peninsula.

European wars made commerce so hazardous during these years that a lack of quicksilver curtailed mining operations. Peace was celebrated in 1698, but it was only a brief interlude. Early in March, 1701, a black-clad messenger bearing a banner of the same somber shade, who paused each half-hour to fire a salute to the departed king, brought to Mexico City the news of the long-expected death of Carlos II.

Despite the fact that Carlos II had been in poor mental and physical health for much of his life, with unfortunate consequences for the Spanish empire, his demise was acknowledged in a fashion befitting an emperor. The courier who brought news of his death also carried instructions concerning the ceremonies which were to be performed. Two ministers were appointed to make the arrangements, and officials of the various towns were given detailed instructions. To prevent unscrupulous merchants from profiteering in the sale of black cloth required for the occasion, the viceroy set the price and invoked severe penalties against violators. On the appointed day a procession formed at the cabildo. With muffled drums sounding, the deliberate march began. The mace-bearers, dressed in black, led the way, followed by the members of the audiencia, the alcaldes, the alguacil mayor, and the remaining dignitaries of the city and the university, each bearing his insignia of office. At the viceroy's residence the king's death was publicly proclaimed, after which the cathedral bell tolled three hundred times. The funeral cortege continued in the same order and manner to the archbishop's house, the Inquisition building, and the cabildo. Other ceremonies were conducted during the following month.

As it was known that the viceroy was opposed to the Spanish throne passing to the French Bourbons, he was soon recalled. Rumors had spread that he planned to secure the independence of New Spain and establish himself as king if the Spanish crown passed to a Frenchman, although there is no evidence that he seriously contemplated such action. According to the will of Carlos II, the Spanish throne was granted to the grandson of Louis XIV of France, and before mourning for the former king had ended, the accession of Felipe V was celebrated. Felipe's new kingdom and empire were not to be acquired peacefully, however, and for more than a decade Europe was plunged into a general war which saw Spain and France pitted unsuccessfully against England, Holland, and Austria. If there existed a genuine desire for independence on the part of New Spain's rulers, conditions were indeed favorable.

XII

The Flowering of Peru

> The post of Viceroy is so exalted and majestic that it might be held by an Infante of Spain, were it a life position; for every year he appoints to over 70 Corregimientos, plus an infinite number of offices, the administrations of Indian communal affairs, the Royal Treasury, naval and military judges, mill inspectors, with authority equal to the King's. He has a guard of halberdiers and is accompanied by the city's nobility whenever he goes out. In church his eminent position is indicated by his brocaded seat of honor on a great rug in the center of the main chapel . . . And the whole Kingdom flocks to see him as they would for the King he represents . . .
>
> ANTONIO VÁZQUEZ DE ESPINOSA *

I N 1600 the viceroyalty of Peru was the more extensive of the two major Spanish jurisdictions in the New World, and because of the rich deposits of silver and gold was also regarded as more important than New Spain. Nominally under the rule of the viceroy of Peru were the kingdoms of Peru proper, Panamá, New Granada, Quito, Chile, and Charcas, which embraced Upper Peru and the towns of Río de la Plata. New Granada was a captaincy-general, while the others were presidencies. New Granada was for all practical purposes independent of the viceroy of Peru, although it was technically under his supervision. Since the problems of New Granada were largely those of the Caribbean area for the period under consideration, it is dealt with in the chapter on the

---

* *Compendium and Description of the West Indies*, Smithsonian Miscellaneous Collections, Vol. 102, Washington, D.C., 1942.

Caribbean rather than with the viceroyalty of Peru. In the lands remote from Lima viceregal authority was slight. The audiencias
especially were assertive in their relations with the viceroys. At the
outset of the century these tribunals existed in Lima, in Chuquisaca,
or La Plata — modern Sucre — in Santa Fé de Bogotá, in Quito, and
in Panamá. Another was to be added early in the seventeenth century in Santiago de Chile, and one was temporarily established in
Buenos Aires. Between the outlying audiencias and the viceroy
there was often little co-operation or harmony.

In the Andean region the problem of communications was a
major obstacle to efficient supervision of provincial affairs from
Lima. Intercourse between Callao and Chile or Panamá could be
carried on fairly easily by sea, but this fact did not improve the
subordination of the officials of those regions. It was not to the
discredit of the viceroys in Lima that they were not well informed
as to what transpired in Asunción or Buenos Aires or Concepción.
The area of the viceroyalty was far too vast and its parts too isolated
for effective rule from Lima.

Since the time of Pizarro Lima had become a moderately large
city, despite the fact that it had not been founded in the midst of a
sizable native population. Lima's wealth came from the silver mines
in the sierra; its prestige from its wealth and the presence of the
viceroy, the audiencia, the archbishop, and the inquisitor-general.
In 1600, of the approximately 25,000 persons living in Lima more
than 10,000 were Spaniards, with a like number of Negroes and
mulattoes, free and slave. The city contained many splendid buildings and gardens, and was noted for the ostentation of its wealthy
inhabitants. Because rain rarely fell on the narrow coastal plain
where Lima was located, tile roofs for houses were unnecessary, and
this typical feature of Spanish colonial architecture was lacking.

The position of viceroy of Peru was regarded as the highest of
colonial officialdom, and after the time of Antonio de Mendoza it
was often the reward of men who had served successfully in the
viceregal office of New Spain. The mineral wealth and political
importance of Peru were reflected in the higher salary paid to its
viceroy. This differential continued to be maintained even after the

mines of Peru were surpassed in output by those of New Spain in the seventeenth century.

The wealth of Lima was displayed not only in the homes of the laity but in the many richly adorned houses of the chief orders as well. Some of the orders maintained academies for teaching, and as elsewhere in Spanish America charity was also their domain. Confraternities operated the various charitable institutions; one was organized to manage the hospital for women, another was concerned with the care of prisoners, and providing lawyers to defend the poor in lawsuits. After it was discovered that the officials appointed by the government to manage the Royal Hospital mismanaged the funds at their disposal, a confraternity was organized to conduct its affairs. This hospital, founded toward the close of the sixteenth century, was one of the largest of its day, providing 500 beds for the sick as well as an asylum for the insane. The Hospital of Santa Ana, dedicated to the care of sick Indians, was also managed by a religious confraternity.

Educational institutions were likewise the domain of the religious orders. Many academies were conducted by them, and Lima boasted the University of San Marcos. In the university as well as the various academies, the principal chairs were in theology, scripture, law and canons, philosophy, and Indian languages. A complaint frequently made in this period was that there were so many men with advanced degrees that there were not enough suitable positions for them, either in law or in teaching.

The eighty Doctors and Masters composing the university's faculty were given an honorable place in the city's processions and celebrations, some of which were held in the university's amphitheater. The granting of a doctorate was one of the imposing spectacles frequently witnessed, although it could not compare in solemnity and awe with the rare and dramatic *autos de fé*.

When a candidate for the doctorate had fulfilled his requirements, the city's nobility arrived at his house with a salute of trumpets to serve as his escort. The procession then began, with the nobility leading the way, followed by the beadles with their maces, the masters and doctors with all their insignia, and the candidate and the dean of the faculty bringing up the rear. The procession marched with great dignity past the important buildings of the city, and repeated the performance on the following day. At the conclusion, the new doctor received his degree in the same manner as in the University of Salamanca in Spain.

The students of the various academies wore distinguishing gowns, which added to the splendor of Lima's processions. Those of the Colegio de San Martín wore gowns of dark gray with red sashes; others were equally colorful. The quality of their instruction, however, was somewhat less spectacular. The primary aim was to train men-of-letters well indoctrinated in the idea of submission to monarch and church.

As elsewhere at this period, Latin was the university language. In 1678, when a chair of mathematics was established at San Marcos, the students showed so little interest in the subject that within a decade the viceroy was disposed to abandon it. The study of medicine likewise did not attract a large following. In 1637, when a discussion was held to consider restoring the chair of medicine, most of the physicians were opposed, alleging the uselessness of studies for members of their profession!

Indians, mestizos, and other castes were excluded by law from attending the university, but the law was not strictly enforced. This aristocratic exlusivism was founded on the fear of educating those who might not prove entirely trustworthy, and who with a little learning might develop heretical or subversive ideas.

Extremely important in the political and social significance of Lima was the Holy Office of the Inquisition, which exercised jurisdiction over all of Spanish South America except New Granada. In the seventeenth century the tribunal's most frequent victims were the 'new Christians' and Portuguese Jews who entered Peru from Brazil by way of Buenos Aires. The rare celebration of an auto de fé was the most impressive ceremony seen in the capital, for even the viceroy assumed what was intended to be a posture of humility. To the accompaniment of trumpets and kettledrums, the event was announced throughout the capital and the neighboring towns.

Work was immediately begun on the stands erected in the principal plaza, and even though all available space was utilized the crowds could not be accommodated. The fact that lumber was scarce and expensive in Lima discouraged the frequent holding of the terrifying spectacle. Sections of the stands were set apart for the city's nobility and dignitaries, and for the wives of high officials. These sections were made more comfortable by stretching ships' sails over them to shield the occupants from sun or rain. The viceroy's box was richly adorned with carpets and cushions.

On the day preceding the auto a procession was made by all the friars of the various orders and the nobility, conducted by the Familiars of the Inquisition. On arriving at the plaza, the friars chanted the 109th psalm in melancholy tones. From this time until the event took place Dominican friars guarded the green cross which had been set up near the tribunal stand by their order. During the night guards composed of gentlemen of the city prevented the eager populace from surging into the section reserved for the viceroy and other dignitaries.

On the appointed day the city was protected from disorders by several companies of cavalry. The cross, veiled in black, was paraded from the cathedral to the plaza in awesome fashion, for the penitents themselves fell in behind the friars. First came those guilty of minor offenses. Last of all came any who were to be delivered to the civil tribunal for the supreme penalty. Every foot of the way was crowded by multitudes of people, some from distant towns, who struggled to get a view of the procession. In the plaza the culprits who were to pay the extreme penalty were reminded of their prospects by being seated in vaults decorated effectively with figures depicted as writhing in flames.

After all were seated one of the secretaries read aloud the Edict of Faith to the viceroy and nobility; all answered, 'Yes, I swear. Amen.' This was followed by a sermon, after which the auto began. The secretary called each penitent by name, and the accused stood while his sentence was read. Last of all were those who were to be turned over to civil authorities for punishment. The ordinance was drawn up immediately, and announcement made of the penalty of the pyre. The condemned were then placed on packsaddles on the

backs of mules and paraded through the streets once more, this time
to the *quemadero* or place of execution, while the town crier proceeded them proclaiming their sins. The others were absolved in accordance with their sentences, which ranged from penance to service
in the galleys. The pyre for the extreme cases was located outside
the city, where the sentence was carried out by civil officials. Fortunately for the Indians, the Inquisition's authority did not embrace
them.

A short distance from Lima was its seaport, Callao, a town of some
700 Spaniards and multitudes of Indian and Negro laborers and
servants. A thriving commerce was carried on with New Spain,
Central America, Panamá, other regions of the Pacific coast, and
Spain. Callao was the port of entry of most of the commerce of the
interior, and the most traveled route in South America was that between Lima and Buenos Aires. It must be pointed out, however,
that much of the commerce which came over this route from the
Plata region was contraband, and actually detracted from the traffic
of Callao.

Early in the century Callao had little to offer in the way of defense against sea marauders. The voyages of Sir Francis Drake and
Cavendish along the Pacific coast in the late sixteenth century
caused alarm, but little action in preparing defenses was taken until
the advent of the Dutch around 1600. The Dutch fleets were considerably larger and more dangerous than the English squadrons had
been, and their appearance caused consternation in Lima and
Callao because of the lack of defenses. Viceroy Luis de Velasco,
forewarned of the Dutch designs, made hasty preparations to defend
Callao, but the Dutch fleet dispatched in 1599 was scattered by
storms and failed to fulfill its threat. In 1615 the viceroy, Francisco
de Borja y Aragón, the Prince of Esquilache, again faced a Dutch
invasion. He began the construction of two forts to be armed with
cannon cast from Chilean copper, and enlarged the naval squadron.
The Dutch defeated his fleet, however, and entered Callao. The
invaders soon departed and, after looting Huarmei and Paita, sailed
from the coast of Peru. Other forts were added to Callao's defenses
by succeeding administrations, and powder mills were established

to supply the artillery. The defense of Lima was strengthened by the addition of thirty-two companies of militia composed of Spaniards, and several others of free mulattoes and Negroes.

The port of Arica was the principal gateway for the commerce with the famous mining town of Potosí in Upper Peru. Many ships visited the harbor, bringing quicksilver from the Huancavelica mines to be used in processing the silver ore, and merchandise for the miners. Most of the few hundred Spanish residents of Arica were engaged in the carrying trade, and maintained the mule trains used in the traffic.

North of Lima was the presidency of Quito, which included the district of Popayán in modern Colombia. San Francisco del Quito, the capital, was situated in a densely populated region, and contained about 3000 Spaniards, and countless Indians, mestizos, Negroes, and mulattoes. Within a short distance of the city were more than forty Indian villages which supplied food and labor. Gold and silver mines were operated profitably, while sugar plantations, cattle and mule ranches, and cacao farms were numerous. Textile mills such as those of New Spain and Peru supplied coarse cloth for local trade.

Like Peru, Quito was geographically divided into two radically differing regions, the coastal plain and the mountainous interior. Guayaquil, in many respects the best harbor on the Pacific coast, enjoyed a large volume of trade despite endemic diseases which made it notorious as a graveyard of Spaniards. Hemp, lumber, cordovan leather, and great quantities of cacao passed through Guayaquil on the way to Peru, Central America, and New Spain. Not far from Guayaquil were the ruins of Túmbez, the Inca city visited by Pizarro on his first visit to Peru. By 1600 Túmbez had been reduced to a small Indian village, although other Incan cities had survived in a happier condition.

Cuzco, the ancient capital of the Incas, represented in the seventeenth century much greater fusion of races and civilizations than Lima. The dominant group in the city was the Spanish population of about 3000. An unknown number of mestizos and about 14,000 Indians, as well as some Negro and mulatto servants, composed the bulk of the population. Many of the mestizo descendants of the

Inca nobility and the conquerors had risen to high positions in society and were regarded as creoles.

In Cuzco there was a great number of Indian artisans — silversmiths, carpenters, tailors, and similar craftsmen. The city was an important trade center, for it lay on the road to the mining regions of Upper Peru. The city contained the usual religious institutions, as well as a famous hospital for Indians built by contributions of the conquerors. In the late sixteenth century a university was established at Cuzco, with a curriculum similar to that of San Marcos in Lima.

The chief products of Peru, in addition to the fabulous amounts of silver and other metals, were sugar, wine, cereals, beans, coca, and textiles. Lumber and cordovan leather were imported from Guayaquil, while Central America furnished pitch and sailcloth. Silks and other oriental goods were obtained through the illegal trade with Acapulco. Because of the great demand for mules in the mining operations and the interior trade, vast numbers were brought each year from New Granada and the Plata region. After 1687, when Peruvian wheatfields were destroyed by volcanic eruptions, wheat from Chile was imported.

Among the remarkable obstacles to life in the entire Andean cordillera were the recurrent earthquakes which caused the destruction of entire towns and the loss of thousands of lives. Frequently the shocks lasted for days, and in some instances were accompanied by volcanic eruptions and tidal waves. One especially destructive series of shocks in 1600 lasted for fifteen days, during which time the sky was obscured by dense clouds of ash and smoke. Eight inches of sand rained down on the town of Arequipa and vicinity. Tremendous roars from the volcano added to the terror and misery of the inhabitants, most of whom were convinced that their day of judgment had arrived and found them unprepared. Religious processions were held and a nude hermit from the desert marched through the town striking himself with a stone in contrition. By the time that the eruption and quakes had ceased, sand and ashes had destroyed crops and vineyards over a wide area and had wiped out entire villages of Indians. Other famous earthquakes during the seventeenth century occurred in 1618, when Arica was inundated by a tidal wave, 1630, 1647, 1650, 1657, 1660, and 1687. The last was felt from New Granada to Chile. Many others were recorded throughout the century, and the reconstruction of damaged cities was an almost constant problem for colonial officials.

Upper Peru, or modern Bolivia, was within the jurisdiction of the Audiencia of Charcas. La Plata, or as it was better known by its Indian name, Chuquisaca, was the seat of the audiencia and the archbishopric. The city contained only a few Spaniards, but a large number of Indians and mestizos, who were able to labor at the high altitude far more effectively than Europeans or Africans. Parts of Upper Peru were dissected by deep valleys called *yungas*, which made travel slow and difficult. The yungas were remarkable for the variety of climate they afforded. Tropical crops were raised at the lower levels, while the inhabitants of the villages on the heights saw frost every morning.

The mining towns of Upper Peru were characterized by the same boisterous, flamboyant, and violent life typical of mining towns throughout the New World. In 1607, when a noteworthy strike was made at San Felipe, miners and traders and ruffians rushed to the scene from great distances; in a few weeks the town had a population of more than 1000 Spaniards. Twenty mills were constructed to grind the ore, and both smelting and the quicksilver amalgamation process were employed in extracting the metal.

Most of the mines were manned by Indians serving under the mita system, although there were a few which depended entirely upon voluntary, hired laborers. To operate the famous mines in the mountain of silver at Potosí, the king authorized the use of more than 13,000 Indians under the mita. Assembling these laborers and filling the allotment of the mine-owners was the responsibility of the corregidor at Potosí. Each year the natives of the Indian villages chose an official whose duty it was to conduct them to the mine and oversee their activities. By law the distance which Indians could be taken from their homes was limited, but enforcement was lax, and as the native population within reach declined, the interpretation of the law was modified. The proportion of men who could be taken from a village during the year was also specified by law, but the demand for miners was too strong to permit proper compliance, with the result that some Indians were kept constantly at the mines. The native population declined seriously in the mining regions, owing not only to those who died as a consequence of the labor, but also to the disruption of family life.

In addition to the Indian miners under the mita, there were about 4000 *mingados* or free laborers who worked in the mining and smelting operations by choice. Those who performed the task of extracting the ore from the earth entered the tunnels on Monday each week and did not emerge again until Saturday evening. An enormous quantity of tallow furnished by the Indians was consumed each year in the candles which lighted the galleries. The ore was carried to the surface by hand in baskets; the ladders from one landing to another were crudely made, and fatal accidents were frequent. From the mouth of the mine the ore was taken to the mills on the backs of llamas, and 8000 of them were used daily in this task. The transporting of the ore outside the mines was carried on entirely by mingados rather than mita Indians.

Water mills for grinding the ore were arranged in succession along an incline so that the same water could be used. The scarcity of water, which necessitated this arrangement, was alleviated somewhat by the construction of reservoirs and aqueducts, yet in unusually dry years the mills were forced to suspend operations. After the mills had ground the ore to a powder, it was mixed with brine and quicksilver, a process which caused a high mortality among the unfortunate Indians employed in it. The conglomeration was washed so that only the combined silver and mercury remained, and the residue was placed in clay pots and heated until the mercury had vaporized and passed off.

The silver thus acquired was melted into bars and, if legal channels were followed, was taken to the assayer to determine its quality. When this had been done the bars were stamped and the king's fifth set aside. Between the years 1545 and 1628, 326,000,000 pesos' worth of silver was taken legally from the mines of Potosí alone, not counting the unknown quantities taken out illegally to avoid payment of the quinto. Some Spaniards estimated that the amount taken out illicitly was greater than that which passed through the hands of royal officials.

Potosí, long the most famed mining town in the Americas, had at the beginning of the century a turbulent population of about 40,000 Spaniards, many of whom were of the troublesome type usually attracted to mining camps. In addition to these some 80,000 Indian laborers and their families lived in the suburban wards of the city. An account of Potosí in this period would not be complete without mention of Doña Clara, one of the gayest members of the city, whose wealth and charms were fabulous; or of Claudia, who also helped to make life in Potosí intensely exciting; or Doña Catalina Erauso, the Nun Ensign. Dressed as a man she fled from adventure to adventure throughout the Andean towns, and won great fame by her success in duels. Her strange career ended in New Spain, where she spent the last years of her hectic life as a mule-driver.

To supervise the mining activities and to settle the multitudinous controversies which arose, an *alcalde mayor de minas* was appointed, and his difficult duties made the position an especially responsible one. Officials who treated the *potosinos* in a highhanded fashion in the early years usually died violent deaths, while more reasonable and compromising ones shared in the general wealth. In the early seventeenth century a seat on the cabildo of Potosí sold for as much as 18,000 pesos, and the office of alguacil mayor for more than 100,000 ducats. Since the salaries received by these officials were but a small proportion of the purchase price, the temptation to accept gifts and bribes from grateful mine-owners and smugglers must have been strong. It is true, however, that here also wealthy men occasionally purchased offices merely to add to their prestige.

The mint at Potosí produced silver coins which were used in Peru, Chile, the towns of Río de la Plata, and Central America, where they were taken by traders. In the mining regions prices were excessively high, for everything that was needed had to be brought great distances on the backs of mules.

In the seventeenth century the mines of Potosí began to play out, for their richest veins were nearly exhausted. In 1626 one of the reservoirs broke through its walls and the water deluged the lower mills and the town, causing havoc and consternation. Twenty mills were completely ruined, and five others badly damaged. Many persons were drowned in the flood, and the property losses were reckoned at four million pesos. This was a serious blow to the mining industry, for it came at a time when unprofitable methods and poorer veins were already causing some of the mines to be abandoned. By mid-century the production of silver at Potosí had dropped off drastically through exhaustion of the richest lodes and of the supply of Indian miners.

South of Upper Peru and still within the jurisdiction of the Audiencia of Charcas, was the district of Tucumán, which included the towns of Jujuy, Salta, La Rioja, Tucumán, Santiago del Estero, and Córdoba. The region was sparsely settled, and contained only about 700 Spaniards, half of whom held Indians in encomiendas. Most of the remainder were merchants and artisans. In 1607 about 24,000 Indians were employed by the encomenderos, but this number declined during the remainder of the century. The mestizo population was large, and contained the forerunners of the gauchos; many of the mestizos were engaged in killing and skinning wild cattle, or cattle whose owners were not in the immediate vicinity.

In the early seventeenth century a strenuous effort was made to improve the condition of the Indians of the Plata region by an oidor of the audiencia in Charcas, Francisco de Alfaro. Among the many ordinances which he issued on the subject were those repeating the earlier abolition of personal service on the part of the Indians, and substituting instead tribal assessments. Alfaro represented the spirit of Spanish jurists and theologians of the time of Las Casas, and his well-intentioned efforts struck a severe blow at the encomenderos. Because his detailed ordinances were not in keeping with the needs of the few Spaniards in the region, they could not be enforced. The cabildos of all of the towns of Río de la Plata and Paraguay sent protests to the king along with requests for modification of the more obnoxious ordinances. Some of the towns even sent agents to Madrid to convince the king and council of the justice of their cause. The principal complaints were that the Indians preferred service in lieu of payment of tribute, and that the ordinances so weakened Spanish authority that the Indians would become vagabonds, and all gains in civilizing them would be jeopardized. In these arguments the cabildos were generally supported by the clergy. Even the bishop of Tucumán, who had written the king in 1609 that he would prefer almost anything to the perpetuation of the abominable practice of personal service, changed his mind after the ordinances of Alfaro were issued. In 1612 he wrote again to the king that the Indians lacked the capacity to live in complete freedom, and that the situation was much worse than before. Few sincere attempts were made to enforce the ordinances because of the apparent ruin to the encomenderos and the settlements.

The Indians of the Plata region ordinarily were engaged in tending herds of cattle and mules and in weaving. The number of those held in encomiendas was reduced drastically during the century because of lives lost in uprisings and in epidemics of diseases believed introduced by the Negro slaves taken through the port of Buenos Aires, over the trails across the plains to Tucumán, and eventually to Peru.

Córdoba and Tucumán were the most important of the interior towns of the Plata area, for they lay on trade routes between Buenos Aires and the west-coast cities as well as Upper Peru. The mining towns of Upper Peru furnished the most accessible and profitable markets, and most of the traffic was turned in that direction. Coarse cloth, foodstuffs, and mules were the most prominent articles of commerce. In 1622 a customs-house was established in Córdoba, and the town was also the seat of a university established by the Jesuits in 1610. This university, the only one in the Plata region, was famous throughout the colonial period. The only other institution of higher education within reach was San Francisco Xavier, which the Jesuits founded in Chuquisaca in 1624.

Asunción, the capital of Paraguay and Río de la Plata, was larger but less prosperous than Córdoba. The 250 encomenderos of the city employed their charges in the production of sugar, for which there were 200 mills, and in wine-making. Asunción was surrounded by Indian villages which supplied laborers for these enterprises. Although the city had enjoyed early prestige as the first permanent settlement in the region, its extreme isolation and the restrictions on trade undermined its importance, and the recently founded port town of Buenos Aires forged slowly ahead.

The rise of Buenos Aires, however, was not rapid. In 1600 it was still a small, impoverished village struggling to defend itself against marauding Indians. The greatest handicap was not troublesome natives, but the closing of the port except to occasional licensed ships. Commerce with Brazil was permitted from 1602 till 1608, after the repeated urgings of the bishop, who pleaded the poverty of the inhabitants. The amount and kind of goods which could be carried over the land route to Peru was exceedingly limited, so the *porteños*, people of the port, were desperate whenever ships did not arrive with the articles they needed. The establishment of the customs-house in Córdoba rather than on the coast was a blow to Buenos Aires, for merchants who brought goods into the interior from the port were required to pay a duty of 50 per cent. The porteños of necessity found ways to circumvent the regulations; Portuguese traders in Brazil were co-operative, as were the Dutch and English. Only a few officials steeled their hearts to the importunings of the inhabitants and tried rigorously to enforce the restrictions. Most governors permitted contraband trade even if they did not participate in it themselves.

Although Buenos Aires had little wealth to attract raiders, it was frequently threatened from the seaward. In 1607 English, French, and Dutch corsairs entered the estuary with impunity, for the port had no defenses, and seized ships found there. In 1628 Dutch ships made soundings in the channel, an act which seemed a harbinger of future visits. In the following year the viceroy of Peru warned the governor of the expected arrival of forty Dutch ships, which happily for the inhabitants did not arrive. A few years later news that French ships were on their way to Buenos Aires also produced alarm. On a few occasions the town was attacked by corsairs, but there was little to be gained from its capture.

The porteños meanwhile complained vigorously of their exposed condition, pointing out that the most effective means of assuring their security was to permit commerce to flow liberally through the port and thus build up its population. The oidor Alfaro regarded this as a specious argument; greater commerce would merely attract more attention, and after all, it was in the king's interest to concentrate on the defense of the Caribbean mainland. Little attention was paid to the frequent suggestions of the porteños. After 1640, when Portugal became independent, the fear of the Portuguese was great among officials in Río de la Plata, and measures were taken to disarm those living in Buenos Aires. Of the 1500 inhabitants of the city at this time, 370 were Portuguese, many of whom held important positions in civil life or in the army. They were ordered to register with the governor, and to withdraw twenty leagues from the coast.

One of the most remarkable colonial officials in the Plata region during the seventeenth century was the creole Hernandarias de Saavedra, who served several times as governor. What made him unusual was the strictness with which he enforced the laws, even those which he saw as ruinous to the region. When Buenos Aires was closed to commerce, he rigorously prosecuted *contrabandistas*. A friend of the Jesuits, he encouraged members of the order to come to the Plata region and was influential in having the Guaraní country assigned as a Jesuit province in 1607. Although his jurisdiction included Paraguay as well as Río de la Plata, like most of the governors from the 1590's on he resided in Buenos Aires. He endorsed the proposals made by his predecessors to separate Paraguay and Río de la Plata, as the area was far too extensive for one man to govern. In 1617 the separation was carried out, and Buenos Aires became the capital of the newly established province. In 1620 a bishopric was created in Río de la Plata, marking another step in the decline of Asunción.

The governors of Río de la Plata generally did not share the enthusiasm for enforcing the distasteful laws of Alfaro and Hernandarias de Saavedra. In their reluctance to proceed against smugglers they were motivated by powerful reasons. If they cut off contraband trade the inhabitants under their jurisdiction must inevitably suffer. Another reason for their attitude also appeared when their residencias were held. Time after time the outgoing governors were found guilty of having participated in the illicit traffic themselves, and severe fines were assessed against them. The bishops seem to have been similarly engaged, and their competition was not always received by the governors in a friendly spirit. In 1627 a serious rift between civil and clerical officials occurred when one of the regidores, a partisan of the bishop, was arrested for engaging in contraband trade and then forcibly freed by his friends.

Cuyo province in western Argentina was still a part of Chile. The province was governed by a corregidor appointed by the governor of Chile, and who resided in the town of Mendoza. Some 15,000 Indians were held in encomienda at the outset of the century but the number dwindled to about 5000 by 1650. The main economic pursuits were wine-making, textiles, and a little mining, in addition to the usual pastoral activities. Mendoza was connected by road or trail with Buenos Aires, Córdoba, and Santiago de Chile. A trip to Buenos Aires usually took two months; to Córdoba about twenty days' travel was necessary, while the trip across the Andes to Chile required about one week.

The last region under the nominal rule of the viceroy of Peru was the kingdom of Chile. The Chilean cities, like those of the Plata region, were small and far from prosperous. Most of the encomenderos were concerned with ranching and farming, although the market for their products was limited. The Indian wars of southern Chile were more serious than those of the Plata region in the seventeenth century, for the Araucanians continued to defend themselves with skill and courage, and to take the offensive whenever the Spaniards relaxed their vigilance. In 1608 the king granted Chileans the right to enslave Indians waging war against them, but governor García Ramón withheld the edict, and it was not published until after his death. This order merely prolonged the strife. It again became necessary for the king to provide a permanent army for Chile, and to pay for it from royal funds collected in Peru. This provision was a fortunate one for Chileans, for it relieved them somewhat of the usual obligation to serve on campaigns against the Indians, and it provided the region with an income in the form of pay to the soldiers. Warfare against the Indians seemed a permanent problem, incapable of solution.

Attempts were made from time to time to pacify the Araucanians by gentle means and by force. None succeeded. In 1609, when the audiencia was established, the judges were instructed to put an end to the irritating practice of using the Indians for personal service. The unyielding opposition of the encomenderos made it impossible to fulfill the order in Chile as elsewhere. During his brief term as viceroy, the Count of Monterrey had appointed a commission to make a study of the Indian situation in Chile and to offer recommendations. One of the strongest recommendations made by the group was that personal service be abolished gradually over a two-year period, so that employers would have a reasonable opportunity to engage voluntary laborers. The encomenderos simply refused to release their Indians, and there was no force available capable of assuring their compliance.

The continued lack of success in warfare against the Araucanians led to an attempt at peaceful penetration early in the seventeenth century. The author of this plan was Juan de Villela, who pointed out that the main causes of resistance were the severe penalties inflicted by the Spaniards and the mistreatment of the encomienda Indians. Personal service, he declared, was especially unjust and should be suppressed. The king agreed to abolish the encomiendas and personal service in return for payment of tribute by the Indians, and to leave the territory south of the Bío Bío to them. He rescinded the order authorizing the enslavement of Indians captured in war. In 1612 the plan was put into operation, under the guidance of the Jesuit Luis de Valdivia. With other priests of his order he began to proselyte the Araucanians, who at first welcomed them. The Indians soon became suspicious, however, and drove the missionaries away.

Father Valdivia did not fail in spirit or in optimism. Realizing that opposition of Chileans was one of his major obstacles he visited the viceroy and audiencia in Lima, and won their consent to new regulations. He continued to Spain to secure the approval of Felipe III. In 1622, nevertheless, Governor Osores de Ulloa suspended most of the regulations, and a few years later the project was abandoned in favor of a return to warfare. In 1641 a new agreement was negotiated with the Araucanians, and although no more permanent than previous ones, it was the first of a long series providing interludes of peace in the south. In 1655 the Indians took the warpath again, largely because of the cupidity of the governor who, like his counterparts in New Mexico, hoped to profit by the sale of captives. The fiasco so enraged Chileans that they drove him from the kingdom.

Life in Chile was exceedingly simple. The vineyards around Santiago produced a sufficient quantity of wine to meet the needs of the inhabitants. A few woolen mills turned out coarse cloth and blankets, and Chile produced her own flour. Leather-working was an important industry, and cordovan leather was one of the few exports. Educational facilities were not in much demand, for the more fortunate men sent their sons to Peru for schooling. The Franciscans, Dominicans, and Jesuits founded academies, however, and during the course of the century these schools produced a number of writers of sufficient talent to make their works remembered.

The viceroyalty of Peru, as can be seen from the vast and differing areas it included, was not easily governed by a viceroy in Lima. The problems of each area, although some were universal, required strict attention and solutions peculiar to each. Since communications were especially difficult and slow, and because there were sufficient problems in Peru proper to occupy the energy of most viceroys, the more remote provinces suffered from neglect and a lack of appreciation of their needs.

Scarcely less influential than the viceroy was the archbishop of Lima, whose ecclesiastical jurisdiction included the dioceses of Lima, Cuzco, Trujillo after 1611, Arequipa after 1612, and Guamanga after 1615. The multitude of religious establishments, including schools, hospitals, and charitable institutions as well as cathedrals, churches, and religious houses, affected every segment of society. Even the Negro slaves received attention, and religious assemblies for them were held on Sunday afternoons. Those who were required to hold the horses of officials were not neglected, for a priest came out and preached to them. The Indian villages left under the control of native officials also were assigned priests.

The viceroy's court was the center of literary activity. The Prince of Esquilache, who entered upon his duties in 1615, surrounded himself with scholars, and encouraged discussions on scientific, artistic, and literary subjects. He interested himself in the founding of academies for the instruction of Indians of noble birth, for he believed that one of the best ways to bridge the gap between the native civilization and that of the Spaniards was to teach the Indians to speak the Castilian language. Most of the writers and scholars of the era were members of the priesthood; the Jesuits were especially prominent in these activities.

Esquilache's administration was concerned with problems which were to plague his successors increasingly as the century progressed: augmenting royal revenues and defending his realm against foreigners and Indians. By strictly enforcing the various revenue measures which were being mocked by lax officials he was able to accumulate large sums to send to Spain; the hostile attentions of the Dutch caused him to raise and expend additional sums in constructing forts to guard Callao.

The Marquis of Guadalcázar, a former viceroy of New Spain, succeeded Esquilache in 1622. The Araucanian offensive in Chile and the continued visits of the Dutch made his rule difficult. The Dutch, emboldened by their earlier successes, returned to the coast of Peru, and in 1624 the viceroy was forced to call all of the inhabitants of Lima to arms to defend the city. Callao remained under siege for five months, but disease in the Dutch force wrought a destruction which Spanish cannon had failed to accomplish, and the siege was lifted.

Domestic problems were no less pressing, for in the same year a famine caused starvation and great loss of life among the Peruvian Indians. In 1625 a more favorable note was sounded when the warring factions among the miners of Potosí were induced to reach an agreement and resume work in the mines with a prospect of less frequent interruptions in the future. But it was of little use to the king of Spain to have his subjects laboriously empty the mountains of their treasure only to have it fall into the hands of Dutch heretics. In 1627 the viceroy was again ordered to maintain cruisers along the coasts from Panamá to Chile.

During the rule of the Count of Chinchón, who followed Guadalcázar, the use of quinine for curing fevers was first adopted by the Spaniards. The treatment had long been known to the Incas, but it received its first publicity when the bark was used as a remedy for the viceroy's wife. In the eighteenth century the Swedish scientist Linnaeus named the plant which produced the bark *Chinchona* after its famous patient. In the seventeenth century, however, it was known by a variety of names.

Chinchón's administration was no more peaceful than that of his predecessor. Indian uprisings in Chile and Tucumán threatened those provinces, and led him to authorize sending vagabonds and malefactors to serve against the Araucanians. In 1635 he ordered a settlement re-established at Valdivia to guard against the Dutch, who still entered the Pacific from that quarter. He found the Portuguese deeply entrenched in Peruvian commerce and even mining. He attempted to curtail their activities by giving Spaniards monopolies of the *pulperías*, grocery stores, and some other pursuits. Fear of the Portuguese, many of whom were Jews or 'New Christians,' was reflected in the increased activity of the Holy Office in the second quarter of the century. In 1639 an auto de fé was held in Lima which resulted in the execution of eleven Portuguese. In the same year Chinchón sent Jesuits to explore the Amazon valley in search of Portuguese posts and suitable mission sites.

In 1640 the new viceroy, Pedro de Toledo y Leiva, Marquis of Mancera, had to cope with the problems arising out of the revolts of Portugal and Catalonia. He collected the sum of 350,000 pesos to bolster the ailing treasury, and took defensive measures against the Portuguese in Peru, Buenos Aires, and Panamá. In 1643, what appeared to be an unusually grave threat subsided when the Dutch gave up Valdivia after failing to form an effective alliance with the Araucanians.

Mancera's relations with the audiencia in Panamá represent the type of insubordination in outlying jurisdictions which forced vice-roys to become men of tact and diplomacy. The audiencia challenged his right to appoint a governor in Panamá in case of a vacancy. Despite a decree from the Council of the Indies confirming the authority of the viceroy in this question the audiencia remained adamant, and Mancera failed to win the argument.

By the middle of the century the condition of the Indians of Peru had become deplorable, for their decline in numbers had led to a more widespread and unscrupulous search for laborers. *Guatacos*, agents who supplied workers, scoured the land, and kidnapping of Indians was general. Laws inspired in part at least by humanitarian motives, such as Toledo's ordinances governing the mita, became instruments of oppression under officials who connived with mine-owners and other entrepreneurs. Although by law the amount of time each year that an Indian should serve was limited, in practice this restriction was ignored, and the victims had no recourse to justice despite the various official protectors and advocates appointed to defend them. The limitations on the distance that Indians could be taken from their homes for labor in the mines were violated increasingly as the supply of laborers near the mines diminished.

On occasion voices were raised in indignation at the maltreatment of the Indians, and the citizens who thus spoke out generally reproached the priests as bitterly as the civil officials. The complaint was that the civil officials and the priests between them deprived the Indians of everything except the barest necessities. Even though a village might have no able-bodied men left, the remaining villagers were forced to pay the tribute at the former rate. Assessments of this type did not find their way into the coffers of the royal treasury. The fees charged by the priests for their various services were a further and inescapable burden to the natives in many villages. One of those who spoke most violently concerning the plight of the Peruvian Indians in the seventeenth century was Juan de Padilla.

Padilla's protests at length reached the ear of the king, and he ordered the royal judges to make an examination of the complaints. As usual on such occasions, the judges found that long-standing laws were not being obeyed. The king ordered the promulgation of new edicts for the protection of the natives, and some oft-repeated ones were renewed. Hours of work were fixed; employment of aged persons or young children was prohibited; the distance Indians could be taken from their homes to work was limited to two leagues; and finally, wages were ordered paid in the presence of a competent official. Enforcement of these statutes by conscientious administrators might have removed most of the worst abuses, but at the same time work in the mines, on the plantations, and in the obrajes would have ceased. In 1664 edicts to improve the conditions of work in the obrajes were issued, and the use of the hated guataco was prohibited.

The laws, however, were not enforced, and the Indians continued to be deprived of the privilege of choosing to work or not. The economic abyss into which Spain herself was falling made colonial revenues urgent, and edicts for the protection of the natives were not infrequently accompanied by appeals for vast sums of money. Viceroys and other officials seriously concerned about the financial requirements of the royal government could not permit the mines and fields to be abandoned simply because the Indians had not developed enthusiasm for voluntary labor.

Indian uprisings and missionary endeavor continued to characterize life in the pastoral, frontier provinces. After a serious Calchaquian revolt in 1630 had been quelled, the encomenderos of Tucumán were content for a time to follow a more lenient policy. The natives were better satisfied than previously, although they were incited into another conflict in 1657 by a renegade creole or mestizo named Pedro Bohórquez, who pretended to be a descendant of the Inca. The encomenderos were hard pressed to subdue the Indians, and the province was seriously set back. Devastating raids from the wild, unconquered tribes of the Chaco were now added to the difficulties. The practice of enslaving captives taken in the wars helped to prolong the conflict, as in Chile and New Mexico. Repeated orders from the king to liberate the captives were ignored.

The forays of the Chaco tribes nearly destroyed Esteco and Tucumán during the last two decades of the century. Córdoba, which was located in the lands of the docile and skillful Comechingones, was by far the most prosperous city of northwestern Río de la Plata. It did not come within the range of the Calchaquians or the Chaco raiders, and its commanding position on the overland trade routes gave it advantages lacking to the other towns.

Of all the missionary fields of South America the Jesuit operations among the Guaranís of Paraguay were by far the most notable. The Jesuits were fortunate in that the Guaranís were of a higher degree of civilization than most other mission Indians except the Pueblo tribes of New Mexico. They were relatively peaceful, although they made capable soldiers. Another advantage which the Jesuits enjoyed in this region was their comparative success in keeping their charges isolated from Spanish soldiers and colonists, who were often the cause of lament on the part of missionary-priests.

The Guaranís were grouped into towns organized according to royal regulations similar to those which governed the formation of Spanish colonial towns. The civil government was largely in the hands of native officials who conducted their affairs under the paternalistic guidance of the Jesuit fathers. Each Indian received title to land according to his family's needs, and this land as well as its products were his personal property. Common fields were tilled by the men of each town for general needs such as paying tribute.

The Jesuits in Paraguay were never numerous. In the seventeenth century there were never more than 175, and they could not have enjoyed such remarkable success without the co-operation of the Indians. One of their most critical problems from the outset was defending the neophytes against the rapacious paulista slave-raiders, who carried off an estimated 60,000 mission Indians between 1627 and 1631. Powerless to resist these well-organized campaigners, who caused the complete abandonment of nine missions, the Jesuits led their converts on a thousand-mile hegira below the Iguassú river to the banks of the Paraná and Uruguay. The raids, nevertheless, continued, and by mid-century twenty-six of the forty-eight reductions had been destroyed. In remaining ones there were approximately 40,000 Indians.

To aid the Jesuits and Guaranís in the face of these invasions which Spanish diplomacy could not exorcise, the king granted the natives the unusual right to use firearms. In 1644 Indian troops were armed, trained, and led by Spanish officers; later on the Guaranís were able to furnish their own military leaders. They were permitted to use 150 arquebuses at first, but as the conflict continued the number of firearms was raised to 800. In 1661 Felipe IV authorized the general use of weapons when occasion demanded, but a few years later the order was rescinded. In 1676 one of the most terrible of the paulista invasions occurred, and the king belatedly permitted the possession and use of arquebuses and muskets sufficient for the defense of the missions.

As the military prowess of the Guaranís became known the Jesuits were frequently called on to furnish troops for various campaigns, and occasionally for the defense of Buenos Aires. Three thousand Guaranís participated in the assault which took Colônia do Sacramento from the Portuguese in 1680; between 1664 and 1766 the Guaranís took part in at least a hundred expeditions in the name of the king. Their service to Spain was extraordinary, and their cost to the royal exchequer was slight. Their unusual role in the defense of the Plata area was acknowledged occasionally by Spanish kings.

In addition to their military value the Guaranís provided the Plata region with many craftsmen, artists, and sculptors. Among them were a few writers of history, religious works, and drama. The Jesuits introduced a printing press, and in 1700 the first book printed in the Plata region was produced in Paraguay. All of these accomplishments were made under difficult circumstances, and they are a high tribute to the ability and energy of the Jesuit missionaries as well as the adaptability and intelligence of the Guaranís. The Jesuits were not so highly complimented by their contemporaries, however, for the encomenderos resented the fact that the missionaries apparently were not concerned with preparing the Indians for transfer to rule by lay officials, but intended to keep them in perpetual tutelage.

Despite the separation of Buenos Aires and Paraguay into two provinces in 1617, the governors of the former town failed to check illicit commerce as expected. The occasional licensed vessels which entered the port were too few to supply the demands of the inhabitants. Illicit trade with Portuguese in Brazil was fairly simple while the king of Spain held the Portuguese crown. After Portugal's independence in 1640, the traffic became more difficult but continued to flourish. Few of the seventeenth-century governors of Buenos Aires were not accused of allowing or participating in contraband trade, but the severe fines imposed in their residencias did not seem to dissuade their successors from the same practice.

In 1661 an audiencia was established in Río de la Plata, in hope that it could succeed where governors had failed. Buenos Aires was probably the smallest town in which an audiencia was located, for its Spanish population numbered less than 1000. The houses were primitive, of clay with roofs of straw. The streets were either a series of mudholes or choking with dust, according to the season, and it was not unusual for marauding Indians to slay citizens within the confines of the town. It is not surprising that the audiencia failed in ten years to suppress the smuggling trade, and was itself withdrawn in 1671.

In order to facilitate the contraband trade as well as to fulfill their ambition to make the left bank of the Plata the southern boundary of Brazil, the Portuguese established themselves at a post called Colônia do Sacramento late in 1679. Governor José de Garro of Buenos Aires took immediate action without awaiting instructions from Lima. He raised a force of porteños and Guaranís, expelled the intruders, and destroyed their post. But within a few years the Portuguese were back on the scene, and Garro's action had been disavowed by Spain.

The return of Colônia to Portugal reflected the low state of Spanish diplomacy and Spain's humble position in Europe. The Banda Oriental, in which the Portuguese had secured a foothold, was clearly on the Spanish side of the ancient Line of Demarcation. And although Spain did not uphold Garro, that energetic official was promoted to the governorship of Chile. The history of Colônia, a smugglers' mart athwart the natural gateway to southern South America, was one of intermittent strife and continued Spanish humiliation. That Colônia remained a Portuguese possession for nearly a century despite its frequent capture by Spanish troops was the result of England's growing weight at the council table.

With the establishment of Colônia contraband trade improved, for it was much simpler to arrange meetings and exchanges from a near-by base than from Brazil. English, Dutch, and French merchants also found the port convenient. That they did indicates that the porteños and residents of other towns in the Plata region found Colônia a valuable asset as well. After 1680 Buenos Aires was divided into two opposing factions over the existence of Colônia. On the one hand were a few royal officials who were for ejecting the Portuguese because of their smuggling activities and consequent damage to royal revenues and the interests of the merchants of Lima and Seville. Vigorously opposed were those who wished the post to remain in Portuguese hands because of the market which it provided. To these men dependence upon illicit commerce was far less distasteful than doing without necessities or relying upon the exorbitantly priced items which came by way of Lima.

In Chile the intermittent wars with the Araucanians continued to be an insurmountable obstacle to most governors. The lack of success in the attempts to subdue the fierce tribes and the absence of hopes for gain on the part of the troops hampered the Spanish cause. The use of prisoners and vagabonds as soldiers was also a drawback, for martial enthusiasm and patriotic fervor could hardly be expected of such troops. In 1692 the Araucanians were persuaded once more to admit priests into their lands, and hopes soared again for a pacific and permanent settlement of differences. The Indians readily listened to the exhortations of the missionaries, but their attitude toward Spaniards in general, forged in the long and cruel wars, remained firm. Troops which approached their villages were furiously attacked. By 1700 the project was abandoned, and the Araucanians remained completely outside the Spanish sphere of authority. Despite these difficulties Chile continued its slow growth, and the army stationed in the kingdom contributed to the formation of the mestizo population, if little else. By the end of the seventeenth century the mestizos composed the most numerous class.

Piratical raids on Chilean coastal towns occurred occasionally during the second half of the century. The most destructive attack was that of Bartholomew Sharpe on La Serena, in 1680. After failing to extract a ransom of 100,000 pesos from the inhabitants

Sharpe and his men sacked the town and set fire to the buildings.

In 1700 the population of Chile was upward of 100,000, the majority of whom were mestizos. Santiago had some 12,000 inhabitants, most of whom were encomenderos, priests, traders, artisans, and soldiers. The homes, like those of Buenos Aires, were far from pretentious and the streets were narrow, muddy lanes crossed by ditches which served as sewers. No system of streetlighting had been introduced, and at dusk a curfew was sounded for Indians and Negroes. A few hours later another signaled that it was time for all citizens to be in their homes. Water was supplied to the city by a narrow canal which emptied into a pool in the central plaza. Amusements were simple and like those of other provincial towns, gambling in some form being the most common diversion. Many of the local industries were conducted by Jesuits, who were permitted to engage in such worldly pursuits for the support of their establishments.

The viceroys of Peru in the seventeenth century were most frequently troubled in their domestic affairs by the anarchy prevailing in the remote but essential mining communities such as Potosí. The opening of new mines of Laicacota in 1657 enriched a few mineowners, and a large population of lawless individuals gathered around the mines to share the good fortune. Armed strife broke out. The disorder reached such serious proportions that the viceroy, Count of Lemos, went to the mines in 1668 to restore order. He succeeded by means thought especially severe even in that turbulent age. Forty men, including the owner of the richest mine, were executed, and many more were imprisoned. Others fled, and at the viceroy's order the town of Laicacota was razed. The mines were neglected. Lawsuits over the viceroy's acts lasted for years, and his decisions eventually were reversed.

The Count of Castellar, who became viceroy in 1674, found the royal treasury in Lima in a state of chaos. Many persons were indebted to it for public offices sold on credit. The treasury had an annual deficit of more than 200,000 pesos. By introducing a rigorous system of personally inspecting receipts and authorizing expenditures Castellar changed the financial situation drastically. His agents inspected the various outlying offices of the royal treasury and discovered many abuses. The treasurer of La Paz, who had defrauded the king of 400,000 pesos, was summarily hanged, while other delinquent officials were punished in keeping with their crimes. The mounting treasure in the royal coffers which resulted from these efforts was matched by a growing number of enemies, and Castellar's opponents finally succeeded in bringing about his downfall. The charge which caused the king to order him replaced was that he permitted a ship to carry quicksilver to New Spain and return with Chinese goods brought by the Manila galleons. According to the merchants and the consulado, this shipload of merchandise nearly ruined the trade of Portobelo and Peru, although the trade had been carried on illegally for a century. Immediate recall was the reward of a viceroy who, during his four-year administration, had sent to Spain more than four million pesos, provided seven million more as salaries and supplies to various parts of the viceroyalty, and who left more than two million in a treasury which he had found empty. He was replaced in the viceregal office by Archbishop Melchor Liñán y Cisneros, with whom he had quarreled over the patronato.

As viceroy Liñán concerned himself particularly with the discord prevailing among the religious orders, but he gained little success in bringing about lasting agreements. His successor, Melchor de Navarra y Rocaful, Duke of Palata, revived efforts to improve the situation of the Indians. In 1684 he issued an edict aimed at preventing the clergy from inheriting the property of Indians or from charging excessive fees for marriages, baptisms, burials, and other ceremonies. Palata's efforts, however, not only were in vain but they brought down on his head the wrath of the archbishop. In a series of bitter sermons Palata was denounced for provoking the anger of God and bringing upon Peru the calamities such as the earthquakes and the visitations of foreign pirates. After the terrible earthquake of 1687, the archbishop refused to co-operate in the rebuilding of the damaged churches.

Because of the sacking of Veracruz, New Spain, in 1683, Palata feared for the safety of Lima. The project of building a wall around the city had been discussed for many years, but nothing had been done. Palata called upon the consulado, the university, and the various religious orders to join in the work, and each agreed to construct or finance a part of the wall. Within three years a brick wall between eighteen and twenty-five feet in height, with seven gates and thirty-four bastions, had been nearly completed.

Another accomplishment of Palata was the establishment of a mint at Lima. In this he had to overcome the opposition of the officials of Potosí, who feared the competition. At the conclusion of his term of office Palata expressed strong opposition to the residencia, as various viceroys of New Spain had already done.

The Count of Monclova, Melchor Portocarrero, succeeded Palata in 1689 and ruled Peru until his death in 1705. As he came to Peru from New Spain, where he had also been viceroy, he spent the last nineteen years of his life as the king's chief representative in the two viceroyalties. In Peru he undertook the reconstruction of Lima and Callao after the earthquake of 1687. He continued work on the wall begun by his predecessor, and added several vessels to the naval squadron which patrolled the Pacific against raiders. The city of Trujillo was also walled. These measures did not prevent occasional losses to foreign pirates, but these were not serious threats to the Spanish empire in America. The gradual growth of Spanish and part-Spanish populations had given many regions the strength to defend themselves and to expel foreign interlopers. Even in the Banda Oriental, where the Portuguese succeeded in establishing and maintaining Colônia do Sacramento, Spanish officials did not lack the power to retake the land. The failure to expel the Portuguese from the Banda Oriental was determined not by the weakness of Río de la Plata but by the decline of Spain herself.

XIII

The Consolidation of Brazil

When one thinks of the obstacles of every kind which the back-
country people had to conquer at the head of their herds and
cattle, and the bandeirantes in their expeditions through the
back country hunting the Indian or seeking gold fields, one
cannot fail to recognize in this stupendous movement of territorial expansion the robust foundations upon which, in the
interior, there began to rise the structure of the nation.

FERNANDO DE AZEVEDO *

WITH the expulsion of the French from Rio de
Janeiro and the subsequent embroilment of
France in religious wars, Portugal's hold on Brazil seemed greatly
strengthened. French adventurers, it is true, still paid visits to the
northern coast and the Amazon area, but they represented no concerted effort to dispossess the Portuguese of their plantations. Even
with the French threat gone, however, Brazil, with its scattered population of some 25,000 persons of Portuguese ancestry and its 18,000
Indian and Negro slaves, invited competition. Not long after the
French menace had subsided a new and more determined rival appeared in the form of Holland.

Although the Spanish Netherlands and Portugal had traded
amicably as parts of the Spanish empire, the Dutch rebellion against
Spain had far-reaching consequences for Portugal. Since the latter
country was still under the Spanish crown, the Dutch regarded

* *Brazilian Culture*, translated by William R. Crawford, The Macmillan
Company, New York, 1950, pp. 51–2.

Portuguese possessions as fair game. For a time it seemed that Holland would deprive Portugal of all her overseas possessions. Before considering the Dutch invasion of Brazil a few words on the conditions prevailing in the colony are necessary.

By 1600 the Portuguese of Brazil no longer relied heavily on Indians to defend them, and Indian slavery was common. In line with previously established policy, Felipe II of Spain had decreed in 1595 that no Indians should be enslaved except those taken in 'just' wars. Brazilian slave-hunters regarded resistance to themselves a just war, and the law was ineffective. The tribes living in the interior, having escaped the smallpox epidemics that destroyed the coastal Indians, were aroused to savage reprisals by the slave-raiders. The Aimorés caused serious damage to Ilhéos and Pôrto Seguro before they were pacified and, like their predecessors, weakened by disease.

Early in the seventeenth century the Portuguese colonial administration was changed to make it conform more closely to that of Spain. In 1604 the *Conselho da India,* patterned after the Spanish Council of the Indies, was established in Lisbon. Previously colonial administration had been carried on largely through various regular Portuguese councils. The Conselho da India went through vicissitudes, but in 1642 and 1643 it was revitalized and renamed *Conselho Ultramarino* or Overseas Council by the new monarch, João IV, and it enjoyed a more vigorous life thereafter. In 1609 a high court was established in Bahia to lessen the need for appeals to Lisbon. A few years later the office of *Administrador das Minas do Sul* or Administrator of the Southern Mines was created, although mining was not yet an important industry.

During the seventeenth century Brazil's territorial limits were largely defined. At the outset the Portuguese population occupied only a narrow coastal strip, but a movement along the coast toward the Amazon valley was soon under way, and the paulistas began their irresistible drive into the interior of the south. These two movements culminated in Brazil's claim to the Amazon valley and a vast area bordering on the Plata colonies of Spain. At the same time cattlemen were advancing the frontier from all Brazilian settlements.

In the north, settlement of Ceará began in 1608, while interest in
Maranhão was spurred by efforts of French Huguenots to establish
a colony there in 1612. In 1615 this colony, Saint Louis, was taken by
the Portuguese, who retained its name in their language as São Luís.
Belém was founded a few years later, and from it Portuguese expansion proceeded into the Amazon valley.

In 1621, to bolster the defenses of Maranhão against Indian attacks, colonists were brought from the Azores. In the same year the
captaincy of Maranhão, including the area from Cabo São Roque to
the Amazon, was created an entity separate from Brazil. The reason
for a separate jurisdiction was that prevailing winds made it easier
to maintain communications by sea between Maranhão and Portugal than between Maranhão and Brazil. The region did not prosper,
and slave-hunting became the chief occupation. The arrival of
Jesuit priests threatened this livelihood, and protests were so violent
they were forced to agree not to interfere.

The year 1621 also marked the organization of the Dutch West
India Company, which threatened more solid encroachments than
those of previous years. The West India Company was inspired by
the success of its eastern counterpart against Portuguese holdings in
the Orient. The states-general of Holland generously granted the
western company a monopoly of trade with Africa and America and
between them, and offered support in case of war. Since this trade
was to be with jealously guarded possessions of other powers, warfare was expected, and the company organized military and naval
forces. Its officials hoped to gain complete control of African slave
traffic, at the time a monopoly of Portugal because of her hold on
Angola. The Spanish government was aware of Dutch ambitions,
but Olivares and Felipe IV could see merit in operations which
would weaken restive Portugal. Portuguese Jews who had taken refuge in Amsterdam advised the company to seize Brazil, and they furnished information as well as capital needed for the undertaking.

In 1624 a Dutch fleet captured São Salvador and a short time later
Piet Heyn, one of the company's most famous admirals, took Angola.
The threat was more serious than complacent Spanish officials had
realized, and a combined Spanish-Portuguese fleet was sent to re-

cover São Salvador. In 1625 the Dutch were forced to surrender the prize not long before one of their own squadrons arrived with reinforcements. The following year Piet Heyn entered Bahia and sailed away with a fleet of merchant ships already loaded with sugar. After 1628, when the same admiral captured the treasure fleet from New Spain, the company had ample means for expanding its activities in Brazil.

The success of West India Company squadrons against Spanish and Portuguese shipping soon diminished this source of profit, and the company began seizing colonial settlements. In 1630 Olinda and Recife (Pernambuco) were taken, and in the following year a Spanish fleet was defeated off the coast of Brazil.

But for the fact that the Dutch were Protestants and that their methods were far from tactful, their rule might have been preferred by Brazilians to that of Spain. Religious differences in that epoch loomed large, and the Dutch further stimulated opposition by seizure of property. The feeling against the Dutch grew intense as plantations were sequestered. Opposition to them mounted also as a consequence of the Portuguese revolt against Spain in 1640, for Brazilian sympathies were with Portugal.

The colonizing efforts of the Dutch were jeopardized by the company's primary interest in immediate profits. The seizure of fazendas forced influential Brazilians into the opposition, and with the aid of Jesuit priests, who regarded the intruders as heretics, the dispossessed fazendeiros organized bands of Indians and free Negroes to carry on guerrilla warfare. Especially renowned for his destructive raids on Dutch forces was a free Negro named Henrique Dias, one of the principal heroes of the resistance.

The losses suffered by the company in these campaigns convinced its officials that they must make themselves masters of the country in order to profit from their Brazilian enterprise. In 1636 the company sent able and enlightened Count Jan Mauritz of Nassau to Brazil as general in charge. His rule was the most memorable aspect of the Dutch occupation, and he won the respect of many Brazilians. He encouraged the fazendeiros to return to their lands, and promised full religious freedom. Nassau hoped to found a lasting colony under

Dutch rule. In this aim he differed from the company directors, who were loath to invest money in long-range projects. His frequent requests for colonists and for the removal of trade restrictions were coolly received in Holland.

Nassau carried out several of the desired campaigns to extend Dutch power in Brazil, and the captaincies northwest of Recife were brought under control. By 1639 Dutch rule was established from Sergipe to Ceará, and two years later it included Maranhão.

Pernambuco was the most valuable Brazilian region conquered by the Dutch, but its sugar production fell off sharply from the closing of many engenhos. Nassau was especially interested in building up the cities. He sent to Holland for artists and scholars; the works of art and scientific studies of these men are of great interest today for a study of seventeenth-century Brazil.

The condition of Portugal during these years of Dutch encroachment was so precarious that little attention could be paid to the conflict in Brazil. Foremost among Portuguese aspirations was independence from Spain. A feeble effort was made to aid Brazil in 1639, but the fleet which was sent accomplished little. In the following year Portugal severed her Spanish ties, and was no longer able to assist her colony. Her first problem was to prepare for expected reprisals, and this required aid from Spain's enemies, the chief of which was Holland. Brazil became a political liability, for while Portugal was seeking Dutch support in Europe Brazilians were battling Dutch troops in America. Holland's officials displayed no intention of withdrawing peacefully from Brazil; on the contrary, they took advantage of Portugal's weakness to compel her to halt Brazilian attempts at reconquest.

In 1641 a ten-year truce was signed by Portugal and Holland which both believed would give time to improve their positions with regard to Brazil. While the truce was being negotiated company officials ordered Nassau to extend his conquests quickly, especially in the direction of Bahia. Dutch troops failed to take the captaincy, and Brazilians saw the act as a breach of faith. Nassau's hopes of founding a Dutch empire in Brazil were doomed to failure. While he was preparing an expedition against Buenos Aires, revolts in São

Tomas and Maranhão diverted his forces; and he had to cope with the destructive raids of Negroes from Palmares. With the beginning of the Dutch wars many slaves escaped to the interior, where they established colonies known as *quilombos*, of which Palmares was the largest.

In later years wars with Palmares became a severe problem for the captaincy of Pernambuco, for the coastal population was weakened by smallpox epidemics. Palmares, with a population of perhaps 20,000, took the offensive and looted towns and fazendas. A trade in merchandise thus acquired was carried on with Portuguese at other parts of the coast who supplied the former slaves with the munitions necessary for their forays. The military strength of Palmares prevented the governor of Pernambuco from attacking it, and the situation grew so critical that he reluctantly requested aid of the paulistas. In 1695 a paulista force assaulted Palmares and destroyed it; the survivors were returned once more to a life of slavery.

Insurrections against the Dutch broke out in many areas in the 1640's, and the Dutch tried desperately to restore order by repressive acts. In the guerrilla fighting no quarter was given on either side. Soon the Brazilians had recovered Ceará and Maranhão. Nassau, seeing his efforts to establish a lasting colony useless, resigned in 1644.

The hold of the Dutch on Brazil weakened rapidly after the departure of Nassau. The independence of Portugal stirred Brazilians to acts of emulation, and the daring sorties of Henrique Dias and other partisan leaders raised hope for a final victory over the invaders. Attacks on Dutch posts were co-ordinated by a fazendeiro, João Fernandes Vieira, who engineered the widespread revolts of 1645.

Within a short time Olinda had been retaken and the Dutch were forced to abandon all posts south of Recife. The West India Company, faced with financial difficulties, failed to provide adequate reinforcements and left its troops to carry on with little hope of victory. While the Brazilians were slowly winning back their land in the desperate fighting, Dutch diplomats pressed Portugal to cede the contested provinces.

Portugal's independence was still insecure, and the need for powerful allies outweighed all other considerations at the moment. Holland, a bitter enemy of Spain in recent years, was a logical ally; the fact that the Dutch were completing the rape of the Portuguese empire was merely an unfortunate complication. As a price for assistance Holland demanded an additional part of Portugal's overseas domain. In 1646 Dom João reluctantly ordered Brazilians to surrender Pernambuco to the Dutch, in the belief that it was better to lose half of Brazil than to risk loss of all. The company's resources could not support a long war, however, and time began to run in favor of the Brazilians. João Fernandes Vieira refused to obey the king's command and the fighting against the Dutch continued.

In Lisbon the most astute counselor of Dom João was the Jesuit priest Antônio Vieira, who had spent most of his life in Brazil until 1640. Before leaving for Lisbon Vieira had been one of the foremost agitators for resistance to the Dutch. He advised the king to delay while the wars in Brazil were going favorably. When it was necessary to placate Holland by apparent willingness to cede parts of Brazil and Africa, Vieira knew how far it was wise to be conciliatory. At the same time he urged secret aid for the rebels of Pernambuco, for it was through them that Brazil might be preserved. Dutch expeditions were sent to Brazil in 1646 and 1648, but they were wasted in futile campaigns. In the latter year Portugal recovered Angola in Africa.

Aware that Portugal still urgently needed her support Holland now pressed for cession of all Brazilian territory held at the time of the truce of 1641, her African conquests, and a large indemnification. Fear of reconquest by Spain caused Vieira to advise the king to agree to Dutch demands though it meant an inglorious abandonment of Brazilians. He expected that conditions would change in favor of Portugal, and that the loss of Pernambuco would be temporary. The Portuguese were fortunate both in that Holland was in no hurry to settle the issue and that the expected blow from Spain did not fall.

Vieira's recommendation that two commercial companies similar

to those of the Dutch be organized in Portugal was partially fulfilled with the creation of the Brazil Company. He insisted that
Jews and 'New Christians' be protected against the Inquisition and
confiscation of their property, for he was certain that the success of
the companies depended upon the willingness of these groups to
participate and to furnish part of the needed capital. In 1649 the
Brazil Company's first fleet was sent out, and it returned safely despite Dutch efforts to intercept it. Anglo-Dutch maritime rivalry
now began to occupy Dutch attention, and the war in Brazil approached its conclusion.

In 1653 the company's fleet was employed in preventing Dutch
aid from reaching Recife, while Brazilians invested the city by
land. In January, 1654, this last Dutch post fell to Brazilian forces.
The Dutch retaliated by seizing Ceylon, most valuable of Portugal's
remaining oriental possessions. Dom João now advised his family to
move to Recife should the threatened war with Spain go badly for
Portugal.

After the death of João IV in 1656, the Dutch renewed their demands on the queen-regent. Spain assumed a more threatening
attitude, and the outlook was dark except for the growing rivalry
between England and Holland. Although the Dutch accepted Louis
XIV as mediator of the dispute, they dispatched a fleet to Portugal
with a peremptory demand for immediate cession of all lands between the Rio São Francisco and Ceará, as well as a heavy indemnity. Portuguese officials delayed, arguing that they could not legally
alienate national territory during the minority of the king. In 1657
the Dutch declared war, and the Brazilian merchant fleet narrowly
escaped capture. Another squadron was sent against Portuguese
shipping the following year, but Holland was now involved in disputes with Denmark and Sweden.

Portuguese fortunes improved when Charles II of England hinted
that his country might become a party to the conflict if it was not
settled, and when Louis XIV interfered more energetically. In 1662
the Dutch agreed to accept an indemnity of four million cruzados in
exchange for territorial claims. This was the last time Portugal was

in danger of losing Brazil to European enemies. The retention of the colony had been accomplished as much by the Brazilians as by the mother country.

While the wars with the Dutch went on in the north the southern captaincies pursued their various interests, that of São Paulo being the search for mines and slaves. The paulista bandeirantes probed deeper and deeper into the interior until they came upon the Jesuit reductions among the Guaranís, where they found thousands of docile Indians already trained in useful occupations. The paulista raids have already been mentioned in connection with the Plata region. From the Brazilian point of view they provided additional laborers and a claim to lands in the south and west.

Elsewhere in Brazil the gradual expansion into the interior followed the advancing cattlemen, who pushed back or destroyed the fluid barrier of hostile tribes. Behind the cattlemen came the farmer and merchant. The cattle industry was especially suitable for occupying vast areas with few people, and its role in the westward movement of Brazil was of great importance. The names of many towns in the interior indicate their origins; among them are such names as Vacaria, Curral, Campo Grande, Pouso Seco, and Pouso Alto.

After the expulsion of the Dutch the treatment of Indians in Maranhão became an acute problem. João IV ordered that all Indian slaves be freed, but the governor sent to enforce the decree was greeted by an angry mob, and prudently ignored his duty. Similar incidents occurred in other towns of the region, for the temper of the inhabitants precluded freeing Indian slaves without a powerful military force.

The Jesuits, as the chief protectors of Indians in Brazil, faced constant hostility and even expulsion. Father Antônio Vieira returned to Brazil in 1652 to dedicate his life to improving the condition of Indians in Maranhão. Since he enjoyed the complete confidence of the king, Vieira was able to write him frank letters concerning the plight of both Indians and colonists. Religion was completely neglected, he wrote, for there were only two priests in the entire captaincy, and they were more interested in the slave trade than in their spiritual duties. One difficulty was that the region was under the bishop of Bahia, and the only means of communication with him was by way of Portugal.

The treatment of Indians was especially deplorable, none being more abused than those who lived in villages near towns or fazendas. Neither the governor nor the capitão mór was interested in their welfare, for they were not private property. Many of these Indians preferred to give themselves into outright slavery, for there was then more reason for their masters to protect them. The remedy Vieira proposed was that no governor nor capitão mór should be permitted to engage in cultivation for the purpose of trade nor to allot free Indians for work other than in the king's service. Vieira's first sermon in São Luís made a profound impression, and in a moment of piety some persons freed their Indian slaves. This attitude proved temporary, and conditions remained unchanged despite repeated commands from the king.

In 1654 Vieira recommended appointing a *Procurador Geral* or Advocate General for the Indians in each captaincy, and that Indians be placed exclusively under control of the priests. A *Junta das Missões* or Missionary Board was formed to achieve co-operation among members of the various religious orders in support of the missions. A royal decree ordered that all Indian villages of Maranhão be placed under direction of the Jesuits. Vieira, as Superior of the Missions, was authorized to control all expeditions to the interior and to locate villages of 'reduced' Indians.

While Vieira was in Maranhão the king asked his advice on the desirability of two capitães mores or one governor; to which the sagacious priest replied that two thieves were a greater problem than one, and that one honest man was easier to find than two! He added that the governor should be from Brazil rather than Portugal, as the reinois would simply exploit the country and then leave it. This advice was not followed, probably because there were too many faithful followers in Lisbon claiming such an opportunity in reward for past services.

In carrying out his system for protecting the Indians Vieira met strenuous opposition not only from fazendeiros but from priests as well. When Indian captives were brought before a board composed

of priests and laymen to determine if they had actually been 'ran-
somed from the cord' — rescued from cannibals — or illegally seized,
other priests consistently voted against Vieira. Despite these difficulties Jesuits visited the wild tribes and employed their famed powers
of persuasion in reducing the Indians to village life. By 1655 there
were already more than fifty Jesuit reductions in the captaincy, and
the Indian problem seemed nearer solution than at any time since
the region was settled. The main livelihood of the inhabitants was
still traffic in Indian slaves, and owners bitterly resented the interference of the Jesuits.

In 1661 the Portuguese residents of Maranhão complained to the
king of their poverty, which they attributed to his restrictions on
Indian slavery. They argued that free Indians living in villages under
the Jesuits were useless, for they detested labor and did not volunteer
their services. Vieira reminded the aggrieved that it was far better
to have the Indians living peacefully if indolently than to suffer
their raids. The dissatisfaction of the populace was too intense to be
assuaged by argument and the Jesuits were driven from Maranhão.
A new governor came from Portugal to punish the offenders and
restore the priests.

Maranhão continued to be disturbed over the Jesuit efforts to protect the Indians. In 1684 the missionaries were expelled once more.
The region remained poor; one of the obstacles to its prosperity
was the practice of retaining privileges pertaining to commissions in
the militia, even though the period of service was only three months.
Because of the prestige assumed by the many former officers, they
were disinclined to engage in productive enterprises.

In 1662 Brazil, having maintained her freedom from the Dutch,
now paid a large share of Portugal's annual indemnity to Holland.
This sum, together with Brazil's contributions for the dowry of the
Infanta Dona Catarina for her marriage to Charles II of England,
amounted to 140,000 cruzados a year. Bahia offered to raise 80,000
cruzados, the remainder to be divided among the other captaincies.

At mid-century Rio de Janeiro was still an unimportant city,
although in 1658 it became the seat of a separate government for the
southern captaincies. A few years later a smallpox epidemic spread

along the coast from Pernambuco to Rio de Janeiro with great mortality, especially among the Africans. Many fazendas lost all of their slaves, and it was years before the region recovered.

In 1668 Spain acknowledged Portuguese independence and ended the fear of reconquest which had made the crown rest so uneasily on the heads of the Braganças. The danger of invasion over, the Portuguese were able to continue their expansion into the back country of Brazil and into territories claimed by Spain.

Since the restoration of 1640 Brazilians had been eager to re-establish their former commerce with Buenos Aires. In 1643 Salvador Corrêa de Sá recommended construction of a fort near the mouth of the Río de la Plata in order to protect such commerce as might be carried on illicitly. Vieira urged a more drastic step — the conquest of the Spanish settlements in the Plata region. These proposals anticipated Portuguese intrusion into the Banda Oriental, modern Uruguay, in 1680. In the 1670's the prince-regent accepted as his doctrine that all land south to the left bank of the Río de la Plata belonged to Portugal. A justification of this claim was lacking, but in 1676 papal action seemed to support Portuguese pretensions. Rio de Janeiro was raised to a bishopric, and the southern boundary of the episcopal see was extended to the Río de la Plata.

Late in 1679 an expedition sailed from Santos for the island of San Gabriel near the mouth of the Río de la Plata, where Portuguese officials decided to erect a fort. Leaders of the force changed the proposed site to the mainland, and began work on Colônia do Sacramento. In August, 1680, Colônia was assaulted and taken by a force of Guaranís and Spaniards before reinforcements arrived from Brazil. Despite the dubious claims of Portugal to the region, great indignation was manifested in Lisbon, and rumors of war with Spain were common. With England as mediator war was avoided and Colônia was returned to Portugal.

For nearly a century Colônia remained an object of contention between the Iberian nations. That Portugal retained the outpost so long was a defeat for Spanish diplomacy and a reflection of the growing maritime power of England. Spain was ruled by Carlos II, last and weakest of the Spanish Hapsburgs, and the feeling of despondency permeating his regime made humiliating concessions acceptable. After the death of Carlos II, when Felipe V ascended the contested Spanish throne, Spain preferred to preserve Portuguese neutrality rather than push her claims to Colônia.

While the Portuguese were contemplating entering the Banda Oriental the paulistas renewed their invasions of the Guaraní country. In 1651 four columns were repulsed by the missions on the Uruguay river. It was at this time that the Jesuits were permitted to arm and train the Guaranís for the defense of the missions. The paulistas continued their search for precious metals, and toward the close of the century the gold strikes in Minas Gerais gave the Spaniards and mission Indians a welcome respite.

In the northeast the plantation economy suffered after the expulsion of the Dutch, not only from the damages occurring during the fighting, but also because of new competition in the sugar industry. The Dutch took with them Negroes familiar with the planting of cane and management of engenhos, and introduced sugar production into French and English islands in the Caribbean. Brazil's former advantage was lost, for the market was ruined by overproduction. Recife and Olinda suffered particularly.

Even as capital of the southern captaincies Rio de Janeiro was a far from imposing city, for most of the houses were located on low lands bordering swamps. Until the close of the century, when the discovery of rich gold deposits in interior Minas Gerais vastly improved the coastal city's economic position, its development did not rival that of Bahia. It was Rio de Janeiro's fortunate position at the terminus of mule trails to the mining region which made the city important in the Brazilian economy.

Throughout the seventeenth century Brazil's population was primarily rural. The better cities, Bahia, Olinda, Recife, Rio de Janeiro, and São Paulo, were poor in contrast to the estates of the wealthy fazendeiros. The solidity of social structure in the tightly knit fazenda society gave it greater influence than that of urban communities. Count Mauritz of Nassau's development of Recife and Olinda gave Brazilians a taste for cities independent of the great fazendas, but urban growth was slow until Minas Gerais was settled.

That the outlook of Brazilians corresponded to that of Portuguese was the firm opinion of Father Vieira. He caustically described Brazil as the very image of Portugal. In Brazil, he wrote, there were preparations for war without men or money; full harvests of vice without reformation; unbounded luxury without capital; and all other contradictions of the human mind.

In some of the cities slaves outnumbered free whites as much as twenty to one. The engenhos of Bahia and Rio de Janeiro were operated on a large scale and employed as many as a hundred slaves, while in Pernambuco smaller works were conducted where forty slaves were sufficient. The constant influx of Africans at a time when Indians of the coastal area were disappearing resulted in lasting social, economic, and ethnic influences.

Fazendeiros were not the only employers of slaves. Many persons with no agricultural lands bought slaves to hire out or to make their own arrangements in exchange for a sum to be paid weekly. If these slaves failed to earn the prescribed amount or, as often happened, they gambled it away, they had recourse to robbery. The vast number of such individuals made it hazardous to travel the streets after dark. Early in the century Brazilian towns were teeming with naked Indians and Negroes; in later years most of them were forced to wear at least some simple garment for the sake of modesty.

Toward the end of the century the dress of the Portuguese was patterned after that of the French. Black was the prevailing color worn by men; their dress was not complete without a Saint Anthony medallion suspended around their necks and a sword and dagger in their belts. Women were seldom seen away from home except going to and from church and attending the more important festivals. Since it was considered debasing to travel on foot, a number of man-powered conveyances such as sedan chairs were used, the women being shielded from sight by curtains. The custom of secluding women was so prevalent that married women were not permitted to sit at the table with their husbands when guests were present.

Criminal law in practice applied only to slaves; for the Portuguese offended pride was avenged by the dagger. Since the time of João II it was customary for kings to excuse homicides of this type; in

Brazil the saying was, 'Kill, for the king pardons.' The courts were notably venal; one Brazilian declared that the wands of justice would bend double if four chests of sugar were placed on them.

The governors, who were charged with seeing that the Portuguese in Brazil led exemplary lives in order to aid in civilizing the natives, found that the ships arriving from the mother country brought as colonists criminals in irons. Only petty offenders were permitted to remain in Portugal. Making model citizens of convicted felons was beyond the power of most governors, and too frequently the example of high officials was not conducive to better behavior in others. Every governor brought with him from Lisbon a number of friends who made the voyage for the sole purpose of enriching themselves quickly and returning home. Even among the priesthood there was laxity with regard to certain vows. A current saying of Brazilians was: 'As fortunate as the son of a priest.'

Except at the highest level of society there was little distinction of caste, and as in Spanish America most of the old families were mixed with Indian stock. Free Negroes and mulattoes were not degraded by law, nor was public opinion generally hostile toward them. The amalgamation of races which proceeded from the time of Caramarú helped secure Brazil from riots based on racial antagonisms. During the genesis of a new race formed of Portuguese, Indians, and Negroes, a Brazilian spirit was produced by this varied ancestry. Its flowering was delayed by the scarcity of educational institutions and the absence of effective Brazilian literature. Most Brazilians could not have read literary works had these been produced in their land.

The most notable event after the expulsion of the Dutch was the discovery of a rich mining region in the interior. The search for minerals had been continuous since the settlement of Brazil, and mines were worked in São Paulo at the beginning of the century. This mining was sufficiently important in 1618 to inspire royal regulations, a code similar to that of the Spanish colonies reserving a fifth part of minerals as the king's share. To possess unstamped gold was punishable by death.

In 1692 a rich strike was made by paulistas near the headwaters of the Rio São Francisco in modern Minas Gerais and a 'rush' to the region began. Adventurers crowded into the area from all parts of Brazil. Fazendeiros who were ruined by the fall of the price of sugar abandoned their engenhos and took their slaves to the gold fields. Dozens of mining camps sprang up, and although most of them were deserted when the placer mines were exhausted, a few survived to become important cities.

The paulistas, as discoverers of the mines, regarded all others as intruders, and desperate battles were fought for possession of the mining region. The paulistas were greatly outnumbered, and despite their renowned martial prowess, the outsiders triumphed. While gold-seekers continued to come, the paulistas resumed the search for mines farther west. Within a few years the population of Minas Gerais had swelled to 40,000.

As a result of the exodus from the coastal plantations to the interior the ailing sugar industry was badly disrupted. The sudden increase in the amount of gold in circulation brought a rapid rise in prices, especially in São Paulo and Rio de Janeiro. Early in the 'Age of Minerals' gold was extracted only by placer mining in the beds of streams, and the population was mobile and scattered. Not until 1720 did vein mining begin, bringing with it stability of population. The turbulence and tax evasion which were to characterize the mineiros throughout the eighteenth century were already evident by 1700.

Coins in circulation in Brazil required the constant attention of officials, for the ancient practice of clipping reduced their value and hampered their use in commerce. In 1694 the king ordered the minting of money for circulation in Brazil only. The mint was first set up in Bahia; when this region was supplied with coins the mint was moved to Rio de Janeiro, and later to Recife.

Contraband trade with Upper Peru became a profitable occupation in the seventeenth century, and many peruleiros made fortunes in the clandestine traffic in silver. One of the men who outfitted the expeditions, Father Guilherme Pompeu, grew so wealthy he was able to maintain a luxurious home and to provide for guests 'a hundred beds, each with its curtains and fine Breton sheets, and a silver basin under each of them.'

In 1697 an attempt to improve the administration of justice caused the introduction of magistrates of higher rank and responsibility than previous ones. Laws protecting the Indians began to be effective as the Indians decreased and Negro slaves became plentiful. In all the old captaincies except São Paulo an Indian was declared free on demand. The evils of Indian slavery were simply transferred to the Negroes, who bore hard physical labor with less mortality.

During the seventeenth century the geographic and economic definition of colonial Brazil was completed. The social and economic forces that previously adhered to the coast were now dispersed far into the interior. Expansion into the hinterland occurred from Maranhão in the north to São Paulo in the south, and at the same time the Portuguese established a precarious foothold near the Río de la Plata. Most of these regions were beyond the old Line of Demarcation, but later, when Spain and Portugal agreed to settle their boundary problems on the principle of each keeping what it already occupied, the expansionist tendencies of Brazilians made their country enormous.

One of the most impressive accomplishments of Brazilians in the seventeenth century was the expulsion of French and Dutch invaders. It was the Brazilians who by force of arms determined that Brazil should not be separated from the Portuguese empire. They were conscious of their achievement, and although local agitation appeared occasionally, the majority of Brazilians did not contemplate the rejection of Portuguese authority. For Portugal, the loss of prized possessions in the Orient left Brazil as her most valuable colony, and her interest in Brazil grew in keeping with this situation.

SUGGESTED READING

A. G. Barcia Carballido, *Barcia's Chronological History of the Continent of Florida*, Gainesville, Florida, 1951.
H. E. Bolton, *Rim of Christendom*, New York, 1936.

———— *Spanish Exploration in the Southwest, 1542–1706*, New York, 1916.

W. W. Borah, *Early Colonial Trade and Navigation between Mexico and Peru*, Berkeley, 1954.

———— *New Spain's Century of Depression*, Berkeley, 1951.

C. R. Boxer, *Salvador de Sá and the Struggle for Brazil and Angola, 1602–1686*, London, 1953.

W. E. Dunn, *Spanish and French Rivalry in the Gulf Region of the United States, 1678–1702*, Austin, 1917.

T. Gage, *A New Survey of the West Indies*, 1648, Various editions.

R. B. C. Graham, *A Vanished Arcadia: Some Account of the Jesuits in Paraguay, 1607–1767*, rev. ed., London, 1904.

C. H. Haring, *The Buccaneers of the West Indies in the XVII Century*, New York, 1910.

———— *Trade and Navigation between Spain and the Indies in the Time of the Hapsburgs*, Cambridge, Mass., 1918.

M. Kiemen, *The Indian Policy of Portugal in the Amazon Region, 1614–1693*, Washington, 1954.

J. T. Lanning, *The Spanish Missions of Georgia*, Chapel Hill, 1935.

I. A. Leonard, *Don Carlos Sigüenza y Góngora, a Mexican Savant of the Seventeenth Century*, Berkeley, 1929.

J. P. Moore, *The Cabildo in Peru under the Hapsburgs*, Durham, 1955.

B. Moses, *The Spanish Dependencies in South America*, 2 vols., London, 1914.

M. Morner, *The Political and Economic Activities of the Jesuits in the Plata Region*, Stockholm, 1953.

A. P. Newton, *The European Nations in the West Indies, 1493–1688*, London, 1933.

J. H. Parry, *The Spanish Theory of Empire in the Seventeenth Century*, Cambridge, 1940.

P. W. Powell, *Soldiers, Indians, and Silver*, Berkeley, 1952.

W. Roscher, *The Spanish Colonial System*, New York, 1904.

F. V. Scholes, *Church and State in New Mexico, 1610–1670*, 2 vols., Albuquerque, 1937, 1942.

E. R. Service, *Spanish-Guaraní Relations in Early Colonial Paraguay*, Ann Arbor, 1954.

A. Vázquez de Espinosa, *Compendium and Description of the West Indies*, Washington, 1942.

R. C. West, *The Mining Community in Northern New Spain*, Berkeley, 1949.

III

MATURITY OF EMPIRE

XIV

The Enlightenment, International Rivalry, and Latin America

All for the people, but not with the people.

IN 1701 the Bourbon heir to the Spanish throne, Felipe V, entered upon his new duties. His accession produced a renewal of dynastic leadership, but it also inaugurated an initial period of turmoil and warfare destructive of manpower, commerce, and resources. The long-run consequences were nonetheless salutary. A new spirit was injected into Spanish life, due in no small part to the influence of French and Italian advisers with whom the Bourbon kings surrounded themselves at Madrid. The alien viewpoints and ideas struck responsive chords among the Spaniards themselves, who stirred from the lethargy that had gradually overcome them in the preceding century. Out of the resulting synthesis, Spain emerged once again as a world power, recovering much of the ground lost in the intellectual and economic stagnation under the Hapsburgs of the late seventeenth century.

Commerce between the mother country and the colonies improved, agricultural production revived, notable creations were produced in literature and the arts, and in the political arena Spain regained some of her lost prestige. As it was for Western Europe generally, the eighteenth century was for Spain the age of the enlightenment.

Within Spanish America the new developments were more in the nature of a culmination than a revival. Social and political forces at work for two centuries began to bear fruit. The frontier culture of the conquest and settlement now gave way to the culture of the sedentary life of great cities. The gradual admixture of races and reproduction of Spanish family lines in the colonies were creating new social groups the size and outlook of which made them potential masters of the social balance of power. The enlightenment served at once as stimulus for Spain to tighten the bonds of empire and regularize its organization and for the new American social classes to assert their inherent equality and demand a more fitting place within the scheme of Spanish social and political organization. In the end, the forces loosed by these movements came into conflict, and the eighteenth century closed in antagonisms that could only end in independence for the American peoples. Before the forces became irreconcilable, however, the Iberian world experienced a regenerative surge that added many pages to the chronicle of its achievements.

The Spanish branch of the Hapsburg family vacated the throne in the fall of 1700 when its last representative, Carlos II, died without heir. In his will Carlos bequeathed the crown to his grand-nephew Philip, Duke of Anjou, grandson of Louis XIV of France, and a representative of the French Bourbon family. The naming of this man as successor marked a victory for French diplomacy, but a victory that it proved necessary to verify on the battlefield. England and Holland were unwilling to accept what appeared as a drastic threat to the existing balance of power in Europe, and they joined with Austria in the support of the Hapsburg claimant to the Spanish throne, Archduke Charles of Austria. The war, which commenced in 1702 and is known as the War of the Spanish Succession, lasted for over a decade. Peace was re-established by various treaty agreements among the participating parties in 1713–15, but only after the Austrian claimant, Archduke Charles, succeeded to the imperial throne of the Holy Roman Empire and Austria, leaving Felipe V in undisputed possession of the Spanish crown.

The war proved to be a costly affair for Spain, for by the peace of Rastatt (1714) Felipe was forced to cede to the Holy Roman Empire all the remaining Spanish possessions in Flanders, Luxembourg, and Italy. From the standpoint of the empire in the Americas, Spain's loss of European territory, in some cases permanently, proved advantageous, for in the vicissitudes of European politics Spain had been overextended. Much Spanish manpower and treasure had been squandered in behalf of Hapsburg dynastic interests in areas in which the Spaniards themselves were in no sense vitally concerned. Thus the loss of non-contiguous European territory enabled the new Spanish rulers to concentrate their attention increasingly on internal and empire affairs while at the same time the likelihood of involvement in Central European wars was diminished. On the other hand, other losses, more vital to the empire, were incurred. Gibraltar passed under English control, as did the island of Minorca off the Spanish Mediterranean coast, and the English were granted the exclusive right to import slaves into the American colonies. The *asiento*, as the slave-importation franchise was called, was to prove an important wedge in the opening of the empire to British trade. At the same time, the possession by Britain of Gibraltar, together with the family ties existing between the Spanish and French ruling houses, created between Britain and Spain points of continual friction. These factors made almost impossible any rapprochement that could serve to lessen the tension between the two powers as colonial rivals in the Western Hemisphere.

As stated previously, the accession of the Bourbon family to the throne proved to be a favorable development for Spain, but it was not until the second half of the century that any real improvements became apparent. It took some time for the new ruling family to become oriented to the Spanish environment. Felipe V surrounded himself first with French and then with Italian advisers whose interests were inseparable from those of the countries from which they came. Isabel Farnese, Duchess of Parma, whom Felipe married some time after the untimely death of his first queen, María Luisa, was in no small measure responsible for the continued attempts of Felipe to regain and hold control over the Italian peninsula. While such a policy was followed, involvement in European wars was inevitable. However, by the time of Felipe's death in 1746, a change had set in. Capable Spaniards had gradually replaced the foreign advisers, and internal and empire reform received more and more attention. Felipe's two sons, Fernando VI and Carlos III, who ruled in that order, were both men who centered their interest in Spain itself and who were determined to avoid if at all possible further entanglements and wars in Europe. Both contributed measurably to the restoration of Spain's former strength and importance. Carlos III, who came to the throne in 1759, earned for himself an enviable record of good government and enlightened leadership. He was Spain's enlightened absolutist and under his rule the country reached its zenith of strength and development in the eighteenth century.

Portugal underwent a parallel development, but the period of ascendancy was much shorter. João V, who ruled from 1706 to 1750, brought his country to the verge of complete degeneration by the neglect of his responsibilities and the corruption of his administration. The discovery of gold and diamonds in Brazil had placed considerable wealth at the disposal of the monarchy, but the returns from this bonanza were squandered uselessly. Thus when José I succeeded to the throne in 1750 his task was enormous. He called as his prime minister Sebastião José de Carvalho e Melo, later the Marquis of Pombal, one of the most energetic administrators Portugal has ever produced. Under Pombal's leadership strong action was taken to ferret out corruption and to place government finances in order. A number of social reforms were introduced particularly in Brazil, where the legal distinctions between the Indians and the Europeans were eliminated. The reforms of Pombal were in most respects salutary, but they were short-lived and ineffective. His international intrigues and particularly his aggressive policy in the Plata region involved his country in difficulties with Spain. His reforms created many enemies at court. When, in 1777, José I died, Pombal was dismissed. In Portugal the spark of the enlightenment had burst forth suddenly and died out quickly. Pombal's dismissal signaled the return to corruption and neglect.

The enlightenment, as the intellectual awakening of eighteenth-century Europe has been called, produced great changes on the Iberian peninsula, particularly in Spain. In many respects, however, these changes were shallow. Seldom do intellectual movements produce great lasting effect unless they permeate down through the social and economic structure or unless they surge upward from the lower classes. Herein lies a point of contrast between the mother countries and the colonies. In Spain, and to a lesser degree in Portugal, the enlightened rulers took important steps to promote the well-being of their subjects at home. Economic societies were organized to teach the skilled trades and improve the level of artisanship. The Spanish government built textile and glass factories to stimulate light industries. It embarked upon a program of agricultural resettlement to improve the lot of the farm laborers and to increase the quantity of agricultural production. It even moved weakly to put an end to the system of entailed estates that had produced enormous concentrations of land ownership in the hands of a small number of wealthy families. Viewed against the background of the entire Spanish economic and social structure, however, these measures cannot be regarded as impressive, for their effect was limited. The bulk of the population remained impoverished, unskilled, and illiterate. The conditions that prompted the industrial revolution in England were largely absent in Spain, and in spite of the progressive measures of the Bourbon monarchs the country remained predominantly manorial. Had the programs of Fernando VI and Carlos III been continued over a long period of years, a greater change might have been wrought, but this was not to be. In Portugal, change was even more ephemeral.

In the American colonies of both countries, in contrast, the changes of the eighteenth century were much more profound. The reforms coming down from above were met by an upsurge from below. Generations of racial and social intermingling in a frontier society had produced racial, social, and economic pressures that could not long be contained within the restrictive systems of Spanish and Portuguese imperial control. This became increasingly evident as the end of the century approached and incipient revolts broke out in Peru, Brazil, and New Granada. The American continents, rich in resources, had reached a state of development that permitted them to embark upon independent courses. More and more the Spanish and Portuguese restrictions upon the movement of goods, upon the introduction of foreign literature, and upon the free movement of persons were observed by their breach. Contraband flourished. Spain and Portugal, never able to supply the economic wants of their dependencies, were increasingly unable to meet the demand for cultural and intellectual leadership. Consequently, the fertile land of the colonies was much better prepared to nurture the seeds of social and economic reform than was the arid soil of the Iberian peninsula.

To the increasing manifestations of colonial strength and independence the shrewd ministers of Carlos III and José I responded, cautiously at first, by application of the new ideas that were the product of the enlightenment. Many of the restrictions on commerce were abandoned, the fleet system was terminated, and trading companies were organized in various parts of Spain for the development of commerce with designated areas of the empire. For the first time the colonies were permitted to trade quite freely among themselves. A number of the more troublesome taxes were modified or abolished and replaced by a simpler *ad valorem* duty collected in Spain. Definite steps were taken to end the forced labor of the Indians, and the system of corregidores was legally terminated. In Brazil, the Jesuit aldeias were secularized and the Indians freed from the control of the religious orders.

All of these measures had rather immediate consequences. They permitted the tide of colonial development to surge onward more rapidly — so rapidly, in fact, that the feeble efforts of the mother countries to keep pace by internal reform proved quite inadequate. Neither Spain nor Portugal could continue to remain a center of the civilization she had fostered. True, trade between the Iberian countries and their colonies increased enormously — several hundred per cent within a few years — evidence indeed that the former mercantilist policies of the Spanish empire had been excessively restrictive in spite of heavy contraband trade. Nevertheless, the swelling commerce notwithstanding, Spain and Portugal both remained primarily entrepôts — transfer points through which trade was carried on by the colonies with other parts of Europe. England, France, and Holland were the principal beneficiaries.

The enlightenment produced other effects of an entirely different nature. By the middle of the eighteenth century, all of Western Europe was the scene of great intellectual ferment. Much more was involved than the ivory-tower scribblings of a few intellectual giants — Voltaire, Montesquieu, Raynal, and others. On all sides, conventional concepts were under attack. Mercantilism, monarchy, the class system, religion, all were subjected to the challenge of intellectual investigation. The stimuli were many and varied. The rise of the nation-state with its overtones of patriotism threatened the dynastic practices of the past which had permitted land and peoples to be handed back and forth as the personal property of royal sovereigns. Such an international institution as the Roman Church found in the nationalistic movements a challenge to its authority which by nature had imposed at least theoretical limitations upon the concept of the national state. Within the states the commercial classes were rapidly replacing the feudal landholders as the most important economic and political factors in the population. The ever-increasing wealth of the European monarchies made possible the continuation of a tendency, already apparent in the preceding century, to strengthen the position of the royal chiefs of state. Dependence upon representative bodies of nobles for financial support of governmental functions had been all but eliminated on the continent as taxes upon commerce and the lower classes provided monies for the crowns. Royal absolutism reached its climax in Spain, France, Portugal, and Prussia. All of these developments represented change, and change provoked uncertainty, restlessness, and inquiry.

The intellectual awakening carried far beyond the justification and acceptance of a new state of affairs. The whole process had only begun to run its course in the eighteenth century. One might say that a door was merely opened, and through the aperture a new and boundless universe invited inspection. Soon virtually all conventional concepts were under attack. Many refused to see one type of authority simply replaced by another. The splintering effect of the Reformation and the religious controversies of the two preceding centuries now bore fruit in outcries against all ancient systems, creeds, doctrines, whatever the source. Such outcry was strongly supported in many cases by scientific discoveries that threw a shadow of doubt over all sorts of previously accepted explanations of the universe, the world, and the society of people that lived thereon. In reality, the enlightenment represented not so much a sudden increase in the store of human knowledge as a growing receptiveness to new ideas and a willingness to question the validity of the old ones.

The New World contributed immensely to the whole process of European intellectual development. Whereas the spirit and the ideas that characterized the age of enlightenment flowed from the Old World to the New, the very discovery of America and its indigenous population profoundly influenced the thinking of the British, German, and particularly the French writers who are most frequently associated with the broad intellectual currents of the eighteenth century. The real or imagined life among the indigenous American peoples served as basis for attack upon the artificialities, class distinctions, and even the religious concepts of European society. It was trade with the New World upon which the mercantile system was founded. The competition for that trade and for the dependencies which made it possible prompted in considerable measure the rise of national states. It was the gold and other wealth flowing from the Americas that made possible the gradual industrialization of Europe, providing a means of exchange and a market for the products of a manufacturing economy. Thus in a broad sense, the Western Hemisphere had much to do with the European awakening.

On the other hand the influences that were moving westward upon the Americas by the second half of the eighteenth century were equally significant, for the vast colonial domains of the European powers were in a receptive mood. Carried across the Atlantic in books, pamphlets, newspapers, and in the minds of travelers, the anti-authoritarian ideas of equality and liberty took hold in spite of the many efforts to suppress them. They struck responsive chords among the repressed creole classes of Spanish and Portuguese America who saw in them a possible salvation from their unhappy state. They even held out hope to those few mestizos and Indians who were in a position to appreciate their impact upon the colonial social and economic systems.

In assessing the import of eighteenth-century liberalism in Latin America, it must be understood that the entire movement was essentially destructive rather than constructive. It tore away the curtain of superstition and ignorance revealing society in all its naked imperfections. It undermined the church and the empires, encouraged rebellion against the *status quo*; but it offered no substitutes and solved few problems. All this was not immediately apparent, and as the end of the century approached the Latin American empires of Portugal and Spain enjoyed the fullness of their development in splendor and strength. Only the most discerning sensed that the foundation had been gradually weakened to the point where the structure might readily collapse.

What, indeed, were the sources of weakness? Actually, they were many and varied. Highly important were the gradual intellectual reorientation away from Spanish and Portuguese leadership, and the weakened position of the church. To these must be added the greatly increased freedom of commerce, the realization of independent strength and self-sufficiency in the colonies, the negative effect of administrative reforms, and the inability of the Iberian powers, Spain in particular, to achieve any permanent success in their diplomatic struggles with the other European nations. Of these factors, the first two were directly related to the intellectual awakening in France and the remaining four were most intimately associated with the colonial rivalry between Spain and England.

The center of the eighteenth-century intellectual attack upon conventional institutions was France. True, there were major contributions from other quarters, but the French thinkers dominated the scene, tearing away at the very foundations of a decadent social order. Rousseau's was unquestionably the most influential pen in Europe as far as America was concerned. Quite ignorant of conditions in the Western Hemisphere, he nevertheless based many of his ideas upon what he supposed to have been the idyllic life of the aboriginal Americans before their debasement by the conquest. Other

Frenchmen, equally ignorant of the virgin continents, also turned their vitriolic pens against a system that sanctioned the subdivision of mankind into classes and racial groups for the purpose of subjugation and domination. Such were Voltaire and Raynal. Noting that the staunchest defender of the old order was the Catholic Church, the French writers waxed strongly anti-clerical. The activities of the Jesuits were singled out for particularly violent criticism. As the works of these men filtered into the libraries of the upper classes in America, even into those of the clergy, many of the intellectual elite of the great American cities, Mexico, Lima, Buenos Aires, and Bogotá, turned increasingly from Spain to France for their inspiration. Paris was emerging as the center of the intellectual world.

The reorientation was one that Spain could ill afford, for it weakened the bonds that held the colonies to the mother country. The shift was too subtle, perhaps, to be immediately appreciated. Travelers to Europe from the colonies, however, found in the French capital much more of interest than Madrid had to offer. There were the finest buildings, the best plays, the greatest works of art, the most lively interchange of ideas. These facts served only to reinforce in the minds of the colonists the growing suspicion that Spain was no longer mistress of the Latin world.

Caught up in the spirit of reform that was so widespread in the second half of the eighteenth century, Carlos III and his ministers took what steps seemed to them proper to increase the well-being of the state and strengthen the weakening bonds of empire. The same was true of Pombal in Portugal. The courts of both countries were carried along in the intellectual currents flowing from France. Aranda, Carlos' First Minister, and Pombal were equally under the influence of Voltaire and other French leaders in the attack upon the reactionary internationalism of the church. They saw in the great power of the Jesuit Order not only a source of much intrigue in the European capitals, but also an alien element within their empires posing a threat to the supremacy of civil authority. The idea was conceived that it would well serve the interests of the monarchies to exclude the Jesuits from all of the vast domains in which they had become so powerful.

Opposition to the Jesuits had other bases as well. In America their power over the Indians and their long defense of the Indians against economic exploitation aroused the jealousy of many who viewed the native population gathered in the mission reductions as a potential labor supply. Certainly too, the Jesuits had themselves used the labor of the Indians to the great economic advantage of the Order. In both the Iberian countries and their colonies the Jesuits had come into possession of enormous areas of the most productive land. As entrepreneurs in many fields of activity they controlled the manufacture of various commodities, driving lay competition out of existence. In Chile, for example, the Jesuits monopolized the meat industry, operating slaughter houses and retail stores. They even built small vessels, engaged in the manufacture of lime, pottery, and other articles, and trafficked in drugs and medicines. They possessed similar economic interests in other parts of the Americas, and their wealth increased steadily as devout followers lavished benefits upon them. Such favorable worldly status naturally aroused jealousy and antagonism, not only among secular business people and landholders who felt their opportunities limited by the power of the Order, but also among other religious orders less fortunately situated.

An attempted boundary demarcation between the Portuguese and Spanish possessions in America centered much attention on the Jesuits in the decade between 1750 and 1760. By a treaty signed in 1750, seven Jesuit reductions in the Paraguay region were to be handed over to Portugal. The Indians refused to move from territory that they had regarded as their own for nearly a century, and it proved necessary to send a joint Spanish-Portuguese military expedition against them to bring about compliance. Unfortunately for the Jesuits, they were accused of having incited the Indians to revolt, and the exaggerated tales of their disregard for civil authority lent credence to the assertions of their opponents in Europe that they constituted a dangerous empire within an empire. Unfounded as many of the charges were, they nevertheless had their effect at the Spanish and Portuguese courts and made easier the subsequent decision to expel the Jesuit Order from all parts of both countries' possessions.

The decision of expulsion was taken first by Portugal in 1759. Eight years later Carlos III took the same step with respect to the Spanish domains. France too ordered expulsion, and the Bourbon monarchies then turned to the papacy to secure abolition of the Jesuit Order. On the whole, the departure of the Jesuits was most orderly, in spite of the extreme rigor with which the decrees were carried out. Most important, however, were the later consequences of this move.

The Jesuits had long served as a firm bond of union between the Iberian kings and their empires. They were the defenders in the colleges and universities of the established order and the most able opponents of the liberal social and political philosophies emanating from France and England. In their mission outposts they were to the Indians not only apostles of the Christian religion, but they represented and sanctified the authority of the king as well. Their disappearance left a vacuum that no others were able to fill. The orderly Indian communities fell into decay, and many of the well-tilled fields and orchards reverted to tropical jungle or barren wasteland. Other of their confiscated properties came into the hands of rising creole and mestizo families. Those who were fortunate thereby secured a better economic footing from which to oppose the peninsular Spaniards who had dominated the political and economic scene in the colonies from the days of the conquest. Schools and colleges were shut down or deprived of their ablest teachers, and education in the colonies, limited and imperfect as it had been, received a setback from which it had not recovered by the time of independence. Thus did the forces of the enlightenment combine with material considerations to deprive the Spanish and Portuguese monarchs of one of the most important unifying bonds with their colonial subjects.

It is not to be thought that Spain and Portugal failed entirely to give political leadership to their colonies in the eighteenth century.

Spain was particularly active in administrative reform. The reforms took on a number of aspects, each significant for its later effect upon Spanish American political development. First, the Bourbon kings introduced a substantial degree of territorial decentralization within the empire, and second, they effected a high degree of administrative centralization. In addition, there were tax reforms, changes in the methods of collection, and attempts to strengthen the military defenses of the colonies. While it would be unjust to ascribe all of these reforms to the desire of the Spanish kings to protect the empire from English encroachments, the dictates of empire defense were an ever-present consideration. Whether a change involved a shortening of the lines of administrative communication or a more efficient method of bringing revenues into the royal treasury, the constantly growing power of England imposed a real urgency upon the Spanish rulers in finding means to protect their vast domains. Portugal found the problem much less acute, for, caught between the two colonial giants, she was able to play one against the other to her occasional advantage. Portugal's success, however, was due not so much to the shrewdness of her policies as to the fact that she allowed herself to be used as a pawn in the hands of the English. For Spain no such easy solution existed. She could only take advantage of Britain's preoccupation with France to prepare for an eventual onslaught.

Under the Hapsburg monarchs, the empire of Spain in America was divided into two great viceroyalties, those of Peru and New Spain. The disadvantages of ruling so vast a region as all Spanish South America (with the exception of a coastal section of present-day Venezuela) from Lima was apparent in the preceding century, but it remained for the Bourbons to make the necessary changes. The first additional viceroyalty to be created was that of New Granada — eventually embracing the modern countries of Colombia, Venezuela, Ecuador, and Panamá. Final separation from Peru was achieved in 1739, following an earlier separation between 1717 and 1722. Then in 1776, Buenos Aires was made the seat of a viceroyalty, largely to strengthen the Plata region militarily during a series of conflicts with the Portuguese in Brazil over the Banda

Oriental. British interest in this region was also a major factor. In addition to the creation of new viceroyalties, new captaincies-general were established in Caracas, Santiago, and Habana, as well as in New Orleans when the vast Louisiana territory was ceded to Spain by France in 1763. The captaincies-general became increasingly independent of the more important viceroyalties to which they were nominally attached. In most matters they maintained direct communications with Spain, they possessed their own audiencias, and their relationship with the viceroyalties came to consist of little more than financial dependence and subjection to a vague military supervision. These territorial subdivisions effected by the Bourbon monarchs laid the basis for the independent states that were to arise in America when the Spanish empire collapsed.

Administrative centralization, an aspect of Bourbon policy in the latter half of the century, was achieved primarily during the reigns of Fernando VI and Carlos III. Some of the ideas were French in origin, however, and had been imported by Spain when Felipe V sought advice and assistance from neighboring states just after ascending the throne. Centralization had as its principal objectives the strengthening of empire defense and the improvement of financial administration. A corollary factor was the elimination of corruption and dishonesty prevalent among colonial officials, and replacement of many vested prebend-holders with men of more certain loyalty to Spain. Loyalty, strangely, was thought to be determined largely by the place of birth. The gobernadores, corregidores, and alcaldes mayores, many of whose titles were looked upon as proprietary rights, were separated from their posts and replaced by *intendentes* and *intendentes subdelegados*. The new officials combined within their authority financial, judicial, and military functions, and they were given wide responsibility for stimulating the agricultural and commercial development of their respective jurisdictions. The intendentes were given exclusive control over the collection of revenues. The system of tax-farming, whereby some private or semi-private organization undertook to collect the king's revenues for a fixed percentage or a guaranteed cash settlement with the treasury, had already begun to disappear by the middle of the century. The establishment of the intendant system put a virtual end to it everywhere.

The replacing of one group of officials by another did not in itself centralize administration, but in actual practice a considerable centralization was achieved. In the first place, the number of local government officials was greatly reduced, and those who were left under the new system no longer enjoyed the prestige and limited perquisites of official position with little responsibility. Instead the intendentes and subdelegados found themselves arranged in a definite hierarchy of responsibility, culminating in the *super-intendente general* in the various colonial capitals. The problem of divided authority soon made it necessary to combine the latter post with that of viceroy, but the basic pattern remained essentially changed, and the various officials carried on their duties with uniform and well-defined instructions. Most received regular salaries instead of the incidental perquisites and graft upon which their predecessors had depended. The salaries were generally too low, however, to relieve the official of the necessity of adding to his income by questionable means in order to maintain himself.

Secondly, whereas the former local government officials had come to be largely creole appointees of the viceroy, or people who had purchased their offices, the new officials were royal appointees and for the most part were sent out directly from Spain.

The intendant system was not adopted throughout the empire at one time, but was applied first in the captaincy-general of Cuba in 1764. It was later extended piecemeal to other parts of the Americas, and not until 1790 was it in general operation. Its effects upon government administration and upon the empire generally were shortlived, for it came too late to be given a fair trial. Undoubtedly some improvement resulted, as long-standing abuses were corrected and revenues flowed in increased amounts to the royal treasury. On the other hand, imposition of the system served to accentuate existing social grievances. The creole classes were in many instances eliminated from offices that they had come to regard as their own, and their already sharp embitterment against the peninsular Spaniards was thereby increased. Thus in one respect at least, imposition of the intendant system produced a negative reaction, alienating rather than strengthening the allegiance of Spain's colonial population.

Complaints against peninsular domination were partially counteracted during the latter part of the eighteenth century by the wise selection of colonial officials by Carlos III. Capable viceroys such as Ceballos, Arredondo, Bucareli, Azanza, and the second Revillagigedo did much to improve relations between the mother country and the colonies. They devoted considerable attention to the needs of their subjects, took steps in the fields of sanitation, physical improvement, and commercial development and showed concern for honest administration and provision of justice. Under the leadership of such men, colonial culture and society flourished, the cities were beautified, and new roads were constructed. In fact, so great had been their general progress by the end of the century that Mexico City and Lima had come to surpass Madrid as centers of beauty, scientific achievement, and cultural diversion.

At the same time the lifting of many of the restrictions upon commercial activity, climaxed by the issuance of the *Reglamento* of Free Commerce in 1778, had a pronounced effect in aiding colonial development. While trade was still nominally reserved to Spanish subjects, by 1790 virtually all Spanish American ports were open for trade with each other and with all parts of Spain. Duties on many articles had been greatly reduced or removed altogether and an enormous increase in commercial activity had already been recorded.

The policy that brought about these changes was due in large part to the urgent need for Spain to revitalize the trade upon which she depended for the benefits of empire and to retain her position as a major European power. Wise counselors, giving heed to the deplorable poverty that prevailed throughout the Spanish domains in the early part of the century, urged the stimulation of commercial activity as a remedy. Then too, Spanish goods in the colonies, overpriced because of the heavy taxes and restrictions of the mercantile system, were increasingly unable to compete with the lower-priced contraband goods brought in by the British, French, and Dutch merchants. Unwilling to see her merchants priced out of their own protected market, Spanish statesmen saw the most effective remedy in a general reduction in the price of Spanish goods. This could be achieved only by lifting many of the trade restrictions.

Increased commercial freedom successfully raised the extent of commerce in Spanish America to a new high, but Spain was unable to reap the full benefit of her actions. Her navy was unequal to the task of keeping open the lines of communication during the warfare that engulfed the colonial powers toward the end of the century. Within ten years after 1790 Spain was forced to open colonial trade to all neutral vessels. In the meantime, however, the general prosperity that prevailed in the colonies with the great increase in commercial activity created the realization that the American regions possessed an economic importance independent of their relationship with Spain.

As has already been indicated, international rivalry played a major role in determining Spain's policy toward her American colonies in the eighteenth century. Having entered first in the contest for colonial territory Spain enjoyed a great advantage, an advantage that protected her for more than two centuries. During the period of her greatest weakness in the seventeenth century, Spain was never in serious danger from the greedy ambitions of her European rivals. French interest was concentrated upon central Europe, and England was involved in internal dissensions and revolution. Neither Holland nor Portugal was strong enough to constitute any real danger. True, pirates and privateers preyed upon the great merchant fleets moving along the Spanish Main, picking off stragglers and otherwise annoying Spanish traders. Occasionally cities, such as Cartagena, were attacked and sacked by raiders. The very nature of such hit-and-run depredations, however, is a clear indication of the relative weakness of Spain's colonial rivals. Not even the English were in position to endanger seriously the Spanish empire by full-scale attack with a view to appropriating it to themselves.

Early in the eighteenth century, however, Spanish statesmen realized that such favorable conditions no longer prevailed. English sea power was an ever-increasing threat, and the prospering British colonies in North America came to be viewed as a powerful outpost from which attacks might be launched upon the Spanish regions to the south and west. Under Felipe V and Fernando VI steps were taken better to fortify the more vulnerable and strategic points in the Indies, and they added many ships to the Spanish fleet. These measures were for the most part successful, and Spain was able with vigorous colonial support to endure without serious loss the hectic years preceding the Napoleonic wars.

Throughout the century, however, friction between Spain and England was continuous. The British were arrogant and aggressive, and the attitude taken at London left little doubt that the Spanish dominions were looked upon as ripe plums which must sooner or later fall from the parent tree into the waiting hands of the rising mistress of the seas. Other problems occupied Britain, however, the foremost of which was her rivalry with France in North America and India and upon the European continent. For a time Spain was able to hide behind this rivalry, remaining aloof from definite commitments involving either nation. Between 1739 and 1748 Spain was involved in her first war with England in which the principal scene of conflict was the Western Hemisphere. Known as the War of Jenkins's Ear, the struggle demonstrated that Spain's colonies were far from helpless when it came to defending themselves. It resulted in a stalemate between the colonial contenders, and postponed any final decision. The war did serve to indicate to Spain the extent of her danger, and to cause Spanish leaders to think increasingly of making common cause with the French in defense of their colonial possessions. Such a course had its disadvantages. It could involve Spain in useless wars in defense of French interests. At the same time, it was not altogether certain that France herself was devoid of any interest in the Spanish possessions, and should her neighbor emerge victorious in her struggles with England, Spain would be more or less at her mercy.

In the face of these hazards, Fernando VI chose to continue a policy of non-commitment; but after his death, his brother, Carlos III, reluctantly chose what seemed the only other course open to him. In 1761 he entered into the Family Compact with France. The Compact created an offensive and defensive alliance between the two powers and immediately plunged Spain into the colonial war that France had been waging with England since 1754. Peace was made in 1763, but the war had gone unfavorably for both Compact powers. England captured Habana and Manila, and successfully ejected the French from Canada. Both Habana and Manila were restored in the settlement, but Spain was forced to cede to England Florida and all Spanish territory in North America east of the Mississippi river. In a secret agreement, however, France turned over Louisiana to Spain, a gift that proved to be far more of a liability than an asset. Not only did Spain have to take the region by force of arms, but she then found herself possessed of a long, ill-defined frontier with the British North American colonies — an excellent source of further conflict with Britain.

A chance to recover their losses was soon presented the Bourbon powers. The revolt of Britain's North American colonies forced her to concentrate her military and naval resources upon that struggle. Both France and Spain recognized their opportunity but were uncertain how to take advantage of it without risking more than might be gained. The colonial revolt was in fact a double-edged sword. An English victory would strengthen enormously that country's position in the Western Hemisphere, and from the Bourbon point of view was therefore most undesirable. On the other hand, neither France nor Spain stood to gain much by a victory of the rebellious colonies, for neither could hope to take possession of a region strong enough to hold the British at bay. Any territorial gains that might be exacted from the English would therefore have to be chosen from some other quarter. More important still was the reluctance, on the part of Spain in particular, to aid in establishing the undesirable precedent of colonial independence. Spain's flourishing colonies could not fail to take careful note of a successful overthrow of British domination in North America.

For a time Spanish leaders considered the possibility of using Britain's temporary preoccupation as an opportunity to conquer Portugal and put an end to long-standing differences with her Iberian rival, but France was cool to this proposition and it was abandoned. France was the first to come to a decision, and entered the war on the side of the colonists. Thereafter Spain had little to gain and perhaps much to lose by remaining neutral, and she entered the war in 1779. Unlike her French ally, however, Spain gave little direct support to the British colonies, but instead acted quickly in pursuit of her own immediate interests. She reconquered Florida, overran the British outposts in the Bahama islands, and expelled the enemy from their logging establishments in Honduras. An attack on the British in Gibraltar was unsuccessful. In the peace settlement of 1783 Spain regained once again her ancient dominion over Florida, but restored the Bahamas to England and granted to her recent enemy a limited right to continue economic activities in Honduras. For Spain the war was only moderately successful. The United States of America had been launched upon her independent career, thus creating the unwelcome precedents not only for colonial revolt but for republican government as well.

Spain's policy throughout the eighteenth century was essentially defensive. Her empire was threatened and occasionally under attack, and her military and diplomatic efforts were devoted largely to meeting the general threat and repelling these attacks. The empire was rounded out, mature, complete. True, there remained frontier areas in which considerable expansionist activity centered. In northern portions of New Spain, Indian attacks were a constant menace to the mission settlements and military outposts, but gradually the frontier was pushed northward into what is now the western portion of the United States. California was settled and presidios and missions established there. The northernmost permanent occupation was in the region around San Francisco Bay, just south of the Russian outpost at Fort Ross. The settlement of Upper California was, in fact, the most ambitious and extensive colonizing enterprise undertaken by Spain in the eighteenth century.

Other frontier areas also presented problems. In southern Chile the Araucanian Indians continued to create disturbances and prevented the Spanish from completely subjugating the region. Throughout the entire century a constant struggle went on with the Portuguese in Brazil over the Plata basin, and the constant pressure exerted by the paulistas on the Jesuit settlements in Paraguay gave rise to numerous military campaigns. Finally, while British aid was denied Portugal during the revolution of the North American colonies, Spain once again conquered all of the Banda Oriental, and this time she kept it in the peace settlement that followed.

The high-water mark of empire was reached in the year 1790. This was true in several respects. The empire was at peace, prosperous, and well governed. It embraced the greatest extent of territory it was ever to attain. Its important cities had become centers of art, culture, literary activity. Beautiful buildings adorned the public squares. Important events which were to change the course of history had not yet been felt to the detriment of the peace and stability of the realm. In France social revolution was raging, but Spain had not yet been drawn into its vortex. Carlos III was dead, but the weakness of his successor, Carlos IV, had not yet had time to manifest itself in political degeneration.

The year before, 1789, a Spanish naval expedition captured two British vessels at Nootka, near what is now Vancouver, British Columbia, claiming that the unsettled territory belonged to the king of Spain. The incident produced an international crisis, bringing Spain and England to the verge of war. Failing to receive satisfactory support from the French revolutionary government under the terms of the Family Compact, Spain was forced to accept a humiliating and disadvantageous settlement with England. The year was 1790. The climax of empire had been reached and passed. In the years that immediately followed all the latent and pent-up pressures that had been building for so long were to break forth and tear the whole imperial structure asunder. Spain and Portugal, overrun by the armies of Napoleon, were left helpless to deal with the mounting demands of their mature and now articulate colonies. The era of independence was at hand.

XV

New Spain and the Caribbean Area

> After a hundred years of the Bourbon revolution New Spain
> was on her way toward taking her place among modern nations.
> She was certainly the most solvent nation in the world. She
> not only paid her own way and had no debt, but remitted
> twenty million pesos a year in revenue to the Spanish crown.
>
> LESLEY BYRD SIMPSON *

GEOGRAPHICALLY speaking, New Spain was the logical center of Spain's North American empire. From the City of Mexico, high on the plain of Anáhuac, two figurative arms stretched outward; one reached south and east toward Panamá, the other north and then east toward Florida. Between them, they embraced that most romantic of historical seas, the Caribbean. Not only was the geographic setting conducive to the pre-eminence of New Spain; in that kingdom were also to be found the largest population, the highest cultural development, and the greatest mineral wealth of colonial America. In the years of discovery and conquest and in the period of empire consolidation that followed, the many advantages of this favored region over much of the rest of Spanish America were not at first realized. Even later it was not fully appreciated. The islands of the Caribbean were the first centers of attraction for the Spaniards coming to the New World, but the discovery of the wealth of the Aztecs quickly drew the conquerors from the islands to the mainland. There remained, how-

* *Many Mexicos*, University of California Press, Berkeley, copyright 1941, 1946, 1952, pp. 179–80.

ever, the lure of as yet unconquered regions and dreams of oriental wealth, and it did not become apparent immediately that New Spain would one day become the most valuable single possession of all the great empire of the Catholic kings.

By the end of the seventeenth century the years of consolidation and development had gradually brought the region into its proper perspective. The century of maturity that followed only served further to clarify the factors that marked New Spain's pre-eminence. The administrative changes effected in the latter half of the century by the Bourbon monarchs produced a remarkable fragmentation of the once great Peruvian viceroyalty in South America; but despite reforms in North America as well, the vast area dependent upon the viceroy in Mexico actually expanded. By 1790, the renowned Revilla-gigedo could look upon his extensive domains as stretching from Cartago in the south to the Great Salt Lake in the north, and from San Francisco in the west to the Mississippi river in the east. Silver from his treasury subsidized the island governments of Santo Domingo and Cuba. Ships from his Pacific ports carried silver to the Far East and returned laden with oriental merchandise. His capital was the most attractive city in North America, the largest, and the most highly developed in the arts. True, some of these regions within his purview were ruled by captains-general and audiencias that paid him little heed. Nevertheless, none could deny that he was the king's first representative in North America.

The very size of the vast region surrounding the Gulf of Mexico and enclosing the Caribbean on the west and north suggested marked internal variation. Indeed, the pattern presented was anything but homogeneous. The Caribbean islands, Puerto Rico, Santo Domingo, and Cuba, threshold areas of Spanish colonization in America, languished in neglect at the opening of the eighteenth century, serving primarily as way points for the treasure fleets from the mainland. Their mineral wealth exhausted, their Indian population vanished, and their agricultural potentialities undeveloped, these islands were of little economic use to Spain. Their blue waters and their desolate coasts were the frequent haunts of pirates and privateers who preyed upon the remains of what had once been a great

Spanish colonial trade. It remained for other European powers, France, England, and Holland, to make the most of the opportunities afforded by rich soil, pleasant climate, and slave labor in the Caribbean islands. From Jamaica, Curaçao, Martinique, and Saint Domingue, Spain's competitors conducted an illegal commerce with her island and mainland possessions and challenged her hegemony in the central part of the hemisphere. Only Cuba, because of its strategic location, excellent harbors, and developing sugar production, showed signs of keeping pace, during the eighteenth century, with the wealth-producing islands of Spain's rivals.

North of Cuba, Spanish Florida remained primarily a military outpost and mission frontier, useful only as a buffer against the increasingly troublesome British settlements in Georgia and the Carolinas. Louisiana was in the hands of the French throughout most of the century. When this vast and potentially valuable region fell to Spain after the peace settlement of 1763, the Spaniards saw in it only a burden and source of trouble with Great Britain and her colonies.

West of Louisiana and north of Mexico lay the great plains, the rugged mountains, and the fertile but arid valleys that now constitute the southwestern part of the United States. At the opening of the eighteenth century much of the region remained without permanent settlement and some sections had not even been explored. Santa Fe was the northernmost town of importance within the Spanish domains and remained so until several outposts were established in California near the end of the century. The vast region was populated by Indian tribes whose members, with the exception of the Pueblos, generally showed little inclination to accept the political and ecclesiastical domination of the Spanish king. So great was their reluctance, in fact, that from the time of Coronado the northern frontier of New Spain remained highly fluid and almost never peaceful. During the eighteenth century the tenuous boundary was shoved haltingly northward, and an enormous section of territory was effectively added to the great viceroyalty. Permanent settlements were founded in Texas as well as those already mentioned in California, not so much because of any expansionist drive from Mexico as from the desire on the part of Spanish political leaders to forestall French and Russian penetrations. Inasmuch as these activities continued to meet native opposition, the northern section of New Spain remained a decidedly wild frontier.

Finally, southeast from Mexico lay the long, crooked isthmus of Central America. Organized politically into the captaincy-general of Guatemala, with its own audiencia, its inhabitants and officials had little to do with the viceregal court in the capital of New Spain. Lacking accessible mineral wealth and possessing a climate that spawned malaria in the coastal regions, Central America did not attract a large Spanish population. In spite of the general development that characterized the empire in the eighteenth century, the Guatemalan captaincy-general remained predominantly Indian, primitive, and impoverished. A few of its cities — Antigua Guatemala, León, Granada, Cartago — exhibited some of the progressive tendencies that were to be observed throughout Spanish America during the era of empire maturity, but they never became foci of commercial and industrial activity as did the principal population centers of Mexico. Antigua, the ancient Guatemalan capital, did achieve a high degree of artistic and architectural splendor. The beautiful government and religious buildings, abandoned when the severe earthquake of 1773 forced a transfer of the capital to its present site, remain outstanding examples of the baroque style in Spanish colonial architecture scarcely equaled in any other part of the hemisphere.

In its total aspect, the viceroyalty of New Spain comprised a vast, sprawling empire of continental proportions. Its outlying provinces and dependent jurisdictions were loosely bound to the central authority, but the superiority and leadership of the viceregal capital were acknowledged. The major cities of central Mexico — Puebla, Guanajuato, Pachuca, Toluca, Valladolid, Guadalajara — all contributed to the splendor that was Mexico, but no region dependent upon the Mexican viceroy came at any time to rival the capital or pose an economic or political threat to its dominance.

In South America, on the other hand, rather than gaining in power and prestige within the empire, the great colonial capital of

Lima and the region of Peru generally were losing their pre-eminence. New Granada, Chile, the Plata region, all were becoming centers of their own culture, commerce, and political life. By way of contrast, the figures of the German naturalist, von Humboldt, concerning population distribution are both startling and enlightening. At the opening of the nineteenth century von Humboldt reported that the region of New Spain proper, excluding Central America and the Caribbean islands, possessed approximately half the white population, a third of the mestizo population, and half the Indian population of Spanish America. Economic pre-eminence was no less marked. New Spain was the source of more than half the gold and silver produced annually in all of America, and her agricultural production exceeded by a substantial margin the value of her mineral products. As late as 1791, New Spain exported more than six times the amount of cotton exported by the United States, and without dependence on slave labor. The invention by Eli Whitney of the cotton gin, however, and its rapid use by growers in the United States soon put an end to Mexico's previously favorable position in the world's cotton markets.

New Spain attained her position of empire pre-eminence only toward the latter half of the eighteenth century. When the period of Bourbon rule opened in 1701, the viceroyalty shared with its South American counterpart the general social stagnation and economic impoverishment that had come to characterize all Spanish possessions under the later Hapsburgs. The Bourbon reforms had much to do with the reinvigoration of New Spain.

The first consequence of dynastic change to manifest itself in New Spain was a marked attention to matters of defense. A change in viceroys was effected to allay any suspicion as to the loyalty of the new king's representative, and shortly thereafter preparations were made at Veracruz to defend the port against an expected foreign attack. The urgency of these measures was emphasized by the loss of a treasure fleet to the enemies of France and Spain in the fall of 1703 and by British attacks on Spanish outposts in both the Atlantic and Pacific. Fear that the War of Spanish Succession would involve major military and naval activities in the Americas proved un-

LATIN AMERICA AT THE
END OF THE BOURBON ERA 1790

DISPUTED

VICEROYALTY OF

Commandancy General of
the Interior Provinces

Presidency of
Guadalajara
o Guadalajara

CAPTAINCY GENERAL

Havana

o Mexico

Acapulco o o Veracruz OF CUBA

SAINT DOMINGUE FR.

CAPTAINCY GENERAL
OF GUATEMALA

Santo Domingo

N E W

o Guatemala

CAPTAINCY GENERAL
OF SANTO DOMINGO

S P A I N

CAPTAINCY GENERAL
OF CARACAS

Santa Fé de Bogota

VICEROYALTY
OF NEW GRANADA

GUIANA

Presidency
of Quito

Pará o

VICEROYALTY OF

Lima o

Presidency of Cuzco

Presidency
of
Charcas

VICEROYALTY
OF BRAZIL

Bahia

VICEROYALTY

CAPTAINCY
GENERAL
OF
CHILE

OF

Rio de Janeiro

Santiago

LA PLATA

P E R U

Buenos Aires

o CAPITAL CITY

SPANISH VICEROYALTIES

NEW SPAIN

NEW GRANADA

PERU

LA PLATA

PORTUGUESE VICEROYALTY

BRAZIL

ADMINISTRATIVE UNIT TYPES
VICEROYALTY
CAPTAINCY GENERAL
Presidency, Commandancy
0   MILES 800

ALLEN K. PHILBRICK

founded; but it was well that efforts were made to improve defenses, for they had long been woefully neglected. The attention to military matters had the effect of strengthening internal control in the colony and also made possible the expulsion of the British from the region of Tabasco where they had secured a foothold on the island of Carmen.

Of the procession of viceroys that Felipe V sent to Mexico City, few were outstanding. Each in turn struggled with the problem of increasing the flow of revenue to Spain — a principal mark of success in Madrid — and in so doing undertook to bring some order and morality into the chaotic and corrupt administration. That none succeeded too well is evidenced by the fact that in writing the required instructions to their successors nearly all dwelt at length on the dismal state of affairs encountered upon arrival. Nevertheless, modest accomplishments may be credited to the efforts of a number of the local rulers, and the total of these accomplishments is indicative of a gradual but steady improvement in virtually all aspects of business and public affairs.

The suppression of brigandage and piracy and the modernization of social life and customs marked the era of Francisco Fernández de la Cueva Enríquez, Duke of Albuquerque, from 1702 to 1711. The long reign of Juan de Acuña, Marquis of Casafuerte, from 1722 to 1734, saw the re-establishment of Spanish authority and missionary activity in eastern Texas, a region that previous officials had allowed to fall into neglect and abandonment after early colonization. During this same period, two periodicals were established in the viceregal capital, and their publication marked an important cultural advance. A general improvement in the volume and value of commerce enabled several viceroys to remit substantial revenues to the homeland. Juan Antonio de Vizarrón y Eguiarreta, who governed from 1734 to 1740, is credited with having sent more treasure to Spain than any previous viceroy, and the first Count of Revillagigedo, Juan Francisco de Güemes y Horcasitas, 1746–55, also had a commendable financial record in spite of the fact that he used his public office for such obvious personal enrichment that his illicit activities became the subject of public scandal.

The first half a century of Bourbon rule was not without its difficult moments, however. The British in Georgia threatened Spanish outposts in Florida, and in Central America their logwood colony at Belize proved more than the Spaniards were able successfully to cope with. Numerous raids were made on coastal cities, and Spanish treasure ships were in constant danger. Portobelo was sacked by Admiral Vernon in 1739, and although defeated at Cartagena in 1741, the British commander vented his frustration by a fruitless raid on Habana while returning to England. In 1735, an uprising of Negro slaves at Córdoba disrupted the internal peace of the realm, and a year later a serious epidemic ravaged the population of central Mexico. In general, however, conditions in New Spain were considerably better economically and politically by mid-century than they had been when Felipe V ascended the Spanish throne.

Far more important changes were in the offing. In 1760 Joaquín Monserrat, Marquis of Cruillas, was appointed viceroy, and during his administration was inaugurated one of the most outstanding *visitas* in the history of the empire. Carlos III came to the Spanish throne in 1759, and although his predecessor had done much to revitalize the military and naval establishments of the empire, the measures taken by the new king soon set him apart as perhaps the most progressive of all Spanish monarchs. Carlos' reform measures brought about great changes in Spain proper, but the king viewed the empire in its totality and he saw clearly that the resurgence of Spanish power depended upon development in the colonies as well as on the peninsula. One of his first measures was to undertake a review of conditions in America by the time-honored visitation process. For the inspection of New Spain, he sent José de Gálvez, one of the most able of Spanish administrators.

José de Gálvez was sent to New Spain in 1765 with delegated authority far exceeding that of the viceroy, Cruillas, who was soon replaced. He interested himself in every phase of administration from treasury management and internal defense to the status of the Indians and the economic monopoly of the consulados. To secure better viceregal co-operation, he arranged for the appointment of Carlos Francisco de Croix, Marquis of Croix, who throughout his incumbency served as the pliable agent of the visitador. The results of Gálvez' activities were far-reaching, but not all his recommendations were immediately put into effect. His most important suggestion was that the intendant system, already in use in Spain, be utilized in New Spain. This involved the creation of a much tighter hierarchical structure presided over by an intendant-general in Mexico City, who was to supervise twelve intendants with specific territorial jurisdictions throughout the viceroyalty. The intendants, in turn, were to exercise supervision over sub-delegates who replaced the former alcaldes mayores and corregidores. The intendant-general and his subordinates were to assume responsibility in four broad categories of governmental activity: revenue administration, police, economic development and regulation, and administration of justice. The most significant aspects of intendancy rule were not the re-ordering of the organizational structure or the retitling of the chief administrative posts; rather, they were the clarification of responsibilities that had long been confused and diffused and the injection of new administrative blood into the system. Under the new organization, Spaniards from the peninsula were to replace creole and mestizo officials at the local level. It was felt, and with considerable reason, that local government had become corrupted by long association of the alcaldes mayores and corregidores with community interests adverse to those of the crown. Far too many had yielded to the temptation to line their pockets at the expense of the ignorant and helpless Indian on the one hand and of the royal treasury on the other.

The intendant system was not inaugurated in New Spain until 1786, long after Gálvez' departure. But he was responsible for its form and content and, indeed, for its implantation. He was made minister of the Indies at the close of his mission in New Spain, and from that advantageous position he was able to make certain that virtually all of his recommendations were eventually adopted.

Of more immediate consequence than the intendant system were some of the military and economic measures that the visitador initiated. To stimulate commerce and industry, New Spain was permitted to trade freely with other parts of the empire. In addition, import and export duties were sharply reduced. These changes in commercial policy had the effect of breaking the old commercial monopolies and producing a marked increase in trade volume. At the same time, improvements in the system of revenue collection and administration made possible a considerable improvement in the position of the treasury. What Gálvez had seen was a revenue structure so complex and oppressive as to be self-defeating. It had depressed commerce and invited evasion. By easing the burden and improving administration, commerce and the crown both benefited.

In military matters, José de Gálvez did much to solve the age-old problem of stabilizing the northern frontier. Two matters concerned him. One was the Indian situation in the northern part of the viceroyalty. The other was the increasing attention being paid by Britain and Russia to the northern Pacific coast. To cope with both problems at the same time, Gálvez stimulated further exploration and settlement along the Pacific coast and organized the frontier provinces into a separate jurisdiction known as the commandancy-general of the interior provinces. The new jurisdiction included Lower California, Upper California, where new settlements and permanent mission stations were established, Sinaloa, Sonora, Coahuila, Nueva Vizcaya, and the modern regions of Texas and New Mexico. Presidios were relocated and new ones established so as to create a chain of frontier military outposts from the Gulf of Mexico to the Pacific. The occupation of Monterey Bay in 1770 and the founding of San Francisco in 1776 marked the northernmost advance of the Spanish land occupation. Further exploration by sea carried the Spaniards to Nootka Sound in 1788 and 1790, but conflict with the English and fear of war with that nation brought about a withdrawal.

To man the new military establishments with Spanish regulars would have required far greater forces than Gálvez and the later viceroys had at their disposal. The same problem was faced throughout the Spanish domains where similar expansions in defense facilities were under way. Carlos III, his military and diplomatic policies linked to those of France by reason of the Family Compact, foresaw an inevitable clash with England. His only recourse lay in strengthening Spain and her empire economically, administratively, and particularly militarily. To increase the available manpower, consequently, he adopted the expedient of creating colonial militia to man the defenses of the empire. In New Spain, native Americans were recruited and organized into militia units officered by creoles and mestizos. Many of these units underwent their baptism of fire on the northern frontiers where strenuous efforts were made to bring the hostile Indian tribes under effective control and subjugation. Little did the king realize what the creation of a colonial military force might mean for the future of the empire, but in any case the prospect of British conquest left him little alternative.

The reform measures instituted by the great visitador might well have come to naught had there not followed a succession of able viceroys in New Spain. Antonio María Bucareli was transferred to the high post from the captaincy-generalship of Cuba in 1771. During the eight years of his rule were carried out the important colonization and defense measures along the northern Pacific coast. In spite of his firm adherence to the policies of fiscal regularity laid down by Gálvez, Bucareli proved immensely popular with his subjects, and his untimely death in 1779 was a matter for great mourning among the people. There followed a period of confusion during which Gálvez, now minister of the Indies, sought to place his brother in the viceregal chair. At first unsuccessful, Gálvez finally saw his brother take possession of the office in 1783 only to learn of his death within a year. In rapid succession the viceregal post was held by José de Gálvez' nephew, Bernardo, the archbishop of Mexico, Alonso Núñez de Haro y Peralta, and Manuel Antonio Flórez, under whose administration the intendant system was finally inaugurated. In 1789, the second Count of Revillagigedo, Juan Vicente de Güemes Pacheco de Padilla, assumed office. He earned the reputation as the greatest viceroy since Mendoza and Velasco in the sixteenth century.

Revillagigedo was appointed to office after the death of Carlos III and José de Gálvez. The viceroy's selection and his work nevertheless represented the culmination of the efforts of these Spanish leaders to achieve revitalization in the empire. Revillagigedo carried into operation the new system of intendancies, and his careful attention to fiscal affairs, to honest and impartial enforcement of the revenue laws, enabled him to achieve the highest degree of administrative success. While he undertook major programs of physical improvement, particularly in the capital, and maintained the defense establishment at peak efficiency, he was still able to remit to the homeland larger surpluses than had ever been received from any part of the empire at any time in its history. In addition to these achievements, Revillagigedo, by reason of great attention to the needs of his subjects, gained a popularity that few viceroys ever enjoyed and that served to cement relations between the colony and the homeland to a degree never again attained.

Several factors favored the great viceroy. The death of Gálvez had permitted an alteration in the intendant system making the system workable. Under the original plan, an intendant-general, as superintendent of the treasury and chief administrative officer of the system, would have replaced the viceroy as chief officer of the realm. The position of viceroy would have been reduced to that of ceremonial figurehead and presiding officer of the audiencia. Dual leadership in the colonial capital could have led to nothing but conflict and frustration. Foreseeing this difficulty, Bucareli delayed inauguration of the new system. Upon Gálvez' death, a modification was introduced which combined the position of intendant-general with that of viceroy, and it was under the revised plan that Revillagigedo put the new organization into operation.

Another factor favoring the viceroy was the general confusion prevailing in Spain upon the death of Carlos III. His weak successor, Carlos IV, was the victim of court intrigue that undermined his political leadership and his marital prerogatives. The viceroy of New Spain ruled his domain with a minimum of interference from the peninsula. He enjoyed a free hand fully in accord with his high concept of viceregal leadership. Attention in Spain was focused on the struggle at court and upon the ominous cloud of revolution visible beyond the Pyrenees. Revillagigedo made good use of his opportunities. Under his guidance, New Spain became truly pre-eminent in the Spanish system.

In spite of the many advances made during the eighteenth century, life in Spain's North American colonies remained one of difficulty and hardship. Sanitary facilities were poor or non-existent, and the incidence of disease was high. Medical care was, in general, available only to the wealthy, and the quality of professional practice left much to be desired. In these respects, New Spain differed little from the mother country or from other parts of Europe, for the mentioned difficulties attended the state of scientific knowledge of the era. On the other hand, other conveniences that were becoming commonplace in the Old World were notably lacking in the New. Few cities in New Spain enjoyed anything approaching adequate police protection; protection of life and property was essentially a matter of private concern. Those of wealth continued to bar their windows and doors, build high walls, and keep large and ill-tempered dogs, just as they had done in centuries preceding. Travel by night was undertaken only in circumstances of great urgency, and the traveler did well to provide himself with suitable arms. Street lighting was inaugurated in Mexico City only in the latter part of the century, and even then it was extended only to a few of the wealthy sections.

It is one thing to note that there were great improvements in commerce and industry in New Spain in the latter half of the eighteenth century. It is quite another to consider what such improvements meant in the lives of local inhabitants. First of all, they meant higher production in virtually all commodities. More people worked in the mines, more entered the *trapiches*, or textile shops. Larger numbers engaged in the enormous task of transport, loading and driving the long trains of mules and burros that constituted the principal carriers of goods over the endless trails of the mountainous countryside. Often there was hardship, for mining was a difficult and thankless task for the miners, the textile establishments were crowded, poorly lighted sweatshops to which the workers were herded like slaves, and the pack trains provided a wearisome existence for man and animal alike.

Economic improvement benefited many, however. Once the old monopolies were broken by greater liberality in trade and taxation policy, new elements in the population entered into the production and distribution of goods. Many new fortunes were made and the distribution of wealth became less concentrated geographically.

New Spain was greatly handicapped by her rugged terrain. The high mountains, the unhealthful climate of the tropic lowlands, and the wide dispersal of mining and commercial centers created tremendous problems in communication and transport. Consequently, few roads were built upon which wheeled vehicles could travel. The principal high road was from Veracruz to Mexico City. Other roads connected the capital with a few of the larger cities of the high central plateau. Beyond this area, however, traveler and cargo had to take to the back of an animal to go any great distance. Thus it was that New Spain constituted a loosely knit kingdom with little land contact with such remote territories as Guatemala, Cartago, Texas, and California.

The same difficulties that impeded communication and transport placed serious limits upon agricultural development. Today only a very small per cent of the area of Mexico is considered suitable for agriculture — possibly as little as 15 per cent. Mexico has suffered greatly from soil erosion in the past century and a half, but the area available for tillage in the time of the viceroys could not have been much greater than it is now. Much of the badly eroded area lies on the sides of mountains where cultivation should never have been undertaken. In addition to the lack of suitable farm land, the pattern of rainfall was unfavorable. It either rained too much and too hard or too little and too hard.

In spite of these difficulties, New Spain achieved greatness economically in the eighteenth century. The wealth of the Aztecs exploited by Cortés and his followers was as nothing compared to the steady stream of silver poured forth by the mines of the viceroyalty during the period of Bourbon rule. Production increased steadily decade after decade until output in the last years of the era was four times greater than a century before, averaging better than twenty million pesos annually. The mines were scattered over a fairly wide area in the central highlands, but the biggest producers were those in Guanajuato, San Luis Potosí, and Zacatecas. Increased pro-

duction was the result of close co-operation between producers and
the crown. Mexican mine-owners united their efforts to organize
a school of mines in Mexico City, and the government supplied its
chief instructor and director in the person of Fausto de Ilhuyar, a
well-known European expert who had discovered tungsten and who
was commissioned to introduce a newly developed silver amalgamation process in Mexico. Ilhuyar's arrival in Mexico and his assumption of the posts of director of the school and director-general of
Mexican Mines preceded only slightly the arrival of the second
Revillagigedo as viceroy. Under the stimuli of intelligent government interest and the application of scientific knowledge and techniques, the mining industry of New Spain expanded perceptibly. By
1790 New Spain, producing more than half the world's annual output of silver, employed thousands of people in the extraction of
mineral wealth and enjoyed a high degree of prosperity as exports
expanded and purchasing power increased.

Not only did the production of silver enrich those who owned an
interest in the mines, but indirectly many others also benefited.
Numerous service activities were to be found in each mining district. Quicksilver had to be imported, food produced, rope made,
and various kinds of leather goods provided. Intendants and sub-
delegates took the initiative in opening new roads between the mining districts and the capital and in protecting the mule trains from
the depredations of highwaymen. The raising of mules was in itself
an important activity, as the demand for animals in transportation
services almost always exceeded the supply. Much silver was retained in New Spain to be coined at the mint or to be made into
various kinds of jewelry and decorative goods for which the region
was and remains justly famous. Thus mining was a matter of great
economic importance and both directly and indirectly accounted
for an important segment of those factors which gave New Spain
its eminence in the Western Hemisphere.

It is easy to assume that mining in colonial Latin America dominated all other activities. The search for precious metals was certainly a paramount factor in the colonization and settlement of
much of both western continents. Never, however, did the extractive

industries account for more than a small portion of the economic activity of the Iberian colonies. Perhaps the greatest concentration of energy and manpower in the mines took place in Upper Peru during the sixteenth and early seventeenth centuries, but thereafter the importance of mining declined relatively in respect to the amount of human effort devoted to other productive enterprises. In New Spain, where the absolute importance of mining increased as time went on, agriculture, manufacturing, and commerce kept pace with the extractive industries in the total economy. Thus, when the silver mines of New Spain were at their peak of production in the late eighteenth and early nineteenth centuries, the value of agricultural products surpassed that of mineral output year by year. It was the precious metals, of course, that gave to the New World its early fame. Throughout the colonial era they constituted the bulk of the exports in terms of value and occasionally in terms of tonnage. Their extraction formed the hard core of economic activity upon which other industry depended. Nevertheless, to emphasize unduly their importance is to mislead. In New Spain, as elsewhere in Latin America, great value was extracted from the earth with relatively small capital investment and with the use of limited manpower. The great majority of Europeans who migrated to the Spanish colonies and a great majority of the native population never saw a mine nor participated in any phase of the mining industry. On the contrary, they lived out their lives unobtrusively and unspectacularly engaged in the traditional activities of their forefathers, agriculture and the minor handicrafts.

A clear indication of colonial maturity was the increasing economic self-sufficiency of New Spain. As already noted, the colonial or mercantile system of economic organization upon which the Spanish empire was founded was predicated upon the idea that the colonial regions of the world would send raw materials and minerals to the technically advanced mother country in exchange for manufactured and processed goods. Spain employed the system with only limited success, and by the second half of the eighteenth century it was particularly inappropriate as applied to New Spain. Aside from the inability of the mother country to keep open the lines of communication with her colonies — indispensable to successful operation of the mercantile system — New Spain possessed an internal economy nearly as industrialized as that of the mother country. Just as a long period of neglect favored the development of local industry in Britain's North American colonies, the weaknesses of the Spanish trading system encouraged local industry in New Spain and other regions farther south.

Spain herself failed to achieve any substantial degree of industrialization. Her dependence upon England, France, and Holland for goods to send to the colonies in trade plus the complete domination of that trade for so many years by a small group of favored monopolists resulted in restricted supply and exorbitant prices. Only the wealthier classes were served by this trade. A large unsatisfied demand existed for certain basic commodities that were not supplied by import. In New Spain the concentration of population on the high central plateau to which access from the seacoast was difficult meant the addition of sizable transportation costs to such European goods as reached the inland cities and the far-flung northern mining centers. The Jalapa fair near Veracruz was a famous commercial institution, but it was far removed from Guadalajara, Durango, or Saltillo. In these circumstances, to which must be added the presence of such basic raw materials as cotton, wool, hides, and maguey fiber, it would have been strange if New Spain had not developed important manufacturing activity.

By the middle of the eighteenth century there were extensive textile establishments in operation throughout the central part of the viceroyalty. Wool and cotton goods were produced in considerable quantity in such diverse places as Guadalajara, Puebla, Texcoco, and Saltillo. The quality of cloth was generally poor and many of the weaving establishments were but small home shops. Other manufactured goods included ropes and cables, pottery, china, and glassware, and all sorts of leather products. The alcoholic beverage, pulque, made from the sap of the maguey plant, was widely produced, and tobacco was grown and processed for cigars and cigarettes in government-monopoly plants. Excellent furniture was locally manufactured.

Virtually all the articles mentioned were domestically consumed and entered into export trade only when carried to Guatemala or some of the Caribbean islands. These manufactures were of vital importance to the economy of New Spain, for they supplied the wants of a great majority of the population, not only for items of everyday life, but for the few luxuries that the lower classes could afford.

New Spain benefited materially as a strategic transfer point in Spain's oriental commerce. From the sixteenth century onward, the port of Acapulco on the Pacific Coast served as the western terminus of the famed Manila galleons. Sailing annually, these ships brought spices, silks, and other eastern goods in exchange for silver. Guadalajara, as well as Acapulco, enjoyed the advantages of this commerce and the related carrying trade by which oriental merchandise was transported across the continent for reshipment at Veracruz. An added benefit was the Peruvian business attracted to Acapulco by the opportunity to participate in the trade fairs that took place upon the arrival of the galleons. The practice of sending Peruvian ships to Acapulco was long illegal, but continued in open violation of the law until authorized by the liberalization of Spanish trade policy in 1784. The importance of the oriental trade is indicated by the fact that Chinese currency came to be based upon the Spanish, and later the Mexican, silver peso. Likewise, Peruvian participation can be measured by noting that there were times in both the seventeenth and eighteenth centuries when Peruvian-minted pesos in circulation in New Spain exceeded in number those from the local mint. Repeated efforts by the crown on behalf of the Cádiz and Veracruz monopolists were unavailing in the attempt to keep the Acapulco trade within legal bounds. For many years the Manila galleons were limited to two annually, but this restriction was circumvented by building larger ships. Some of the galleons were for their time the largest ships afloat.

New Spain's principal artery of commerce was, of course, the high road from the capital to Veracruz, the monopoly port for trade with Europe. By the middle of the eighteenth century, however, the manner in which goods entered Veracruz was undergoing a revolution. The old flota system became increasingly unsatisfactory, and finally it was abandoned altogether. The number of *registros* — ships licensed to sail without convoy — increased steadily. The quickening tempo of commercial intercourse had much to do with this, for merchants were more and more unwilling to endure the delays and irregularities that attended the movements of the flotas. Large-scale ship movement was repeatedly interrupted by the frequent wars, not only because of the risks of capture by enemy naval squadrons but also because Spanish men-of-war and merchant vessels could not always be spared from other activities to undertake the long voyage across the Atlantic and back. Thus it was that during the entire era of Bourbon rule, little more than a score of flotas entered the port of Veracruz.

Substitution of the registro for the flota system encouraged the development of a much more varied commercial pattern. Individual ships were far more difficult to control than were the escorted fleets, and many took advantage of the more liberal sailing arrangements to stop at forbidden ports and trade in contraband merchandise. Much to the discomfiture of the Veracruz merchant guild, many cargoes were unloaded at Tampico and Campeche. By the time of José de Gálvez' famed visita, the entire Caribbean region was beginning to swarm with individual trading vessels of many nations, and it was obvious that the old system of monopoly was on its way out.

French merchants in particular were able to establish themselves as regular suppliers of the Spanish colonies, due in part to the tendency of the Spanish Bourbon kings to wink benignly at the irregular activities of their French cousins. Habana was a favorite port for British as well as French vessels, and the Central American ports south of British Honduras were all but monopolized by English traders after 1713. By the end of the century, United States merchants entered the picture and were particularly active in the Caribbean islands and in Louisiana and the Floridas. Not only did the United States provide a new source of supply of various manufactured goods, but the new nation furnished a ready market for sugar, hemp, indigo, and mineral products — all items that the merchants of New Spain and its insular dependencies were happy to sell.

In her period of maturity, New Spain was strong. Her productivity was great, her trade balance favorable, her domestic industries flourishing. Dependence upon the mother country was waning rapidly as new commercial links were forged and as her own militia assured the defense of the region and quelled the lawless Indians along the northern frontier. Spaniards continued to dominate the government, and particularly the civil administration. They still held the chief offices in the church and dominated commercial life of the chief ports and the capital. But now they were supported and their role supplemented by creole elements that dominated the miner's guild, the Tribunal de Minería, the merchant guilds in the outlying cities, and the intellectual life of the capital. Creole aristocrats owned the vast landed estates, and their sons provided a good portion of the officer corps of the colonial militia. Together these elements, Spaniard and creole, gave to New Spain its class, its brilliance, and its prosperity. Their accomplishments in government, in science, in commerce, in art, and in the social graces brought New Spain to the apex of her colonial glory.

Below the surface accomplishments of the viceroyalty and those who benefited from them, life for the common Indian changed hardly at all. A serious drought in 1784 caused widespread crop failure and famine stalked the land. Untold suffering was endured with the stoic passiveness of those who had no hope apart from the charities that a paternalistic state and church were able to provide. After centuries of ignorant exploitation, the impoverished and eroded land of New Spain was giving warning of serious trouble ahead, but in the social and economic climate of the times there were none to be found who could view the causes and take remedial action. For such problems the scientific minds in Mexico had no solution or even time for consideration.

With the gradual suppression of encomiendas and the end of the commercial repartimiento that accompanied the establishment of intendancies, the Spanish officials hoped to eliminate some of the more pronounced abuses among the Indians. The caciques and corregidores of Indian villages had long been among the worst exploiters and oppressors of the native masses, and the new intendants were specifically charged to bring about the termination of the system that had fostered such evil. The elimination of one form of personal service, however, was gradually followed by another — debt slavery on the hacienda. By paying miserable wages and charging the Indian for food, clothing, lodging, and tribute, landholders and their foremen kept the workers hopelessly in debt and thus bound them to the estate. Debt peonage was well in evidence during the last quarter of the eighteenth century, and it became the principal form of Indian exploitation passed from colony to republic.

The condition of the illiterate masses greatly disturbed the viceroy, Revillagigedo II. He abhorred the miserable huts and crowded slums that surrounded his capital and saw in them breeding places of disease as well as street urchins. To discourage the raggedness and nakedness so common in the streets of the capital, he had ordinances passed forbidding people so clothed or unclothed to appear in public places. That his concern extended to doing something about the cause is indicated by the fact that he ordered government monopoly enterprises to clothe their workers and deduct the cost from their wages. The viceroy was at least partly correct in his assumption that ignorance and lack of self-respect were as much causes of the difficulty as was poverty.

In contrast with life on the high plateaus of Mexico, the northern plains, and the sleepy mountain villages of Guatemala, the teeming port cities and vast sugar plantations of the Caribbean presented a quite different picture. Here the Negro was everywhere in evidence. During the eighteenth century the slave trade was at its height, and thousands upon thousands of the unhappy blacks were marched off the stinking slavers to the auction blocks of Habana, Port Royal, and Cap Français. Upon their labor was developed one of the most intensive sugar economies that history records. The plantation system became all-important in the British colony of Jamaica and in French Saint Domingue, the western third of the island of Española. In Cuba too, sugar gradually became the first crop, but coffee and tobacco were likewise important, as they were also on the island of Puerto Rico. Saint Domingue became the most productive of all Caribbean sugar colonies and a prototype of the colonial slave-holding society.

By 1785 it is estimated that there were over half a million slaves in Saint Domingue, a large portion of which were African born. Because of the arduous conditions of toil under the tropical sun, the unsatisfactory conditions of sanitation and housing, and particularly because of the inhumane treatment accorded them, the mortality rate among the Negroes was extremely high. The supply of slaves had to be replenished continuously. A small number of French planters, some creole and others European born, owned and directed the huge labor force. They occupied fine homes on their plantations where their furnishings and social customs were in emulation of those of pre-revolutionary French nobility. Mulattoes too were present, a few as plantation owners, but more often employed as labor foremen and farm managers, from which middle position they envied and hated the whites while flaunting their superior social and economic status over the slaves. Class and racial tensions on the Spanish mainland, or even on the neighboring Spanish islands, were as nothing compared to the powder keg that was Saint Domingue.

In 1789 the French Revolution broke forth in Europe and quickly engulfed the Caribbean colony in all its fanatical extremism and social upheaval. Within two years Saint Domingue was plunged into a bloody racial conflict that reduced the once prosperous island to a shambles. French control was broken, and although years of vicious warfare were necessary to confirmation of the Negro victory, a new republic, Haiti, took its place as the second American nation to throw off the yoke of the mother country.

The revolution in Saint Domingue had its repercussions in Jamaica where bloody Negro uprisings had already occurred. Untroubled at home, the British succeeded where the French had failed and held their colony fast. Only the most rigorous repression, however, prevented a repetition of the holocaust of Saint Domingue. In the Spanish island colonies, where slaves were much less numerous, the threat of Negro uprisings scarcely existed. The Spanish in their treatment of slaves were generally more easy-going than either the French or the British, and they were far more liberal in permitting the Negroes to gain their freedom. As a consequence, strong incentives to revolt were lacking. Spain may have governed badly, but she did so very well.

Between 1701 and 1792 New Spain had come a long way. In common with other parts of the Spanish empire, the viceroyalty and its outlying dependencies had profited from able rule, economic development, and marked liberalization in the commercial policies of the mother country. In José de Gálvez, Bucareli, and the second Revillagigedo, the vast kingdom had seen the best administrative talent that the Bourbon era produced. The momentum generated by their combined efforts and the renewed vigor of the Mexican upper classes carried into the succeeding years, but already there were indications that the future would be less bright. With the death of Carlos III, leadership from the metropolis terminated, and able men were replaced by fawning courtiers whose lack of comprehension of imperial affairs was exceeded only by their lust for power. The high point of empire had been reached. Imperceptibly but surely, the bonds of empire fell slack. Only a sudden jerk was needed to break them asunder.

VICEROYS OF NEW SPAIN, 1700–90

1701–2	Juan Ortega y Montañez, Archbishop of Mexico
1702–11	Francisco Fernández de la Cueva Enríquez, Duke of Albuquerque
1711–16	Fernando de Alencastre, Duke of Linares
1716–22	Baltásar de Zúñiga, Marquis of Valero
1722–34	Juan de Acuña, Marquis of Casafuerte
1734–40	Juan Antonio de Vizarrón y Eguiarreta, Archbishop of Mexico
1740–41	Pedro de Castro y Figueroa, Duke of la Conquista
1741–2	Audiencia
1742–6	Pedro Cebrián y Agustín, Count of Fuenclara
1746–55	Juan Francisco de Güemes y Horcasitas, first Count of Revillagigedo
1755–8	Agustín de Ahumada y Villalón, Marquis of Amarillas
1758–60	Francisco Cagigal de la Vega (ad interim)
1760	Audiencia
1760–66	Joaquín Monserrat, Marquis of Cruillas
1766–71	Carlos Francisco de Croix, Marquis of Croix
1771–9	Antonio María de Bucareli y Ursúa
1779	Audiencia

1779–83   Martín de Mayorga (ad interim)
1783   Matías de Gálvez
1784–5   Audiencia
1785–6   Bernardo de Gálvez
1786–7   Alonso Núñez de Haro y Peralta, Archbishop of Mexico (ad interim)
1787–9   Manuel Antonio Flórez
1789–94   Juan Vicente de Güemes Pacheco de Padilla, Count of Revillagigedo
1794–8   Miguel de la Grúa Talamanca y Branciforte, Marquis of Branciforte
1798–1800 Miguel José de Azanza
1800–1803 Félix Berenguer de Marquina
1803–8   José de Iturrigaray
1808–9   Pedro Garibay
1809–10   Francisco Jamier de Lizana y Beaumont, Archbishop
1810–13   Francisco Jamier de Venegas
1813–16   Félix María Calleja del Rey
1816–21   Juan Ruiz de Apodaca
1821   Juan O'Donojú

XVI

The Emergence of New Granada

> The number of those who feel the want of reading is not very considerable, even in the Spanish colonies most advanced in civilization.
>
> ALEXANDER VON HUMBOLDT *

NEW GRANADA was settled more slowly than many of the other regions of Spanish America. Early explorers encountered great difficulty in simply penetrating the vast jungle and mountain fastnesses. Hostile Indian tribes were more persistently troublesome than in regions such as Peru and Mexico where the aboriginal civilization was more highly developed and authority centralized upon a sedentary basis. In New Granada and in northern South America generally the Indians formed groups unto themselves, and it proved impossible to impose Spanish rule by conquering the seat of native power, for there was no such seat. Each group had to be subdued, one by one, or by the use of such combinations and alliances as the Spaniards were able to employ to their advantage. Thus the process of conquest and settlement was a slow one, and many a town was established only to be abandoned in a few years when the native population melted away or rose up and crushed the few European settlers who had made it their home.

By 1700 the entire region of New Granada was still very much in a frontier state. Although there were few areas into which some

---

* *Personal narrative of travels to the equinoctial regions of the new continent, during the years 1799–1804,* London, 1814–29, 7 vols.

intrepid soul had not penetrated in the search for wealth and adventure, there were large sections devoid of white settlement. As elsewhere in Latin America, the Iberian peoples in New Granada were prone to base their permanent settlements upon the presence of native population. The Indian peoples were essential, for their labor made the mines and the agricultural lands produce. Thus when the Indian groups were small and prone to mobility, white settlement was difficult.

As noted in an earlier chapter, the Spaniards, upon entering the area known as New Granada, moved up and down the great river valleys of the Magdalena and the Cauca. The permanent settlements were established generally along these arteries or their tributaries and at favorable points along the sea coast. Such was the pattern to be found in the region at the opening of the eighteenth century. There were many populated places, but most were small and lacking in the elements of convenience and comfort that might be found in other more favored regions of the Americas at this time. A city of such modern importance as Medellín had been in existence less than half a century and consisted of little more than a small cluster of crude houses surrounded by the more primitive habitations of the Indians. The vast eastern region beyond the cordillera, although entered by exploring parties in preceding centuries, held few if any attractions for the Spaniards and remained entirely without important settlement.

The same factors that made settlement difficult hampered communication. The Magdalena river was the principal highway of the region, though navigable only in portions of its length. Once one left the river the rugged mountains imposed a considerable barrier; and communication across the mountains rather than up and down the valleys was consequently neglected. Isolated outposts remained without contact with other parts of the country for years at a time. Throughout the seventeenth century, hostile Indians frequently made hazardous such lines of communication as did exist, and native hostility continued to be a menace during the early part of the eighteenth century.

To these difficulties, which stemmed largely from the topography of the area and the character of the Indian population, must be added others which were external. Cartagena had early been designated one of the three trading ports of Spanish America, due in large part to the amount of gold and other mineral wealth exported from the region to Spain. Thus European goods brought into the colony directly were not subject to such enormous costs of overland transport as was the case with goods shipped to colonies farther south. This very fact, however, together with the proximity of Portobelo, the similarly favored port on the Isthmus of Panamá, attracted to the entire coastal region large numbers of foreign interlopers. These were both pirates and enemies of Spain. Frequently they came to engage in illicit commerce, but on numerous other occasions they came to pillage and destroy. In the period just preceding the opening of the eighteenth century these raiders were particularly active, and they made of Cartagena the most frequently besieged city on the Spanish Main. Not only did this serve to discourage commerce and development, but — coupled with the general decline of commercial activity between Spain and her colonies in the late seventeenth century — it caused excessive expenditures to be devoted to military defense at a time when these outlays could ill be afforded. Available funds were devoted to the coastal region and the vast hinterland was neglected. In fact, surpluses were drawn from the upland cities to finance the measures required for the defense of the sea ports.

The many difficulties flowing from problems of settlement and communication, relations with troublesome Indians, and defense of the coastal towns all combined to relegate the region of New Granada to a condition of extreme poverty and decay by the end of the Hapsburg era. From the time of conquest the region had never experienced a vigorous development or a high degree of economic prosperity. Once the early discoveries of gold were exhausted, interest in the region declined, and while mining continued to be the most important economic activity, most of the population came to depend upon some form of subsistence agriculture. The discovery of emeralds and additional gold in the region of Antioquía served to stimulate commerce on the rivers during the middle of the seventeenth century, but other parts of the country remained un-affected, and intense depression prevailed. More than some other parts of the empire, New Granada suffered from the general stagna-tion that immediately preceded the opening of the Bourbon era of Spanish development.

General poverty continued long into the eighteenth century. The mother country was involved in the War of Spanish Succession and for a period of twelve years after the opening of the century only one fleet sailed from Spain to the Isthmus and the adjacent ports of New Granada. After peace was re-established in Europe, conditions began slowly to improve. No great progress was made, however, until 1717. In that year New Granada was raised to the status of a vice-royalty.

The preceding years had been marked by almost complete politi-cal turmoil in the colony. President Diego Córdoba Lasso de la Vega, who was appointed to the chief executive office of the colony in 1703, spent only part of his administration in the capital at Santa Fé de Bogotá. He went to Cartagena in 1710 in anticipation of a military expedition against the port by Spain's enemies, and there he remained until he returned to Spain in 1712. In the mean-time, government of the upland region was passed back and forth between the audiencia and the archbishop. Even after the president departed and a new one arrived, conditions remained chaotic be-cause of disputes between the executive and the audiencia, and authority again passed from one interim ruler to another until An-tonio de la Pedrosa y Guerrero arrived as the first viceroy in 1718. Stability was not achieved even then, for within a year a new vice-roy, Jorge Villalonga, was appointed.

Several factors prompted the creation of a viceroyalty in New Granada. Nominally attached to the viceroyalty of Peru, New Granada could not properly be controlled from so distant a point as Lima. Not only was communication too uncertain, but few ties linked the two regions together. Economically New Granada fronted on the Caribbean into which all its important rivers discharged. On the other hand, Peru depended entirely upon the Pacific for its in-tercourse with the empire and the world; goods moved by way of the troublesome Isthmus of Panamá or clandestinely through the Strait of Magellan or around the Horn. Thus commercial ties contributed in no way to a welding of the two regions. Under the circumstances, it was hardly to be expected that the viceroy in Lima would devote much of his effort to coping with New Granada's many problems. He had many of more immediate consequence in Peru, Upper Peru, and Chile, to say nothing of those in the Plata basin. In addition, the practice of making all important political appointments directly from Spain left the Peruvian viceroy with little means to exercise direct supervision over the New Granada authorities, for he did not appoint them. Thus not only the lack of geographic and economic ties, but also the failure adequately to delegate governmental authority to the viceroy weakened that official's control over such distant parts of his realm as New Granada, far removed from the capital in Lima. No doubt also the increasing problem of the defense of the ports of Cartagena and Portobelo indicated the need for direct viceregal supervision in the region that strategically constituted a cornerstone of the Spanish empire in the Indies.

The first viceroyalty in New Granada was short-lived. Villalonga was unfavorably disposed toward it from the time he took office in 1719 and repeatedly recommended its abolition. While he entered actively into his administrative tasks he nevertheless felt that the cost of maintaining a viceregal court at Santa Fé was unjustified. Within four years his judgment prevailed, and in 1723 the viceroyalty was suppressed and the region of New Granada returned to the status of a captaincy-general.

The region embraced by the first viceroyalty included the areas of the modern republics of Ecuador, Colombia, and Venezuela. Thus the Audiencia of Santo Domingo lost control over the coastal regions of Guayana, Cumaná, Caracas, and Maracaibo. The presidency of Quito was suppressed and authority over the entire area was centered in Santa Fé. The only exception was Panamá, which was left as a presidency and remained nominally dependent upon Lima. Administratively, there was much to recommend this arrangement. Santo Domingo had long since ceased to exercise effective jurisdiction over the coast of Venezuela, and the Quito region had become intimately linked militarily and commercially with Popayán, Pasto, and Cali. In fact, the Popayán area had originally been occupied from the south by Benalcázar coming north from Quito, and ties with the latter center had remained strong for many years. It is interesting to note that the administrative organization of the church foreshadowed that of the civil government. The jurisdiction of Santa Fé had been raised to the rank of archbishopric, equivalent to that of Lima, as early as 1564.

There is little to indicate that the presence of a viceroy in Santa Fé for so short a time had any marked effect on the status and development of the region. When the viceroyalty was abolished and former jurisdictions restored, the country remained poverty-stricken and underdeveloped. The captain-general of the colony, Antonio Manso Maldonado, in his report to the crown upon leaving office in 1731, pointed to the deplorable poverty that prevailed, the lack of commercial activity, and the evil economic consequences of the long-continued system of forced Indian labor in the mines. Nevertheless, New Granada and the adjacent regions of Caracas and Quito constituted far too important and strategic an area within the empire to be neglected indefinitely, and in August of 1739 the viceroyalty was re-established. Outside pressures were not wholly absent in this move, for England had just gone to war with Spain over disputes in the Indies, and attacks upon the Spanish cities of northern South America were certain to form a part of British military strategy.

As a result of the 1739 reorganization, Santa Fé de Bogotá again became the administrative center of a vast region. Included were the same territories assigned in 1719, plus the territory under the jurisdiction of the Panamá audiencia. On the other hand, neither the presidency of Quito nor that of Panamá was suppressed; each was permitted to continue functioning, subject to the viceroy at Santa Fé instead of the one at Lima. Minor adjustments in the governmental arrangements were still to be made, however. The Caracas area had become sufficiently developed to require special arrangements, and the need for strong independent military leadership there suggested the end of dependency upon Bogotá. This was effected in 1742. Likewise, judicial appeals from that region were taken to

Santo Domingo as in the past rather than to the audiencia at Santa
Fé, a procedure easily justified by the ease of ocean travel as compared with land transportation and communication. At the same
time, while the prominence of Caracas was increasing, that of
Panamá was on the decline. Termination of the galleon trade and
the Portobelo fairs and the growing ship traffic around the Horn to
the west coast of South America all cut deeply into the commercial
activity at Panamá. The isthmian region could no longer be regarded as the great pivotal point of Spanish commerce for South
America. In 1751 the presidency came to an end and the functions
of the audiencia were transferred to Santa Fé. Twenty-six years
later, in 1777, the captaincy-general of Caracas was created, embracing essentially what is today the territory of modern Venezuela. The
political jurisdictions of Spanish America were approaching a more
rational pattern.

The viceroyalty of New Granada was forced to undergo a baptism
of fire almost immediately upon its reconstitution. The British did
not fail to carry the war to the Spanish colonies, and the Portobelo-
Cartagena area was singled out for the principal attack. Admiral
Vernon captured Portobelo in 1739 with little difficulty, much to
the delight of his countrymen to whom he had boasted that the port
could be taken with a handful of ships. Vernon then made several
fruitless passes at other coastal points and retired to Jamaica to
await reinforcements.

By the spring of 1741, a large British fleet had been assembled
and Admiral Vernon attacked Cartagena in force. A slight initial
success filled the Britisher with such great confidence that he sent
word homeward announcing his 'victory.' After over a month of victorious attack he retreated in defeat to Jamaica, his troops decimated
by Spanish bullets and bayonets, and by dysentery and malnutrition. Vernon climaxed his string of 'victories' by still another defeat
at Santiago de Cuba later in the same year.

Accounts differ widely as to the number of ships and men involved in the attack on Cartagena, the British minimizing and the
Spanish tending to expand the figures. Whatever the size of the
attacking and defending forces, the outcome of the battle marked

a signal defeat for the British and gave strong indication that the revival of Spanish military power was under way. More important still, it demonstrated that at least one unit of the empire was capable of assisting in its own defense and strong enough to turn back a powerful British squadron. This was significant not only in terms of the immediate competition between Britain and Spain for control of the Western Hemisphere, but significant also for future relations between Spain and her maturing colonies.

The victory over Vernon furnished an auspicious opening for the second viceregal period in New Granada. The viceroy who participated in the direction of the defense was Sebastián de Eslava, a high officer in the Spanish army who had arrived at Cartagena the year before. During the period of his incumbency, Eslava remained in Cartagena, never venturing up to the capital at Santa Fé. He never exercised his function as president of the audiencia, but devoted the major portion of his energies to maintaining the defenses of the coastal region in anticipation of such other attacks as Spain's enemies might see fit to launch. That Eslava was considered an able viceroy and an excellent public servant is attested to by the fact that after nine years in office he was appointed viceroy of Peru, a post that he renounced in order to return to Spain. Certainly Eslava's military success helped to establish his reputation as an able viceroy, but there were other factors as well. In spite of a limited knowledge of his vast domain, he tried to deal with some of its more pressing problems. He devoted energy to improving communications and strengthening some of the more exposed frontier regions against Indian attack. When he left office the viceroyalty was firmly established as one of the major jurisdictional areas of the Spanish empire.

In the years that followed, the New Kingdom of New Granada, as the viceroyalty was called, was favored by a series of able administrators whose measures added greatly to the increasing importance of the region. The period coincided with that of the reigns of Fernando VI and Carlos III in Spain, monarchs whose careful attention to the welfare of their realms resulted in a substantial raising of the level of governmental officialdom throughout the empire. A few of the more noteworthy viceroys in New Granada were José Solís Folch de Cardona, Pedro de Messía de la Cerda, Manuel Guirior, and Manuel Antonio Flores.

Solís, who took possession of office in 1753, devoted his entire energies and his fortune to the interest of the New Kingdom. Among his notable achievements were the taking of a census and the construction of a number of important roads and public buildings. In spite of the fact that he was forced to struggle throughout his administration against jealous officials and a high degree of public apathy, he remained attached to his subjects. Particularly notable is the fact that, upon retirement in 1761, he donated his worldly possessions to charity and joined the Franciscan order, spending the remainder of his life in the country. This was a far cry from the actions of so many of his fellow officials, who, sent out from Spain like himself, considered their assignment only as an unpleasant interlude to be terminated as soon as possible by return to the peninsula.

Viceroy Messía, who followed Solís, took important steps to regularize the collection of revenues, to establish such local industries as would enable the country to produce basic military necessities such as gunpowder, and to promote agricultural development. It was during his administration that the Jesuits were expelled from the Spanish dominions. Messía carried out the expulsion order with the same calm firmness and restraint that was the general rule throughout the empire, but the event was an unhappy one for New Granada in many respects. Many historians have pointed to the great loss in the field of education. True, the Jesuits had over a dozen schools of one kind or another in the kingdom, and a large number of students were enrolled in them. On the other hand, the spirit of inquiry was notably lacking and the growing body of scientific knowledge had little or no part in the curriculum.

A greater loss stemmed from the abandonment of missionary and colonizing enterprises in the frontier region. Particularly in the plains of the Meta did the expulsion cause great damage and loss. The Jesuits, almost alone, had gone into this region of what is now eastern Colombia and southwestern Venezuela and established Indian reductions which with much effort were made to function as prosperous agricultural centers. Withdrawal of the Jesuits resulted in an almost immediate abandonment of the entire region to savage Indians and harsh nature. The productiveness of the region was thus lost to the kingdom.

In 1763, a volcanic eruption and severe earthquake in the presidency of Quito caused serious disruption in the southern part of the viceroyalty. The region, which had long been ravaged by natural disturbances at rather frequent intervals, was virtually paralyzed for several years. The town of Ambato was almost totally destroyed. Over the course of a year and a half, the tremors moved northward, eventually effecting the region around Popayán, seriously interrupting the productive mining enterprises in that part of the kingdom.

Such disturbing movements within the earth, together with those that were taking place on the surface — particularly a series of Indian uprisings — placed a serious strain on the colonial treasury. When, in 1773, Manuel Guirior succeeded Messía as viceroy, he was faced with the pressing necessity of placing the treasury in order. Guirior correctly recognized that the situation called for measures to stimulate production and commercial activity. If the country were prosperous and revenues honestly collected, the condition of the treasury could not fail to improve. Consequently, Guirior began by reducing duties on various articles and by giving preferential treatment to those native products which were most essential to the development of local industry. He then applied vigorous measures to collect the taxes of all kinds that formed the basis of the king's patrimony. When he handed over the government to Manuel Antonio Flores in 1776, the beneficial results of his actions were already to be noted.

Events soon conspired to bring discredit to the name of Flores, events for which the new viceroy was only partially responsible. It is difficult to see how he could have avoided the actions taken without having his loyalty to duty questioned. In 1779 Spain went to war against Great Britain, thus indirectly aiding Britain's North American colonies to gain their independence. By that very fact, Spain set in motion a train of events that raised the first serious sign of colonial revolt in her own dominions. In order to carry on the war

Spain undertook to augment revenues from the colonies. Viceroy Flores, in spite of considerable effort to improve the economic welfare of his dominions in the first three years of his incumbency, was regarded by the crown as not sufficiently zealous in collecting funds for the treasury. Consequently, a visitor-regent was sent from Spain to straighten out the financial situation in New Granada, and at the same time to install the new intendant system. The presence of the visitador, Juan Francisco Gutiérrez de Piñeres, also made possible a division of responsibility in the administration during the period of the war. Flores was able to assume military command of the coastal region with headquarters in Cartagena, leaving Piñeres in charge of the civil government in Santa Fé de Bogotá. It proved an unhappy arrangement.

Piñeres showed himself to be short-sighted, irresponsible, and cowardly, although properly zealous in the king's behalf. The measures he took to increase the revenues were drastic, and eventually self-defeating. One measure, while reasonable, was misunderstood. He attempted to secure the separate collection of two taxes which in the New Kingdom had become confused, the alcabala, or sales tax, and the armada de barlovento, a lesser transactions tax imposed originally to raise funds for the naval defense of the Windward Islands. The public came to believe that they were in fact being forced to pay a new tax, which was not the case. New taxes were also imposed, however. A forced contribution that amounted to a head-tax was levied. Of particular moment was the exploitation of the government monopolies: salt, tobacco, and alcoholic spirits. Prices were doubled on some of these items in the effort to increase revenues, and the production of tobacco was restricted to keep the price high and to simplify control over entry of the golden leaf into the market. The country, already overburdened with taxation, refused to accept the new measures, which were made the more unpalatable by the arrogance of the tax collectors and the well-founded belief that a very substantial portion of the king's revenues never got closer to the king than the collector's pockets. In the face of the measures adopted by Piñeres the people of the New Kingdom rose in revolt.

The first uprisings took the form of public protests and were held in northern New Granada late in 1780. Things took a more serious turn in the spring of 1781 when, on March 16, the people of Socorro became more violent, tore down the tax edicts, and formed a large mob which paraded through the streets shouting 'death to the visitor-regent.' The crowd was temporarily pacified by suspension of the new tax regulations in Socorro; but the revolt continued to spread quite spontaneously. In other towns the government monopoly ware-houses were assailed and tobacco, stamped paper, and other monop-oly items burned. Government liquor was poured out, no doubt reaching the conventional destination. In the middle of April a large assembly was convened in Socorro and a *común* or junta was constituted to conduct the struggle against the regent. The chief of the group, Juan Francisco Berbeo, became a somewhat unwilling leader in what amounted to a revolt against royal authority. The series of uprisings and skirmishes that followed is known as the Comunero Revolt, the name arising from the title assumed by the directing body.

The revolt was short-lived. The outcome resembled Admiral Vernon's 'victorious' defeat. In the military activities of the uprising, Berbeo and his capable lieutenant, José Antonio Galán, were highly successful, although the few encounters were scarcely to be classed as battles. At the height of his success in early June, Berbeo presented the audiencia at Santa Fé a series of demands, which involved pri-marily tax reforms and abolition of monopolies. Rather than see the revolutionary forces enter Santa Fé, the audiencia capitulated and its commissioners signed, although not without having first taken the precaution to swear before a notary that they were accepting under duress. In the agreement was a provision that Berbeo should become regidor of Socorro, and also a statement that American-born subjects should be favored for certain official posts over Europeans. To give sanctity to the agreement, the archbishop held High Mass in honor of the occasion. Their objectives achieved, the Comunero forces withdrew from the field.

The leaders of the uprising were naïve in the extreme to believe that success could so easily be attained. Fearing that his life might be in danger, the visitor-regent had fled from Santa Fé to Cartagena at the first indication that the revolutionary forces were planning to move on the capital. From Cartagena the viceroy, Flores, made clear that the agreement was unacceptable; and he provided a trained force of 500 men who went to the capital to protect the returning visitor-regent and to free the legitimate authorities from any further threat of armed resistance. The agreement was denounced and the revolutionary leaders captured and punished. The Comunero forces were unable to rally for a second serious uprising, and the movement was crushed.

The entire affair presented many confusing features. The uprising was scattered and almost entirely spontaneous. No strong leadership emerged capable of giving the movement definite social or political orientation. At no point was independence from Spain considered as an objective, although there were a few outside opportunists who seized upon the conflict as an opportunity to voice such a desire. Participants were primarily creoles and mestizos, although certain Indian groups in the remoter regions were led to believe that the movement was part of a general uprising to overthrow the Spanish domination and re-establish the Inca empire. Credence was lent to the latter delusion by reason of the fact that the Comunero revolt in New Granada coincided in point of time with the Tupac-Amaru insurrection in Peru. The whole series of episodes has been overemphasized by those who would see in it an important premonition of the wars of independence. Certainly the Comunero movement indicated that there was a point beyond which an arbitrary government could not go and still retain the support and obedience of its subjects. It indicated that property holdings, even among the lower creole and mestizo classes, had become sufficiently important to arouse their owners to desperate measures for their preservation. It also represented a common but often forgotten tendency in social behavior. When constituted authority is seriously questioned for whatever cause, scores will seize the opportunity to commit acts of violence and destruction with only the dimmest social or political objectives, or with none at all.

The entire region of Spanish America underwent an enormous development during the eighteenth century, but that of the northern viceroyalty was particularly impressive. This development was by no means confined to New Granada proper, but extended over into the Caracas and Cumaná sections as well. In terms of its early exploitation and settlement, the northern coast of South America east from Santa Marta and Río de la Hacha was long neglected. The immediate coastal zone was in many places swampy, hot, and unhealthful. The back country, while higher and somewhat more attractive, was peopled by Indians of a nomadic bent and generally retarded state of social and economic development. Important mineral wealth was not a feature of the area so far as the Spaniards were able to determine, and few settlers were attracted to the section. Two centuries before, in the early years of the sixteenth century, a German banking family by the name of Welser had attempted colonization in the province of Venezuela in an effort to develop trading activities, but the effort proved a failure and was abandoned. In the years that followed there was little to encourage other entrepreneurs to undertake ventures there.

It is not to be inferred that the Venezuelan region remained without settlement, for small towns existed at various points along the coast dating from the first settlement efforts. But life was hard and the Spanish government did little to ameliorate the adverse conditions of the population. Few ships were allowed to trade along the coast and products of the region did not enter importantly in the commerce of the Caribbean. Governmentally, the Venezuelan province remained under the administrative jurisdiction of the audiencia at Santo Domingo for virtually all but military purposes until well into the eighteenth century. This was indeed an indication of disinterest and neglect, for Santo Domingo itself had come to receive almost no attention from Spain. Years would pass during which no ship from the homeland troubled the calm waters of the island harbors, and contact with Venezuela was ill maintained.

At the opening of the century, permanent settlements existed at La Guaira, Caracas, Puerto Cabello, and Maracaibo. Trade with the area was based almost entirely on the exportation of cacao, of which Spain and the Netherlands were virtually the sole consumers. The Spaniards did not themselves participate in this trade, however, for practically all of the product was bought up by Dutch merchants from Curaçao who openly — though illegally — traded along the coast, carried the product to Europe, and sold it to the Spaniards at exorbitant prices.

Felipe V, as the first Bourbon monarch of Spain, determined to make a new effort to bring Venezuela within the orbit of Spanish commerce and make the region produce some benefit to the treasury in place of the annual deficit that had been recorded year after year. A privileged trading company was organized in northern Spain, known as the *Real Compañía Guipuzcoana de Caracas*, and it was given a monopoly of commercial activity along the Venezuelan coast. It began operations shortly after its creation in 1728 and functioned for over half a century, being one of the few successful governmentally sponsored trading companies in the history of the Spanish empire.

The activities of the Guipúzcoa Company were many and varied, and its highhanded methods aroused intense antagonism among the older families. Nevertheless, to its achievements the region owed a great portion of its rapid development and increasing prosperity. The illegal trading operations of the Dutch merchants were brought to a standstill, the production of cacao was expanded greatly, and new crops were introduced and successfully grown for export. Coffee, cotton, and indigo became valuable staples of the rapidly growing agricultural industry. In the llano regions of the interior cattle raising loomed as the principal activity, a few large-scale ranchers marketing thousands of head each year. By the end of the century the cattle population was estimated at around one million head, approximately one-twelfth the number in Argentina and one-sixth the number in France at the same period.

The vigorous and effective methods of the Basques from Guipúzcoa almost produced a miracle in Venezuela, and the wealth pouring back to the homeland did equally well for the owners in Spain. The company did not long limit its activities to economic enterprise, however, for its leaders became the political bosses of the colony. The company possessed its own ships which moved independently about their business, even in the face of British naval opposition that isolated other parts of the empire for years at a time. In a word, the company became the government of the region, acting with an assurance that brooked no interference from nominally superior jurisdictions, such as those at Santo Domingo or Santa Fé. Ample influence at court guaranteed the outcome of any conflict precipitated by anyone foolish enough to challenge the power of the Guipúzcoans.

There were those who did challenge the company, nevertheless. Aided by Dutch merchants from near-by Curaçao, a zambo or Indian-Negro, Andresote, first raised the standard of rebellion; but he was quickly and effectively put down. The most serious uprising took place in 1749 and was led by Francisco de León, a well-to-do creole who had the misfortune to possess a public office considered desirable by a Basque. When he was dismissed and the company's man attempted to take over the post, León resisted, first passively and then by raising a band of local landowners and marching on Caracas. Whereupon there followed a series of maneuvers not unlike those that were to take place in New Granada thirty-two years later: paper concessions by the Spanish authorities, naïve acceptance by the irresolute creoles, disillusionment, complete defeat of the rebels after the authorities had made good use of their time to clear the proper channels to the crown and bring in necessary military assistance.

The Guipúzcoans came as aliens to the Caribbean shore, and the readiness with which they made themselves masters of the economic and political life of Venezuela speaks well for their resourcefulness and enterprise. Their disregard for existing prerogatives and commercial and governmental relationships caused them to be hated and feared, and, above all, envied. Coming from Spain and bearing the approval of the Spanish crown, by their very success they widened the breach between the creoles and the European born. Many of them were absorbed into the local population, losing their peculiar identity and coming to form a part of the greatly increased population of Venezuela by the end of the century. Nevertheless, the process was one that well prepared the region for separation from the mother country. It gave it strength, vitality, development, a sense of power, and a bitter, deep-seated conflict concerning who should exercise that power.

At the opposite end of the viceroyalty, in Quito, a similar antagonism prevailed between the American-born population and the Spaniards who had come to the colony to rule or engage in business. As early as 1765, an outbreak occurred in which unruly mobs were able to dominate the situation temporarily and demand the exclusion from the city of recently arrived Europeans. Taxation and monopolies were largely to blame, the Europeans occupying favored positions that enabled them to exploit their less fortunately born brethren. The outbreak in Quito, like those elsewhere in the viceroyalty, was symptomatic of a maturing colonial society in which inequality of economic and social status based on the accident of European or American birth was beginning to wear thin the bonds of empire unity and solidarity.

XVII

The Decline of Peru

In Cuzco they draw the sword
To fight for a righteous thing:
To shake off the foreign king
And to crown their native Lord.

SONG FROM ORURO QUOTED BY SALVADOR DE MADARIAGA *

LIMA was the capital of Spanish South America. This great city, erected by the conquistadores and their successors a few miles from the shores of the vast South Sea, became the most important of all Spanish capitals in the New World. Unlike Mexico City, its North American rival, Lima was not located on the site of a more ancient capital of Indian civilization. The great Inca stronghold of Cuzco was situated at too high an elevation and was too inaccessible to serve the Spaniards as a great colonial center. Consequently, Lima presented a more European cast than most Spanish American cities. There was less of the aboriginal atmosphere and the Indian population was relatively smaller. It consisted primarily of those drawn from the uplands to perform the menial tasks of personal service or to engage in the 'degrading' manual trades.

Lacking the large numbers that the presence of indigenous population gave to Mexico City, Lima remained a comparatively small community. Its inhabitants numbered only about 30,000 at the opening of the eighteenth century, and of these a relatively large

* *The Fall of the Spanish Empire in America,* The Macmillan Company, New York, 1948, p. 303.

percentage were of European blood. As a small city, Lima was nevertheless well supplied with imposing buildings, and it presented an air
of urbanity and importance. It was laid out rectangularly, and the
streets were wide, straight, and the more important ones paved.
Houses were low and generally spacious, fronting directly on the
streets. Within the walls, open patios gave light and air to the
various rooms that surrounded them. The patios also provided plots
for the planting of flowers and vines. The beauty and cleanliness of
the city made it attractive, and the presence of the viceroys with
their courts made Lima the center of colonial social and intellectual
life. It was not improperly referred to therefore as the 'City of Kings'
for reasons quite apart from the fact the city had been founded on
'El Día de los Reyes Magos,' or Epiphany.

Lima was distinctively a government city. The other areas dependent upon its political leadership created its importance. It was
not a port, there were no mines there, it was not an agricultural
center; but as the political headquarters for all Spanish South
America, all ports, all mines, all agricultural and commercial activity
in His Majesty's continental dominions were controlled from its
administrative offices. As time wore on, this became a strained and
artificial situation. It bespoke well the lack of geographical knowledge and administrative acumen at the Spanish court of the later
Hapsburgs. The regions to be controlled were too vast, the distances separating them too great, and the physical barriers too imposing for any centralized direction from Lima to be effective. By
the end of the seventeenth century, this was well realized by many
of the imperial officials in the far-flung outposts of Chile, Paraguay,
Buenos Aires, and Santa Fé; but the distracted degenerates of the
once illustrious Hapsburg line took no heed of the issues that
threatened the very source of their wealth and power.

Lima flaunted the essence of all that was artificial in the colonial
system of the Hapsburgs. The presence of the viceregal court attracted the petty aristocracy, the hangers-on, the seekers after royal
favor. In the colonial capital they might enjoy the pomp, the
spectacles, the ostentatious but barren social life that no other
American city afforded. In Lima were also gathered the favored mer-

chants and monopolists whose principal interest was the preservation of their economic stranglehold upon South American trade. Restricted in their outlook by the fallacious commercial theories of their time, they sought to reap a rich harvest of profits by means of a restricted supply of goods marketed at exorbitant prices. The possibility of making a still larger profit by turning over a much greater volume of goods at low unit price in an expanded market was completely alien to their thinking, and so it has remained in much of Latin America to this day. All of this was artificial, for its survival depended upon the maintenance of ill-considered commercial policies in Spain and the suppression of the more healthy competition of the open market.

The narrowness of outlook that characterized Lima's social and economic life carried over into the religious attitudes and beliefs of the populace. In no other Spanish city of the New World was the use of the Inquisition carried to such excesses as in the capital of the great Peruvian viceroyalty. Trials for religious deviation were common, and frequently during the seventeenth and on into the eighteenth century large numbers suffered the punishments meted out by the Holy Office in the name of religious orthodoxy, although the number of those condemned to the pyre was small. Lima was a city of excesses and extremes, of outward piety and righteousness, beauty and finery, all of which masked the underlying crudity, corruption, and artificiality.

As might be expected in such an environment, great store was placed in purity of blood and noble lineage. Elaborate social ladders have been worked out by many historians in an attempt to show the numerous rungs by which people were classified. At the bottom were the Negro slaves, and on the uppermost rung the pure white, Spanish-born noblemen. The very existence of the many levels between top and bottom bespeaks the futility of classification. The many degrees of racial intermixture present ample evidence that all classes and types found a common meeting place, if not in the ballroom or confessional, at least upon the lowly bed.

As the headquarters of a great colonial domain, Lima exemplified the dual basis upon which the empire had been founded. The ex-

ploitative and commercial activities on the one hand were counter-
balanced by the many religious activities on the other. The city was
full of churches, and the robed representatives of the various orders
were everywhere in evidence. Religious ceremonies and processions
were daily occurrences, and they served as a major form of diversion
for the lower classes. Education was firmly in the hands of the church
at all levels, and intellectual and artistic activity was molded in a predominantly religious cast. Ecclesiastical affairs occupied a great
portion of the viceroy's time. He was almost constantly called upon
to intervene to effect a settlement of some dispute within or between
the orders, or between the latter and the secular clergy. The disputes
and wrangles which claimed this attention were in part due to the
great corruption that prevailed among the religious. Many had long
since forgotten their vows and given themselves up to a life of lustful ease in the colonial capital. In the back country and on the
frontiers, many a friar joined with the local corregidor in exploitation
of the poor Indian, and the great missionary zeal of the early fathers
became largely the forgotten stimulus of a bygone era. Truly the
Kingdom of Peru had fallen upon hard times.

Indeed, times were hard at the end of the seventeenth century.
Peru reflected, more than regions less dependent on empire commercial and military activity, the decadence of Hapsburg Spain. Few
Peruvians probably realized it, but the once great Spanish navy now
numbered little more than a dozen warships. The homeland treasury
was empty, and the demented monarch was unable to raise an army
worthy of the name. Peruvians did realize, however, that Spanish
fleets seldom anchored at Panamá with their cargoes of high-priced
merchandise for the colonies. They saw other European vessels, those
of the French, the English, and the Dutch, sail into the Pacific ports
without fear of Spanish arms. Not only did the viceroys take no steps
to drive the interlopers away, but rumor connected the mounting
wealth of more than one such royal representative with the illicit
commerce. Royal authority was at low ebb. Not even the clamor of
the Cádiz monopoly agents was effective.

If the royal treasury was depleted, that of the viceroyalty was in no
better state. The loss of revenues attendant upon the rampant con-

traband activity caused the exchequer to operate in the red. Administrative corruption also took a heavy toll, and what little resources there were quickly melted away. What boded ill for the future, however, was the fact that the great mineral wealth of the Andes, which had once made Peru the richest of Spain's overseas possessions, was slowly but surely running out. At least so it appeared, for the known veins of silver were becoming exhausted.

The impotence of the Lima government was bound to be reflected in a weakening of the bonds that held the viceroyalty together. The outlying jurisdictions of the realm, Buenos Aires, Chile, Sante Fé de Bogotá, even Charcas, were all conducting their own affairs with an ever-mounting independence. In the century that followed the death of the last Hapsburg monarch, new leadership gave rise to the rebirth of Spanish power and prestige, and in the empire things took a turn for the better. The new rulers were abler men and better administrators. The decentralization of Spanish authority in South America was continued. New viceregal jurisdictions were hewn from the once vast Peruvian realm. Lima maintained much of its old atmosphere, its extreme contrasts, its uncompromising adherence to the glories of the past. But as the great center of a continental empire, its role had been played. In the eighteenth century the scenery was changed and new actors with a different play appeared upon the stage.

The struggle over the succession to the Spanish throne did not cause much furor in Peru. Communication with Europe was too poor to permit the colonial population to follow the course of events in the war; and, for the most part, the new Bourbon ruler was accepted without serious question. No immediate change in administrative officials was made, and the elderly Count of Monclova continued as viceroy until 1705. His death left the audiencia in charge, and for two years the great viceroyalty was virtually without governmental leadership. The audiencia was unable to act. Its members could not agree among themselves, and the issue of suppressing the contraband trade presented it with a problem of considerable magnitude. The body reached no solution but instead it struggled with the merchants and with the clergy. By the time a new viceroy arrived, the audiencia had brought complete discredit upon itself. Thus were matters allowed to drift in the colonies while Felipe V struggled to make secure his new throne in Europe.

Gradually it became apparent that a change was under way. The viceroys appointed by Felipe V were more vigorous than their Hapsburg-appointed predecessors, and many of the measures undertaken by them were intended to strengthen royal authority. The Marquis of Casteldosrius, who took office in 1707, strongly supported the new monarch and worked to break the power of the contraband merchants. His attempts to create a literary circle at his Lima court and his interest in the secular theater caused him to be ridiculed by the cynical and disliked by the clergy. He was followed by others who created less of a commotion but who were equally anxious to further the interests of the new dynasty. Two were members of the clergy, a bishop of Quito and an archbishop of Lima. Both strove to benefit the church by their presence in political office, and many religious houses received special grants and favors. This was of course to be expected, for church and state were inseparably united.

During the first quarter of the century, Peru was troubled by several events of considerable importance. In terms of broad historical significance, 'importance' is hardly the word to use. The events are important because the people living in Peru so considered them and so recorded them. The mention of these happenings and the reaction to them serves to give some indication of the temper and spirit of the times. The attitude of the people had changed little since medieval times, when similar incidents caused similar reactions. Perhaps that which aroused and disturbed the people most was the theft, in 1711, of the sacred hosts from the cathedral. The loss of these was a public calamity. Not only was the act of vandalism an outrage against public morals and decency, it was an affront to Almighty God for which all, in some measure, feared the consequences. The viceroyalty might well expect the visitation of some plague or other token of divine wrath. The search was long and diligent, and finally the administration of the sacrament by an unauthorized practitioner led to the discovery of the sacred hosts buried in the ground. Thousands came to carry away bits of the soil made holy by their contact with the hosts, and a new church was immediately constructed on the site where the recovered articles had been buried.

A few years later a great scandal broke upon the city. A Chilean resident of Lima committed suicide, leaving a note that promised his soul to the Devil provided the latter would take vengeance on the Chilean's wife and the friar with whom she was sleeping. The suicide and the note were in themselves serious matters, but when within a period of five days after the Chilean's death, the bodies of his wife and the friar were found one morning in an alley, the terror that reigned among the ignorant populace may well be imagined. Months later, a serious epidemic broke out and raged throughout the central section of the viceroyalty. For over two years it continued, and the deaths exceeded the facilities for burial. No one knows how many were involved in the final toll, but the matter became so serious that Felipe V ordered an immediate end of the forced mita service in the mercury mine of Huancavelica. The epidemic brought mining operations to a virtual standstill. As might have been expected, the displeasure or wrath of God was viewed as a major factor in such calamitous events.

In 1726 Don José Armendáriz, the Marquis of Castel-Fuerte, was named viceroy of Peru. Don José was an old soldier and a rough one. Not only was he disinclined to tolerate the many disorders and the general lack of respect for Spanish authority all too evident throughout the realm, but he saw no reason why the capital city of the viceroyalty should not conform to the standards of a disciplined military establishment. Consequently the ten years that he remained in office were years of turbulence and strife. Don José set about to restore order, respect for authority, the prestige of the crown, and respect for the power and might of Spain. It was Don José who forced the issue with the Comunero revolutionists in Paraguay, who strove to gain control of the audiencia at Charcas in order to reverse its support of José Antequera, and it was he who forced through the trial, conviction, and execution of that gentleman against great opposition from the populace and most of the clergy. Only the

Jesuits demanded the death penalty for the Lima aristocrat who had dared to fight their reduction system in Paraguay, and the viceroy gratified their wish.

Don José had trouble with the clerics generally. He had little use for their petty squabblings, in which he sometimes intervened with a firm hand. He vigorously opposed the immorality that was so openly in evidence among members of the orders, and he had little patience with the religious exploiters of the Indians on the frontiers. So violently was he disliked by many of the clergymen that the ecclesiastical cabildo went so far as to direct a letter to the king after the Antequera affair, and in the letter the possibility of excommunicating the viceroy was mentioned. The monarch, however, supported his American agent.

The Marquis of Castel-Fuerte was not known for the quality of his justice, but rather for its sureness. His principal objective was the restoration of respect for authority, and he was shrewd enough to realize that vacillation and lack of decisiveness would defeat his purpose much quicker and more certainly than a few miscarriages of justice. Consequently, when the Indians rose against the mistreatment they were suffering at the hands of the corregidores, the rebellious natives were severely punished. Many were executed. He took vigorous action against the Araucanian Indians of southern Chile, who were again causing the settlers much loss of life and property. Whatever the issue, his procedure was to make a quick decision and then enforce it no matter how great the opposition and popular clamor to the contrary. The viceroy was not an arbitrary tyrant, however. His effort was directed toward enforcement of the laws of the Indies; and if for many his measures seemed oppressive, it was largely because the laws were themselves oppressive and had long gone unenforced.

The viceroy's heavy hand was felt particularly in the economic sphere. Long unenforced tax laws were made effective and the taxes collected. A strong campaign was directed against the contrabandists, and illegal traffic with foreign vessels at Pacific ports was interrupted. The chief losers at the time were the Dutch, for the English enjoyed their special right of asiento and the French were usually able to find means of dealing with their Bourbon cousins. In spite of all his efforts, however, the viceroy was unable to control the illicit traffic at the extremities of his realm. Contraband activity continued unabated at Buenos Aires and Cartagena. Even the Chilean ports could not be effectively policed. An earthquake and tidal wave that destroyed the city of Concepción in 1734 were far more effective than the viceroy's inspectors. The greatest difficulty lay in the fact that there were no Spanish traders to replace the foreign interlopers. The long ineffective flota system provided no real commercial opportunities in the colonies, and the crown was disposed to take the completely negative measure of suspending the sailing of commercial fleets until contraband had been curtailed and the merchandise of earlier fleets sold. Thus did the Lima merchants make effective their influence at Madrid.

The Marquis of Castel-Fuerte was the first really strong and forceful viceroy appointed to Lima after the Bourbons came to the Spanish throne. His efforts to restore the former prestige and glory of the viceroyalty are worthy of special note, not only because he achieved some success, but also because his struggle is illustrative of that conducted by many another Latin American leader in later years — a struggle to bring order out of chaos, self-respect out of degradation, and yet to retain a humanity and a balance through it all. Had he not had a strong king behind him, his subjects would undoubtedly have made short shrift of him and his measures. As it was, his efforts were little appreciated, and his successor, a much weaker man, soon allowed matters to drift into their former deplorable state.

The years just prior to 1740 were crowded with events portending the death of the old regime. During these years came recognition that the old commercial and administrative systems could no longer suffice, and the time-worn expedients of the Hapsburg monarchy were cast aside. In 1737 there was sent from Spain to Panamá the last of the flotas. Small though it was, when it arrived at Portobelo the merchandise that it carried could not be sold. The market was already glutted with cheaper contraband goods, and the Lima merchants were unable to get together sufficient colonial products to provide an adequate exchange. The products of the viceroyalty had already been drained off in the contraband trade. The flota system had received its final blow as far as the isthmian trade was concerned. In 1740 it was legally terminated and the system of individual registered vessels was extended to provide for handling the trade of the South American continent. The older system was revived briefly a few years later with respect to trade with New Spain, but this did not affect Peru. Without the flota system and the Portobelo fair, isthmian trade came to an end. The registered vessels reached Peru by rounding the Horn; fewer and fewer ships dropped anchor at Panamá. In 1751 the audiencia there was suppressed. Gradually the jungle reclaimed the old mule trails and the ancient fortresses decayed to ruins.

With the change of the commercial system came an important political change. In 1739 the viceroyalty of New Granada was created, combining the major provinces of Spanish South America bordering on the Caribbean sea. The vast and wealthy region, never successfully administered or controlled from Lima, was strengthened militarily and financially and given its own viceregal court at Santa Fé de Bogotá. Inexorable forces were reducing Peru to the status of a minor kingdom. Even the reduction of the royal quinto on silver, from 20 to 10 per cent, while stimulating commerce, failed to effect any great improvement in affairs at Lima. Indian warfare against the white settlers and military outposts in the trans-Andean region went unchecked, and when a major uprising occurred in 1742, the attempts to suppress it only brought financial collapse to the treasury.

In 1735 an expedition was sent out from Spain to measure a degree of longitude at the equator. The scientists spent much of their time in and around Quito where their strange instruments were viewed with suspicion. Priests in particular were inclined to exhort their followers to acts of hostility against the strangers. Two of the members of the expedition were of outstanding ability. In addition to carrying out their scientific investigations, Jorge Juan and Antonio de Ulloa took general stock of affairs in the northern part of the viceroyalty, and upon their return to Spain they rendered a secret report to the king on what they had seen. The document,

known as the *Noticias secretas*, proved to be an invaluable source of
first-hand information on the status of affairs in the colonies during
the time in question. The ignorance and superstition that prevailed
everywhere among the population could not escape the notice of
such observers. The university at Lima was a sham and a fraud, with
more faculty than students, the former being purposely made numerous in order that the election of rector might be controlled. Degrees were seldom earned. Rather, many were owned by the illiterate
who had secured them through purchase. Bigotry in religious life
still took violent form. As late as 1737 the Holy Office condemned a
woman for the practice of Judaism and she was burned at the stake.
Indications are that she, having failed to obey the Judaic law concerning adultery, was falsely denounced by her scorned lover. All
indications point to the fact that government was ineffective and
corrupt, commerce was disorganized and much of it conducted in
violation of the law, and social and intellectual life was tawdry and
artificial. The stern measures of the Marquis of Castel-Fuerte had
proved of little avail.

In 1745 another strong viceroy came to Lima. He was José Manso
de Velasco, Count of Superunda. He had been governor of Chile
for a number of years and knew the problems of the region well. By
firm measures he was able to restore the finances to some semblance
of order. He then attempted to bring heavier military pressure to
bear upon the rebellious Indians of the llanos who were still uncontrolled. No victory was achieved, however, for not only was the
task well nigh impossible, but the military forces were found to be
worse than useless. There was no discipline, no equipment, no
morale. The unpaid rabble who passed for soldiery were corrupt
beyond description and lived only to prey upon the society they
were supposed to protect. Real law and order simply did not exist.
The Count of Superunda set about to correct all this.

Unfortunately, the count had no opportunity to measure the
effect of his efforts by the results. In fact, all effort came to a standstill on October 28, 1746. On that date Peru suffered the greatest
earthquake recorded in her history. Lima was especially hard hit. A
huge tidal wave rushed in from the sea and swept away the port

city of Callao, drowning nearly all the inhabitants. The few who survived spread panic in Lima where thousands fled from the shambles in terror lest the sea reach them too. Estimates have placed the total loss of life at around 16,000, but no really accurate count was possible.

The entire western region of South America has been subject to severe earthquakes throughout the recorded history of the area. The great cordillera of the Andes is a geologically young mountain formation and earth movements are frequent and severe. Time and again mountain cities and villages have been wiped out by the tremors or the landslides which the earthquakes have caused. Furthermore, the ocean region bordering the continent has been subject to frequent upheavals of the ocean floor, and tidal waves have not been uncommon following upon the heels of these sharp earth movements. Several violent tremors were experienced during the second quarter of the eighteenth century. Lima was shaken in 1725, but damage was not severe. Then in 1734 a heavy earthquake was felt in southern Chile, and a tidal wave rushed in to destroy the city of Concepción. Other severe quakes had occurred in the previous century.

Once the Limeños had recovered from their fright, returned to the city, and searched out the bodies of their friends and relatives, and once they had been properly reminded by the priests that the calamitous events represented a visitation of divine wrath for the licentiousness of their living habits, the work of reconstruction was begun. As is often the case when a city is visited by substantial physical destruction that necessitates the rebuilding of vast portions of the metropolis, the new city that emerges is much better built and arranged than the old. So it was with Lima. In the rebuilding, more thought was given to the beautification of the parks and avenues, to the architectural quality of the civic and religious structures. The new Lima was a finer city than the old. The work of reconstruction was not accomplished in a day, however; years were involved in the slow and expensive process.

After the middle of the century it became increasingly apparent that important changes were taking place in the Spanish colonial system. These changes were to be noted in Peru as well as in the

areas of rapid growth and development, such as La Plata and New
Granada. Many of the changes were liberalizing in their effect; others
were the opposite, consisting primarily in a tightening of administrative control that rendered effective measures that had long
gathered dust in the statute books. The period was one that stirred
men's emotions, roused people from their lethargy, and awakened
an interest in the destiny of colonial states.

No area of human activity was more forcefully affected than that
of religious practice. Viceroys for years had experienced great
difficulty maintaining peace among and within the many religious
orders. The orders became so concerned with internal political
maneuvers that less and less attention was given ministry to the faithful and conversion and training of the Indian. Increasingly the orders
were looked upon with distrust. In the end, steps were taken that
greatly changed the picture of religious life in Latin America. In
Peru, reduction of the power of the orders began with the secularization of preaching in 1753. Thus the role of the secular clergy was
enlarged and strengthened. The orders continued to remain powerful, nevertheless, but the exercise of their power was viewed with
increasing dissatisfaction. Lima was blessed with more than a score
of religious houses, and the number of regular clergy stretched into
the thousands. They were present in the halls of government, in the
marketplace, in the streets, and even in the brothels. They still controlled education completely, dominated intellectual life, and were
increasingly important in the field of commerce. Thousands of acres
of the best agricultural land had come under their ownership, and
while much of it was put to useful exploitation, it was effectively
removed from the competitive market and worked under conditions
of special privilege that placed the private owner at an ever-increasing disadvantage. Enjoying the benefits of tax exemption, the religious became the chief growers, slaughterers, and distributors of
meat in Chile, and their activity in this commercial field was great
in many parts of the viceroyalty. There was scarcely any economically
profitable field of activity in which the orders did not engage.

Throughout all Latin America the most active order was the Society of Jesus. Most of the educational institutions were in Jesuit

hands, particularly those of higher learning, and this order was the most active in commerce and agriculture. The Jesuits were on unfriendly terms with the other orders as early as the execution of José Antequera in 1731. They demanded and secured the death of this popular favorite against the opposition of the other orders, the secular clergy, and the populace in general. In the years that followed, nothing healed this breach in Peru. On the contrary, it grew wider and wider as the wealth and power of the Jesuits grew. When in 1767 the order for their expulsion from the empire was received in Lima, there were many who felt no sorrow at their departure. In Peru proper, that is, in the area subject to the jurisdiction of the Lima audiencia, the Jesuits left over 5000 slaves, more than a dozen colegios in as many different places, and nearly a million pesos in liquid assets, to say nothing of the value of their real property. In Chile their departure was attended by an almost complete revolution in the commercial life of the colony.

Dissension within the religious ranks served to weaken the church. The Roman Catholic religion itself was little affected. But if one could oppose the Jesuits with the blessing of the Dominicans or the Franciscans, or all of the orders with the support of the secular clergy, it was not too heretical to oppose the political and economic influence of all the religious. Thus anti-clericalism, unthought of a century before, became an important factor in the political life of the colonies. Many anti-clericals were later to become prominent revolutionists.

Important economic changes were effected in Peru. New sources of silver were discovered in Charcas and new products and manufactures were introduced. In 1752 a government tobacco monopoly was established in Lima. It proved so lucrative that it was soon extended to Chile. A separate mint was built in Santiago, and other indications of the gradual development of the southern captaincy were evident. The granting by the king of permission for individual registered vessels to sail round the Horn greatly enhanced the economic and commercial importance of Chile. The vessels called at the Chilean ports before going on to Peru. Residents of the dependent region began at last to reap the benefits of their better geographic position. As noted, the end of the flota system spelled the doom of isthmian trade, but it gave to Chile its first real opportunity for commercial development.

In spite of the growing importance of other Pacific ports and the virtual end of the Lima trade monopoly, commerce within the viceroyalty and between the viceroyalty and other regions increased. Many factors were responsible for this. The world as a whole was experiencing a great commercial development, Spain was undergoing a national revival under the more able leadership of the Bourbons, and, while far from enjoying free commerce, Peru found that the registro system provided far better opportunities for the interchange of goods than had the old flota system and the Portobelo fairs. Peru continued to be concerned primarily with the exportation of silver, but gradually agriculture emerged as another important factor in the export trade. Alpaca wool, cotton, cacao, balsam, and medicinal herbs entered into the export column. Peru was no longer the emporium of Spanish South America, but economically the country was better off than when it had been.

There were many other signs of progress and development. Peru's most able eighteenth-century viceroy, Don Manuel Amat y Junient, was appointed to the Lima post in 1761 after having governed well for several years in Chile. During his administration a number of important measures were again undertaken to strengthen royal authority and restore the kingdom to its former position of power and prestige. The military and naval forces received much attention. To curtail corruption he issued an order preventing military men from being corregidores while active in the service. Military pay was brought up to date, soldiers were subjected to rigid discipline, and they were supplied with adequate arms. A naval expedition was sent to the Pacific islands to clear the region of the British, but none were encountered even though the Peruvian fleet sailed as far as the Marquesas islands.

The viceroy had particular designs on recovering for his jurisdiction the presidency of Quito, for the port of Guayaquil was becoming increasingly valuable. As a source of naval supplies it was of major importance. At one point an uprising in Quito against the enforcement of tax measures gave the viceroy at Lima an opportunity to send a force against the region and to occupy Guayaquil, even though he was infringing upon the territory of the viceroyalty of New Granada. The uprising was suppressed without the necessity of a march upon Quito, and the Peruvian forces finally retired from Guayaquil without effecting any change in the territorial distribution of viceregal jurisdiction.

A most important administrative improvement was made by establishing a regular customs station at Callao, the port of Lima. Immediately, the revenues derived from import duties mounted almost incredibly. In the space of ten years they were increased by more than twenty times. This was fortunate, for local administrative costs were also rising and the pressure from Spain for larger and larger payments to the homeland was insistent. The great struggles between France and England had enmeshed the Spanish monarchy by reason of the Family Compact, and the almost continuous warfare was a constant drain on the Spanish treasury.

In his fifteen years as viceroy, Don Manuel Amat y Junient effected great progress in the physical development of the Peruvian kingdom. Streets were paved, bridges were built, and Lima was made one of the cleanest cities in Latin America. Laws were enforced, order was maintained, and life was made much more secure. On the other hand, the Jesuits were expelled and the entire religious and intellectual community disturbed thereby. The Indians of the higher mountain regions were particularly affected by the departure of the black-robed fathers who had been their strongest defenders against the mercenary machinations of the corregidores and other exploiters. The viceroyalty had progressed, but it had been profoundly shaken by some of the changes.

The last years of Don Manuel's incumbency were disturbed by the hopeless struggle to maintain the integrity of the realm. The entire Plata region was on the point of being stripped from Peru and established as a separate viceroyalty as New Granada had been some years earlier. Lima merchants and officials viewed this possibility as an abomination. In Charcas, however, the possible advantages of a more rational territorial organization were foreseen, and the audiencia there was favorable to the move. When the division was finally made in 1776, Peru was left in the status of a minor kingdom. Even Charcas was taken from it and given to La Plata. Only Chile remained as a major dependent area, and it had been stripped of its trans-Andean territory, Cuyo. Nevertheless, Peru retained the responsibility for maintaining the military garrisons in Chile, on the island of Chiloé, on the island of Juan Fernández, and at Panamá and Tarma. This proved a heavy financial burden.

Thus the viceroyalty of Peru, after some progress during the middle of the century, approached the remaining years deprived of its great and extensive jurisdiction over the continent. The loss of Charcas was a particularly serious blow, for it meant the loss of an important part of the silver production. Exports that formerly moved westward to the port of Callao would now be sent eastward through Buenos Aires. Gradually the artificial commercial relationships that had made possible the maintenance of the elaborate social and governmental paraphernalia at Lima had been stripped away, leaving only the trappings.

Perhaps the true nature of the situation was not realized in Europe. Carlos III was indeed hard-pressed for funds to maintain the more important role that he was leading Spain to play in international affairs. It was natural that the empire should be called upon as often before to tighten up its revenue administration and produce larger surpluses for the crown. What indicated a failure to understand the weakened status of Peru was the continuous attempt to augment the revenues from that kingdom while other regions were not subject to nearly the same amount of pressure. The result was an explosion.

Don Manuel Guirior was viceroy when the pressure reached its climax. He had been transferred to Lima from Bogotá in 1776 and had devoted his efforts to the physical improvement of the capital. There was then suddenly appointed a superintendent-general of finance with the dual authority of visitor-general. This powerful official set about tightening revenue administration as soon as he arrived at Lima. José Antonio de Areche soon became famous, or perhaps the word infamous would be more appropriate. It is true that many taxes had gone uncollected for long periods of time, and one can feel little sympathy for the chronic evader who complains loudly when the law finally catches up with him. Complaints nevertheless arose loudest from many of the socially important and wealthy families. It seemed impossible to satisfy the visitador, however. His motto was 'when in doubt, collect.' Consequently, he collected tribute from the Negroes, he required the Indians to pay the alcabala or sales tax, even though both groups were respectively exempt from these exactions. Guirior tried to intervene by countermanding Areche's orders, and he was summarily dismissed for his pains. Areche became the master of Peru, and his one aim was the raising of revenue.

Areche failed to take into consideration the condition of his subjects. He ignored the exploitation of the Indian by the priest and corregidor that had gone on for so long. His increased pressure upon the impoverished and exploited lower classes roused them to resistance. The conflict that broke out, known as the revolt of Tupac Amaru, centered around the activities of a particular corregidor in one of the mountain valleys. A well-educated lineal descendant of the Inca kings, José Gabriel Condorcanqui, became the leader of the revolt and united the Indians in open resistance to Spanish oppression. The corregidor was murdered, Spanish authority overthrown, and an Indian army put in the field to resist any attempt on the part of the authorities at Lima to re-establish the ancient tyranny.

Condorcanqui took the Inca name of Tupac Amaru II and established control in the mountain fastnesses south of Cuzco. Accounts of the vicious struggle that followed are relatively clear as to the events, but there is little consistency in the recording of motivations. Hope of establishing a new Inca empire in the mountain fastnesses of the Andes must have seemed as absurd to the leader, Tupac Amaru, as it does to the modern chronicler. The Spaniards were quick to assign imperialistic and atheistic, or heathen, motives to any native movement that presented a challenge to their rule. A dispassionate view would probably reveal no such motives on the part of the Indians. Certain members of the clergy actively supported them and attempted to bring about a peaceful settlement on terms favorable to the Indians, thus placing in serious doubt charges that the revolt was inspired by anti-religious sentiments. In reality the activities of certain corregidores had simply gone beyond the point of Indian endurance; and once violence was invoked, fear of reprisal drove the leaders to seek safety in better organization and larger numbers. Thus full-scale warfare became inevitable.

The revolt started in November of 1780. Nearly three years passed before peace was again restored. Thousands of Indians were killed in the bloody battles that took place on the rugged mountainside and in the deep Andean valleys. Treachery on the part of Areche enabled the Spaniards to capture Tupac Amaru, and the Indian leader was publicly tortured and then drawn and quartered. The violent treatment meted out to this man as well as to other members of his family inspired the Indians to still further resistance. In the end the revolt was crushed, the leaders were executed, and the descendants of the royal Inca line were either murdered or sent as prisoners to Spain. Even the Inca Garcilaso's famous *Royal commentaries* was burned by the authorities, so bitter was the reaction against all things Indian, however worthy and time-honored. Then and then only did the Spanish authorities relax some of the oppressive measures of their colonial system in Peru. The end of forced labor and the repartimiento system was decreed. These were the evils against which the Indians had struggled at the sacrifice of their lives. Their abolition came too late to prevent a horrible slaughter, and even when it came it was little more than a paper change. Debt labor quickly replaced the slavery of the repartimiento system.

The Inca revolt served as fair warning that the vicious practices of the colonial system could not endlessly be maintained. It must be recalled, however, that this particular uprising was against the worst excesses to be found in the Spanish American dominions. Nowhere else had forced labor imposed such hardships as in the mines of Charcas and Peru. In no other region is there record of such degeneracy on the part of the corregidores and the clergy who supervised or ministered to the Indians. The departure of the Jesuits had

left the native population with few defenders, and there was little
escape from the endless exploitation to which it was subjected. As
mentioned earlier, Peru was a land of excesses and extremes, and
the revolt of Tupac Amaru was a part of the natural harvest of such
an environment.

As the Indian revolt was drawing to a close, a distinct administrative change was introduced by the establishment of the intendant
system. Royal decree made it effective in Peru in 1785 during the
viceregal reign of Teodoro de la Croix. A chief advantage was the
replacement of the former corregidores, governors, and alcaldes
mayores with new officials, sub-intendants. The introduction of new
blood could not fail to produce some improvement, for not only
did it bring about the elimination of those officials in whom still
burned the flame of rancor lighted by the recent revolt, but it would
take the new administrators some time to become as corrupt as their
predecessors.

The bitter struggle had caused the viceroyalty a great deal of expense. At the same time it disrupted the economic life of the region
by shutting down the mines and cutting the channels of communication between the interior and the coast. In spite of these losses,
conditions in Peru continued to improve gradually. Physical improvements were made in the cities, particularly in Lima. A police
lieutenant by the name of José Engaña instituted a number of innovations. He named the streets and numbered the houses, at the
same time dividing the city into barrios and cuarteles for easier identification. Street lighting was initiated and it became safer to be
about the city at night. The university was reformed with the
introduction of new courses in the exact sciences, a great advance
over the curriculum of the past. Another improvement was the
creation of a new audiencia and its location at Cuzco, for the
difficulties of carrying litigation from the former Inca capital to
Lima had worked great hardship upon the residents of the mountain
city.

The eighteenth century was for Peru a period of adjustment. The
viceroyalty did not expand and mature as did New Spain, La Plata,
and New Granada. True, great physical improvements took place

and to a certain extent commerce did expand and develop. But the important reality was the long period of readjustment to a position of lesser importance in the empire. Industrially, Peru experienced no significant changes. This is in a sense attested to by the fact that as late as 1789 the largest tax revenue was from Indian tribute, a sad commentary on the condition of the once great colonial kingdom.

Intellectually, Peru had developed. As in the other principal cities of the empire, literary societies were formed to promote the arts and sciences; and a Peruvian scholar, José Hipólito Unánue, wrote a history of the later years of the viceroyalty. In 1791 the *Mercurio peruano de historia, literatura y noticias públicas* began publication. This journal, most appropriately classed as a newspaper, was issued three times a week by the literary and scientific club, the *Sociedad Amantes del País*. One of the outstanding periodicals to come out of colonial Latin America, the *Mercurio* devoted its pages to all manner of subjects of cultural interest to an intelligent citizenry. Lima's scientific and literary awakening was of minor consequence, however, in comparison with the achievements of such leaders as José Antonio de Alzate y Ramírez and Manuel Antonio Valdés of New Spain, both of whom published useful journals over a considerable span of years, or José Celestino Mutis and Francisco José de Caldas of Bogotá, who made outstanding contributions to the knowledge of natural history and botany in the New World. Alexander von Humboldt, the famous German naturalist who traveled extensively throughout the Spanish empire in the later years of the colonial period, remarked upon the limited cultural development he encountered in the principal capitals of northern South America, including Lima, in contrast to the much greater development of Mexico. Even in South America, Lima could not boast the great advancement in the late colonial period that was to be noted in Bogotá and Buenos Aires, even though the seat of the ancient viceroyalty might still possess a strong intellectual element in its society.

In its basic social character, Peru was little affected by the great population expansion and the concomitant breakdown of some of the older class barriers that was taking place elsewhere in the Spanish dominions. Where vigor and virility characterized the life of the booming regions of New Spain and the Plata basin, Peru's social structure had become increasingly brittle and effete. At the end of the century, Peru was still rigidly conservative, blindly dogmatic, and staunchly absolutist. It was well fitted to remain the stronghold of royalist supremacy in an empire that was on the point of falling apart into republican states.

VICEROYS OF PERU, 1705–1816

1705–7	Audiencia
1707–10	Manuel Oms de Santa Pau, Marquis of Casteldosorius
1710–16	Diego Ladrón de Guevara, Bishop of Quito
1716–20	Carmine Nicholás Caracciolo, Prince of Santo Bono
1720–24	Diego Morcello Rubio de Auñón, Archbishop of Río de La Plata
1724–36	José de Armendáriz, Marquis of Castel-Fuerte
1736–45	Antonio José de Mendoza, Marquis of Villagarcia
1745–61	José Antonio Manso de Velasco, Count of Superunda
1761–76	Manuel de Amat y Juníent
1776–80	Manuel de Guirior
1780–84	Agustín de Jáurequi
1784–90	Teodoro de Croix
1790–96	Francisco Gil de Tabada y Lemos
1796–1801	Ambrosio O'Higgins
1801–6	Gabriel Avilés, Marquis of Avilés
1806–16	José Fernando Abascal

XVIII

Development of the Plata Region

La Plata colonial economic life was based on the cow, the horse, and the mule.

MADALINE W. NICHOLS *

W ITH the opening of the eighteenth century, the Plata region stood upon the threshold of a new era. This would scarcely have been apparent to the casual visitor, however. The previous century had been one of continuous frustration for the inhabitants of the region, and decline or general stagnation had characterized the colonial life of the Plata area. Harassed by hostile Indian raids, encroached upon by the paulistas from Brazil, and demoralized by subservience to Peruvian trade monopolists on one hand and by continuous contraband trade on the other, no section of the vast region made much progress socially or economically. Buenos Aires was still a miserable little settlement of a few thousand sickly people and filthy mud huts along a marshy river front. Although a provincial capital, there was no semblance of the wealth and grandeur, the culture and sophistication, the pomp and circumstance that characterized older colonial centers such as Lima and Mexico City and even Bogotá. Instead life was crude and rough as befitted a frontier community. Even political importance was lacking. The governor was subordinate to the viceroy in Lima, as were his equals in Asunción and Tucumán, and the audiencia with jurisdiction over

* The Gaucho, Duke University Press, Durham, 1942, p. 26.

the region was a thousand miles away in Charcas. Even the strategic importance of the city, located as it was at the mouth of one of the great river systems of the world, was counteracted by the presence of Colônia, the Portuguese outpost and center of contraband trade on the opposite bank.

Several factors were at work, nevertheless, to alter the miserable picture of Spanish settlement in the Plata area. Some of these factors were local, such as the rapid growth in cattle herds on the Argentine pampas and the gradual extension of farming and related animal industries out onto the rich plains. Other factors presented themselves from far afield. The reawakening of imperial life brought about a general surge of colonial enterprise and resulted in the expansion of the colonial holdings into the vacuum areas still to be found at the northern and southern extremities of the great Spanish system in America. The increased tempo of colonial rivalry between Spain and Portugal, France, and England stimulated the Spanish monarchs to plug the obvious gaps in their colonial defense, and one of the greatest gaps was the relatively weak hold maintained in the Plata basin. Finally, the general movement for greater economic freedom that was beginning to permeate the thinking of the leading European economists, and the constant warfare that made greater economic freedom essential to the welfare of the colonies began to bear fruit in the loosening of the binding restrictions on colonial trade. All of these factors soon combined to work a transformation in the Plata region, and these changes that came about enabled the area, over a period of little more than a century, to become one of the strongest and most important of Spanish possessions on the American continent.

One of the gravest problems confronting the Spanish settlers in the Plata region was that of controlling the Indians. From the beginning of the conquest the Indians there proved particularly hostile. Unlike the sedentary Incas and Aztecs, who were quickly brought under Spanish domination, the various tribal groups encountered on the vast plains of the pampas, in the Chaco, and along the various tributaries of the Plata river were semi-nomadic, prone to attack and retreat into the wilderness in much the same manner as those Indians encountered in the western part of North America by the English settlers moving toward the Pacific. The system of encomiendas, successful in Mexico and Peru, although attempted in the Plata region was never particularly successful there. The Jesuit reductions among the Guaraní tribes of Paraguay produced a remarkable pacification, and the Spaniards were even able to arm these people and make use of their military abilities against their mutual enemy, the Portuguese. No such happy solution attended the efforts of the Spaniards to deal with the more nomadic tribes of the Chaco, pampas, and the Andean foothills. Instead, almost constant warfare was the rule. Spanish settlers living out on the land in the country around Tucumán, Jujuy, Catamarca, and even Córdoba found life and property rendered most insecure by reason of the frequent Indian depredations. Communication between Buenos Aires and these inland population and commercial centers was also seriously affected, rendering even more unpalatable the artificial trade routes that the Spanish monarchy attempted to maintain between the 'closed' seaport and Peru. During the first half of the eighteenth century rapid strides were made to end this difficulty. In 1710–11 and again between 1730 and 1742 rather extensive campaigns were conducted by the inhabitants of the western cities against the Chaco tribes. These campaigns, extended and fraught with hardship, placed a heavy burden upon the manpower of the country, so much so, in fact, that eventually La Rioja and Catamarca openly refused to send more militia to fight on the Chaco frontier. By the middle of the century, however, the Indian danger in the north and northwest was largely overcome. This was of considerable importance, for it paved the way for a more rapid economic development and speeded the gradual reorientation of this region away from Peru and toward the more natural relationship with Buenos Aires and other river or coastal centers on the Atlantic.

That the ties between the coastal and Andean foothill cities were becoming stronger was evidenced by changes emerging in the social pattern. Many new immigrants from Spain found their way to Tucumán, Córdoba, Catamarca, and other population centers in western Argentina. These newcomers, primarily from the artisan classes of Spain, entered by way of Buenos Aires. Chroniclers of life in the Andean country decried the changes that were brought about by the influx of these people, noting that the older families, the descendants of the conquistadores, were being swallowed up in the wave of new population. The number of encomenderos diminished sharply, and of those that remained few possessed more than a handful of Indians entrusted to their care. Immigrants, however, rather than pursuing the trades of their homeland, sought quick riches in commerce or on the land, and the simple trades remained the province of the Indian, the mestizo, or the Negro. Spaniards, from whatever walk of life in Europe, upon arriving in America insisted upon a certain superiority as to trade or profession, disdaining the manual activities that would prevent them from claiming the status of gentlemen. This was true even in this remote region where the shortage of skilled tradesmen was acute and where the breakdown of the encomienda system and Indian service made it increasingly difficult to surmount the first rungs of the social scale.

On the other hand, the Indian was actually being replaced. Increasingly, the European population was coming to depend upon the Negro slave for menial service. The number of Negroes and mulattoes in the Andean foothills had increased steadily during the late seventeenth and early eighteenth centuries. An estimate made in the *gobernación* of Tucumán in 1778 places the number of people of Negro blood at more than 44,000, larger than the number of Spaniards, and greater even than the number of Indians. About a fourth of the Negro population lived in slavery. This is of course a measure of the extent to which the importance of the Indian was declining. It also indicates how ineffective were the attempts of the Spanish government to keep closed the river ports of the Plata to foreign commerce. Negro slaves were brought in, illegally in many cases, in large numbers and found their way to the inland cities of the Argentine.

While the lines of communication to the interior were being strengthened and the Indians driven back to the plains and forests of the Chaco, the population centers along the Plata were engaged with difficulties of their own. The establishment of the Portuguese outpost of Colônia do Sacramento opposite Buenos Aires in 1680 posed many problems for the Spanish crown and added many complications to the lives of the porteños. For those interested in the contraband trade, the presence of the Portuguese outpost was a blessing. No longer was it necessary to meet contraband boats out at sea or in the estuary; instead, goods could be unloaded at Colônia and transferred across the river at leisure. On the other hand, the presence of the Portuguese created a political and military threat to the Spanish colonies. While the Hapsburg kings in Spain had long neglected the entire Plata region, forcing it into a ridiculous economic dependence upon the rich Peruvian merchants, there was little to indicate that the Portuguese monarchs were so obtuse. On the contrary, Portuguese actions, backed by the benign machinations of the English, gave definite indication that Portugal would have considered the entire Plata region a most appropriate addition to the already vast territory of Brazil.

Peaceful relations between Portugal and Spain having broken down upon the accession of the Bourbon, Felipe V, to the Spanish throne, war was declared by Spain, and in 1704 an expedition was organized under the leadership of the new governor of Buenos Aires, Alonso Juan de Valdés e Inclán, for the purpose of taking Colônia for the second time. As had been the case in the time of previous military projects in the region, Guaraní Indians from the Jesuit mission reductions were called upon to supply a sizable body of troops. After a siege of several months, the Portuguese colony fell to the Spanish forces in the spring of 1705. The Portuguese fortifications were promptly razed. Nevertheless, by the Treaty of Utrecht ten years later, the colony was restored to the Portuguese, much to the disgust of the governor and military leaders in Buenos Aires. These men found it difficult to understand why achievements of the colonial military forces should for a second time be nullified by the ineffectiveness of Spanish diplomacy in Europe. Nevertheless, in order to control the Portuguese advances in the immediate vicinity of Colônia, the governor of Buenos Aires, Bruno de Zavala, was ordered to fortify and settle colonists at the site of Montevideo and Maldonado on the same side of the river as Colônia. This order was issued in 1716, but it was not until 1724 that an expedition was actually sent to accomplish the project, and in the meantime the Portuguese had already extended their activities to Montevideo. They retired in the face of the Spanish advance, however; and the Buenos Aires government was able to establish itself permanently on the other side of the river.

Such a situation as then existed could not, under the circumstances, resolve itself peacefully. Hostilities were resumed in 1735 when a new attempt was made to take over the Colônia outpost, but this time without success, although the city was under siege for nearly two years. Again, events in Europe were the deciding factors, and the conflict was brought to a conclusion by an agreement signed in Paris in 1737 which left Portugal in possession of the controversial locality. A complete reversal took place, however, when a new treaty between Spain and Portugal signed in 1750 transferred to Spain the much contested city of Colônia in exchange for territory occupied by seven Indian reductions on the Uruguay river. The ramifications of this agreement were much broader than the mere contest for a minor colonial outpost and the desire of the Spanish government to suppress contraband which the maintenance of that outpost had aided and abetted. It brought into focus the series of events that had been transpiring in the up-river country for the previous thirty years and which had caused no small concern to the Buenos Aires governors, the viceroy in Peru, and the Spanish court itself.

During the late sixteenth and early seventeenth century the importance of Asunción as a center of Spanish settlement in the Plata region had declined sharply. This decline was due in part to the fact that shortly after 1580 a number of new settlements were established, such as Corrientes, and these new towns were for the most part founded by people going out from Asunción, thus draining leadership from the older settlement. Buenos Aires possessed a much more favorable location strategically and economically, and as time went on, newcomers from Europe, including

governors who had jurisdiction over Asunción, established themselves in the growing city at the mouth of the river and saw little
to attract them in the more inaccessible region of Paraguay. The
inland river town might still have maintained commercial importance had free commerce prevailed in the Plata region; but
the closing of the ports to ocean commerce and the enforcement,
ineffective as it was, of the Peruvian trade monopoly sounded the
death knell of Paraguayan development.

When the Jesuit mission reductions were established and the
Guaraní Indians were concentrated in the various reduction settlements under the tutelage of the Jesuit fathers, a further blow was
struck at the Paraguayan settlers. The principal source of cheap
Indian labor was virtually monopolized. There arose a bitter enmity
between the white settlers and the Jesuits who had charge of the
reductions and who exercised great care to prevent the Indians
from being drawn away from the communal religious life. In spite
of numerous representations to the viceroy in Lima and to the
crown in opposition to the reduction system and to the complete
closing of the reduction areas to white settlement, the governmental
authorities in the peninsula and in America continued to support
the religious system.

Deprived of their labor supply and excluded from some of the
best land in the region, the residents of Asunción had little love
for the Jesuits. The attempted enforcement of the ban on direct
commerce with the Plata region, and the incipient depopulation
of the Paraguayan settlements to create other communities and
to engage in military campaigns against the Indians and the
Portuguese, seemed to prove that the Spanish government had little
interest in the welfare of the Asunción settlers. Indeed, realization
of royal preference for their religious competitors seemed inescapable. Thus neglected, the residents of Asunción became increasingly embittered. In 1721 events occurred which soon produced an
open challenge to constituted authority.

The governor at the time of the uprising was Diego Reyes. He
was generally unpopular and was unable to get along with the
Asunción cabildo. Apprised of the difficulties that the governor was

encountering, the audiencia at Charcas sent José Antequera as visitador to survey the situation. The visitador ordered Diego Reyes seized and assumed the governorship in his place, a move supported by the cabildo but regarded by the viceroy in Peru as a usurpation of authority. The viceroy supported Diego Reyes, but in view of the complexity of the situation he sent still a third person as the new governor. The cabildo, now formed as a cabildo abierto at the call of Antequera, determined to oppose the new governor. The difficulty was eventually resolved by the intervention of Bruno de Zavala, governor of Bueno Aires, who brought troops to pacify the region. Antequera was later executed in Lima and the authority of the Peruvian viceroy upheld. This first intervention took place in 1725, but it did not end the difficulty.

Basically, the unrest in Paraguay was deep-rooted. It stemmed from dissatisfaction with the policies of the Spanish crown, from the economic restrictions that left the residents of Asunción at the mercy of distant trade monopolists and the near-by religious authorities. The unhappy condition was aggravated by the absence of clear-cut administrative responsibility, a situation that permitted two distant governmental authorities to pursue opposite and contradictory courses in an attempt to bring about a settlement of the disagreements. Furthermore, the limits of cabildo power were not clearly defined.

Within a short time the issue was revived with the arrival in Asunción of a former friend of Antequera, Fernando Mompó, who proceeded to espouse the cause of local autonomy. Viewing the community as a self-contained and self-regulating political unit, he talked of the *común* as a local governing body with authority derived from the people it represented, authority to determine the destiny of the community. Thus the name of *comuneros* was applied to Mompó's followers. Under his leadership, the people of Asunción opposed the authority of the new governor sent from Lima, asserting that he was favorable to the Jesuits. Open strife followed with considerable rioting, and again Bruno de Zavala, now relieved of his post of governor in Buenos Aires, was sent to restore order.

It is clear that the general idea of asserting local authority against unpopular appointed leaders was attractive to the colonists. In 1762 similar demonstrations of community rebellion took place in Corrientes where a lieutenant-governor was imprisoned by the populace when he attempted to carry out conscription orders to raise troops for campaigns in other sections of the region. Again, the question of secular versus Jesuit authority was raised, indicating that the matter of conscription was only one issue that divided the constituted authority and the leaders of the community.

The comunero movement and related disturbances in the Plata region were of considerable significance in that they pointed up distinct weaknesses in the Spanish imperial system, and they became part of the complex of changing conditions that eventually caused remedial action to be taken in Madrid. They brought more clearly into the open the religious-secular conflict centering around the Jesuit activities in America than any previous series of events had done. They also called attention to the unfortunate consequences of the economic policies that had so long favored the powerful merchant pressure groups in both the older colonial centers and in Spain. Finally, they brought into better perspective the anachronistic administrative system that permitted so vast a region as Spanish South America to be administered from the single governmental center of Lima. That these disturbances may be considered as forerunners of the independence movement is far less certain. They did indicate that when neglected long enough or pressed hard enough any people is apt to take matters into its own hands. More significant perhaps than the possible implications of independence from Spain is the relatively clear indication of dissatisfaction with a governmental system that by reason of preoccupation elsewhere was inclined to ignore the problems of the remoter frontier outposts of civilization. This, indeed, may be considered of importance when viewed in the light of the later refusal of Asunción to throw in its lot with Buenos Aires in the struggle for Argentine independence.

In the early months of 1750, a new and unexpected problem presented itself with respect to the future of the Plata region. As al-

ready indicated, Spain, by a new treaty with Portugal, secured
the cession of the city of Colônia do Sacramento in exchange for
territory occupied by seven mission reductions maintained by the
Jesuits on the upper Uruguay river. This treaty would have the effect
of pushing the Portuguese back northward, but would have permitted them to spread out to the west in territory long under the
control of Spain. A special commission was to make a survey and
determine the boundary between the possessions of the two colonial
powers. The treaty, merely another phase of the long maneuvers
of European international politics, was not lightly received in America. It was made in almost total ignorance of conditions in the area
affected, conditions which made compliance virtually impossible.
All of the Guaraní Indians living in the reductions were to abandon
their homes, their lands, and their towns and move out of the territory. The Indians, estimated to have numbered around 30,000,
had lived a sedentary life of relative security in the reductions for
several generations, and to thrust them suddenly into the wilderness to begin anew to accumulate the trappings of civilization
would have submitted them to inestimable hardship. Naturally the
Indians resisted, and with more reason than the inconvenience and
hardship which the move would have caused them. Few native
peoples in the annals of the Spanish empire had demonstrated
greater loyalty to the Spanish monarch or a greater willingness to
serve the interests of the king. Time and time again the governor
at Buenos Aires had called upon the Indian villages for soldiers to
assist in the campaigns against the Portuguese at Colônia and
against hostile Indian tribes that were threatening the frontiers,
and always large numbers had been sent and had acquitted themselves well in battle. The treatment to which they were now subjected could hardly be considered fair recompense for such loyalty
and service, particularly when they understood that their lands
and homes were to be turned over to those they had been taught to
consider as mortal enemies, the Portuguese.

Naturally the Jesuit fathers could hardly be expected to view
with equanimity such a turn of events. Clearly they expressed their
opposition to compliance with the treaty, sending remonstrances

to the important colonial officials including the viceroy in Peru and the audiencias at Charcas and Lima. Certainly they communicated their feelings to the Indians; but the many charges that they incited the Indians to armed resistance have never been substantiated, although later events indicated that the Spanish monarchy accepted the authenticity of such charges.

In order to carry out the agreement of 1750, instructions were issued that the Indians should be moved to other localities, far less favorably situated. The Jesuit leaders pleaded for time and counseled restraint and caution; the Guaranís refused to move. By 1754 it was seen that a forceful eviction would be necessary, and the Portuguese and Spanish conferred to organize a joint military expedition into the reduction country. The governor of Buenos Aires, Andonaegui, led one body of troops and Gomes Freyre headed the Portuguese forces. The difficulties encountered by the troops were substantial, and at first little progress was made. Lack of supplies and unfavorable weather caused the armies to bog down long before any important encounters with the Indians took place. No doubt the Spaniards missed their hardy Guaraní contingents. The failure to achieve immediate success gave rise to a series of wild rumors circulated in Europe to the effect that a great Jesuit-led Indian army had been organized which was capable of defeating the combined forces of the Portuguese and Spanish. In the rumors, an Indian king, Nicolás I, was even identified. Nicolás Nanguiru, the reported 'King of Paraguay,' was in reality an aged and somewhat enfeebled old man who had long been corregidor of the town of Concepción, and who, from all reliable reports, in his impoverished state never so much as dreamed of royal status for his humble person.

Finally, early in 1756, the principal skirmish of the war took place and the poorly equipped and ill-led Indian forces were hopelessly defeated. Shortly thereafter, all of the reduction towns were occupied and the Indians submitted to the Spanish authority. This was the War of the Seven Reductions in which, as one historian, Francisco Bauzá, put it, 'the Spaniards fought bravely to promote the interests of the Portuguese, facing hardships and dangers in order to carry out a boundary treaty that dismembered their territory and weakened their military and political power in America.'

Military conquest of the Guaraní reductions, unfortunate as it was from every conceivable standpoint, did not result in fulfillment of the treaty obligations. By the time resistance to the forced migration had been quelled, neither the Spanish government nor the Portuguese cared to see the treaty terms carried out. The Portuguese decided that Colônia, which they had never evacuated, was of more value than the Indian lands; and the Spaniards were not inclined to force the issue, being better apprised of the difficulties involved. Furthermore, the Spanish position in Europe had improved to an extent that permitted the use of greater firmness in dealing with Portugal. The issue languished for several years, and in 1761 a new agreement restored the rights of the respective powers to their former status.

The Guaraní affair was not without its further implications. At the time, the role of the Jesuits was far from clear. The charges against them, however exaggerated, were coupled with the long complaints and grievances of the secular and lay interests in Asunción. All seemed to be part of a pattern to be fitted together like a jig-saw puzzle with complaints against the Jesuits in other parts of America and Europe, where the wealth, the commercial dominance, and the intense activity of the religious order had aroused a great wave of antagonism. The new Spanish monarch, Carlos III, was further predisposed against the order by reason of its ultramontane views concerning the authority of the state over the church and because of his having embraced many of the religious ideas of the French 'enlightenment.' The order of expulsion, issued in 1767, might have come in any case, for France and Portugal had already taken such a step; but the recent events in Paraguay and the way in which they were interpreted to him certainly confirmed in the mind of the monarch his fears of the 'state within a state' and speeded the fatal order on its way.

As in other parts of the Spanish empire, the removal of the Jesuits was carried on in Río de la Plata with firmness and resolution, and before the year was out virtually all of the more than three hundred Jesuits in the region had been rounded up and dispatched by ship for Europe. The last to be removed were those Jesuits in charge of the Guaraní Indian reductions, for it was feared that the Indians might be stimulated to open hostility and resistance. Rather elaborate steps were taken to prevent such an eventuality, but this proved unnecessary; and by the end of 1768, the missionaries from the reductions were on their way. It is to be noted that Buenos Aires was used as a major concentration center for the priests and missionaries prior to their embarkation. Jesuits from Cuyo and Charcas were removed from this port as well as those whose work had been carried on in the more immediate vicinity. Furthermore, the orders from Spain for the expulsion had first been transmitted by Count Aranda to Bucareli, the governor of Buenos Aires, for retransmittal to the viceroy in Peru. This would seem a clear indication of the changing orientation of Spain toward the geographical reality of South America, and the mode of procedure foreshadowed by only nine years the administrative adjustment that gave recogniton to the growing unity and administrative importance of the Plata region.

Naturally, the exclusion of the Jesuits meant the end of the entire Indian reduction system in Paraguay. There was no one to carry it on, nor would any newcomers have been welcomed by the white settlers of Asunción. It seems particularly significant that for generation after generation the Jesuit fathers had worked to teach the Guaraní population the skills and trades of domestic life in organized settlements, but within a few years after the religious had departed the villages were abandoned, the fields were uncultivated and unplanted, and little remained to indicate that man had toiled there so long. This indeed, was the history of Indian reductions throughout Latin America, whether in Paraguay, Lower California, or interior Brazil. Indians were viewed as children to be taught the rudiments of the Christian religion and a few necessary agricultural and industrial skills, but all directive and administrative responsibilities, civil and spiritual, remained the exclusive domain of the missionaries themselves. Tribal chieftains there were, but their authority and responsibility were nominal. As a consequence of such arrangements, native leadership did not develop, even after a great many generations, to a point sufficient to enable the Indians to carry on their own organized village activities after the black-robed fathers had departed. Gradually they returned to the semi-nomadic life of their ancestors or found their way into white settlements to work as menial servants.

As in other parts of the empire, removal of the Jesuits from the Plata area disrupted educational activities. Within a few years, however, schools that had been conducted by the Jesuits were being operated by other orders. Toward the end of the century greater liberality in curricular offerings and more attention to the newly developing sciences were introduced.

One of the most important changes made in empire administration during the later years of the eighteenth century was the redistribution of viceregal jurisdictions. In terms of future effect on the areas concerned, the change was far more important than the institution of the intendant system, which, in the last analysis, did little more than alter in a not too major way certain governmental procedures. The creation of the viceroyalty of La Plata was one of the principal steps in jurisdictional reform, for it brought together under a central administration located within the region the various segments of a vast and rapidly developing civilization.

Several factors were responsible for the creation of the Plata viceroyalty. Probably the most important was the increasing need for a more effective defense of the region. Certainly the Portuguese encroachments in the Banda Oriental were an influence, as was the ambition of certain Spanish leaders to extend the area of Spanish control northeastward into Rio Grande do Sul. But the Plata residents had shown themselves perfectly capable of holding their own in competition with the Portuguese by repeatedly dislodging their Iberian rivals from Colônia by means of military expeditions from Buenos Aires. Of far greater consequence was the changing balance of colonial power in Europe. French and British colonial activity was at its height, and recent activities by both powers in the Islas Malvinas off the coast of Patagonia had revealed the interest of these rivals in the Plata region. France, to which power Spain had recently allied herself in the Family Compact, had suffered a serious reversal at the hands of the English with the loss of Canada and parts of India in the war terminating in 1763. As a result of that struggle, England had emerged as the dominant sea power of the world, and Spain faced the gloomy prospect of seeing the British fleet interpose itself between her Indies possessions and the homeland. Thus it became essential that the various American colonies be prepared to defend themselves and stand on their own feet, if necessary, through prolonged periods of severed communications with the mother country. Of all the important Spanish possessions, those in the Plata region were the most vulnerable, for the Portuguese were already established there to provide bases for the enemy, and the key river ports were open to attack by sea. Thus, the necessity of strengthening the military forces was evident, and creation of sufficiently powerful governmental authority to cope with possible invasion was clearly imperative.

Another factor of great importance was the demonstrated difficulty of governing so vast and important a region from far distant Lima, the seat of the Peruvian viceroyalty. The uprisings in Asunción earlier in the century, the difficulty with the Guaraní Indians over the execution of the 1750 treaty with Portugal, the continual problem of Indian raids in the inland regions, and finally the ever-present problem of lawless contraband trade, all pointed to the need for a higher degree of administrative centralization. In addition, more than negative control was involved. Positive direction by high authority was needed to bring about a greater development of the area, to establish a firm hold in Patagonia, to stimulate commerce and industry, and to make the region more genuinely productive of benefits for the homeland.

Finally, the logic of the situation impelled the creation of the new viceroyalty. Here was a great geographic entity, united by its system of rivers and its great plains, and physically separated from the Pacific possessions of the Spanish crown by the high mountain chain of the Andes. In spite of all efforts to the contrary, the economic life of the region had come to focus more and more on the port city of Buenos Aires. The wine and other products of Tucumán, Catamarca, Córdoba, and Mendoza moved eastward rather than north and west. Even the silver of Charcas found its way in large quantities into the Plata commerce, and, quite naturally, turned up eventually in the commerce of Brazil. In order to take advantage of the growing importance of the region, in fact to prevent the Plata colonies from drifting gradually into a state of economic and possibly political autonomy, it was essential that the Spanish monarch take steps to make the administrative situation conform to the reality of the times.

The installation of the new viceroyalty was accomplished with considerable ostentation. A large military and naval expedition was organized at Cádiz and set sail November 13, 1776. Accompanying the expedition was Pedro de Cevallos, the new viceroy, clothed with the broadest of powers and exempted from a number of the usual restrictions and obligations that usually went with royal appointments. He was relieved from payment of the media anata, a tax imposed upon the first year's income of new appointees, and no residencia was to be held at the termination of his assignment.

The appointment of Cevallos was fortunate. He had already demonstrated his ability as a colonial administrator while governor of Buenos Aires from 1756 to 1766, during which incumbency he had led another militarily successful but politically futile expedition against Colônia do Sacramento. His first important task was to repeat the capture of that Portuguese outpost. This he accomplished with little difficulty after a brief siege in the spring of 1777, and this time the result was final. The Portuguese were swept from the Banda Oriental, the city of Colônia demolished, and the defenders removed to Brazil. The civil population was transported and resettled in the inland cities of the new viceroyalty, primarily in the vicinity of Tucumán.

The new viceroy moved as a man confident of the support of the power that had appointed him, and he was not disillusioned. To him had been given jurisdiction over all of the vast Plata region, including the former Chilean province of Cuyo and the territory included in the audiencial district of Charcas. To secure the benefits of the inclusion of the Potosí mines, he ordered the restriction of silver exportation from that city to Lima, thus legally channeling that important commerce through Buenos Aires. He removed the many restrictions on trade with his new capital, opening the port to licensed ships, an act subsequently verified by royal order. He even turned his attention to various socio-economic problems, at-

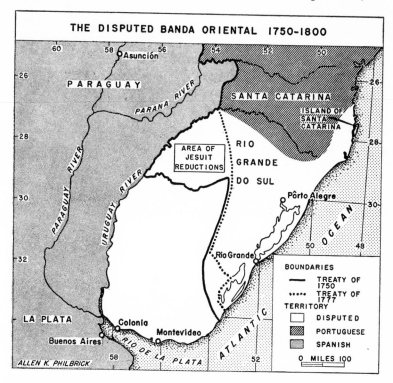

THE DISPUTED BANDA ORIENTAL 1750-1800

tempting to regulate the working conditions and wages of agricultural laborers in the field. Nothing that he did, however, including the elimination of the Portuguese from the Banda Oriental, so rapidly advanced the welfare of the new viceroyalty as the opening of the port to commerce.

As early as 1720 registry ships had been permitted an occasional visit to Buenos Aires, but the legitimate commerce had never been large. After 1777 a considerable change took place, for the new viceroy's orders permitted the entry of registered vessels on the same basis as they were admitted to other 'open' ports in the Indies. In the years that followed still more liberal concessions were made in favor of neutral vessels of foreign powers, this being necessary because of the long blockades during the almost continuous warfare in the last quarter of the century. To control the commerce and to make certain that the royal revenues were collected, a customs-house was established in Buenos Aires, and its receipts soon surpassed those collected in Lima. To stimulate further the commercial activities within the empire and to eliminate some of the unfortunate consequences of the former restrictive policies, the general declaration of free commerce of 1778 eliminated or reduced sharply many of the taxes and special assessments that had burdened Spanish commercial intercourse and driven profitable business into illegal channels for so many years. The Plata viceroyalty profited greatly by all these liberalizing measures.

Nevertheless, there are few changes that do not bring misfortunes to some or create new and unforeseen problems. During the long period of restricted commerce and contraband activity, the high prices that resulted and the very restriction itself created a certain economic balance in the Plata region. A fairly high degree of internal diversification prevailed in the production of agricultural goods. Cuyo was a wine center, and great mule trains carrying wine casks moved more or less regularly at their slow pace across the pampas to Buenos Aires and along the foothills to the other western cities. Grain was produced in Tucumán and distributed internally in the Plata region. For a time cotton production had loomed as a potential industry, but the absence of a sufficient labor force caused this activity to fade to insignificance, to be replaced by wool growing. Most important, however, was the hide industry. The exportation of hides had been a principal feature of the *asiento* trade with the English and a major factor in most of the clandestine commerce with the Portuguese and other foreign traders. Each of these industries or agricultural activities was affected by the opening of the port of Buenos Aires. Cuyo wine could no longer compete with that imported from Europe. It was found to be cheaper to bring wheat in from the United States than to raise it domestically. And the rapid increase in cattle slaughter to satisfy the foreign demand for hides soon threatened to depopulate the cattle herds of the pampas.

The problem of maintaining the cattle herds had been faced earlier, and the feeble measures of various governors of Buenos Aires had been generally unavailing. After 1776 the seriousness of the problem became increasingly evident. The hide industry had been and still was exceedingly wasteful. Cattle and horses were slaughtered where they were found by the roving gauchos, their hides removed, a small chunk of meat cut from the carcass for the meal of the hide-gatherer if he were hungry, and the rest was left for wolves and vultures. In fact, the wolves lived so well and multiplied so rapidly that they too became a menace, killing off the young cattle while the gauchos took care of the mature animals. Perhaps at no time in modern history has a more wanton destruction of useful animal life taken place on such a scale, comparable only to the destruction of the bison herds on the plains of North America a century later.

Various measures were attempted to restrict the wasteful slaughter, but in spite of all such actions, hide exportation increased tenfold in the twenty years following 1776. It has been estimated that the average number of animals slaughtered for their hides during this period was somewhat over one million annually. A note of caution should be injected, nevertheless. The cattle industry of the Plata viceroyalty was, for its time, a most important activity; but the area devoted to the raising of cattle was relatively small. The herds roamed wild, and no fences restricted their movements. The animals were public domain, for no system of ownership as yet prevailed. In other words, it was not a systematic industry as is the case today. Large portions of the Argentine plains which today produce thousands of well-bred cattle were beyond the frontiers of European settlement, and hostile Indians were to be encountered by those who ventured too far afield in pursuit of the lucrative cowhide. As a matter of fact, Indian raids in the vicinity of Buenos Aires were known as late as the 1780's.

Shortly after 1780, a major change was introduced in the cattle industry with the introduction of meat salting. By this process it was possible to preserve meat for overseas shipment, thus opening an entirely new export market. By the same token it was possible to avoid at least a part of the enormous waste of the hide industry. Within a short time cargoes of salted meat were on their way to Habana and Spain, the former furnishing the largest market for the new product. In the long run, this proved beneficial from the standpoint of preserving the Plata livestock, for cattle came to have a greater commercial value and the establishment of individual ownership of herds was fostered. With such ownership came eventual control over production and slaughtering of the animals.

In spite of the benefits that were derived from the opening of the Plata port and the rapid extension of commerce in the region, the trade balance of the new viceroyalty gradually shifted from positive to negative. That is, whereas in the period prior to these important changes the value of exports had surpassed that of imports, now the value of imports came to exceed that of exports. Several developments account for this. First, the establishment of the new viceroyalty made necessary a considerable number of physical improvements if the viceregal capital were to compare with other such capitals in the empire. In turn, the standards of convenience and luxury were raised. Such improvements necessarily involved the importation of new and expensive articles. Second, articles and commodities formerly produced domestically under the protection of the trade restrictions began to be imported due to the better quality and lower prices that characterized the imported articles. Finally, the availability of larger amounts of European-made goods played an important role in the shifting trade balance. The problem did not become serious during the period of the viceroyalty, but in the years immediately following independence the new country was forced into the position of a debtor nation for several decades.

Prior to the establishment of the viceroyalty, the entire Plata region had languished culturally and socially. The most prominent cutural center during the period of the governors was Córdoba, the reason being that the Jesuits had established there the most advanced school in the region. The *Colegio Máximo* and a seminary were of recognized importance in the educational field. Schools were maintained by the religious in other cities, including Asunción and Buenos Aires, but their total impact on the culture of the Plata region was slight. On the contrary, few people were touched by these institutions, and the general frontier atmosphere was hardly conducive to great attention to learning. Furthermore, the displacement of the Jesuits had thrown the educational activities of the Plata region into almost complete chaos for a time, and recovery had not been achieved by the time the viceroyalty was created.

The establishment of the viceroyalty changed much of this. The second viceroy, Juan José de Vértiz y Salcedo, who took office in 1778, did much to stimulate intellectual activity. During his administration the first printing press was put to use in Buenos Aires. It was brought from Córdoba where the Jesuits had employed it for religious purposes. A theater was organized and opened, and the proceeds from both the theater and the press went to the support of a foundling hospital that was also of new creation. The Academy of San Carlos was founded and soon became the most important institution of higher learning in the viceroyalty. A corps of physicians was organized and vaccination introduced.

The institution of the viceroyalty likewise resulted in significant improvements in the new capital. Sidewalks were constructed and two of the principal streets were paved. These were important improvements, for the soft soil of the river delta upon which Buenos Aires was constructed became a quagmire during the rainy season, making the streets all but impassable. Houses were flooded for lack of adequate drainage, and the difficulties of movement about the city were great. No mention need be made of the miserable sanitation conditions that prevailed.

The decision to create a viceregal jurisdiction in the Plata region was a provisional one. Once the step was taken, however, any move to return the great region to its former status was unthinkable. Nevertheless, Peruvian interests were greatly displeased by the entire affair, especially by the economic measures taken by Cevallos and his successors. The opening of the port to commerce, the restriction on the movement of uncoined silver from Potosí to Lima, and the introduction of mercury from Spain into the port of Buenos Aires for use in the silver extraction process, all were detrimental to the Peruvian commercial monopoly. In fact, they destroyed it. Protests to the Spanish court were unavailing, however. The decision had been made, and the wise ministers of Carlos III, including José de Gálvez, were clearly aware of the many advantages of the new arrangement, and its permanence was assured. Between 1778 and 1782 the intendancy system was applied in the viceroyalty, with an intendant-general in Buenos Aires and intendants in Paraguay, Salta del Tucumán, Córdoba, Cochabamba, La Paz, Charcas, and Potosí. Military districts were established in Montevideo and various of the mission regions. At first the intendant-general was given jurisdiction over only the functions of army and the royal treasury, but later the other branches of justice and police were brought within the system. As elsewhere in the empire, the position of intendant-general was found to present difficulties with respect to relations with the viceroy, and the functions were soon combined, with the viceroy assuming the duties of the suppressed position of intendant-general. The installation of the intendant system did not mark a great change over the previous system. The principal advantage was derived from the regularization of the subordinate administrative organization and the injection of new blood in the lower levels of the hierarchy. Coming as quickly as it did after the establishment of the Plata viceroyalty, however, the intendant system became a part of the general administrative reform so that the results and benefits of one change cannot realistically be separated from the advantages derived from the other.

The period between 1776 and 1796 was one of great progress and development in the entire Plata area. The stimulus of the great changes that the viceroyalty brought about was felt in all branches of the social and economic life. Domestic and external trade increased enormously, government revenues mounted, and social and cultural life experienced a new birth. This was in reality the birth period of the Argentine nation. For the first time the great region was brought together in a single political entity with capable and aggressive political leadership. The action of the Spanish monarchy in centralizing this jurisdiction and sweeping away the economic restrictions that had prevented its previous integration was one of the most important strokes of governmental wisdom that may be attributed to the enlightened rule of Carlos III.

The year 1796 marked a turning point, however, for it was the year that initiated the long struggle that was to determine whether the creative efforts of the Spanish ministers and the able viceroys were to survive. The genius of Carlos III had been laid to rest, and the ineptness of Carlos IV had taken its place. More concerned with the maneuverings of European politics than with the welfare of the vast overseas dominions upon which his power really rested, Carlos IV entered upon a series of wars that proved the undoing of the Spanish empire. In 1796 Spain went to war with England, a move that proved disastrous in many respects. Especially did it damage relations with the colonies, for England controlled the seas. For six years virtually no commerce could be carried on between Spain and her American empire, for the British navy maintained a rigid blockade of the Iberian peninsula. In Buenos Aires a great surplus of merchandise for export collected on the wharves and in the warehouses, and the scarcity of European goods became acute. To resolve the difficulty, Spain permitted the colonies to trade with neutral nations, but with the provision that the neutral vessels engaged in such trade were to call at Spanish ports. The commodities to be exchanged in such trade were also narrowly limited. Such limitations were absurd. Neutral ship captains had no inclination to run the British blockade to enter Spanish ports.

Eventually the dam broke, and for their own survival the Spanish colonies were forced to engage in whatever commerce was available to them, illicit though it might be. The viceregal authorities were forced to take measures into their own hands, governing quite independently of the homeland with which so little communication was possible. The first steps toward independence were being taken, and the Plata viceroyalty, dependent as it was upon the exchange of commodities for its welfare and prosperity, led the rest in the independence of its actions.

VICEROYS OF RIO DE LA PLATA

1776–8	Pedro Antonio de Cevallos
1778–84	Juan José de Vértiz
1784–9	Nicolás del Campo, Marquis of Loreto
1789–95	Nicolás de Arredondo
1795–7	Pedro Melo de Portugal
1797–9	Audiencia; Antonio Olaguer Feliú
1799–1801	Gabriel Avilés de Ferro
1801–4	Joaquín del Pino y Rozas
1804–6	Rafael de Sobremonte
1806–9	Santiago Liniers
1809–10	Baltásar Hidalgo de Cisneros

XIX

Colonial Preparation for Brazilian Nationhood

> Brazilians from every part found Coimbra a common meeting
> ground, a more fertile field of nationalism perhaps than any
> in Brazil itself. While it would not be correct to think of
> Coimbra as a hothouse of revolutionary ideas, it is true that
> Brazilians came into closer contact with the ideas animating
> Europe and America than if they had remained at home.
>
> BAILEY W. DIFFIE *

PORTUGAL'S hold upon her American empire
was tenuous at best. Of all the great colonizing
powers of Europe, the kingdom of the Braganças was certainly the
weakest, for it was scarcely able to maintain its own independence
from Spain. Only the internal difficulties of her neighbors and the
mutual jealousies of her colonial rivals made possible Portugal's
survival as an overseas power. Throughout the seventeenth century
her financial debility had made most difficult the struggle to hold
Brazil. She had not been able to organize strong military expeditions
or to protect with her limited naval forces the lines of communication to America. It had been the colonists themselves who had
seized the initiative and who had been responsible for the defeat
of the Dutch West India Company. Such action constituted a
remarkable display of self-reliance on the part of the settlers. They
were, however, a hardy lot, inured to the difficulties of frontier life,
and they had been able to recruit a considerable number of Indians

* From *Latin American Civilization*, The Stackpole Company, Harrisburg,
1947, p. 715. By permission of the publisher.

and Negro slaves to assist them in the protracted and desultory battles. Such colonial self-reliance did not necessarily inspire confidence in the minds of the governing officials in Lisbon, however. That very initiative might well be taken as an indication of the difficulty to be encountered in any attempt to maintain a rigid control over the developing empire.

The nature of the American settlements accentuated Portugal's problems. The vast area to be defended and held stretched for more than 4800 miles along the coast of the Atlantic. The populated areas were few and widely separated, and all were clustered along the coastline where they might be easy prey to any foreign naval power. Communication between the different localities was almost non-existent, and no central administrative authority in America bound them together. In this respect, the Portuguese settlements in Brazil were similar to the British colonies in North America at the same period.

Each of the various population centers of Brazil constituted a largely autonomous colonial entity, with its captain or governor who held his authority directly from the king. These officials conducted themselves as befitted the proprietors of private estates, as indeed some of them were. A governor-general resided in the capital at Bahia, and after 1717 he was given the title of viceroy, but he had no way of making his more general authority felt beyond the borders of his own immediate territory, and had he tried to do so support from the king would have been doubtful.

By 1700, the economic life of the Brazilian settlements had become generally stabilized. Virtually all wealth and affluence were to be found in the north where the large sugar plantations and the extensive cattle ranches provided a surplus of local commodities for export. Each engenho or fazenda tended to constitute a community unto itself, largely self-sufficient in the basic necessities of life. Luxuries were imported from Portugal, but their use was restricted to the owners of the great estates and their families. Settlements in the south were of lesser importance. The agriculture practiced in the São Paulo region was more diversified and on a much smaller scale. Little was available for export and the inhabitants were generally poor, less settled in their mode of living, and frequently lawless. Much energy was devoted to replenishing the supply of Indian slaves at the expense of the Jesuit Indian reductions in the neighboring Spanish colonies, where the paulistas were considered a scourge. The marauding bandeirantes were a law unto themselves in the back country, but they were responsible for pressing the frontier of empire ever southward against their Iberian neighbors. To them is due credit for the great discovery of mineral wealth that was to convert Brazil overnight from a neglected group of frontier settlements into a great flourishing community and the backbone of the Portuguese empire.

Gold was discovered by a small group of paulistas in the inland valley of the Rio das Velhas in 1698. Minor discoveries had been made previously, but it soon became apparent that this was an important find. The gold fields were extensive and rich. As soon as the discovery became known, a fever of excitement gripped the whole Brazilian coast, spreading to the homeland and to foreign regions as well. Soon thousands of people were on the march. From the sugar plantations of the north, from the cattle ranches of the São Francisco valley, from the steamy port cities of Ceará, São Luís, and Pernambuco, from Rio de Janeiro and Santos, people of all classes streamed into the gold-bearing highlands. Slaves deserted their masters; the masters left their sugar engenhos and cattle fazendas and followed, all participating madly in the struggle for sudden riches. Many were successful, but far more perished amidst the hardships encountered in the great rush.

The paulistas were at first possessive about their strike and viewed the mobs of strange prospectors with marked hostility. Bitter enmity between the discoverers and the interlopers ensued, and in 1709 a vicious struggle took place over mining rights. Already, however, the many gold-seekers from afar had so populated the region that the paulistas were outnumbered and in pitched battles they were quickly defeated. Thereafter, the mining region was open to all comers and organized attempts to monopolize the fields largely terminated.

Soon new discoveries were made, not only in the tributaries of the São Francisco river, but in the more distant region known as Goiás and even farther west in the wilderness of Mato Grosso. In 1729, to the discovery of gold was added that of diamonds, and again it was found that the supply of the new wealth was considerable. The world was soon to learn that Brazil was one of the most richly endowed areas on earth in mineral and many other natural resources.

The influx of population to the gold districts was most pronounced in the ten or fifteen years immediately following the first discoveries, but it did not die down to modest proportions for several decades. Each new discovery revived the fever of excitement and stimulated a new flood of migration. Nevertheless, in spite of the great waves of people who spread out over the hills and mountains of Minas Gerais, as the mining district came to be called, the manpower shortage was acute. Everyone, of course, wished to work for himself. Those who established claims and set about exploiting them quickly turned to slavery as the answer to the shortage of workers. Indians were first pressed into service, but they proved inefficient, unable to withstand the rigors of labor and disease, and prone to desert at the first opportunity. As rapidly as possible, Negroes were brought into the mining section and, as on the northern plantations, they proved much more satisfactory workmen. In the long years of placer and other forms of mining activity that followed, the Negroes, slave and free, performed the bulk of the work.

From the outset, life in the gold fields was hard. At the time of the first discoveries, the remote wilderness to which the treasure seekers rushed was utterly primitive back country in which no means of subsistence was available. Food was extremely scarce or not to be found at all. In the first years, death from starvation was an ever present possibility, provided one survived the brawls, feuds, venereal disease, and decimating epidemics that scourged the whole turbulent region. Life was brutally crude and primitive. Prices of all commodites suffered an enormous inflation, and the amenities of civilized life became available but slowly. Eventually, however, mule trails were opened from the port city of Rio de Janeiro and sporadic communication was established along the rivers leading to the hinterland. The cattle herds of the São Francisco valley proved a great boon, for they provided a meat supply without which the death rate from starvation would undoubtedly have been much higher.

The effects of the great gold-rush were felt throughout the whole Brazilian territory. So great was the exodus from the northern plantations that crops were neglected, sugar mills shut down, and cattle left to stray aimlessly over the fields. Even outside the mining area food shortages threatened. Proprietors and civil authorities attempted to restrict the movement of the laboring classes by establishing road blocks, taxing migrants, and severely punishing such runaways as were caught. These measures were of little effect. The dream of riches could not so easily be dispelled. In the end, a great population shift was effected and the entire settlement pattern of Brazil was changed.

As already indicated, prior to 1700 the center of Portuguese settlement in Brazil was the northern coastal region, with Bahia designated as the colonial capital. Economic and social activity was focused in this area. Explorers had penetrated far into the Amazon basin, and in the south the paulistas had carried their slave-hunting expeditions deep into the interior, but no permanent settlements of any importance had been established back from the coast. The discovery of mineral wealth changed all this. The center of economic activity shifted southward, and for a time at least the mining and related enterprises more than balanced the sugar and cattle industries of the older coastal provinces. Rio de Janeiro, as the coastal outlet of the mining region, became the most important city in Brazil; and the captaincy of Minas Gerais, established in 1720 to provide a political organization for the mining territory, became the most populous of the Brazilian subdivisions. The principal city of the new captaincy, Vila Rica do Ouro Prêto, became a brawling, bustling town, and other mining communities experienced similar concentrations of population. Naturally these changes represented more than a mere shift of those already in the colonies. The total population was augmented tremendously by new settlers from Europe and new slaves from Africa.

All these changes encouraged settlement inland and away from the coast. Minas Gerais, while not a coastal province, was separated from the coast by only a small strip of land, much as the state of Pennsylvania in the United States is separated from the coast by the state of New Jersey, without benefit, however, of the excellent river communication available to Pennsylvania. Had the treasure-seekers ended their search in Minas Gerais, the vast hinterland would still have remained untouched. Such was the lure of gold and diamonds, however, that many pushed on into Goiás and into the great Mato Grosso territory, the latter having an area five times that of the state of Texas, and lying deep in the heart of the South American continent. Many areas were explored where no European had ever before set foot. In nearly all sections some mineral discoveries rewarded the relentless searchers. As a consequence, Brazil experienced a great spreading-out upon the land. Small permanent settlements sprang up in the distant westward regions where groups of miners and prospectors, tired and unsuccessful in their difficult hunt for the glittering dust or the little hard pebbles, settled down and turned their efforts to agriculture.

These events were of great importance to the Portuguese empire. In Brazil they produced a social and economic upheaval. By reason of the wider distribution of the population, a greater unity emerged; old cleavages and social caste structures were undermined. The tendency toward racial mergers was accentuated, for in the crude frontier life of the mine fields differences in pigmentation lost their sharpness. The foundation of a great Brazilian nation was being laid.

Portugal too stood to profit greatly by the sudden good fortune. However, the small Iberian kingdom derived a minimum of lasting benefit from the exploitation of the colonial mines. The ruling monarch, João V, delighted with the unexpected riches placed at his disposal, became an easy dupe for those smarter than he, of whom there were many. Taking no thought for the development of his empire, the king lavished his wealth upon the ladies, upon the many ingratiating courtiers, and especially upon himself. For a payment to the Pope he was granted the title of Most Serene Majesty, a designation which well suited him, for he was serenely oblivious to the welfare of his subjects. Others were not so foolish. By the Methuen Treaty of 1703 the British took Portugal under their diplomatic wing, and soon they enjoyed a virtual commercial monopoly in the Brazilian trade. This relationship was to prove beneficial to both the British and the Brazilians in many ways. Under the protection of the world's greatest sea power, Brazilian goods moved securely across the Atlantic without serious interruption during the many wars that so disrupted the trade of other nations during the latter part of the century. Portugal, however, apart from the preferential treatment accorded its wines in England, was left the empty role of intermediary. Tax benefits she might receive, but even her aspirations for a textile industry were sacrificed on the altar of British friendship.

Portugal's stake in the mining activities of her colony was made effective by the 'royal fifth,' the tax imposed upon extracted mineral wealth. The tax proved extremely difficult to collect for evasion soon became an almost exact science. Collection effort generally centered around the royal mint and bullion stamping offices, but it was found necessary to go directly into the fields and attempt collection from the miners at the location of the diggings. Diamond production was subjected to government control on a different basis. Once the extent of the diamond fields was realized, an effort was made to limit mining activity to those authorized by an official government contract. This system was inaugurated in 1740, but was found to be a quite ineffective method of control. Unauthorized diamond miners were active in all quarters, and many achieved legendary fame for the size of their finds and their skill in evading the royal agents. Rigorous punishment was meted out to those who were caught, and hatred for the mining officials became widespread and bitter. In 1772 the government established a royal monopoly for mining diamonds, but this failed utterly to put an end to the activity of the surreptitious workers and smugglers.

Nevertheless, royal income from the Brazilian mining activities was tremendous, and the Portuguese kings used it to further the cause of absolutism and free themselves from dependence upon parliamentary generosity.

It is not possible to indicate exactly how productive were the gold fields and diamond beds of Brazil during the period of Portuguese control. Rough estimates place gold production in the neighborhood of 1000 metric tons, approximately one-half the world production, during the first century after discovery of the rich deposits. Diamond production was somewhat over two million carats, possibly as high as three million. Such figures are probably high. Nevertheless, it is impossible to determine what percentage of the gold and diamonds escaped control and taxation. The total must have been large, particularly in the early years before the Portuguese government was able to set up the necessary administrative machinery to make control effective. Diamonds, of course, were easy to conceal, and the general anarchy and lawlessness that prevailed in the areas of the diggings made control at the source difficult. As for preventing the illegal export of either gold or diamonds, this too was almost impossible, for expert smugglers abounded, and many were the goldsmiths who counterfeited the stamp of the royal mint.

Eventually the Portuguese crown was able to establish a more rigid tax system in the principal gold-bearing districts, and intendants were placed in charge of the diamond regions to prevent illicit traffic and to act as the principal crown administrative officials. The government agents were extremely unpopular, not only because the taxes were burdensome, but because the control laws to be enforced were rigid and severe, and particularly because administrative authority was exercised in a highhanded and arbitrary manner. There was no practical possibility of appeal to higher authority. These conditions eventually led to an attempt on the part of the *mineiros* — residents of Minas Gerais — to take the law into their own hands.

To consolidate her rapidly expanding Brazilian domains, Portugal made a number of administrative changes, creating new captaincies as the need arose. São Paulo and Minas Gerais were combined in one such unit in 1709, but the rapid expansion of mining activity in the northern region made desirable a further division, and the two areas were separated in 1720. Still later other areas, Goiás in 1744 and Mato Grosso in 1748, were separated from the São Paulo captaincy.

At the same time that Portuguese power and authority were being pressed westward, expansion to the far south was undertaken. Settlements were begun in what is now Rio Grande do Sul and Santa Catarina, the newcomers moving ever nearer to the Spanish centers in the Plata basin. Santa Catarina was made a separate captaincy in 1735. Struggles with the Spaniards for control of the Plata port of Colônia do Sacramento continued. The Portuguese realized, however, that final victory would in the long run depend upon effective possession and consolidation of settlements in the territory that lay between the far river outpost and the more densely populated Portuguese territory to the north.

Each new settlement to the west and south raised potential legal questions, for the old line of Tordesillas, established in 1494 as a dividing line between Portuguese and Spanish possessions in the new world, was being crossed with impunity. The question was more or less academic, for the Spaniards had not seriously raised the issue except with regard to the Plata region, and even in that area no one was certain exactly where the line was supposed to run. The Portuguese wisely rested their claims upon other grounds, those of possession made effective by actual occupation. They strove to have territorial claims recognized on this basis. The idea of effective possession is embodied in the oft-repeated and frequently misused legal term 'uti possidetis.' Finally, in the treaty signed at Madrid in 1750, the Portuguese succeeded in getting the Spanish government to deal empirically with the boundary question and to discard all appeals to more ancient or higher authority. However, the treaty is a remarkably poor example of the application of 'uti possidetis,' for by its terms each country disregarded the status of actual possession and agreed to a mutual exchange of effectively occupied territory. Colônia was traded for the territory occupied by the Jesuit Indian reductions east of the Uruguay river. Thereafter no one bothered about the ancient mythical line, nor did the Spaniards question Portugal's claim to the vast western regions of Brazil which had so recently revealed their secrets of mineral wealth.

As already noted, the treaty of Madrid was never effectively executed, in spite of the War of the Seven Reductions in which Portuguese forces joined the Spaniards in crushing the resistance of the Guaraní Indians. Instead it was abrogated by Carlos III in 1761. Nevertheless, the willingness of Spain to deal on other than historical grounds could be taken as tacit acceptance of a new order in the Western Hemisphere, an order in which the Portuguese in Brazil might expect no serious opposition to their westward expansion as long as actual Spanish occupation was not disturbed.

Under the impetus of mineral discovery, internal population movement, and new migration from Europe and Africa, Brazil became a nation, destined soon to surpass in importance the mother country. It was largely the activity of the enterprising Brazilians themselves which resulted in the new settlements and explorations that rounded out the boundaries of the Portuguese possessions. Other evidences of a remarkable growth began to appear. Many new buildings were constructed, among them a large number of fine churches. New commercial houses were opened in the port cities to handle the growing volume of import and export trade. New fortunes were made, both in mining and commerce, and the relative power of the northern plantation owners declined accordingly. A natural diversification gradually emerged, inevitable in a country so vast in extent and so richly endowed with resources. This was to prove a fortunate stabilizing factor in later political life.

It is not to be assumed that Brazil's tremendous development after the discovery of mineral wealth made life in the region much more bearable than before. On the contrary, the press of humanity in the principal cities strained every facility of urban existence. The viceregal capital, Rio de Janeiro, was a pest hole of narrow, filthy streets and miserable hovels. Public squares and market places teemed with scantily clad Negroes and Indians while the wealthy rode about uncomfortably in hand-carried sedan chairs and similar conveyances. The deference accorded the ladies and gentlemen in their sweat-stained finery was hardly apparent on the teeming streets where the crowds gave way only to a common household slave known as 'the Tiger,' who made his way to the public dumping grounds or the nearest stream with a great jug balanced on his head. In later years, the Tiger was replaced by municipal sewerage systems.

Even in the cosmopolitan atmosphere of the larger cities, all ladies of class were jealously guarded. They seldom left their homes except to attend Mass, and those who dared learn to read or write were considered risqué and perhaps even of doubtful virtue. When a woman became ill enough to require the attention of a medical practitioner, every precaution was taken to protect her from the prying eyes of the physician. Diagnosis was based upon a discussion of complaints with the husband or father. Given the state of medical science in that time and place, the absence of contact between patient and doctor was no doubt salutary for reasons other than those intended.

At mid-century, Portugal was finally rid of her indolent and self-indulgent monarch. The new king, José I, was not a particularly able ruler. He enjoyed many of the same vices as his predecessor. Unlike João, however, who was content to let the business of state pile up on his desk while he amused himself elsewhere, José I called to his assistance someone who proved only too willing to relieve him of the tedious duties of administration. The assistant, Sebastião José de Carvalho e Melo, later Marquis of Pombal, presided over the affairs of state throughout José I's reign of twenty-seven years. So great an impact did he have on the government and diplomacy of the Portuguese empire that this period has come to be known as the 'Age of Pombal.'

Pombal was an able and ruthless man, self-reliant and egotistical. He dominated the Portuguese government by the force of his personality and by constant intrigues against his enemies. He had few friends. He molded the king to suit his pleasure and to carry out his policies and schemes. Returning one night from a clandestine tryst with a lady-love, the king found the gates of the palace closed, and while trying to enter through a rear portal he was fired upon and wounded. Pombal convinced the king that this attack was due partially to the Jesuits, whom he considered his bitter enemies. This and other pretexts were used by the king to exclude the religious order from all his great dominions. Pombal played well upon the weaknesses of his associates.

As a younger man, Pombal had lived in England where he had come to admire and envy the growing industrial power of that country. It was his wish that a similar industrialization take place in Portugal in order that she might occupy a more important role in trade with the colonies. He particularly wished to stimulate the manufacture of textiles. Unfortunately, the British merchants and manufacturers were opposed to such an undertaking, seeing a possible threat to the virtual monopoly which they maintained in the introduction of manufactured goods in Portuguese commerce. The Portuguese wine market in England, which they controlled, proved the lever with which they were able to make effective their opposition to Pombal's dreams of industrialization.

Pombal saw, as did Carlos III and his adviser Jovellanos in Spain, that the Iberian colonial powers had lost the battle for control of the commerce of their dominions. The wealth of raw materials and minerals that flowed in from America passed on through their hands into those of the English, French, and Dutch manufacturers who alone were able to supply the finished products the colonial population was so eager to possess. Neither Spain nor Portugal was able to change the pattern that had already been established. They might tax the goods as they moved to and fro, but substantive participation in the commerce had long since been lost. The colonists were soon to realize the futility of this arrangement and were to deprive the mother countries of even this role of intermediary.

In the meantime, Pombal took steps to strengthen the political hold of the Portuguese in Brazil. A rationalist philosophically, as befitted a leading figure in the 'age of reason,' the Portuguese minister set about to rationalize the colonial administrative system. He moved to put an end to the anomalous private captaincies and privileged administrative entities in Brazil. He made of the whole region a single viceroyalty, destroying the autonomy of the captains-general and submitting them to the central authority of the king's chief representative. He transferred the capital from Bahia to Rio de Janeiro, a change in keeping with the great population shift and the new economic emphasis that the development of Minas Gerais had produced. He tightened up the tax administration, converted the diamond industry into a royal monopoly, and tried to reduce smuggling. In contrast to the neglected frontier community of the past, Brazil became a well-controlled and rigidly exploited colonial possession.

Under Pombal's guidance, commercial companies were organized to develop and exploit more fully the economic potentialities of the overseas region. Sugar and cattle production, both of which had declined somewhat after the discovery of gold, were now revived and made prosperous activities. New mining methods were introduced that enabled the richer veins to be exploited by underground shafts, and the output of gold reached its height during the period of Pombal's ministry. New and important products were added to Brazil's export column. Among these were coffee, cacao, tobacco, cotton, and indigo. Some of these, notably coffee and tobacco, were grown in the southern captaincies and marked the entry of those areas into the great export market. Brazil became intensely prosperous. Exports consistently surpassed imports, frequently by substantial ratios. Increased quantities of European luxury goods flowed into the great colony and the standard of living rose appreciably.

There were other important indications of Brazilian progress. As the increasing population spread out upon the land and moved into new territory, the religious authority of the church went with them. Ecclesiastical organization kept pace with political organization, and in some areas, such as the Amazon valley where Jesuit missions among the Indians were particularly active, it took precedence. This was of great importance, for the intellectual life of the colony depended heavily upon the church. Such schools as existed were created and maintained by the religious orders. As elsewhere, the Jesuits were particularly active, and from their midst notable figures emerged of whom the most outstanding was undoubtedly Father Vieira of Bahia, who in the previous century, gained wide recognition as a man well versed in the arts and humanities. Toward the end of the eighteenth century, other intellectual leaders claimed attention, particularly in Minas Gerias.

As elsewhere in Latin America, educational institutions received a sharp set-back with the expulsion of the Jesuits in Brazil. More so than in many of the Spanish colonies, the Jesuits had dominated teaching activities in the Portuguese possession. Their departure meant the closing, at least temporarily, of many schools. Pombal was the primary figure in the Jesuit expulsion, and to him must go a large portion of the credit or blame, as the case may be. As a rationalist intellectual, Pombal viewed what he considered to be the ultramontane dogmatism of the Jesuit order as an abomination. In an age when the state was being elevated to a position of all-embracing importance, the Jesuits stood as a bulwark of internationalism, insisting upon the existence of higher earthly authority than that of the 'divine right' monarch. That they would dare to oppose the dispositions of two such exalted kings as José I and Fernando VI in order to protect their Paraguay Indian reductions was more than an absolutist such as Pombal could swallow. This and other grievances, real or imagined, led the Portuguese minister to press the king for their expulsion. In 1755 the Jesuit aldéias were broken up and in 1759 the expulsion order was issued.

It would appear, however, that departure of the Jesuits made a much less marked impression upon the inhabitants of Brazil than it did a few years later upon their contemporaries in the Spanish colonies. For one thing, the Jesuits lacked the economic power in Brazil that they possessed in such Spanish centers as Santiago de Chile or Lima. Their advocacy of Indian rights had made them many enemies among the Portuguese settlers in the early days, but after the substitution of the Negro for the Indian as the chief Brazilian laborer, much of this animosity had been forgotten. Lacking control over a valuable labor supply and not being firmly established in commercial activity in Brazil, the black-robed fathers left in the wake of their departure little semblance of the wild scramble for confiscated wealth which characterized their expulsion from the domains of Carlos III. Then too, Brazilian society was at the time more virile, more fluid and flexible. It was undergoing a great metamorphosis, and one additional shock, more or less, was of little importance. Finally, one may be permitted to speculate that the rank and file of the Brazilian populace was somewhat less religiously submissive, more independent, less concerned with religious problems, for Brazil was a polyglot compound of Portuguese, African, Indian, and various grades of intermixture.

All of the great changes that came over Brazil in the eighteenth century tended to promote a more mature society, one fully able to compete on a basis of equality with that of Portugal. However, no such equality was forthcoming. In the eyes of the Portuguese, Brazil was a vast and interesting place, a source of wealth and power for the empire, but in no sense an equal or entitled to a participating role in the councils of public affairs. Native-born Brazilians were not selected for high office, even when they had pursued their higher education in Portugal or elsewhere in Europe. A few of the minor offices might fall to scions of the better families, particularly positions on the municipal councils; but the higher positions were reserved for the king's Portuguese favorites. In this respect, the Portuguese were even more rigid than the Spaniards, for the latter occasionally conferred high administrative posts upon the creoles. Thus there arose a natural jealousy of the *reinois* on the part of the native Brazilians, a jealousy in no sense lessened by the knowledge of how important a role Brazil had played and was playing in the development and prosperity of the empire.

The efforts of Pombal to effect administrative reform and a tighter control did not improve family relations between Portugal and her step-children. Brazil was given a more effective government and undoubtedly a better one, but the colonials had long enjoyed the liberties of a frontier community, and the new measures were viewed with mixed feelings. In the mining regions especially, antagonism gradually mounted. The heavy taxes and the inability of the taxpayers to secure redress in the frequent cases of abuse on the part of the crown officials caused great dissatisfaction. Eventually a conspiracy against the Portuguese developed, the leaders of which clearly advocated the independence of Minas Gerais as an interior republic.

The first independence movement in Brazil, commonly referred to as the *Inconfidência* or act of disloyalty, followed but a few years after the establishment of independence by the British colonies in North America, an event which profoundly impressed many Brazilians. In reality, the Brazilian Inconfidência predated any genuine separatist movement in the neighboring Spanish colonies, although evidences of unrest, particularly among the Indians of Upper Peru, had become apparent. Several factors account for the earlier movement in Brazil. Brazil, accustomed to a rather lax administrative and economic control during the previous century, experienced a general tightening of the bonds during the eighteenth, especially under the ministry of Pombal. In contrast the Spanish empire, during the reign of Carlos III, experienced a degree of relaxation in the economic sphere, even as more rigorous administrative controls were being established. At the same time, the Spanish colonies were favored by the appointment of a remarkably able set of viceroys who saw fit to exercise their delegated authority in behalf of their jurisdictions. Thus while tensions mounted in Brazil, they tended to diminish in most of Spanish America. Furthermore, Brazil, strong, economically prosperous, conscious of its history of independent action and self-help, supported on the seas by a friendly Britain, had little need of Portugal. The Spanish colonies, drawn by the mother country into the continuous wars of the eighteenth century, open to attack from the sea by both England and France, were less certain of their ability to stand alone.

Brazilian separatism became popular among a small group of young intellectuals of Minas Gerais. Thus it was not the case of a downtrodden man who, when his burden has become unbearable, lashes blindly and viciously at his oppressor. Those who led the movement acted with the enthusiasm and conviction of immature students. The principal figure in the conspiracy was a young lieutenant of militia, Joaquim José da Silva Xavier, commonly known as *Tiradentes* ('Toothpuller'). Other and more important leaders were involved, but few were so outspoken, and none was so quick to accept responsibility for what followed. Tiradentes was an ardent supporter of the new republican regime in North America, and he freely preached a gospel of independence and a similar status of self-government for Brazil. In 1789, words threatened to become action when it was decided to stage an uprising, the pretext being an attempt on the part of the government to collect a sizable amount of back taxes on gold. Feeling ran high over the anticipated collection, for the arrears were large; and some lent their support to the conspiracy solely in the hope that the tax enforcement measure would be abandoned. In reality, the entire plot was crude, poorly planned, and there is no indication that it received much popular support. The conspirators, including several high-ranking military officers, were careless in their utterances and the plot was discovered and crushed. Trials were held and a number of persons convicted and sentenced to varying degrees of punishment. Several were to be executed. However, the Portuguese court diminished the severity of the penalties, and only Tiradentes paid with his life, although Claudio Manuel da Costa, one of Brazil's leading literary figures, committed suicide.

Many Brazilians have ascribed considerable importance to the Inconfidência as the first significant move toward national independence. The harsh penalties decreed by the trial court, even though ultimately softened, produced an unfavorable reaction in the colonies. Joaquim José da Silva Xavier became a martyr and popular hero in the eyes of Brazilian nationalists. As a move toward independence, the conspiracy was insignificant. It had no chance of success. Its leaders were naïve and visionary men who acted not because of immediate grievances but through conviction, gained in part by the conversation of one member with Thomas Jefferson, that a republic was an extremely desirable political system. Nevertheless, the story of the incident and its hero served as a rallying point in future years for the staunch liberals of Minas Gerais who, when circumstances were more propitious, stood in the vanguard of the independence movement.

The events of the Inconfidência took place after the dismissal of Pombal, for the term of the much-discussed autocrat did not survive that of his patron, José I, who died in 1777. Pombal had few friends and many enemies. Queen Maria I, who assumed the reins of government at her father's death, had no use for the aging minister. She had long regarded the anti-Spanish and pro-English policies of her father's favorite with abhorrence. She moved quickly, not as a reigning sovereign, but as a weak woman seeking to avoid the horrors of war. Spain and Portugal experienced a rapprochement.

Left without the guiding hand of the great Pombal, Portugal drifted. The retired minister, rejected and unwanted, the butt of calumny and ridicule, lived only to see his work undone, his best efforts turned to naught. The new queen, fanatically religious, unstable, tormented with fear, moved rapidly across that vague line that divides the rational and the irrational, the sane and the in-sane. For fifteen chaotic years the monarchy tottered on the brink of royal disaster. Only after the demented queen suffered an epileptic fit early in February of 1792 was her son João made regent.

The changes taking place in the court at Lisbon had little direct effect upon the great Brazilian colony in America. In some ways, they proved beneficial. A general relaxation of the stern policies of Pombal eased some of the pressures and permitted a greater economic freedom. The two trading companies which the minister had been responsible for establishing were abolished, much to the satisfaction of the Lisbon merchants and the English commercial houses. Commerce continued to flourish in spite of a sharp drop in the production of the mines. Britain's demand for Brazilian raw materials, augmented by the loss of her own colonies in North America and by constant warfare in Europe, provided an ample market for virtually all that could be produced. As a consequence, increased attention was given to agriculture. The rising demand for agricultural products in Europe and the difficulty of securing adequate markets for Portuguese products caused the ill-advised queen to issue, in 1785, an order for the destruction of industries and factories in Brazil in the hope that this move would force more workers into agriculture and decrease the competition that native manufactured goods presented to Portuguese products. Such a measure solved nothing, however; it could only anger the Brazilians, and there is little indication that any serious attempt was made to enforce it. Natural economic forces stimulated higher agricultural production, particularly of sugar and cotton. The importance of mining, while still great, declined relatively, forcing the exploitation of mineral wealth to play a less spectacular role in the economy of the country.

The rapprochement with Spain permitted settlement of the territorial question in the Plata basin, with Colônia being definitely left in the hands of the Spaniards. The question of territorial rights in this region did not seriously trouble the river waters again until after the struggle for colonial independence set in motion in the former Spanish viceroyalty the centrifugal forces that tossed the Banda Oriental once more into the outstretched hands of the Portuguese.

Of far greater significance for Brazil were the events taking place north of the Pyrenees mountains. The forces of the down-trodden had raised in France the bloody banner of 'Liberty, Equality, and Fraternity' and thereby set in motion a chain of events that were soon to drive the Portuguese royal family from European soil and overnight to convert Brazil from a dependent and exploited colony to the homeland and capital of the empire.

VICEROYS OF BRAZIL

BAHIA

1714–18	João de Lencastro, Marquis of Angèja
1718–19	Sancho de Faro, Count of Vimieiro
1719–20	Junta
1720–35	Vasco Fernandes Cesar de Menezes, Count of Sabugosa
1735–49	André de Mello e Castro, Count of Galvêas
1749–54	Luís Pedro Peregrino de Carvalho de Menezes e Ataíde, Count of Atouguia
1754–5	Junta
1755–60	Marcos de Noronha, Count of Arcos
1760	Antônio de Almeida Soares e Portugal, Marquis of Lavradio
1760–63	Junta

RIO DE JANEIRO

1763–7	Antônio Alvares da Cunha, Count of Cunha
1767–9	Antônio Rolim de Moura
1769–78	Luís d'Almeida Portugal, Marquis of Lavradio
1778–90	Luís de Vasconelos
1790–1801	José Luís de Castro, Count of Resende
1801–6	Fernando de Portugal e Castro, Marquis of Aguiar
1806–8	Marcos de Noronha, Count of Arcos

SUGGESTED READING

H. Bernstein, *Origins of Inter-American Interest, 1700–1812*, Philadelphia, 1945.

H. E. Bolton, *Outpost of Empire*, New York, 1931.

—————— *Texas in the Middle Eighteenth Century*, Berkeley, 1915.

J. W. Caughey, *Bernardo de Gálvez in Louisiana, 1776–1783*, Berkeley, 1934.

L. E. Fisher, *The Intendant System in the Spanish Colonies*, Berkeley, 1929.

V. W. von Hagen, *South America Called Them*, New York, 1945.

W. Howe, *The Mining Guild of New Spain and Its Tribunal General, 1770–1821*, Cambridge, Mass., 1949.

R. D. Hussey, *The Caracas Company, 1728–1784*, Cambridge, Mass., 1934.

J. Juan and A. de Ulloa, *Voyage to South America*, 2 vols., London, 1807.

J. T. Lanning, *Academic Culture in the Spanish Colonies*, New York, 1940.

B. Moses, *Spain's Declining Power in South America, 1730–1806*, Berkeley, 1919.

C. G. Motten, *Mexican Silver and the Enlightenment*, Philadelphia, 1950.

H. I. Priestley, *José de Gálvez, Visitor General of New Spain, 1765–1771*, Berkeley, 1916.

J. R. Spell, *Rousseau in the Spanish World before 1833*, Austin, 1938.

A. B. Thomas, *Teodoro de Croix and the Northern Frontier of New Spain, 1776–1786*, Norman, 1941.

A. P. Whitaker, *The Huancavelica Mercury Mine*, Cambridge, Mass., 1941.

—————— *Latin America and the Enlightenment*, New York, 1942.

—————— *The Spanish American Frontier, 1763–1795*, Boston, 1927.

IV

THE REVOLUTIONARY ERA

XX

Genesis of the Independence Movement

> While there remains in Spain a bit of land governed by Span-
> iards, that bit of land ought to rule Spanish America; as long
> as there is a single Spaniard in the Indies, that Spaniard should
> rule the Spanish Americans.
>
> BISHOP BENITO DE LUE Y RIEGO TO THE CABILDO OF
> BUENOS AIRES, 1810

N O single cause or event aroused the desire for
independence in Spanish America. Indeed, it
would be difficult to demonstrate that the desire was widely held
in the disturbing years between 1790 and 1810, and even after 1810
independence as such became an accepted aspiration throughout
Spain's American dependencies only gradually. Nevertheless, there
can be no doubt of the existence of strong common sentiments regarding the imperative need to strengthen the status of the American realms within the empire and of the Americans as loyal Spaniards capable of exercising administrative authority on an equal
footing with their European-born brothers. That such sentiments
were advanced with considerable vigor in all portions of the
empire is amply demonstrated by both the uniformity and spon-
taneity of municipal action that followed immediately upon the
French occupation of southern Spain in 1810. In region after
region the local cabildos stepped suddenly to the fore and seized
the reins of government from the faltering hands of royal officials
whose home government had just ceased to exist. The outbreaks
may be likened to individual and isolated tinder boxes being ig-

nited by a single spark — a spark struck from the forge of Napoleon's boundless ambition. But the tinder boxes had been prepared over a period of many years by the endless suppression of creole political and social ambitions.

Brazil's passage from colony to empire was accomplished gradually and by peaceful stages, so that it was in no way an ordeal by fire as was the conflagration that soon engulfed Spanish America. The coming of the royal family to Rio de Janeiro in 1808 ended Brazil's colonial period, but fortunately the new nation did not try to make its way alone until 1822. In Spanish America, on the other hand, no royal court appeared. The Spanish kings, both Carlos IV and his son Fernando, had abdicated in favor of Napoleon's brother, Joseph; and the only remnant of a truly Spanish government was a peripatetic junta that finally came to rest in Cádiz. There, denounced by the former Spanish monarch, ringed about with French bayonets, and protected only by the guns of British naval vessels, the junta shouted defiance at the world, proclaimed its control over the Spanish empire, and dissolved itself.

It was during the reigns of Carlos IV of Spain and Maria I of Portugal that the frayed bonds of the two great American empires began to separate. Although actual disintegration came during the rule of the sons of these monarchs, the process had already achieved considerable momentum. After 1788, Maria was no longer mentally able to rule, and in 1792 her oldest surviving son, Dom João, began directing state affairs as regent. In 1788, Carlos IV succeeded his far more able father to the throne of Spain, and his unfortunate rule was to last almost to the day Napoleon ordered his legions into Madrid. Affairs outside the peninsula were of such great portent that the Portuguese and Spanish governments were converted into mere straws to be swept this way and that by the cold gale from the more northerly portions of Europe.

In 1789, the Estates-General were convoked in France to deal with a national financial crisis, but it was soon obvious that their leaders were bent on reforming the whole political structure of the nation. Tension mounted, and while King Louis XVI tinkered with his locks the Paris mob stormed the Bastille, the old fortress symbol of royal despotism. France was soon convulsed in fratricidal social revolution, and it rapidly became clear that the ideas of the radical Jacobins could not be turned back at the Pyrenees by a royal frown. Bound by the Family Compact, pressured by England to help preserve the concept of royal authority in Europe, Carlos IV felt impelled to declare war on the French Republicans in 1793. From a military standpoint, the war brought disaster to Spain, for her troops that invaded southern France soon fled homeward through the mountain passes. They were followed by battalions of the French citizen army, and it became necessary to sue for peace in order to get the enemy troops off of Spanish soil. By the Treaty of Basle, signed in 1795, Spain ceded to France her portion of the island of Española, known as Santo Domingo, the birthplace of the Spanish empire in America. Only by this concession was peace restored and France induced to remove her military forces to the other side of the Pyrenees.

From the beginning of the French Revolution, Spain's subservience to France brought increasing domestic complications. The flood of revolutionary propaganda that poured across the border into Spain threatened to undermine the monarchy. It was more feared than outright warfare. The Spanish minister of state, the Count of Floridablanca, whose views were regarded as inimical to the French revolutionary cause, fell from power owing to the machinations of French agents at Madrid. His successor, Aranda, fared little better, although his replacement by Manuel Godoy was at the queen's insistence. As first minister, Godoy attempted to save the life of Louis XVI without involving Spain in war with France; the failure of this attempt led directly to the war of 1793-5, whose unfortunate consequences for Spain have just been mentioned. The internal political structure of Spain was greatly weakened, and competent officials were brushed aside in favor of less able men who were more interested in mixing in the intrigue of European power politics than in preserving the integrity of Spain and its empire.

During the brief war with France, Spain found herself an ally of England, but the experience was not a happy one. Britain showed

only contempt for her Iberian partner, and her anti-Spanish attitude was in no small part responsible for the restoration of co-
operation between Spain and France and for its continuance
through the early years of the Napoleonic era. Even as Spain made
peace with France at Basle she prepared for war with England,
and the latter's indignation over the desertion of her ally made
renewed Anglo-Spanish conflict a certainty.

In the summer of 1796, Spain became once again the active
partner of France, and war with England began in November. The
British attacked various of the Spanish outposts but were generally
unsuccessful. The island of Trinidad, however, was captured and
subsequently remained a British possession. In the peace negotiations following the war, all powers except France and England
were excluded from the council table, and Spain's interests were
almost totally disregarded. In the meantime, the French won
Godoy's dismissal because they feared his intention of seeking an
alliance with England. When the war was shortly resumed again,
France made repeated demands for use of the Spanish navy, but
failed to aid Spain in the recovery of possessions lost to England.
Carlos IV seems to have been motivated largely by his fear of the
French Directory, but his intimidation was even greater after 1799
when Napoleon dismissed the Directory and proclaimed himself
First Consul. A new treaty was made in which France promised to
aid Spain in the extension of the Duchy of Parma in exchange for
Louisiana and six warships. To such absurdities were the Spanish
officials carried by their fear of their ally.

In 1801 Spain issued an ultimatum to Portugal demanding that
the Portuguese close their ports to British ships; the ultimatum
was rejected and Godoy led an army into Portugal. After a few
indecisive battles, peace was restored, with Portugal promising to
close her ports in return for a Spanish guarantee of the territorial
integrity of the Bragança kingdom. Napoleon was indignant at the
hasty termination of the conflict, for he had hoped to see Portugal
crushed because of her traditional friendship for England. He declared that if the war were not continued, the last hour of the Spanish monarchy was near. He was dissuaded from taking hostile action,

however, by an increased indemnity from Portugal, and in 1802 a general peace was secured by treaty at Amiens. Spain recovered Minorca, but Trinidad was ceded to England. Little more than a year later warfare was once more resumed.

Spain's alliance with France was characterized by mutual distrust and constant recrimination. Napoleon retained his grip on the Spanish monarchy by threats and promises. He accused Spain of double dealing at the very moment he was selling Louisiana to the United States, yet to secure Louisiana he did not hesitate to promise Spain that the vast American territory would never be relinquished to any nation other than Spain. The Spanish indemnities owing to France were meanwhile greatly increased, much to the anger of the English who attacked Spanish squadrons without a prior declaration of war. Napoleon now planned an onslaught on England with the joint Spanish-French navies, but his plans miscarried because of the incompetence of the French admiral. The little Corsican's sharp criticism of the admiral led to an ill-advised sailing of the fleet from Cádiz in the face of Nelson's squadron, and to its nearly complete destruction off Cape Trafalgar in October, 1805. The English victory was to be exceedingly important to the Spanish American colonies a few years later, for it left England unchallenged on the sea. The naval defeat was a crushing blow to Spanish morale and deprived Spain of the means to enforce her authority in her overseas dependencies. England became the arbiter of overseas disputes, and thereafter no nation could seriously consider launching an attack on the Western Hemisphere countries without courting her acquiescence.

While external affairs were forcing Spain into an inglorious international position, the regime of Carlos IV greatly increased domestic demoralization. The scandalous conduct of members of the royal family — Godoy won the highest ministerial post by demonstrating his virility in the queen's bedchamber — and the failure to solve internal problems gave Spaniards little reason to anticipate future reforms. The blow suffered at Trafalgar, however, roused the Spaniards into a desperate policy of opposition to the demands of Napoleon. Godoy opened cautious and secret negotiations with England, yet French successes on the continent intimidated him. But Napoleon had already resolved upon the overthrow of Carlos IV. Fernando, the heir-apparent, was a willing party to his father's humiliation.

In 1806, Napoleon and the Spanish government agreed upon the conquest of Portugal and the partition of that kingdom, and in the following year Marshal Junot brought a powerful French army into Spain to co-operate in the project. The Spaniards were happily unaware that this force was destined for use against them also. Godoy and Fernando, while plotting against one another, revealed their secret designs to Napoleon who employed both men for his own purposes. On November 30, 1807, Junot seized Lisbon, but too late to capture the Portuguese royal family, which with the aid of the British fleet had fled to Brazil. Portugal had been the announced victim, but now the shadow of Napoleon's tri-cornered hat was cast over the entire peninsula.

Napoleon's true intentions now became apparent even to the most gullible Spaniards, for French troops, rather than returning home, quickly seized many of the fortified towns of northern Spain. Godoy asked the Royal Council to demand the removal of the alien army, but this request, together with his personal resignation which followed it, was refused. Napoleon now demanded title to all of Portugal as well as to certain provinces of northern Spain. The Corsican's shadow now darkened even the queen's bedroom, and Godoy urged the king to imitate the Portuguese royal family and flee to America. The king and queen began the journey, but before they could make good their escape an insurrection had broken out, led by the fernandistas. The downfall of Godoy and the abdication of Carlos IV followed rapidly. Napoleon, taking advantage of this turn of affairs, ordered General Murat to occupy Madrid and to withhold recognition of Fernando VII. By threats and promises Bonaparte induced both Carlos and Fernando to come to Bayonne for conferences. There he forced Fernando's abdication in favor of his father and that of Carlos in favor of himself. In exchange, the French dictator promised that Spain should remain independent under a ruler that he would name, and that the Catholic religion should be respected as the only one in Spain. Joseph Bonaparte, brother of the emperor, was handed the Spanish crown. Napoleon, whose contempt for Spaniards was based upon the recent conduct of their government and of their royal family, completely underestimated the reaction which was to follow.

While Carlos and Fernando abjectly yielded to the demands upon them, popular opinion in Spain was intensely aroused. Riots broke out spontaneously at several cities. The most decisive uprising occurred at Madrid on May 2, 1808. On that day the war for Spanish independence began, without encouragement from the departed monarchs and almost without leaders. News of the resistance in Madrid spread rapidly, and soon all Spain was in arms against the French invaders.

The Spanish uprising marked a new turn of events in the Napoleonic wars, for previously no people had dared make such a bold move against the all-conquering emperor. The actions of the Spaniards, people whom Napoleon still held in contempt, were cited as an example to follow by the leaders of other conquered peoples. They became an important factor in the emperor's eventual downfall. The French troops in Spain won countless battles, yet Spain remained unconquered.

The story of the Spanish resistance to Napoleon is a tremendous epic in itself. Daring and ingenuity proved remarkable substitutes for equipment, training, and organization. Arms captured at night from unwary outpost garrisons were effectively turned against their original French owners. Again and again Napoleon's generals pressed for the open pitched battle, in which superior power and equipment would quickly assure them victory; but just as persistently the Spanish guerrillas eluded the marching columns and escaped into the mountains only to reappear again where least expected. Inevitably, however, the French grip on Spain tightened as Bonaparte, determined to prevent the interruption of his long string of victories by small groups of Spanish irregulars, poured more and more men through the Pyrenees passes. Every important city fell to the invader until only Cádiz remained. To Spaniards in the overseas dominions, deprived of contact with the homeland

and largely unaware of the heroic resistance of their peninsular compatriots, it appeared that Spain as an independent kingdom had reached the end of the road.

With Spanish power seemingly broken, consternation spread throughout the American empire. The reins of government, so long firmly held by the hands of peninsular Spaniards, suddenly went slack. Deprived of support from the homeland, royal officials were entirely dependent upon their own resources to maintain their precarious status. They could count as allies their European-born compatriots whose economic and social privileges were open to challenge by the increasingly restive creoles. They could expect support from the higher officials of the church hierarchy whose deep-seated devotion to monarchical institutions and political absolutism caused them to fear and hate the republican liberalism of creole intellectuals. They could hope to sway the ignorant masses in their favor, but to do so they needed a rallying point and a program. For some time they had neither, and time was of the essence.

Creole groups were faced with equally complex problems. For years they had sought social and political equality within the empire, and by the first half of the eighteenth century many had achieved local administrative offices that were both lucrative and important. But the Bourbon reforms, beneficial in many ways, had abolished many of the traditionally creole positions and instituted in their place a new hierarchy of offices under the intendant system — offices filled by a host of new administrators from Spain. Creole political opportunity had been reduced to participation in the cabildos, except in the relatively infrequent cases where wiser colonial administrators had secured the appointment of able creoles to seats in the audiencia or to important intendancies. Now for the first time an opportunity was presented for the American-born Spaniards to move upward into control of their own countries. Few, however, thought of independence, and scarcely anyone would have advocated rebellion against Spain. The real crisis was produced by the action of Napoleon's armies in overrunning Spain and leaving throughout the empire a host of officials whose right to rule was of questionable validity. In this situation, many of the long-suppressed yearnings of a recently matured colonial society came to the surface. Trees of independent nationhood sprouted in every cabildo chamber.

Creole leaders, nevertheless, had no simple choices before them. Overt acts against the homeland would undoubtedly bring severe retribution should Spain recover her independence and be able once more to deal freely and directly with her American possessions. There was the danger that if Spain's apparent demise should prove genuine, other European powers, particularly England, might attempt to replace her as lord and master of the American continents. There was ample evidence that the British did not as yet regard the independence of the United States as necessarily permanent; and when, in 1806 and 1807, British forces twice occupied Buenos Aires in an attempt to establish a firm foothold in the Plata region, it was made painfully clear that England's designs upon the Spanish colonies emcompassed more than a desire to engage in friendly commerce. On the other hand, the fact that creole troops rallied and threw the enemy into the sea demonstrated both a strong attachment to Spain and a high degree of colonial self-sufficiency.

The extension of French influence over the Spanish colonies presented still another possibility. France represented far more than the country from which Napoleon's armies emanated. Paris was the intellectual capital of the Latin world, the home of revolutionary republican doctrines, the city in which the now famous slogan of 'Liberty, Equality, and Fraternity' had first been raised in defiance of the political and social absolutism of the Old Regime. French influence had long been strong in Spain, stemming in part from the French ties of the Bourbon ruling family, but even after the revolution in 1789 and the overthrow of Louis XVI, Spain's close association with its French ally was only briefly interrupted. Spain had many *afrancesados*, intellectuals who embraced French philosophies, French styles, and French manners. The term hardly conveyed flattery, particularly after Napoleon's soldiers were stalking the Iberian peninsula, but French sympathizers were common, and they were able to play effectively upon the Spaniards' long-standing hatred for the English. Their influence in the colonies was less marked, but it was nevertheless present. Indeed, many a creole intellectual boasted a French education, while others had read avidly the works of Rousseau, Voltaire, and Montesquieu. Some, such as Francisco Miranda of Venezuela, saw service in Napoleon's armies, while many more had fought side by side with the French in the long struggles with England. The very success of Napoleon captivated men's imaginations and, when coupled with the social doctrines of the revolution, stirred deeply the Latin world.

Napoleon himself was not insensitive to the effect of his Iberian conquests upon the Western Hemisphere. Even before the Spanish monarchs had pusillanimously delivered themselves to him at Bayonne, he had dispatched agents to win the good will of the colonies. After the abdication of Fernando and Carlos, early in May, 1808, he sent another group of agents to inform colonial authorities of the change of dynasty and to keep Spanish America free of English influence. Napoleon's ministers were slow in transmitting this important information to America, while England acted with greater dispatch. In the meantime, Spanish Americans were almost without news from any other source. Venezuela, for example, had received no reports from Spain since the fall of Godoy in March. News of the stirring events — the Bayonne captivity and the resistance in Madrid — was finally received through copies of the London *Times*, obtained in Trinidad and translated into Spanish by Andrés Bello. The agitated Spanish officials refused to believe what they read until a French ship arrived in July with Napoleon's commissioners aboard. The perturbation of the officials increased, for they correctly surmised that creole leaders would refuse to swear fidelity to Napoleon and would use the Bayonne *coup* as an excuse for independent action. Similar crises occurred elsewhere when the news from Spain arrived. Calmness, tact, and firm control were required; instead, most of the colonial officials were panicky, vacillating, and either weak or ruthlessly severe.

Over most of Spanish America, the response to Napoleon's overtures was spontaneous and similar. Peninsulares were divided in their reactions, some inclined to accept Bonaparte's new regime and others resentful to the point of acquiescing to creole pressures to follow a more independent and defiant course. Creole leaders for the most part took the view that if the French were permanently to occupy the peninsula the American colonies must seek independence, perhaps with Fernando as a ruling monarch in America. In the meantime, they intended to imitate the conduct of the Spanish people themselves and form local juntas of self-government in the name of Fernando, preparing to defend themselves against the attack from France which they expected to come.

For Spanish Americans the peninsular war for Spanish independence was an excellent opportunity to free themselves, although independence from Spain was the first thought in the minds of but a few. The devotion to the unworthy Fernando, who applauded French victories over patriots fighting in his name on Spanish soil, became manifest in Spanish America as well as in Spain. This emotional loyalty to an absent king gave the real planners of independence an excellent shield behind which to set in motion the independence movement.

In December, 1809, Napoleon declared that he was not opposed to the independence of the Spanish colonies, because it was necessary and just, and in the interest of all the powers. His main concern was assurance that once independent, Spanish America would look to France rather than England for political leadership and commerce. He apparently feared that Joseph would not be able to maintain the Spanish empire and that the safest solution was to encourage the colonies to become independent with the benign blessing of France. Napoleon's agents in South America gave an added impulse to the movement for independence by issuing proclamations, apparently emanating from Joseph, offering the colonies their freedom.

The actions of creole-dominated cabildos from New Spain to La Plata were much the same, each taking a stand against French domination, swearing allegiance to the deposed Fernando, and

setting up local governing juntas to control the colony until the
absent king should be restored or come to America. Viceroys and
captains-general yielded or resisted, depending upon their personal
convictions and courage. In Peru the creole effort was ruthlessly
suppressed. In New Spain a bitter social revolution was precipitated.
In Buenos Aires, power passed from the viceroy to the local governing junta with relative tranquility. Nowhere, with the exception
of New Spain, did the events take the form of a popular uprising
against a despotic and repressive colonial rule. The great mass of
the colonial population, the mestizos and the Indians, paid little
heed to the dramatic events transpiring across the seas and in their
own homelands. They would eventually be moved to participation
in the battles to come, but at the outset they were passive and for
the most part ignorant of the significance of what was taking
place.

The revolutionary events of 1810 marked the first major effort
by the creole classes to assert their right to equal status with the
peninsular Spaniards. The attempt to link themselves to the royal
person of Fernando was natural and in some ways quite appropriate.
Centuries before, imperial theory treated each of the major colonial
entities as a separate kingdom ruled by the Spanish king, and a
separate royal council had concerned itself with the affairs of the
Indies as a region apart from peninsular Spain. By this theory,
now conveniently remembered after a century of imperial centralization under the Bourbons, the empire did not belong to Spain;
only the king could claim dominion over it. Throughout the
centuries following the first Spanish settlements in America, this
peculiar relationship was never entirely forgotten. The king could
do no wrong, although his ministers might. The problems of
government were problems of communication — getting through
to the king could not fail to produce the desired result. Hence the
oft-repeated cry of the tumulto, 'Down with bad government! Long
live the king!' Thus many of the local uprisings of the late eighteenth century, such as that of the comuneros in New Granada,
were in a sense throwbacks to a more ancient period. Inspired to
resistance by the more efficient law enforcement produced through

Bourbon reforms, the local population in the colonies clamored for return to the more easy-going days of the past. The king would surely sympathize with this desire, for he could not wish to see his American realms exploited by the greedy officials from Spain. Attachment to paternalistic monarchy was firm and deeply imbedded in the social and political outlook of Latin Americans. It was not to be easily overcome by the shoutings and clandestine preachments of a few creole radicals who parroted the views of French and North American philosophers and revolutionaries.

The political and social outlook of most creole Americans can hardly be described as radical. The small groups of firebrand intellectuals such as Miranda, Andrés Bello, and Antonio Nariño assumed an important role in the independence movement because they were willing to act while others hesitated in impotent indecision. But even these, whose ranks were augmented in the period of crisis by such able men as Bernardo O'Higgins in Chile and Simón Bolívar in Venezuela, viewed their mission to be that of setting up independent American states under creole leadership of an essentially aristocratic caste. The 'rights of man' were considered in a quite different light than in France or even in Spain. They were hardly thought of as pertaining to the lower classes of Indians and mestizos even though their significance in France was irrevocably linked to the uprising of the Parisian proletariat. Thus, with the exception of such men as the priest Hidalgo in New Spain, the Spanish American revolutionaries were essentially conservative and aristocratic in their political leanings. The great majority of the creoles, less well educated and far more provincial than the men just mentioned, were disinclined toward any move that might upset the social order. They sided with the independence leaders because Spain had been overrun and because of their class interest in displacing the Spaniards who ruled in America. By stressing their continued allegiance to the king they salved their consciences and at the same time stated their general acceptance and support of the old aristocratic social structure in which they now hoped to play a more prominent role.

The conservatism of the independence movement became increasingly clear as events unfolded in Europe. In Cádiz a regency was formed which soon gave way to a Cortes claiming to represent the Spanish people in both Europe and America. Some American delegates presented themselves, but the Cortes viewed the creation of self-governing juntas in the colonial capitals as acts of treason and ordered them suppressed. In turn, few American leaders wished to have any dealings with the Cádiz body. Those who aspired to independence preferred to ignore the Cortes, for it presented the possibility of maintaining peninsular domination throughout the empire. Others, hopeful that the bonds of empire would not be permanently severed, were quickly alienated by the radicalism which the Cortes displayed. Decrees and resolutions embodied in the Constitution of 1812 clearly indicated that the Cádiz body was dominated by men who had drunk deeply of the heady wine of French republicanism. The king was to become a mere figurehead subservient to the legislative body, the authority of the church was to be greatly curtailed, many class privileges were to be abolished, and a host of so-called civil rights were to be guaranteed and emphasized. American adherents to the old regime were aghast at the evidences of Spanish radicalism, and many threw their support behind the local creole governments which at the moment seemed to represent the lesser of two evils.

In the meantime, confusion prevailed in virtually all quarters. Forces loyal to Spain opposed the creole juntas in Venezuela and Peru, and from Peru loyal armies crushed revolutionary movements in Quito and moved against those in Chile. In New Spain, attempts to create a local government failed, and loyalist forces engaged in bloody combat with the riotous Indian mobs of Hidalgo. In Spain, supported by a British expeditionary force, patriot forces recovered from what appeared to be complete disaster and began driving the armies of Napoleon northward. The tide of events shifted, and even as the French emperor was forced to relinquish his grip on the Iberian peninsula, he met bleak defeat on the wintery plains of Russia. Early in 1814, Fernando returned to the throne of Spain. Not once had he shown any sympathy for the patriot forces of Spain in their bitter struggle with the French. He had distrusted — and not without reason — their republicanism and their radicalism. Promptly he set about the hopeless task of turning back the clock. The Constitution of 1812 he brushed lightly aside and reconstituted himself as absolute monarch. He restored all the ancient rights and privileges of the aristocracy and the church, suppressed civil rights, reinstituted the Inquisition, and closed such hotbeds of radicalism as the universities and theaters. He even ended the publication of all newspapers other than the official gazette. At the same time, Fernando set about destroying the revolutionary governments in America. Armies were sent to Venezuela and Colombia, and garrisons were reinforced in New Spain and Peru. All possibility of reconciliation between Spain and the empire ended as opposing forces faced each other across a bloody gulf that grew steadily wider and deeper. The issue of independence was brought clearly into the open, and no one any longer pretended that there were other alternatives than complete independence or complete subjugation to Spain.

For a time the Spanish armies were victorious. They overran Venezuela and New Granada and drove the principal creole military leader, Bolívar, into exile. Chile was reconquered. In New Spain, loyalist troops, supported by creole conservatives and the principal religious leaders, dispersed the Indian armies of Hidalgo and captured the rebellious priest and put him to death. Only in the great Plata basin did the independence forces remain unchallenged by Fernando's legions. In all other regions vengeance stalked mercilessly across the land. Thus was guaranteed the eventual independence of Spanish America.

Again events in Europe came to the aid of the creole patriots. The harsh measures of Fernando produced their own domestic reaction. Freemasonry had for years been growing rapidly among Spanish intellectuals; now the lodges became the centers of antiroyalist conspiracy. Cupidity and corruption in Fernando's administration drained the treasury and left the army unpaid. Opposition to the continuous expeditions to America spread throughout the land as it became increasingly obvious that they were mismanaged and had as their ultimate objective the complete suppression of colonial liberties. A plot was hatched in Andalucía, where Masonic leaders joined with the officers of an expeditionary force destined for American service and turned the army against the government. On January 1, 1820, Colonel Rafael del Riego proclaimed the restoration of the Constitution of 1812 and proceeded to take command of the local district. The revolt spread quickly, and almost without bloodshed the king was forced to capitulate, call the Cortes into session, and swear allegiance to the constitution he found so repugnant. The Spanish government had done an about face and the radicals and intellectuals of 1812 were again in power. Spain's faltering grip on America weakened further as the new leaders concerned themselves with problems of internal reform.

The resurgence of Spanish liberalism struck no responsive chord in America. The bitter and bloody struggle between Spanish and creole forces in northern South America had opened a gulf too deep and too wide to be bridged by any structure that Spain might now attempt to erect. Liberal forces in America, concerned above all else with the issues of empire organization and independence, had lost all meaningful contact with their Iberian counterparts. The latter had shown little regard for colonial sensitivities during their earlier brief period of control in Spain. In New Spain, where the first revolutionary efforts had taken on many of the aspects of a social upheaval, those who had crushed the Indian mobs of Hidalgo viewed the 1820 Spanish *coup* with consternation. Conservative creoles and Spaniards alike preferred independence to restoration of the 1812 Constitution and all its doctrinaire liberalism and anti-clericalism. Quickly old loyalties were reshuffled. The moderate independence forces, which had been gradually losing ground, were suddenly joined and overwhelmed by the conservative and reactionary elements whose military leader was Agustín Iturbide. New Spain became the independent Mexican Empire, with the opportunistic general at its head. Spain's North American empire had been undone by the forces of counter-revolution. When, in 1823, Fernando was once again able to crush Spanish liberalism and restore his absolutist rule, New Spain had been irretrievably lost and an independent Mexican nation had superseded the ancient viceroyalty.

After 1822, the liquidation of Spain's last continental outposts in America was but a matter of time. Only in Peru were loyalist forces still powerful, but against them Bolívar conducted a vigorous and increasingly effective campaign which ended in the utter defeat of Fernando's troops in 1824. For a time after the restoration of absolutist rule in Spain, the monarch harbored hopes of securing French and Austrian support for a gigantic effort to reconquer all his lost American possessions, but these hopes were dashed asunder by Britain's refusal to acquiesce in any such scheme. Indeed, the British foreign secretary, George Canning, sent word to the Congress of Verona, assembled in 1822 by the Austrian chancellor, Metternich, to plot the restoration of absolutism throughout Spain and her former colonies, that England would insist upon the right of peoples to set up whatever form of government they thought best and to be left free to manage their own affairs. More directly France was informed of Britain's opposition to an American venture by the allied absolutists of continental Europe. Inasmuch as Britain controlled the seas, the land-bound powers were helpless to do more than talk.

Then in December of 1823, when Fernando was once again firmly the master of Spain, President Monroe of the United States issued a statement in his message to Congress that reinforced the position already taken by England. After stating that the United States had not mixed and did not intend to mix in the affairs of Europe, but that it was concerned with matters affecting the Western Hemisphere as a factor in its own defense, President Monroe added: 'We owe it, therefore, to candor, and to the amicable relations existing between the United States and those powers [Austria, Russia, Prussia, and France], to declare that we should consider any attempt on their part to extend their system to any portion of this hemisphere as dangerous to our peace and safety. With the existing colonies and dependencies of any European power we have not interfered and shall not interfere. But with the governments who have declared their independence and maintained it, and whose independence we have on great consideration and on just principles acknowledged, we could not view any interposition for the purpose of oppressing them or controlling in any other manner their destiny by any European power in any other light than as the manifestation of an unfriendly disposition toward the United States.' The United States had already recognized the formal independence of Colombia, Chile, Argentina, and Mexico. Shortly after Monroe's declaration, which subsequently became known as the Monroe Doctrine, Great Britain formally recognized the independent nationhood of Mexico and Colombia. Thus the Anglo-Saxon powers, the one a great imperial nation and the other a struggling new republic, indicated their similarity of views with respect to the independence of Spanish America. The friend-liness of these views did not go unnoticed in the struggling new nations.

While Spanish authority in America was being tested on the battlefield from Mexico to Chile, Brazil achieved independence from Portugal almost without recourse to military action. When the Bragança family fled the homeland to escape Napoleon's invading armies, the royal court was established in Brazil in such a manner as to bring about dramatic changes in the status of that colony. Portugal alternated between French and British domination for several years, but finally a corrupt regency came to exercise nominal control while the actual government was in the hands of British army officers. The royal family, however, raised Brazil to the rank of a kingdom and continued to reside in Rio de Janeiro. For a time the Brazilians were dazzled and pleased by the pomp and affluence of their new role as the capital of the Portuguese empire. Gradually, however, prominent and ambitious creoles became increasingly jealous of the many Portuguese hangers-on at the royal court, and irritation mounted when Napoleon's downfall in Europe posed the prospect of the royal family's returning to Europe and leaving Brazil once more in the status of a colony. Return of the king, Dom João VI, could not long be delayed if Portugal was to remain part of his kingdoms, for liberal elements in the homeland were bent upon creating a constitutional monarchy and perhaps even a republic. A constituent assembly was called which abolished many of the feudal vestiges and drew up a constitution guaranteeing all citizens equality before the law, as well as freedom of the press. Such radical changes were not universally popular, and aroused bitter antagonism among the clerical party. It became imperative for João to return lest he lose the Portuguese crown. Portuguese jealousy of Brazil made it impossible for the European kingdom to accept any solution other than a return of the American realm to its former status of colonial subservience, but any such outcome was just as unacceptable to the Brazilians. It was obviously impossible for both kingdoms to have the same king residing in its capital at the same time. Since no compromise was possible, separation became merely a matter of time.

Dom João read well the temper of the times. He remained in Brazil until 1821 when, leaving his elder son, Dom Pedro, in Brazil as regent, he set sail for home and the unhappy turmoil of Portugal which soon produced his early death. Before leaving, however, he made clear to his son that if preservation of the dynasty should make necessary the independence of Brazil, Pedro should take the necessary step. In little more than a year Brazil was independent and Dom Pedro was its emperor.

In a number of respects, the independence of the Latin American nations was precipitated prematurely by events in Europe. Although the principal viceroyalties were maturing political entities with social and economic institutions rivaling those of Spain and Portugal, dissatisfaction with the colonial relationship had not reached a point where independence was at the forefront of men's minds. The increasing laxness of Spain's mercantile system — particularly after 1790 when almost continuous warfare interrupted communications between Europe and America — served both to ease the burden of Spanish domination and to awaken the colonies to the advantages of unrestricted commercial intercourse and to the strength of their own economic position. Brazil, long a participant in British commerce, was further awakened to her important role by becoming the seat of the Portuguese court. Viceroys in Buenos Aires, such

as Cevallos and Vértiz y Salcedo, openly advocated a greater freedom of commerce within the Spanish system, and merchants
throughout the Americas debated with considerable warmth the
advantages of free trade, brandishing Adam Smith's *Wealth of
Nations* to lend greater force to their words.

Spain's European involvements likewise cast a major portion of
the burden of empire defense upon the colonies, and colonial
militias came into being with numerous creole officers commissioned in the king's service. Colonial troops acquitted themselves
well against the English at Buenos Aires in 1806 and 1807, but
the very existence of large numbers of armed American troops
portended the strength of revolutionary armies that could be turned
against Spain as well as against Spain's European rivals.

Finally, by 1810 the American possessions of both Spain and
Portugal had produced a generation of able intellectuals which
was readily caught up in the vortex of social, intellectual, and political rationalism that swept both Europe and North America. Many,
inspired by the example of the United States, nourished in their
own breasts the dream of a great new political order. Nevertheless,
an inherent loyalty to the king and to the Spanish and Portuguese
systems still prevailed among the majority of Spanish and Portuguese Americans. Reformists were to be encountered everywhere,
but true advocates of outright independence were prominent by
reason of the radical views they expressed and the martyrdom they
frequently suffered rather than because of their great number. Even
after the few planners had decided upon independence as their
goal, it was generally necessary for them to conceal their intentions
from their countrymen. The idea of embarking upon warfare admittedly against the king was even more abhorrent in the eighteenth
and early nineteenth centuries than in the time of Gonzalo Pizarro.
That the Spanish Americans were able to set in motion their
movements for independence in 1810 without frankly showing their
separatist intentions, which surely would have alienated many of
their followers, they owed to the memorable aspirations of the
celebrated Corsican, Napoleon Bonaparte. Brazilians could thank
the same gentleman for driving their royal family to American

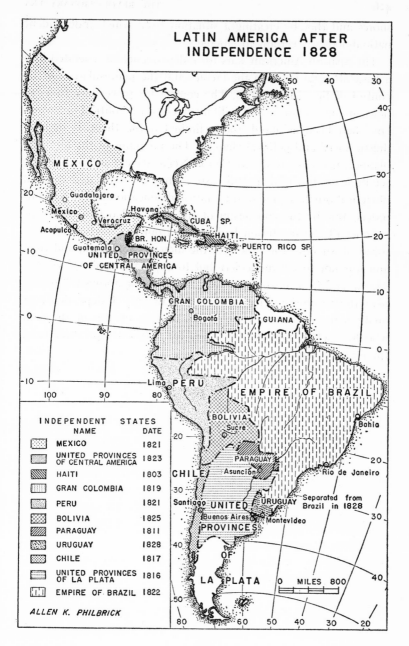

LATIN AMERICA AFTER
INDEPENDENCE 1828

MEXICO

Guadalajara

Mexico

Acapulco

Veracruz

Havana

CUBA SP.

HAITI

BR. HON.

PUERTO RICO SP.

Guatemala

UNITED PROVINCES
OF CENTRAL AMERICA

GRAN COLOMBIA

Bogotá

GUIANA

Lima PERU

EMPIRE OF BRAZIL

Bahia

BOLIVIA

Sucre

PARAGUAY

CHILE

Asunción

Rio de Janeiro

Santiago

UNITED

URUGUAY

Separated from
Brazil in 1828

Buenos Aires

Montevideo

PROVINCES

OF

LA PLATA

INDEPENDENT STATES	
NAME	DATE
MEXICO	1821
UNITED PROVINCES OF CENTRAL AMERICA	1823
HAITI	1803
GRAN COLOMBIA	1819
PERU	1821
BOLIVIA	1825
PARAGUAY	1811
URUGUAY	1828
CHILE	1817
UNITED PROVINCES OF LA PLATA	1816
EMPIRE OF BRAZIL	1822

O   MILES   800

ALLEN K. PHILBRICK

shores and thereby creating a situation from which independent nationhood was certain to emerge.

The Spanish American wars for independence degenerated into a basic struggle between the creoles and the peninsulares for the control of Spanish America. The contest for power and fruits of office among the successful military chiefs, once political independence had been achieved, soon eliminated the theorists desiring drastic social and political changes. The programs of the idealistic planners had embraced abolition of Negro slavery and involuntary servitude by the Indians and castes. They contemplated the end of clerical privileges and of the control of education by the religious orders. But by the conclusion of the long and destructive wars, conduct of the revolution had passed from the intellectuals and social planners to the caudillos, the men on horseback, and their aim was not to reform society but to enjoy the spoils of victory. The later Mexican aphorism was not without aptness: 'thinkers plan the revolutions; bandits carry them out.' Independence as finally achieved little resembled the utopian dreams of the men who first set in motion the forces for political separation from the mother country.

XXI

The Wars of Independence in the South

> In Buenos Aires itself there were not lacking creoles who viewed
> our enterprise with loathing; some believed that it could not
> be accomplished because of the strength of the Spaniards;
> others judged it to be the madness and delirium of untrained
> leaders; others, in brief — and these were the most pious —
> viewed us with compassion, not doubting that in a few days
> we should be the victims of Spanish power and fury in castiga-
> tion of our rebellion and infidelity against the legitimate sov-
> ereign, lord and proprietor of America.
>
> CORNELIO SAAVEDRA *

N O Spanish colony fared better in the late years
of the empire than the viceroyalty of Río de la
Plata. Other sections of the Spanish king's vast possessions enjoyed greater wealth and they consequently received a greater
share of royal attention. To a remarkable degree, the Plata region
was permitted to shift for itself, and in the late eighteenth and
early nineteenth centuries this proved highly advantageous. With
the creation of the viceroyalty and the lifting of many of the
centuries-old trade restrictions, conditions were created which
sharply stimulated both economic and social development. Trade
flourished as Buenos Aires became a bustling port through which
passed not only the agricultural and pastoral products of the hinterland but also an increasing share of the mineral wealth of Charcas.
Manufactured goods and luxury items from Europe poured into

* *Memoria Póstuma.*

427

the river city as Spain's Atlantic commerce gave way to British, French, Dutch, and even North American merchantmen. New fortunes were made and all phases of life in the viceregal capital quickened. The ostentatious display of wealth became increasingly commonplace as rich landowners and merchants built fine homes and imported expensive coaches in which to ride through the muddy streets which some effort was now made to pave. Public buildings, many of which had remained uncompleted for years, were finished and others constructed as viceroys gave attention to beautifying their capital. In a city that had long been considered drab socially, elaborate private entertainment provided a marked change in the pace of social activity.

The viceroys and their courts initiated a much wider range of public functions. In addition to the traditional round of religious festivals, various political celebrations were introduced to mark important events in the life of the monarchy. The festivities that attended the swearing of allegiance to Fernando VII were particularly elaborate and involved a great deal of special preparation to provide public entertainment in the central square. At such times, the various government bodies and officers, as well as private enterprises and individuals, undertook to construct elaborate decorations and to entertain the populace with music and ceremonies. The great popular sporting event, the bullfight, was developed into a highly colorful spectacle in which important officials and the wealthy classes took part at the opening ceremonies with great formality and display. Indeed, so much time was given over to bullfights, holiday festivities, and other ceremonies that concern was occasionally expressed that such events kept the laboring classes from their work. The development of the theater, musical events, and educational facilities added much to the intellectual life of Buenos Aires, and the capital city came to rival in its tone and sophistication the more mature colonial capitals of Lima and Mexico City.

As the economy of La Plata expanded, so of course did the demand for its principal item of export, the hides of cattle that roamed the pampas. Hundreds of thousands of hides were shipped each year, gathered by roving bands of gauchos from the estates of the great hacendados. Living in the wilds with none of the amenities of civilization, the gaucho became a legendary figure and a symbol of the vast plains that stretched southward and westward from the population centers along the great river chain. Uneducated and crude in the extreme, these men, usually mestizos, fought the Indians, the elements, and each other in a primeval struggle for survival and for the cattle whose hides were the sole source of income to purchase the few meager pleasures they enjoyed. The hide trade was immensely destructive, for the meat of the cattle had no useful value other than to satisfy the appetites of the gaucho rovers. The carcass was often left where the animal fell, to be consumed by wild beasts and birds of prey.

The burgeoning activity of the Plata basin and the great plains beyond did not fail to attract the attention of Spain's rival colonial powers. British statesmen had turned an attentive ear to such renegade Spanish colonials as Francisco de Miranda, who urged the English to undertake the liberation of Spanish America. Indeed, Great Britain, having lost much of North America, showed great interest in recouping her colonial fortunes in other parts of the world. Every advantage was taken of the war against Napoleon's continental system to seize the colonies of those European nations under the Corsican's thumb. After the defeat of the French and Spanish fleets at Trafalgar in 1805, the seas were clear for British colonial expeditions, and several were soon forthcoming.

Early in 1806, an English force under Admiral Sir Home Riggs Popham invaded and conquered the Dutch settlements at the Cape of Good Hope in South Africa. The British commander, who had participated in earlier conversations with Miranda and who had been led to believe that the Spanish colonists would receive the British with open arms, then turned his attention to the Plata basin and sent an expedition there under command of William Carr Beresford. On June 25, 1806, the English force disembarked on the coast and marched on Buenos Aires, taking the capital city two days later. The cowardly Spanish viceroy, the Marquis of Sobremonte, interrupted in the midst of a theater party given in honor of his future son-in-law, fled 'over the hill' to Córdoba. His action, in addition to providing the residents of Buenos Aires an excellent opportunity to invent puns and derisive limericks, earned no respect for Spanish authority.

The English commander quickly took steps that seemed clearly aimed at converting Buenos Aires into a British colony. He guaranteed property, the Roman Catholic religion, and the administration of justice; he also opened the port to commerce on the same footing as other British colonies. These actions failed to rally the local inhabitants to his support, however; and soon creole leaders were plotting Beresford's overthrow. Santiago Liniers, a Frenchman serving in the Spanish navy, and Juan Martín de Pueyrredón, a creole patriot, organized a resistance force. Pueyrredón with a company of peasants launched the first attack and was defeated. Liniers, however, was able to recruit assistance from Montevideo, and joined by the remnants of Pueyrredón's force, he attacked the capital and routed the British completely. Beresford was captured, as were over 1000 of his men, together with all their equipment.

Important events immediately took place which considerably altered the complexion of government in Buenos Aires. Viceroy Sobremonte insisted on retaining his prerogatives, but a cabildo abierto had taken action in his absence and appointed Liniers as a lieutenant to act in his behalf. Furthermore, a local militia was organized and a force of some 8000 men was placed under arms, a little more than half of whom were creoles. The creole troops selected their own officers, and a new spirit of self-reliance suffused the entire colony.

In the meantime, the British government, apprised of Beresford's conquest of Buenos Aires, sent additional forces to consolidate the foothold already gained and to conquer Montevideo and Santiago de Chile. The collapse of Beresford's force took place before the British reinforcements could arrive. When the loss of Buenos Aires became known to them, the English changed their strategy. A force under General John Whitelocke undertook to recapture the viceregal capital after the English seized Montevideo in February of 1807. Viceroy Sobremonte, who had taken charge in Montevideo before the attack, again fled from his duty and his people. Liniers, supported by a cabildo abierto, took over the government as acting viceroy, with governing authority nominally vested in the audiencia. Sobremonte was declared 'ill' and unable to govern. Actually he was deposed and made prisoner.

In June, 1807, General Whitelocke attacked with an army of some 12,000 men. Liniers, commanding little more than 8000, most of whom were ill-trained militia, undertook to defeat the English in open battle, but was unable to do so. British forces entered portions of the capital, which the alcalde, Martín Alzaga, had fortified on his own initiative. As the battle progressed, the British were gradually overwhelmed as various local militia units attacked from all possible quarters. The population was so completely hostile that the British could find no support in any quarter. Finally, General Whitelocke was forced to surrender, accepting Liniers' terms of abandoning the country and restoring to Spanish control the city of Montevideo. Local resistance triumphed completely.

The defeat of the British at Buenos Aires virtually inaugurated the revolution against Spain. The Spanish government had been of no help whatsoever, and its chief representative had proved himself such a witless coward that the local population had deposed and imprisoned him. At the same time, the creole leaders and the local militia had proved themselves capable of organizing a government, developing a defense force, and defeating highly trained British regulars in battle. Certainly the viceroyalty was capable of standing alone.

The years from the defeat of the British in 1807 to the first indications of open revolt in the Spanish colonies in 1809 constituted a period of intense unrest in Buenos Aires. Pueyrredón was in Spain sending reports of anarchy and chaos to his friends at home. A would-be revolutionary, Saturnino Rodríguez Peña, plotted with the alcalde of Buenos Aires, Martín Alzaga, to bring Princess Carlota, sister of Fernando VII, to La Plata as ruling monarch of an independent nation. His enthusiasm was whetted by the presence of Carlota in Rio de Janeiro as wife of the Portuguese regent, João. However, with Liniers as viceroy, the creole element did not feel a great urgency to action. Instead, fear spread among the royalists that the local government was drifting away from its attachment to Spain, and early in 1809 a feeble and fruitless effort was made to depose Liniers. Soon, however, the arrival of a new viceroy, Baltásar de Cisneros, was announced. No man could have undertaken a less desirable assignment. Plots were on foot to resist Cisneros long before he ever set sail for America, and from the day of his arrival he was constantly reminded of the fact that Spain was without an effective government and that a self-governing junta would be most appropriate in Buenos Aires.

Cisneros tried manfully to pacify the creoles without bowing to their demands, and for a time he was able to resist. He himself had little assurance that his course was the correct one, for he knew the weakness of the Seville junta that appointed him. When finally it was forced to flee before the French, the viceroy tried to suppress the news, but that proved impossible. Reluctantly, on May 18, 1810, Cisneros announced the Spanish debacle, accompanying his statement with a request that law and order be upheld. Royalists made an abortive attempt to keep the viceroy in control of the government, but the tide of creole self-determination could no longer be held in check.

Cisneros received insistent demands that a cabildo abierto be summoned to decide upon the course to follow. Fearing the consequences of such a move, he temporized as best he could, but finally he yielded and called the meeting for May 22. The majority of those assembled on that date voted to depose the viceroy and to establish a junta responsible to the people, but the official cabildo of the city refused to yield completely to the popular demand. Rather, it attempted to name a junta, of which the viceroy was to be a member, that it could dominate. This arrangement proved unacceptable, and with patriot crowds gathered in the streets two resolute young men entered the council chambers on May 25 and presented the cabildo members with a list of people to be named to a junta. The mob outside the cabildo chambers was insistent, and threat of military action was raised if the popular demands were not met. Finally the cabildo capitulated. The junta which it appointed contained no royalists, nor was the viceroy retained as a member. Cornelio Saavedra was named president and Mariano Moreno secretary. Other members were equally prominent patriots responsive to creole desires and ambitions for self-government. Nevertheless, in spite of its composition and the popular support which it enjoyed, the new junta, upon taking over the government, made no open gesture toward independence. Rather, it tried to protect itself against unforeseeable calamities by solemnly swearing to preserve the land for Fernando VII. Its actions otherwise belied the oath, for the members quickly took steps to prevent interference by the audiencia or other pro-royalist elements. Moreno, famed for his economic treatise in behalf of the cattlemen, became the dominating figure.

In Chile, where viceregal rule had rested fairly lightly since 1778, similar events were taking place. In 1808, the death of the governor, Muñoz Guzmán, tempted the patriots to bid cautiously for power. A royal decree of a few years earlier had named the highest ranking military officer to succeed the governor in such a contingency. The audiencia, following an older practice, named its president to the post. The army officers, urged on by various creoles, refused to accept this decision, and declared in favor of Colonel García Carrasco. The audiencia was forced to capitulate and recognize the colonel as provisional governor and captain-general.

Since García Carrasco was little interested in routine administration, he left many decisions to his secretary and chief adviser, Dr. Juan Martínez de Rozas, one of the creole intellectuals who aspired to see Chile independent. The governor was persuaded to enlarge the cabildo of Santiago, unaware of his secretary's plan to employ it to counteract the audiencia. When the radical nature of the cabildo members became obvious, García Carrasco reduced its size and acquired a new secretary. His earlier quarrel with the audiencia was still exploited by the creoles, however, for it kept their chief opponents bitterly divided. The audiencia denounced the governor as unfit, while he appealed for help to the authorities of Lima and Buenos Aires. The patriots meanwhile entered into communication with their counterparts in the latter city, and were greatly encouraged by the course of events in the Plata region. On May 25, while the porteños were deposing the viceroy, García Carrasco arrested three of the reputed conspirators in Santiago. A cabildo abierto was immediately assembled, and it summarily ordered the governor to appear. Although cries for his deposition were heard, the cabildo was satisfied with his acquiescence to its demands for freeing the prisoners and submitting his acts to it for approval.

Martínez de Rozas, after his dismissal by the governor, had returned to Concepción, where he continued to promote the cause of independence. Knowing his countrymen's innate loyalty to the king, he argued that they should follow the example of the patriotic juntas in Spain, as these governed merely in the absence of the king. Many Chileans, including some royalists, were persuaded to this point of view. Bernardo O'Higgins was already pledged to the cause of independence, and was among the most enthusiastic organizers of the movement.

Once the immediate crisis had passed, García Carrasco refused to comply with his promises made under duress. He sent the prisoners secretly to Lima, and established a special junta to oppose the conspirators. Because of many Chileans' belief that in opposing the governor they were actually supporting the king against the French, the royalist acts appeared in an unfavorable light. The citizens of Santiago became aroused, and a large force assembled to demand the formation of a junta similar to that of Buenos Aires. The audiencia acted to prevent the assertion of authority by the cabildo, and replaced García Carrasco with Mateo de Toro Zambrano, the venerable Count of the Conquista, who was persuaded to call a cabildo abierto. The threatening aspect of the multitude which assembled induced him to offer his resignation. He was nevertheless named president of the junta, for he was popular and respected, and too old to stand in the way of creole plans. The resounding ovation for Martínez de Rozas on his arrival in Santiago to take his place in the junta made it clear where the authority lay.

The similar courses which were followed in the Plata and in Chile facilitated the formation of an alliance between the patriots of the two regions, for the porteños realized that Chilean independence was necessary to their own security. The common interest in the struggle against Spain became the basis for warm and sympathetic relations between the future nations, a situation more unique than usual in Spanish America in the half-century after independence.

The immediate problem of the junta of Buenos Aires was to win support in the other provinces of the former viceroyalty, a task hampered by the hostility born of earlier commercial regulations. Animosity toward the porteños was evident in Asunción; Montevideo, Tucumán, and Córdoba contained royalist groups which, because of the undercurrent of feeling toward Buenos Aires, were able to organize resistance to the junta. Upper Peru remained strongly royalist. And in both Buenos Aires and Santiago, there appeared a sharp cleavage among the creole patriots themselves.

One reason for the immediate rifts in the patriot ranks was their lack of an accepted program of action. Other than a cautiously advanced objective of ultimately securing independence, no agreement had been reached as to the general type of government which should be established, and there were substantial and irreconcilable differences of opinion on this matter. The example of the United States won proponents of a federal republic. Some patriot leaders, however, were equally convinced that a centralized monarchy was most appropriate for their countries. Lack of political experience was a severe handicap in discussion, for the spirit of compromise was feeble. With the threat of reprisal from Lima or Madrid hanging like a threatening sword over the patriot deliberations, any attempt at government by the inexperienced champions of independence was indeed an adventure. Military defeat frequently preceded a fall from power. Inexperience, immoderation, and personal ambition fragmented the patriots into contentious factions which threatened not only the success of the immediate contest with Spain but the future welfare of the nations they hoped to create.

The Chilean patriots were not even agreed on their goal, some holding back from a complete severance of Spanish authority while others demanded an immediate declaration of independence. Martínez de Rozas was interested primarily in securing reforms such as freedom of commerce. The junta issued an edict granting such freedom in February, 1811, but with royalist cruisers sailing before the principal Chilean ports, the reform meant little. Martínez de Rozas preferred to achieve the desired changes without openly declaring independence, but royalist resistance and the agitation of extremists of his own party dashed his hopes. Father Camilo Henríquez, one of the most articulate of the patriot leaders, called for complete separation from Spain. In April, 1811, a royalist counter-movement was put down, the audiencia was dissolved, and Chile was left without any vestige of imperial rule. An election for provincial deputies to a general congress was held without incident, and Chile's abortive first attempt at self-government was launched. No declaration of independence was attempted; rather, the congress took the usual oath of loyalty to Fernando VII.

In Argentina the cleavage between factions was far more serious and deep-rooted than in Chile. Issues involved the ancient antagonism between the interior provinces and Buenos Aires and the divergent views regarding monarchism and republicanism, centralism and federalism. The porteños, who had begun the rebellion and deposed the viceroy, were convinced that they should dominate the new government, but only with difficulty could any of the other cities be won over. The creoles of Asunción and Montevideo remained aloof and suspicious. Paraguay even expelled a force sent from Buenos Aires to co-operate against the royalists. To many people in the remote regions, fear of Buenos Aires loomed larger than the threat from France or Spain, and the interior provinces opposed the porteño junta more effectively than did royalist agents.

Actual royalist resistance in the Plata area was soon confined to Montevideo. The greatest danger to the patriots was not from that quarter, however, but from Peru, for the way was open through Upper Peru to invade northwestern Argentina. The first patriot force dispatched in that direction won a triumph at Suipacha; but in July, 1811, the Argentine army was routed at Huaqui, and the royalists remained in control of the silver mines of Upper Peru. The repulse at Huaqui had repercussions far from the field of battle, for the first governing triumvirate in Buenos Aires fell from power as a result. It also meant that Upper Peru, the richest province of the former viceroyalty of Río de la Plata, was not to be a part of the future Argentine nation. The loss of the silver mines was a damaging blow to the impecunious junta, and at the same time it gave the royalists of Peru the means for continuing their resistance. Northwestern Argentina, furthermore, was in immediate danger of invasion.

The failure of Huaqui subjected the junta to acrimonious criticism, and the assembly of delegates from the provinces was strengthened in its opposition to porteño rule. The most articulate spokesmen for the anti-porteño groups were the clerics Gregorio Funes of Córdoba and Juan Ignacio Gorriti of Jujuy, who were agreed in their desire for independence and their support of regional interests against Buenos Aires. As a result of their efforts an act was passed early in 1811 which transformed the former intendancies into provinces and gave them a semblance of equality with Buenos Aires.

Independence from Spain was only one of the problems facing Paraguay and the Banda Oriental. Both had been within the viceroyalty of Río de la Plata, and the porteños hoped that both would remain within the new nation to be formed. Soon after the movement for self-government was initiated, the intendants and cabildos of the viceregal area were invited to send representatives to a general congress in Buenos Aires. In response to this invitation, the leading citizens of Paraguay, who were uncertain as to the immediate future, tried to ride three horses at once so as to be certain of the eventual winner. They announced their obedience to the council of regency in Spain, in case Spanish arms should triumph. They resolved to maintain a cordial solidarity with the junta of Buenos Aires, without conceding its supremacy. Finally, they created a similar body of their own to maintain the defense of

Paraguay. Thus carefully protected against the vicissitudes of war, they quietly set about establishing an independent state. But when the porteño junta sent a military force under Manuel Belgrano to aid in the deposition of royalist officials, the aid was forcibly rejected. Paraguay did not, however, become a center of royalist resistance, for once the porteño intrusion had been met, the long-standing separatist tendencies came to the fore, and creoles took over the government.

In the junta of self-government created in Asunción in 1811, Dr. José Gaspar R. de Francia became the leading figure. He envisioned Paraguay as an independent republic, and his views prevailed. By 1814 he had assumed dictatorial powers; and since Spain made no serious effort to restore her authority in Paraguay, and because Francia was superior to his opponents in the struggle for power, 'El Supremo' was able to rule the little nation until his death in 1840. His regime, however, falls largely in the national period, for Paraguay took no direct part in the independence campaigns beyond her borders.

The Banda Oriental, on the other hand, was the arena of a triangular struggle that greatly hampered the effectiveness of the creole patriots, led by José Artigas. For a short time the *orientalistas* and porteños co-operated against the Spaniards in Montevideo, but as the Spanish menace disappeared, Artigas became the champion of the federalist provinces against Buenos Aires. Then Brazilians replaced Spaniards as an outside threat, and for a number of years the patriots of the Banda Oriental found themselves in a position of running with the herd and hunting with the pack.

Early in 1812, before the porteños had made much progress in organizing an army, José de San Martín arrived in Buenos Aires to dedicate his services to the independence of Spanish South America. Although a creole, he had been a professional soldier in the Spanish army and was a veteran of the war against the French in the peninsula. It was a crucial moment in Buenos Aires, for the serious fighting was still ahead, and discord was already fragmenting the patriot ranks. In Lima the Spanish viceroy was preparing to stamp out the insurrections one at a time. Independence was still not the avowed intention of the patriots, and many people expected to see royal authority restored. The lack of a solid program on the part of the rebels, the divided opinions of their leaders, and the threat of invasion from Upper Peru made the hopes for independence seem chimerical. Into this discordant and disorderly scene came San Martín, bringing his solid character and his exceptional talent for training combat troops. Both qualities were invaluable to the patriot aims.

San Martín's experiences in the Peninsular campaigns against the French had convinced him of the value of intensive training and thorough discipline. His regiment of mounted grenadiers became the model for the entire army; his patient, inspired leadership gave his troops a passion for duty which, coupled with their rigid training, decided the issue on many a battlefield.

In 1812 the viceroy of Peru prepared expeditions for the subjugation of Chile and Argentina, and one was sent toward Tucumán. The defeat at Huaqui had left the road to that city open, but Belgrano was ordered to withdraw with what remained of his army. Nevertheless the people of Tucumán urged him to make a stand and offered their fierce gaucho squadrons to serve as his cavalry. Belgrano disregarded his prior instructions and won a sizable victory. However, the danger of invasion remained, for the royalists reassembled at Salta and sent for reinforcements.

In June, 1813, Belgrano again invaded Upper Peru. Within a few months his army had suffered a serious defeat followed by a disastrous rout. Neither the patriots nor the royalists had discovered that conditions of terrain and altitude made successful invasion from the altiplano to the lowlands, or the reverse, impossible. In either case, troops going to the region with an altitude vastly different from that to which they were accustomed soon became incapable of the strenuous action demanded by combat.

Other efforts of the porteños to unite the former viceregal territory under their government fared little better. In 1813 an invitation was extended provincial representatives to assemble in Buenos Aires. Artigas sent delegates from the Banda Oriental armed with peremptory demands that the congress make an unequivocal declaration of independence from Spain and that it create a government of republican form under a constitution which guaranteed autonomy to the confederated provinces or states. Such ideas were far from welcome among the porteños, who envisaged a centralized government under their own domination and who were not yet ready to declare formal independence. Artigas' delegates were denied seats in the congress on a technicality. This foolish action turned the orientalista leader into a bitter opponent of the porteños and precipitated a sanguinary federalist-centralist conflict. Artigas became a spokesman for the provincial leaders. He withdrew from the siege of the small loyalist garrison remaining in Montevideo and turned his attention to consolidating provincial opposition to the former viceregal capital. His troops overran Entre Ríos and Corrientes, and from Santa Fé they threatened Buenos Aires itself.

Early in 1814, a new figure, Gervasio A. Posadas, became director of the porteño government. He organized a naval squadron under the command of an Irishman named William Brown. Brown attacked the few remaining Spanish ships in the estuary, dispersed them, and renewed the siege of Montevideo. The isolated loyalist garrison soon surrendered and the last Spanish troops were removed from the Plata region. But with Artigas in open opposition, the Buenos Aires government was in little stronger a position than before. The Plata region was torn by factional strife.

In Chile, too, violent factionalism had begun to undermine the movement for independence. The return of José Miguel Carrera, an erratic though gifted young creole who had served in the Spanish army against the French, introduced a discordant element. Carrera's espousal of independence and republicanism brought him quick popularity, but his lust for power made his services more costly than beneficial. In September, 1811, he seized the government, dividing the patriots into hostile groups just when they were in greatest need of unity. Royalist groups still held southern Chile and the archipelago of Chiloé, and the viceroy in Lima was determined to make the Chilean oath of loyalty to Fernando VII a reality instead of pretense.

Viceroy Abascal hoped for a quick and easy pacification of Chile so that Chileans could be employed in restoring royal authority in Argentina. He sent veteran troops under Antonio Pareja to Chiloé. This force, augmented by militia, captured Talcahuano from the patriots, and Pareja began the march on Santiago.

Internecine strife jeopardized the Chilean defense. In February, 1814, after a year of bloody fighting a new junta was formed which deposed Carrera and removed him from command of the army. The partisans of Carrera divided the army, now under command of O'Higgins, and diminished its effectiveness. The royalists were being forced back to Talca, nevertheless, when the European situation changed abruptly. In May Fernando VII was restored to his throne, and he displayed immediate determination to recover his former colonies at any cost. The popularity of the patriot cause waned rapidly, for the ostensible reasons for conflict had vanished.

At this stage, the English commodore, James Hillyar, offered his services as mediator in Chile. His offer was accepted, and the Treaty of Lircai was drafted. Chile was to return to her previous condition, under the temporary rule of a provisional junta. Royalist troops were to be withdrawn within a month. The viceroy rejected the treaty, for veteran regiments from Spain were arriving, and his bargaining position was vastly improved. In the interim a mutiny in the patriot army restored Carrera to power. While the patriots disputed among themselves, General Mariano Osorio marched northward with a powerful loyalist force. O'Higgins was defeated at Rancagua, while Carrera kept a large force out of action near by. The battle was followed by an exodus of Chileans across the Andes. Repressive royalist control was inaugurated in Chile, and known patriot leaders were sent to languish with the goats and turtles on Juan Fernández Island, the locale of Defoe's *Robinson Crusoe*.

In Argentina at about this time, San Martín reached the conclusion that the war against Lima could not be conducted successfully by way of Upper Peru. The only alternative was an attack by way of the sea, and Chile was the most likely base for such an expedition. In 1815 San Martín began preparation for carrying the war to Chile. He withdrew from the Argentine army and was appointed governor of Mendoza province, in western Argentina. He set about recruiting, training, and equipping troops for the Chilean campaign at the most inauspicious moment of the wars of independence. His success in raising a large army was remarkable, for it occurred at a time when Argentina was torn by factional strife and threatened with invasion. Indeed, the struggles for independence had reached their nadir. By 1815 the revolt of Hidalgo and Morelos in New Spain had been crushed. Bolívar had fled from the continent, and Chile had been reconquered. The Argentine 'Army of the North' had suffered an overwhelming rout at Sipe Sipe in Upper Peru, and it seemed only a matter of months before a royalist force from Peru would reduce the Plata provinces to submission. But while Spaniards confidently celebrated the end of the wars, San Martín resolutely and calmly pursued his program for the final destruction of royalist authority in southern South America. The defense of northwestern Argentina was left to Martín Güemes and the formidable gauchos of Tucumán, who proved more than equal to the task.

The only offensive action of the patriots in 1815 was a privateering expedition from Buenos Aires to the Pacific coast, led by William Brown and Hipólito Bouchard. A number of Chilean refugees, including Ramón Freire, took part in the expedition. San Martín used this and other opportunities to spread terror in Chile by permitting the governor, Francisco C. Marcó del Pont, to seize dispatches telling of a vast patriot army to be landed on the Chilean coast. By these means he deceived the royalists into dispersing their troops to guard the sea approaches, leaving the Andean passes weakly defended. The cruise of Brown and Bouchard produced little in the way of immediate military gains, but its value was great for other reasons. Patriot morale was improved; communications between Peru and Chile were interrupted; Spanish naval strength in the Pacific was tested and found to be weak; and the project for invasion of Chile was enhanced by convincing the royalists that a maritime campaign was planned.

On July 9, 1816, the Congress of Tucumán declared the independence of the United Provinces of Río de la Plata, but it could not come to a decision as to the form of government. In the debates between those favoring a monarchy and those holding out for a republic, a unique proposal was made — that a Peruvian Inca be placed at the head of the new state! This plan, which its supporters hoped would recover for the United Provinces the silver wealth of Upper Peru, was seriously considered. The congress, for want of agreement as to the form of government, left the question for the future and named Juan Martín de Pueyrredón as Supreme Director. For San Martín, the choice was fortunate, for his plans had been endangered by the prevalent belief that Lima could be taken by way of Upper Peru. His friend, Pueyrredón, now permitted him to continue with his project and gave him what assistance and encouragement he could afford.

The administration of Pueyrredón marked a time of trial for the United Provinces. Artigas still maintained his Liga Federal against Buenos Aires, and Dom João of Brazil once more sent Portuguese troops into Montevideo. With internal unity still beyond attainment, the United Provinces were in no position to resist Brazilian encroachments. And after San Martín crossed the Andes with a large part of the army, Pueyrredón was hard pressed to cope with Artigas. In 1819 Pueyrredón resigned, and the central government was no more. Provincial governments attempted to fill the vacuum, but a state of near-anarchy prevailed. In 1820 Artigas, succumbing to the mounting pressure from Brazil and the continued hostility of Buenos Aires, sought refuge in Paraguay. The next year Brazil annexed the Banda Oriental as the Cisplatine province.

While the former viceroyalty of Río de la Plata was disintegrating into independent and warring provinces, beyond the Andes San Martín's plans bore fruit. In January, 1817, his Army of the Andes was ready to march. It was divided into three divisions to cross the mountains, and a force was sent to the south under Ramón Freire to seize Talca while the main body was emerging near the plains of Chacabuco.

On February 12, the patriot army won a tremendous victory, and the royalists abandoned Santiago. The battle of Chacabuco was a turning point of the wars. It initiated the first well-planned campaign for the overthrow of royalist authority at Lima; its stimulus to patriot morale was tremendous, while the hopes of the royalists suffered a corresponding decline. It was a remarkable feat from any point of view, and it indicated the high degree of efficiency which San Martín had instilled in his heterogeneous troops. From this time forward the aspect of the wars changed, and the gloomy prospects of 1815 and 1816 gave way to the optimistic campaigns of 1819 and 1820. From the Spanish side it became apparent that the time remaining for the reconquest of Spanish America was fast running out. Joaquín de la Pezuela, who had succeeded Abascal as viceroy of Peru, had attempted to divert San Martín's army from invading Chile by a royalist attack on Tucumán. The redoubtable gauchos of Salta and Jujuy effectively blocked the road with their lances, and San Martín's passage of the Andes forced the viceroy to withdraw his troops. The Argentine invasion of Chile left the Plata area safe from attack by way of Upper Peru.

After the patriot victory at Chacabuco the events in the Plata region had little direct bearing on the final outcome of the wars, although the Army of the Andes fought its share of the battles until ultimate victory had been achieved. What mattered now was the struggle for Chile and the proposed campaign against Peru. The heavily fortified port of Valdivia in southern Chile was still held by royalists, and capable officers were in the field. San Martín and the Chileans prolonged the danger by not marching against them immediately after Chacabuco, when conditions were favorable. The viceroy's naval squadron enabled him to communicate with his commanders in Chile, and reinforcements were sent when circumstances permitted.

Early in 1818 fresh royalist troops were landed at Talcahuano, and General Osorio again attempted the reconquest of Chile. In a night battle at Cancha Rayada the patriots were put to flight, and the cause of Chilean independence hung in the balance. San Martín calmly reorganized the defeated army and restored its confidence.

On April 5, the fate of Chile was decided by the overwhelming patriot victory of Maipú. Losses were heavy on both sides; of more than 5000 royalist troops engaged, less than 1000 escaped. The principal casualties on the patriot side were among the battalions of former Negro slaves recruited in Cuyo province, who shed their blood freely at both Chacabuco and Maipú. After the defeat of his army, the viceroy abandoned his attempt to reconquer Chile and began preparations to defend the viceroyalty itself. Maipú was another milestone in the bloody struggle for independence.

In 1818 the major military problem remaining for San Martín was the invasion of Peru. Between the victories of Chacabuco and Maipú, Chile had already begun to acquire the naval squadron needed for the enterprise, and Spanish cruisers no longer appeared off Chilean ports with impunity. English and American naval veterans and ships were recruited for the Chilean service. The bulk of the seamen, however, were Chileans for the most part without maritime experience, but capable and eager for service. The formation of a naval force from such dissimilar elements was a tremendous task, yet the Chilean squadron swept the Spanish warships from the South Pacific. The hero of this often discouraging undertaking was Lord Thomas Alexander Cochrane, a dynamic Scot who had gained recognition as one of the most brilliant naval tacticians of all time by his exploits in the English navy during the Napoleonic Wars.

Cochrane's career in the British navy had ended in dismissal, owing to financial peculations of his relatives with which he had little concern. Declining a commission in the Spanish service, he accepted Chile's offer and arrived at Valparaiso in November, 1818. Under his aegis the Chilean squadron cleared the seas of Spanish ships and opened the way for an invasion of Peru. After an unsuccessful attempt to destroy the Spanish warships in Callao by means of rockets, Cochrane sailed south to Valdivia, the most heavily fortified royalist port in the Pacific. In January, 1820, he entered the harbor with two ships, landed a few companies of marines and soldiers at sundown, and by daybreak was in possession of Spain's last base of operations on the coast of Chile. The daring action was characteristic of the Chilean squadron during the time of Cochrane, and it is not surprising that the viceroy preferred to keep his warships anchored safely in Callao rather than expose them to certain destruction.

In 1819, while Cochrane and San Martín were engaged in their naval and military preparations for the invasion of Peru, the Spanish government was making a last effort to organize a force capable of reducing the former colonies to subordination. News of the massing of troops in southern Spain helped precipitate Pueyrredón's fall from power, and patriot leaders in Santiago were apprehensive lest the blow should fall before their plans had matured. Fortunately for the Spanish colonies, they received respite from an unexpected quarter. In January, 1820, the Spanish expeditionary force mutinied. The plans for military expeditions against the former colonies had to be abandoned, and the royalist forces in Peru were cast adrift.

The passing of the immediate threat from Spain did not relieve San Martín of his obligations to the government of Buenos Aires. When the tenuous truce between the central government and the provincial caudillos collapsed in federalist-centralist dissension, the porteños lacked the military power to enforce governmental authority. San Martín was ordered to return with the Army of the Andes. To abandon the campaign against Peru and to see his veteran troops consumed in civil strife was a sorrowful prospect for San Martín. After weighing the issues, he decided that his duty lay in pursuing his project. He assumed a grave responsibility in disobeying the orders of his government, and although some of his contemporaries condemned his insubordination, the judgment of posterity has been favorable to his course. It is difficult to conjecture what might have happened in Argentina had he returned with the army and established porteño authority throughout the land by force.

In August, 1820, San Martín's Chilean expedition departed from Valparaiso for Peru. The force was composed of only some 4000 troops, whereas the viceroy, Joaquín de la Pezuela, commanded more than 20,000 men. San Martín's intention was merely to aid the Peruvians in winning their independence and thereby remove any further threat to Chile and the Plata region on the part of Spanish forces. He viewed the campaign as an extended one and declared that the fate of Peru should not be decided by the outcome of a single battle. For a time his plan seemed to be succeeding. He occupied Pisco and set about recruiting Peruvian regiments. Large numbers of Spanish soldiers deserted to his cause. As time went on, however, and San Martín did not invade the royalist stronghold in the highlands, delay and inactivity undermined the morale of his troops. He perhaps counted on the isolation of the viceroy's army, deprived as it was of all possibility of reinforcement, to produce an eventual surrender; but in this hope he miscalculated the determination of royalist officers to resist to the bitter end. Early in 1821 Viceroy Pezuela was ready to give in and declared that it was useless to continue the struggle, but he was promptly deposed and replaced by General José de la Serna, whose energy and leadership saved the royalist army from disintegration.

Even with a change in leadership, the royalist cause seemed definitely lost by the middle of the year. In the struggle for northern South America, Bolívar won a decisive victory at Carabobo, near Caracas. In July, José de la Serna evacuated Lima and permitted San Martín to enter the city without opposition. Blockaded by Lord Cochrane and besieged by San Martín, the port of Callao capitulated. Royalist armies were soon confined to Upper Peru and a few scattered outposts. The prospect of aid from Spain was little better than it had been when Pizarro and his adventurers entered Cajamarca nearly three centuries earlier. Nevertheless, the army of independence faltered.

Throughout the Peruvian campaign, residents of the viceroyalty had shown little enthusiasm for independence. No popular acclaim welcomed San Martín and his army, although neither was the populace particularly hostile. Rather, the Peruvians seemed indifferent. The wealthier classes, Spaniard and creole alike, feared the social consequences that might follow in the wake of a victory by San Martín's citizen army. Consequently, with the occupation of Lima, followed by the brief siege of Callao, military action came to a halt. Energies which should have been employed in prosecuting the war were wasted in the trials of forming a government upon which San Martín could depend for support. Personal ambitions and enmities increased the difficulties, and discord became general. Lord Cochrane and San Martín quarreled, the former urging action and the latter patience. They disagreed over the payment of Cochrane's forces. Finally, the doughty admiral sailed away to the north and left the general to his own devices. Little progress was made either in creating a suitable government in Lima or in terminating the war. Soon a reaction in favor of the royalists, or at least against the alien patriots, developed; in its turn San Martín's army was diminished by desertions. The general, who assumed the title of 'Protector of Peru,' was suspect both as a foreigner and for his belief that a monarchy was the most fitting form of government to replace the quasi-monarchial viceregal regime.

Until 1822, the movements for independence in the north and south had remained quite distinct. With the fall of Quito and Guayaquil to Bolívar, the two currents merged in Peru. Bolívar appeared on the Peruvian scene at a moment when San Martín's star was sinking rapidly. His troops were inactive and restive. Disease and desertion had gravely weakened their fighting power, in spite of some reinforcement from Chile. When Bolívar proposed a conference between the two liberating generals, San Martín was quick to accept. On July 26, 1822, the two leaders conferred privately in Guayaquil. No record was kept of what they said, for during much of the conversation, which lasted a number of hours, they were alone and unattended. Accounts of what each man said to the other are almost all pure speculation; neither ever completely revealed his feelings about the meeting, although San Martín later hinted at disillusionment. However, the result of the conference was clear. They did not join forces to complete the conquest of Peru as had been suggested prior to the conference. Rather, San Martín returned to Lima where he soon surrendered his command and withdrew to Chile, leaving the destiny of Peru in the hands of Bolívar.

Even while San Martín was absent from Lima on his journey to Guayaquil, an insurrection against his government had broken out. The revolt was directed primarily against the ministry of Bernardo de Monteagudo, who was regarded by many ambitious Peruvians as an odious tyrant. Monteagudo was, like San Martín, an Argentinian, and the uprising reflected the anti-foreign sentiment which was strong throughout the country. Bolívar's regime enjoyed no greater popularity.

The junta which replaced San Martín upon his resignation at first declined Bolívar's offer of assistance. In the latter part of 1822, however, the loyalist general, José Canterac, inflicted a serious defeat on the Peruvian independence army. By the following year, the Peruvian government reluctantly accepted the Liberator's proffered aid, for no improvement in the military situation had come about and royalist forces were growing stronger.

Before Colombian troops were able to take up the battle in Peru, the royalists recaptured Lima, and in February, 1824, a mutiny of the troops at Callao gave the viceroy control of that vital port. Lima was soon evacuated again, for its possession conveyed little military advantage. Canterac returned to the sierra with his army intact and, indeed, strengthened as a consequence of his victories.

Antonio José de Sucre, Bolívar's ablest field commander, marched against the royalist forces in the highlands with an army composed of Argentine, Chilean, and Colombian troops. General Andrés Santa Cruz also entered the mountains to converge on the royalists with an army of Peruvians. In August, 1824, Sucre's army came to grips with that of Canterac on the plains of Junín. The patriot army shattered royalist prestige, and the viceroy's forces were rapidly weakened by mass desertions. The royalist general, Canterac, was himself greatly discouraged, for there was no source of reinforcements. However, the timely arrival of Spanish warships at Callao gave the royalists temporary naval preponderance and aroused new hopes of effective resistance. Lord Cochrane had retired from the Chilean service in 1822, and Peru had only a small squadron under William Guise which was no match for the Spaniards.

The royalist resurgence proved brief, however. Viceroy La Serna attempted to cut off and destroy Sucre's army in the valley of

Ayacucho. On December 9, 1824, the two armies locked in desperate battle to decide the fate of Peru. When the day ended, the patriot forces had won a decisive victory. The triumph at Ayacucho was the culmination of years of sacrifice on the part of Spanish American patriots. It was fitting that in the final battle Argentine grenadiers, Peruvian hussars, and Colombian lancers fought side by side with Chilean artillerymen to win the victory. Also conspicuous on the battlefield, at the head of a regiment of cavalry, was William Miller, former artillery officer and former commander of the Chilean marines under Lord Cochrane. The patriot success at Ayacucho was the crowning achievement of fourteen years of strife, highlighted by the feats at Chacabuco, Boyacá, Maipú, and Carabobo.

After the battle, only the forts of Callao and the archipelago of Chiloé remained in royalist control. It was not until 1826 that the Peruvian port city was surrendered and the Chilean islands were freed by a special expedition from the mainland. The war was for all practical purposes ended at Ayacucho, but neither Chile nor Peru could feel completely secure until the last Spanish outposts had been liquidated.

While final victory over the Spaniards was being won in Upper Peru, political affairs in both the Plata region and Chile deteriorated. In Chile, O'Higgins ruled for a time as a heavy-handed dictator, bent on social and moral reform as well as the establishment of a strong republican government. Eventually he was forced to resign and seek permanent exile in Peru while revolution and anarchy disrupted the peace of his homeland. The great Chilean patriot never returned, but died on foreign soil. In Buenos Aires, the government was directed for a considerable period by Bernardino Rivadavia, a capable leader who tried in vain to instill a feeling of nationalism in the country and restore some semblance of national government throughout the area of the former viceroyalty. His liberal reforms brought him into conflict with the church and with the more conservative elements among the laity. Most of the changes he proposed were effected by later generations, but in the 1820's the time was not yet propitious for sweeping social reform.

External problems also contributed to Rivadavia's difficulties. Early in 1826 a congress of the United Provinces was momentarily restored, and it voted to support a Uruguayan patriot, Juan Antonio Lavalleja, in an effort to recover the Banda Oriental from Brazil. The war proved a costly undertaking for the disunited provinces, and despite initial successes against Brazilian forces on land and sea, the federation could not muster enough strength to win a final victory. The envoy of Rivadavia at Rio de Janeiro agreed to acknowledge Brazil's claim to the Banda Oriental in order to terminate the war. An angry outburst in Buenos Aires forced Rivadavia to denounce the treaty, but the chief executive's prestige had been damaged beyond repair. He resigned the presidency in July, 1827. His attempt to resolve the capital question by federalizing the city of Buenos Aires contributed to the bitterness of the porteños. Buenos Aires preferred to follow a solitary course rather than yield to the demands of the other provinces.

By 1830, the former viceroyalties of Peru and Río de la Plata were broken up into the new nations of Peru, Bolivia, Chile, and Paraguay. The provinces of Río de la Plata were hardly a nation, but constituted a loose confederation in which Buenos Aires was always the dominant power but never fully recognized as such by the other members. Also in 1830, Uruguay became an independent state whose status was guaranteed jointly by Brazil and the Argentine provinces, an arrangement worked out largely through the mediation of England and France in an effort to terminate the fruitless warfare over the Banda Oriental. The process of empire disintegration had run its course in southern South America, but the new states that emerged coincided remarkably in territorial extent with the former imperial jurisdictional units of the late Bourbon era. The viceroyalties had fallen apart, but the lesser entities, the captaincies-general and presidencies, had become the new nations of the independence era.

XXII

The Wars of Independence in the North

> They worked with courage and good faith, and in that disper-
> sive, disruptive, explosive way which is typical of Spain, as it
> is of the pomegranate. And the Empire, born as a pomegranate
> bursting forth and dispersing its grains of life thoughout a con-
> tinent, died also as a pomegranate strewing the continent with
> its grains in helpless dispersion, to be pecked at will by the
> eagles of power.
>
> SALVADOR DE MADARIAGA *

IN the wars for Spanish American independence,
New Spain produced vestment-clad social vision-
aries who died as martyrs; La Plata sent forth a somber, silent
general whose military ability was matched only by his self-effacing
refusal to leave his chosen profession to enter the political jousts.
Chile contributed the grim statesman whose dogged perseverance
kept the patriot flame alive through the darkest hours of defeat
and reconquest. It remained for Caracas and New Granada, however, to produce the glamorous heroes who well bestrode a white
horse, who combined a daredevilish military acumen with great
personal valor and unbounded political egotism. Here as in no
other part of the empire was the creole intellectual called upon to
step forth from his discussion society and from behind his editorial
desk to lay his fortune, his freedom, and his life upon the altar of
independence.

* *The Fall of the Spanish American Empire,* The Macmillan Company,
New York, 1948, p. 378.

The roster of revolutionary heroes began accumulating names at an early date in New Granada. While numerous predecessors, many of them unnamed and unknown to history, espoused the cause of liberalism and the enlightenment in Bogotá, Quito, Caracas, and other cultural centers of the viceroyalty, none stood out for his leadership as did Antonio Nariño. In 1794, Nariño was a young and well-to-do creole of Bogotá whose home provided a popular meeting place for a group of able men of radical persuasion — men who took a keen interest in the political and social doctrines of the French Encyclopedists, as well as those advocated by the founders of the new republican government in North America. Virtually all those in Nariño's circle were to figure prominently in the independence movement, and a number were to give their lives for it. Other regions had their patriotic societies and liberal discussion groups, their radical publicists and scientists who rejected the old order and defied the despotism of the Holy Office; but seemingly in no other capital of the empire was the spirit of scientific inquiry and free political discussion so assiduously cultivated at so early a date as in Bogotá. In one sense, intellectual activities of the younger creole element were a continuation of currents and trends apparent in the closing years of the reign of Carlos III, but the French Revolution had created a new background against which a now reactionary Spanish regime could not fail to view the propagation of liberal views as subversive and heretical. The creole patriotic groups of Bogotá soon found themselves in trouble with the authorities.

Nariño took the audacious step of translating and publishing the revolutionary French Declaration of the Rights of Man. For this act he was arrested, tried, and found guilty of sedition and condemned to exile in Africa. He was able, however, to escape his captors and flee to England. There he remained for many months, but not long enough to escape the consequences of his action. Nariño returned to Bogotá in 1797 and was promptly imprisoned. He was released by the viceroy, Mendinueta, in 1803. Nariño's role in the revolutionary movement had hardly yet begun.

There were many other evidences of the vigor of creole intellectuality. The eminent scholarship prevailing at the College of El Rosario, at the Seminary of Popayán, and at San Bartolomé in Bogotá attested to a spirit of inquiry that could not be restrained by imperial legislation or impeded by religious doctrine. A tendency toward open discussion gave rise to the publication of a number of newspapers. That none survived for long is indicative of a lack of adequate financial backing, lack of sufficient response in the literate populace, and the absence of the modern advertiser. Those who undertook to air their views through the medium of publication would form an imposing list of independence leaders, however. Among those most prominent were Jorge Tadeo Lozano, Manuel del Socorro Rodríguez, and Francisco José de Caldas. The period in which these and other intellectual leaders assumed great prominence ranged over twenty years, roughly between 1790 and 1810. Thereafter came the period of action.

As in other parts of the empire the Napoleonic conquest of Spain made deep inroads in the authority of the constituted Spanish officials in New Granada. Spaniards, of course, were prompt to acknowledge the pretensions of the Junta Central at Seville as spokesman for peninsular rule in the absence of the king. Creole groups generally ignored the claims of the rump Spanish government and seized upon the legalism by which the various viceroyalties were held to be independent kingdoms of the Spanish crown, not integral parts of Spain as the Seville government declared. By asserting the independent status of each kingdom, creole leaders were in position to set up their own juntas and for the first time to exercise political authority in their homeland. In South America, the first creole junta was established in Quito on August 10, 1809. The action was premature and unpolitic for several reasons. The quiteños abolished the royal audiencia and pretended to assume authority over Popayán and other territories to which no valid claim could be made. If the independent kingdom argument was to have any validity at all, it had to be asserted by the jurisdiction as a whole, not by one of its lesser cities. Thus while supporters of the Quito movement were to be found in Bogotá and other cities of the viceroyalty, many creoles also felt that the upstart junta at Quito was trying to assume prerogatives that more properly belonged to the capital or to a junta representative of the entire territory. Likewise, creole leaders in Bogotá and other cities were not yet ready to take the course chosen by the Quito leaders, and they were unprepared to provide support.

The creation of the independent Quito junta alarmed Spanish officials in all northern South America. In New Granada repressive measures were taken against known liberals such as Nariño, who was thrown into prison again. In Peru the viceroy took matters firmly in hand and sent a military force into the southern part of New Granada to oust the creole junta at Quito. His efforts were successful, for the first creole government was crushed and Spanish authority restored.

In Santa Fé de Bogotá as in Mexico City, creole forces found the cabildo the only institution of government through which they could officially and legally express their views, and they quickly availed themselves of it by pressing the viceroy to call a cabildo abierto, an open meeting in which prominent citizens and the various public corporate bodies would be represented. The viceroy, Amar y Borbón, undecided as to what he should do, gave in to creole pressure and the assembly was called. It met late in 1809, but accomplished nothing. The time was not yet ripe.

In the nominally dependent eastern portion of the viceroyalty, the captaincy-general of Caracas, the groundwork was also being laid for a creole effort to assume control of the government. Caracas had had one ardent revolutionist for a long time, a man who had devoted many years of his life to trying to gain foreign support for a colonial revolt against Spain. This man was Sebastián Francisco de Miranda, son of a local creole family that always fell just short of making the social register. Miranda left Caracas in 1772 to serve in the Spanish army. He was a soldier in Africa first, and later he fought in Florida and the West Indies against the English during the revolution of the British North American colonies. Miranda got into difficulty, however, as a result of participation in certain transactions violating the commercial laws of the Indies. He was arrested, tried, and found guilty. Rather than spend his sentence of ten years in a Spanish jail, he effected escape and entry into the United States. From there he went to England, and eventually traveled throughout most of central and northern Europe. In France he became a general in Napoleon's armies and fought in the campaigns in the Low Countries.

Francisco Miranda was, in many ways, more of an opportunist than a patriot. He shifted allegiance from Spain to 'South America' gradually and under circumstances that suggest anger with the Spanish authorities over his legal difficulties and need for cash had quite as much to do with the matter as a burning concern for the welfare of a country he had literally forsaken. Miranda wandered around Europe representing himself as a nobleman, which he was not, and selling information about Spanish defenses in the New World to the English, which traitorous action he justified by extracting vague promises of military support from the British in a campaign for Spanish American independence. Shrewd but at times naïve, Miranda was used by the British Prime Minister, Pitt, and then cast aside. Returning to the United States, the self-exiled Venezuelan planned an expedition to South America, secured assistance from ignorant American officials by telling them he had the support of President Jefferson, and eventually sailed from New York with an outfitted ship, the *Leander*.

Reinforced by two smaller vessels, Miranda's expedition arrived off the coast of South America in the spring of 1806. He was promptly defeated by a Spanish squadron and retreated to Barbados, where British aid was requested. By the end of the summer, Miranda was ready for a second try, and with a British naval escort he succeeded in landing on the Venezuelan coast and in capturing the small town of Coro. With Coro as his headquarters, he issued a call to his countrymen to rise against their oppressors. No one rose except the captain-general at Caracas, who prepared to throw Miranda into the sea. Disgust on the part of Miranda's British supporters may well be imagined, for after an absence of over thirty years he had assured them that patriots in his homeland were seething with revolutionary fervor and would throw off the Spanish yoke if given the merest opportunity. His expedition was a hopeless failure, and by the end of the year he had withdrawn to Trinidad and disbanded his forces.

Miranda was a precursor of independence for northern South America in the sense that he was a chief advocate of the cause in England and the United States long before actual revolution got under way. How he was able to plead his cause in so many high places is a tribute to his ingenuity, his eloquence, and the receptiveness of his listeners to the idea of separating the Spanish empire from Spain. At one point or another he was in direct communication with Alexander Hamilton, Thomas Jefferson, William Pitt, and the empress of Russia. He became a well-known figure to the enemies of Spain, but few of his own countrymen had ever heard of him except as a shadowy conspirator with whom other conspirators occasionally communicated.

By the spring of 1810, the fortunes of Spain were at their lowest ebb. The junta at Seville had fled to Cádiz, and then given way to a regency whose future status was very much in doubt. A cabildo abierto met in Caracas, and in response to popular clamor the captain-general, Vicente de Emperán, resigned and was replaced by a junta. Other provinces threw in their lot with the creole government, but three remained loyal to Spain and furnished a foothold for development of a counter-revolutionary force. For a time, however, fortune smiled upon the creole leaders. Suddenly throughout virtually all New Granada local juntas sprang into existence. Cabildos selected representatives to a central junta meeting in Bogotá, which, aided by the cabildo in the capital, drove the viceroy and the audiencia into exile and took over administration of all departments of government. All this, of course, was done in the name of that empty symbol of royal authority, Fernando VII.

The course of self-government was far from smooth. Perhaps the Spanish officials had been too easily excluded and creole leaders failed to realize the seriousness of the steps they had taken. Perhaps their efforts were not deeply enough rooted in popular support. Ignorant of their peril, the Venezuelan cabildos elected members to a congress which early in July of 1811 declared complete independence from Spain. At the same time, efforts to form a government in New Granada were hopelessly bogged down by regional differences and the demands of local loyalties. Cartagena led the opposition to Bogotá and the pretensions of the Bogotá junta to speak for the entire viceroyalty. The leaders in the capital in turn tried to maintain a centralist domination, and, failing that, formed a separate government with the name of Cundinamarca and invited adjacent provinces to join. The disunity of New Granada was on the point of being institutionalized.

The leaders in Bogotá were Jorge Tadeo Lozano, the first president of Cundinamarca, and Antonio Nariño, a member of the Bogotá city government. The latter was an outspoken advocate of unitarian political structure and strong executive authority, and he vigorously attacked the federalist inclined government of the president. A constitution had been proclaimed denominating Cundinamarca a monarchy with the president acting as viceregent for the king, Fernando VII. The poignant attacks of Nariño through his newspaper, *La Bagatela*, aroused great opposition to the government of Jorge Tadeo Lozano, and shortly it fell, the monarchist constitution with it. Nariño became president of a republican Cundinamarca.

At the very moment Nariño assumed the presidency of Cundinamarca a federal congress was meeting in Santa Fé de Bogotá for the purpose of forming a general government of New Granada. Delegates from the various provinces, Antioquia, Cartagena, Casanare, Chocó, Neiva, Pamplona, Socorro, Tunja, and Cundinamarca, did indeed arrive at a pact of federation by which was created the United Provinces of New Granada. Under the pact, of which the principal author was Camilo Torres, each province was to retain its own administration. To the central government, consisting of a congress, were assigned powers over military matters and foreign affairs. The entire arrangement was generally displeasing to Nariño, and so bitter did the disagreement become that the congress moved from Santa Fé de Bogotá to Ibagué to avoid the unpleasant interference of the *bogoteños*.

For a time Cundinamarca joined in the confederation of the

United Provinces, but as a result of disagreement over jurisdictional boundaries, Nariño withdrew his government. Actually, during most of 1811 and 1812, two opposing governments existed in New Granada; and in the fall of 1812 open warfare existed between them. Nariño, as a liberal revolutionist and able patriot leader, was a popular hero and effective dictator in his centralist state formed around the ancient viceregal capital; but he was quite unsuccessful in his efforts to overcome the opposition of regionalist leaders who insisted upon virtual independence for each province. While New Granadans quarreled among themselves, the fortunes of Spain took a turn for the better. Aided by the British, Spanish armies drove the legions of Napoleon northward, a liberal government was formed at Cádiz, and the task of recovering lost colonial territory was successfully initiated in Caracas. At no time had the loyalist Spanish element been thoroughly discredited in the initial stages of the independence effort. Spanish officials had indeed been forced to leave both Caracas and Bogotá; but at the moment of their departure they had no home government capable of giving them support. Even the most ardent Spaniard and royalist had no assurance that an independent Spanish government would soon again arise in the homeland. Stunned, he remained relatively quiet and awaited developments. But the moment Spanish power re-emerged in Spain, the loyalist element came to life in all parts of New Granada. From Quito and Popayán loyalist power spread northward, and in Caracas it surged like a returning tide over the feeble republican structure which Miranda had returned to head after the uprisings of 1810.

A powerful factor in the loyalist resurgence was the steadfast adherence of the clergy to the old regime. Priests there were who supported the creole cause, but no Hidalgo appeared as in New Spain to sway the Indian masses and lure the mestizos into the independence camp. On the contrary, the first real resistance against the Miranda government was spearheaded by the clergy at Valencia; and when early in 1812 an earthquake destroyed with tremendous loss of life the creole strongholds of Caracas, Mérida, and Barquisimeto, the religious promptly seized upon the catastrophe as proof of divine wrath at the rebel cause. Such a representation had a telling effect, for loyalist cities had somehow been miraculously spared. The confusion of the disaster and the impotence of the Miranda government in the face of it discouraged many who were not persuaded by the arguments of the clergy, and desertion to the Spanish cause became general. In July of 1812, Miranda gave in to the loyalist army of Juan Domingo Monteverde and fled with a few of his aides to La Guaira preparatory to leaving the country. In La Guaira Miranda was accused of having betrayed the independence cause and turned over to the Spaniards. He spent the remaining four years of his life in one dungeon after another, and the cause which he had pursued so long passed to other and abler hands.

There had already appeared upon the patriot scene a man who, while only in his middle twenties, amply demonstrated his capacity for leadership in the government of Miranda at Caracas. Simón Bolívar y Palacios was born into a well-to-do creole family of Caracas in 1783. Educated under the guidance of an able tutor, he went to Spain as a youth to complete his education and to acquire the social graces, polish, and experience becoming a young man of the creole aristocracy. Not only did Bolívar enter successfully into the social life of the Spanish capital, but he also went through a period of philosophical metamorphosis during which his outlook became one of defiance to the dogmas, superstitions, and prejudices of the old order and the imperial system that maintained it. He traveled in France and Italy and saw the French Revolution transform itself into the empire of Napoleon. He saw the weaknesses of Spain's political leaders. At the same time, embittered by the early death of the young wife he had taken in Spain, Bolívar developed a zest for sowing wild oats that he never overcame and which added a particular spice to the aura of a figure soon to become legendary.

Upon returning to America in 1807, Bolívar visited briefly in the United States, but then journeyed on to Venezuela and occupied himself for a time in caring for his family properties. Soon he was involved in revolutionary intrigue, and in 1810 accompanied Andrés Bello and Luis López Méndez to England in the hope of soliciting support for the independence cause. There he first became associated with Miranda, under whom he was later to serve as a military commander in the first effort to establish Venezuelan independence.

With the collapse of the first creole government in Caracas, Bolívar escaped from Puerto Cabello and went to Cartagena, at which point he began to raise his sights and to see the need for combining the efforts of all patriot elements of the New Granadan viceroyalty. The revolutionary junta in Cartagena accepted Bolívar's services; and soon, in command of a small force, he took over for the patriot cause most of the cities and towns along the lower Magdalena river. These initial successes attracted stronger support, and in 1813 the town of Cúcuta, situated on the border between New Granada and Venezuela, was occupied by the patriot army. In tribute to the new-found military leader, both the New Granadan government of the congress and Camilo Torres and the Cundinamarca government of Nariño came to Bolívar's aid. He was made a citizen of New Granada, given an official military command, and authorized to undertake a campaign eastward into Venezuela.

It is remarkable indeed that Bolívar received such strong support from the disorganized and divided authorities in New Granada and Bogotá, to say nothing of the isolated junta at Cartagena. There was fear of a Spanish invasion from the south, from Quito and Popayán. The coastal port of Santa Marta was captured and shortly lost again to royalist forces who used it as a base of operations and a landing point for fresh Spanish troops from Europe. Thus to many Bolívar's campaign into Venezuela must have seemed ill-advised and fraught with peril for the safety of New Granada proper. Fears were at first pushed aside, however, as Bolívar's initial efforts were crowned with success. He swept all before him, and in August of 1813 entered Caracas. In the midst of the campaign, the daring young general had proclaimed a *guerra a la muerte*, or war without quarter; and the war from that point on took a bitter turn that rendered impossible any thought of reconciliation between the Spanish and creole forces. This, of course, was what Bolívar wanted, a break so sharp that it could not be repaired, even with the fine patching cement of the Spanish liberals and the revolutionary Constitution of 1812.

Bolívar re-created a patriot government in Caracas, with himself at its head, but his string of victories was running out. Royalist forces under José Ceballos began to move, and in the early summer of 1814 they defeated Bolívar and entered Caracas. The Venezuelan leader fled once more to New Granada where he re-entered actively the military and political controversies that still divided the entire region. Bolívar's association had been and continued to be primarily with the confederation, whose member provinces one by one had declared their independence from Spain during 1813 and 1814 while the general from Caracas was engaged in the Venezuelan campaign. Nariño's government at Santa Fé de Bogotá had assisted in supporting the military activities of Bolívar, but with the confederation no peace seemed possible, and during 1814 the foremost New Granadan patriot was himself removed from the scene.

Spanish forces coming up from Peru captured Popayán and continued on northward up the Cauca valley. Nariño set out to meet them, and in the battle that ensued the patriot forces from Santa Fé were badly defeated. Nariño was captured and promptly transported to Spain and condemned to languish indefinitely in a Cádiz dungeon. The royalist forces continued northward to threaten Antioquia. In the face of this situation, the struggle between Cundinamarca and the confederation continued; but now the confederation took steps to increase its own effectiveness by delegating supreme executive authority to a junta of three men, none of whom was from Santa Fé de Bogotá. Furthermore, the confederation called upon Bolívar to bring an end to the ridiculous internal dissension by subduing Cundinamarca. This he did, capturing Santa Fé in December of 1814. The capital of the confederation was transferred there almost immediately, and for the first time since the initiation of the revolutionary movement, New Granada was constituted a single nation with a single source of political authority.

Too long had the New Granadans played the fool and allowed

the *patria boba*, or foolish homeland, to continue on its course of self-destruction. There was a Spanish army before every door. Early in 1815 a large army of regulars arrived from Spain under the command of Field Marshal Pablo Morillo. Establishing himself first in Caracas, Morillo moved westward by sea against Cartagena, which fell late in 1815 after a long and desperate siege. Bolívar, disillusioned by his inability to bring about unity in New Granada even after his campaign against Santa Fé, had resigned his command and gone into exile in Jamaica. With Bolívar gone and Cartagena in the hands of the Spaniards, the confederation took the last desperate measures of a dying regime. It conferred virtually all authority upon one man, Dr. Camilo Torres. But this act of desperation was to no avail; Morillo marched upon Santa Fé and captured it easily.

The re-establishment of Spanish rule in New Granada was accompanied by a reign of terror unprecedented in the history of the region. In April of 1816, Fernando VII decreed the re-establishment of the viceroyalty and named Francisco Montalvo viceroy and captain-general of New Granada. The audiencia was likewise re-created, and the Holy Office of the Inquisition, more and more an instrument of state under the Bourbons, was revived. The viceroy and the audiencia remained in Cartagena; but the army under Morillo, as military governor of Santa Fé, and under his successor, Juan Sámano, roamed the interior engaged in acts of vengeance and recrimination. Hundreds, possibly thousands were hanged or shot, among them Camilo Torres and other prominent leaders of the patriot forces. Decrees of amnesty were issued only to lure additional patriots into the open and to their torture and death. The Spaniards systematically went about destroying the last vestiges of hope that the viceroyalty might be peacefully reunited with the mother country. The military despots seemed bent on alienating even those who a few weeks before had welcomed the returning Spanish armies with open arms.

Bolívar's retirement to Jamaica was anything but a withdrawal from the independence struggle. Rather, the time spent in exile was used to good advantage to consider the future, to plan the military reconquest of northern South America and the political system to be established once independence was a reality. Bolívar was a prolific letter writer, and many of his letters have been preserved not only for their value as a key to the man's character but also because of their outstanding quality as political essays. Never did he write so prophetically, however, as from his temporary island home. Bolívar understood well the political and intellectual climate of the time and place; and in that milieu his own views were strongly progressive and indeed liberal, yet at the same time tempered with a realization of the social and political realities that were to make living with independence more difficult than attaining it.

From his island retreat, Bolívar had some difficulty getting a new campaign launched. His first attempt, a move against eastern Venezuela, ended in defeat and the return of the patriot leader to Haiti, which republic had given him supplies and munitions. The second effort, undertaken at the beginning of 1817, produced more lasting results by the creation of an independence force that the Spaniards never again were able to drive from the mainland. Joined by another patriot leader, José Antonio Páez, Bolívar captured one town after another as he moved westward from Cumaná and Barcelona. Before the gates of Caracas, however, the patriot generals faced the Spanish general-in-chief Morillo, who had rushed from Santa Fé de Bogotá to oppose the patriot revival. In the ensuing engagement Morillo was successful, and the patriots fell back toward the Orinoco valley.

From defeat Bolívar now rose to conduct one of the famous campaigns of military history. Instead of throwing his forces again and again at Caracas, as less imaginative men might have done and as Morillo certainly expected him to do, Bolívar took an army of 2500 men up the Orinoco river and over the Paya pass of the Andes to descend suddenly upon Bogotá. The maneuver itself was exceedingly difficult, and the loss of equipment and life in the freezing altitude was heavy. Early in August, 1819, after surprising and overwhelming the outlying Spanish outposts, Bolívar's army met and defeated the main body of royalist forces at

Boyacá. The road to Bogotá was open and the remaining Spanish officials there fled hastily toward the lowlands and Cartagena. The viceregal capital was quickly occupied and the republic of Colombia proclaimed.

The war was not yet over, of course. Morillo was still in Caracas, Panamá was in Spanish hands, and the entire southern part of the former viceroyalty was held firmly by royalist troops. Three years of sporadic fighting were yet required before even Caracas was freed. A major battle was fought at Carabobo in June of 1821, a battle in which Bolívar again distinguished himself and in which recruited soldiers from the British Isles played an important role. But after Bolívar captured Bogotá in 1819, the issue was never seriously in doubt, for early in 1820 the liberal revolution in Spain crippled Fernando's military effectiveness and literally caused him to concentrate his attention on regaining some measure of his former authority at home.

The victorious patriot leaders moved quickly to form a new republican government after the capture of Bogotá. Late in 1819 a congress was held at Angostura, a congress dominated by the ideas if not the person of the liberating hero, Bolívar. The liberator was at once a realist and a visionary. He realistically aligned himself on the side of a strong central government with full administrative authority as opposed to the hopeless weakness and internal contentiousness of confederation. As a visionary, however, the nation he strove to create he pictured as a large one embracing all of northern South America. The congress at Angostura voted to make of Venezuela, New Granada, and Quito a single national state to be known as Colombia. Regions still in Spanish hands, as was the case with both Quito and Panamá, as well as parts of Venezuela, would be added when liberated. A constituent assembly was called to prepare a constitution for the new government and Bolívar was chosen president and military commander-in-chief. As a concession to the vastness of the territory and the traditional administrative separation of the two major regions of New Granada and Venezuela, it was thought best to provide a separate vice-president for each who would direct the civil administration. Thus Bolívar was left free to continue his military activities and rid the entire region of Spanish armies.

Many of the arrangements made at Angostura were temporary and intended only to provide a basis for political organization until a formal constitution could be drafted and adopted. In May of 1821 a constitutional convention opened at Cúcuta with delegates in attendance from all parts of New Granada and Venezuela. The meeting was a memorable one in many respects. Both major regions of the former viceroyalty had been successfully freed of Spanish control and their representatives had come together to build a great new republic on the prepared foundation of an illustrious Spanish colonial kingdom. Regionalism and its attendant drive toward a confederation of autonomous provinces had for the moment been eclipsed by the unifying victories of the creole armies and the obvious benefits derived from pooling resources in the joint struggle against Spain. Able men with respect for each other's views formed the assemblage, and not the least of those present was Antonio Nariño, freed from a Spanish prison as a consequence of the liberal revolution of 1820.

For long months the delegates deliberated, and when finally a constitutional document was adopted on August 30, 1821, it was clear that no small men had met and worked together. The fundamental law was bold and visionary, yet it embodied a sufficient element of realism to indicate that divergent points of view had been ably compromised. A new state of Gran Colombia was formed claiming jurisdiction over all the territory embraced by the former viceroyalty of New Granada. The government was to be representative, unitary, and for the exercise of power divided into legislative, executive, and judicial branches. The legislature was created as a bi-cameral body with four senators chosen by electors from each of six departments and representatives chosen by electors from provinces, the number so chosen to be based upon population. Executive power was conferred upon a president who was to serve a four-year term and who would be ineligible for immediate re-election. Provision was also made for an elected vice-president and a council of government, the latter composed of the vice-president, one justice of the supreme court, and the secretaries of state. Justices of the supreme court and secretaries of state were to be appointed by the president, the former subject to legislative confirmation. As in the case of members of the legislature, the president and vice-president were to be chosen indirectly by electors. Suffrage was restricted by requirements that voters be able to read and write (after 1840) and that they own real property of an unencumbered value of 100 pesos or be engaged in a useful business, trade, or profession. It was also required that a person be twenty-one years of age or married in order to vote. One need only consider the social and economic structure of the country to understand how greatly restricted was the suffrage by these rather mild limitations. No mention was made of women voting, nor was it considered necessary to put their exclusion from the polls in writing.

The constitutional provisions herein mentioned point to the rather decided influence of the United States Constitution upon the framers of the 1821 Constitution of Gran Colombia. Also they are characteristic of many contemporary and subsequent constitutions adopted by Latin American constituent assemblies. In two particular respects, however, the constitution adopted at Cúcuta provides a basis for consideration of the political controversies to follow, not only in Colombia, but in Ecuador and Venezuela as well. First, no mention was made in the constitution of the Roman Catholic religion or of relations between state and church. In such time and place, the omission constituted recognition of freedom of worship and religion; and this was indeed the intention of many of the liberal-minded framers. Clerical and conservative interests were quite unwilling to let the matter rest, however; and the omission became a matter of prolonged and bitter controversy. The second, and equally controversial point, was the high degree of centralization provided in the constitution. No genuine element of federalism, to say nothing of confederation, was even implied. All levels of political and administrative jurisdiction were creatures of and entirely dependent upon the central government. While the historic provinces were continued in existence and electors chosen in them selected representatives to the lower house of the legislature, the provinces were provided with no popularly elected local legislative or administrative officers. Each was governed by an official called a governor who was responsible to a departmental intendant, but who, together with the intendant, was appointed by the president directly. The six departments were artificial creations combining various provinces, and likewise had neither popularly chosen legislative bodies nor administrative officers. Even the municipalities were stated to be creatures of the national legislature, which by law could establish them, determine their powers, and alter their jurisdictional limits.

There were good reasons why a highly centralized political organization seemed desirable to the constitution makers of Cúcuta. The frustrations and confusion of the recent and unsuccessful New Granadan confederation were fresh in the minds of all, as was of course the long struggle between that confederation and the autonomous government of Cundinamarca. Furthermore, strong leaders at the time, such as Nariño and Bolívar, were ardent centralists. Bolívar did not participate in the deliberations of the convention, but his views were well known and carried great weight. He was at the peak of his popularity, and many were carried along by his dream of a powerful new state embracing all of northern South America. They were subsequently brought back sharply by the stark reality of localism.

In Gran Colombia the centralists were from the early days of the revolution liberals and radicals with respect to such matters as relations between church and state, freedom of the press, suffrage, and similar components of a political philosophy. The royalists, the pro-Spanish elements, the church, and the ultra-conservative classes were not anti-centralist by conviction; on the contrary, the old regime which they espoused had been highly centralist. In 1821, however, these groups found the centralist stage already occupied by the revolutionary liberals. To oppose the new and powerful elements by whom their special prerogatives were threatened, the privileged groups of the old order now threw their support behind the separatists and confederationists. Thus while in many parts of Latin America, and as was the case originally in

Anglo-Saxon America, liberalism and local autonomy marched hand in hand, in Gran Colombia as in the Plata region liberalism and centralism formed a union, and the conservative oligarchs crawled unhappily into bed with those who most of all rejected any interference by a central authority with the local dispensation. A few years later such a combination did not seem strange; but in the period immediately after independence the centralism of the church and the opposition of the old aristocracy to all forms of local self-government frequently forced centralism and conservatism into alliance to protect themselves from the inroads of religious liberalism and social and economic reform. Gran Colombia was a marked exception to this alignment, as was Argentina.

With adoption of the new constitution leaders of the new government did not sit down to the orderly affairs of peaceful administration. Bolívar was chosen president, but he accepted the position on condition that he be permitted to take an army south to free the remaining portions of the former viceroyalty still occupied by Spanish troops. Civil administration was left in the hands of Francisco de Paula Santander, the newly elected vice-president. Santander had been a participant in the revolutionary movement for a number of years, had served as a military commander under Bolívar in the famous campaign across the Andes to Boyacá and Santa Fé de Bogotá. As a native of New Granada he provided a proper balance in the new administration to President Bolívar, a Venezuelan. With Bolívar gone off to the wars, responsibility for governing under the new constitution fell directly upon Santander's shoulders.

For a time Santander seemed equal to the task confronting him. The new government organized its public services, collected revenues, and undertook to obtain recognition abroad. Both Great Britain and the United States recognized the independence of Gran Colombia rather promptly, the latter in 1822 and the former in 1825; but from Spain and her continental allies there came only threats of reconquest.

As might have been expected, the least satisfied region of the new state was the former captaincy-general of Caracas, the department of Venezuela. There the revolutionary hero, General José Antonio Páez, chafed by the bonds of subservience to the central government, spoke like a supporter of local autonomy, and for this he was removed from the position of military commander of the department. He appealed to his old friend, Bolívar, but the absent president instructed him to obey the legally constituted government, and for a time the conflict seemed to subside. Other problems plagued Santander's government, however. Conservatives and clerics opposed him strenuously, and everywhere there was dissatisfaction with the jurisdictional subdivision of the country and the lack of local authority to oppose the sometimes arbitrary efforts of the intendants. Gradually disillusionment and unrest crept like a fog over the countryside, blanketing the isolated valley settlements and leaving only the mountaintops to bask in the glorious idealism of the new nation.

In the meantime, Bolívar was far afield. In 1821, his lieutenant, General Sucre, had swept the Ecuadorian highlands of Spanish loyalists and taken possession of Quito. Then Bolívar himself undertook to extend the benefits of independence to the coastal residents of Guayaquil. There, as already discussed, the Colombian leader held his famous discussion with the Argentine liberator, José de San Martín, who then retired from active participation in the independence wars and returned to the south and to eventual exile in Europe. Bolívar's next step was to carry the war southward into Peru and Bolivia, the latter state being named after its liberator. All these efforts and campaigns, while successful from a military and political standpoint, were a continuous drain on the Gran Colombian treasury and they deprived the struggling new state of its able president at a time when he was most needed. Bolívar's enemies — and any prominent political leader has many of them — were quick to criticize the liberator for his absence while using that absence to full advantage in furtherance of their own political fortunes. The cost of supporting Bolívar's southern campaigns was a perfect issue for argumentation in the legislative halls at Bogotá, and once the threat of Spanish armies no longer alarmed the residents of Gran Colombia, it was easy to forget that any remaining

Spanish foothold on the continent was in reality a point of national danger.

Bolívar's very existence had unfortunate consequences in the political life of the nation. For all those who quarreled with their compatriots he remained an almost unreal figure who upon his return would certainly side with them and thus set all things right. The enemies of Santander particularly relied upon this legend, and they used it as an excuse for obstructionism and disloyalty to the man upon whose shoulders rested all the burdens of state but not the insignia of rank. The vice-president's administration became increasingly ineffective, and the clamor for Bolívar's return grew to a veritable din.

With the final defeat of Spanish forces in Upper Peru and the formation of the independent nation of Bolivia, the liberator's military work was done. He remained, however, and prescribed the Bolivian constitution of 1826 before undertaking a triumphal return to his own country. Finally he started upon the home journey and entered Gran Colombia at Guayaquil. The return was not that of a chief of state, however. Instead, Bolívar's gradual approach to the capital was like that of a man who had issued a *pronunciamiento* against the government and was leading a revolutionary movement to overthrow the existing regime. City after city vested in him dictatorial powers as he passed through, indirectly rejecting the government of Santander and the national congress. It is hard to picture a more difficult position in which the vice-president could have been placed.

In a sense, Bolívar had indeed 'pronounced.' He had done so in the new Bolivian constitution which was alleged to embody his philosophy of government and to provide the basis for making needed reforms in the constitution signed at Cúcuta in 1821. General Páez was in revolt in Venezuela, furthermore, and although Bolívar admonished him to submit to the authority of congress, it was obvious that Páez was a recalcitrant nationalist who represented in part a sectional opposition to Bogotá. It was a problem that Bolívar could not ignore. By addressing himself to the people and calling upon them to restore order or to abide by the order that he would restore, and by indicating his support of the Bolivian constitution, Bolívar set himself against those who had long and with great difficulty upheld the constitutional regime of Gran Colombia.

As Bolívar assumed the reins of authority he took upon himself powers not clearly vested in him by the constitution. He modified administrative arrangements in the subordinate governmental units, he limited the freedom of citizens to assemble and petition, and, when he shortly went to Venezuela, he played fast and free with the revenue system as though he were both congress and executive of an autonomous state. In reality, of course, the Cúcuta constitution left the department of Venezuela no authority to establish and modify taxes; Bolívar's action in restoring the alcabala and other old Spanish imposts was entirely extra-legal.

Bolívar stayed in Bogotá only a few days after his return from Bolivia. He went almost immediately to Venezuela to bring about an end to Páez' insurrection, but he succeeded only by confirming Páez in his usurped authority and in reality joining the Venezuelan nationalists in their defiance of the Gran Colombian congress. It could not fail to occur to the Bogotá officials and congressmen that Bolívar had two loves: the country of his birth, and the new countries to the south which he had so recently liberated and with whom a general confederation was now proposed. Santander and those around him stood firmly for upholding the legal order established at Cúcuta and the full authority of the Bogotá government. A wave of dissatisfaction and confusion swept across the country. The liberator still possessed tremendous prestige, but he no longer showed himself skillful in using that prestige either to his own advantage or to that of the country. His influence divided rather than united, and even military groups were inclined to enter the political arena on one side or the other by issuing statements and pronouncements of what they would or would not tolerate.

In 1827, the congress of Colombia commenced its sessions in May, and one of the early orders of business was a presidential resignation presented to the legislative body by Bolívar. Three times previously the liberator had offered to resign, conducting himself like a petulant child who demands attention and tries to get it by threatening to pick up his marbles and go home. As before, a sufficient number were persuaded of the indispensability of the president to assure a favorable vote for his retention; but this time 24 out of 74 votes were cast for letting him go. Santander, who also offered to resign, was retained by a greater margin. The congress then proceeded to call a constitutional assembly to meet the following year at Ocaña and reform the Cúcuta constitution.

The convention at Ocaña was an utter failure. From all parts of Gran Colombia came delegates committed to this or that change in the governmental structure, but the basic issue was the extent of executive authority. Bolívar in his public statements voiced moderation, but his supporters proposed an arrangement that would have made him dictator and eliminated the vice-president from all effective participation in the administration. The convention was composed, however, of those who in the majority opposed dictatorship and saw no need for fundamental change in the legal order established at Cúcuta. Faced with defeat, Bolívar's supporters withdrew, leaving the convention without a quorum. Those remaining had no alternative but to adjourn.

Shortly before the Ocaña convention the break between Bolívar and Santander became fixed and open, and the failure of the convention was in part attributable to the vigorous struggle between supporters of the two men. With failure at Ocaña all hope for the continuation of Gran Colombia died. The intendant of Cundinamarca provoked an uprising against the established government and advocated the vesting of full dictatorial powers in Bolívar. Bolívar accepted this *coup d'état* and during the summer of 1828 assumed complete authority; he suspended the constitution until 1830 when it was intended that a new constituent assembly would meet. In taking these steps, Bolívar misjudged the temper of his people. In New Granada at least, sentiment was running in support of the old constitution and the Santander faction that favored abiding by it. There quickly came a resort to violence. On September 25 an attempt was made on Bolívar's life as part of a plot to overthrow his government. The liberator narrowly escaped and the plot failed, but the end was now rapidly approaching. He took repressive measures to maintain order, and dealt severely with the conspirators. Even Santander, who could not be linked to the plot, was sentenced to death; but the sentence was commuted to exile.

Now revolution broke out in many quarters. Bolívar had left his able assistant, General Sucre, in Bolivia as president of that country, and Sucre was supported by Colombian troops. This arrangement proved increasingly unsatisfactory to Peru, where Colombian troops had also been stationed until Bolívar's authority was overthrown during the liberator's absence. Finally, in major part instigated by hostile Peruvian officials, an uprising occurred in Chuquisaca that nearly cost Sucre his life. Peru used this as an excuse to intervene in Bolivian affairs, and soon all Colombian troops in the southern republics either joined with the Peruvians or returned to their own country. Sucre himself resigned the presidency of Bolivia and went to Guayaquil and then to Quito. These events took place during the spring and summer of 1828 when conditions in Bogotá were far from peaceful, but Bolívar accepted the challenge and declared war on Peru. Fighting broke out with the invasion of the southern Colombian provinces by an army under command of the Peruvian president, General José de La Mar. Early in 1829, Colombian forces under General Juan José Flores and General Sucre scored a decisive victory that brought about the capitulation of La Mar and the eventual signing of a treaty of peace between Colombia and Peru. The result of all these difficulties was to remove completely Bolívar's influence over both Bolivia and Peru; also, by distracting the liberator's attention from domestic matters, it gave his enemies at home encouragement to strike further blows against the now weakening dictator. Scarcely were affairs settled with Peru when a former revolutionary general, José María Córdoba, raised the standard of rebellion in Antioquia and occupied Medellín. Córdoba's forces were defeated and the general killed, but once again peace was disrupted; confidence in the government approached the vanishing point.

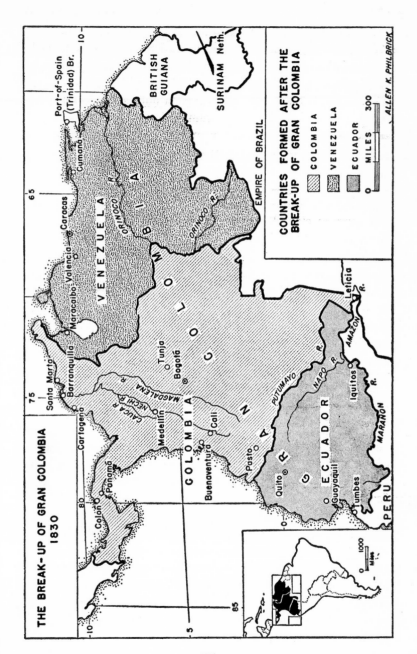

THE BREAK-UP OF GRAN COLOMBIA
1830

COUNTRIES FORMED AFTER THE
BREAK-UP OF GRAN COLOMBIA

COLOMBIA
VENEZUELA
ECUADOR

0   MILES   300

ALLEN K. PHILBRICK

VENEZUELA

COLOMBIA

ECUADOR

PERU

EMPIRE OF BRAZIL

BRITISH
GUIANA

SURINAM Neth.

Port-of-Spain
(Trinidad) Br.

Cumaná

Caracas
Valencia
Maracaibo

Barranquilla
Santa Marta

Cartagena

Colón
Panamá

Medellín

Buenaventura

Cali

Pasto

Quito

Guayaquil

Tumbes

Iquitos

Leticia

Tunja
Bogotá

ORINOCO R.

ORINOCO R.

MAGDALENA

CAUCA R.

NECHI R.

PUTUMAYO

NAPO R.

AMAZON R.

MARAÑON R.

0   1000
Miles

475

In January of 1830, Bolívar returned to Bogotá from the south after his successful efforts to put an end to the strife with Peru. Broken in health, he appeared an old man no longer able to bear the burdens of public life. He insisted upon his separation from public office but was induced to remain until a new constitution could be drafted and a new government formed. In the meantime, an independent Venezuelan government was organized under the leadership of Páez, a government that expressed its ingratitude by denouncing Bolívar as the cause of all Gran Colombia's troubles. In the south, a separate Ecuadorian government took shape under the leadership of Flores. A new constitution was drafted at Bogotá, and congress elected Joaquín Mosquera president; but the best efforts of Sucre failed to bring about acceptance of the new government in Venezuela, and Sucre's ambush and assassination on the way back to Quito signaled the end of Colombian control in the southern departments. 'Those who have toiled for liberty in South America have plowed the sea,' Bolívar wrote. Suffering from tuberculosis, he felt his strength slowly ebbing while anarchy descended upon his beloved country. He made an effort to leave for Europe, but was too ill to depart. In December of 1830, broken in spirit, he died quietly on the estate of a friend near Santa Marta.

Many of the chronic ills that beset the new governments formed from Gran Colombia were clearly apparent in the closing years of Bolívar's rule. With the Cúcuta constitution there was no satisfaction, but this basic law was hardly at fault. Nor could the ills of the body politic be remedied by adoption of a new charter in which the same words had been rearranged slightly. The most difficult system of government to make work is one involving the complexities of federalism or confederation and decentralization of authority to local legislative bodies. The Cúcuta constitution provided for a highly centralized system with ample authority vested in the chief executive. The structure was simple; it should not have been blamed for the failure of men.

What indeed were the difficulties that caused people to clamor for change and a new constitution? Basically they were an empty national treasury, the absence or failure of government services, unmet payrolls, disorder and brigandage on the roads, and the management of local affairs in a manner more arbitrary and less efficient than citizens had been used to under the Spaniards. To these problems Bolívar gave little thought, nor did Santander concern himself with them particularly. These revolutionary men saw in public office the glory and prestige of successful military effort and the honor of leading a new and independent nation. They accepted the hardships that constant political activity and frequent military effort imposed. They could not, however, sit down at a desk and devote long and tedious hours to assuring themselves that the affairs of government were well administered. This part of their responsibility they neither understood nor cared for, and they neglected it.

True, the founding of a new nation through a long struggle for independence and the creation of a new political system created demands upon men that only the ablest could hope to satisfy. Bolívar, Santander, Páez, Sucre, Nariño, and many others met the basic tests and more. They placed their lives and their fortunes on the altar of independence and self-government, and in doing so they achieved immortality in the annals of history. That their dreams were not fully realized is a measure only of how grand were those dreams.

XXIII

The First Mexican Revolution

> Let the government weaken again and the country would blow
> up like an overheated boiler.
>
> LESLEY BYRD SIMPSON *

SPAIN'S last great statesman died in 1788. Eventually the effects of that death sifted through the chinks of empire like a cold wind. New Spain did not feel the benumbing chill until 1792, when a weak hireling of Godoy arrived to replace the great Revillagigedo as viceroy. But the Marquis of Branciforte was but the first in a line of Mexican viceroys whose abilities bore no resemblance to those of their able predecessor. Their ill-timed and unstatesmanlike measures were poor recompense for the vast treasure that New Spain continued to send to the homeland year after year. Old hatreds and passions, deadened somewhat by the social progress and economic prosperity that attended the Bourbon reforms, now returned with greater vigor, for the weakness at home was increasingly apparent and the smoke of revolutionary fires was wafted on every breeze.

Hard on the heels of the revolution in France came the direct effects of that revolution in the most important of the French colonies in America. In Saint Domingue, republicanism, separatism, and racism were poured into the same cauldron and stirred by Jacobin commissioners; and the mixture overflowed in an orgy of

---

* *Many Mexicos*, University of California Press, Berkeley, copyright 1941, 1946, 1952, p. 180.

violence that not only accomplished the independence of Haiti and the abolition of slavery in the island, but profoundly shocked the conservative and propertied interests throughout the Americas. In an important sense the revolution in Saint Domingue provided obvious lessons for all who would learn. It demonstrated the dangers of stirring up the unbridled passions of the impoverished masses, it foreshadowed the end of slavery, and it provided a tangible demonstration of how even the best of European armies — one of Napoleon's own — could be defeated by ill-armed and ill-trained irregulars in the jungles of tropical America.

By early 1801 the French had lost all control of their errant colony, and Toussaint L'Ouverture, the victorious Negro general, had extended his dominion to include the eastern or Spanish portion of the island of Española. The stage had been set for this move by the Spanish minister, Don Manuel de Godoy, who had without hesitation thrown this loyal colony to the French in 1795 in an effort to further his European schemes. By reason of their difficulties in Saint Domingue the French had been unable to take possession of the Spanish portion of the island, but in January of 1801 Toussaint did. The French were not yet finished, however, for Napoleon sent a large expedition under General LeClerc which was successful in occupying the entire island and shipping Toussaint to Europe in chains. Shortly yellow fever and guerrilla warfare took their deadly toll, and French authority literally died out. Haiti was abandoned to the Negro forces of Dessalines, and a lonely French general, Ferrand, remained in Santo Domingo as a symbol of Napoleon's authority until 1808, when the Dominicans took matters into their own hands and returned the colony to the Spanish crown.

All these events were profoundly disturbing to Spanish interests in the Caribbean. Spain's preoccupation with events in Europe was clearly manifest, as was the willingness of Spanish leaders to trade away lesser portions of the empire to improve their standing vis-à-vis their European neighbors.

If Spain's ineptness in maintaining her position in the Caribbean was cause for concern, events in Europe could not fail to confirm whatever doubts already existed. The Spanish navy was sunk off Trafalgar, and French armies marched through Spain to attack Portugal. Then suddenly Charles IV abdicated in favor of his son Fernando; both Spanish kings became prisoners of Napoleon; and Joseph Bonaparte assumed the throne. In an era of slow and difficult communication, these happenings most certainly confounded official and ordinary subject alike, in New Spain as elsewhere in the Spanish overseas dominions. Most disturbed were those whose social, economic, and official status depended upon continuance of the old regime.

Many saw in the events on the peninsula a rare opportunity for readjusting the power relationship between creoles and gachupines. Could not a creole-dominated junta in New Spain exercise authority for the king during his captivity just as well as a junta in Seville having no better claim to legitimacy? The same question was asked almost simultaneously throughout all Spanish America. In New Spain, the one corporate political body largely in the hands of creoles was the municipal cabildo. Other political or semi-public governmental entities, the audiencias, consulado, and various guilds, were entirely controlled or at least dominated by European Spaniards. Thus the lines were drawn, and only a most able viceroy could successfully prevent the conflict from being brought into the open. The viceroy in Mexico City, José de Iturrigaray, hardly qualified. An opportunist in the manner of his patron, Godoy, he attempted to keep a finger to the breeze and an ear to the ground without asserting himself. The breeze told him that the peninsular patriots could not stand against Napoleon; from the ground he detected rumblings of an independent Mexico, and he dreamed of himself as its head. At the insistence of the Mexico City cabildo, Iturrigaray authorized the calling of a junta in August of 1808. Members were to be selected by the different municipal councils. The provisional government idea proved a failure. The creole element was of course dominant, but support from the provinces was at best lukewarm due to the presumptuous centralism of the Mexico City cabildo. Strong opposition was expressed by both the Mexico City audiencia and that of Guadalajara, and all Spanish elements rallied to the support of these venerable institutions of the empire. The arguments presented by the opposing factions are interesting if only to demonstrate how political combatants strive to conceal their true motives behind clouds of legal precedent and cited authority. In justification of its right to act for all of New Spain, the Mexico City cabildo cited royal edicts dating as far back as 1523, when, of course, Spain's tenuous foothold in North America consisted of nothing more than Cortés' control over the Aztec capital. Lest anyone be considered disloyal to the empire, all parties vociferously proclaimed their allegiance to Fernando VII; but the true issue was the desire of the creoles to seize and the gachupines to retain political power, and claims of loyalty and citations of ancient authority were but thin screens behind which the real battle lines were drawn.

The creoles of Mexico City lacked genuine support in the viceroyalty, and with one eye cocked toward Spain and the other toward their jealous fellows in the provincial capitals, they failed to note the threat on their flank. Perhaps they reposed too much confidence in the support and sympathy they received from the irresolute Iturrigaray. The gachupines, on the other hand, certainly had everything to lose and nothing to gain by the presumptuous actions of the creoles. Alarmed by the growing unrest and the obvious trend toward independence, the Spaniards struck on the night of September 15, 1808. Don Gabriel Yermo, a wealthy sugar planter from Cuernavaca, was persuaded to lead the *coup d'état*, and, the way paved for them by bribery, the small group of armed men which he had organized entered the viceregal palace and seized Iturrigaray and proclaimed a feeble old general viceroy in his place. As might have been expected, the audiencia promptly approved Yermo's action, and the Spanish faction sat firmly in the saddle. The Mexico City creoles' bid for power was at an end. The cabildo busied itself in the dullness of routine and the revolution passed to other hands.

In spite of having wrested the initiative from the creole cabildo the Spaniards were unable to consolidate their position. The usual difficulties of collegiate rule plagued the audiencia and its figurehead viceroy. No leadership emerged to give the country a program, orientation, or hope. Government was hopelessly weak, and its single purpose was the continuance of a holding action to maintain the Spaniards in power and await developments in Spain.

One fact seldom noted concerning this turbulent period in the closing days of empire was the almost complete ineffectiveness of Napoleon's efforts to popularize the artificial Spanish regime of his brother Joseph. Spaniards and creoles alike swore allegiance to a captive king, to the Junta Central at Seville, and to local juntas and provisional governing bodies in the Americas. Virtually no one supported Joseph, for neither group had any stomach for rule by the French. At the same time French doctrines of a different sort spread to creole intellectual circles throughout New Spain. Clandestine clubs and societies sprang up everywhere, and the views expressed at their meetings were those of the French political and social theorists and the more active Jacobins. The themes were social reform and independence, both inevitable consequences of a creole seizure of power.

The Mexican revolution had not as yet really begun, but it was close at hand. By 1810 there existed in Querétaro an active literary and social club headed by a creole officer who commanded the local militia, Ignacio Allende. Prominent members of this group included Juan Aldama, Miguel Domínguez, a former corregidor of Querétaro, and his wife Josefa María. Also active in the club was a priest of the little village of Dolores, Father Miguel Hidalgo, a creole past his middle fifties who had done nothing to distinguish himself except to grow forbidden fruits, thereby arousing the displeasure of royal officials who came one day and cut down his trees and tore out his grape vines. No doubt the humble priest had been ambitious, but he had seen others, perhaps less able than he, move upward in the hierarchy of the church while he remained behind, forgotten in a minor parish because of his irregular life as well as his lack of a peninsular birth record. For these slights the Spaniards were to pay, but the Indians were to pay more.

The Querétaro club became a center of intense revolutionary

activity not aimed openly at independence, but dedicated to the downfall of the gachupines and vigorous social reforms. Gradually its influence spread, and the leaders made plans for a widespread revolt against which the greatly outnumbered Spaniards would not be able to consider serious resistance. Naturally, no such general uprising could be planned without the Spaniards getting wind of it. That quick disaster did not befall the plotters was owing largely to disbelief on the part of the loyal officials that there was really any danger. Finally, on September 13, 1810, some of the chief conspirators were seized and their small supply of arms was confiscated. This should have ended the matter, but from his small parish of Dolores, Father Hidalgo decided otherwise. Summoning his parishioners as to religious congregation, Hidalgo proclaimed the revolution and announced that the day to overthrow the gachupines had arrived.

The ignorant Indians needed little urging. Seizing upon the Virgin of Guadalupe as the symbol of their cause, they assembled in hordes and marched upon Querétaro shouting the *Grito de Dolores*, 'Long live Independence! Long live Our Lady of Guadalupe!' To this chant was quickly added 'Death to the Gachupines!' The cry of death was far more comprehensible to the aroused mobs than the cry of life, and slaughter of the Spaniards and plunder of their homes and estates became major objectives of the more riotous elements. Hidalgo and Allende soon discovered that they were caught in a tremendous current over which they had little control. They could only direct it from one city to another.

With Querétaro easily captured the hordes of Hidalgo marched on Guanajuato, where a considerable number of Spaniards were gathered for protection in a large stone warehouse used for storing grain. The angry mobs promptly stormed the building, forced an entry, and slaughtered most of the defenseless Spaniards they found inside. This well-known incident was the first major act of violence performed by the revolutionary forces, but others equally violent if less spectacular became commonplace. Soon all New Spain was terrorized by the rebels.

Everywhere that Hidalgo went, thousands of ignorant Indians

rose to join his motley forces. Even without his leadership, rebel forces seized many of the cities and towns of northern Mexico. Eventually, after Querétaro and Guanajuato, Valladolid (Morelia), Guadalajara, Toluca, and even San Luis Potosí and Saltillo fell to the revolutionists. Wherever the priest's wild forces triumphed Spaniards died, their homes and estates were sacked and burned, and the cities were opened to general rapine and pilferage. Quickly the creole elements of the viceroyalty began to understand what sort of an uprising Hidalgo was leading. This was no struggle for independence, nor even really a battle against the gachupines. It was an uprising of the Indian and mestizo masses led by ignorant fanatics who had lost all control of the forces they had turned loose upon the land. The specter of Saint Domingue visited creole and gachupín alike. All who possessed status and property were in similar danger, regardless of the accidental differences of place of birth. New Spain was convulsed by a bloody social revolution.

In such circumstances the conflict between Spaniard and creole was quickly laid aside. The militia was called out and trained forces put in the field. All those who valued law and order rapidly deserted the rebel cause and lined up with the established government.

Hidalgo never had an army worthy of the name. He simply had thousands of Indians, mestizos, ruffians, and highwaymen armed primarily with machetes. Captain Allende and his armed troop were the only real soldiers supporting the rebel cause, although the vain and suddenly pompous Hidalgo bestowed high-sounding titles on a host of his immediate subordinates. In the few months that he was in the field, Hidalgo on several occasions commanded forces numbering up to seventy or eighty thousand, many times more men than were present in the largest militia bodies used against him. Hordes such as this, poorly armed and undisciplined, traveling without equipment and living off the land, could be kept in the field only by frequent and repeated satisfaction of their lust for victory and plunder. Inevitably, the rebel forces, successful in the north and west, moved on the capital, approaching from the direction of Toluca. On October 30, Hidalgo's army of 80,000 reached the pass at Monte de las Cruces and quickly swarmed around a force of 7000 regulars and militia sent against them by the viceroy. Well-disciplined and adequately armed, the small loyalist army under General Torcuato Trujillo decimated the ranks of the rebels and when night came fought their way through the opposing forces and fell back on Mexico City. Trujillo's troops had suffered such losses, however, that the capital was almost defenseless.

At this point Hidalgo wavered. Undoubtedly he could have loosed his Indian followers upon the capital and possessed it easily. The destruction they would have wreaked upon the unhappy populace is frightful to contemplate. Apologists for Hidalgo assert that the rebel priest turned away from this possibility to avoid the wanton sacking of the capital. Those less charitable attribute his delay and eventual retreat toward Guadalajara as an indication of inept leadership, demoralization of the Indian army, or fear of the loyalist general, Félix María Calleja, who approached from the north with a fresh force. Whatever his reason, Hidalgo turned back, and in doing so lost his one great chance of victory. His army melted away in the demoralization of defeat. The excitement of conquest was over, and few of his followers had any incentive to continue a war of attrition.

On January 17, 1811, defending his headquarters of Guadalajara, Hidalgo put another army in the field, and with a large force met General Calleja on a hill above the Río Lerma. Outnumbered perhaps twelve to one, the military skill of Calleja and their better training and discipline enabled the Indians and mestizos of the loyalist army to overcome Hidalgo's hordes. Hidalgo's insurrectionist forces collapsed and the rebels fled Guadalajara in all directions. The priest himself, together with his military leaders, fled northward toward Coahuila, but near Saltillo they were surprised by a former insurgent officer turned loyalist. Hidalgo and his principal associates were captured and handed over to Spanish authorities at Chihuahua. The Hidalgo rebellion was over.

In spite of the fact that hundreds of local priests at one point or another threw in their lot with Hidalgo, and a number were with him when he was finally captured, the position of the upper clerical hierarchy was never for a moment other than strictly loyalist. Hidalgo's activities brought him prompt excommunication. In the hands of the loyalists he could not immediately be executed as were Allende and other military leaders; first he had to be defrocked. Condemned to death he was given a final opportunity to recant his heresy. He turned again to the arms of his faith, admitted the error of his ways, and wrote an admission of guilt that is one of the most stirring testimonials of the ruinous course he had followed. But by rejecting his own revolution, abjuring independence, and seeking the mercy of those against whom he had fought with such fanaticism, Hidalgo turned his back on the Mexican Revolution and those who had and were yet to die in its name. To the loyalists Hidalgo was already a hated social revolutionist and enemy of the faith; to the forces of independence he became a traitor who in the face of death turned his back on his own followers. These judgments were perhaps correct, but they both overlooked the fact that Hidalgo was at once a symbol of the hatreds and frustrations of a downtrodden people and a weak little man who lost his head in the fever of his own sudden power, and in so doing turned loose upon society most of the evil passions of primitive mankind.

New Spain did not return to peaceful days upon the death of Hidalgo. Throughout much of the great viceroyalty law and order had ceased to exist, and the Spanish government in Mexico City was too weak to restore them. The lure of stolen riches and rapine had brought forth a host of would-be revolutionary heroes. That is, the cause of revolution became their ready-made excuse for an endless round of guerrilla activities. Petty chieftains arose in every province, and outside the capital New Spain was in a state of anarchy. From this chaos the country would not really escape for over half a century.

Shortly the revolutionary movement came to life anew, and some semblance of order reappeared in the movement. One of Hidalgo's followers was another priest, José María Morelos, who had been sent south into the territory that now comprises the state of

Guerrero. As Hidalgo's star faded, that of Morelos rose. Around him rallied many of the defeated followers of the executed cleric, including remnants of the insurgent government. In addition Morelos proved himself quite capable of attracting followers of his own. Among them were many persons of humble estate, but also others of prominent creole families. Few were his supporters from the wealthy classes, however, for Morelos had a program that involved not only independence from Spain, but social and economic reform as well. The program of Morelos differed from Hidalgo's plan in many respects, for it was well conceived and orderly, embracing popular sovereignty, elected officials, the ending of special castes and privileges, and the breaking up of large landed estates. Hidalgo had preached social revolution, but his objectives had been vague and his personal role that of an autocratic demagogue. Morelos conducted a relatively well-planned and disciplined campaign against the loyalist regime while at the same time he attempted to create and maintain a government selected and organized in accordance with the principles he had undertaken to establish in Mexico. For himself he selected a modest role, subordinating himself to the public authority of his own creation.

Throughout 1812 and 1813 Morelos was a power to be reckoned with, and the loyalist general, Calleja, spent a good deal of his time attempting to do so. The insurgent forces came, nevertheless, to dominate most of southern Mexico. From Orizaba in the east to Acapulco on the Pacific, they threatened to overrun the viceroyalty. Puebla, Veracruz, and the capital Morelos was never able to capture, but at various times he threatened all three. More remarkable than the territory he was able to occupy was the fact that within that territory he succeeded in enforcing order and maintaining some semblance of an administrative organization, which, among other things, collected taxes. What a contrast to Hidalgo's roving, plundering mobs!

In 1813 Morelos called a congress of delegates from territories under his control to meet at Chilpancingo. There he propounded his view of the proper social, economic, and political organization for a free and independent Mexico. His program of land reform and dispossession of the church of its non-religious properties became part and parcel of Mexican revolutionary and liberal doctrine for a century to come. Under his guidance was drawn up the first Mexican constitution, that of Apatzingán, completed in 1814. It was for the time a liberal republican document worthy of the efforts of able governmental theorists.

In the meantime, changes had taken place in the loyalist ranks. Upon recall of the viceroy to Spain, General Félix María Calleja was appointed to the post. His selection was both a reward for his diligence in tracking down and subjugating the guerrilla and revolutionary bands and an effort to give his demonstrated shrewdness and ability broader scope in the hope of restoring peace and order throughout the realm. In crushing the rebel forces, including those of Morelos, Calleja was remarkably successful. A rising young loyalist officer, Agustín de Iturbide, succeeded in driving Morelos from the gates of Valladolid and inflicting upon his forces one defeat after another. Soon Morelos' republic was overrun by loyalist armies, and the great rebel chieftain was himself captured while attempting to divert his opponents from members of his fleeing government. He was promptly unfrocked by the church, as had been Hidalgo, and his condemnation and execution for treason quickly followed. Morelos remained steadfast in his cause to the death. He did not recant, ask forgiveness of the church, or in any way weaken; calmly he laid down his life three days before Christmas, 1815.

Thus closed the first stages of the revolution for Mexican independence. The revolt failed, yet in an important sense the first stages were more significant than those that followed and which finally produced independence. By the abortive efforts of Hidalgo and Morelos there came into existence a set of ideals upon which the Mexican nationalist-liberal-revolutionary tradition has rested firmly ever since. These ideals, most clearly expressed prior to independence by Morelos at Chilpancingo, were successively taken up and acted upon as a positive program by Juárez, Madero, Carranza, Obregón, Cárdenas, and a host of lesser figures who slowly, painfully, and sometimes with bloody strife succeeded piece by piece in making of the early patriots' dreams a reality.

The early revolts failed in part because they were not truly independence movements; their objectives were social and economic not only by declaration but by manifestation. The provisional authority of the Spanish junta was rejected not because it was an alien or foreign authority, for it was not, but because it represented and perpetuated a social and economic system that was no longer acceptable in the New World. Because the movements went far beyond independence, many who favored independence and political reform were alienated and encouraged to seek redress of their grievances within the framework of the Spanish empire, which, if nothing else, at lease provided some guarantee of order and protection of property. Thus such able men as Miguel Ramos Arizpe worked diligently in the cause of empire reform, collaborating in Spain with the Spanish liberals who called the constituent assembly at Cádiz in 1812 and who there drew up Spain's first constitution. There appeared hope, for a time at least, that imperial political reform would make possible participation by such important kingdoms as New Spain in the determination of empire policy, and that the universal domination of colonial political and economic life by gachupines would be ended. For the wealthier creoles the attainment of these objectives would have been sufficient. Events were to prove that a Spanish liberal was a Spaniard first and a liberal second, and that even as the second he generally placed the pecuniary interests of Spanish monopolists above any tendency he might otherwise have had to apply his theories to colonial mercantile policy. In 1812, however, hopes for an improved empire relationship were still high, and many a creole was wont to endure the gachupines rather than risk life and economic well-being by associating himself with the revolutionary aspirations of an Hidalgo or a Morelos. As disorder grew apace between 1808 and 1815, the independence movement lost support; it retained popularity primarily among the thinning ranks of intellectual idealists and among the mestizos and Indians who had everything to gain and nothing to lose by its success.

With the release of Fernando VII in 1814, the American colonies at last had again the king in whose name so many contradictory actions had been taken. Little had the man learned while in Napoleon's custody. His every act bespoke an utter disregard for the efforts in his behalf on the part of loyal subjects, both in Europe and America. With the constitution of 1812 he would have nothing to do. Absolutism was restored absolutely, and all who had participated in the liberal movement were severely persecuted or hounded from the country. The Mexican creole who would have maintained the empire through imperial reform, Ramos Arizpe, languished in jail for his efforts. So did others who had pursued a similar policy of moderation. The Inquisition, which the 1812 constitution had abolished, was now restored, and Fernando made it clear that he intended to restore the old imperial system in its every aspect. Morelos, whose rump government had declared Mexican independence in 1814, was now vindicated, but too late. Creoles, faced with the alternatives of independence or acquiescence in gachupín domination, were too disorganized and too weary of strife to take up the battle where Morelos left off.

Two of Morelos' followers still held out after lesser guerrilleros had been captured and destroyed. Vicente Guerrero continued to hide out in the mountains with a small body of loyal followers. The other, Félix Fernández, deserted and alone, lived as a hermit in the mountains above Veracruz, a price upon his head. Apart from these and a few lesser figures, active opposition to the Spanish viceroy in New Spain had ceased.

Neither the uprising of Hidalgo nor the independence efforts of Morelos had direct repercussions beyond the immediate confines of central Mexico. A few venturesome Americans from the United States toyed with the possibilities of assisting the revolutionary elements in Mexico, partly in the hope of further expanding the territory of the United States. Aaron Burr's difficulties and his trial for treason involved a group exerting their efforts along these lines in the time of Viceroy Iturrigaray. The United States government was far too engrossed in its maritime difficulties with France and England to bother particularly about the internal affairs of

a neighboring Spanish colony. That certain of the Mexican revolutionists looked upon the United States as a potential source of
assistance, however, is indicated by the attempt of Hidalgo and
his army remnants to flee northward into Texas after defeat in the
south. An emissary had been sent ahead to procure American aid
if possible. In the northernmost provinces of New Spain, remote
California and the regions stretching from there eastward to Santa
Fe, the revolutionary seeds failed to take root.

Southward from Oaxaca and eastward beyond Tehuantepec, the
happenings in Mexico were but irregularly reported. The efforts of
the patriot priests aroused no genuinely responsive chords. True,
events in Spain were of great interest to creole intellectuals in
Guatemala, San Salvador, and León. Between 1809 and 1814 popular protests and tumultos occurred from Chiapas to Granada, but
they produced no adherents to the causes of Hidalgo or Morelos,
and no real insurrection took place. For a time the ayuntamiento
of Guatemala withheld recognition from the Junta Central at
Seville, but the hesitancy was only temporary. By and large the
point of view in Central America was exactly what might have
been expected of a somewhat isolated region that by reason of its
isolation enjoyed considerable autonomy and not too severe
gachupín domination: wait and see. The more remote the region, the more steadfast were the inhabitants in their aversion to
independence and in their loyalty to Spain. Indeed, the Costa
Ricans were a case in point; for, far removed from both intellectual
and commercial main currents in Central America, they lived
to themselves in peaceful isolation. Few saw any advantage in
change, and when the course of independence was eventually
chosen, the decision was made with reluctance after all other avenues of action had been blocked off by decisions made in Mexico,
Guatemala, and Nicaragua, on each of which in a sense the Costa
Rican province was dependent.

Likewise in the insular territories dependent upon the viceroy
in Mexico, little revolutionary fervor was aroused. Favored in commercial status, the Cubans had little incentive to revolt, whereas
the Puerto Ricans, isolated and without means for their own de-

fense, were reasonably satisfied with Spanish rule. An independent republic was, of course, something virtually without precedent. The United States was indeed independent, but only after a long colonial war which had seen both France and Spain come to the aid of the struggling colonies in their battle with England. A mere island was no nation nor could it hope to become one. Any move to separate from Spain was certain to result in subjugation by France, England, or some other European power. Haiti, to be sure, had for the moment escaped foreign control, but no one viewed the Haitian situation as a happy one, nor did Cubans and Puerto Ricans wish to risk the social upheaval that had given Negro ex-slaves control of the miserable island of Española.

Creoles of both Cuba and Puerto Rico responded with favor to the liberal 1812 Spanish constitution, for by its terms the American territories were admitted to representation in the Spanish Cortes. Too, they enjoyed such freedoms of press and speech as the constitutional regime promised. The return of Fernando VII and his abolition of the constitution promptly disappointed all liberal elements in Spain as well as in the colonies. But in every overseas territory there were those, creole as well as Spaniard, who saw in the 1812 constitution an abomination and a radical denial of the prerogatives of royal and religious authority. Thus in both Cuba and Puerto Rico the return to the old regime was viewed with mixed feelings. Liberals in Puerto Rico were sufficiently incensed to plot the overthrow of the government, and unrest continued for several years following 1814. In the end, however, the conservative view prevailed and would likely have remained without serious challenge had not the 1820 restoration of the Spanish constitution given new impetus to the liberal cause.

In the neighboring island of Santo Domingo, that is, the eastern part of Haiti, the Spanish government continued to show little interest. After the French army of LeClerc overran the island and captured Toussaint L'Ouverture, Negro power was decidedly weakened. The eventual defeat of LeClerc's army failed to bring about a reassertion of Negro domination in Santo Domingo. Dessalines, who became the principal Negro leader after Toussaint was transported to France, had problems enough in the west end of the island without undertaking to repeat the conquests of his predecessor. Thus it was that a nominal French control over Santo Domingo was retained. In 1808 this control was easily broken by a local uprising of the Spanish inhabitants who immediately restored the colony to its former status in the empire.

In the meantime, in October of 1804, Dessalines converted Haiti into a kingdom and was crowned Jacques I, Emperor of Haiti, partly at least in imitation of Napoleon. Dessalines' rule was short, for his repressive measures aimed at the restoration of order produced an uprising in which he was killed. His death in 1806 signaled the division of the country into two warring factions. Alexandre Pétion set himself up as life president of a nominal republic proclaimed in the south, with its capital at Port-au-Prince. Pétion ruled as a dictator, but he was not a vigorous taskmaster and most Haitians preferred his easy-going regime to that which prevailed in the north. There King Henri Christophe, using the title of Henri I, had converted the entire region under his control into a military labor camp. Under the supervision of soldiers former slaves returned to a familiar servitude in the fields and cities of the small kingdom. The sugar they produced brought money again to the island, and by the strength of their backs and arms they built for Henri two remarkable buildings, the palace of Sans Souci at Cap Haitien and a huge citadel high on a mountain top back from the coast. Although the citadel is difficult of access, it is of immense interest even in its present state of ruin because of its dramatic and massive construction effected without the aid of even rudimentary machinery. Henri managed to keep his austere and despotic regime going for twelve years. More and more, however, his subjects sought refuge in the more relaxing atmosphere of the republic to the south, where Jean Pierre Boyer had succeeded to the presidency upon the death of Pétion. Many of those unable to make good their escape died in the fields and on the mountain of the citadel struggling to perform the exhausting and inhuman tasks that had been assigned them. Finally, Henri's subjects rose in revolt, and the emperor, frustrated and unbalanced, killed himself.

Two events tied Haiti and Santo Domingo to the revolutionary occurrences of the neighboring continental territories. In 1815 the great Simón Bolívar sought refuge in the Haitian republic when his fortunes on the mainland were at lowest ebb. Here he was supplied with arms and a temporary base of operations until he could gather strength for a renewed campaign. Here too he found time to ponder the future of his Spanish world beyond the mere conduct of successful military campaigns; and from the near-by island of Jamaica, where the English also played him host, he wrote what was to become the most famous of his many letters, a letter setting forth his political philosophy and his dreams for a great Spanish American republican system.

The other event was a republican revolt in Santo Domingo, which on November 30, 1821, succeeded in overthrowing Spanish rule in the colony. The leader, José Núñez de Cáceres, promptly asked Bolívar to incorporate the island territory into Colombia. He felt, and quite correctly as events soon proved, that Santo Domingo could not stand alone. Colombia was in no condition to undertake protection of a Caribbean island, and Bolívar could not be reached in time anyway. Instead, protection was quickly forthcoming from the mulatto president of Haiti, Jean Pierre Boyer, who denied the existence of two separate political entities on the island and sent his troops to occupy Santo Domingo, which they did scarcely two months after the tie with Spain had been broken. The Cubans and Puerto Ricans could not fail to note the prompt demise of independent Santo Domingo.

Strangely, Spanish North America remained within the imperial fold throughout the disturbing conquest of Spain by the French, throughout the bitter struggle over constitutionalism and the reassertion of the royal prerogative and the old order by Fernando VII. True, the foundations of imperial relations had been severely jolted; in New Spain, at least, successful social revolution had been averted by the narrowest of margins. Territorially, Spain lost a great deal by being forced and tricked into sale of the vast Louisiana region to France for immediate resale to the United States, a resale prohibited by the terms of the Spanish-French agreement.

But the region was more a liability than an asset in Spain's over-extended condition; yet it would have been better to have disposed of it honorably as she was subsequently able to do with Florida. That old Spanish colony was sold to the United States by negotiations conducted in 1821 and 1822. Nevertheless, in 1820 Spain was still in full possession of the viceroyalty of New Spain, including the Caribbean islands nominally under the viceroy's jurisdiction. Only in South America had successful defection been accomplished.

Now suddenly the locus of conflict shifted to Spain proper where the repressive measures of Fernando VII had stirred up strong undercurrents of unrest. An army that had fought side by side with Wellington and supported the liberal constitutional assembly at Cádiz in 1812 was loath to support a king who wished to turn the clock back a century or more. The Masonic order likewise had taken hold among thinking people at various social levels, and to them the extreme clericalism of Fernando and the re-establishment of the Inquisition were anathema. Plots and counter-plots were the order of the day, inciting the despotic king to ever more rigorous and repressive measures. Fernando understood not at all the temper of his people.

As already noted, the weak fabric of royal despotism collapsed suddenly in the spring of 1820. On January 1, a little known colonel, Rafael del Riego, had proclaimed the constitution of 1812, and response from all sections of the country supported his move. A broad plot was underway and Riego was its spokesman. For two months Fernando's government seemed paralyzed; then early in March the king summoned the Cortes and announced that, in accordance with the general will of the people, he would swear allegiance to the constitution of 1812.

In the weeks that followed, government was virtually wrested from the king's hands by provincial and municipal juntas, and when a new Cortes and a new Ministry were formed they were highly liberal in sentiment, anti-clerical, and bent upon reducing the position of the king to that of a mere figurehead. All those enjoying privileged and special status were in danger of losing such benefits. The new government hastened to have the constitution proclaimed in the overseas dominions, and in New Spain it was proclaimed on May 3. The loyalist and conservative victory of Calleja and his followers and successors had been undone from the homeland.

In the dying days of the viceroyalty, few men fought for country or for love. It was a bitter struggle for status, power, and bread. In such circumstances, loyalty to the homeland had little place; and when it became clear that the liberals had triumphed in Spain, continuance of the imperial relationship became impossible for the privileged oligarchy. Those who now favored independence were not the liberals of Mexico, the creoles, the mestizos, and the Indians. Under the constitution these elements would have achieved many of the objectives for which they had fought under Hidalgo and Morelos. In reality, however, remnants of the Mexican liberal and revolutionary movement were taken unawares. They were disorganized, discouraged, unable to take advantage of the apparent fortune that had befallen them. Again, the conservatives were the first to act.

Those who in 1810 had abhorred independence now suddenly demanded it. The royalists, high church officials, the audiencia, the propertied class, creole and gachupín alike, all urged separation from a Spain that had gone radical and established a government contrary to their every interest. Promptly they looked for a deliverer; and in Colonel Agustín Iturbide, Calleja's former field commander, they found one. Though a mestizo, Iturbide came from a family of wealth and intense religious fervor. His views coincided exactly with those he had served and would continue to serve. Iturbide did not switch sides; he was always with the conservative aristocracy and the religious oligarchy, and, of course, he pursued his own opportunistic interest.

Promptly Iturbide made a deal with General Vicente Guerrero, the determined but simple soldier who still carried on Morelos' guerrilla activities in the back country. The forces of the two men were merged under a plan — the Plan of Iguala, named after the place where the two men met early in 1821. The plan proclaimed complete independence from Spain, the supremacy of the Roman Catholic religion, and equality of rights for Spaniards and creoles alike. These promises, known as the Three Guarantees, were supposed to be fulfilled by Iturbide's army, thereafter known as the Army of the Three Guarantees.

Dutifully the Spanish viceroy, Apodaca, opposed this move; but royalists and conservatives generally moved to Iturbide's support. So did thousands of creoles and liberals who now came out of hiding and joined what appeared to be a middle-of-the-road course leading to independence from Spain and equality, at least, with Spaniards. Gradually the Iturbide forces gained momentum. The *Trigarante* army swelled in size. Old Félix Fernández, now calling himself Guadalupe Victoria, came out of hiding and joined in a victorious march on Puebla. No more propitious moment could have been selected for a new viceroy to arrive at Veracruz, at least from the standpoint of the independence armies. In July of 1821 Juan O'Donojú did indeed arrive at the port, where he was promptly besieged and forced to accept the Plan of Iguala. Only then was he permitted to join the independence army in its triumphal march on the capital, entered September 27.

Spanish outposts now quickly capitulated, and by the end of the year Mexico was free, the conservative cause had triumphed, and the great internal schism had, temporarily at least, been healed. As might have been expected from the conservative and royalist side, however, Mexico was not proclaimed a republic. It was still a monarchy, and for a time there was even talk of bringing the beleaguered Fernando from Spain. As Iturbide began to realize his power, however, thoughts of European royalty were quietly put aside. An American 'prince' — even a mestizo 'prince' — would do just as well.

In the captaincy-general of Guatemala independence was also proclaimed, first in the capital and then echoed in San Salvador, León, and Tegucigalpa. For the time being the isthmian provinces would follow Mexico's lead, but with misgivings and reservations and a clearly expressed intention to wait and see.

Thus ended the struggle for independence in Spanish North

America. O'Donojú's agreement with Iturbide was rejected by the Spanish government, but the rejection did not render Mexico and Central America any less independent. No Spanish army came to re-establish peninsular rule. The revolution against liberalism had won the day.

XXIV

Brazil from Colony to American Empire

In the time of Dom João VI, when the movement which resulted in the independence of the land was in progress, proclaimed in 1822 by Dom Pedro I, one may say that Brazil was
already unified and made one. The moral factor of religion, the
work of penetrating and peopling the territory, the contact and
mixture of peoples to which it gave rise, the fundamental unity
of customs and traditions, the unity of language which became
established, and the conflicts with the mother country, had
in fact formed, on the conquered soil possessed in common, all
those elements which constitute, by binding together different
environments and social types, the organic and moral solidarity
of a nation.

FERNANDO DE AZEVEDO *

I N the European wars which followed the French
Revolution and the rise of Napoleon Bonaparte,
Portugal's role was neither prominent nor voluntary. In most of the
conflicts she appeared among the allies of England, which position
exposed her to frequent threats from France and Spain. Brazil,
on the other hand, profited immensely from the growing demand
for sugar, cotton, tobacco, and hides. Indeed, as early as 1785
the Brazilian economy had begun to recover from the doldrums
caused by the playing out of the mines after 1760. Commercial
activity took the place of mining, and trade with Europe, the
United States, the Spanish colonies, Africa, and the Orient grew

---

* *Brazilian Culture*, translated by W. R. Crawford, The Macmillan Company, New York, 1950, pp. 99–100.

steadily. The almost continuous European conflicts after 1789 greatly augmented the demand for Brazilian products. Agriculture was revived, and the over-all effect on economic life was generally more fortunate than when minerals were the main source of wealth.

By 1800 the population of Brazil numbered between three and four million inhabitants, of whom some 800,000 could be classed as whites, while Negro slaves were about twice as numerous. The remainder of the population was composed of free Negroes, mulattoes, Indians, and a variety of combinations. The management of farms, mills, and mines was frequently left entirely to slaves. Every trade was occupied by Negroes and mulattoes who, according to the comments of English visitors, displayed greater initiative and intelligence than their masters.

Rio de Janeiro, Bahia, and São Paulo were the principal cities. Rio de Janeiro was the largest and most active commercially, for it served as the market for Minas Gerais, São Paulo, and Goiás. It was a common sight to see a thousand mules on the trail to and from the mining districts. During the Napoleonic wars the city was overstocked with English goods. Rising prices of colonial products coincided with the period. English visitors protested that the house rents of Rio were as high as those of London.

Bahia still maintained a pre-eminent position in Brazilian economic and social life. When the royal family arrived there en route to Rio de Janeiro, the city made an attempt to regain its former political position by offering the prince regent a palace to be built at the city's expense if only he would remain.

In southern Brazil the old interest in the Plata region was still alive, and whenever opportunity afforded the paulistas were ready to step in. One opportunity came in 1801, after Spain, under French pressure, had declared war on Portugal. When news of the war reached Rio Grande do Sul, the governor sent several columns of troops against Spanish settlements. Because of the shortage of soldiers, he promised to pardon any prisoner who would serve. Spanish posts at Chuí and Jaguarón and other isolated places were taken. Another Portuguese column entered the region of the Seven Guaraní Missions. By convincing the Spanish commander that his was only the advance body of a large force, the Portuguese officer persuaded his opponent to withdraw without giving battle. In the meantime, peace between Portugal and Spain was re-established at Badajoz. The Portuguese, however, declared that the mission area had not been included in the restoration agreement, and planned to retain it. The issue was not immediately settled, and Portugal's appetite for the Banda Oriental was in no way diminished.

Such military activity was another manifestation of the now time-honored effort of the Portuguese in Brazil to extend their holdings southward, an effort fostered as often as not by the Brazilians themselves rather than by the royal government in Lisbon. Brazilians had not, however, awakened to their growing power as a nation. The events of the Inconfidência in Minas Gerais were almost forgotten, and such early nationalist writers as Tomás Antônio Gonzaga, one of the ablest of the 'Mineiro school' of publicists of the late eighteenth century, resided in African exile. For the most part, any new currents of Brazilian political thought and national consciousness were scarcely to be observed. Most of the population slumbered in the doldrums of the colonial epoch, unaware of the sudden transformation that fate was soon to deal it. What education was available still prepared men for letters and eloquence only. In 1798 a new seminary was established in Olinda, with courses of study that reflected the changing European outlook. Its impact upon Brazil was not great, but it was at least partially responsible for some of the liberal movements that broke out in the north during the first half of the nineteenth century.

In 1807 the Napoleonic wars affected the course of Brazilian history in a most striking fashion. In July of that year Napoleon demanded that Portuguese ports be closed to English shipping, and Spain joined in the ultimatum to Lisbon. Since he doubted that Portugal would comply, Napoleon sent Marshal Junot across northern Spain with an army for the occupation of Portugal.

The idea of taking refuge in Brazil should Portugal become untenable was one which had occurred to various members of the Bragança family for more than a century. The prince regent, João, later João VI, considered the possibility, and accepted an offer by England to give him naval protection for the crossing. Vessels were prepared for the trip well in advance, though João's customary procrastination made it appear a hasty decision.

João gave fate ample opportunity to intervene in his behalf before he undertook the long voyage to Brazil. But when no disaster befell Junot, João reluctantly carried out the plan. On November 29, 1807, with the thunder of Junot's cannon audible in the streets of Lisbon, the royal family embarked. The departure of the monarch, coupled with the ominous roar of French artillery, suddenly gave most of the Portuguese court a compelling urge to travel, and in a matter of hours the ships were loaded far above capacity. The crossing was an ordeal which João never forgot. Food was scarce, and the shortage of water made bathing impossible. The ladies had to shave their heads to combat vermin; this led some Brazilian women to dispose of their own locks to be in fashion, before discovering that shaved heads were not ordinarily worn at court!

The removal of the Portuguese court to Rio de Janeiro was one of the most important episodes of Brazilian history. It ended the colonial regime immediately and it set Brazil apart from her Spanish American neighbors for nearly a century. Political maturity and economic prosperity were accelerated. Because of this event Brazil was to purchase her independence at a cost far lower than Spanish American colonies paid, a saving not only in money but in life and property, law and order, and political and moral wellbeing.

The prince regent, who ruled in the name of his demented mother, Maria I, was made welcome in Brazil. The respect and esteem he was accorded was far greater than any he had received in Portugal, and he was won over by his Brazilian subjects. His wife, Dona Carlota Joaquina, sister of Fernando VII of Spain, was less favorably impressed by Brazil. She avowedly detested the land from the moment she arrived, and her domineering manner made her a severe trial for her hosts. She was, perhaps, more able and energetic than her slothful, good-natured husband, but she was more interested in the welfare of Spain than of Portugal. She was approached by agents from Buenos Aires on the possibility of her accepting a crown over Río de la Plata. It was an opportunity to preserve the land for Fernando, but her absolutist outburst at the suggestion of a constitutional monarchy ended the discussion.

On January 28, 1808, Dom João issued a decree opening Brazilian ports to trade with the rest of the world. The immediate effect of the decree was the anglicization of Brazilian commerce, for England was the only commercial nation in a position to take advantage of it. Brazil was soon flooded with English goods. Another and more lasting consequence of the opening of the ports was social and cultural rather than political or economic. Intellectual relations with Europe were now greatly facilitated, and commerce expanded rapidly, especially once the Napoleonic wars were ended. In 1807, ninety ships visited Rio de Janeiro. In 1808, the number increased to 420. Ten years later, upward of 2000 vessels put in at Bahia alone.

The coming of the royal family gave Brazil a strong and stable government and the basis for future orderliness. Since it was impossible to rely upon Portugal for aid of any sort, it was necessary for Dom João to create the tribunals, police, and military forces necessary for Brazilian security. Among the Brazilians were many who had been educated at Coimbra and who were not inferior in ability to those who had accompanied the royal family. Their acquaintance with local conditions was also valuable. But exceedingly few of them were called upon to help govern their country.

In addition to his efforts in the above fields, Dom João promoted the growth of academies and colleges. In 1808 schools of medicine and surgery were created in Bahia and Rio de Janeiro, and a school to train military engineers was located in the latter city. The Royal Press — Brazil's first printing press — was put into operation. The Public Library, the Royal Museum, the Royal Garden (later the Royal Botanical Garden), and similar institutions of a cultural nature were sponsored.

Agriculture, mining, and industry were assisted in various ways, especially by the repeal of old restrictive laws which were now seen to be detrimental. In 1808 the Bank of Brazil was founded to issue paper money for the expenses of the government. Its novelty for Brazilians did not end quickly, and it was accepted only with reluctance. It served an important role as the only source of credit, however, and it successfully met the ordinary requirements of business. All of these new institutions were unstable and without deep roots. Brazil was not immediately transformed by them, for nothing was done in the way of basic reforms in education to offset the colonial preoccupation with letters and oratory.

The international affairs which were uppermost at the time were concerned with English commercial enterprise and Brazilian interest in the Plata region. England demanded, and João was in no position to refuse, extraordinary commercial privileges giving English merchants a supremacy in Brazilian commerce that was not soon challenged. In Brazil a judge was appointed for the sole purpose of attending to cases involving English merchants. The English repeatedly pressed for abolition of slavery and the slave trade on the part of slave-owning peoples. The questions concerned with slavery and the slave trade were to plague Brazilian governments almost until the end of the empire, but most of the difficulties developed after Dom João had returned to Lisbon. In 1808 João declared war on Napoleon, and although he was unable to influence the course of the wars in Europe, he sent his troops into French Guiana.

Portuguese intervention in the Plata region, and especially in the Banda Oriental, was already an ancient story by 1810. Dom João, like his predecessors, watched for an opportunity to make the left bank of the Río de la Plata the southern boundary of Brazil. In 1811 Portuguese troops were sent into the Banda Oriental to aid the royalist governor, Francisco Javier de Elío, who was besieged in Montevideo. In October, Elío and the junta of Buenos Aires signed a truce, and João was persuaded to withdraw his army. He continued to watch affairs of the Banda Oriental, and the struggle between Artigas and the porteños created numerous opportunities for interference.

In December, 1815, Brazil was raised to the rank of kingdom, and another step was thus taken in the direction of Brazilian nationality and independence. The act was bitterly lamented in Lisbon, for it made Brazil's voluntary return to her former colonial status exceedingly unlikely. The outcome of the Spanish American wars for independence was still not clearly indicated, and the Portuguese regretted any action which might raise Brazilian ambitions. A clamor was raised for Dom João to return to Lisbon. João's powers of procrastination seemed to have been little damaged by his stay in tropical Brazil, and once more he delayed his departure until the last possible moment.

Dom João's regime in Brazil coincided in part, at least, with the 'age of discovery' for European natural scientists. The wanderlust characteristic of the sixteenth century, when the geographers came of age, now infected the scientists. A multitude of them from many European countries swarmed over Brazil, where for years their peregrinations took them from one end of the land to the other. They collected, investigated, and reported on their findings, their works filling literally hundreds of volumes. A partial catalogue of these men should include the German naturalist, Prince Wied-Neuwied, who visited Brazil in the years 1815–17; the Frenchman, A. de Saint-Hilaire, 1816–22; the Bavarians, Martius and Spix, who came with the nuptial train of Archduchess Leopoldina of Austria in 1817; the Englishmen Swainson, Gardner, and Darwin, and countless others. Geologists and geographers also found Brazil a fascinating hunting ground. But while this procession of eminent men in the various sciences passed through their land, the Brazilians themselves remained almost wholly in the role of slightly amused and somewhat bored spectators.

One of Dom João's diplomatic triumphs while in Brazil was in securing the Hapsburg Leopoldina Josepha Carolina of Austria as a bride for his son, Dom Pedro. The political connection with Vienna helped to offset the predomination of Brazil's stepmother, England, and served to give even an independent American monarchy political respectability on the European continent.

Dom João's imperialistic ambitions with regard to the Plata region continued unabated, and he vigilantly awaited an opportunity to intervene with more certain success. After the return of

Fernando VII to the Spanish throne, the Argentine patriots abandoned their pretense of loyalty to him and proclaimed their independence. Not all of the former provinces of the viceroyalty of Río de la Plata joined the confederacy. Paraguay isolated herself, and José Artigas fought to preserve the Banda Oriental against both Spain and Buenos Aires.

Owing to the chaotic state of affairs in the Banda Oriental, it was not surprising that violence against the Portuguese should occur. Raids across the Brazilian border offered Dom João a suitable pretext, as did the ambitions of Artigas to include the region of the Seven Missions in his domain. Assured of Argentine neutrality, João once more ordered his troops into the Banda Oriental, and in January, 1817, they entered Montevideo. In 1820 Artigas was put to flight and his forces scattered. In the following year Brazil annexed the Banda Oriental as the Cisplatine Province.

In the meantime, the prolonged absence of João from Portugal had serious consequences for the Bragança dynasty. For his part, João preferred to remain in Brazil, but in 1816, after the death of his mother, he accepted the Portuguese crown as João VI. Brazil had undoubtedly benefited from his rule, but opposition began to appear. The expensive war in the south had been unpopular, and while João had been occupied with extending his domain, a group of radicals in Pernambuco revolted against 'the infernal monster of royal tyranny.' The movement was both nationalistic and liberal in sentiment, and had as one of its aims the expulsion of the Portuguese from the kingdom. The leaders, a group of priests and Freemasons, were well versed in French ideas of political liberty and English concepts of economic freedom.

The rebels of 1817 proclaimed a provisional government, republican in character. The federative spirit which appeared in Pernambuco this year and again in the outbreak of 1824, was a carryover of the localism of the hereditary captaincies expressed in terms of resistance to the unifying tendencies of the imperial administration. These revolts, like the Inconfidência, were 'revolutions of college graduates,' and except for their expression of anti-Portuguese feeling were not popular movements. The uprising of

1817 was quickly and severely crushed by troops from Bahia, for Brazilians were still not prepared to accept radical changes. Liberal agitation in Portugal not long after this event indicated that liberalism had small followings in both kingdoms, and in both instances the Masonic order was involved.

The temporary success of the Riego revolt in Spain, in January, 1820, and the restoration of the liberal constitution of 1812 encouraged the Portuguese liberals to make a similar bid. The constitutionalist revolt which began in Oporto later in the same year quickly spread to Lisbon and other parts of the kingdom. The Cortes was called to draft a constitution, while the Brazilian liberals watched with growing interest. The idea of a constitutional monarchy seemed a welcome compromise to many Brazilians, for only a small segment of the population thought in terms of a more revolutionary break with the past.

News of the successful movement in Portugal reached Brazil in February, 1821. Dom João, whose great gift for temporizing had enabled him to delay his return for many years, now realized that the time had come. This was true especially in view of the fact that Pará had adhered to the constitutional regime. If he did not return soon a new king would wear the Portuguese crown if it was not to be relegated to a museum. Even before he had announced his intentions, furthermore, Portuguese troops in Brazil demanded his support of the constitutionalist movement in Portugal. On February 26, he published a declaration approving the not yet written Portuguese constitution as the basic law of Brazil.

The next step was the election of Brazilian delegates to the Portuguese convention. The recently established Brazilian newspapers pressed for liberal reforms, and for the first time, the desirability of Brazilian independence was openly debated. From London, the journalist Hipólito da Costa conducted a fiery anti-Portuguese campaign. The Rio de Janeiro electors, distrusting the king, demanded that he immediately swear his acceptance of the Spanish constitution of 1812 as a provisional measure, and ordered the troops to detain the royal family by force if necessary! Disorder spread rapidly through the kingdom, and João saw an opportunity to restore his authority. He forcibly dissolved the electoral college and denied the measures to which he had submitted under duress. In order to quell the rising spirit of insubordination he appointed his son, Dom Pedro, as regent of the Brazilian kingdom, and reluctantly prepared for the unpleasant voyage to Portugal.

The royal family embarked from Rio de Janeiro on April 24, 1821, leaving the government of Brazil to twenty-four-year-old Dom Pedro. Before departing, João reputedly gave his son some sound, fatherly advice: that should Brazil break away from Portugal, he should assume the lead, and thus retain his throne.

Within a month after the departure of Dom João, seventy delegates to the Lisbon convention were elected. Not all of them made the voyage to Portugal, nor did all of those who reached Lisbon participate in the assembly. The declaration of principles which the convention made on May 9, however, was accepted by Dom Pedro for Brazil.

A constructive but fruitless sidelight to this affair was the set of instructions sent to the delegates from São Paulo, and probably written by José Bonifácio de Andrada e Silva. Among other measures, the delegates should press for a federal monarchy, the reorganization of secondary and higher education, and the creation of a university in São Paulo. The university should have a faculty of philosophy, in which the physical and natural sciences and pure and applied mathematics would be required subjects.

As the Spanish liberals had done earlier on their rise to power, the Portuguese liberals now changed their attitude toward their New World possessions. Far from welcoming the Brazilians to an equal position in the Portuguese empire, the assembly showed a determination to undo the progress made in Brazil since 1808 and compel the country to return to a subordinate place. To weaken the position of Dom Pedro the assembly declared the provincial governments independent of the central authority at Rio de Janeiro, and ordered the armies of Portugal and Brazil combined. The law courts, commerce commission, treasury department, and other institutions created by João were to be abolished. The crowning blow was an order to Dom Pedro to return to Portugal to complete his political training.

Dom Pedro at this time was an impulsive young man of twenty-four years. Although lacking in formal education, he was intelligent and well informed, especially in international affairs. Unfortunately, he lacked an ability to co-operate and compromise, and he regarded those who disagreed with him as outright enemies. He was in the paradoxical situation of being a man of moderately liberal leanings who had been brought up in the school of absolutism. In many of the crises which arose, his autocratic impulses triumphed over his fundamental belief in constitutional rule. His personal life, unfortunately for his popularity, was scandalous. The list of those who shared the royal couch and the offspring of these affairs was astonishingly long. It was not so much Dom Pedro's unusual conduct that angered Brazilians, but the fact that he caused suffering to his wife, Leopoldina, who had won the hearts of her adopted people.

Dona Leopoldina had identified her interests with Brazil immediately, and she soon became widely beloved. Her influence in European circles, because of her Hapsburg connections, was of considerable benefit to Brazil. Her support of Dom Pedro in his resistance to the demands of the Lisbon assembly was an important service, for it encouraged the wavering prince regent in his refusal to submit.

The demand that Dom Pedro return to Portugal rapidly united the divergent political groups in Brazil, and the liberals came to see that independence was the only way in which liberal reforms might be introduced. The Brazilian Masons rallied to Dom Pedro's support. The grand master of the order, José Bonifácio, became the chief adviser of Dom Pedro and the chief architect of Brazilian independence. Under his influence, Dom Pedro became a member of the Masonic order in August, 1822. Not long after this he was raised to the rank of grand master.

Despite the support of the Masons, Dom Pedro still did not see his course clearly, for he had to reconcile loyalty to his father with Brazilian desire for independence. He and many others would gladly have compromised with Lisbon on the basis of Brazilian equality with Portugal, but the adamant attitude of the Portuguese made this solution impossible. The spirit of republicanism was alive in Brazil, and Dom Pedro was not certain what independence might mean in the way of governmental organization. But when the idea of a dual monarchy had to be discarded José Bonifácio chose Dom Pedro as the instrument for achieving independence while avoiding the sordid tumults that were taking place in the former Spanish colonies.

While the matter of Dom Pedro's return was still being debated, a petition signed by upwards of 8000 persons, urging him to remain in Brazil, was presented to him on January 9, 1822. It was accompanied by a subtle suggestion that if he returned to Portugal, the separation of Brazil would follow. Dom Pedro chose to remain, in defiance of the Lisbon assembly. A ministry was organized on January 16, with José Bonifácio as chief minister and unquestionably the outstanding figure. Brazilian independence for practical purposes dates from this act, but since widespread popular support of the movement was essential, a more dramatic gesture was needed. The adherence of the Masons was assured, but republican sentiment was strong in Minas Gerais, while other regions were doubtful. A minor test of provincial attitudes came in February when Dom Pedro issued a decree calling for the creation of a council of representatives to advise him. The southern provinces quickly endorsed the plan, while those of the north opposed it or failed to designate their representatives.

In order to win the confidence of provincial leaders in himself and his plans, Dom Pedro traveled through Minas Gerais. His trip was a resounding success. By this venture the threat of a republican movement in the vital province was removed. The Masons now instigated a movement to offer Dom Pedro the title of 'Perpetual Defender of Brazil,' which he accepted on May 13. The fact that this date was his father's birthday was not overlooked by Brazilians. From Rio Grande do Sul and from Ceará in the north, came insistent demands that independence be declared. Their requests for summoning a constituent assembly, however, were temporarily postponed by Dom Pedro, for he wanted to know the attitude of other provinces. By the time the first three provincial representatives had reached the capital, the situation had become clear, and Dom Pedro no longer hesitated. When the three men went into session without awaiting the arrival of the others, their recommendation that a constituent assembly be summoned met with immediate approval. All that was lacking was a declaration of independence, and the opportune moment for it was not far off.

In Lisbon the meeting of the Brazilian provincial representatives was regarded as an act of rebellion. Plans were made to bring to trial those who were participating in it, and to send reinforcements to Portuguese troops in Brazil. Brazilian delegates in Lisbon informed their friends at home of the Portuguese attitude. Even before the official decrees had arrived in Brazil, Dom Pedro, on August 6, issued a 'manifesto of the prince regent to friendly governments and nations,' which censured the colonial regime and invited foreign nations to maintain diplomatic relations with Brazil. This was not, as it might seem, a declaration of independence, but a demand for equality with Portugal.

Within a few days after the appearance of the manifesto, Dom Pedro set out for São Paulo on a tour similar to the one he had made through Minas Gerais earlier in the year. His reception on this occasion was not as flattering as before, although the Masons were actively engaged in stirring up enthusiasm for independence. While Dom Pedro was absent, despatches from Portugal aimed at chastising the 'rebels' arrived in Rio de Janeiro. Dona Leopoldina sensed that the dramatic moment was at hand. She immediately assembled the ministry, and all agreed that Brazil was at the crossroads. The time was ripe to make a resounding bid for popular support for independence, before the Lisbon assembly could repent its haste and make gestures at reconciliation. A messenger sped south with the despatches; he overtook Dom Pedro at Ipiranga in São Paulo. A hasty glance at the documents convinced Dom Pedro that the stage was at last set for his entrance. Tearing the Portuguese colors from his sleeve, he exclaimed: 'Independence or death!' September 7, 1822, marked the official birthday of the Brazilian Empire.

Of all the Latin American nations, Brazil was the most fortunate in the conditions which prevailed when she achieved independence. At the time of the 'Grito de Ipiranga,' as Dom Pedro's declaration was called, some Spanish American countries were still engaged in the struggle against Spain. The Spanish American wars of independence left most of Spanish America in social, political, and financial chaos. The Brazilians experienced little difficulty in expelling the Portuguese troops, with the astute aid of Lord Cochrane. The Napoleonic wars and the civil strife following the rise of the liberals had left Portugal nearly prostrate and quite unable to hold Brazil by force. The last Portuguese stronghold in America was in Montevideo, where loyalist troops held out until February, 1824. Independence cost Brazil little in comparison to the price paid by her neighbors. The political reorganization of Brazil offered greater difficulties, yet this problem was met under extremely favorable circumstances.

Despite the apparent unanimity with which Brazilians supported Dom Pedro in his defiance of Portugal, friction and disharmony soon appeared. Lack of political experience on the part of his ministers and Dom Pedro's irritation at opinions differing from his own jeopardized the stability of the nascent empire. José Bonifácio, too, was unfortunately unable to brook criticism and opposition, and he did not hesitate to take drastic action against those who challenged his views.

The constituent assembly called for in the decree of June, 1822, met in April of the following year. The delegates were composed of lawyers, priests, and landed proprietors, all with lofty notions of their own abilities and rather limited knowledge of the problems of government. The Andrada brothers were the most influential members, which proved, in some ways, unfortunate. Lack of harmony in the ministry caused José Bonifácio to resign, and he launched a bitter, partisan attack upon the government in the constituent assembly. In this explosive situation little progress could be made. Early in November, 1823, Dom Pedro led troops into the chambers of the assembly and personally ordered the members to disperse. This unfortunate act was followed by a promise to grant Brazil a genuinely liberal constitution. José Bonifácio and his brothers were exiled.

A council of state named by the emperor continued work on the constitution, and after it had been approved by the town councils, it was promulgated, on March 25, 1824. The emperor kept his promise, and the constitution was durable enough to continue in force throughout the existence of the empire. Brazil was declared to be a hereditary, constitutional monarchy under the Braganças. Roman Catholicism was declared the official religion, although others were permitted.

One curious innovation in the constitution was the creation of the moderative power. With the exception of this feature the constitution was similar to the one begun by the elected assembly. The moderative power permitted the emperor to select the senators from lists submitted to him, to appoint ministers of state, to convoke the legislature and approve its laws, and gave him other prerogatives which were to bring him into constant conflict with the lower house.

The constitution of 1824 established a legislature composed of a Senate, in which the members served for life, and a Chamber of Deputies, whose members were elected for four-year terms. The Council of State, with which the emperor was to consult whenever the moderative power was employed, also served for life. The ministry was responsible to the emperor rather than to the legislature. The country was divided into provinces, each having an elective assembly with consultative powers only, and a president appointed by the emperor.

The success of the new government was immediately endangered, for the Chamber of Deputies took up the quarrel of the constituent assembly with the emperor. The period of strained relations which followed was not entirely owing to Dom Pedro's political shortcomings, although these were responsible for his inability to compromise with his opposition. He came to govern without regard to parliamentary majorities, and rarely chose his ministers from the Chamber of Deputies. As opposition to him grew, interest in the republican form of government was revived.

The most serious of the many repercussions resulting from this conflict was an uprising in the north, where Pernambuco, Ceará, Rio Grande do Norte, and Paraíba tried to create a federal republic in 1824. The Confederation of the Equator, as it was called, set up a provisional government based on the constitution of New Granada. The rebellion was crushed within six months, but not without damage to the emperor's prestige and the display of sympathy for the rebels.

In international affairs the emperor faced two immediate problems: that of recognition of Brazilian independence and that which concerned the Banda Oriental. Regarding the first of these matters, he was fortunate that his wife's father, Emperor Francis I of Austria, was interested in the welfare of Brazil. Missions were sent to London, Vienna, Paris, and Washington. José Silvestre Rebelo, who visited the United States, easily persuaded President James Monroe to acknowledge Brazilian independence. Since the only immediate threat to Brazilian security might come from Europe, where the Holy Alliance contemplated restoration of the Iberian colonies, recognition by England was of the greatest political importance at the moment.

Obtaining English recognition was complicated by many factors, not the least of which was that nation's determined opposition to the slave trade. England's friendly relations with Portugal was another complication, for the Napoleonic wars had again demonstrated forcibly the value of a foothold on the continent. The Portuguese succession was sure to raise additional obstacles, for Dom Miguel aspired to wear his father's crown, and nearly succeeded in snatching it in an absolutist counter-revolution.

England and Austria were both in favor of an amicable settlement between Portugal and Brazil, but beyond that their views diverged sharply. By urging moderation Austria neutralized the opposition of the Holy Alliance to Brazil, while the determination of England that a pacific solution be reached made the possibility of intervention by the Holy Alliance appear hazardous for European peace. The outstanding Brazilian diplomat involved in these delicate negotiations was Marshal Felisberto Caldeira Brant Pontes, who won over the English foreign secretary, George Canning. For this successful conduct of the affair Marshal Brant was ennobled, as the Marquis of Barbacena.

Portugal's attitude toward Brazil remained adamant; there was no likelihood of her conceding Brazil an equal position in the Portuguese empire. After exhausting the possibilities of peaceful debate as well as his patience, Canning concluded that the points of view were too far apart to render further discussion profitable. The action which he took left Portugal with no choice but to bid her wayward colony farewell. Sir Charles Stuart was sent to Lisbon, where he explained to Portuguese authorities that he was en route to Rio de Janeiro for the purpose of announcing England's official recognition. The English government, he gently pointed out, hoped that English recognition would follow or accompany that of Portugal. After fruitlessly deliberating this matter in search of some means of escape, Portugal yielded, and Sir Charles proceeded on his circuitous voyage as the representative of both countries, empowered to acknowledge Brazil's independence and to negotiate a treaty between the mother country and her errant offspring.

The agreement signed between Brazil and Portugal on August 29, 1825, was extraordinarily fortunate for the newly founded state. No Spanish American nation was recognized by Spain for more than a decade after this date. Brazil was spared the extra hazard to domestic peace engendered by the threat of reconquest. The treaty did not, however, settle the problem of the Portuguese succession. Brazil assumed a large share of the Portuguese debt, to the chagrin of many Brazilians, especially the opponents of Dom Pedro. There is little doubt, however, that the Brazilian diplomats acted wisely, and that the treaty was in reality a triumph for Brazil.

Despite his success in establishing Brazilian independence, Dom Pedro faced rising hostility at home. Criticism of the emperor became more personal and less objective; very little that he did met with wide approval, and his actions were often deliberately misinterpreted by his enemies. A part of the difficulties leading to his abdication concerned the Portuguese succession, for his role in this affair gave some credence to the charges that he was more interested in Portugal than in Brazil.

Shortly after the peace treaty had been signed Dom João died. He had not officially named his successor, but his choice was known to be Dom Pedro. Ignoring the dubious legality of accepting the Portuguese crown, Dom Pedro assented to the arrangement in order to secure it for his oldest daughter, Maria da Glória. After granting a constitution to Portugal and declaring general amnesty, he abdicated in her favor. The matter did not end there, for Dom Miguel soon usurped his niece's crown, and Dom Pedro remained entangled with Portuguese dynastic problems. In this affair as in the financial arrangements of the treaty of 1825, he was assailed by his opponents for sacrificing Brazil's interests to those of Portugal. His growing distrust of Brazilian statesmen and the increasing favor that he showed to his more subservient Portuguese councilors seemed to support their criticism.

The treaty signed with England in March, 1827, gave further cause for dissatisfaction among Brazilians, for it embodied an inescapable clause promising the cessation of the slave trade within three years, and made commercial concessions to English merchants. Brazilian agriculture, and especially the sugar industry, depended upon slave labor, and the fazendeiros could not contemplate changing their ways. Many Brazilians were angered by the treaty, but what was even more odious was the fact that the negotiations were carried out in secret and the final result presented to the legislative body only after ratification. Thus Dom Pedro drew upon himself the total blame for any errors, when he might easily have shared it with the Chamber of Deputies.

The unpopular war with the United Provinces of Río de la Plata was also regarded as evidence of Dom Pedro's great interest in his Portuguese heritage. The war began soon after Juan Antonio Lavalleja and his 'Thirty-three' crossed the Paraná and raised the standard of revolt in April, 1825. Thousands of Uruguayans joined them, and in four months they declared Uruguayan independence from Brazil and incorporation into the United Provinces. In October the United Provinces voted in favor of incorporating Uruguay, and in so doing deeply offended the Brazilian emperor. On December 10, he replied to the insult by imperial decree and a declaration of war. It was regarded as the emperor's war, for most Brazilians opposed it. They preferred to let Uruguay go.

Dom Pedro barely escaped similar criticism with regard to Upper Peru, and he did not get off without injury to the imperial dignity. After the battle of Ayacucho had ended royalist resistance and the Republic of Bolivia had been established, the governor of Chiquitos province remained in opposition to the new regime. He sent agents to the near-by Brazilian province of Mato Grosso for aid, and Brazilian troops marched into the province. Upon receiving news of this precipitous action Dom Pedro and his ministers immediately saw the danger of an invasion of Brazil by the anti-monarchist patriot heroes, Bolívar and Sucre. He hastily ordered the troops back to Mato Grosso. Coming at a time when the empire was involved in the unprofitable Uruguayan venture, Dom Pedro's action undoubtedly saved him from far more serious complications. His undignified retreat, however, did not improve his popularity, despite the fact that he had not been responsible for the march into Bolivia.

The death of Dona Leopoldina in December, 1826, was another blow to his prestige, for the emperor's flagrant affair with the Marchioness of Santos was generally believed to have caused the popular empress grief and hastened her demise.

The war against the United Provinces took an unfavorable turn when it appeared that England was contemplating establishing a protectorate over Uruguay to create a buffer state between Brazil and Argentina, and to provide England with a needed naval base. The Brazilian blockade of Montevideo was not successful, and it brought frequent complaints from England, France, and the United States. On July 26, 1826, a French squadron sailed into the harbor of Rio de Janeiro and delivered a forceful demand to modify the blockade. Other protests were lodged, but the French gesture was the most humiliating, and the emperor bore the blame for this shameful injury to national pride.

On land the inadequate Brazilian troops fared little better, despite the strenuous efforts of the Marquis of Barbacena. He suffered a serious defeat in February, 1827. By this time both Brazil and the United Provinces were suffering acutely from the cost of the war, and no more large-scale battles occurred.

In May, 1827, it appeared briefly that the emperor's policy might succeed. The treaty was signed with the envoy from Buenos Aires in which the United Provinces agreed to Uruguay remaining as the Cisplatine Province of Brazil. But when, as already noted, the terms of this treaty were made known in Buenos Aires, a popular clamor caused its immediate rejection, the disavowal of the envoy, and the resignation of the president.

Neither country was able to consider continuing the war with any optimism. The widespread opposition to the blockade, the further injury to Brazilian economy which prolongation of the war would entail, and the increasing dissemination of republican propaganda in southern Brazil made the emperor pause. A new envoy came from Buenos Aires, and on August 27, 1828, another treaty was concluded.

By the terms of the second treaty Brazil agreed to withdraw her troops, while the United Provinces promised not to incorporate Uruguay. Both pledged themselves to guarantee the independence of their former battlefield, and the republic of Uruguay was born. The treaty, far from assuaging the criticism leveled at Dom Pedro, merely hastened his downfall. When the war on which he had insisted was over, Brazil was left with nothing but casualty lists and financial deficits.

All aspects of Dom Pedro's rule were by no means negative, despite the increasing unwillingness of Brazilians to appreciate his actions. Of far-reaching importance for Brazilian cultural development was the creation, in 1827, of two schools of law. One was located in São Paulo, and the other, until 1854, in Olinda. It is perhaps symbolic that these schools first met in former convents, for through them the ecclesiastical spirit of education was replaced by a juridical spirit. The influence of these colleges on nineteenth-century Brazil is difficult to measure, but their role was unquestionably a powerful one. Through them the ideas of the English, French, and German philosophers penetrated Brazilian thought. The student bodies of both, and especially of São Paulo, were foremost in every liberal movement.

By the creation of these law schools Brazilian culture was virtually liberated from Portuguese influences; the University of Coimbra no longer served as the molding-board of Brazilian intellectuals. The law colleges became the key educational institutions, and Brazilians relied on them to furnish supplementary cultural training.

The study of law became a standard procedure for the educated members of society outside the field of medicine. Training in law became the avenue to politics, journalism, literary careers, and teaching. Politics and academic life were constantly embroiled. The law colleges were also important for their role in advancing national unity, for they were attended by Brazilians of all classes and regions.

The study of medicine was also promoted during Dom Pedro's regime. In 1826 the two schools of medicine and surgery that Dom João had established at Bahia and Rio de Janeiro were authorized to grant diplomas in surgery. But the study of medicine was pursued with far less intensity than law, and the greatest influence of the medical schools came only late in the imperial period.

Since the governing classes of the several succeeding generations were to be composed largely of graduates of the law schools and members of the landholding class, few of the imperial administrators were prepared for making innovations in fields other than law. Few statesmen were prepared to find realistic solutions to the technical problems of national economic development. Commerce and industry, science and research, seemed more the concern of foreigners than of Brazilians.

It was not the fault of the statesmen alone that the colonial outlook could not be banished from the realm by a technically correct law. There was little on which to build, and few men were deeply concerned with material and economic development. As early as 1803 Dom João had spoken enthusiastically of creating a school of mines to revive the floundering mining program. The matter was discussed in Brazil with no feeling of urgency, and in 1832 a law was passed creating a course of mineralogical studies in Minas Gerais. It was 1876 before this law was finally put into effect.

In the period of transition from colony to empire, the pattern of Brazilian culture changed from one dominated by the ecclesiastical outlook to one colored by the professional character of the educated elite. The love of letters so common among the educated men of the colonial regime was not, surprisingly enough, killed by the concentration on legal training. No professional man was satisfied unless he was at the same time a member of the literati. The poets, orators, and scholars of the epoch which followed independence were, for the most part, men trained in law.

The reign of Dom Pedro I also witnessed the advent of French influence in literature and art. In 1816 an artistic mission came from France, and its members conducted the Royal School of Sciences, Arts, and Crafts. In 1826 they were incorporated into the Academy of Fine Arts. The efforts of the French painters, sculptors, and architects to replace Brazilian liturgical arts with French secularism met with strenuous resistance and only partial success. They did succeed in modifying Brazilian art, and they trained and inspired a number of Brazilian artists, who carried on the contest.

In 1828 the Supreme Court of Justice was established, making it possible to dispense with the old tribunals carried over from the Portuguese system for want of anything to replace them. Work on a new criminal code was begun, and when it was put into effect in 1830, Brazil made an important break with the past.

Industry and commerce also showed some substantial gains in the time of Dom Pedro, but not to the fullest extent possible. In 1829 the Bank of Brazil was abolished, for Brazilians had never become aware of the importance of this institution in providing credit for business operations. National finances went from bad to worse, owing not only to mismanagement but to the costly war. The issuance of easily counterfeited copper coins at a face value above their actual worth led to difficulties, and the government eventually was forced to call them in.

Dom Pedro's differences with the legislature and his partiality toward the army led the former body to weaken the latter whenever possible. Co-operation between the army and the legislature has been rare in Brazil since that day, for the ill-will engendered during the war against the United Provinces lingered on. When the second legislature met, its relations with Dom Pedro were marked by even greater hostility than had been those of its predecessor. In this heated atmosphere the only calm words heard above the din were those of a newspaper which first appeared in 1827.

This paper, the *Aurora Fluminense*, under the guiding hand of a bookdealer named Evaristo Ferreira da Veiga, aimed at a dignified and impersonal discussion of Brazilian problems. It had an important part in the formation of a small but powerful group of political leaders whose point of view was midway between the extremes of absolutism and republicanism. Other newspapers were less objective; of the thirty-three published in Brazil in 1830, more than half were opposed to the government. These covered a wide range of political opinion, and supported vastly different solutions to national problems. The editor of the *Aurora* and his associates perceived the dangers of some of these panaceas and endeavored to keep Brazil on an even keel.

His sensitivity to criticism as well as the dynastic problems of Portugal induced Dom Pedro to rely to an unfortunate degree on his Portuguese friends in Brazil. In 1828 he sent his daughter to Europe, accompanied by the Count of Barbacena, with the intention of placing her under the protection of her maternal grandfather, Emperor Francis I of Austria. When they reached Gibraltar, Barbacena learned of Dom Miguel's usurpation of the Portuguese throne. He proceeded to London with Dona Maria da Glória and persuaded the English government to acknowledge her rights. On his return to Brazil he brought a new bride for Dom Pedro, Amélia de Leuchtemberg. Dom Pedro's immediate attachment to her made many forget his past aberrations, but his general popularity could not be restored.

The return of José Bonifácio and his brothers from exile temporarily improved the political situation. They and Barbacena convinced Dom Pedro of the urgent need to dismiss his Portuguese advisers and to replace them with Brazilians. The new ministry which was formed in December, 1829, and headed by Barbacena, was the first genuine attempt at parliamentary government in Brazil. Dom Pedro promised to abide by the constitution, and he permitted Barbacena to expel a group of his unofficial Portuguese advisers. The emperor did not, however, cease communicating with them, and they worked to bring about Barbacena's resignation. Dom Pedro soon reverted to his former policies, and before long the situation was as acrimonious as ever. News of the overthrow of Charles X of France in July, 1830, was a welcome stimulus to Brazilian liberals, and strengthened the opposition to the emperor.

In 1831 Dom Pedro essayed to quench the republican sentiment appearing in Minas Gerais by a tour through the province similar to the one which he had made shortly before the Grito de Ipiranga. Another purpose of the trip was to aid the re-election of one of his principal supporters, José Antônio da Silva Maia. In Minas he met overwhelming antipathy to his rule. The recent assassination of an Italian journalist was blamed on his attacks on the government. The failure of the government to bring his assassins to justice produced a profound impression among the mineiros, who focused their resentment on the emperor.

On his visit to Minas in 1822 Dom Pedro had been reassured in his decision to declare Brazilian independence. His reception on his visit nearly a decade later likewise caused him to reach a revolutionary decision; this time it was to abdicate the Brazilian throne. The greeting which met him on his return to Rio de Janeiro only reinforced his idea of abdication: 'Long live the emperor provided he abides by the constitution.' A series of street clashes between his opponents and his supporters foretold grave disturbances for the future. At this point further troubles were temporarily abated by the astute suggestion of Evaristo da Veiga that the nationalists wear as a symbol of their solidarity the national colors, green and yellow. The immediate appearance of this patriotic emblem on the sleeves of thousands of Brazilians gave pause to the emperor's adherents, and street fighting subsided.

An open threat to Dom Pedro soon followed. Headed by Senator Vergueiro, a group of twenty-four men calling themselves the 'Aurora Fluminense,' presented the emperor with an ultimatum: obey the constitution and forbid his followers the use of violence or face the loss of his crown. Failing to receive a reply, they prepared a bill for the Chamber of Deputies which would declare the emperor deposed. Some members of this group even advocated proclaiming a republic, but calmer heads prevailed. Members of the army became involved in the projects of the emperor's enemies, and it was obvious that he was fast losing one of the most vital bulwarks of his throne.

Although the cause was not entirely lost Dom Pedro could not bring himself to follow the only course left to him. On May 19, 1831, he seemed to be taking a step in that direction, but it was merely a hollow gesture. On that date he appointed a new ministry composed of Brazilian moderates. Some were not, however, members of parliament, nor did he consult with that body. When his action was challenged as a breach of the constitution, Dom Pedro seems to have given way to anger. On April 5, he replaced the moderates with a ministry of Brazilian absolutists. Rumors of further unconstitutional acts circulated rapidly, and popular feeling rose to a fever pitch. A mob gathered; in it were many soldiers. Belatedly, the emperor regretted his intemperate actions. He sent a message promising to obey the laws, but this tardy concession only strengthened the resolution of the tremendous throng. His message was trampled into the dirt, and he received a demand to recall the ministry.

Dom Pedro's refusal of this demand was followed by a general desertion of his remaining supporters. Even the troops joined the mob in large numbers. No violence to the royal family was threatened, but the end of Dom Pedro's reign was obviously at hand.

On April 17, he abdicated in favor of his young son, Dom Pedro II, and embarked for Europe with the remainder of his family. Portuguese influence on the destiny of Brazil was at an end. The political problems of Brazil, however, had only begun.

SUGGESTED READINGS

S. Alexis, *Black Liberator*, New York, 1949.

H. Angell, *Simón Bolívar, South American Liberator*, New York, 1930.

J. Armitage, *History of Brazil, 1808–1831*, 2 vols., London, 1836.

V. A. Belaunde, *Bolívar and the Political Thought of the Spanish American Revolution*, Baltimore, 1938.

A. S. M. Chisholm, *The Independence of Chile*, Boston, 1911.

T. Cochrane, *Narrative of Services in the Liberation of Chile, Peru, and Brazil from Spanish and Portuguese Domination*, 2 vols., London, 1859.

S. Correa da Costa, *Every Inch a King*, New York, 1950.

T. E. Cotner, *The Military and Political Career of José Joaquín Herrera, 1792–1854*, Austin, 1949.

T. B. Davis, Jr., *Carlos de Alvear, Man of Revolution*, Durham, 1955.

L. E. Fisher, *The Background of the Revolution for Mexican Independence*, Boston, 1934.

R. B. C. Graham, *José Antonio Páez*, London, 1929.

C. C. Griffin, *The United States and the Disruption of the Spanish Empire, 1810–1822*, New York, 1932.

A. Hasbrouck, *Foreign Legionaries in the Liberation of Spanish South America*, New York, 1928.

A. von Humboldt, *Personal Narrative of Travels to the Equinoctial Regions of the New Continents during the Years 1799–1804*, 7 vols., London, 1814–29.

———— *Political Essay on the Kingdom of New Spain*, 4 vols., London, 1811.

R. A. Humphreys, ed., *British Consular Reports on the Trade and Politics of Latin America, 1824–1826*, London, 1940.

———— *Liberation in South America, 1806–1827*, London, 1952.

W. Kaufman, *British Policy and the Independence of Latin America, 1804–1828*, New Haven, 1951.

S. de Madariaga, *Bolívar*, New York, 1952.

———— *The Fall of the Spanish American Empire*, New York, 1948.

G. Masur, *Simón Bolívar*, Albuquerque, 1948.

J. J. Mehegan, *O'Higgins of Chile*, London, 1913.

B. Mitre, *The Emancipation of South America*, London, 1893.

B. Moses, *The Intellectual Background of the Revolution in South America, 1810–1824*, New York, 1926.

———— *South America on the Eve of Emancipation*, New York, 1908.

A. H. Noll and A. P. MacMahon, *The Life and Times of Miguel Hidalgo y Costilla*, Chicago, 1910.

J. F. Rippy, *Rivalry of the United States and Great Britain over Latin America (1808–1830)*, Baltimore, 1929.

W. S. Robertson, *France and Latin American Independence*, Baltimore, 1939.

———— *Iturbide of Mexico*, Durham, 1952.

———— *The Rise of the Spanish American Republics as Told in the Lives of Their Liberators*, New York, 1918.

R. Rojas, *San Martín: Knight of the Andes*, New York, 1945.

J. Rydjord, *Foreign Interest in the Independence of New Spain*, Durham, 1935.

A. Schoellkopf, *Don José de San Martín, 1778–1850*, New York, 1924.

G. A. Sherwell, *Antonio José de Sucre*, Washington, 1924.

J. F. Thorning, *Miranda: World Citizen*, Gainesville, Fla., 1952.

J. B. Trend, *Bolívar and the Independence of Spanish America*, London, 1946.

H. G. Warren, *The Sword Was Their Passport*, Baton Rouge, 1943.

C. K. Webster, ed., *Britain and the Independence of Latin America, 1812–1830*, 2 vols., London, 1938.

A. P. Whitaker, *The Mississippi Question, 1795–1803*, New York, 1934.

———— *The United States and the Independence of Latin America, 1800–1830*, Baltimore, 1941.

V

THE STRUGGLE FOR POLITICAL

STABILITY

XXV

The Responsibilities of Nationhood

> The land, it is true, belongs to large proprietors, but they do
> not form a class of men who, having a common and solid inter-
> est in the country, constitute a sort of natural aristocracy, con-
> cerned to preserve order, and make the government stable . . .
> What is wanting in these countries is a sufficient number of
> citizens who have no personal ends to secure, and nothing to get
> out of the government, except good administration . . .
>
> JAMES BRYCE *

THE independence of the Latin American nations
was achieved by a substantial amount of mutual
aid and co-operation. Had such co-operation been lacking, the
various national uprisings might well have been crushed one by
one. As it was, Argentine troops participated in the liberation of
Chile and then, with Chilean aid, moved north against the Spanish in Peru. Colombian and Venezuelan units struggled together
against the large armies that Spain sent to hold the viceroyalty of
New Granada, and once victory had been attained they turned
southward toward Quito, Lima, and the final defeat of the Spaniards at Ayacucho. Only in New Spain, Brazil, and Argentina
were the battles for independence won without substantial aid
from some other portion of the revolting colonial domains. A
further exception must be made for Haiti and the Dominican Republic. There, at one point or another, both British and United

* *South America, Observations and Impressions,* The Macmillan Company,
New York, 1929, pp. 532–3.

States forces became involved in the independence movements as a result of conflict with the French; but both island republics in the final struggles achieved independence without direct foreign aid. A few regions, Central America, Paraguay, and Argentina, were not visited by the main bodies of European troops sent to hold the colonies. They owed their good fortune, however, to the successful action of the independence forces in those other areas where Spain, in particular, chose to concentrate her efforts to retain or reconquer her vanishing dominions.

Political and military co-operation was highly informal, however. No joint congress met to give orientation and central direction to the forces fighting in the field, or even to decide upon a declaration of independence. No commander-in-chief was chosen to lead the armies. Well-planned and co-ordinated military campaigns were the exception and not the rule. When the last important battle had been fought and the last Spanish flag hauled down, no precedent or firm basis for political co-operation had emerged, to say nothing of the possibility of political union. Instead, the colonial jurisdictional divisions — viceroyalties, captaincies-general, and presidencies — became the natural entities of separate statehood. This outcome, lamented by many Latin Americans at the time, was inevitable. Those who looked with envy upon the union effected among the former British colonies of North America failed to take into account the relative homogeneity of those neighboring states fronting upon the North Atlantic. They underestimated the centrifugal political forces arising from the scope, diversity, and grandeur of the vast domains that had belonged to the kings of Spain and Portugal. They overlooked how closely the North American union had come to failure in spite of geographic proximity and community of interest. Likewise, few at the time noted the comparative finality of Latin American independence, once it had been achieved.

The United States began its independent existence surrounded by potential foes. To the north were the British settlements in Canada and Quebec. To the west and south were the possessions of Spain in Louisiana and Florida. France was known to have designs on Louisiana even after its transfer to Spain. To the east, across the Atlantic, was the erstwhile mother country, still powerful and still the mistress of the seas. Her failure to evacuate forts in the western territories as she had agreed to do and her constant agitations among the Indians raised serious questions as to whether reconquest might not be attempted should England find herself momentarily relieved of the pressure exerted by her traditional foes in Europe. The actions of British naval commanders on the high seas in forcing American sailors to serve under the royal flag did nothing to dispel the fears of the new republic.

With the defeat of the Spanish army at Ayacucho, on the other hand, the reconquest of Latin America became unlikely. No continental foothold remained to the Bourbon monarch. Neither Spain nor Portugal, nor even France, possessed a suitable base in the Western Hemisphere from which an attack upon any of the continental nations might be launched with any hope of real success. Except for minor outposts in the Guianas, in Honduras, and in those Caribbean islands still in the possession of European powers, Latin America formed a single geographic unit north to the Mexican border, a unit surrounded only by water. And on the water Britain stood guard, openly opposed to any move that might be undertaken by a concert of European powers against the independence of the Latin American states. Thus freed of any immediate peril to their new status, the new nations lacked external stimulus to cohesion and union. The independent peoples had far more to fear from each other than from alien encroachments from across the seas.

Naturally, the refusal of Spain, Portugal, and France to grant immediate recognition to the independence of their former colonies continued to be cause for some concern and left open the question of their eventual intentions. Such vague uncertainties were of little consequence, however, in influencing the political evolution of the new states. The political fragmentation that characterized the continents by 1830 became a fixed pattern, except in Central America where the forces of disunion had yet to run their course. External pressures receded ever further into the background and internal problems came to occupy the center of the stage.

By far the greatest internal problem throughout all of Latin America was political, that of government. Each of the new states was more or less free to decide for itself the nature of its future governmental structure once the yoke of the mother country had been cast off. Nevertheless, many problems attended the making of this decision. What groups in the state were to be heard from? Who was to speak for these groups? Where were the voices to be heard? What were the principal choices and alternatives? To none of these questions were immediate answers available, except in Brazil, where independence caused no break in the continuity of government. In many respects, answers must be sought in the nature of the revolutionary movements and the course of the ensuing struggles, for these factors and events predetermined in major part the character of future political institutions and at the same time rendered academic many of the issues raised in the polemics of the era.

As far as the Spanish colonies were concerned the first revolutionary undertakings stemmed directly from the Napoleonic invasion of Spain. Uprisings were originally oriented toward the maintenance of legitimacy with respect to the ruling family. Submission to the usurper, Joseph Bonaparte, was regarded as impossible. Had Fernando VII in 1808 followed in the steps of the Portuguese regent, João, and transferred the seat of his authority to the Western Hemisphere instead of submitting to the French invaders, it might have been possible to maintain intact the institution of monarchy in the colonial kingdoms, regardless of the outcome of events on the peninsula. Fernando, it has been noted, made no such move, but, along with his father, became the captive of the French emperor and turned a deaf ear to the clamor of colonial cabildos and juntas declaring their allegiance to him and renouncing the authority of the French-dominated government in Madrid.

Once restored to his throne Fernando made it perfectly clear that he had no intention of treating his American kingdoms as other than the subject colonies of Spain. The die was thereupon cast not only for independence, but against monarchy as well. The revolutionary juntas of Spanish America had separated, far more sharply than their forerunners in British North America, the two issues of submission to the mother country and her internal governing bodies and submission to the royal authority of the monarch. Both the British and the Spanish colonies reached the position at one point in their respective controversies where co-equal status with the mother country under a common monarch was regarded by many as a desirable solution to the conflicts arising out of colonial-metropolitan relations. The point was much clearer in Spanish America because the legitimate ruler had been deposed by a foreign interloper and the mother country conquered by the invader's troops. The monarch could simply have moved to another of his kingdoms. When, however, Fernando identified himself irrevocably with Spain and upheld her jurisdiction over the empire in the relationship of master to subordinate, the two issues merged as they had in British North America and independence from both mother country and king became the point of controversy.

A few revolutionary leaders favored the establishment of republican governments in Spanish America from the outset. An important republican movement existed in Brazil when independence was declared in 1822. In spite of the North American precedent, these people must have been considered extremists by a sizable percentage of their contemporaries, for the monarchical system was deeply rooted throughout the civilized world, and in Latin America it had the powerful sanction of religion to support it in the minds of even the humblest citizens. Consequently, it is not surprising that early steps were taken to preserve the institution of monarchy even though the Spanish king was rejected. Popular sovereignty was a useful theory that had taken firm hold upon the minds of many Latin American intellectuals, as is evidenced by the widespread use of the argument that once the monarch had been deposed sovereignty reverted to the people. Few, however, understood its real connotations or were willing to see the theory applied to domestic political life. Monarchy was still favored as a governmental form even by many who espoused popular sovereignty in theory and who had just participated in the overthrow of a king with the best of family credentials. Particularly was this the case with such thinking leaders as Bernardo Monteagudo, Manuel Belgrano, and José de San Martín of Argentina, Bernardo O'Higgins of Chile, and Lucas Alamán of Mexico. These men looked about them and perceived signs of social and political disintegration on all sides. In the establishment of a strong constitutional monarchy they and others thought they saw the possibility of arresting the steady drift toward social convulsion and political anarchy.

No sooner was the question of new monarchies seriously raised than the hopes of the monarchists were dashed to the gound. Eligible scions of Europe's royal families saw better than did their American supporters the risks and hazards, if not the utter futility, of accepting an American throne. A delegation from La Plata received a cold reception upon its arrival in Europe for purposes of negotiation with the royal houses. No one wished to set up his kingdom in a land where popular factions had shown their willingness to take government into their own hands. Neither were potential candidates anxious to fly in the face of the Spanish king by accepting the throne of one of his rebellious dominions. As the wars of independence dragged on and the republican forces of Bolívar possessed themselves of one Spanish stronghold after another in South America, the question of monarchy failed to hold much interest. In Mexico, the unhappy experience with the would-be emperor, Agustín Iturbide, served to demonstrate the futility of such a system both to the Mexicans themselves and to potential monarchs in Europe. By 1830 the issue of monarchy was quite dead and republicanism was triumphant in every country except Brazil.

The impossibility of maintaining a monarchical form of government in the new Spanish American states by no means meant that democratic republics were to be established. It meant, on the contrary, that for decades to come Latin America was to constitute a remarkable proving ground for costly experiments in self-government. These experiments again and again ended in failure in that they did not succeed in providing stable and effective political systems. Of course, it cannot be assumed that under a monarch the new states would have fared any better. Brazil under monarchy did achieve a comparatively stable and effective political system and was able to make the transition from colony to independent statehood with ease. The fact that Brazil was blessed with two able leaders of the Bragança line gives no assurance that any other American country would have been equally fortunate, however. Thus, while the form and nature of the Spanish-American revolution did extirpate the seeds of royal authority, this in itself cannot be looked upon as a misfortune nor as a prime reason for the political confusion that followed. Indeed, thereby was eliminated a bone of contention that remained a disturbing factor in European political life for yet another century.

If kings were not to rule in Latin America, who was? To this question the revolutionary wars provided a real though temporary and not very satisfactory answer. In the early days of the revolutionary movements, cabildos and juntas formed of the prominent citizenry of the various communities assumed the reins of government. These bodies could hardly be called democratic or even popular, for their composition favored the well-to-do, the military, the religious, and the intellectual elements to the exclusion of virtually all others. They were status rather than elective bodies. They soon gave way, however, to the military leaders who conducted the campaigns and fought the battles against the Spaniards. These were the real governors who emerged to rule the new nations of Latin America. But these too soon passed from the scene and political life descended to a brutish struggle for power among those who could muster sufficient military support to compete. This was the sorry picture coming into focus in Latin America by 1830.

The factors that made the road toward effective self-government in Latin America so tortuous are numerous and complex. Any listing of them is certain to be incomplete, and few will agree as to which were primary and which secondary in importance. Also, in retrospect, it is easy to confuse the issues of stable government and democracy, the basic requirements for which are not necessarily the same. In 1830, few Latin Americans were concerned with the practical application of the democratic ideal. It would have been enough if government could have been rendered stable and tolerably benevolent, minus the trappings of royalty and foreign domination. Thus such commonly mentioned problems as large unassimilated Indian groups, general illiteracy, and lack of popular experience and education in self-government did not in themselves make stable government impossible, although they did present a milieu in which popular democracy was out of the question. This was well recognized by most of the revolutionary leaders, and few indeed were the serious advocates of handing political power over to the masses of the people.

Probably the greatest single factor predisposing the new republics to unstable government was the absence of a real sense of responsibility at any point in the social structure after Spanish authority was withdrawn. The social system was, during the colonial period, essentially manorial, and so it remained after the independence wars were over. Wealth and social status were based upon the possession of land, large tracts of land upon which the aboriginal classes toiled in virtual servitude to the owners. The system, fostered in the days of the encomienda, nevertheless lacked many of the attributes of European feudal life. The pattern of property relationships did not constitute an articulated system once the Spanish monarch was removed from the picturè. More important, however, was the fact that the possession of property had not, under the Spanish administrative system, carried with it political responsibility. Authority had been centered in the hands of peninsular Spaniards sent out to the colonies to enjoy the benefits of the chief administrative posts, and creoles, while they might and did become wealthy landlords and property owners, were excluded from most positions of political leadership. The cabildos, where the creoles were permitted participation, were of almost no importance, for their activities were so circumscribed by the rigid detail of Spanish legislation that the posts of regidores came to be regarded as largely honorific and were sold to the highest bidder, thus subverting not only the elective nature but the representative function of these municipal government bodies. In marked contrast to the native-born aristocracy of British North America, the creole aristocracy of Latin America played little or no political role in the colonial government. Its status was safeguarded for it by royal authority, and its only important struggle was against that very authority for a more generous share of royal benefices.

As already indicated, it was the creole aristocracy that furnished the leadership in the movement for separation from Spain. It was the cabildo, the political body in which they were represented, that first took up the question of self-government when the Napoleonic armies overran Spain, and the cabildos served as the legislative bodies of many of the colonies during the long struggle for independence. This proved, however, to be little more than a passing phenomenon. Leadership quickly passed to the chief military figures, and when the wars were over it was they who were calling the tune. The creole aristocracy, seemingly natural successors to political authority, were in utter confusion as to their political role. This upper layer of the social structure was itself unstable, a class ill-prepared to govern. It lacked experience, yes; but much more important, it lacked cohesion, purpose, and above all, a sense of responsibility.

The wealthy creole families made major sacrifices and substantial contributions in both men and money to the cause of independence. Sons and heads of families proved their courage on the battlefield and became popular heroes with the lower classes as a consequence, but few indeed were those willing to sit down to the gruelling task of giving their country an honest, effective government. There was perhaps more tragedy than wisdom in the statement of San Martín upon leaving Peru that 'the presence of a fortunate soldier, however disinterested he may be, is dangerous to newly established states.' An even greater danger to such states existed in the tendency for those who had shown constructive leader-

ship during the revolutions to relinquish that leadership when
the glory and glamour was past, letting it fall into the hands of
those less capable and far less disinterested.

The wars of independence tore out by the roots the stabilizing
influence of royal authority, leaving in its place a vacuum that the
creole aristocrats were unable to fill. How quickly the revolutionary
leaders passed from the scene. By 1830 virtually all were dead or in
exile, either forced or self-imposed. In country after country government passed into the hands of lesser military chieftains whose
principal interest seemed to be that of imitating the former Spanish rulers and amassing fortunes for themselves. The wealthy, the
educated, the able, retired to their estates, eschewing the responsibility that their place in the social system and their role in the
revolutionary wars had cast upon them.

This was a well-nigh fatal mistake if stable government were to
prevail in the new republics. In 1830, and for several decades thereafter, virtually every country paraded military leadership in government; but the leaders were not those who had commanded the great
revolutionary armies. Instead, they were the lesser officers, trained
in violence, captivated by their own importance and the attractive-
ness of their uniforms, but lacking the noble purpose and the broad
outlook of the principal figures who had directed the course of the
revolutionary struggles. They did not form a corps of officers inured
to the rigid disciplines of European military castes. The chaotic
revolutionary struggles had not molded men into disciplined forces.
Rather the wars had placed a premium on independent action,
personal glory, and heroism for its own sake. Thus the young
militarists were extreme individualists, in most cases incapable of
working together with others of their own kind, and they were
motivated by an intense interest in politics and a desire to exercise
political power. The rough and undisciplined heroism that had
characterized the Spanish struggle against the Moors and the
early battles of the conquest centuries before was reborn in the
new republics, and no stable forces, political or social, raised a hand
to restrain it.

The rigidity of the social caste system posed further difficulties

that delayed the establishment of stable government. The distinction between the poor and the wealthy was too great, the gulf too
wide to be easily crossed; no strong middle class existed to bridge
the gap. Latin America was and has continued to remain essentially
rural. City dwellers were composed in part of the land owners
who resided away from their land, but whose interests remained irrevocably attached to the soil that constituted the source of their
wealth; in part of the commercial people engaged in supplying the
needs of those who could afford to buy; in part of small shopkeepers
and hand manufacturers; and finally of vast numbers of hand
laborers and servants whose livelihood was gained from the work
they performed in the homes and shops of those more fortunately
situated. Race joined with Old World social values to stamp in-
delibly upon these groups their respective roles in social and political
life. The Indians predominated on the lower rungs of the ladder;
and in the middle, seldom rising above the status of shopkeeper
or small merchant, were to be found the mestizo and the poor
white immigrant. The lines separating these social and economic
groups, indistinct as they were in some cases, were not easily
crossed. Had the lower or even the middle-level groups dared assert
themselves, there were no channels of peaceful political expression,
and a benign priesthood lost little opportunity to instruct the ignorant lower classes in the virtue of accepting their miserable lot.

In the countryside, the social and economic differences were even
more sharply defined. There existed only the large estates and the
ill-fed and ill-housed Indians who worked on them. In the more
primitive regions were the Indian communities from which the
corregidores of the past had long since extracted the last measure
of self-respect in the interest of the tribute, the mita, and their own
pocketbooks. Enforced military service in patriot and royalist armies
during the revolutions only added one more burden to the already
overburdened aborigines.

In such a social environment constructive political leadership
was lacking unless the creole upper classes were to furnish it. When
they did not, other forces took over. The military was regarded as
a noble profession. It offered an avenue to advancement that car-

ried none of the social stigma associated with the trades and commerce. One did not have to be wealthy to enter it. In the new republics it was not sufficiently well organized to have an established hierarchical structure with the officer class at the top open only to the wealthy and the well-born. Personal valor and strength and above all, the ability to command others and attract a following offered promise of success. Coupled with a sortie into the political arena, military life even offered the possibility of wealth and social recognition for those who could never make the grade by any other means. Many were those who chose such a course, and great was the chaos they created and the havoc they wreaked upon their long-suffering countrymen.

Thus the political atmosphere of the new Latin American nations was charged with unrest. Those who might have provided stability and leadership shirked their responsibilities. Men schooled in the violence of the revolutionary wars, who were avid for power, who were seeking a means to break through the arbitrary restrictions of the old social order, these possessed themselves of the political power of their states. Government became a plaything in their hands, albeit a lucrative one provided they could successfully meet all challengers and maintain their positions of authority.

It was inevitable that the struggles of the military chieftains centered around the office of president. It was the office that controlled the military forces, the office from which appointments were made for the entire public administration, the office that dominated all government activities. With the death of the revolutionary cabildos, the role of legislative bodies in government became a mockery. Membership in the various national congresses was dependent more often than not upon the whim of the executive, and such bodies as did attempt to exercise legislative prerogatives soon learned that silence was the better part of valor. Legislative strength can exist only where strong and politically conscious groups seek expression of their interests through representation, and for this no precedent was to be found in Latin America. Furthermore, since no balance of social forces existed, the interests of the powerful and wealthy were better served by means other than debate. Without the participation of the prominent citizenry, the congressional discussions of national problems on the part of those with little social or economic power could be nothing more than a waste of breath. Thus the executive was left supreme.

Backed by the army and the police, ignored or patronized by the wealthy, the military officer who achieved the top executive office could propose and dispose as he saw fit. If the imprudence of his actions caused alarm, some other caudillo could easily be found who by means of intrigue and violence would take his place. In the meantime, the power of the state and usually its treasury were at his disposal. He might leave his office rich and respected, as a few were shrewd enough to do. More likely he would end his days in exile and poverty because he did not pick the opportune moment to retire. Nevertheless, more than one Latin American family owes its fortune and prestige to the fact that some obscure ancestor chose the military road to the presidency of his country.

It is a dark picture painted of a dark era. The years between 1830 and 1860 were far from happy ones for most of Latin America. They were years of retrogression and chaos, of almost constant warfare, both international and internal. The names of Santa Anna in Mexico, Santa Cruz in Bolivia, Carrera in Central America, Flores in Ecuador, and Rosas in Argentina will long be associated with the turbulence of this unfortunate epoch. These were the more successful. Many did not last long enough to be remembered except by the most meticulous historian.

Interwoven in the pattern of power struggles throughout the Latin American countries during the first decades of independence were the conflicts over ideas, rights, and status. The problems that gave rise to these conflicts too had their roots deep in the soil of colonial life and were nurtured by the blood of patriots during the independence movements. The revolution from Spain, while perhaps prematurely consummated because of conditions in Europe, was no accident. Nor were the wars themselves simple struggles between creole and native forces on the one hand and Spanish soldiery on the other. Large American elements were active in both camps, and when the wars were over the opposing groups still remained. Issues that had divided the colonies on the question of independence continued to divide the new nations in their domestic politics. It would be absurd to assume that the influence of the French and American revolutions terminated once independence had been achieved and new governments established, for the ideas of individual rights and human liberties espoused in all three great revolutions were given constitutional embodiment throughout Latin America. The status of Latin American society, characterized as it was by great social and economic inequalities among the people, made the application of these ideas hazardous, difficult, and to some extent impossible. Nevertheless, most leaders gave at least lip service to equalitarian and democratic principles, and in spite of the great turmoil that prevailed in government and in part because of it, step after step was taken to break down the bastions of the old order. These steps did not create political democracy, but they eliminated a number of the legal and social impediments to democratic development.

The Spanish regime had been a centralist regime in which local interests had frequently been subordinated to the interests of larger units and to the empire as a whole. Independence was a signal for the local interests to assert themselves, as was clearly indicated by the pattern of statehood that emerged. The tendency to seek the smallest possible political denominator did not terminate at the confines of the new political jurisdiction, however; in many localities it carried to an extreme localism, justified and defended by reference to the successful federalism that had so recently come into being on the North American continent. In many cases, such as that of Brazil, Mexico, Argentina, and Colombia, vast territory and poor communications, coupled with considerable local variation in economic activity and tradition, made some form of local political autonomy seem most appropriate. Where conceded, and in the absence of strong national representative institutions, it had the disastrous effect of providing unimportant military chieftains a natural base for getting their feet firmly under them before undertaking the stepping-stone march to the national capital. At the same time, because government was hardly representative at any level, local autonomy did little to aid the cause of democratic development. It did provide the basis for much political disagreement and all too often for internal warfare.

Almost from the day of independence in each country, internal cleavages appeared as to what the role and power of the church should be. Aside from constituting a theoretical question stemming from eighteenth-century religious controversy, it was a very practical question. During the period of the empire, the viceroys had exercised the ecclesiastical patronage in the name of the king. Now there were neither kings nor viceroys. Upon whom would the duty fall? Ultramontanists asserted that the prerogative reverted to the Pope and his ecclesiastical representatives while others firmly espoused the natural carry-over of the regalist doctrine that the authority once held by the king passed on to the new state as his successor. Few were concerned with the possibility of a separation of church and state, for the functions of the two were inextricably intertwined. With a few very notable exceptions, the representatives of the church had supported the Spanish crown against the colonies in the independence struggles. They had opposed the revolutionary doctrines upon which the new governments were founded, for they foresaw that those doctrines would inevitably give rise to a challenge of the many privileges and special rights enjoyed by the church. Thus, in the eyes of many, the organization of the church was a carry-over from the empire, an extension of the system that the revolutions had been fought to extirpate. The slowness of the Vatican in recognizing the independent governments and the insistence of papal representatives on upholding the authority of the Pope in matters of church patronage did much to confirm this view. Consequently, many joined in attacking the church, some sincerely and from conviction, others in the hope of profiting from any steps the state might take to restrict the power and wealth of the religious organization. Vast numbers supported the church, believing in its sacred role and opposing the revolutionary ideas that in their minds verged on heresy. Many saw their own rights and privileges challenged along with those of the church, and common interest caused them to cast in their lot with the clerics. A major division of opinion ensued, an inextricable factor in the politics of the new republics.

Because no benefices could be filled until the Vatican recognized the new republics, and because many of the incumbents died or fled, there was a serious shortage in the clerical hierarchy, with disastrous effects on the lower clergy. In some areas the church's influence never was fully restored.

Under the conditions that prevailed after independence, all factions engaged in controversy naturally sought to widen the orbit of their influence and to affiliate or form alliances with other factions of similar or related interests. The maintenance of order through strong government seemed a more certain protection for the church than risking anarchy as a consequence of weak central authority. On the other hand, such major cities as Buenos Aires and Bogotá turned out to be strongholds of political liberals and anti-clerical intellectuals who, when in power, utilized the central authority of the state to attack church privileges and prerogatives. Consequently, church alignments with other groups engaged in political controversy tended to vary with local circumstances. Strong central authority was favored if those in power were political conservatives sympathetic toward the church. If, as was the case in Colombia and the Plata region, the centralists were anti-clerical, the church without hesitation threw its influence behind the more conservative advocates of federation from the provinces. In Central America, where federation was a centralizing tendency as contrasted with the separatism of the several states, the church opposed federalism and supported the separatists, for the federal or liberal party under the leadership of Morazán showed itself strongly anti-clerical. As time went on, a pattern emerged showing two opposing groups — a pattern encountered generally throughout Latin America. One group was centralist in political orientation, somewhat liberal in its social outlook, and anti-clerical in its religious views. The other was federalist, conservative, pro-clerical, and highly militaristic. However, in the considerable number of countries where liberalism had little foothold and anti-clericalism was but a minor issue, the church commonly supported the strongest and most dictatorial of centralist regimes. This arrangement most closely resembled the old order with royalist central authority and church power supporting and complementing each other.

The manifestations of developing political factions, while general, were not universal. Caudillismo, which emerged during this period and has continued in some regions of Latin America to the present day, was virtually dead in Chile by 1830, scarcely appeared at all in New Granada, and did not establish itself in Venezuela until a later epoch. The problem of centralization and decentralization in government was a most important issue in Mexico, Central America, New Granada, and Argentina, but of much lesser importance elsewhere, except in Brazil where the existence of a fairly stable monarchy tempered the issue measurably. In almost all areas the church issue was beclouded. Nowhere did anticlericalism at first mean anti-Catholicism, much less opposition to religion, although as the struggle continued, anti-Catholicism emerged. Opposition to the church meant opposition to certain aspects of its activities or to some of the activities themselves: the conduct of business enterprises, preoccupation with politics, the enjoyment of special legal privileges, control over the civil status of individuals and over education. Within the church the secular branch clashed with the religious orders, particularly with respect to the operation of schools. Ardent anti-clerics and members of the Masonic lodges in Mexico and Brazil experienced no great difficulty in upholding the Roman Catholic religion even though the bishops were denouncing the lodges to which they continued to belong as heretical and ungodly. Latin America was experiencing an era of confusion characterized not only by political chaos but by chaotic thinking as well. Very little was clear, well-defined, or concise.

Much of the turmoil, however, was on the surface. History is written about those who make history, who bring about change and alter the course of human events. Little is said about those who continue at their daily tasks generation after generation in the humbler levels of society. The few years of revolutionary warfare had not erased the work of centuries. The adoption of new constitutions did not improve the living standard of the impoverished Indian or Negro, nor did it reduce the incidence of dysentery, tuberculosis, or venereal disease, which continued to decimate the population. The Indian continued to toil in his field or in the field of his hacendado, using the same methods of cultivation, the same tools, and reaping the same harvest as had his ancestors in the centuries preceding. The cobbles of the streets in the cities continued to resound to the crunch of the big wooden wheels of the oxcarts. The miserable waifs of the villages continued to huddle in the church doorways to protect themselves from the chill of the night. Religious processions proceeded regularly from the doors of the churches, made the rounds of the village streets, and returned to the churches followed by long streams of faithful adherents, some in the finery to which their status entitled them, others in the rags of the poor and humble. The strong current of every-day life flowed on, but its pace did not quicken.

In the three decades following the end of the revolutionary wars, little material progress or development was experienced in most of Latin America. Life was too hard and insecure to leave a margin for development and new construction. Enterprise languished, and everywhere men were on the defensive against the depredations of the political and military demagogues. In Mexico, the great silver mines that had poured forth their treasure in the days of the Spanish viceroys now stood idle, their shafts filled with water. In Central America, the orchards and fields, the indigo plantations, the rich lands of the monasteries grew weeds while the conscript armies of Morazán and Carrera roamed the countryside in a seemingly endless struggle for military and political supremacy. Venezuela and New Granada were all but prostrate after the devastating wars against the armies of Fernando VII. The wealth and prestige of the once great viceroyalty of Peru was gone, and the national treasury was reduced to dependence upon the sale of bird manure. The bleak highlands of the altiplano saw only the dust of the mounted legions and barefoot stragglers that formed the army of

Santa Cruz. Argentina lay benumbed under the heavy hand of Rosas and his secret police.

Not only were social and economic life stagnant; the same was true of intellectual activity. Education and the arts were neglected, forgotten in the all-consuming struggle for political mastery. Able men from Argentina and Venezuela found refuge in Chile where the stimulus of their intellects contributed substantially to the welfare and development of that haven of stable government and national progress. Others fled to Europe from whose cultural centers they were able to return and contribute the more to their national literature by reason of their foreign experience.

During the long era of colonial rule, and particularly toward the latter part of the eighteenth century, the Spanish monarchs had shown much interest in the fostering of intellectual and cultural achievement in the Americas. They and their viceroys founded universities, patronized the sciences and the arts, encouraged the beautifying of cities and the construction of public buildings. During the wars of independence such things were quite naturally neglected. In the confusion that followed thereafter, an attitude of neglectfulness tended to become characteristic of many of the new governments. The new political leaders frequently had no interest in such matters, and those who did found little opportunity to exploit that interest. They were too busy maintaining themselves in power, and their public treasuries were drained by the corruption of their administrations and by the necessity of maintaining their military forces.

Any real progress was difficult for other reasons. Most decisions of policy were of necessity negative; that is, they were decisions of status rather than decisions of action. Economic development was 'fostered' if export duties on some product were lowered, or if import duties were raised in protection of some local industry. Education was 'fostered' if schools, closed during the revolutions, were permitted to reopen, or if teachers were permitted to teach with greater freedom than the previous regime had permitted. Finances were 'reorganized' if the public debt was refunded, or, for that matter, if public monies were honestly collected and disbursed for a short time. Progress consisted of words, legislative declarations, speeches, outlined objectives, meaningless reports — seldom of achievement. When a government did undertake some progressive measure, such as the construction of roads or the improvement of port facilities, the ancient bureaucratic machinery carried over from the colonial era often stood in the way. Designed as it had been to protect the king's patrimony from the machinations of wayward administrators, it served effectively to delay and block constructive activity by those who were honest, but it left the door of the treasury wide open to those who cared nothing for the rules or for the interests of the nation. In part these difficulties indicated that while the external yoke of Spain had been cast off, many of the administrative vices of the old regime still insidiously bound the new republics; in part they reflected the dearth of competent leadership.

In Latin America, as in most other parts of the world, including the United States, government in the last century was not viewed as having a positive role to play in the economic or social affairs of the average citizen. It was expected to maintain order, provide a stable currency, uphold justice and the law, conduct foreign relations, and defend the homeland. These were minimum objectives and accorded well with the theory that the least government is the best government, a theory quite different from that of extreme paternalism espoused by the majority of Spanish monarchs. Reaction against the Spanish system and the reluctance of the propertied classes to participate in or accept responsibility for government made the minimum objectives seem adequate to important segments of the population. Unfortunately, when even these limited functions proved to be beyond the abilities of the struggling new nations, private enterprise and initiative could hardly be expected to venture into the field of national development. Conditions were too unstable and the risk of armed depredation and plunder was too great.

In a region where church and state were closely linked, chaos in government could not fail to react upon religious life and religious

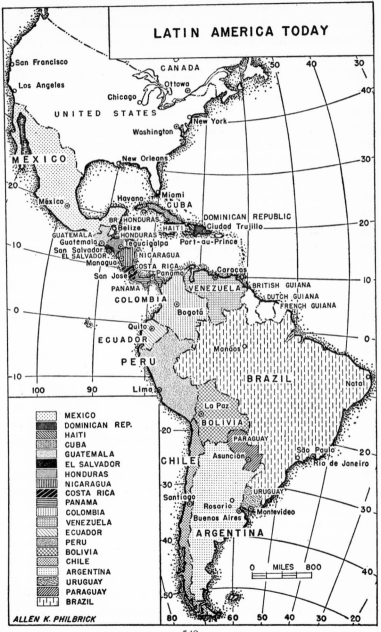

LATIN AMERICA TODAY

San Francisco
Los Angeles

CANADA
Ottawa
Chicago
UNITED STATES
Washington   New York

MEXICO

20

México   Havana   Miami
                          CUBA
BR. HONDURAS   DOMINICAN REPUBLIC
Belize   HAITI   Ciudad Trujillo
GUATEMALA   HONDURAS   Port-au-Prince
Guatemala   Tegucigalpa
San Salvador   NICARAGUA
EL SALVADOR
Managua
San Jose   COSTA RICA
            Panamá   Caracas
PANAMA   VENEZUELA   BRITISH GUIANA
COLOMBIA   DUTCH GUIANA
        Bogotá   FRENCH GUIANA

Quito
ECUADOR

PERU
            Manáos

        BRAZIL   Natal

Lima
La Paz
BOLIVIA
            PARAGUAY
CHILE   Asunción   São Paulo
                          Rio de Janeiro
        Santiago
        Rosario   URUGUAY
        Buenos Aires   Montevideo
        ARGENTINA

New Orleans

MILES   800

Legend

- MEXICO
- DOMINICAN REP.
- HAITI
- CUBA
- GUATEMALA
- EL SALVADOR
- HONDURAS
- NICARAGUA
- COSTA RICA
- PANAMA
- COLOMBIA
- VENEZUELA
- ECUADOR
- PERU
- BOLIVIA
- CHILE
- ARGENTINA
- URUGUAY
- PARAGUAY
- BRAZIL

ALLEN K. PHILBRICK

institutions. Whether it willed it or not, the church was inevitably drawn into political controversy. Its resources were at stake and its control over many traditional functions was threatened. To the complaints against it arising from its attitude during the revolutions were added those created by its support of fallen caudillos, opposition to Masonry, and insistence upon the maintenance of special courts and other privileges. In a number of countries the government turned upon the church and stripped it of much of its authority and no small portion of its property. Treatment was far from uniform from one country to another, but among the measures taken affecting the church were the abolition of special church taxes, abolition of church courts, confiscation of commercial and agricultural properties, secularization of cemeteries, and secularization of education. Many of these steps were justified and in the long run beneficial from the standpoint of those favoring the reduction of the political power of the church. On the other hand, certain important and useful activities suffered in the process. The maintenance of primary and secondary educational institutions had long been considered a church function throughout Latin America. Likewise, the church, together with private charities, was expected to maintain hospitals, and to create and maintain the institutions for the helpless and the aged, for the poor and the destitute. While this was true elsewhere as well as in Latin America, the great social and economic distinctions and the very size of the lower classes, particularly the large impoverished Indian population, made the problems so great that the church could not begin to cope with them even under the best of conditions. The attacks upon the church and the depletion of its resources meant the inevitable curtailment of its service and educational activities at a time when the chaotic national governments were ill-disposed and in no way prepared to meet these important needs with state resources. Thus these functions, too, languished and atrophied.

However, the mid-nineteenth century was not a period of total gloom. At least two countries were fortunate enough to escape most of the difficulties that have just been described. Political stability was achieved at an early date, and during the years under discussion a firm foundation was laid for future development and national progress. This was true of Brazil and Chile, and to a lesser degree of Paraguay. Still another nation, Colombia, or as it was then known, New Granada, while convulsed by internal dissensions and repeated fruitless attempts to overthrow the government, nevertheless moved steadily forward in developing its national consciousness, in clarifying divergent political points of view, and in experimentation with organizational devices to meet the needs of a complicated geographic diversification that strained the very bonds of union time and again.

Both Brazil and Chile met well the rigorous tests of nationhood. Firm and enlightened leadership made possible the surmounting of early disorders in spite of the discordant clamors of numerous rebellious spirits. Brazil was indeed fortunate in that independence was accomplished gradually and without long and bloody warfare with Portugal. The country became virtually independent with the transfer of the Portuguese monarchy to Rio de Janeiro, so that when independence was proclaimed fourteen years later by the young Dom Pedro, no interruption in the affairs of internal government was necessary. Neither was there created by the severance a generation of self-seeking ex-soldiers to lead ignorant followers in endless struggles for power. Battles there were over local autonomy, but no single leader was strong enough to challenge seriously the Bragança kings, and those who might have united to overthrow the empire in the hectic days of the second Dom Pedro's infancy saw in the maintenance of royal authority the one firm hope of national solidarity, and to this they gave their support.

Chile, although the scene of extended and bitter revolutionary warfare, drew the early support of its prominent citizenry who were unwilling to cast the hard-won prize of self-government before the feet of self-seeking military demagogues. Astute and able men whose fame and fortunes were not made on the battlefield stepped to the helm and gave to their new state a stable political order that soon became the envy of the rest of the continent.

By mid-century, the independent Latin American nations had endured their most critical and difficult years. Encroachments from North America there had been, and as a result of these Mexico had lost half of her national territory. But the danger of permanent European conquest or domination was long since past. The principal problems were domestic, and toward the solution of these some of the countries had made important strides. In others internal disorder had become so fixed a pattern that it would take years to eradicate it. Such disorders had led and would lead again to international warfare among these nations of common Iberian ancestry. They had brought about and would again bring incidents and punitive intervention by European powers and by the United States. A foolish French emperor was yet to take advantage of chaos in Mexico to establish a short-lived satellite empire there. But these difficulties were part of the long process of achieving national stature. The future held vast possibilities, and those states that had passed their crisis and achieved the creation of a national consciousness were ready to move forward to the building of healthy and stable societies. They could now begin to give meaning to the philosophical concepts of liberty and equality about which so much had been said and written and so little done.

XXVI

The Stability of Moderation: Chile, Brazil, and Paraguay

> Regardless of the form of government, republican society had changed but little in the twenty years which followed the beginning of the revolution; it continued to be almost the same as colonial society during the last years of Spanish control.
>
> LUIS GALDAMES *

OF all the Spanish American republics, only two achieved a relatively stable political structure shortly after independence. These were Chile and Paraguay. For Paraguay, the problem was simple, for old Doctor José Francia simply assumed the role of father and ruled the relatively small population of the isolated river republic as though they were his children. He accepted no interference, not even by the church, whose ultramontane manifestations he ignored and over whose officials he assumed powers greater than those formerly exercised by the Spanish viceroy in Buenos Aires.

Several factors account for the docility with which the rule of Francia was accepted. The man himself was an active leader whose local development programs produced results and whose stern demeanor inspired both respect and fear among the mestizos and Guaraní Indians who formed the bulk of the population. His army, recruited from the lower classes, developed an intense loyalty

---

* A History of Chile, translated by I. J. Cox, University of North Carolina Press, Chapel Hill, 1941, p. 244.

to the old caudillo and provided an ample force to check the ambitions of any creole landowners who might contemplate change in the political arrangements. Of significance also was the remarkable isolation in which the Paraguayans lived and which the paternalistic Francia did everything in his power to strengthen and perpetuate. Paraguay became almost completely self-sufficient, raising its own food and meat and manufacturing such clothing, utensils, and other light products as were necessary to carry on the rather primitive economy to which the people were accustomed. Foreign trade along the great river system that led to Buenos Aires and Montevideo was rigorously restricted to those goods and carriers in which the old dictator saw direct advantage to his continued domination of the country. This is not to imply that Francia was either an exploiter of his people or engaged in amassing a personal fortune. On the contrary, the dictator feared involvement in the warfare and strife that raged all around him in Uruguay and Argentina. He strove to protect the independence of his country and its peaceful existence. In his personal life he preferred the rigors of an almost spartan regimen.

Francia could scarcely be called a benevolent ruler. His was a personal despotism made somewhat tyrannical by the neurotic xenophobia he exhibited in all contacts with the outside world. Initiative and independence were crushed in the dictator's effort to maintain Paraguay as a hermit republic.

In 1840, Francia died. For a time it was not clear just how a peaceful transfer of authority might come about. For almost a year a military junta ruled the country pending the assembly of a congress and the selection of a new chief executive. Congress, reaching for executive stability without tyranny, saw fit to create a two-man executive similar in nature to a consular arrangement by means of which Francia had years before risen to power. As before, however, a strong man emerged to dominate. Carlos Antonio López, one of the pair of executive officers, assumed the leadership and shortly had congress place the government on a more formal basis with a written constitution providing for a president with a ten-year term of office. In 1844, López was elected under the new constitution and the country moved into a more progressive era without having suffered disruption or revolution during the transitional period following Francia's death.

The political situation in Chile stabilized far more slowly than in Paraguay. As already noted, the period following independence was one of intense strife and almost continual bloodshed. Bernardo O'Higgins had been an able revolutionary leader, and no one has ever seriously questioned his sincere devotion to the welfare of his country. He was not, however, the proper man to soothe the fevered spirits of his fellow-citizens and calm the troubled waters of factional disagreement. Not only were his personal enemies numerous, but he viewed the needs of his country in such a puritanical frame of reference that he alienated many who would otherwise have been his friends. To pacification of the nation and the establishment of political stability he attempted to couple vigorous moral reforms. To restore law and order O'Higgins created strong police units to function over the countryside as well as in the cities, but their instructions were to suppress the use of alcohol as well as to put down sedition and arrest those involved in common crimes. The Chilean president was shrewd enough to realize that speed and sureness of punishment were strong deterrents to would-be criminals and insurrectionists alike. His system of drum-head courts dispensed a rapid and vigorous if sometimes not-so-just justice. But gambling and cock-fighting were considered to be serious crimes along with robbery and rebellion. By his puritanical efforts O'Higgins made himself the butt of many a joke and stirred up a fog of minor indignation. Far more serious consequences resulted from other reform measures that the president fostered, as when he attempted to secularize cemeteries and prohibit the entailment of estates.

All in all, the great Chilean patriot was no politician. His interference with burials angered the church, which was already ill-disposed toward the new republic and its independence leaders. His attempted abolition of entailments struck at the very core of the landholding system of the great families. Chile, perhaps to a greater extent than any of the other new republics, was characterized by an essentially feudal social and economic structure, resembling in many respects that of medieval Spain. Mineral wealth remained largely undiscovered and undeveloped during the long period of colonial rule, and an agrarian society came into existence in the great central valley. Lacking exportable products and cut off from the main stream of Spanish commerce, Chilean landholding families developed a high degree of self-sufficiency on the great estates that became their feudal domains. The crude agricultural implements which were used to till the soil were fabricated on the hacienda, as were household furnishings and much of the cloth in common use. The maintenance of law and order became the duty and the prerogative of the wealthy *patrón*. So did care for the well-being of the *inquilino* and his family. The inquilino was the peasant of Chile, tied to the estate on which he was born by the tenant relationship to the patrón, or landholder, and the bonds of tradition, family life, and personal dependence. When the inquilino or members of his family became ill, it was the patrón who saw to the necessary care. In time of death, marriage, or childbirth, the landholder and his family took care of the necessary amenities, providing for mourning or festivities as the case required. In contrast with other parts of Latin America, the laboring class was of essentially the same racial stock as the wealthy hacendado; for the native Araucanian Indian resisted conquest from the outset and moved southward into the forest lands beyond the Bío-Bío river rather than submit to the invader. Mestizos there were, to be sure, but in Chile the sharp racial distinction between the white proprietor and the Indian laborer existed to a far lesser degree than in Peru, Colombia, or Mexico, for there were far fewer Indians living within the area of white settlement.

The stability of the social structure and the wealth of the landholders depended on holding the large estates together. This was accomplished through the process of entailment whereby a stated heir, usually the oldest son, inherited the property and could not legally dispose of any portion of it. By the time of independence, the best land was monopolized and the system of ownership had come to constitute an economic and social evil depriving would-be agriculturists of any opportunity to acquire suitable land, even though much of it might not be in use. Consequently, O'Higgins' desire to institute reform in the system of land ownership was indicative of his farsighted statesmanship, but he attempted to do too much too rapidly. His puritanical attempts at moral reform lost him the support of the poorer classes, for they interfered with a cherished personal freedom. The inquilino cared little about the system of entailment, but he valued the pleasures of the cockfight and enjoyed an occasional bout with the demon alcohol.

Finally, O'Higgins committed a most serious mistake. His failure to give adequate attention to the collection and disbursement of revenues resulted in a financial deficit that left the soldiery unpaid. Only respect for a great revolutionary figure and the stern measures O'Higgins used to maintain law and order persuaded the populace to endure his government. The endurance proved temporary.

Between 1818 and 1831, constitution making became nearly a profession in Chile. Everyone of political importance had a hand in it. O'Higgins called a convention to draw up a constitution in 1822, and by controlling the selection of the delegates he was able to dictate almost the entire contents of the charter that emerged. Unfortunately, the document pleased only O'Higgins and it never became effective. Rebellion broke out in both the north and the south. Finally, an opposition group in Santiago gained sufficient strength and courage to call upon the now despairing leader to resign. O'Higgins went into exile in Peru, from which point he was able to judge the lasting effects of his revolutionary efforts and assess the failures and mistakes of his adventures as a politician and administrator. He continued in exile until his death in 1842. His place in Chile was taken by Ramón Freire, a military leader who was able to establish his authority and shortly undertake the creation of another constitution. This time someone decided that federalism was the cure for Chile's ills. The idea had no basis in political precedent or reality, however, and no federalism resulted. Instead, the country was thrown into a new turmoil out of which emerged a new convention and a new constitution in 1828. Constitution making had by now become an avocation, and as might have been expected the new piece of paper that fluttered in the 1828 breeze served only as another issue over which the many politicos and military factions could contend.

The period following O'Higgins' resignation and departure was an era of violence as well as an era of political uncertainty and administrative chaos. Until a major battle was fought at the Lircay river in April of 1830 — a battle that ended with the complete defeat of Freire and his departure from the Chilean scene — there seemed little hope of rescuing the new nation from the hands of competing caudillos. Independence had come to mean anarchy. Several important stabilizing factors were emerging, however — factors that were to make possible eventual peace and stable national development. For one thing, the issues that divided the politically articulate elements of the population were gradually clarified. Basically there were those who wished to preserve society and national life much as it had been prior to independence, making only those changes that the maintenance of separate nationhood demanded. On the other hand were those who saw in national independence an opportunity to create a new order in society, to bring to fruition the ideals and aspirations of European and North American revolutionary extremists. This latter group proved that it well deserved the derisive title of *pipiolos* (novices) that the conservatives gave it by espousing just such causes as federalism in a country where regional or sectional differences and traditions scarcely existed and certainly had no significant political meaning. Likewise other changes that they advocated were doctrinaire in the extreme, considering the time and the environment and the basic necessity of establishing independent nationhood.

The *pelucones*, or bigwigs, as the conservatives were called, were the realists of revolutionary Chile. Whatever one may think of their politics in retrospect, they were the group that best recognized Chile's immediate needs and they set about to create a governmental system that would provide the necessary stability, respect for law and order, and an increased though limited amount of individual freedom. In 1833 a new group met to revise the 1828 constitution, a group dominated by Diego Portales, a conservative businessman who had moved from a ministerial position into effective dictatorship of the country in the period following Freire's military defeat and exile. It proved impossible to arrive at a satisfactory revision of the 1828 fundamental law, and the convention ended by drafting an entirely new document. The fact that the new constitution went into effect and endured for over ninety years may be taken as an indication that the framers performed their service well. However, one needs only to compare the new document with the older ones to realize that the differences were of little consequence. Any one of the charters might have become the favored instrument had it been launched under the proper auspices and at a time when the populace was in a properly receptive mood. The key to the success of the conservative effort was the fact that strong leaders adopted moderate yet firm policies that were in basic accord with the reality of social and economic conditions as they existed in Chile in the 1830's.

Diego Portales was a most important factor in effecting the transition from the chaos of military caudillismo to progressive conservatism. As the head of Portales, Cea, and Company, the dominant mercantile house in Valparaiso and Santiago, he felt more sharply than the conservative landholder the need for a stable political system within which the commercial activities of the country could be expanded and developed. Likewise, he lacked many of the personal ties that linked many of the wealthy hacendados to each other and to various of the factions in the armed forces. Portales was, in reality, an upstart, a *nouveau riche,* whose great financial power gave him status that he could not claim by reason of birth or education. He had other attributes that stood him in good stead. He possessed boundless energy, firm decision, and courage. As is so often the case with successful businessmen he distrusted the intellectual and the theorist. In Chile in the year 1829, this distrust was also in Portales' favor; the intellectuals had proved they could talk and fight, but they had yet to demonstrate that they could administer a government.

Portales entered political office as a minister of several cabinet portfolios, including foreign relations, war, and navy, during the regime of a temporary junta created by congress in 1829. He quickly assumed a position of direct dominance of the government, and between 1829 and the inauguration of the new constitution in 1833, he was effectively dictator of Chile. His first major effort was to reduce the military to size by ridding the armed forces of all liberal-tinged officers who had supported either Freire or O'Higgins, as well as any others who might become troublesome to his civilian government. Then the entire public service was similarly purged. Liberal writers and the liberal press were silenced, and a conservative, aristocratic oligarchy moved to the ascendancy in public life. The regime continued to be dominated by Portales, but its policies accorded well with the desires of the church and the conservative landholders of central Chile. The constitution approved in 1833 was highly centralist, restrictive as to suffrage, and paved the way for strong presidential leadership of a conservatively oriented, two-house congress.

General Joaquín Prieto was the first Chilean president elected by the stable conservative regime. For a time Portales remained in the cabinet, but once Prieto was firmly in control of the government, he resigned and returned to live in Valparaiso where, as governor, he continued active in politics and proved a bulwark to the new administration. Prieto, at the insistence of Portales, adopted policies designed to make of Chile a strong commercial power in South America. The port of Valparaiso was greatly improved and its dock facilities enlarged. Favorable tax treatment was also used as a device to lure foreign merchants into the developing Chilean port first and, if possible, to the exclusion of the Peruvian port of Callao. The financial position of the government improved greatly with political stability, and for the first time since independence, Chile began to take on the characteristics of developing nationhood.

The reversion to a strongly centralized regime dominated by a conservative oligarchy was not a change that liberal elements could be expected to accept without question. A period of consolidation was required during the early stages of which the country might easily have been thrown again into bloody inter-party strife. Two factors worked strongly in favor of the conservatives, however. First, Diego Portales had been remarkably thorough in his early efforts to centralize control over the army in the government at Santiago and to destroy the loose relationships that enabled military commanders to develop what amounted to personal armies within the military establishment. Second, the government which Portales and Prieto provided was remarkably honest and reasonably efficient. Liberal sympathizers might decry the suppression of free expression and bemoan the absence of social and economic reform measures, but they could nevertheless take pride in a government whose positive and constructive measures gave tangible evidence of sincere devotion to the nation. Furthermore, opportunity soon arose to utilize the unifying cement of conflict against a common foreign enemy.

From Peru the ousted Freire plotted to overthrow the conservative government in Chile; but by the time his aspirations had reached the military stage the government was too well seated to be lightly brushed aside. Freire was soon defeated and became one of the political exiles on Juan Fernández island, far out in the Pacific. But Freire had received aid from the Peruvians, and had been conveyed to Chilean soil by Peruvian warships. Portales, now returned once more to Prieto's cabinet as minister of war, viewed with alarm the conditions he perceived beyond the desert and mountains of the northern frontier. One of Bolívar's old campaigners, General Santa Cruz, had made himself dictator of Bolivia, and in 1835 he brought about the unification of Peru and Bolivia under his authoritarian rule. Weak as were both Bolivia and Peru, their southern neighbors, Chile and Argentina, viewed this combination as a disruption of the balance of power and the potential threat of a more ambitious unification program. The support given by Santa Cruz to Freire, even though indirect, provided tangible evidence that the Bolivian dictator might view his role in history to be that of reconstituting as a single political entity the new republics that had once formed the viceroyalty of Peru. In any case, Portales counseled war, and late in 1836 Chile issued the declaration.

One can only speculate as to what elements constituted the complete matrix of Portales' interest in the conflict. Perhaps he and Prieto viewed a foreign military adventure as an antidote for internal political ills. Perhaps he was enraged by Peruvian measures aimed at blocking Valparaiso's development into the chief Pacific port of South America. Perhaps the desire to put an end to the potential threat of Santa Cruz was his and Prieto's only consideration. In any case, the military undertaking was viewed in Chile with strongly mixed feelings. No doubt some feared defeat, for the combined forces of Peru and Bolivia were far superior numerically to those of Chile. Others saw no threat in Santa Cruz and felt that their government was embarking upon an unprovoked military aggression. Feeling in opposition to the war ran sufficiently high that when martial law was declared it provoked considerable clamor and open sedition in some quarters. There was mutiny in the army, and Portales fell a victim of the tumult he had created, assassinated by soldiers of his own country.

The shock felt throughout the nation as a consequence of Portales' murder was profound. Portales had never been popular, but his ability and resourcefulness had earned him great respect. His death, quickly attributed by his friends to an enemy plot, served to rally the Chilean public behind the government. Prieto continued the struggle with renewed vigor, and by 1839 his field commander, General Manuel Bulnes, defeated the Bolivian dictator. The victory of the Chilean army promptly brought the downfall of Santa Cruz and collapse of the Peru-Bolivian confederation. Chile had been aided early in the war by an Argentine force sent into Bolivia by Rosas, but the final victory was achieved by Chileans alone after the Argentine forces had departed in defeat. Thus Chile could claim for herself full credit. The southern republic was well on the way to the development of a strong military tradition, and a new pride was engendered in the body politic.

Prieto had been elected to a second term in 1835, and thereby a tradition as to presidential succession was established; the 1833 constitution permitted the re-election of a president for one additional term after his initial five years in office, but further re-election was prohibited. Prieto took advantage of the full electoral opportunity permitted him by law, and for several decades others followed this same pattern without interruption. General Bulnes succeeded Prieto by the outgoing president's choice. Bulnes in turn, after ten years in office, secured the election of Manuel Montt, his minister of education. Every five years, of course, the constitutionally provided election was held; but the restrictions upon the suffrage, the good times that prevailed, and the general popularity of the outgoing president assured his re-election or the election of his chosen successor. Thus Chile was ruled by a conservative self-perpetuating oligarchy. Perhaps it might more appropriately be called an aristocracy, for it ruled generally in the interest of the nation. Political morality was maintained at a high level, finances were soundly managed, and the national and international credit of the country was firmly established.

Chile's conservative leaders were not so conservative that they took no interest in social progress and gradual change, even when change meant a shift in the old political and social order. As early as Prieto's administration there was an active interest in education and a special administrative department of the government was created to foster it. Only higher education was involved, however, for elementary instruction remained a function of the church just as it did elsewhere in Latin America and in a major portion of the United States. Even greater progress in education was made during the administration of Bulnes when Manuel Montt was Minister of Education. The latter set about founding numerous new educational institutions. Included were a reorganized National Institute in the capital, various secondary schools, and even a considerable number of primary schools. Institutes for study of the special trades were also created for the lower classes. As was true everywhere at the time and in many places throughout the world even today, few were able to take advantage of the educational facilities thus created. There were neither schools nor teachers in sufficient number to approach even remotely mass education. The Lancastrian method of instruction, introduced in Chile during the presidency of Freire, had as one of its principal innovations the extension of educational opportunities to larger numbers of students by enlisting the aid of the more advanced to instruct the beginners. It involved primarily, however, a change in the mechanics of teaching that made possible the better utilization of talent where instructors were too few. It did little to change the social philosophy that recognized little value in educating the ignorant masses beyond the rudimentary formalities of Christian doctrine. Manuel Montt and a few other Chilean leaders were far advanced in their social outlook, and they carried Chile ahead of her neighbors in the educational field, but even after the progress of the 1840's and 50's a genuine system of universal public education was something only dimly perceived in the far-distant future. There is little to indicate that the liberal politicians of Chile had any broader view of the educational role of the state than did Montt and his conservative supporters.

Bulnes and Montt, in contrast to Portales and Prieto, had little fear of new ideas or free expression of old ones. Under their administrations the restrictive measures of Portales were relaxed and ignored. Chile became a mecca for the intellectuals of other lands where the political environment did not favor their efforts. Andrés Bello of Venezuela was one of the first outstanding educators who identified himself with Chile and contributed in a major way to the intellectual climate of Santiago. There he for a time served as director of a colegio, edited a government periodical, and exerted his influence on behalf of cultural advancement and development. During the 1840's many more men of letters came to Chile, refugees from tyranny in other lands. They included such outstanding figures as Domingo Faustino Sarmiento and Vicente Fidel López of Argentina, Juan García del Río of Colombia, and Andrés Antonio Gorbea of Spain. Under their influence Chilean intellectual life was stimulated and a generation of native scholars prepared to move to the fore in the years to follow.

Chile made considerable progress economically under the stable rule of the conservative aristocrats. The restrictive alcabala tax was eliminated and tariff laws were revised so as better to accord with Chile's economic needs. Mining became an activity of increasing importance owing to the discovery and exploitation of rich silver veins. Of greatest importance, however, was the tremendous increase in commercial activity. In late colonial times and on into the period of independence Chile had produced considerable agricultural wealth. Large sections of the country were ideally suited to orchard crops and much fruit was grown. The marketing system of the region was extremely poor, however. Not only was adequate transportation lacking in the matter of roads and waterways; marketing was simply not an organized activity. The large estates were virtual feudal manors subsisting upon their own products and the meager manufacturing skills of the workmen who resided there. Only the rich owners purchased in a wider market, and these purchases consisted largely of the luxuries imported from Europe. Prieto, Bulnes, and Montt each gave support to progressive measures aimed at tying the country together economically and opening the interior to commerce. Construction of roads was undertaken, and eventually, during the administration of Montt, the first railroads were built. Paralleling the development of land communication facilities was the development of ocean commerce. Extensive warehousing facilities built by Portales had lured many ships to Valparaiso during the 1830's. Then, in 1840, an American, William Wheelwright, started a steam navigation line between Chile and Peru. This same engineer was instrumental in beginning construction on the first rail lines a decade later. These commercial and facilitative improvements were of great importance, for by mid-century Chile was fast becoming a country of considerable commercial standing. Independence and able statesmanship strengthened a trend already under way in the closing days of the empire for Chile to replace Peru as the chief commercial center of western South America.

The discovery of gold in California in 1848 proved a tremendous boon to Chile. The many ships that now rounded the Horn on their way to the 'treasureland' of California stopped at the Chilean ports. Not only did Chilean products provision these vessels, but great quantities of foodstuffs were shipped to San Francisco to feed the hungry population there. The reopening of isthmian commerce and the construction of a railroad at Panamá eventually caused a sharp reduction in the importance of Chile's new-found market, but the country had enjoyed a great commercial stimulation which left lasting benefits in terms of national development.

Forty years after independence, Chile had achieved much. The country was unified and relatively prosperous. Cultural life was well advanced; no other Spanish American republic could boast of an educational system comparable to that of Chile. The southern republic had engaged in successful foreign warfare and acquitted itself well. Political life, while subject to occasional violence, was remarkably stable. The ruling aristocracy passed the reins of presidential power from one leader to another decade after decade through the process of peaceful election, restricted and controlled though the suffrage was. Chile had taken the first important steps toward national maturity: the achievement of a stable social and political order. The republic prospered, and by mid-century new immigrants flocked in from Europe to share the benefits that it provided and to make their contribution to the developing nation. The newcomers were primarily Germans of a liberal bent who fled their homeland as a consequence of the social and political unrest attending the 1848 uprisings and subsequent repressive measures of the German principalities. The immigrants settled primarily in southern Chile around the city of Valdivia, and soon the countryside blossomed forth with new agricultural products — products grown on middle-class farms rather than on the grand estates of wealthy hacendados. A new and stabilizing element had been introduced in Chilean society.

On a much smaller scale and with a considerably more primitive political system, Paraguay moved forward under the rule of Carlos Antonio López. As had Bulnes and Montt in Chile, so López encouraged educational development in Paraguay. The restrictive isolationism of Francia was replaced by a policy of commercial intercourse with the country's river neighbors. Wagon roads were cut through the jungles and the river ports were opened to all nationalities. Communications were further improved during the 1850's by construction of a telegraph system and the building of a short railroad.

Paraguay's problems were substantially different from those of Chile, or, for that matter, from those of almost any other of the new Latin American republics. The region had stood still or retrogressed in the late colonial period and there was little left of the creole population that had once made of Asunción a major river outpost of Spanish civilization. There were few great estates and few wealthy hacendados; much of Paraguay had been built originally on the basis of communal Indian settlements operated by the church, and these, disrupted and abandoned as a result of the intrigue between Portugal and Spain in the late colonial period, had reverted to wilderness. Paraguay did well to claim and to uphold its independent status, for it possessed few of the elements of nationhood. Nevertheless, López did a remarkable job of building a Paraguayan nationality upon the base prepared by Francia. One of his more important methods of welding the country together was through a widespread primary education system whereby the children, Indian, mestizo, and creole alike, gained the rudiments of an education. Hence came the oft-repeated boast of the Paraguayan of that era: 'I am Paraguayan: I can read.' Lacking in Asunción, however, was the intellectual flowering in the arts and sciences and in literature that became characteristic of Chile. Instead, the country came increasingly to resemble a great hacienda of which the president was the owner and whose interest in development was essentially that of improving one's own property and estate.

López had his problems, however. In 1855 a colony of French founded a settlement called Nuevo Burdeos at the edge of the Chaco region. López found himself in difficulties with France, which country protested the treatment received by the colonists. With Brazil López had a boundary dispute; with the United States there was an incident involving an attack upon an American naval vessel engaged in a river survey. With Argentina there was continuous difficulty, for the dictator Rosas refused to recognize Paraguay as an independent nation. In anticipation of an eventual attempt to conquer the region by either Brazil or Argentina, López set about to build and equip a sizable army and a small navy to sail on the river system. López developed a rather formidable little fighting force, and true to the patrimonial system of which he was the head, he placed his son, Francisco, in charge of it and made him minister of war. Thus Francisco was groomed to succeed his father and given the means of guaranteeing his domination of the country in the event of his father's death. In 1862, Carlos Antonio López died, and the congress assembled to elect Francisco for a ten-year term. Francisco was soon to destroy all that his father had created and to bring his race and his country very near to extinction. The patrimonial system had made possible an early stability in Paraguay, but it provided no broad basis for democratic development. There had been no institutionalization of law, order, and progress such as the Chilean conservatives had achieved.

Just north of Paraguay, but far across the continent from Chile, another recently liberated nation had advanced at least as spectacularly as had Chile. Externally the conditions under which that progress was made were quite different. Brazil was a monarchy, the only monarchy in the Western Hemisphere. In contrast to the narrow and extended coastal strip that formed the Chilean homeland, Brazil was a vast and diverse continental region far larger than the United States in 1830 and still larger than the great North American nation after the latter had filled out its continental frontiers at mid-century. Brazil was a land of marked regional variation, not only in the sense that geographic extent and difference in latitude and elevation created regional peculiarities, but also in the sense that the many population centers, remote from each other and poorly linked by non-existent or inadequate communication facilities, had each developed its own peculiar interests and outlook. Chile, on the other hand, while extended over many degrees of latitude, was characterized by a concentration of population within the confines of a relatively limited area of the central valley that paralleled the coast. Major centers were linked by ready access to ocean communication. Both countries, however, had by mid-century achieved remarkable political and social stability and were to be regarded as centers on the South American continent of cultural and intellectual advancement. No other Latin American countries could claim such achievement.

Brazil owed much to its erratic monarch, Pedro I. In spite of his many weaknesses, his devotion to the pursuit of the opposite sex to the neglect of duties of state and the good name of the monarchy, his autocratic refusal to permit more than a figment of popular participation in government; in spite of these drawbacks and to some extent because of them Dom Pedro I served as a rallying point for Brazilian patriotism. He it was who declared the independence of the Portuguese American state and who maintained the pomp and elegance of a European court amid the tropical splendor of Rio de Janeiro. He it was who held the Brazilian state together in the hour of its independence and who provided a unified and effective government in the years that followed. Then too, in spite of the raised eyebrows, the whispered rumors and the open criticism that Pedro's amorous antics caused, there can be little doubt that behind the façade of piety existed a frank admiration for the monarch's virility and bedroom accomplishments.

Dom Pedro's downfall was largely attributable to those whom he assumed to be his friends, the Portuguese gentry with whom he surrounded himself. If the Brazilians were to have a monarchy and pay the price of supporting it, they should at least enjoy the emoluments of office and the tokens of prestige that monarchy afforded. Suspicion grew as the years went by that the real interest of Pedro's friends, if not of the emperor himself, lay in the Portuguese homeland and the possibility of reconstituting a single realm. Likewise, the refusal of Dom Pedro to permit a broader participation in the affairs of state fortified republican sentiment, strengthened the adherents of federalism, and aroused a general animosity against the insolent favorites of the imperial court. The final cabinet crisis and desertion of the army that led to Dom Pedro's abdication was basically a reassertion of Brazilian nationalism and independence far more than a rejection of the emperor himself or of the institution that he represented.

Dom Pedro's position in the early days of April, 1831, just prior to his abdication, was weak. Nevertheless, he might have aroused sufficient support to put up a defense and attempt to retain his throne. The fact that he chose not to do so is to his credit, for his eventual defeat would have been only a matter of time and the institution of monarchy certainly would have gone down with him. As it was, by choosing self-denial and exile, the emperor was able to preserve the monarchy and to pass on to his young son the Amazon throne, giving to Brazil in the act of his abdication the most able executive leader in its history.

Dom Pedro II was less than six years of age when he became emperor, and it was necessary to name a regent. At first a committee was formed, but after four years of executive confusion the committee gave way to a single regent, a priest named Diogo Antônio Feijó. Padre Feijó was a powerful figure who had dominated the government as minister of justice since the abdication, but as regent he was less successful. He resigned after two years in office and was replaced by Pedro de Araújo Lima, a leader of the Conservative party.

The period of the regency was a period of great stress and strain for the young monarchy. It was virtually an interregnum, for no single firm hand was at the helm of state. The tides of republicanism and caudillismo surged about the infant prince and only by a thread was the empire held together. Even the monarchists were divided, for a strong group favored the recall of Pedro I to act as regent for his son. The possibility of the exiled emperor's return was never very real, and there is little to indicate that Pedro himself ever seriously considered such action. All his failing energies were devoted to securing for his daughter, Maria da Glória, her title to the Portuguese throne, a title usurped by Pedro's brother, against whom the exiled monarch plotted in Paris and whom he eventually ejected. Shortly after his successful campaign in Portugal, Pedro died, thereby removing one of the divisive factors in Brazilian politics. His American adherents joined their forces to those of the *moderados* who were supporting the constitutional monarchy and the regency. The new Conservative party that emerged from this union greatly strengthened the hands of those who were working to retain centralized government under an imperial court at Rio de Janeiro.

More of a threat to the monarchy than the out-and-out republican faction were the various proponents of federalism. The federalist principle found expression in two ways. Both the *exaltados*, a branch of the Liberal party, and the republican elements clamored for federalism in the press, and the former group used every opportunity to advocate it in congress. More serious were the provincial manifestations that expressed themselves in open rebellion. Revolt sputtered feebly in Pará and died out; but in Rio Grande do Sul it burst into open flame and consumed the resources of the province and the central government for over a decade. Intermittent strife broke out in Bahia and Minas Gerais. In the face of such opposition, the regency, conservative and centralist in political alignment, moved cautiously but effectively. In the congressional maneuvers at the capital it gave way. In 1834 the now famous *Acto Adicional* was adopted, granting representative legislative bodies to the provinces in place of the former consultative councils. The new assemblies were given considerable local authority, including the right to levy taxes and disburse funds. Provincial presidents continued to be appointees of the crown, however. The Additional Act, as an amendment to the Constitution of 1824, proved to be a sufficient concession in the direction of provincial autonomy to make possible a clearing of the air, and the issue of federalism gradually faded as a matter of immediate political significance.

The constitutional change might have proved quite ineffective in achieving stability had not the regency taken firm military action in the provinces at the same time that concessions were being granted in the capital. The efforts to put down forcibly the rebellion in Rio Grande do Sul were not immediately successful, and the struggle dragged on until five years after the new emperor had ascended the throne and taken up the reins of state. Finally, military pressure and increasing fear of Rosas in Argentina caused the *farrapos* (residents of the southern province) to consider the advisability of a reconciliation. Elsewhere, however, the regency was more immediately successful in meeting the seemingly never-ending crises of local insurrection. One by one rebellious movements in the provinces were crushed, and the supporters of federalism were forced to take what satisfaction they could in the limited local self-government provided them in the Additional Act.

Neither the concessions to local government nor the military successes served to quell the general feeling of discontent with the regency. The regency was an expedient made necessary by the infancy of the monarch, but it suffered the additional weakness that it was exercised not by a member of the royal family, but by a politician whose claim to the role rested upon personal prestige and the continued support of a conservative coalition. A steadier hand was needed, a hand with less personal interest in what it touched. Consequently, early accession of the young monarch was postulated by members of the opposition, led by Antônio Carlos de Andrada, a leading figure in the house of deputies. At first the regency opposed the move, fearing loss of control by the Conservative party. In the end, no other move seemed possible and the national assembly declared young Pedro of age and proclaimed him emperor of Brazil. Late in July of 1840, while still but fourteen years of age, Dom Pedro II took the oath of office and swore to uphold the constitution. Once again Brazil had a reigning monarch.

Had the new Brazilian emperor proved as autocratic as his father or as prone to play favorites, his accession to the throne would have provided little relief from the country's political difficulties. But Dom Pedro II was an entirely different kind of man. Young as he was, he was remarkably mature both physically and intellectually. That he was able to take the reins of government firmly in his hands and deal vigorously with the experienced politicians who surrounded him and who continued to struggle for national leadership was a great tribute to his common sense, his astuteness, and above all to the confidence he enjoyed in the eyes of the people. The new monarch did not allow affairs to continue drifting as they had in the last years of the regency. He set about to establish order in the provinces by military action and by political manipulation, and within five years even the dissident elements in Rio Grande do

Sul had submitted to firm imperial rule. He replaced many provincial presidents with strong men of his own choice who were pledged to uphold law and order, yet he was generous in granting amnesty to those who had taken up arms against the regency.

Under Dom Pedro Brazil enjoyed many of the benefits of democracy, yet there was little doubt as to who was the real ruler. Life and property were reasonably secure, and personal liberty was certainly as great or greater than in any other country of Latin America. Popular participation in government was hardly to be expected on any significant scale, however. This was true not so much because the country was a monarchy, nor even because of any disposition on the part of the nation's leaders to prevent popular participation. Rather, the machinery of popular government was undeveloped. In a vast country of mixed races, dispersed population, and great ignorance and illiteracy, government remained the province of the aristocratic few. In the absence of a tradition of local self-government, there was little soil in which popular political forces could take root. Brazil experienced no counterpart of the democratizing movements that swept political control from the hands of the tideland aristocrats in the United States during the 1830's. Under a monarchy, of course, the stakes of political victory were not so high; and the centralized government of Brazil necessarily limited the advantages of political success at the provincial level.

Dom Pedro was shrewd enough to form no permanent alliances with either of the principal political factions. The liberals rode to power with the monarch's accession to the throne, but the conservatives were soon again in control of the national assembly — a control, however, to which they were unable to lay permanent claim. The emperor played one faction against another, one leader against opposing leaders; and while seeming to hold himself aloof he succeeded in keeping the balance of power firmly in his own hands. He did not provide great leadership in bringing about social or economic change, but he provided a stable political environment that facilitated sound national development on many fronts. Brazil was still a pioneer country, a rough country in which the pomp and display of an imperial court contrasted almost obscenely with the primitive crudity of life in the back country where the raucous influence of the gold-rush days was still to be felt. The anomaly of a stable monarchy in a frontier wilderness guided serenely along its course by a firm, kindly, unpretentious scion of a European royal family was not lost upon contemporaries. The crowned heads of Europe looked on and wondered.

The imperial court at Rio de Janeiro under the second emperor presented a marked contrast to the gaudy display of earlier days. Three years after ascending the throne Dom Pedro took as his wife an Italian princess, daughter of King Francis I of the Two Sicilies. Married by proxy, the young woman soon made the long journey to the royal husband she had never seen. She was warmly received by her new subjects as well as by the emperor, who took his marriage vows far more seriously than had his father. Throughout his long reign, Dom Pedro's domestic life was exemplary and the court gossips found little about which to waggle their tongues. The simple modesty that characterized family life at Guanabara Palace was also typical of state affairs. Dom Pedro had little interest in regal display, seldom appeared in uniform, and made little or no effort to popularize himself with the tools of glamorous exhibitionism so skillfully wielded by his parent. So lacking in color was he that in later years of his reign he was often referred to as the 'gray' emperor. What the emperor lacked in flashiness and popular appeal he made up in other ways. He was a native Brazilian with no ties to the fawning Portuguese nobility who in former years had sapped the substance of the royal treasury. The Brazilians were his people and were treated as such, and none had cause to question the honesty and sincerity of the emperor's concern for their welfare.

Perhaps during the first half of the nineteenth century Brazil was still too much of a frontier country to devote much attention to literature and the arts. Perhaps the transition from colonial status to national independence was too easily accomplished to evoke the talents of men who might have taken up the brush or pen in portrayal of the longings, sufferings, and aspirations of the people. The fact remains that little literary or artistic effort was forthcoming in the early days of independence or in the years that followed. Dom Pedro II was noted for his intellectual accomplishments and his interest in the sciences and arts. As a patron of intellectual and artistic pursuits he did much to raise the stature of Brazilian social life in the capital. But his efforts bore fruit in later years, and at mid-century the country could not claim, as could Chile, important strides in literature and education. As a home of exiles from all over the continent, Chile profited by the influx of talented men. Brazil attracted few such people. The country was absorbed in the physical aspects of living, the conquest of the wilderness, the mixture of races, the advent of new settlers from Europe.

In common with Chile, however, as well as with the United States, Brazil enjoyed during the early years of independence the concern and devotion of a public spirited aristocracy. These leaders, conservative in outlook, were at the same time progressive in their approach to national development and realized that only through a government characterized by stable and orderly processes could the welfare of the nation be secured.

XXVII

Tyranny and Confusion: The Dictatorship of Juan Manuel de Rosas

> . . . for this is not the first time in history when prodigality in the distribution of honors has stimulated public men until they reached the level of tyrants.
>
> JUAN MANUEL DE ROSAS

THE first twenty years of independence were disastrous years for the Plata region. All the perils that seemingly could have attended the establishment of a new and independent nation proved mighty rocks upon which the Argentine ship of state pounded and crashed, apparently bent upon utter disintegration. One by one outlying provinces of the former viceroyalty slipped away to form independent governments of their own, aided in their escape by the constant warfare that raged across the pampas, up and down the great river valleys, and across the turbulent waters of the great estuary. Brazil was an avowed enemy; Britain was unfriendly and had aided in securing the independence of Uruguay; but most devastating of all was the turmoil that prevailed in the heart of the homeland. The struggle that divided the centralists and federalists seemed endless and hopeless. Neither side could gain a permanent advantage, and no leader emerged strong enough to unite the warring factions and turn the effort of the populace into constructive channels. The downfall of the centralist regime under President Bernardino Rivadavia spelled the end of porteño leadership. Federalists disliked Rivadavia and his policies at best, but his agreement with Brazil granting independence to the Banda Oriental and the loss of the Charcas region to the Bolivarian forces of Generals Sucre and Santa Cruz provided the opportunity to discredit him completely.

The situation in the Plata region in the late 1820's and early 1830's was far more confused than is generally pictured. Only in recognition of this fact can otherwise apparent contradictions in motivations and events be explained. In a country with no developed sense of nationality and over-all unity, how could the granting of independence to a disputed frontier province prove so unpopular? Was not the federalist objective a high degree of autonomy or near independence for all provinces? Why would an ardent supporter of the federalist cause subject the country to the most tyrannical of centralist rule once he held the reins of power? Mere opportunism?

In reality there were four Argentinas. The first, and that which dominated the colonial viceroyalty and sparked the independence movement, was the port area of Buenos Aires. Its commercial and political interests favored continuation of the pre-eminent role enjoyed by the city prior to independence. As the center of political and intellectual leadership, Buenos Aires succeeded in directing the course of the new state after expulsion of the viceroy in 1810. For a time the intellectuals, the distinguished gentlemen of the assembly halls, the revolutionary leaders, had their day, but the chaos that was Argentina in the 1820's testified to their failure. No other Latin American country embarked upon the road to independent nationhood with such an array of distinguished leadership, yet lack of success in bringing about national unification and domestic tranquillity indicates only too clearly that the Argentine nation was as yet a dream founded upon a colonial administrative jurisdiction that had not stood the tests of time, community of interest, and mutual dependence. The sense of nationality lay buried deep beneath the soil of the pampas, and only a strong metamorphism could bring it to the surface. The porteño leaders were unable to provide the experience of transformation, for they could not see far beyond the interest of the capital.

The second Argentina lay far to the west in the sunny valleys along the foothills of the Andes mountains. This region, a principal population center in the early colonial period, had ceased to count for much politically or commercially during the previous century, but it still had its military leaders, or caudillos, who by giving support to one or another of the other factions were in position to influence the outcome of interregional struggles. The third Argentina was the river country north and west of Buenos Aires and including particularly the province of Santa Fé. This region was an increasingly important stronghold for the adherents of provincial autonomy and opposition to the domination of Buenos Aires. Finally, there was the fourth region, the province of Buenos Aires south from the port city. This area was gradually being wrested from the inhospitable Indians by the owners of large cattle estates, who with their gaucho followers conducted a more or less continuous campaign to push the frontier ever southward. These were the four Argentinas, each of which had its own peculiar interests and policies which it sought to protect or further. The degree to which unity among the four regions was lacking is attested to by the fact that foreign relations and commercial policy were largely in the hands of Buenos Aires, whereas internal taxation, education, and other matters lay within the control of each province, and military forces were largely the personal armies of the various provincial caudillos. General Sucre aptly wrote in 1825, in a letter to Bolívar, that no one could tell 'which people, which order of government was in control in Buenos Aires.'

The struggle between federalists and centralists was by no means a clear-cut conflict between the porteños and the provinces. On the contrary, there were ardent federalists in the erstwhile viceregal capital who saw in centralism a threat to the favored position of Buenos Aires. Centralism could mean, as Rivadavia had wanted it to mean, a single national budget and a single national tax structure that would have forced the capital city to share its resources and particularly its customs receipts with the other sections of the national territory. Though certainly a minority, there were men in the provinces who would have given up a measure of local autonomy for the benefits of participation in the economic assets of the capital. The strategic position of the port city was crucial, for it enjoyed a near monopoly in foreign trade and provided the principal market for provincial products. The economies of the hinterland regions could be benefited or strangled depending upon the trade policies of the great river port. Consequently, the federalist-centralist issue was obscured by the more basic question of who was to control Buenos Aires.

Following the resignation of Rivadavia in the summer of 1827, there was little immediate effort to hold the country together. The question of ultimate political organization was an open issue, and for the time being the various provinces went their own separate ways. Principal attention was focused upon Buenos Aires, province and port city. There in 1829 a strong figure appeared upon the scene — the figure of a crude but rugged man of the plains, an avowed federalist and by political orientation a conservative. Juan Manuel de Rosas was not a gaucho. He came from the city of Buenos Aires and from a fairly well-to-do family. When as a boy he went to live on a cattle ranch in the far south of Buenos Aires province, he went as the son of the owner and not as a wandering cowboy of the plains. Nevertheless, Rosas' early development was that of a frontiersman accustomed to the rugged life of a cattle raiser, and while still a young man he had achieved the distinction of being recognized as a prominent cattle baron and the master of grand estates. His frequent battles with the plains Indians, conducted at the head of his gaucho employees and fellow ranchers, brought him prestige and a reputation as a military leader.

Wealth and military prestige soon made Rosas a man to reckon with in provincial politics, and, coupled with his willingness to enter into the power struggles of the political leaders at the capital, gave him an importance in national affairs that could not lightly be dismissed. Rosas was a caudillo, a leader on horseback, a potential restorer of law and order in a conflict-weary and disturbed country.

Rosas first emerged upon the political scene to participate in the struggles that took place upon the return of the unhappy troops which had been engaged in the Uruguayan war ending in

1828. He had previously supported a former provincial governor in crushing a minor uprising, but after the murder of Governor Dorrego by Lavalle, a disgruntled unitarian officer back from the wars, Rosas took a leading part in the general movement that unseated the usurper and drove him from the country. The legislature thereupon elected Rosas governor of the province for a three-year term. As governor the rising caudillo found himself plunged into a bitter civil war that raged for nearly two years between unitarians and federalists. It was a war that he knew how to win, and eventually Rosas restored peace in the province. He was also able, by agreements with the leaders in other provinces, to establish a pattern of inter-provincial relationships that ignored the question of whether or not there should be a national government. Before the world Buenos Aires province spoke for the Argentine confederation, but its authority to do so rested upon what were essentially personal agreements between Rosas and the caudillos of other provinces, such as Estanislao López in Santa Fé. Efforts of dissident federalists to secure the convocation of a confederation congress were skillfully blocked.

On governing the province for the first time, Rosas firmly altered the policies of the liberal *unitarios* whom he had succeeded, but his acts were generally characterized by moderation and gradualness. He abolished free trade and imposed tariffs on imported flour and grains, thereby favoring the wheat growers in his own province and Santa Fé. At the same time he opposed the idea of Argentina's need for new settlers and liquidated the colonization program of Rivadavia, who had established a special commission to attract northern European settlers to come to the country and take up farming. Rosas was himself the owner of a large estate, and his inclination was to build an economy based upon great landed properties belonging to the wealthy families that were his friends. Rosas' interests were still largely personal, however. His chief concern was for the maintenance of law and order in his own province and for the expulsion from public office of those whose policies of liberal reform and political unity betokened interference with the feudal independence of his own peculiar kind of society. With the unitarios defeated and driven into exile, Rosas resigned the governorship and returned home. Hostile Indians were stealing his cattle and overrunning his estates, and the owner's attention was required. For over two years Rosas, aided by his supporters and followers, waged a relentless campaign of extermination against the Indians of southern Buenos Aires province. As a consequence the frontier was pushed far to the south and vast tracts of Indian land were opened for new cattle estates.

Beginning in 1834, however, a new effort was made to bring Rosas back into politics. The provincial government was weak, and such governors as General Balcarce and General Viamonte were unable to maintain order or to hold the respect of the provincial legislature. In June of 1834 the legislature named Rosas governor again, but the caudillo was ill-disposed to accept. In fact, he stood firmly by his resolve through four successive offers. Others also refused, and finally the president of the legislature, Manuel Vicente Maza, took the position of chief executive on a provisional basis. In the meantime, affairs throughout the country went from bad to worse. The caudillo leaders of the other provinces warred among themselves, Tucumán and Salta in particular being in open conflict as a result of the rivalry of their governors. In March of 1835, Maza gave up all effort to govern in Buenos Aires, and for the fifth time since his retirement from office, Rosas was again offered the governorship, this time as absolute dictator in possession of all public authority and with no limit upon the term of office. Rosas agreed to accept, but on condition that a plebiscite be held to obtain approval by the people of the extraordinary delegation of authority that the legislature offered. Promptly the vote was taken in the city of Buenos Aires, and Rosas was confirmed in his position of absolute dictator of the province.

Quickly all aspects of Argentine political life changed. Rosas was dictator of but one province; but he soon made himself master of the entire confederation. By force, by intrigue, by alliance and compact, supported by a strong popular following among the middle and lower classes, Rosas was able to make his will prevail and his policies dominant. No one challenged his leadership.

Many have sought an explanation of the factors that motivated Rosas in his exercise of power and authority. A man of wealth and power at the outset of his political career, cajoled into the acceptance of public office, it was hardly to be expected that he would exercise the functions of governor and dictator in so arbitrary and ruthless a manner as history records that he did. Rosas was no intellectual and he had only a minimum of education. Apparently he distrusted those whose backgrounds were more genteel than his own. Yet he was one of those rare individuals who inspire in their followers an extreme loyalty to their persons but who at the same time drive from them and fear all those capable of exercising independent thought and judgment. Rosas rapidly became a tyrant. Political opponents were crushed and driven from the land, as were many others not engaged in politics but who found the atmosphere stifling and the risk to life and property too great to endure. Chile, Uruguay, and even Bolivia became refuges for an increasing number of Argentine citizens.

Rosas entered upon political life as a federalist, and a federalist he remained in name. Nevertheless, his rule provided a degree of centralism that the most ardent unitarian would have balked at imposing. Rosas' centralism was one of terror and fear. The efforts at repression and confiscation were at first directed at the unitarians, and the battle-cry of his regime, 'Death to the unitarians,' was adhered to closely. Death was meted out to thousands of Rosas' political opponents. But soon no one stopped to question whether the proposed victims of Rosas' tyranny were indeed unitarians; it was enough that they had incurred the wrath of the dictator or of his fanatical followers. Rosas' adherents were organized into political clubs in the various cities, and the dictator created a secret police known as the *mazorca*.* Rosas was a monolithic figure and he built for himself a monolithic state.

To those who have witnessed the political developments of the twentieth century, the Rosas regime can hardly appear strange, but it certainly belonged to the wrong epoch and the wrong

---

* An ear of corn, used as a symbol of earthy unity. Rosas' enemies were prone to use the term, *más horca*, meaning 'more gallows.'

continent. Never before in the Western Hemisphere and scarcely since has there existed such a political system with all the trappings of totalitarianism. In the mazorca existed the secret organization of the party elite bound together by a cult of adherence to Rosas. Terrorism and denunciation produced death and exile for those who fell under official disfavor or who were unfortunate enough to possess property coveted by one of the cultists. Those who wished to protect themselves swore allegiance to the regime, displayed the red party colors, and featured the picture of the political leader prominently in their homes and places of business.

As might have been expected after the years of political chaos, the church supported Rosas from the outset. Not only did he give promise of restoring order and suppressing the anti-clerical measures taken by Rivadavia, but he was known to favor the closest possible relationship between church and state. Once in power, Rosas did embrace the church as a political ally; he nearly suffocated it. He restored many of the privileges that the church had lost during the long period of confusion following the revolution when Argentine political leaders had been wont to bargain with the papacy for diplomatic recognition of the new republic. He permitted the re-establishment of various religious orders that had earlier been excluded, including that of the Society of Jesus. He did not for a moment, however, relinquish his policy of regalism by which he, as head of the state, exercised authority over the church as well as over the civil government. During the period of his rule he literally purged the ranks of the religious in the interests of his government. Mariano Medrano, bishop of Buenos Aires, became the dictator's willing tool, and the clergy were forced to uphold the 'federation' and denounce the unitarians in the pulpit and in the confessional. Only the Jesuits showed an inclination to resist and adhere to the ultramontane view of religious organization. For failing to conform they were promptly excluded again from the country. Soon the church altars displayed Rosas' red colors, and his likeness appeared beside those of Christ and the Virgin Mary in the sanctuaries.

Rosas ruled Argentina from 1835 until 1852. His only real program was law and order for those who supported him and death and confiscation for those who dared raise a hand in opposition. His was a civil regime, for the military had no voice. The symbolism which he deftly utilized appealed to the masses and, supported by the church, Rosas enjoyed a considerable popularity among the ignorant of the lower classes. Foreign residents, pleased with the outward appearance of law and order, generally regarded his regime with benign toleration. Nevertheless, thousands of Argentines did not adhere to Rosas' government. Many sought refuge in Montevideo, from which neighboring river city they plotted Rosas' overthrow and attempted to rouse support for their cause in the Banda Oriental. The younger generation of Argentine liberals, however, attempted to work within the country through secret societies such as the Association of May, dedicated to fulfilling the political objectives of the May Revolution of 1810 for a free society and a liberal democratic government. One by one, however, the youthful leaders discovered that life in the Argentine capital was unhealthful for them, and their literary and intellectual abilities came to flower in Santiago and Montevideo where they joined earlier refugees from Rosas' despotism.

Outstanding figures in exile were such men as Bartolomé Mitre, Domingo Sarmiento, Juan Alberdi, and Esteban Echeverría. These men, each of whom contributed in a major way to the development of political liberalism in Argentina, were, with the exception of Echeverría who died prematurely, to play an important role in the creation of an Argentine nation once the era of confusion and disunity under Rosas had come to an end. They had little to do, however, with bringing the federalist dictator's regime to a close. Action and strong allies were required to accomplish this feat. For the most part, the eligible leadership in the foreign capitals was disinclined to adopt tactics of violence, and the exiles were fearful lest an invitation to a foreign power to help in the overthrow of Rosas might be construed as an invitation to remain active in Argentine affairs long after Rosas was gone. Consequently, it was Rosas' own policies and actions that eventually brought about his downfall. His aggressive attitude toward neighboring Uruguay and Paraguay aroused not only the antagonism of those countries, but that of Brazil as well; and it created a situation in which it eventually proved possible for rival caudillos to draw support from these neighbors against the dictatorial regime in Buenos Aires.

Rosas' accomplishments were meager indeed. Twentieth-century dictatorships of the totalitarian variety have characteristically distinguished themselves by undertaking programs of physical improvement and by inauguration of measures designed to improve the economic lot of the lower classes, albeit at the expense of some scapegoat group. Upon such programs has rested the popularity of these regimes. Rosas provided a circus, but little bread. The country deteriorated during his rule in almost every way. Physical development languished and higher education virtually ceased as a number of institutions were closed and others subjected to a rigorous censorship. Economic life stagnated as investment capital turned elsewhere and potential immigrants sought more pleasant lands. Repeated blockades of the river capital by French and British warships in an effort to counteract Rosas' intervention in Uruguay did nothing to improve the trade situation; and even though the over-all trend of commercial activity was upward during the Rosas era, there were years in which it came to an almost complete standstill. In the end, Rosas' popularity faded and even his favored henchmen joined in plotting his destruction.

Rosas was aggressive in his foreign policy, but remarkably ineffective. In the first period of his governorship he attempted to make good the Argentine claim to the Malvinas, or Falkland islands, in the Atlantic. A small settlement was established there and an effort made to prevent sealers and fishermen from the United States from using the islands as a base. The result was a retaliatory attack upon the settlement by an American naval vessel. The Argentines withdrew and shortly the British arrived to make good a claim arising from an earlier coerced arrangement with Spain. The British stayed in spite of Rosas' protests, and the

United States rejected the dictator's claim for indemnity for damage done the Argentine settlers on the ground of the disputed possession of the islands.

In 1837, Rosas joined with Chile in declaring war on the Peru-Bolivian confederation of General Santa Cruz, but his efforts were largely verbal owing to preoccupation with Uruguay and the absence of any real interest among the Argentine provinces in an Andean war. It was in the Banda Oriental that Rosas concentrated his military efforts, but even there he was not notably successful. Rosas claimed to be a federalist, and though his regime bore little resemblance to a federal system of government, the pretense served his purposes. Within the 'federation' were provinces that resisted his control. Among these Rosas numbered Corrientes, Paraguay, and the Banda Oriental, or Uruguay. Subjugation was in order and could be undertaken as a domestic rather than a foreign war. The possibility of reuniting the Banda Oriental to the former Spanish viceroyalty was a far more attractive undertaking, however, than the conquest of Corrientes or the isolated patriarchy of Doctor Francia; likewise, the possibilities seemed better, for Uruguay was torn with internal strife that Rosas could employ to advantage. Consequently, the struggling buffer state across the river was marked for special attention.

Uruguayan independence had been nurtured in Buenos Aires during the years that the Banda Oriental formed the Cisplatine Province of Brazil. When Uruguay's famous 'Thirty-three Immortals' landed on the eastern soil in April of 1825 to raise the standard of revolution and liberty, unification with the Argentine provinces was clearly in their minds. In an assembly held in the little town of Florida, the revolutionists declared the eastern province incorporated into the United Provinces of the Río de la Plata, as Argentina was then known. The war that followed this invasion and declaration witnessed strong Argentine participation against Brazil, and the general success of the Spanish-speaking allies seemed to assure that incorporation would take place. Great Britain, ever concerned with the future of commercial activity in the Plata region, viewed with misgiving the possibility of an Argentine victory that would place that country firmly astride the mouth of the great river in position to shut off all river trade not beneficial to Buenos Aires. At the peace conference in 1828, the British representative, acting in the role of intermediary, insisted that the disputed territory be set up as an independent nation with no direct political attachment to either of its powerful neighbors. This arrangement was provided in the terms of settlement, and to assure that all parties were in agreement, both Brazil and Argentina were induced to approve the constitution of the new state. Thus did Britain seek to prevent further struggle over the region and, incidentally, of course, establish for herself a quasi-protectorate on the great Plata estuary.

By the time Rosas had assumed power in Buenos Aires, the Uruguayan leaders, Juan Antonio Lavalleja and Fructuoso Rivera, had proved their basic similarity to the rest of mankind by engaging in armed disagreement as to who should rule the new republic. By 1836, a third contender, Manuel Oribe, placed in the presidency as a compromise choice, had shown sufficient attachment to the Lavalleja faction to spur Rivera to organized revolt. A permanent pattern of factional disagreement was emerging. Into this struggle stepped Rosas.

Rosas threw his support behind the *blanco* * faction of Oribe. The blanco leader, following in the steps of Lavalleja, was at least friendly to Argentine overtures of union, particularly when he found himself in need of Rosas' support against the *colorado* † forces of Rivera. Unfortunately for Oribe, Rosas' assistance proved of negative value. The revolt had begun in 1836, and in 1837 Rosas had serious difficulty with the French over his highhanded treatment of certain French nationals and their property. As a consequence of the dispute, a French fleet was sent to blockade Buenos Aires. Rosas' new European enemies were delighted to have the opportunity to deal him a further blow by aiding the rebellious colorado forces of Rivera in Uruguay, and they made available more modern arms and ammunition. By October of

* So known for their party color, white.
† Likewise so called for the party color, red.

1838 Oribe was obliged to resign and flee the country, taking up residence with his mentor in Buenos Aires. Rivera became president of Uruguay, promptly declared war on the Argentine dictator, and with the assistance of French troops drove all of Rosas' army back across the river.

Rosas' downfall was eventually sealed in the Banda Oriental. The long struggle over this region, begun in the early days of colonial rule in the Plata basin, seemed destined to continue unabated far into the republican era. The British effort to erect a buffer state resulted only in the creation of a power vacuum into which the competing forces of Argentina, Brazil, and even Paraguay were drawn. Rosas, as many a colonial governor before him, threw countless human and material resources into the battle, and in doing so he lost his hold on the parent country. Constant warfare raged from 1839 until 1852, and the latter part of the period is known in Uruguayan history as that of the Great War. It was characterized by a nine-year siege of Montevideo by the combined forces of Rosas and the Uruguayan blancos supporting Oribe. Ranged against the blancos and their Argentine allies were the Uruguayan colorados and the Argentine province of Corrientes, joined later by forces from Santa Fé and Entre Ríos as the grip of the dictator in Buenos Aires began to slip. Numerous battles were fought, and for a time it looked as though Rosas might succeed in subduing his recalcitrant 'province,' but in the end the tide surged strongly against him.

Rosas was particularly inept in dealing with the two European powers that showed most interest in the Plata region, England and France. The motives of both powers were certainly open to question, and there can be little doubt that they were willing to take what advantage they could of disturbed local conditions for the benefit of themselves and their nationals; but by his arbitrary actions and by over-extending himself in relation to his resources, Rosas placed himself at their mercy. During the siege of Montevideo, the two European nations jointly blockaded the mouth of the Plata river with their fleets, supplied the beleaguered citizens of the Uruguayan capital, and forced their way up the Paraguay and Uruguay rivers to open the hinterland to their commerce. Such action destroyed much of the effectiveness of Rosas' military measures, encouraged the river provinces to slip out from under Rosas' domination, and made virtually impossible a complete victory over the Uruguayan colorados.

The Uruguayan war carried on by Rosas was much more than a simple struggle undertaken to subdue a wayward 'province.' It was a conflict affecting the entire Argentine federation in a direct military way. Rosas' ability to dominate provinces other than Buenos Aires was subject to continuous challenge. Montevideo was a hotbed of intrigue on the part of Argentine centralists in exile from the day that Rosas established his dictatorship. Various Uruguayan politicians and military leaders participated openly in plots against the dictator, and soon they were in league with federalist recalcitrants from the back country provinces along the foothills of the Andes. During the long conflict governors of Corrientes, Tucumán, Salta, Catamarca, La Rioja, and Jujuy, all at one time or another joined in the efforts to overthrow the government in Buenos Aires. General Juan Lavalle was a principal leader in the 'liberation' forces, and organizing an army with the aid of President Rivera in Montevideo, his movements ranged throughout the northern provinces and westward as far as Córdoba. There, in November of 1840, he suffered a major defeat at the hands of General Oribe, the ousted blanco president of Uruguay and principal commander in Rosas' army. Clearly, the conflict was all mixed up. Leaders on both sides of the river made common cause with allies on the opposite side, and throughout the war Argentines and Uruguayans alike fought for each other's causes and in each other's armies with little or no distinction. It was one big civil war among a people whose provinces were too disunited to form a nation but sufficiently well united to make common cause in an effort to settle the problems and determine the fate of all. Uruguay was scarcely yet a nation, nor did its people really so regard it. It was, during the wars of the Rosas era, for all practical purposes just another province neither more nor less closely linked to the Argentine confederation than Corrientes,

Santa Fé, or Córdoba. Time and the experience of working together had not yet created in the minds of the people the concept of separate nationality.

The long struggle was finally brought to an end by a combination of circumstances that produced the resignation of Rosas and his exile to England. The most important blow was dealt the dictator by Justo José de Urquiza, long-time follower of Rosas and governor of Entre Ríos province. Urquiza, a strong man politically and a provincial caudillo in his own right, turned against his dictatorial superior in Buenos Aires and allied himself with the Uruguayan colorados. His official pronouncement was made on May 1, 1851, after a long period of ever-mounting disagreement between the Entre Ríos governor and Rosas over control of commerce by the porteños. The proclamation itself set forth the idea that the high hopes for peace and order with which the Argentine people had greeted the advent of Rosas had been dashed to the ground by the evil actions and sinister intentions of the dictator. A call was issued for 'liberty, organization, and war against despotism.' Quickly Urquiza formed his alliances for the inevitable struggle. Corrientes was already with him, as were the colorados of Uruguay; but now Brazil too was brought into the compact in exchange for minor boundary concessions along her frontier with Uruguay. This time the forces against Rosas were determined to succeed, even though it meant incurring the risk of further Brazilian intervention in the Banda Oriental.

Urquiza soon raised a large army with units from each of the compact members, including Brazil. First he moved to relieve the siege of Montevideo, a feat accomplished with no great difficulty. Then with an army of some 30,000 men he negotiated a difficult crossing of the Paraná river at Diamante and moved on into Santa Fé province. In February of 1852 the major battle of Urquiza's campaign was fought at Monte Caseros, where after intense fighting Rosas' army fled in defeat. Urquiza's victory was complete, for the dictator's military forces disintegrated as an organized body, and only straggling units of disgruntled soldiers fell back upon the capital. They would fight no more. Rosas took pencil in hand and wrote his resignation and promptly departed for England, where by reason of the confiscation of his properties he lived in poverty until his death in 1877. Unlike his more modern imitators, he had not taken the precaution to establish a sizable bank account abroad.

General Urquiza occupied Buenos Aires and appointed a new provisional governor. He then set about the difficult task of organization that confronted him in his effort to establish a federal government. Most of the extraordinary powers over foreign affairs, vested in the Buenos Aires governor by the federal pact of 1831, were assumed by Urquiza, even though his only official position was that of governor of Entre Ríos province. This arrangement was displeasing to many in the port city, where the victor of Monte Caseros was regarded not only with suspicion but also with a considerable amount of contempt. He was, after all, only an up-river provincial who insisted on continuing to wear Rosas' red colors. The pot continued to boil, and it rapidly became evident that Buenos Aires was hardly the place to lay the foundation for a new federal system. In accordance with an agreement drawn up by the provincial governors in May of 1852, a constituent congress assembled in Santa Fé in November of that same year. No delegates from Buenos Aires appeared.

Gradually the air was beginning to clear. Urquiza, as one of his first acts after the overthrow of Rosas, had declared a general amnesty, and many of the exiled unitarians swarmed back to Buenos Aires. They gradually took over control of the city and province, and although they rebelled against Urquiza they were in no position to contend with him at Santa Fé. Instead, they remained aloof, setting up their own independent state while the remaining thirteen provinces of Argentina worked out a new political organization. The centralist porteños were determined to dominate the entire country, and if that was not possible they would go their own way alone. Chief among them was Bartolomé Mitre, who as a deputy in the provincial legislature and later as a principal collaborator of Governor Pastor Obligado provided statesmanlike leadership in the political group that ruled the port city.

In Santa Fé, the federalists were in complete control. Among them were men of outstanding ability and character, Urquiza himself, Juan María Gutiérrez, a poet and literary figure of considerable note, and Juan Bautista Alberdi, an able political theorist. Alberdi, in his book *Bases y puntos de partida para la organización política de la República Argentina,** captured the spirit of strong liberalism within a workable federal system that characterized the Santa Fé constituent assembly's work. Alberdi wrote much of the constitution that was approved by the assembly in 1853, patterning his basic concepts after those of an earlier American political theorist, Alexander Hamilton. The constitution was to endure for many a year.

The era of Rosas was now past. Gone were the oppression, the mazorca, the little red flags, and the stultifying condemnation of intellectual independence. Nurtured in exile and tempered by the bitter strife of civil war, the Argentine spirit was free once more to soar above the bloody pampas and the misty marshes of the great rivers. Able and dedicated men still allowed their personal jealousies and petty regional interests to divide them. More battles would be fought, to be sure, but it was only a matter of time until a great and united Argentine nation would emerge, for the one valuable heritage of the Rosas dictatorship was a sense of Argentine nationality.

* *Bases and Points of Departure for the Political Organization of the Argentine Republic.*

XXVIII

Caudillismo and Anarchy: The Bolivarian Republics

Del rey abajo ninguno — Below the king, no one is better than I.

OLD SPANISH PROVERB

WITH the death of Bolívar all the liberator's dreams of a great and powerful nation in northern South America were dashed asunder by localism and petty self-interest. Each of the major segments of Gran Colombia went its own way to form a separate nation. Venezuela succeeded to the territory formerly governed by the Spanish captain-general in Caracas; Ecuador claimed jurisdiction over the region of the former presidency of Quito; and New Granada was formed from the central territory of the earlier viceroyalty. Peru was already a separate nation having no further tie with the northern neighbor from which the forces of its liberation had emerged. Bolivia, too, stood forth in the ragged garb of her independent statehood, but for a time political and military links with Peru were maintained as efforts to achieve stability encouraged a certain amount of mutual intervention.

In New Granada the transition from the larger to the smaller state was made less difficult by continuation in office of much the same group of public officials in power at the time of Bolívar's death. Nevertheless, for a period of two years it appeared that a sort of national lethargy might permit the republic to suffer almost total dismemberment. General Juan José Flores, a former military leader under Bolívar, headed the movement to make Ecuador independent, and he became the new country's provisional president. After a centralist constitution was adopted in 1830, Flores was elected to a four-year term as president by the new congress; and, as virtual dictator, he set about establishing a northern frontier that would include in his jurisdiction as much of southern New Granada as political persuasion and military conquest could make possible. Flores invaded the Cauca valley; he occupied Pasto, Popayán, and Buenaventura. These areas had been represented in the Ecuadorian constituent assembly held at Riobamba. For a time it appeared that the highland valleys, part of which had been included in the old Quito presidency, would merge peaceably with Ecuador, and largely by their own choice. There was little to indicate that anyone in Bogotá was remotely interested in the fate of the southern regions of Gran Colombia. The province of Chocó voluntarily declared for union with the Flores regime. Eventually, however, the New Granadans awakened to the fact that they were in peril of losing some of their richest provinces, and sent an army against Ecuador. Flores might have achieved victory had his own position been more secure; but so unsettled were conditions in Quito and so tenuous a hold did the general have on Guayaquil that he was obliged to disengage his forces and return to the capital to suppress his political opponents. There followed a series of diplomatic negotiations in which Flores was bested. The Cauca region was recognized as belonging to New Granada and the Carchi river was established as the boundary from the mountains to the coast.

New Granada was too weak and disunited to press further any attempt to reincorporate the Quito region in the larger republic, nor was there any serious interest in so doing. A new constitution, adopted in 1832, proclaimed the territory of New Granada to include the disputed southern valleys, but it laid no claim to Quito or Guayaquil.

During the crucial period of controversy with Flores, New Granada was ruled by a constituent assembly and by a provisional vice-president, Dr. José Ignacio Márquez. To Márquez fell not only the difficult task of securing a settlement of the southern boundary question, but also that of organizing the government under the new centralist constitution. The provisional president, chosen by the constituent assembly, was Francisco de Paula Santander who was at the time residing in exile in New York. Santander now returned to New Granada and a popular election confirmed him in the post of president for a four-year term. Don Joaquín Mosquera became his vice-president and Márquez retired from his provisional role. Thus at last Santander was president in his own right and assumed the duties he had so long exercised in Bogotá as vice-president of Gran Colombia during Bolívar's absence in the south. Now, however, the country was greatly reduced in size and suffered from bitter factionalism brought on by Bolívar's final debacle and the political disintegration that followed.

Santander as president was a man of stern aspect and rugged determination. In popular appeal he was almost the antithesis of Bolívar. He was admired and respected for his integrity, his devotion to duty and to the program he fostered in the interest of the young nation over which he presided. He demonstrated almost none of the flamboyant gallantry and social grace, however, that had constituted so basic a feature of Bolívar's appeal. Perhaps disillusionment and frustration had soured Santander. Certainly the crucial break with his old and trusted friend, Bolívar, had come about only after great emotional crisis — a crisis that could not fail to leave a deep mark on the sensitive and somewhat introverted statesman. In any case Santander ruled with a sober determination and inflexibility of principle that left no room for frivolity. Indeed, the harsher aspects of his character emerged and seemed to dominate his conduct in office. Political enemies, the former supporters of the late liberator, were offered no token of conciliation or gesture of forgiveness. Neither were they permitted any role in the new government. Exile or the firing squad was their reward for renewal of political activity. Santander's efforts to purge the army of sympathizers with the late president produced a bitter reaction that finally erupted in plots to overthrow the government.

These Santander suppressed and in 1833 a number of the conspirators were publicly executed in the main square of Bogotá. Soon it was obvious that the ranks of the president's enemies were growing rapidly. A general factor in addition to the harsh measures taken against the Bolivarian factions was the unwillingness of the chief executive to take advice. Suggestions were interpreted as personal criticisms, and criticism became, in Santander's mind, synonymous with treason.

In spite of the many difficulties faced by the president, including that created by his own personality problems, Santander's administration produced a number of notable achievements. A peace agreement was worked out with Ecuador and Venezuela whereby each recognized the independence of the others and each assumed a share of the national debt of the former Gran Colombia. Ratification of this agreement was delayed until after Santander's retirement, but the basic terms of settlement were worked out through his efforts. The president retained a firm hand in matters of religion, asserting strongly the right of the government to exercise the patronato. Likewise, in the face of considerable clerical opposition, the government embarked upon a program of public elementary education for both boys and girls. Santander, who had traveled both in Europe and North America, had developed a strong interest in all aspects of education, and he fostered in New Granada the Lancastrian system of instruction. Many were happy when Santander's term of office drew to a close, but few could deny that the young nation had made substantial progress toward stability and prosperity under his firm, if rigorous, rule.

To the east, in the new republic of Venezuela, Bolívar's old friend and occasional trouble-maker during the days of Gran Colombia, José Antonio Páez, dominated the political scene. Páez was the first president elected under the constitution adopted in 1830, and his administration was a relatively stable one. Although a conservative he was sufficiently moderate in his views to avoid the bitter animosities that troubled Santander in New Granada. On the other hand, apart from providing an atmosphere in which the pangs of separation from Gran Colombia quickly disappeared, there was little for which the government could claim much credit.

As a successor to Páez, the Venezuelan congress selected the rector of the university as president. In the election no person had achieved a majority of the votes cast, thus throwing the burden of decision on the legislators. The selection of José M. Vargas was not received with great joy throughout the country, not because anyone particularly disliked the distinguished scholar, but because intellectuals simply were not regarded as possessing the requirements of vigor and strength to exercise the prerogatives of chief executive. Military men particularly were distrustful of intellectualism — a phenomenon by no means rare nor limited in its currency to Venezuela. Shortly a military coup ensued and Vargas was forced to turn over his duties and responsibilities to the vice-president and leave the country. A more successful and thoroughgoing revolt was prevented by the intervention of Páez, who, as commander of the government troops, restored order. However, Vargas was not returned to the presidency. Páez' views were not notably at variance with those of his military friends, but he had no wish to see the government become the plaything of military adventurers.

In 1838 Páez was again elected president, and during his second term the country's progress in terms of economic well-being was considerable. International trade increased sharply, thus adding to the government's revenues at a time when expenditures on the military were being reduced. New immigrants came to the country from Central Europe, cart roads were built, a national bank was established, and other tangible improvements were noted. The slave trade in African natives was terminated by agreement with England. The administration of Carlos Soublette, who followed Páez, was likewise marked by general prosperity throughout the country and was unmarred by serious threat to the internal peace.

During the years of relative calm after independence, and particularly during the period that Páez was most active in national affairs, an air of complacency seemed to prevail in most matters of public interest. True, there were advocates and supporters of greater decentralization in government, of withdrawal of state support from the church, of secularization of education, and of many other ideas that would have involved considerable change. By and large, however, no one pushed such matters vigorously, and the attitude of the government was not discouraging to those inclined toward the expression of liberal or radical views. As time went on, however, there emerged a genuine opposition movement, the leaders of which regarded the progressivism of Páez as nothing but ultra-conservatism. Chief spokesman for the liberal group was Antonio Leocadio Guzmán, a publicist and editor of *El Venezolano*, a journal founded primarily as a medium for the expression of political opposition to the leadership of Páez and the conservative families from which he drew his principal support. The liberal group was hardly revolutionary, nor did it associate itself with the liberal impulse that had produced a revolution from Spain and spearheaded the anti-clerical struggles in New Granada. Rather, the liberal movement found expression in carping criticism of the government. In the background lay the jealousies and antagonisms of family factions that more truly than any intellectual differences provided the divisive factors in Venezuelan social and political life.

In 1846 a new family entered the political jousts with the election of José Tadeo Monagas as president. Supported by Páez and the conservative faction, Monagas was expected to continue the tradition of moderate progressivism. He had been opposed in the election by the owner of *El Venezolano*, Guzmán, who became so vitriolic in his attacks that Soublette had had him arrested and condemned to death. Monagas softened the penalty to exile, but shortly the outspoken editor was back and serving as Monagas' vice-president. Some of his friends were appointed to high office. It was apparent that Monagas was joining the opposition. In congress there was talk of impeachment, and as a consequence the legislative body was dissolved and the dissolution enforced by the army. Páez started a revolt, was defeated, and sent into exile in the United States.

Now the era of peace was almost at an end. Páez' grip upon the country was not only weakened; it was broken. Men spoke of liberalism and conservatism, of radicals and oligarchs, but these were mere words. Federalists opposed centralists, but the positions taken reflected the jockeying for power of families and factions rather than sincere convictions of how best the government should be constituted and organized. There was revolution in France, in Germany — a true liberal movement was in progress. It carried into Chile, the Argentine, and into New Granada, wherever genuine intellectualism responded to trends in contemporary thought and political action. Its impact in Venezuela was slight; for there the minds of men were sterile. Intrigue was rife and critics were outspoken, but this was only the froth stirred up by personal rivalries; beneath all this the country plodded on its lethargic way to market and home again. For over a decade the Monagas family directed the affairs of state. The third in line, José Tadeo again, evidenced new ambitions. He forced through the controlled congress a new constitution, centralist in concept and permitting the president to succeed himself to a six-year term. This move united the various factions against him, and early in 1858 he was forced from office and replaced by a provisional junta which called a new constituent assembly.

Soon it became apparent that the various family factions could not agree. Calling themselves 'conservatives' and 'liberals' they struggled over the issue of centralism *versus* federation until debate degenerated into a resort to arms. The country was torn with revolution. In 1861 Páez was recalled from exile to restore order, which he was able to do only after months of bitter fighting. A new constitution was drafted, this one providing for provincial autonomy in a federation. Páez retired again from the scene, and when the new arrangement proved to be no improvement over the former, the aged statesman could no longer summon the strength to return and quench the fires of revolt that flared anew. For ten years the country was prostrated by conflict and warfare, all to no purpose beyond satisfying the personal ambitions of warring caudillos. Finally, in 1872, one man emerged more powerful than the rest. He was Antonio Guzmán Blanco, son of Antonio Leocadio Guzmán of editorial fame. He was to rule as Venezuela's prototype caudillo for the next twenty years. Bolívar's homeland had strayed far from the path of the great liberator. From the grave in Caracas, to which the body of Bolívar had been transferred in 1842, the voice of the great statesman could not be heard.

Far to the south, Bolívar's legacy proved no less a burden than in the successor states of the dismembered Gran Colombia. The failure of the Gran Colombian dream is often attributed, in part at least, to the liberator's absence during the period of greatest crisis. However, the regions favored with his presence during those crucial years of the late 1820's failed even more dismally to live up to the great plans of the Venezuelan general. Bolívar's ultimate aim was certainly the creation of a powerful federation of all the states of northern South America. His many writings and many of his letters and public decrees point to such a goal. Only in the light of such an objective can one make out the elusive explanation of the liberator's extended preoccupation with Peru and Bolivia.

Bolívar's strange constitution, which was foisted on both Bolivia and Peru, provided excellent material for the general's critics and in a sense came to symbolize all that was wrong with his grandiose schemes. The lifetime presidency, coupled to a cumbersome three-house legislative structure, was impossible enough in itself, but when Bolívar assumed the presidency in Peru and his principal general, Marshal Sucre, reluctantly assumed that role in Bolivia, the impracticability of the entire program became patently apparent. To Peruvians and Bolivians alike it seemed that the benefits of their independence were to be enjoyed exclusively by their Venezuelan and Colombian liberators. The continued presence of Colombian armies did nothing to allay such suspicions. Thus when Bolívar was absent in 1827 to deal with the Venezuelan crisis created by the separatist tendencies of General Páez, Peruvians quickly overthrew the provisional government of General Andrés Santa Cruz and established one more to their own liking. Colombian troops, discouraged by irregular pay and long absence from home, joined in the mutiny and were quickly sent home. A new constitution was framed and Peru assumed responsibility for its own government without the aid of a liberator. Soon a struggle was underway with Colombia over title to the border provinces of Mainas and Jaén, and an army was sent to invade Guayaquil. The Peruvians met defeat at the hands of Marshal Sucre, but the last vestiges of friendly collaboration between Peru and Colombia were at an end. The southern portion of Bolívar's dream of federation was already exploded before Gran Colombia fell apart.

It was perhaps no accident that for years following the Bolívar era, the affairs of Peru and Bolivia were strangely intermixed. The two regions had been closely united for centuries until the audiencia in Charcas was attached to the viceroyalty of Río de la Plata late in the eighteenth century. Once Spanish domination was at an end, the old ties were reasserted and Buenos Aires, torn with its own problems, was quickly forgotten. Peruvians sought to dominate Bolivia and Bolivians sought to dominate Peru. The first victim of this development was Marshal Sucre, who, in 1828, was faced with rebellion in Bolivia, invasion from Peru, and mutiny among his own Colombian troops. He was forced to resign and return northward. Sucre, far more than Bolívar, was the creator of the Bolivian nation. As Bolívar's field commander, his was the army of liberation and he the hero of the last great battle with the Spaniards at Ayacucho. He it was who, in opposition to the expressed wishes of Bolívar, called into being the first legislative body of Bolivia and supported its declaration of independence. It was Sucre who with great difficulty persuaded the liberator to accept that decision and endorse Bolivian independence. It was he who gave to Bolivia its first independent government. Had he given up his ties with Bolívar he might have been able to maintain his position as head of the new state; but he wisely refused to regard himself as other than an interim chief executive bound sooner or later to hand over to the Bolivians control of their own destinies. Thus it was that although his departure was forced it was not unexpected, nor was it viewed with bitterness by the great general. He came as a hero and he departed as one, even though wounded in the uprising that precipitated his departure.

With Sucre out of the way, Peruvian forces occupied the principal cities of Bolivia and imposed a number of terms to be complied with before they would leave. One condition, of course, was the departure of all Colombian soldiers from Bolivia, a move that a majority of the Bolivian leaders looked upon with favor. Other conditions involved the acceptance of Sucre's resignation, the calling of a constituent assembly to draft a new constitution, and financial settlements to defray the costs of occupation. It is difficult to determine the exact nature of Peruvian motives at this point. Certainly they wished to see all Colombian influence — meaning that of Bolívar, in particular — eliminated from both Peru and Bolivia. The possible incorporation of Bolivia into Peru was certainly not altogether absent from the minds of Peruvian political and military leaders, and there is little doubt that individual military commanders used the occupation as an opportunity to foment among the Bolivian populace some sentiment for annexation. Before matters could run their course, however, the Peruvian troops quit Bolivia to engage in the war with Gran Colombia and attempt the conquest of Guayaquil. The Bolivians were suddenly left to their own devices.

Neither Peru nor Bolivia was really prepared to undertake self-government. Both owed their independence largely to external forces. Neither had, in the process of gaining independence, developed outstanding leaders and statesmen comparable to those of Colombia, Chile, or Argentina. Rather, they fell back upon those military leaders brought to the fore during the era of Bolívar, and as was the case in Ecuador and Venezuela where similar military leadership prevailed, the legislative branches of government scarcely got off to a start. In Bolivia particularly, several attempts to get action out of the representative assembly after the departure of Sucre ended in such dismal failure and disorder that the body, called into being as a conventional assembly, went down in history known as the 'asamblea convulsional,' the assembly of convulsion. A major and related problem in Bolivia was the absence of any real sense of social or political unity among the Spanish-speaking population, to say nothing of course of the Indian masses who constituted the great majority of the Bolivian people but who had no role whatsoever in public affairs. The various figures who moved in the limited political circle were known as supporters of Sucre or Bolívar, of Peruvian ambitions, or of some other essentially alien individual or influence apart from development of a true Bolivian nationality. The man who finally emerged to bring some semblance of order to Bolivian national existence was a native son who had been a soldier under Bolívar, had headed the Peruvian interim government that ruled for a brief period during Bolívar's absence in 1826 and 1827, and who, when chosen to be president by the Bolivian congress, was in Chile engaged on a diplomatic mission for Peru. Thus in the generation of independence was leadership mobile and transferable. General Andrés Santa Cruz assumed the presidency of Bolivia in May, 1829, and thereupon undertook to stem the tide of anarchy that was sweeping his homeland and his adopted Peru as well.

For two years Santa Cruz ruled Bolivia as a dictator without a constitution and without any more legal claim to his office than his appointment by a congress called into being by a military agreement with Peru. Nevertheless, he enjoyed great personal popularity and the confidence of all elements that were politically articulate in Bolivia. When he took over as president, the treasury was empty, the economy of the country disrupted, the mines unproductive, and law and order non-existent. By 1831 Santa Cruz had been able to replenish the treasury by loans and taxes, to restore mining activity to some degree of productivity, and to build the armed forces of the country into a body capable of maintaining order and defending the country against foreign encroachment. It was then time to elect a constitutional assembly to draw up a new constitution and to place the presidential office on a legitimate basis. This was done. The various actions of Santa Cruz were ratified, a constitution was adopted providing for a two-house popularly elected legislative body, a chief executive assisted by a council of state, and an independent court system. Santa Cruz then set about, through the use of special committees, the development of basic legislative codes, such as the criminal code, code of civil procedures, commercial and mining codes, and others. This was an extremely important step, for a new country without a basic code structure and unused to the system of common law and judicial precedent common in Anglo-Saxon countries, had little or no basis upon which to perform the normal judicial and regulatory functions of government. Santa Cruz and his committees used French and Spanish precedents primarily, as eventually did most of the countries of Latin America, even though much French legislation was neither particularly good nor well suited to the Bolivian situation. Nevertheless, as a result of Santa Cruz' efforts, Bolivia became one of the first newly independent American states to possess a fairly complete codified legal structure.

Santa Cruz took other important steps to give his country some of the basic elements of nationhood. He founded universities in Cochabamba and La Paz, organized the medical and legal professions, and undertook to develop the rudiments of a secondary education system. Such constructive efforts served to add appreciably to the popularity of the president and to justify Marshal Sucre's confidence in the man, for Sucre had recommended him to the Bolivian political leaders at the moment of his retirement from the country. Santa Cruz, however, was a man of broad political convictions whose experience, as already indicated, included intimate association with the affairs of Peru. Like his earlier illustrious associates, he did not wish to be bound by the provincialism manifesting itself in the pattern of national jurisdictions that had emerged in the Andes region. Undoubtedly his success and general popularity in Bolivia influenced Santa Cruz to believe that he could provide the leadership for a grander structure within which both Bolivia and Peru might enjoy the benefits of unification. Conditions in Peru certainly indicated that a guiding hand was needed, for after the Peruvian armies had been turned back from Guayaquil by Sucre, all semblance of stability seemed to have departed the country that had so long served as Spain's principal kingdom in South America. President José de La Mar was shortly overthrown by the outstanding Peruvian army leader, General Agustín Gamarra, but Gamarra in turn was unable to establish himself firmly. By 1833 Peru was in the throes of general disorder and anarchy with rival claimants for power established in various parts of the national territory. These Peruvian difficulties played directly into the hands of Santa Cruz who treated with first one and then another of the Peruvian caudillos in an effort to gain support for his program of federation.

The motives of Santa Cruz have been subjected to severe criticism by both contemporaries and historians. Some assert that he was vain, lustful for personal power, avaricious in a financial sense, and in general a thoroughly reprehensible character. That he ruled Bolivia in a completely dictatorial manner is hardly to be questioned. Nevertheless, there is strong testimonial to the effect that however dictatorial, Santa Cruz' government was both moderate and progressive and only in a minor sense tyrannical. Further, it must at least be stated that his plan of confederation had the distinct merit of uniting Peru and Bolivia without subordinating either of the two countries to the other. True, the plan did subordinate both nations to his own personal rule, but no one can seriously deny that vigorous leadership was needed if the unification plan was to have even a faint hope of succeeding.

Whatever his motives, Santa Cruz requested and received from the Bolivian congress extraordinary authority to embark upon his unification program, and in 1835 his armies entered Peru to support General Orbegoso, one of the Peruvian claimants for power from whom Santa Cruz had received a promise of support in uniting the two countries. In two difficult battles the Bolivian army defeated both Generals Gamarra and Salaverry, and all Peru fell to Santa Cruz. There followed special congresses and agreements, and in the end a confederation was formed uniting north Peru, south Peru, and Bolivia in a three-way confederation. Each unit was provided with its own congress and executive officers, and Santa Cruz was chosen by the plenipotentiaries as protector, or chief executive, of the confederation. His term of office was to be ten years with re-election permitted.

There was much to be said for the confederation in that, had it endured, one of the causes of future international difficulty in the western region of South America might have been avoided. Of prime importance to Bolivia, and a matter of much discussion during the pre-federation maneuvers, was the matter of Bolivia's access to Pacific ports. In this period Bolivia possessed coastal territory between Peru and Chile. The region was largely desert and its harbors were less than satisfactory. It was eventually to prove an important source of nitrate and to attract Chilean investors and developers, thereby creating an international crisis that exploded into war and cost Bolivia her access to the sea. In the time of Santa Cruz, however, the question was one of access to ocean commerce, and the route to Arica and Cobija was not suitable. Commerce might move more easily over the older established trade routes through Peru to the ports of Mollendo and Callao. Peru, however, was inclined to press its geographic advantage and impose severe burdens on Bolivian commerce through its territory. Unification could well have ended such difficulties and made possible the movement of goods by routes uninfluenced by the artificialities of political boundaries. Furthermore, it might well have discouraged subsequent Chilean adventures in the nitrate fields of the Atacama desert. The Peru-Bolivian confederation was not to last, however.

Both Chile and Argentina viewed Santa Cruz' creation with strong disfavor. For a time the Bolivian leader attempted to calm his troubled neighbors with assurances of peaceful intentions, and even when Chilean expeditionary forces were sent against the confederation after a declaration of war, Santa Cruz preferred to negotiate rather than fight. Such efforts were unavailing, however, for Chile in particular was determined that the unification of her two northern neighbors should not endure. At the same time, it quickly became obvious that Santa Cruz had over-extended himself, for with the possibility of Chilean intervention latent opposition to the confederation dictator appeared in all quarters, including Bolivia. Defeated in battle by the Chileans at Yungay, Santa Cruz was quickly discredited. In February, 1839, the whole structure he had created crumbled around him. He fled to Ecuador and the confederation came to an end. Indeed, so bitter were the dictator's enemies that even in Bolivia they expressed approval of Chile's action in breaking up the confederation, outlawed Santa

Cruz, and confiscated his personal property holdings. After contests for power in both countries, General Gamarra took over the presidency of Peru and General José Ballivián assumed the corresponding position in Bolivia. The era of Santa Cruz was at an end.

Not so the struggle for domination between Peru and Bolivia. President Gamarra blamed Bolivia for the problems created by Santa Cruz, and in 1841 he invaded the highland country during a struggle between Ballivián and a rival claimant for the presidency. The rival, General Velasco, immediately united his forces with those of his opponent, and in the battle that followed the Peruvian forces were routed and Gamarra killed. For a time, at least, the Peruvian threat to Bolivian independence was ended, and each country went its own way.

In Bolivia Ballivián was a national hero. He was formally chosen president by convention in 1843, at which time a new constitution was also proclaimed. Ballivián governed the country through a series of insurrections until the end of 1847. He then resigned his position and left the country on a diplomatic mission to Chile. His departure was forced, however, for conditions had reached such a state that he was in constant danger of assassination. Immediately upon his departure, political disorders spread throughout the country. Ballivián was the last of a series of men, beginning with Sucre, who had provided some semblance of orderly and constructive government for the new republic. Indeed, Ballivián accomplished more of lasting benefit in terms of physical improvements and extension of public services than did his more famous predecessors, but even his efforts to set a pattern of progressive national development came to naught in the long period of almost utter chaos and anarchy that began in 1848.

The early history of independent Bolivia is a history of violence, intrigue, and half-way successful efforts by three outstanding men to give the nation leadership in its formative years. Strangely in the background is another figure, almost lost in the shadows of forgotten records and dust-covered documents. The man, Don Casimiro Olañeta, was the nephew of a Spanish general who fought against the independence movement. Perhaps a monarchist at heart, as was his better-known counterpart in Mexico, Lucas Alamán, Olañeta exercised considerable influence in Bolivian affairs throughout the entire period until the departure of Ballivián and even afterward. Now a minister of state, then a court justice, later an ambassador to Chile, Olañeta was deeply involved in the intrigue that marked the rise and fall of each of the three outstanding presidents of the era beginning with Sucre. An educated man, he wrote ably but caustically to persuade prominent men of his day in favor of or in opposition to the chief political figures. He appears to have had few scruples. In the fall of Sucre, his fine hand is seen encouraging the Peruvian Gamarra to invade Bolivia. He supported Santa Cruz and served as his ambassador in Chile, yet quickly and nimbly shifted to the opposition as the Protector's position weakened. In the closing days of Ballivián's presidency, Olañeta's evil pen was at work to bring about the downfall of the last of Bolivia's early constructive leaders. In part, at least, this back-stage detractor was responsible for the numerous sharp and bitter about-faces that came to characterize Bolivian public life and that made it all but impossible to resolve political questions on any other basis than force and violence.

As Bolivia tumbled into the abyss of unrestrained lawlessness, Peru settled down to enjoy the benefits of its first stable government since independence. The death in battle of President Gamarra had touched off a new series of internal struggles for political power that lasted until 1844. In that year, a young mestizo caudillo from Tarapacá, Ramón Castilla, achieved victory over his competitors and control of the government in Lima. The following year he was named constitutional president of Peru for a six-year term, and under his firm and able leadership the country enjoyed a period of relief from internal strife and undertook a number of important economic and commercial improvements. It had been discovered that the accumulated tons of bird excretions that virtually covered the Chincha islands in the bay of Pisco were an excellent source of nitrates. This product came into great demand in Europe, as did nitrates from the enormous salt beds of the Atacama desert region. Overnight, export of guano (bird deposits) became a most profitable business, and this desirable traffic was augmented by activities in the desert mineral fields. Castilla's government extracted and exported the guano fertilizer as a government monopoly and thereby brought millions of dollars into the national treasury each year. Basically an honest man, Castilla put the huge revenues to good use in stabilizing the fiscal system and in making payments on foreign loans contracted during the revolutionary era.

For a time, at least, the stability and financial soundness of the Peruvian economy seemed assured and private investment increased. New buildings arose, roads were constructed, and a railroad line was built linking Lima with the near-by port of Callao. Other improvements of a similar nature were undertaken and the country prospered. Castilla nevertheless occasionally had time to roil the troubled waters of Peru-Bolivian relationships.

At the end of his term of office, Castilla retired and a much lesser man, José Rufino Echenique, was made president. Echenique could not avoid the temptation to convert to his personal use and that of his friends some portion of the handsome government revenue, and soon the whole moral tone of the government service declined. Public confidence disappeared and domestic commerce languished. Soon a revolutionary plot was under way, headed by Castilla, and Echenique was overthrown and exiled. Castilla resumed the presidential office after a *pro forma* election and continued in that position until 1862. Again the country prospered and numerous improvements were fostered, this time in a less material sense. The few remaining slaves in Peru were freed, the Indians were relieved of paying tribute, and a feeble attempt, at least, was made to provide some facilities for public education. Also during Castilla's second term of office a new constitution was drawn up and adopted, providing as had earlier basic laws for a national unitary government of separated executive, legislative, and judicial powers. At the same time the presidential term was reduced from six to four years and immediate re-election prohibited.

The long period or relative tranquility was discouraging to ambitious local political leaders, however. Castilla ruled with a firm and almost dictatorial hand, and he was able to keep things under control until he retired from office. Signs of unrest were apparent when a revolt occurred in Arequipa in 1856, an insurrection in which the Peruvian naval forces joined. Indeed, reduction in the presidential term and the ban on re-election provided by the 1860 constitution were indications that Castilla's long rule was becoming tiresome. His departure from office signaled a return to corrupt and chaotic government.

Farther north, in Ecuador, independence provided no better guarantee of a secure life for the people than it had in Bolivia and Peru. Juan José Flores, the first president, ruled with a heavy hand that offered no relief from the political and religious exploitation that had aroused liberal opposition to the Spaniards in 1809 and 1810. Opposition was ever present, particularly in Guayaquil where separation from Quito seemed to have a continuing appeal. Likewise, outspoken liberals, who wished to curtail the authority of the church and permit greater freedom of expression, posed a constant threat to Flores' regime. The principal liberal leader, Vicente Rocafuerte, who had a strong following in Guayaquil, proved particularly dangerous. Flores arranged with him to alternate presidential terms, and for eight years the agreement was kept. In 1843, however, Flores, after serving his allotted four-year term, broke faith and secured re-election for eight years under a new constitution. Rocafuerte was pacified with a handsome pension, but other liberals were not so easily placated. They revolted and threw Flores from office and into exile, leaving the country without effective leadership. Liberal zealots committed numerous anti-clerical acts and these were reciprocated by acts of violence on the part of church supporters. Soon the country was in complete disorder, racked by widespread and continuous violence. Individual caudillos controlled this or that section of the national territory for brief periods and then lost out to rival claimants. Trouble arose with New Granada and Peru. For fifteen years there existed no Ecuadorian government worthy of the name. Finally, in 1860, Flores saw an opportunity to return from exile and join forces with Gabriel García Moreno, a strange, ultra-conservative intellectual who had formed a movement to restore order in the country and bring about political reform along lines in keeping with the conservative tradition of imperial Spain. Inasmuch as a military effort was needed Flores proved useful, for García Moreno was a writer, a university rector, a lawyer, and a politician, but no soldier. Together, the two men ousted the local caudillo in Guayaquil, who had attempted to turn over that port city to Peru, and moved on to take over the country. Quickly Flores was brushed aside, and the long regime of García Moreno began.

By 1860 caudillo government had become the rule in all the outlying regions touched by the Bolivarian epic. It was government by the military with a vengeance, and it had led to anarchy, violence, and chaos, interrupted for greater or lesser periods by the stable regime of an outstanding man. In none of the countries, Peru, Bolivia, Ecuador, or Venezuela, did substantive issues or programs provide the basis for political activity nor did they significantly influence the selection of men for public office. True, in some of the countries people called themselves conservatives or liberals, but these labels had little bearing on how men thought or acted. More often they distinguished one group of landholders from another. Those whose wealth and influence were concentrated near the capital were centralist and conservative. Those whose power lay in the provinces favored decentralization, which represented a change from the established pattern; they were *ipso facto* liberals. Such matters were essentially personal and proprietary. To the long parade of military upstarts who strutted across the national stage, most of whose family connections were somewhat vague, even these considerations meant little. Power and wealth were their objectives, and the issues that concerned them were the personal battles with their military rivals. Without system or tradition, with no firm rooting in the minds and hearts of men, the republican form of government served only as a phrase written into each succeeding constitution. Who, after all, would constitutionally describe his government as military despotism intermixed with anarchy! As for popular democracy, no one even dreamed of that in a country populated largely by subservient Indians.

One issue, however, did assume significance, not so much in the countries that had formed the outskirts of Bolívar's shadowy empire, but in the heartland of New Granada. That issue was the question of just where the church was to fit in the new order of independent nationhood. The old Spanish empire had been far more than a political system; into its fabric had been woven all the institutions of human society. Once the fabric was torn asunder, the resulting pieces possessed many loose threads that had to be tied firmly back into the cloth lest each segment become completely unraveled. The early Iberian weavers had selected a major portion of their yarn in Rome.

The degree to which church and state had been intermingled in the empire made it difficult for secessionist nations to adjust to their new status. Did the republican governments succeed to the religious prerogatives of the Spanish king, or did the duties and responsibilities of the monarch pertaining to religion revert to the Pope in Rome once the king's voice in American affairs had been silenced? This was a major and all-important question. It had little to do with religious freedom, and most of the traditional discussions of liberalism *versus* conservatism are in large measure irrelevant. Prompt resolution was necessary, however, for the very nature of the new states was involved, as was also the reality of independence. In such areas as Bolivia, Peru, and Venezuela, the lack of political stability and the preoccupation of the caudillos with matters military permitted the issue to be resolved for a time at least by default. The church became the arbiter of its own destiny, and for a military chieftain to challenge its right to do so was to invite disaster. In Gran Colombia and subsequently in New Granada, however, where intellectualism and true liberalism had been outstanding features of late colonial society, the issue was inescapable and was faced almost as soon as political independence was firmly established. The struggle over its resolution permeated all other forms of political controversy for more than two decades after the death of the liberator.

In 1824 a Law of Patronage was enacted by the government of Gran Colombia. By this law, the new government reserved to itself the full patronage authority with respect to the church — that is, the authority to nominate the principal religious officials of the country. Inasmuch as the government was not recognized by the papacy, the actions taken by it in religious matters were in a sense provisional. The Pope could not act upon the nominations or presentations of the Gran Colombian congress without recognizing the legitimate authority of the revolutionary government. Recognition he could not grant without creating a whole set of problems for himself in Spain. The Pope could not appoint the various religious officials himself, however, for he had no way of enforcing his decisions. In these circumstances, the local church hierarchy received and accepted office from the republican government, but papal confirmation had to await an eventual adjustment in relationships between Rome and Bogotá.

The patronage issue was for a time the prime issue of church-state relationships. The clerical group and their supporters opposed government control over the selection of church officials. They would have preferred to have the church free to control within its own organization all religious personnel, their selection, and their advancement. They were in no sense willing to concede the other side of the coin, however, and permit church-state separation. They insisted on continuation of the tithe as a tax and through it financial support of the church by the government. Likewise, they demanded prohibition of non-Catholic religious activity and asserted their exclusive right to continue performing the varied semireligious temporal functions that had historically fallen into the church province. These functions included the conduct of all education, public and private; the performance of all welfare services; operation of hospitals and all institutions for the homeless and aged; control of marriages and funerals; and operation of cemeteries. It must be recognized, of course, that many of these functions have only become uniquely civil rather than religious in the twentieth century. They were, and to some degree remain, church functions throughout the Christian areas of the world. In Spanish America, the union of the Roman Catholic Church and the state had promoted a complete monopolization of the indicated functions by the church and support of the activities by government-imposed taxes paid over to the church. A further matter of no small significance was the extent of economic power exercised by the many religious orders through ownership of land and the conduct of agricultural and commercial activities. The integration of church and state had fostered a high degree of 'socialism.'

Bolívar was in many ways a more conservative Catholic than others of the Gran Colombian political leaders. Santander was the firm and stable statesman who saw clearly the course of moderation and followed it doggedly. He insisted steadfastly upon governmental control of religious patronage, upon the creation of secular educational institutions, and upon limiting the jurisdiction of the special religious courts that exercised control over the clergy in civil matters. He was damned by the clergy as a 'liberal' and by the liberals as pro-clerical. Thus was vindicated the wisdom of his course.

In 1838 José Ignacio de Márquez was elected to succeed Santander in the presidency of New Granada. He believed in freeing education from the restrictions of religious dogma, as had Santander, but he also had strong views concerning the economic power of the church, particularly that of various religious orders. The church itself was divided on this issue, as the secular clergy, that is, those who performed religious services for the public and who did not belong to monastic orders, were jealous of the power and wealth of the various orders. Márquez moved against several missions operated by the orders and transferred them to the secular clergy, and in so doing he had the support of the chief secular prelate in the affected area, the bishop of Popayán. The stroke was aimed primarily at assuring a more definite dedication of the church's resources to religious and educational purposes, but it produced a revolt against the government, led by priests. While the uprising was quickly crushed, and principal political, military, and religious leaders joined Márquez in the effort, the incident was merely the opening shot in a long struggle over the religious issue. Indeed, it soon became questionable whether religion was an issue or a pretext, for caudillos in various parts of the country rose in revolt claiming to be acting in support of the church. Astutely, the bishop of Bogotá, Manuel José de Mosquera, noted in a pastoral letter that religion was being used as a pretense for disturbing the peace and he denounced those who would on such a basis justify revolution. Nevertheless, revolt seethed throughout the country, and for a time Márquez seemed powerless to control it. General Pedro Alcántara Herrán commanded the government forces. Joined with him was another outstanding leader, General Tomás Cipriano de Mosquera. Together, and with the help at one point of President Flores of Ecuador, these men were finally able to restore peace. However, the struggle lasted nearly four years, disrupted the economic and social life of the country, bankrupted the national treasury, and settled nothing but the personal ambitions of a few men. In the midst of the disorders, Santander died, and thus was lost the one great stabilizing figure linking the new republic to the glorious period of the revolution. Also during the conflict, a new election brought General Herrán to the presidency, but for more than a year he was forced to absent himself from the capital conducting military campaigns against the revolutionists.

The administrations of Herrán and Tomás Cipriano de Mosquera, who succeeded Herrán in 1845, were periods of more stable national life. A new constitution was adopted in 1843, centralist in nature, and tending toward parliamentarism in that members of the president's cabinet were given seats in congress and members of congress were permitted to hold positions in the administration. With respect to the religious issue, the bond formed between the government leaders and the secular religious hierarchy during the preceding struggle held firm, and, for a time at least, church and state drew closer. Inasmuch as peace prevailed, commerce revived and flourished, aided by commercial treaties with other countries, including Spain. Roads were built and a treaty with the United States authorized that country to construct a railroad across the Isthmus of Panamá. The national debt was sharply reduced, a new monetary system established, and the Bogotá mint refurbished.

A guiding hand in New Granada's progress was that of Mariano Ospina Rodríguez, a wealthy conservative of an aristocratic Antioquian family. Holding various public offices, he was able to wield tremendous influence on public policy and to do much to further national development. His efforts were particularly significant in the field of education where he was successful in reorganizing university education, founding normal schools in nearly all provinces, and placing the entire educational program of the country on a sounder and more disciplined basis. Indeed, the Jesuits were brought back in 1844 to take over responsibility for much of the revised educational program. In other fields Ospina was able to undertake a program of distributing large tracts of public land to private settlers and landholding companies. Whatever the social wisdom of the new landholding arrangements, much otherwise idle land was made productive, and with the introduction of coffee growing, an important new piece of the foundation was laid for the future economy of the country.

Although anesthetized somewhat by all the obvious material and social benefits produced by the peaceful years of Herrán's and Mosquera's administrations, New Granadan intellectual liberalism was far from dead. Unlike most of the military leaders of other Bolivarian countries, New Granada's presidents and other prominent public figures were for the most part well-educated and widely traveled men. They were aware of and receptive to social and political shifts on the European scene. Many, including President Mosquera, were aroused by the wave of liberal revolutions that swept Europe in 1848. For New Granadan liberals it was a fresh and welcome breeze which, once felt, inspired a rededication to ideals and principles espoused during the days of the American, French, and Spanish American revolutions, but since almost forgotten. Those in control of the government represented the landholding classes, the church, and the military. Their views, although enlightened and generally progressive, were essentially conservative and on some matters reactionary. It was with considerable justice that they called themselves and were referred to by their political opponents as 'Conservatives.' Mosquera was clearly one of these, but in the background of his character was an element of radicalism that gradually came to the fore and caused him to view with some favor the efforts of political and social reformers. Certainly he took no action to suppress or quiet them.

In 1849 congress as usual had to select the president inasmuch as no candidate received an electoral majority. Their choice was José Hilario López, who was supported by virtually all who opposed the older conservative elements. It was a victory for Cundinamarca, the province of the capital, and the port regions over the church-dominated provinces of the south. In the later years of Mosquera's administration the old religious and territorial differences had begun once more to crystallize. Now López set forth upon what was in essence an extremely radical program to break the power of the church. To the consternation of his friends and family, ex-President Mosquera supported this radical move. Within a brief time all manner of measures had been taken to curtail church authority and power. It was cut off from the national treasury, the tithe tax abolished, and it was forced to turn to the provincial governments for support. The Jesuit order was again expelled, the church fueros were abolished, and an official act was passed separating church and state. In other areas, also, López moved to satisfy his radical supporters. All slaves were freed, virtually complete freedom of the press was permitted, and a convention was called to draft a new liberal constitution granting complete religious freedom and providing general manhood suffrage. Other steps were taken, both by statute and constitutional provision, to strengthen provincial and local governments and to increase their financial resources and autonomy.

Naturally, such sweeping and radical changes were hardly to be inaugurated peacefully. In 1854 and 1855 the country was swept by revolt and disorder, but even the conservative ex-presidents came to the support of legitimate government however much they disagreed with its policies. Internal peace was restored. The liberal movement, with considerable popular backing, continued on its course of reform, albeit at a slower pace. The religious issue was still dominant, but at mid-century in New Granada other factors were beginning to emerge as major points of national controversy. A stronger agricultural base underlay the economy, light industry flourished, and economic issues assumed increasing importance. Surrounded by countries in which caudillismo and anarchy prevailed, New Granada had not escaped unscathed from such evil influences. The far richer and deeper cultural and intellectual heritage of the former viceroyalty, however, served to hold men to reason and orderliness. There existed a true sense of nationality and a sense of patriotism for which men were willing to sacrifice personal ambition. This degree of national maturity remained but a vague promise in the other Bolivarian republics.

XXIX

The Age of Santa Anna

> The new rulers of independent Mexico were the military . . .
> Law was their will; assassination and betrayal were their weap-
> ons; their price was the wealth of their country.
>
> LESLEY BYRD SIMPSON *

T HE former viceroyalty of New Spain presented a dreary picture indeed in the decades immediately following independence. Throughout its whole, vast extent there was no order, no peace, no security. The greatest and the richest of Spain's former dominions had become the most miserable of independent states. Probably in no other region of Latin America, with the exception of French Saint Domingue, had the wars of independence so utterly destroyed the fabric of society. In no other place had the excesses of the old order provoked dissenting priests into leading hordes of ignorant and untrained Indians in an orgy of plunder and rapine and to their eventual slaughter at the hands of Spanish soldiery. Nowhere else did the struggle degenerate so completely into a mad mêlée of warring factions fighting without purpose, without understanding, without identification of principles or objectives. A struggle that began as an assertion of freedom from the misgovernment of Spain and the oppression of the military and religious oligarchy became so confused that independence was finally achieved under a counter-

---

* *Many Mexicos*, University of California Press, Berkeley, copyright 1941, 1946, 1952, p. 199.

revolutionary movement in opposition to the 'radical' constitutional system proclaimed by the Spanish monarchy in 1820.

Independence, of course, did not put an end to the difficulties. It only cut the last weak cord that tied the vast region to the rotting tree of empire and the one remaining source of order and stability. Agustín Iturbide, whose defection from the Spanish cause at Iguala turned the tables on Spain, found himself in a very dubious position. An avowed monarchist, he had just thrown his army against the remaining feeble forces of Fernando VII. A strong supporter of the Catholic Church and the privileges of the clergy, he had just allied himself with the anti-clerical republican revolutionaries; and, as an ally of the republicans, he proclaimed the continuance of monarchy and the virtues of the old order. Had Iturbide been a man of great ability and political astuteness, he might have gotten away with his utterly opportunistic anomalisms and united a majority of the factions behind him. He was no such man. On the contrary, he was a vain autocrat of little tact and no patience. His personal ambition led him to believe that with the army behind him he could succeed in any unscrupulous act of deception and betrayal. He overlooked the fundamental difficulty of keeping the support of the army without money.

The aged viceroy O'Donojú had accepted the Plan of Iguala under duress. The Spanish government rejected it. At this juncture, Iturbide found himself looking down what appeared to be an open road to the emperorship of his headless monarchy. He had little support from the Bourbon sympathizers, who could see no sign of the required royal blood in the up-start mestizo. Likewise, the numerous republicans rejected his royal pretensions, for they were in no mood to countenance monarchy whoever the king or emperor might be. But these groups were paralyzed by the lack of either program or leadership. Iturbide was strong enough to form a provisional junta and a committee of regency, both of which he headed. A congress was called into being with due care exercised that the membership was predominantly monarchist in sentiment. Iturbide immediately encountered difficulty with his congress, however, for it was truly a do-nothing legislative body. It failed to provide needed fiscal support for the military and was particularly disinclined to support the ambitions of Iturbide for a crown. Bourbon monarchists and republicans drew together in their common distrust of the regency chairman. There was serious danger that lack of action and general dissatisfaction with the government would bring about the downfall of the regime. Frustrated and desperate, Iturbide decided to move things along a bit in his own way.

The regency chief had sufficient army support to stage in the capital an impressive parade and demonstration. The chanted theme of the participants was 'Viva Agustín Primero.' The cry was soon taken up by the rabble and a large crowd gathered in front of the regency building demanding the appearance of the prospective monarch. The 'reluctant' chief acceded to the popular clamor and consented to accept the crown. The coronation took place in July of 1822.

Mexico's upstart 'emperor' quickly set about strengthening his grip on the country. Congress, which had been frightened by the Mexico City mob into voting for Iturbide's coronation, remained cold to the executive's proposals. It would vote no taxes and it would not work seriously on a constitution. Finally, Iturbide imprisoned fifteen members of the legislative body, dissolved the congress and reconstituted it with fewer and more tractable deputies, but to no effect. Thereupon he began ruling openly as dictator and the sole and final authority in the government.

One of Iturbide's first steps as 'emperor' was to attempt to secure recognition of his authority throughout all the mainland region that had been New Spain. The captaincy-general of Guatemala had proclaimed its independence from Spain in the late summer of 1821 after word arrived of the events transpiring in Mexico. Iturbide had sent an invitation to join in the new Mexican state, and deputies from the former captaincy-general were present in Iturbide's congress. Difficulty arose, however, when it became apparent that a monarchy was to be retained and that Iturbide was to be the emperor, for republican feeling ran strong throughout most of Central America. Adherence to Mexico, furthermore, was by no means an entirely acceptable course of action to all provinces of the former captaincy-general. Leaders in Salvador openly opposed such a step, and those in Honduras, Nicaragua, and Costa Rica were little more enthusiastic. In Nicaragua and Costa Rica, inter-city squabbles loomed large in local affairs and the question of association with the central region of the former viceroyalty received little attention. Iturbide, nevertheless, sent an army to enforce his imperial authority, but it made little headway beyond Guatemala. It was stalled near San Salvador when word came that the 'emperor' had found it convenient to seek employment elsewhere and that a republican regime had been proclaimed in Mexico City. The Mexican army thereupon withdrew, and a general assembly was called in Guatemala City to decide upon a future course of action. At the assembly, the five provinces determined to join in the formation of an independent federation to be known as the United Provinces of Central America. Only the remote region of Chiapas, which had in the past been a part of the Guatemalan captaincy-general, remained with Mexico. Both Mexico and the United Provinces were far too preoccupied with their own internal problems to do more than mark for future dispute the issue of the political fate of the primitive jungle district between them.

Mexico made no move with respect to the Spanish insular possessions, which were left to shift for themselves. Neither Puerto Rico nor Cuba was sufficiently strong to cast off Spanish domination unaided, for the mother country held them far more firmly than she had Santo Domingo, which had been absorbed by Haiti in 1821. As noted earlier, abortive uprisings had been easily crushed in Puerto Rico in 1815; and after Spain in 1820 restored the liberal Constitution of 1812, the privilege of having a colonial assembly and representation in the Spanish Cortes calmed revolutionaries in both Puerto Rico and Cuba. Liberalism in Spain was short-lived, and when, in 1823, the king regained his autocratic authority and restored rigid control over the internal affairs of the colonies, restlessness became rife, particularly in Cuba. Puerto Rico was too isolated to make much pretense of revolt, and Cuba was too heavily garrisoned with Spanish soldiery to leave independence leaders much hope of success.

Mexico was quite unable to provide assistance to any other region of the empire in its struggle for independence, not even to the islands that had formerly been under the nominal jurisdiction of the viceroy at Mexico City. The crusading spirit that brought Bolívar and San Martín together in Peru from opposite ends of the South American continent had no counterpart in the independence movements north of Panamá. The ambitious 'emperor' Agustín was unable to hold the continental realm together; much less was he able to embark upon an insular campaign.

Iturbide's reign was short. Having no claim to regal status, he did his best to make up for this lack by show and extravagance. He created a new nobility whose members immediately became the objects of ridicule and buffoonery. The treasury was already bare, and to finance his pretentious display of imperial pomp, Iturbide turned to the expedient of exacting forced loans from the wealthy — a measure designed to win him few friends. His high-handed methods, his extreme clericalism, his utterly ridiculous pretensions, and his wanton waste of public funds in the midst of poverty converted more monarchists into republicans than the exhortations of political theorists could ever have done. Iturbide even committed the cardinal sin of forgetting his military supporters. Some of them he snubbed; most of them he left unpaid. When the congress would vote him no funds, he flooded the country with worthless paper scrip. Conditions quickly went from bad to worse, and the machinery of state ground to a halt.

Too late did the would-be monarch realize his mistakes and seek to conciliate his detractors. In vain he searched for supporters; none remained. In December of 1822, an able and opportunistic military leader whom the 'emperor' had snubbed, the commandant at Veracruz, saw his opportunity and pronounced against the 'empire.' The commandant, Antonio López de Santa Anna, was a mere upstart, and his pronunciamiento would have appeared absurd had the atmosphere been less volatile. But others were of like mind, and the faltering Iturbide was helpless to check the rising tide of opposition. In February of 1823 he resigned and accepted a pension voted in token of his services to the country and granted on condition that he leave Mexico and not return.

Iturbide went to Italy, but in exile he showed even less wisdom than he had demonstrated at home. He planned to return. Within two years, ignorant of the fact that his enemies were aware of his designs and had moved to forestall him, Iturbide landed on Mexican soil. He was arrested immediately, and his subsequent execution was carried out within a matter of days. Would-be Mexican emperors of the future would have done well to ponder this lesson.

With the departure of Iturbide, Mexico entered upon a period that has come to be known as the 'Age of Santa Anna,' certainly the most dismal period in all Mexican history. Vain, arrogant, shrewd, and beset with a profound sense of boredom that verged on psychosis, Santa Anna amazed the world by his comings and goings, his military exploits, his skill at political manipulation. For over thirty years he dominated the Mexican political stage, and under his guiding hand the once magnificent colonial kingdom reached the nadir of national calamity. In vain have historians and students of government sought to explain the strange hold that this prince of caudillos maintained on the minds and emotions of his countrymen. No less than eleven times did he step to the center of the stage to direct the destinies of Mexico, and eleven times he let his people down. Yet in each new national crisis some fool was always ready to call back the 'hero' of Manga de Clavo.* Perhaps the greatest tribute ever paid the man was the decision of a museum curator to hang his autographed picture upon the wall of the Lee Chapel museum in Lexington, Virginia, where the likeness of the dashing Mexican general looks down upon the skeleton of Robert E. Lee's famous horse.

Santa Anna did not lead the movement that overthrew the government of Iturbide. Although he had been the first to pronounce for a republic, he remained at Veracruz and prepared to flee the country if others did not come to his support. The chief figure to emerge from the chaos of Iturbide's downfall was Guadalupe Vic-

* Manga de Clavo was Santa Anna's estate in Veracruz.

toria, the popular general who had played an important role in the revolutionary army of Morelos. Guadalupe Victoria had broken early with the would-be emperor and had been residing in self-imposed exile in the mountains above Veracruz, but with the first mutterings of revolution he came forth and headed the army of 'liberation.' He became Mexico's first president.

The new congress, summoned after the downfall of the 'empire,' drew up Mexico's first republican constitution. The document represented the views of the extreme liberals who dominated the congress, and provided for a decentralized federal system of nineteen states and several territories. The three branches of government — executive, legislative, and judicial — were patterned closely after those of the United States, except that the president and vice-president were to be chosen by the state legislatures rather than by an electoral college, and the president was not permitted to succeed himself. An important innovation was introduced in that the church was deprived of its monopoly over education.

The new constitution was an absurdity in Mexico. Its idealism was excellent, but the realities of Mexican social and political life belied its underlying assumptions. The states, for the most part artificial creations of the law, were not homogeneous political units. They possessed no traditions of self-government nor had they any experience in the use of legislative bodies. The majority of the population in all the states was composed of illiterate Indians and mestizos accustomed only to a life of servitude and social segregation. Their participation in government as independent voting citizens would have run counter to the fundamental scheme of social existence and to their very outlook on life. They could only blindly respond to the exhortations of the clerics or follow the instructions of the local caudillos and politicos who plied them with pulque and herded them in drunken hordes to the polls. Many, still living in the back-country wilds where the rudiments of the Spanish language had not even reached them, were completely outside the orbit of political life.

Of fundamental importance was the absence of any sort of consensus of political opinion. No group or class seemed willing to place the interest of the new nation above what it conceived to be its own selfish interest. Compromise, the very essence of republican and democratic government, was utterly alien to the spirit of even the most altruistic of political leaders.

Given these difficulties, the new government did remarkably well for the first four years. Guadalupe Victoria, upon being chosen to the presidency, had sufficient military backing to maintain himself in office and serve out his term. He was not strong enough, however, to face realistically the problems that confronted his administration. The most pressing problems were financial. With commerce and industry disrupted by the years of revolution and chaos and with Indian tribute abolished, revenues were wholly inadequate. Expenditures, two-thirds of which were absorbed by a bloated military establishment, far exceeded available resources. Faced with this dilemma, the government under Guadalupe Victoria's leadership turned to a disastrous expedient. It borrowed from abroad. Loans were negotiated with London bankers at exorbitant discount rates and the money squandered in useless military expenditures. Thus was inaugurated a sequence of financial manipulations that created crisis after crisis. Viewed in retrospect, it is difficult to see who were the bigger dupes, the foreign money lenders or the Mexican politicians. The government was seldom able to pay even the interest on its loans, and the foreign investors, unable to collect their accounts, turned to their governments to have political pressure exerted on the irresponsible officials of the Mexican republic. Financial default became the standing issue of Mexican diplomatic negotiations, and in the end it was a major factor in attracting foreign military adventurers to Mexican soil. The consequences of Guadalupe Victoria's policies were hardly to be foreseen during his four-year term of office, but the precedent of irresponsibility in fiscal policy was firmly adhered to by his even more irresponsible successors.

The government's weakness lay in the fact that it was utterly dependent upon the military, and the military were a pack of gluttonous wolves interested only in their regular feed. Victoria's government was opposed by the church, by the landowners, and by the conservative Scottish-rite Masons. The president did not care to risk certain revolution by attempting to tax the wealth of these groups. He found himself in a vicious trap and took what seemed the only course open to him. His path was made much easier by the intrigue of foreign agents. H. G. Ward, the British chargé d'affaires, and Joel Poinsett, the American minister, competed strenuously for influence over the new government. The tactless Poinsett, working in alliance with the York-rite Masons, made himself so obnoxious that his recall was requested, but not until he had become deeply involved in Mexican politics. Lucas Alamán, a powerful conservative aristocrat, was strongly favorable to British interests during the many times he was in the government as a minister of state, and to his pro-British sentiment was due in part the success enjoyed by Ward in tying the new government to the coat-tails of British financiers. The British played a vigorous game of sterling diplomacy, and their interest grew apace with favorable trade agreements and heavy investments in Mexican mining stock and other commercial enterprises. Mexico took her first steps toward becoming an economic dependency of alien powers.

In the election of 1828 General Manuel Gómez Pedraza, a former officer of the Spanish army, was chosen president by the state legislatures. The vote was ten to nine, each state having one vote. Gómez Pedraza was a strong conservative with support from the church and the Scottish-rite Masons, and the liberal-republican opposition whose defeated candidate had been an old revolutionary general, Vicente Guerrero, refused to accept the electoral verdict. Guerrero pronounced against the president-elect.

For four years little had been heard from Veracruz. Now the young commandant decided once again to take a hand in national politics. Santa Anna pronounced in support of Guerrero, insisting that he would not stand idly by and see the Inquisition re-established by the conservatives. Gómez Pedraza attempted to crush the uprising and he might have been successful had he not broadened his attack to crush other political adversaries who were not in revolt. Other factions pronounced and the president-elect left the country. In January of 1829, the retiring Victoria handed over the government to Guerrero. Again Santa Anna had triggered the overthrow of the national government, but his role in the hostilities had been inconsequential. He was not yet a hero.

Santa Anna soon had a better opportunity. Fernando VII noted the chaos prevailing in Mexico, and he decided to send an army to restore order in what he considered still to be his colony. The army was landed at Tampico where it took the fortress, only to be abandoned by the fleet that had brought it. Santa Anna rushed from Veracruz to accept the surrender of a fever-ridden expeditionary force with no line of retreat. Now he was a hero, and the country began to take notice of him.

The Spanish attempt to recover the former colony touched off a new series of reprisals against Spanish-born residents of Mexico City. It was an opportunity for more looting and destruction, and the mob rose to the occasion. A considerable exodus occurred among the Spanish merchant class, and the economy of the country was further weakened by the decrease in commercial activity. Guerrero was unable to maintain order and reaction set in against him. His vice-president, Anastasio Bustamante, plotted his overthrow, and in 1830 a defection of the army permitted Bustamante to take over the government. Guerrero fled, only to be delivered up to the authorities for execution by an Italian sea captain at Acapulco in exchange for 50,000 pesos. Santa Anna talked loudly, but remained in Veracruz.

Bustamante ruled Mexico for two years, but he was a tool of the reactionaries. Lucas Alamán directed national policies, and for the first time since the overthrow of Iturbide the conservatives enjoyed the fruits of office. A military dictatorship was imposed that ruled by terror and violence in the name of religion and the privileges of the military caste. Santa Anna bided his time and when the inevitable reaction set in, fanned by the execution of the revolutionary hero, Guerrero, he made a new pronouncement. Others followed and Bustamante retired, leaving the government in the hands of the man who had been constitutionally elected in

1828, General Gómez Pedraza. In the turmoil that followed during the spring of 1833, Santa Anna was chosen president.

Beginning with his pronouncement against Iturbide in 1822, Santa Anna's campaign for the presidency had been a long one. Perhaps the Veracruz commandant was not really campaigning after all. When the day of his inauguration arrived, he stayed home at Manga de Clavo. His vice-president, Valentín Gómez Farías, took office as acting president, and Santa Anna let him have a free hand, or, more aptly, all the rope he needed to hang himself. Santa Anna was a coquet who enjoyed power only for the sheer love of wielding it. He had no desire to administer the affairs of state, for he had no objectives in view, no program to accomplish. He wished only to toy with the government and with the lives and fortunes of the sycophants who waited eagerly for their cues. He wanted to be begged, wheedled, and cajoled until finally, bored with his flatterers, he would turn and destroy them and look for some new diversion. What a man to choose for president of a struggling new republic!

Gómez Farías was no sycophant. He was an able liberal leader determined to place the Mexican governmental house in order. Supported by a liberal congress, he embarked upon far-reaching reforms. He struck at the resources of the church by making the payment of tithes voluntary, by assuming control over church patronage, by closing the Indian missions in California, and by limiting the jurisdiction of the ecclesiastical courts. Like other 'liberals' he wanted to deprive the church of its prerogatives and still preserve the state's right of patronage. Then he turned to the problem of reducing the military to size, proposing to decrease their number and curtail the special judicial immunities they enjoyed.

Gómez Farías lasted about a year. Santa Anna stood aside and allowed matters to take their course, interfering only occasionally. In the meantime, the conservative political factions became increasingly incensed. Army officers and the church united their voices in the cry of *religión y fueros,* or 'religion and privileges.' Someone must be found to deliver them from the liberal regime that was attacking the very foundation of their privileged existence. They turned, of course, to Santa Anna; and after sufficient coaxing he responded. In the spring of 1834, the 'savior of religion' threw out the man he himself had placed in power and assumed absolute control of the government. All along he had been the master, but every so often he felt called upon to reverse the whole political system lest anyone forget who was calling the tune. So degraded had political life become that Santa Anna had little difficulty in reasserting his power. The liberals who had originally supported him for the presidency were crushed and demoralized. Gómez Farías and other leaders were hounded into exile.

It is not important to detail here all the political shifts and maneuvers that took place in the years immediately following the return to power of the conservatives in 1834. Santa Anna did not long remain in office but retired again to his Veracruz estate. He much preferred to play cat and mouse than to rule the country, always pouncing again just when the mouse was about to make good its escape. One by one the mice died, and the country grew weaker and weaker.

Between 1835 and 1848 conditions in all of Mexico went from bad to worse. The same was true in Central America. It was a period of political fragmentation and economic collapse. There was imminent danger that the entire region would break down into a multitude of anarchic little states, and indeed there were times when even ineffective government virtually disappeared and only roving bands of barefoot soldiery dared venture upon the roads of the countryside.

It is not really surprising that Mexico was unable to retain her vast domains. Every outlying region was lightly held, and the continuous struggle for control of the central government left little time for attention to affairs in the states and territories. It was on the northeastern frontier that the first signs of disintegration appeared. Anglo-Saxon settlers from the United States began to enter the territory of Texas as early as 1824 under a concession granted by the Mexican government to Stephen Austin, an American frontiersman of venturesome spirit who was interested in the

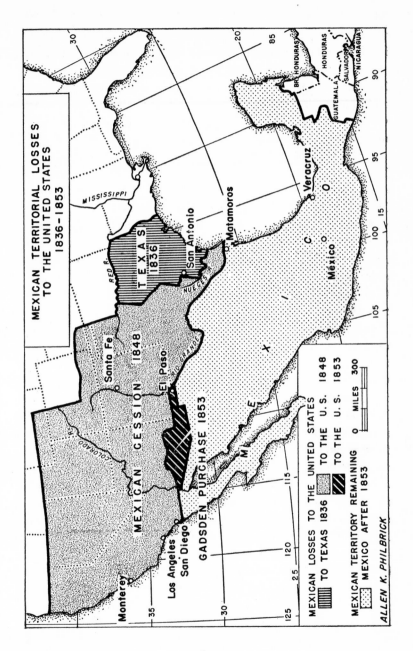

MEXICAN TERRITORIAL LOSSES
TO THE UNITED STATES
1836-1853

MEXICAN LOSSES TO THE UNITED STATES
TO TEXAS 1836
TO THE U.S. 1848
TO THE U.S. 1853

MEXICAN TERRITORY REMAINING
MEXICO AFTER 1853

MILES
0   300

TEXAS 1836

MEXICAN CESSION 1848

GADSDEN PURCHASE 1853

MEXICO

Monterey
Los Angeles
San Diego
Santa Fe
El Paso
San Antonio
Matamoros
Veracruz

MISSISSIPPI
RED R.
NUECES R.
RIO GRANDE
COLORADO R.

BR. HONDURAS
HONDURAS
GUATEMALA
SALVADOR
NICARAGUA

ALLEN K. PHILBRICK

rich land along the Brazos river. Mexico was at first anxious to have its northern land settled, but as time went on the increasing hazard to national sovereignty in the region became apparent. There were few Mexicans in Texas when the original concession was made, and the English-speaking settlers lived unto themselves. They were even exempt from taxation under the terms of Austin's agreement, as well as under those of later grants.

As the alien population continued to mount Mexican leaders began to perceive the danger. Many of the settlers were unruly characters seeking escape from their creditors or from the sheriff in the United States; they could hardly be expected to mend their ways upon becoming Mexican subjects. Others brought slaves with them, even though slavery in Mexico was nearly unknown. An almost constant squabble over land claims gave rise to disorder and caused Mexican officials much concern. Steps were therefore taken to curb the influx of American settlers and restrict the influence of those already established in Mexico.

The Mexican congress enacted several laws intended to discourage further settlement. One enactment abolished slavery throughout the republic and another prohibited the entry of non-Catholics. An attempt was made to collect customs duties at the frontier. When these measures proved ineffective and a survey by a prominent Mexican official indicated that slavery continued to prevail and that non-Catholics were still entering the country in large numbers, more drastic action was taken. In 1830 a decree was issued prohibiting further colonization from the United States, and troops were sent into the Texas region to enforce the law and insure the collection of customs duties. In addition, Mexican settlers were urged to enter Texas to counter-balance the large Anglo-Saxon population. These measures, while more effective than any of those previously taken, had the immediate effect of inflaming the Texas settlers to the point of rebellion.

Mexican leaders had good reason to be alarmed about the future status of the 15,000 or more Americans living inside the Texas boundaries. That prominent leaders in the United States had designs upon the region was well known. While Minister to Mexico Joel Poinsett had indicated the possibility of purchase; others were inclined to argue that the Texas territory was part of the vast tract of land included in the ill-defined Louisiana Purchase which brought the Mississippi valley and land to the west into the United States in 1803. Lucas Alamán was particularly distrustful of the intentions of Mexico's northern neighbor, and his fears were transmitted to many of those around him. British agents and diplomats in Mexico City, ever vengeful in their attitude toward the United States and jealous of the growing power of the former British dominions, missed no opportunity to play skillfully upon Mexican misgivings. The cold fact of the matter was, however, that once settlers from the United States had moved into Texas in large numbers and established their homes there, nothing short of a miracle could have prevented the loss of that region by the Mexican republic. Not even Santa Anna was adept at performing this kind of miracle, although it must be said that he tried.

The inevitable might have been postponed had Texas been granted separate statehood in the Mexican federal system. Stephen Austin realized this and went to Mexico City to argue the case for autonomy, but he was jailed for his trouble. When open resistance to Mexican authority broke out in San Antonio, Santa Anna recruited an army and headed north.

In February of 1836 Santa Anna reached San Antonio in command of an ill-equipped and ill-trained Mexican army. He found the Texans disorganized. Austin, released from prison in Mexico, had rushed to Washington in the hope of securing aid from the United States. A group of 150 settlers and adventurers had formed a defensive force. Too few in numbers to face Santa Anna in open combat, they turned an old mission building, the Alamo, into a fortress and prepared to defend it. The Texans were commanded by William Barrett Travis. Santa Anna surrounded and attacked the Alamo fortress, but was at first repulsed. Finally, after a brief siege, the Mexican army broke through the Texan defenses and a fight to the death ensued — a fight in which every last defender died. No quarter was given, and there is little to indicate that any was asked.

In the meantime, a rump convention held in eastern Texas had issued a declaration of Texan independence. A government was formed and a military commander was named to defend it. The commander was Sam Houston, a true adventurer capable, when sober, of directing frontier warfare in true Western style. Now the issue was finally drawn, and Santa Anna had the choice of returning to Mexico to boast of his accomplishments in San Antonio or of adding to his exploits by crushing rebellion throughout the Texas territory. He chose the latter course and soon came to regret his decision. His first efforts were highly encouraging, for Texans fled eastward before his armies in complete confusion, and it appeared that the erstwhile Yankees might be driven from Mexican soil without so much as a major skirmish. Near the San Jacinto river, however, Houston prepared for battle, and the foolish Santa Anna, confident that he held the initiative, took few precautions against a Texan attack. Shortly before his dinner hour Santa Anna was rudely awakened from a siesta by heavy gunfire and shouts of 'Remember the Alamo!' There was no opportunity for defense, and the Mexican army was quickly decimated or captured while the great general fled the scene of battle dressed in his red carpet slippers.

Santa Anna's defeat was climaxed by his capture the day after the battle and his narrow escape from on-the-spot execution. Finally, however, he was spared and sent to the United States to discuss his problems with Andrew Jackson. Unfortunately for Mexico, the American government finally sent him home. Texas was in fact independent, barred from entry into the United States by northern fear of adding new slave territory to the Union, and separated from Mexico by a gulf of hatred that would endure for years. The Mexican government firmly refused to recognize Texas' claim to independence, but it made no serious effort to reconquer the region by military action. Mexico was encouraged in its refusal by the sorry state of Texan affairs and the failure of

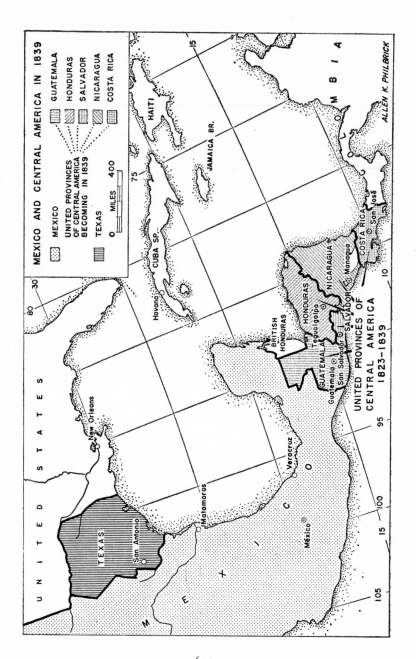

MEXICO AND CENTRAL AMERICA IN 1839

MEXICO

UNITED PROVINCES
OF CENTRAL AMERICA
BECOMING IN 1839

TEXAS

GUATEMALA

HONDURAS

SALVADOR

NICARAGUA

COSTA RICA

0   MILES   400

UNITED PROVINCES OF
CENTRAL AMERICA
1823-1839

ALLEN K. PHILBRICK

Texan military undertakings against Mexican settlements in New Mexico and Tamaulipas. The Texas republic appeared to be destined for a short career.

In other parts of the former Spanish viceroyalty matters were little better. From its inception the confederation in Central America was torn by controversy. At first the major issue was the authority of the church and the relationship it should bear to the republican authorities. Liberalism in religious matters centered in Salvador where efforts were made to secularize education and where a local priest, Matías Delgado, secured the creation of a separate diocese and an appointment as its first bishop. The archbishop at Guatemala City opposed this arrangement vigorously. Manuel José Arce, elected president of the confederation in 1825 as a candidate of the liberal forces, soon indicated that his sympathies lay with the archbishop, and his earlier backers felt that they had been betrayed. In 1826, passions inflamed by the exhortations of the clerics reached the boiling point; the vice-governor of Guatemala, a liberal, was assassinated by an incited mob. Open warfare followed.

There emerged during the ensuing struggle a distinguished yet tragic figure who was to devote his entire life to the causes of liberalism and Central American union. The man, Francisco Morazán, was a Honduran by birth, but in the seemingly endless military campaigns in which he was forced to engage he became increasingly identified with the liberal faction of Salvador. He drew support in varying degrees from Honduras, Nicaragua, and Costa Rica. He had a small group of followers in Guatemala, which he entered in 1829 at the head of a liberal revolutionary army determined to re-establish order throughout the confederation and to expel the archbishop and his supporters — including Arce — who were felt not only to have disrupted the peace within the confederation but to have betrayed the republican movement in interests of the church and restoration of the Spanish monarchy. Morazán became the chief executive of the confederation in fact, and he was officially elected to the presidency by the congress when complete order was restored.

The period between 1829 and 1837 was characterized by tremendous efforts at reform within the confederation. Morazán
ruled as a virtual dictator, but he enjoyed great popularity as a
military hero and vigorous political leader. He was intensely hated
by the church and all the conservative political forces that opposed
the many changes he inaugurated. Under his leadership the liberal
congress decreed the end of all religious orders and dis-established
the church; at the same time he declared that religious freedom
should prevail throughout the confederation. Many buildings and
other properties that had formerly belonged to the church were
taken over by the state and used for other purposes, including
public schools. Efforts were made to bring new immigrants to the
country, and some attention was given to the development of roads.
Even the old Spanish legal codes were revised to accord with the
new republican regime.

Many problems troubled Morazán and his liberal followers in
congress and in the administration, however. The major centers
of confederation activity were in the northwest, in Guatemala
City and San Salvador. Honduras, Nicaragua, and Costa Rica, as
states within the confederation, enjoyed a high degree of autonomy, but their own internal problems increasingly absorbed
their attention and tended to isolate them from the main stream
of central government activity and controversy. Morazán's problems with Guatemala and Salvador were sufficiently vexing to
keep him completely occupied. At one point the capital was
transferred to San Salvador to reduce the influence of Guatemala
and to provide a more central location within the confederation.
This only served to create further friction, and a continuous effort
was necessary to preserve order by putting down incipient revolts
and movements toward secession.

Throughout Morazán's administration the church continued its
battle to influence the minds of the people in favor of restoration
of the old order. Natural phenomena were pointed out to the
ignorant Indians as manifestations of divine wrath at the atheistic
and sacrilegious activities of the liberals. No Indians in Central
America were more ignorant and superstitious and more docile in

the hands of the priests than those of the Guatemalan back country. It was among these Indians that the religious finally found a willing tool and able leader in the person of an illiterate pig-driver. In 1837 a cholera epidemic ravaged the countryside, and unscrupulous clerics spread the rumor that the liberals and foreigners were poisoning the water. Supported by the church, Rafael Carrera left his pigs to assume the role of divine emissary to lead his people against the liberals and foreigners who, he was told, were bent upon destruction of religion and the Indian race.

Soon all of back-country Guatemala was inflamed and Carrera was able to take Guatemala City, where he promptly instituted a reign of terror. Many liberals fled to the old capital, Antigua, where they awaited the coming of Morazán from San Salvador to restore order. At first Morazán was successful. He defeated the Indian forces in the streets of Guatemala City, but he could not reconquer the hinterland. Blocked for the time being, he returned to San Salvador, where he remained until expiration of his presidential term in 1839. The confederation was falling apart, and the states took steps toward secession, encouraged in this move by the federal congress whose members saw little hope of preserving the union.

Morazán was unwilling to see the confederation dissolved. Organizing an army of Salvadoreños, he headed west to do battle once again with Carrera. He set up his headquarters temporarily at Ahuachapán, and near there he inflicted defeat upon a conservative contingent sent against him. Moving on to Guatemala City, he saw his luck run out, for Carrera defeated him badly. Now Morazán's fickle following vanished into thin air. His former friends turned their backs on him and refused him welcome even in San Salvador. After two years of exile in South America he was induced to come to Costa Rica where he was shortly betrayed and executed. The year was 1842; the confederation was at an end and its most able proponent and defender was dead.

With the disintegration of the Central American confederation, each of the five participant states went its own way. Discussions of reconstituting the union were held from time to time by representatives of the affected nations, but they all came to naught. Rafael Carrera ruled Guatemala for over twenty-five years. Possibly well meaning, he was far too ignorant to carry out any manner of constructive program. He was sufficiently shrewd, however, to maintain himself firmly in office and to prevent the conservatives and clerics from dominating him completely. His was a dictatorial regime in which liberalism and liberals had no part, and the country made little progress in any direction.

Internal disorder within any country invites international difficulties. Property becomes less secure, including that held by aliens; and it is common practice for all powers, particularly the major ones, to intercede in behalf of their nationals when the welfare of such nationals is threatened abroad. The disorder prevailing in Mexico and Central America caused serious property loss to many alien residents, and European powers took up the claims of their citizens and attempted collection through diplomatic channels. France made such an attempt in Mexico in 1838.

The question of damage claims cannot be regarded as basic in the many maneuvers of France, England, and the United States in the Caribbean area during the middle of the nineteenth century. The two European countries were predatory hunters after territory, economic and political advantage, and international prestige. Political leaders in the United States were not wholly innocent of pretensions along these lines. The struggle between the slave-holding and the non-slave-holding states of the Union had its international ramifications. Southern leaders looked upon Cuba, for instance, as ripe for annexation to the United States as new slave territory. Efforts were made to puchase the island from Spain on more than one occasion after 1845, and twice, in 1850 and 1851, filibustering expeditions to free Cuba from Spain were organized by Cuban independence leaders on United States soil with financial support from pro-slavery factions within the country. Britain and France furthered their imperialistic designs on a far more official basis, however. Their warships cruised the Caribbean waters and France exerted almost continuous pressure upon Haiti while Britain extended her influence and control southward along the Atlantic coast of Central America from her base at Belize.

In 1838 French warships blockaded the Mexican port of Veracruz in an effort to force the Mexican government to recognize claims of French citizens for compensation for property damage which they claimed to have suffered as a consequence of the general disorder prevailing in the country. One of the claims, and only a very minor one, was for 800 pesos on behalf of a French baker in Tacubaya whose pastries had been confiscated one night by an unruly group of Mexican army officers. The Mexican president, Bustamante, refused payment of what he considered quite correctly an exorbitant claim of 600,000 pesos to cover a variety of minor losses, including that of the baker. Finally the French admiral fired upon the old fortress of San Juan de Ulúa and forced its surrender. The Mexican government declared war upon France, and the famous 'Pastry War' ensued.

No more able leader could be found to lead the Mexican army against the French than Santa Anna. Here was a chance to vindicate himself for the debacle at San Jacinto. The French took the whole affair rather lightly, and from their position in control of the fortress and the harbor they seemed quite content to let Santa Anna control the city. Again the frustrated Santa Anna went to sleep. He was rudely awakened by the approach of a French landing force conducting a small raid into the city. Santa Anna fled in his underwear. Soon he came back as the French were returning to their boats, and at the head of his troops he attacked. Then, as one historian has so incomparably described the event, 'the god of luck took him by the hand and led him into the path of a French cannonball.' * Santa Anna lost his left leg below the knee. Now all was vindicated! San Jacinto was forgotten! Mexico's hero was a hero again.

Guaranteed payment of the 600,000 pesos, the French squadron withdrew. The war was over and Santa Anna was ready for new

* Simpson, *op. cit.*, p. 215.

adventures in the wonderland of political activity. Shortly he was again president of Mexico, and his in-again, out-again approach to the acceptance of political responsibility continued. Each sojourn in the presidential palace, however, cost the country enormously. Increased taxes, illegal levies, forced loans, all produced new funds for the general to squander in personal display and ostentation. True, the dictator undertook some rather important public works activities in Mexico City; but in addition to paving a few streets he also erected a monument to himself and had constructed a costly cenotaph for the severed portion of his leg, which was brought from Manga de Clavo and paraded through Mexico City to its new resting place.

Now once again in the midst of Mexico's distress the issue of Texas came to the fore. Northern resistance to annexation in the United States was weakening, particularly as Britain was showing more than a casual interest in the tottering republic. Finally, in the spring of 1845 annexation was approved by the United States Congress. Mexico promptly broke off diplomatic relations with her northern neighbor, but with an empty treasury and generals 'pronouncing' from every quarter, her ability to wage war was far from impressive. For a time matters drifted without any overt act or a genuine declaration of hostilities. Perhaps the crisis would pass. Those who hoped for peace, however, reckoned without considering the objectives of James K. Polk, the new president of the United States, or the foolhardiness of the 'hero' of San Jacinto, Antonio López de Santa Anna.

Ambitious expansionists in the United States had long looked covetously at the vast expanse of territory stretching westward from Texas and including the far Pacific coast region known as California. Mexico's claim to Santa Fe and the surrounding area of New Mexico dated far back to the early days of Spanish colonization in the New World, but the Pacific coast territory had been effectively occupied and settled only in the latter half of the eighteenth century. California remained sparsely populated with the principal towns located along the line of the mission chain founded by the Franciscan fathers. The missions, following the secularization laws of Gómez Farías, had gone into decline, and Mexico's hold upon the region was tenuous at best.

Life for the scattered cattle ranchers who dwelt in the rolling hills along the Pacific was idyllic indeed. They were few in number and their vast land grants extended for miles in all directions. With the breakdown of Mexican governmental institutions, they ceased to be bothered by arbitrary edicts and exactions of transitory politicians who swarmed in and out of Mexico City. The hacendados conducted their own affairs in autonomous complacency. Such a situation was most inviting to land-hungry European powers, and England particularly showed considerable interest in acquiring California. The possibility of a French venture along the Pacific was not out of the question, and Russia, with numerous outposts in the far northwest corner of the continent, likewise could not be overlooked as a potential west-coast neighbor of the United States. American statesmen, looking into the future and dreaming of a nation of continental dimensions, could not fail to see the disadvantages of any European power acquiring a new foothold along the Pacific coast. If Mexico was too weak to hold California, the better part of wisdom called for the United States to occupy it. President Polk was poignantly aware of the need for prompt action, and the acquisition of California became one of the key objectives of his foreign policy.

The Texas issue played squarely into the hands of the American expansionists. Firmly the United States set about settlement of the Texas issue by linking it to the purchase of California. While diplomatic relations between Mexico and the United States remained severed, President Polk made what he hoped would be a conciliatory gesture and sent to confer with President Herrera of Mexico a special envoy with the rank of minister, John Slidell. His mission was to negotiate a settlement on the various matters of disagreement between the two governments. In exchange for Mexican recognition of the annexation of Texas to the Union and the establishment of a suitable boundary line, he might offer to absorb a considerable amount of outstanding claims by American citizens against the Mexican government and to purchase California for a substantial sum of money that would go far toward replenishing the Mexican treasury.

Polk reckoned with little understanding of Mexican politics and no understanding of a people's patriotic sensitivities. Perhaps he thought that all Mexican presidents had as few scruples as Santa Anna. José Joaquín Herrera had come to the presidency in 1844 as a result of a revolt of the moderates against Santa Anna. Although the 'hero' had been temporarily exiled, Herrera's position was far from secure. He dared not show any sign of weakness, such as a willingness to compromise over the Texas issue. He refused to treat with Slidell, even though there were indications that he would have liked to do so. Slidell was sent home. Even this action did not satisfy the Mexicans, and General Mariano Paredes overthrew the government. He would lead his country to war. But this was a miscalculation; only one man could lead the country to war against the United States. Santa Anna answered the call.

The dismissal of Slidell by Herrera produced a strong reaction in the United States, and American troops were sent to the Río Grande, into a region beyond the Nueces river which the Texans claimed but never occupied. Paredes, then still president in Mexico, regarded this as an act of war and ordered the American advance to be resisted by force. A detachment of American soldiers was attacked and some killed, others captured. President Polk asked Congress for a declaration and the war was on. This was April, 1846.

General Zachary Taylor moved into northern Mexico from Texas. He captured Matamoros and then Monterrey. Saltillo also fell, and there he set up his headquarters. In the meantime, California was taken over by the American navy after a transitory republic was set up under the leadership of John C. Frémont, a visitor from the United States. An expeditionary force prepared to land at Veracruz under the command of General Winfield Scott. Mexico's position seemed hopeless.

In league with Gómez Farías, again returned from exile, Santa Anna proceeded to organize an army by impressment, while funds were raised by a forced levy upon the church. Again Santa Anna headed northward with a large army of untrained and ill-equipped soldiers. In February of 1847 he met Zachary Taylor at Buena Vista, far north of San Luis Potosí. There Santa Anna drove his soldiers into the greatest battle of his life. His men overran line after line of Taylor's defensive network. When night came and a heavy storm interrupted the battle, Taylor and his remaining forces were fighting for survival, for Santa Anna's army was in position to annihilate the invaders. Fortunately for Taylor, Santa Anna did not realize the extent of his advantage. His troops had suffered staggering losses and were ready to drop with fatigue and hunger. Under cover of darkness the Mexican army melted away to the south, but Taylor made no move to follow.

Having returned to the capital claiming victory, Santa Anna turned on Gómez Farías in exchange for support from the church, and then prepared to face Scott who was moving on Mexico City from Veracruz. A skirmish in the mountains ended in Mexican defeat, and the defenders retired to prepare a new line before the capital city. A representative of the United States State Department, Nicholas P. Trist, attempted to negotiate with Santa Anna, but with no success. Finally Scott's army advanced and, after several days of bloody fighting, took the capital. The battle was a bitter one. Many of the Mexican units fought tenaciously, some to the death of the last man. But not Santa Anna. Jealous of his subordinate commanders, he fled the city with a fresh contingent and prepared to carry on guerrilla warfare.

Mexico was tired of war and it was tired of Santa Anna. He was deposed and after being given safe-conduct by the American army, was exiled to Jamaica. A new government, headed by the chief justice of the supreme court, Peña y Peña, established itself at Querétaro and made peace with the invader. By terms of the treaty of Guadalupe Hidalgo, Mexico ceded to the United States Texas, California, and all the territory between them claimed by Mexico. In exchange, outstanding financial claims against the Mexican government were canceled and the Mexican treasury received a payment of $15,000,000. On March 10, 1848, the treaty received final ratification by the United States Senate and the war was over. Mexico had lost nearly half of her national territory — the least populated portion to be sure — and had suffered a humiliating defeat at the hands of her northern neighbor.

Now, indeed, Mexico was near to a state of anarchy. In Yucatán the Indian henequen workers had risen against their masters and bitter racial warfare was in progress. The wild Indian tribes of the northern Sierra raided settlements and villages at will. But the moderates were in power in Mexico City, and there they remained. Herrera was brought back to the presidency, and in 1850 he was succeeded by Mariano Arista, who had been properly elected in the first peaceful transfer of executive power since independence. These men attempted to give Mexico a better government, and they were able to restore some sort of order in fiscal matters. British pressure over defaulted obligations was eased by pledging three-quarters of the customs receipts to bond service, and by attacking the army in its moment of weakness it was possible to bring about a drastic reduction in military expenditures. These measures were scarcely signs of progress; they were in reality manifestations of exhaustion.

Between 1848 and 1857 Mexico began to change drastically. The alteration was deepseated and not at first evident on the surface. With the moderates in power and the constitution of 1824 in effect, the authority of the central government was relaxed and that of the several states grew stronger. This in itself was not significant; what was significant was the change in political leadership at the state level that accompanied this resurgence of state autonomy. A new generation was rising to the fore, a generation that had reached maturity in the midst of national degradation and shame, a generation that had witnessed the perfidy of the revolutionary caudillos, the church, the propertied classes, and the parasitic *agiotistas*, or usurers. These groups had consistently for thirty years placed their own interest above that of the state; they had opposed all social progress in an effort to preserve their privileged status and to profit by the corruption of Santa Anna and his ilk. Had circumstances been a little more favorable they might have sold the whole national territory to the United States to buy the protection and order which they themselves were too selfish or too incompetent to provide.

Liberalism had long had a spokesman in Gómez Farías, but he had proved himself inept at politics, foolish and naïve in his dealings with Santa Anna, and with little real support in any quarter. The new generation would build afresh. In Oaxaca a pure-blooded Indian, Benito Juárez, became governor. This man who came from the hills to the city as a domestic servant had, with the aid of a creole benefactor, procured for himself an education and entered the legal profession. He married well and entered politics. As governor of Oaxaca he earned for himself an outstanding reputation for honesty and efficiency, and particularly he gained a strong following among the lower classes. At no time did he forget his own humble beginning. Juárez was but one of a group of new liberal leaders. In Michoacán another important figure secured the governorship. Melchor Ocampo, an able intellectual, gave evidence of real administrative ability and an understanding of the ills that beset his people. Brilliant literary figures, Guillermo Prieto and Ignacio Ramírez, attracted attention in Mexico City with their poetry and satire, and soon a nucleus for revolutionary liberalism had been formed in the capital. As these new figures in Mexican affairs became articulate, memories of Morelos and Hidalgo stirred in the minds of the people. Clearly something was afoot that boded no good for the conservative oligarchy.

Throughout the long, tragic era of Santa Anna, one able conservative had seen with dismay the steady disintegration of his country. Lucas Alamán had always remained a monarchist at heart. Distrustful of the United States, he had foreseen the loss of Texas and California and attempted to guide Mexico into closer relationships with European powers, particularly England. Now in his declining years, he devised a new plan to achieve a stable political system and at the same time guarantee the preservation of the conservative social and political tradition. Mexico should again become a monarchy and Europe should supply the king. But first, the conservatives must seize power. It was a simple matter to foment a new revolution, for now all the old elements of reaction — the church, the landowners, the army, and the money lenders — were thoroughly aroused by the wave of liberalism that seemed to be sweeping the country. Early in 1853 the government of Arista was turned out of office. Of course, an interim dictator was needed until a European monarch could be found, and of course the old oligarchy turned to Available Antonio. Santa Anna was recalled from exile and installed as president for one year. This time it would be different, for the 'hero' would be carefully watched and Alamán would rule from behind the scenes. The plan worked for almost two months. Then Alamán died. Santa Anna promptly reverted to character, looted the treasury, negotiated new loans, expanded the army, and instituted a wave of terror to drive every liberal from the country. In short order, Ocampo and Juárez found themselves living in New Orleans. As long as the funds held out, Santa Anna was firmly in the saddle.

Shortly the treasury was empty, and true to their history, the great property owners and the church saw no reason to contribute to the support of the regime they had foisted on the Mexican people. Someone else could pay the army's wages, and sure enough the United States came to the rescue. In fixing the boundary by the Treaty of Guadalupe-Hidalgo, the negotiators had failed to take into account the American need for a low pass through the mountains for railroad construction. Claims and counterclaims. Yes, Santa Anna would sell the Mesilla valley for ten million dollars! The Gadsden Purchase was completed in 1853, and Mexico transferred to the United States a portion of land along the Mexico-Arizona border. Now Santa Anna had enough money to keep himself in power for two more years. His action had angered many, however, and provided useful ammunition for his enemies. The sale of national territory is an act ill-suited to enhance the popularity of any politician, but the use to which Santa Anna put the new funds added personal insult to the injury of national pride. He spent it largely on himself.

Truly a revolution was brewing. This time, however, it was not a question of a dissatisfied general. The plotters against Santa

Anna included men from less common walks of life. There was Morelos' former chieftain, Juan Alvarez, and a former customs collector, Ignacio Comonfort. These men, in the spring of 1854, proclaimed at Ayutla a plan for revolution having as its objective the return to power of liberal leaders and the drafting of a new constitution. Santa Anna attempted to crush the movement, but its leaders vanished into the mountains only to reappear in a different location. Now began the process that spelled the end of the re-actionary government. In the northern states political leaders one after another declared for the Plan de Ayutla and expelled Santa Anna's administrative officials. In August of 1855, the man whose political and military adventures had marked an era of Mexican social and governmental decadence departed the presidential office for the last time. In part he was frustrated and bored; more perti-nent, however, his perceptiveness enabled him to predict as had Louis XV, 'Après moi, le déluge.' Santa Anna, fearing that his line of retreat might be cut off at Veracruz, hurried away into exile in South America. Twenty years later he died in Mexico City, having been permitted to return by a stronger man who had no reason to fear a spent old general with a wooden leg.

Three months after Santa Anna's departure, a liberal army under Juan Alvarez entered the Mexican capital and a generation of national ignominy moved rapidly to its bloody climax. Now came bitter civil war — the War of the Reform. The liberal movement of 1855 was of a vastly different character than any such movement since the days of Hidalgo and Morelos. Indeed, it was closely related to the earlier social upheaval that accompanied the struggle for independence. Among those who played leading roles were Indians and mestizos. Representatives of these down-trodden classes seized the reins of government and their numbers filled out the ranks of the armed forces. Alvarez surrounded himself with such men as Melchor Ocampo and Benito Juárez, the former liberal governors of Michoacán and Oaxaca. Other strong liberals included Guillermo Prieto, Santos Degollado, and Miguel Lerdo de Tejada, all men whose assumption of high political office struck terror in the hearts of the conservative landholders and the clergy.

That the new regime was intent upon drastic social change quickly became apparent. In late November of 1855 the new government passed the 'Ley Juárez' ending the privileged ecclesiastical courts of the church. Shortly thereafter came the 'Ley Lerdo,' an enactment intended to force religious corporations to sell all their land. Both laws created a storm of protest, and in the hope of allaying somewhat the fears of the opposition, Alvarez stepped aside to turn the presidency over to the more moderate Ignacio Comonfort. This proved to be a mistake, for Comonfort was too easy with those who plotted his downfall. Finally he fell a victim of conservative intrigue, and his weakness and vacillation enabled the conservative forces to seize the capital and drive the liberal government into the provinces. There followed three years of devastating war.

The liberals adopted a new constitution in 1857 before they were driven from the capital, and the constituent congress that created it wrote in the basic reforms that had first found expression in the Ley Juárez and the Ley Lerdo. It went even farther. It included provisions establishing secular education and allowing nuns and priests to renounce their vows, but it failed to include any provision prohibiting the exercise of religions other than the Roman Catholic. The war quickly became a religious war, for the church, including its temporal head, Pope Pius IX, denounced the constitution and all those who supported it. Excommunication was decreed for all who swore allegiance to the new fundamental law, and from that point onward no compromise was possible.

The entire country was thrown into turmoil when the first president under the new regime, Ignacio Comonfort, was tricked into turning over the government to General Félix Zuloaga, a tool of the conservatives, late in 1857. Benito Juárez became president of the liberal government with headquarters first in Michoacán and later in Veracruz. The conservatives continued to hold the capital, and the battle was joined. Plunder, rapine, assassination, murder of prisoners, and wanton destruction of property were practiced by both sides. It became impossible to carry on the economic life of the nation, and soon hunger joined the struggling armies to assist in the slaughter. Each side was forced to desperate measures, and the extreme views that came to characterize the opposing forces served only to intensify the conflict. Now the church poured treasure into the conservative coffers and the liberals took the only retaliatory measure open to them; they nationalized all real property of the church and abolished the tithe. Other drastic measures were aimed at ending the existence of religious corporations and suppressing all religious orders. These steps gave at least some semblance of legality to the plunder and destruction of churches and monasteries by the liberal armies. For three centuries the church in Mexico had grown rich and powerful. With power and wealth had come corruption and exploitation of the lowly Indian and mestizo masses. With the War of the Reform the day of reckoning finally arrived.

As the war dragged on, the stern, silent figure of the Zapotec Indian, Benito Juárez, became the mainstay of the liberal forces. Forced to flee to Veracruz by way of Panamá, he set up headquarters there and directed the guerrilla activities of his followers throughout the country. Step by step the liberal government under his guidance decreed the Laws of the Reform that stripped the church of its status and legalized the confiscation of its wealth. His position was particularly advantageous, for by holding Veracruz he deprived his enemies in the capital of access to commerce and customs revenues. General Miguel Miramón, the conservative chieftain, failed in his attempts to capture the port, for the liberal defenses were strong and the Indians Miramón brought from the high plateau to attack the port city quickly fell prey to the lowland fevers.

Gradually the tide began to turn. Miramón could not be everywhere at once, and although he won victory after victory, the liberal forces surged back like an incoming tide the moment his back was turned. In the north the liberals triumphed. Under an able liberal general, Porfirio Díaz, they conquered the south. Slowly the conservative armies melted away, and after several sharp defeats Miramón saw that the end was near and fled the country. On January 1, 1861, the liberal army entered the capital and the war was over. Days later, dressed in a black suit and riding in a black carriage, Juárez rode quietly into the city. He had achieved a great victory. Without leading a single army into battle he had unobtrusively guided the liberal government through its darkest hours and held the movement together until victory was assured. Could he, a civilian, now rule the country?

Throughout the war, Mexico escaped foreign intervention by the narrowest of margins. Spaniards openly aided the conservatives in every way possible without getting directly involved. The British had also shown a marked preference for the clerical party and had recognized Miramón's government. Only the United States favored Juárez and the liberals, and supplied them with arms through the port of Veracruz. Now that the war was over the danger of intervention actually increased, for Britain, France, and Spain immediately demanded reparations for loss of life and property by their citizens during the conflict. The British bondholders demanded payments from the customs duties. Furthermore, hope for support from the United States was gone; that country was involved in a bitter civil war of its own.

Now fortune averted her face as Juárez rode by. Never had Mexico been so completely prostrated. The treasury was empty. Customs revenues were pledged to foreign bankers, and internal commerce and industry were so completely disrupted that no revenues were to be derived from taxing those sources. The great wealth of the church had been dissipated in the bitter war, and a tax upon the transfer of its former properties produced little. In fact, the whole reform movement had fallen dismally short of attaining its objectives. The church was temporarily subdued, yes; but its vast property holdings had been snatched up by a new class of wealthy landholders, many of them foreigners. In the outlying states a new set of caudillos had come into existence as a result of having taken for themselves the wealth of expropriated properties. Mexico was no nearer being a country of small independent landholders than before the revolution. Some guerrilla fighting still continued, and within a matter of months Juárez lost two of his most able supporters to the conservative guerrilla, Márquez. Both

Mechor Ocampo and Santos Degollado were captured and shot. Juárez seemed unable to act positively. He would abide by the constitutional processes at all costs, even if those processes tied his hands. Congress talked and talked.

During the war the conservative government under Miramón had engaged in two nefarious financial transactions in a desperate effort to raise money. It had confiscated 700,000 pesos being held for British bondholders by the British legation in Mexico City, and it borrowed 750,000 pesos from a Swiss banker, Jecker, who took as security fifteen million pesos' worth of Mexican government bonds. On the liberal side, Degollado had seized a San Luis Potosí silver train belonging to British mine-owners. The foreign property owners held Juárez responsible for making good these losses, plus a long list of other alleged claims arising out of the conflict. The financial position of the Mexican government was far too weak to stand any such burden. Juárez, though willing to recognize legitimate claims, adopted the realistic position that the creditors would have to wait until the government's financial position strengthened. He declared a two-year moratorium on the payment of foreign debts.

England, France, and Spain, quick to take up the claims of their citizens against a weak foreign power, agreed upon a punitive expedition to remind the irresponsible Mexican officials of the importance of meeting their international obligations. The British had little desire to embark upon military action against Mexico, and they tried to forestall France and Spain by making a separate agreement with Juárez giving British officials supervisory authority over the collection of Mexican customs. The Mexican congress, however, rejected any such arrangement, and the British went ahead under their commitment to France and Spain.

Early in 1862, the allies landed at Veracruz and presented their demands. Quickly it became apparent that the French had more in mind than the collection of a few million pesos. They intended to change the government of Mexico. France now had an emperor, Napoleon III, whose ambition it was to make a place for himself in history equal to that of his uncle, Napoleon I. He might have undertaken to do so by extending French influence and power in Europe, but colonial venture would entail fewer risks.

Other factors were at play. The Mexican conservatives and the church were quite willing to call upon the French to support them against their liberal countrymen. With the triumph of Juárez, Mexican exiles streamed into Paris — a procession of bishops, priests, formerly wealthy playboys, and disgruntled politicians. One had become a favorite of the French empress; another, Santa Anna's old comrade-in-arms, General Almonte, was eager to sell his country to the French in exchange for the Mexican presidency. The exiled 'patriots' were easily duped into believing that the French were their champions and upon successfully occupying Mexico would return to them their confiscated properties and estates. Mexico would again become a monarchy with a genuine European prince upon the throne.

When early disagreement arose among the allies as to the objectives of the punitive expedition, Britain and Spain withdrew. They had no desire to further Louis Napoleon's ambitious undertakings in Mexico. The French, using Almonte as a provisional president, waited in Veracruz for a general uprising of the conservative forces which their patriot informants had promised would take place. Finally, the despotic guerrilla, Márquez, arrived with a small contingent of half-starved irregulars. That was all. The French decided to move on Puebla. There their small force of 6000 men was badly routed by Ignacio Zaragoza, one of Juárez' most able commanders. They fell back upon Veracruz to regroup.

Now Napoleon realized that the 'patriots' to whom he had listened had overplayed their case. He had a real project on his hands. The French promptly dropped their pretense of playing along with the exiles and went about their attempted conquest in earnest. A large force was sent to Mexico and a new commander, General Forey, was placed in charge. Almonte was cast aside and the enlarged French army moved on Mexico City. After a brief siege Puebla fell, and shortly thereafter the invaders entered the capital. Juárez had wished to defend Mexico City, but he had neither an army nor capable generals. Zaragoza was dead of typhoid, and his other able commander, González Ortega, together with Porfirio Díaz, had been captured at Puebla. Juárez and his government fled northward to San Luis Potosí and eventually on to Monterrey. Early in June General Forey entered the capital triumphantly. The church held solemn Masses amidst great rejoicing while the conservative sycophants stood around waiting for restoration of their properties. Both the clergy and the hacendados were amazingly naïve. They failed to note the large number of Frenchmen who had possessed themselves of redistributed property under the Ley Lerdo and the 1857 constitution. Great was their shock when General Forey issued a decree confirming the new property holders in their titles to former church estates. They too had been tricked.

Quickly now the French expanded their conquest northward and westward from the capital. A plebiscite was held to confirm Napoleon's selection of Archduke Maximilian of Hapsburg as Mexican emperor. Time passed, and it was the spring of 1864 before the new emperor accepted his throne and set forth with his wife, the former Belgian princess Carlotta, to establish his court in Mexico City. The whole affair was one grand farce. Napoleon expected to get his investment back, all the various European bondholders expected to get their reward, yet in order to finance the new royal court in Mexico City, Maximilian had to borrow still more heavily in France. Mexico's paper debt grew enormously. Maximilian was a gentle well-meaning tool of the French who had been duped into believing he was assuming a throne at the request of his future subjects. He breathed sweetness and light, but when he arrived in Mexico his breath caught in his throat. The French controlled everything, the customs, the treasury, the army, and the economy of the country. He was helpless and ignorant. He did not understand that the country lacked even the barest rudiments of an administrative machinery, that none of his well-intended enactments as emperor had the slightest chance of implementation. Then he made the same mistake that Napoleon and everyone else concerned had made: he thought that Mexico was rich. It was grindingly poor. There was no Aztec treasure to fill the coffers of Napoleon as it had those of Carlos V, neither was the country productive as in the days of Revillagigedo. Increasingly the French emperor began to rue his bargain, while the Mexican emperor tried desperately to ingratiate himself with his subjects.

In 1865 the Civil War ended in the United States, and mysteriously surplus war matériel began to find its way across the Río Grande and into the hands of Juárez' soldiers hiding in the mountains and along the border. At the same time efforts were made through diplomatic channels to persuade Napoleon of a war hazard should his army be left much longer in Mexico. The French prepared to withdraw their troops and write the entire adventure off as a mistake. Such preparation was by no means retarded by Prussia's quick and decisive victory over Austria in the Seven-Weeks War of 1866 — a war that resulted in Prussia's replacing Austria as the polarizing power for German unification among the South German states. Gradually French troops were withdrawn from the northern regions, and as fast as they left Juárist guerrilla armies sprang into existence behind them. The inevitable failure of the French undertaking was now apparent to all — all, that is, except Maximilian and his wife Carlotta. Carlotta returned to France to beg further assistance from Napoleon, but he could promise her nothing. Desperate, she turned to the Pope in Rome, but he could remember only the property that Maximilian had not restored to the church. Carlotta went rapidly insane and had to be taken home to Belgium.

Early in 1867 the French army withdrew. Every effort was made by the French commander and by Napoleon to persuade Maximilian to leave also, but the 'Mexican' emperor would stay with 'his' people. A small group of conservatives continued to support him in the hope that Juárez' armies could be turned back. But one by one the states and cities fell before the advancing liberal forces until only a few points remained. Maximilian went with his army to Querétaro where the liberal armies under General Escobedo quickly surrounded them. In the meantime, Porfirio Díaz moved up from Oaxaca and captured Puebla. The line of retreat to Veracruz and Europe was cut off.

The emperor might still have escaped, but he chose no such way of ending his reign. Possibly it never occurred to him that in Mexico wars are sometimes deadly serious. Perhaps his recollection of what happened to the would-be emperor Iturbide was a little hazy. Or perhaps, as was said of him, he knew better how to die than to govern. At any rate he would stay. In May the royal army surrendered, and the fate of the emperor, as well as that of the old conservative generals Miramón and Mejía, was placed in the hands of the Zapotec Indian from Oaxaca. These men deserved little sympathy and they received none, in Mexico. Ignoring the pleas and protests of both European and American governments, Juárez carried out the sentence of the Mexican military court: death. The emperor, together with Miramón and Mejía, died before a firing squad in Querétaro June 19, 1867.

Now at long last a calm descended over Mexico. The bloody process of cleansing the country of the evil heritage of Santa Anna and his traitorous supporters was at an end. The church's control of the mental and physical resources of the nation was broken, temporarily at least; and a new generation of property owners had arisen as a result of the land redistribution of the reform. The cleansing process had been thorough; not only had the poor Indian soldiers died by the thousands, generals also died, and so had a Hapsburg emperor. Juárez presided over a prostrate land and a people bled white in the struggle to achieve nationhood.

SUGGESTED READING

M. Burgin, *The Economic Aspects of Argentine Federalism, 1820–1852,* Cambridge, Mass., 1946.

J. F. Cady, *Foreign Interventions in the Río de la Plata, 1835–1850,* Philadelphia, 1929.

F. E. Calderón de la Barca, *Life in Mexico,* Boston, 1843.

R. G. Caldwell, *The López Expedition to Cuba, 1848–1851,* Princeton, 1915.

W. H. Callcott, *Santa Anna,* Norman, 1936.

A. Edwards, *The Dawn: Being the History of the Birth and Consolidation of the Republic of Chile,* London, 1931.

F. García Calderón, *Latin America: Its Rise and Progress,* London, 1913.

J. L. de Grummond, ed., *Caracas Diary, 1835–1840,* Baton Rouge, 1951.

B. Harding, *Amazon Throne, the Story of the Braganzas of Brazil*, Indianapolis, 1941.

W. H. Jeffrey, *Mitre and Argentina*, New York, 1952.

A. K. Manchester, *British Preeminence in Brazil, Its Rise and Decline*, Chapel Hill, 1933.

M. W. Nichols, *The Gaucho*, Durham, 1942.

W. Parish, *Buenos Ayres and the Provinces of the Río de la Plata*, 2 ed., London, 1852.

R. Roeder, *Juárez and His Mexico*, 2 vols., New York, 1947.

W. O. Scroggs, *Filibusters and Financiers: The Story of William Walker and His Associates*, New York, 1916.

J. H. Smith, *The War with Mexico*, New York, 1923.

J. L. Stephens, *Incidents of Travel in Central America, Chiapas, and Yucatán*, New edition, New Brunswick, 1949.

C. A. Washburn, *History of Paraguay*, 2 vols., Boston, 1951.

A. C. Wilgus, ed., *Argentina, Brazil, and Chile since Independence*, Washington, 1935.

—— ed., *South American Dictators during the First Century of Independence*, Washington, 1937.

GENERAL

F. de Azevedo, *Brazilian Culture*, New York, 1950.

S. F. Bemis, *The Latin American Policy of the United States*, New York, 1943.

H. Bernstein, *Modern and Contemporary Latin America*, New York, 1952.

J. P. Calogeras, *A History of Brazil*, Chapel Hill, 1939.

F. A. Carlson, *Geography of Latin America*, Rev. ed., New York, 1950.

A. N. Christensen, ed., *The Evolution of Latin American Government*, New York, 1951.

H. F. Cline, *The United States and Mexico*, Cambridge, Mass., 1953.

A. Coester, *The Literary History of Spanish America*, New York, 1928.

J. A. Crow, *The Epic of Latin America*, New York, 1946.

H. E. Davis, *Latin American Leaders*, New York, 1949.

H. C. Evans, *Chile and Its Relations with the United States*, Durham, 1927.

E. Fergusson, *Chile*, New York, 1943.

—— *Guatemala*, New York, 1937.

—— *Venezuela*, New York, 1939.

A. Franklin, *Ecuador*, New York, 1943.

L. Galdames, *A History of Chile*, Chapel Hill, 1941.

J. W. Gantenbein, ed., *The Evolution of our Latin American Policy*, New York, 1950.

E. Gruening, *Mexico and Its Heritage*, New York, 1934.

J. M. Henao and G. Arrubla, *A History of Colombia*, Chapel Hill, 1938.

M. P. Holleran, *Church and State in Guatemala*, New York, 1949.

R. A. Humphreys, *The Evolution of Modern Latin America*, New York, 1946.

P. E. James, *Brazil*, New York, 1946.

—— *Latin America*, rev. ed., New York, 1950.

C. Jane, *Liberty and Despotism in Spanish America*, Oxford, 1929.

C. L. Jones, *Guatemala, Past and Present*, Minneapolis, 1940.

T. B. Jones, *South America Rediscovered*, Minneapolis, 1949.

F. A. Kirkpatrick, *A History of the Argentine Republic*, Cambridge, 1931.

W. H. Koebel, *Uruguay*, London, 1911.

G. Kubler, *The Indian Caste of Peru, 1795–1940*, Washington, 1952.

A. J. Lacombe, *Brazil, A Brief History*, Rio de Janeiro, 1954.

R. Levene, *A History of Argentina*, Chapel Hill, 1937.

R. W. Logan, *The Diplomatic Relations of the United States with Haiti, 1776–1891*, Chapel Hill, 1941.

C. R. Markham, *A History of Peru*, Chicago, 1892.

W. D. and A. L. Marsland, *Venezuela through Its History*, New York, 1954.

J. L. Mecham, *Church and State in Latin America*, Chapel Hill, 1934.

D. Munro, *The Five Republics of Central America*, New York, 1918.

R. Nash, *The Conquest of Brazil*, New York, 1926.

D. Perkins, *Hands Off; A History of the Monroe Doctrine*, Boston, 1941.

D. Pierson, *The Negro in Brazil*, Chicago, 1942.

S. Putnam, *Marvelous Journey: Four Centuries of Brazilian Literature*, New York, 1948.

A. Ramos, *The Negro in Brazil*, Washington, 1939.

Y. F. Rennie, *The Argentine Republic*, New York, 1945.

P. Romanell, *Making of the Mexican Mind*, Lincoln, 1952.

W. L. Schurz, *Latin America: A Descriptive Survey*, new ed., New York, 1949.

L. B. Simpson, *Many Mexicos*, new ed., Berkeley, 1952.

T. L. Smith, *Brazil: Peoples and Institutions*, rev. ed., Baton Rouge, 1954.

T. L. Smith and A. Marchant, eds., *Brazil: Portrait of Half a Continent*, New York, 1951.

A. Torres-Rioseco, *The Epic of Latin American Literature*, New York, 1942.

—— *New World Literature*, Berkeley, 1949.

H. G. Warren, *Paraguay; An Informal History*, Norman, 1949.

VI

THE FEW AND THE MANY

XXX

Popular Government on Trial

> The patriarchal organization of colonial society has shown . . .
> an astonishing capacity for survival. The economy of all the
> Latin American countries is primarily an agrarian economy in
> which landownership means control of the major instrument
> of production. The dominance of the *hacienda* . . has not
> only fostered the stratification of society; it has tended to
> perpetuate a concentration of political power in the hands of
> small minorities.
>
> ROBIN A. HUMPHREYS *

T HE modern world is possibly obsessed with the
idea of progress. Progress implies change from a
less desirable to a more desirable condition or state of affairs. Life
itself is a process of continual change from childhood to old age;
and inasmuch as throughout the greater portion of his span of years
man's outlook is toward the future rather than the past, the element
of progress is associated with the process of change. The growing
child becomes stronger, more self-reliant; as he learns more about
the world in which he lives, he becomes better equipped to support
himself and to cope with life's problems. Eventually a wife and
family are acquired, possibly a home and considerable property.
Within the commonly accepted framework of human values, each
of these steps marks passage from a less desirable to a more desirable
state of affairs. In certain Eastern cultures, old age is the most venerable state of all; and certainly the pattern of Western Christianity

* *The Evolution of Modern Latin America*, Oxford University Press, New
York, 1946, p. 83.

treats old age as but a final step before progression to an even higher status in the world to come.

Progress has been equated with the acquisition of material goods almost universally, in spite of the fact that certain religions see virtue in poverty. All civilizations of which there is record have been characterized by an unequal distribution of material goods, and invariably those persons possessing the greater amount have been the object of veneration or envy. All humanity strives, however feebly and ineffectively, to increase its material well-being. Success in this endeavor is considered to be a mark of progress, whether achieved individually or collectively.

The idea of progress has long been associated with man's most complex institution, the state. States are held to progress as the peoples who comprise them achieve greater material well-being, as they are enabled to live in greater harmony with one another, as their numbers increase, and as they acquire larger portions of the earth's surface. The concept of progress pervades every aspect of human existence.

As the historian Toynbee has so cogently indicated in his studies of civilizations, however, progress is not a continuous process. There are periods of rise and there are periods of decline in the histories of all civilized societies. The achievements of one people or one nation are frequently gained at the expense of others. Nevertheless, because of the ever greater productivity of modern man and because of his ever increasing knowledge of the physical world and his ability to manipulate it to his seeming advantage, the sum total of human endeavor still seems to accord with the concept of progress.

As already suggested, progress can be measured only in relation to some given set of values. If poverty were truly regarded as a virtue, the acquisition of wealth would be considered an act of retrogression. If productive activity were not regarded as desirable, the man who did nothing would be considered as contributing most to society. It must not be overlooked that in a society where such values as these were reversed, man could not support his present numbers and millions would die. Nature provides sanctions that have conditioned the formation of human values.

Some consideration of values is fundamental to any interpretation of history. Those of the historian are probably far less important than those of the people who made the history. Part of the historian's task is to record faithfully changes in the value pattern of those about whom he is writing. The independence of the Latin American peoples marked a great change in value patterns in that self-government became more desirable than attachment to Spain and all that membership in the Spanish imperial system implied. Many did not make the shift and preferred the old order to what they regarded as doubtful benefits of the new. Thereby was precipitated the conflict and the wars of independence. Once separation from Spain was a reality, further value adjustments were called for and new conflicts arose.

The period from 1860 to 1930 was characterized by deep and far-reaching changes in the aspirations of the Latin American peoples. New sets of values were created and old ones discarded. Progress came increasingly to be measured by the degree to which new scientific developments were put to use in the new countries. The construction of railroads and telegraph lines were tangible evidences of progress that any could see and appreciate. The production of more material goods and the acquisition of wealth through commerce were viewed with favor by many who in times past had thought the ownership of land the only road to wealth and higher status in society. In increasing numbers men attached importance to a more equitable distribution of material goods and to the moral, spiritual, and political benefits of independent nationhood. Progress came gradually to be equated with the extension of education, with greater freedom to express opinion, with the maintenance of law and order without oppression. Finally, the masses of Indians, mestizos, farm laborers, peons, and laborers in the cities began to adopt values similar to those of the upper classes. They sought land, education, economic opportunity, and enough to eat. Progress became a vital consideration of the many, not merely of the few.

Already by mid-century change was in men's minds. The European revolutions of 1848 saw a resurgence of liberalism that once

again battered at the ancient structure of the landholding aristocracy.
The stirrings in Europe were observed and faintly echoed in Latin
America, but they were not understood. Germany and France were
undergoing a basic shift in the locus of economic power as industrialization created a new wealthy class of manufacturers and
businessmen. These alterations in the balance of economic and
political power had affected England somewhat earlier; now they
were manifested throughout Western Europe. They were soon to
appear in the United States and contribute to the fires of a violent
civil war. Latin American liberals stirred uneasily, and although they
came into political power in a number of countries, they proved incapable of doing more than erecting a new façade behind which the
ancient colonial social order carried on as before. There was no
industrialization and no rising new class to challenge effectively the
old oligarchy; instead there were developed new agricultural commodities and new products of the pampas and forests that served
only to concentrate greater wealth in the hands of those who owned
the land. A major difficulty, of course, was the apparent absence of
those basic requirements for industrialization: coal, iron ore, and
power. Missing also, however, was any element in the Ibero-Ameri-
can cultural pattern that placed high value on scientific inquiry, on
mechanical creativeness, or on the practical kinds of knowledge
essential to advance in the age of mechanization which the Western
World was entering.

Although Latin American liberalism somehow remained a fetish
for lack of a broader social and economic base, it was not devoid of
accomplishment. Physical progress was indicated by the construction of roads and buildings, and intellectual development was
achieved through the creation of new educational facilities at elementary, secondary, and university levels. A sense of national consciousness emerged in nearly all countries, and with it came greater
political stability, a somewhat broader participation in government,
and a more extensive use of the trappings of democracy. Nevertheless, as time went on and 'liberalism' and 'conservatism' proved to
be nothing more than labels bandied about by competing groups
with essentially the same social and economic outlook, the gulf

grew wider and wider between the few who governed and the many whose welfare they held in their hands. Gradually a deep current of social unrest became evident, and in Mexico it swept all before it in a vast tide of social revolution carried forward in the tradition of Hidalgo, Morelos, and Juárez. Elsewhere, the same current was in varying degrees apparent, and it was to become a major influence in the modern era.

Europe's social and economic changes during the nineteenth century had other direct consequences in Latin America. Millions in Europe, awakened to the hope of a better life and seeing no possibility of achieving it in the land of their birth, turned to the Western Hemisphere as a land of new and greater opportunity. Soon passage was sought on every available ship sailing for the United States, where, it had been reported, land could be had simply by occupying it. The rise of new and sparsely populated nations had long since excited the interest and imagination of English, French, German, Italian, and Spaniard alike. The chaos which followed the creation of the Latin American nations was disillusioning, however, and few were incautious enough to risk life and property in the face of the political disorders that characterized the region. Most emigrants from Europe preferred to take their chances in the United States. When particular Latin American nations became more stable, and the opening of the great grasslands of southern South America became increasingly profitable, thousands of people migrated to Argentina, Chile, Uruguay, and Brazil. The vital need for immigrant labor and capital was acknowledged by Argentina in particular, and agents were sent to major European capitals to recruit new residents. Alberdi, one of Argentina's great statesmen, expressed a conviction of many of his countrymen when he said, 'To govern is to populate.' An extensive colonization program was developed to open up vast new sections of territory, and the population of Argentina increased rapidly.

At the same time that the southern South American nations were experiencing rapid population increase through European emigration, steps were being taken to rid the great plains and the frontiers of the last remnants of hostile Indian groups. The result was a sharp decrease in the Indian populations of Argentina and Chile while the European component increased. Argentina, Chile, and Uruguay took on increasingly a European complexion, and their resemblance to other Latin American nations decreased proportionately.

Immigrants brought with them new tools and new methods of agriculture. The Germans who settled around Valdivia in southern Chile introduced dairy farming on a sizable scale. The English who came to Argentina not only brought with them capital to build railroads, but they also introduced such inventions as windmills and barbed wire, and soon large sections of the pampas were transformed from open range for swift, lean cattle and fierce gauchos into a land of endless wheat fields and complacent English shorthorns. In the face of these bewildering obstacles to his ancient freedom, the lawless, ungovernable gaucho succumbed, as did the nomadic, buffalo-hunting tribes of the great plains of North America. The result was fortunate for both Argentina and her gaucho tradition. The one grew into a prosperous and fairly stable nation; the other became a subject for literary endeavor. Aided by poetic license and abetted by the enchantment of time and distance, the gaucho became a national hero and the epitome of Argentine nationalism, instead of the bloodthirsty, hard-hearted outcast and skinner of other peoples' cattle which his contemporaries had known him to be.

Other effects of immigration were no less marked. The newcomers, who increasingly were of Italian and Spanish stock in Argentina, to be followed later by sizable numbers of Poles, Swiss, and Germans, soon monopolized many industries and forced creoles to abandon many of their ancient methods of production and commerce. Buenos Aires became a great and cosmopolitan city and the entire nation was faced with serious problems of assimilation. By 1915 at least one-third of the inhabitants of Argentina were foreign born; and in 1930 the proportion was still about one-fourth. By this latter date, however, when restrictions were placed on immigration, the number of newcomers arriving annually had already dropped to an insignificant amount.

Brazil was also affected by immigration, although not with the same final result as in Argentina, Chile, and Uruguay, where the

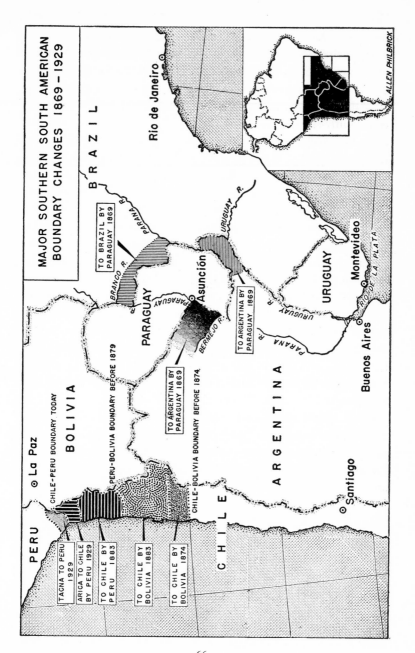

MAJOR SOUTHERN SOUTH AMERICAN
BOUNDARY CHANGES 1869-1929

ALLEN PHILBRICK

BRAZIL

Rio de Janeiro

PERU

○ La Paz

BOLIVIA

CHILE-PERU BOUNDARY TODAY

PERU-BOLIVIA BOUNDARY BEFORE 1879

PARAGUAY

PARAGUAY R.

Asunción

BRANCO R.

PARANA R.

TO BRAZIL BY
PARAGUAY 1869

URUGUAY R.

TO ARGENTINA BY
PARAGUAY 1869

BERMEJO R.

TO ARGENTINA BY
PARAGUAY 1869

CHILE-BOLIVIA BOUNDARY BEFORE 1874.

URUGUAY R.

PARANA R.

URUGUAY

Montevideo

RIO DE LA PLATA

Buenos Aires

ARGENTINA

○ Santiago

CHILE

TAGNA TO PERU
1929

ARICA TO CHILE
BY PERU 1929

TO CHILE BY
PERU 1883

TO CHILE BY
BOLIVIA 1883

TO CHILE BY
BOLIVIA 1874

population was substantially 'Europeanized.' In some Brazilian regions, such as Rio Grande do Sul, immigration played a potent role
in economic development; elsewhere the influence of the new-
comer was less important. Abolition of the slave trade in 1850 stimulated the desire for immigrant laborers, and the imperial government
consistently encouraged Europeans to come to Brazil. The construction of railroads made for an easier adjustment to Brazilian life, but
the abolition of slavery in 1888 removed the greatest obstacle to
settlement by Europeans. The rapid growth of São Paulo and of the
coffee industry in that area was both a product of and a stimulant
to immigration. Brazil's greatest influx, which came after the
abolition of slavery, brought more than a million and a quarter new
residents as contrasted with the six million that were pouring into
Argentina. Brazil's new population came primarily from Italy and
Portugal, although important numbers arrived from Germany as
well. In both Brazil and Argentina, and to a lesser extent in Chile
and Uruguay, the Germans and the English came to exercise an influence far out of proportion to their numbers. They not only introduced more scientific uses of agricultural and mineral resources, but
also exercised dominant roles in banking, commerce, and in commercial transportation.

After the First World War, increasing numbers of eastern Europeans and Orientals entered Latin America. Chinese coolie labor
had been introduced in Peru years before to work on railroad construction projects. Now Japanese colonists came in large numbers to
settle in Brazil, Chinese settled in Mexico and Cuba, and East
Indians emigrated to the southern shore of the Caribbean, particularly to Dutch Guiana and the coastal cities of Venezuela and
Panamá.

Most of Latin America had few advantages to offer the potential
emigrant from Europe. Wherever the large native population included substantial numbers of semi-assimilated Indians, the European was placed at a disadvantage in seeking employment. A large
labor force was already present. If the immigrant desired to farm, as
many did, the best land was already occupied by the owners of
large haciendas. Even in Argentina, where vast tracts of land were

open to the early immigrants, land values rose rapidly; soon new-comers were obliged to become farm laborers or tenants, for un-occupied land quickly disappeared. The size of individual holdings was a major problem, and it became obvious that Argentina was not soon to become a land of small farmers. In general, during the latter half of the nineteenth century the percentage of landless increased in spite of great agricultural expansion throughout major portions of Latin America. In a region that remained predominantly agricultural, this development boded ill for the future.

While large-scale immigration was rapidly giving to the southern countries of Latin America a distinctly European cast, the continuous intermixture of Indian and Spanish races, begun during the centuries of colonialism, was producing a largely mestizo population in Mexico, Central America, and the Caribbean region generally. Brazil, too, became increasingly mixed, but the components were more varied and included a substantial Negro element. In Peru, Ecuador, Paraguay, and Bolivia the process of racial amalgamation was much less thorough, and the large Indian population remained essentially an element apart, racially, culturally, and economically, from the much smaller but dominant European and mestizo groups. In Central America, Guatemala followed the pattern of Peru and Bolivia, with the descendants of the ancient Mayas clinging doggedly to a traditional isolation that even the Roman Catholic Church found frustratingly impenetrable. Various sections of the former Spanish empire were, in the period of independence, growing farther apart from one another racially, culturally, and economically. Political attributes proved infinitely more tenacious.

New residents were not all that approached Latin America from across the seas. As Europe and the United States became increasingly industrialized, the economic power of the leading nations expanded at a tremendous rate. New outlets were sought for the investment of capital, and Latin America appeared to offer excellent possibilities for development. The desirability of investment in the region was considerably heightened by the availability there of raw materials and other resources that were not elsewhere abundant. Argentine hides and beef, Chilean nitrates, Brazilian rubber and coffee,

Paraguayan quebracho extract, Mexican oil, and numerous lesser products were valuable commodities in the markets of Europe and North America, and great effort and money was expended in making them available. Foreign promoters and investors poured large sums into Latin America to construct railroads, telegraph lines, docks and harbors. Others invested in mining, agriculture, and commercial enterprises on a large scale. The introduction of electrification was also the work of foreign entrepreneurs. Technological advance in many regions seemed to accomplish miracles, considering the obstacles which geography, climate, and the shortage of skilled workers presented. Naturally, some regions and some countries benefited more than others, but in all areas the pioneering investor and developer were welcomed by liberal and conservative alike. In most cases, foreign companies relied exclusively upon their own nationals to fill responsible positions, leaving opportunities for Latin Americans only in unskilled or semi-skilled labor. The policy was understandable; extensive training programs in most regions would have been necessary before native managers and technicians could have been made available, and the development projects were not inspired by philanthropy. However, since most of the new industries were extractive in nature, and since Latin Americans found employment in them only as a source of cheap labor, few of the Latin American countries received great direct benefit or found their economies substantially strengthened. As was true of politics, so it was with economic development; it was the few who benefited and the many who looked on with envy, the envy heightened by the realization that the few were frequently foreigners.

Spurred on by the urge for material progress, Latin American governments turned heavily to borrowing. The relative political stability, achieved as the echoes of the wars of independence died out, gave foreign investors an undue measure of confidence in the governments with which they negotiated loans. Borrowed funds were all too often used to erect government office buildings or to pave streets over which only oxcarts rumbled. In such cases productivity was not increased, and neither were the governments' revenues with which to repay the loans.

Economic progress was essential to the welfare of each of the Latin American nations, but few of the statesmen of the period discovered appropriate and beneficial ways of accelerating all currents of economic life. Economic panaceas introduced from abroad were adopted with wholehearted enthusiasm and lack of caution. The apparent prosperity thus created did not permeate the basic economic reality of the poverty of the great majority of the populations, and social progress lagged far behind. Some governments, pathetically eager to benefit from the magic of modern technology, cooperated with foreign entrepreneurs by providing cheap and docile labor. Thus arose the aphorism said of Mexico in the time of Porfirio Díaz: 'She was the mother of the foreigner and the stepmother of the Mexican.'

Other evils were equally costly. Too often the largest part of any loan went into the pockets of the few in power, leaving nothing for the nation but a debt. Government loans had to be repaid like any others, and future generations were saddled with burdens for which there was nothing to show but increased opulence on the part of the favored few.

The impact of foreign enterprise and technological advance was of great benefit in some countries. In the seventy years after 1860 Argentina developed into a great and productive nation, as to a lesser degree did Chile, Brazil, and Uruguay. In each instance, technological improvement and foreign capital played major roles. But in other areas where telegraph lines were erected to link the principal cities and nothing was done to stimulate industry, messages carried by the new communication media were more often of political portent than of commercial interest. Railroad lines in Argentina transported grain and cattle, but in Central America their traffic was more likely to be in troops. Indians carrying their poultry to market now sometimes rode, but for the heavier items the pack mule and the oxcart still were used. It is not to the credit of the mule or the oxen that the steam locomotive failed to drive them out of business.

While the nations of southern South America were experiencing tremendous population influx from Europe and marked transformation of their economies through economic development, less fortunate nations bordering on the Caribbean were being introduced to the fact that economics and international politics are bedfellows. International rivalry in the Caribbean area was as old as European penetration into the region; but in the period immediately associated with the wars for Latin American independence, almost continuous warfare in Europe preoccupied the major powers and precluded their interference in the American revolutionary struggles. With peace re-established in Europe, however, Britain and France turned westward once more; soon the Caribbean was again a major center of international competition. The nature of international competition had nonetheless undergone a change. While land-grabbing colonialism was not entirely discarded, as evidenced by British interest in Texas and along the coast of Guatemala, Honduras, and Nicaragua as well as a renewed French interest in Haiti, penetration by the great powers increasingly took on an economic complexion. Investments and loans preceded political pressure and threats of occupation. Such considerations accounted for French and British interest in Mexico.

The sudden expansion of the United States westward after the war with Mexico added an entirely new dimension to Caribbean rivalry. American interest in the area grew apace with the discovery of gold in California and the great rush of thousands to the Pacific Coast. In the era before railroads spanned the North American continent, travel by sea was by far the simplest, and the long Isthmus of Central America was at once recognized as an obnoxious barrier and an economic challenge. Cornelius Vanderbilt organized a transportation company to take advantage of the San Juan river route across Nicaragua, and soon a treaty between Colombia and the United States made possible construction of a railroad across Panamá. The railroad was built between 1850 and 1855. In the meantime, the United States and Great Britain both sought access to a canal route, with Britain in the forefront by reason of laying claim to a protectorate over the Graytown region of Nicaragua which included the mouth of the San Juan river.

The United States was fearful that a canal route might become the exclusive property of another power and attempted to avoid this possibility by advocating neutralization of any route. In 1850, this objective was achieved in large measure by successful negotiation of the Clayton-Bulwer Treaty with Great Britain. By the agreement neither power was to hold exclusive control over the Nicaragua route or to take dominion over any part of Central America. Any canal route was to be neutralized in time of war or peace and was not to be fortified. No canal was immediately undertaken, and soon attention was focused on other matters.

In the United States the long struggle over the slavery issue began to have international repercussions. In an attempt to retain control over the American congress, slavery advocates became involved with abolitionists in bitter competition to add new states to the Union. Southern glances were cast in the direction of Cuba and Santo Domingo and some fell upon Central America. In 1854, an American filibuster from New Orleans by the name of William Walker organized in San Francisco an expedition to aid the liberals of León, Nicaragua, in a struggle they were having with the conservatives of Granada. Walker had made earlier forays into the Sonora and Lower California regions of Mexico, but had achieved nothing for his efforts. In Nicaragua he was more successful, and soon he was in control of the country and had himself made president. Early objectives seemed to imply an intent to offer the region to the United States for annexation, but any such thought rapidly fled Walker's mind once he found himself in control of the small Central American nation. Walker sought international recognition for his government but could not secure it, even from the United States. Instead, other Central American nations united their efforts to unseat him and destructive warfare ensued. Walker soon made the serious mistake of incurring the disfavor of Vanderbilt and his transportation company and he was forced to flee the country. In 1860 he tried to return but was captured by the British and turned over to the Hondurans who promptly executed him. Although Walker came to no good end, his expedition had struck fear to the hearts of all Central Americans — fear of the United States and what appeared to be its aggressive intentions.

Shortly thereafter France was eliminated for the time being from Caribbean competition by the disastrous consequences of Napoleon III's adventures in Mexico, but British and American interest persisted. End of the slavery issue eased somewhat the risk of American land grabbing, but other forms of imperialism soon appeared. As early as 1854, President Pierce of the United States made an abortive effort to open the possibility of purchasing Cuba from Spain. He sent an agent to Madrid, who, failing there, met with the American ambassadors to Great Britain and France at the city of Ostend in Belgium to discuss the problem of purchase. A declaration was issued by the conference participants that promptly became known as the Ostend Manifesto. It stated in terms clear enough for anyone to understand that if Spain were unwilling to sell Cuba the island would be taken from her by force. The statement was promptly repudiated by the American secretary of state, and soon the Civil War intervened; but the Latin American world had been given notice that Cuba was considered a desirable prize in the United States.

In 1868 Cuba was torn by revolution against Spain, prompted in part by Spanish difficulties at home, but more directly the result of unrest that had been seething in the island for years. The Spanish administration had learned little by the loss of a great empire on two continents, and relations with the remaining American possessions were never smooth. The revolutionists proclaimed independence, and soon American sympathizers, particularly disgruntled soldiers from the recently defeated Confederacy, flocked to their aid. Ships from the United States carried supplies to the rebellious patriots, and the Spanish government retaliated by declaring a blockade of rebel-held sections and capturing a vessel, the *Virginius*, flying the American flag. Although the ship was sailing under American colors illegally, the incident nearly precipitated a break with Spain, for many of the crew were Americans and the Spanish captain-general executed a number of them. Finally the revolution was suppressed; but American interest in Spain's Caribbean possessions did not abate and expansionist politicians continued to advocate seizure of the islands. American investments in nations bordering on the

Caribbean continued to expand even if the 'jingoists' could not promote territorial adventures.

Peace in Cuba did not prove of long duration. Spanish promises
of reform and insular representation in the Spanish Cortes at Madrid proved illusory. Agricultural development of the island favored
peninsular-born landholders, who made huge profits selling sugar to
the United States. Increased investments by American citizens
failed to benefit materially the ordinary Cuban. Dreams of independence continued to fan the embers of insurrection and exiles in
New York, Puerto Ricans as well as Cubans, prepared plans and
solicited funds for a new revolutionary effort. In 1895, Cuba was
once more torn by rebellion. Patriots united under the leadership
of Máximo Gómez, an ardent advocate of independence, and soon
large portions of rural Cuba were in the hands of revolutionists
whose policy it became to strangle their Spanish adversaries by
wholesale destruction of property. The Spaniards concentrated
women and children in the cities and attempted to put down the
insurrection by vigorous forays into the countryside. For over two
years the struggle wore on. Much property, including that of
Americans, was destroyed, and the Spanish government seemed
incapable of bringing the situation under control. All the while sympathy for the patriot cause mounted in the United States, fanned by
reports of the cruelty of the Spanish general, Weyler, and by the
interventionist policies of certain American newspapers, particularly
the Hearst press. The American congress took the lead in advocating
recognition of the state of war in Cuba, an action that would have
given *de facto* governmental status to the insurgents so far as relations with the United States were concerned. President Cleveland
and his successor, McKinley, both held back in an effort to avoid
war with Spain. In January of 1898, however, disorder spread to
Habana, and an American battleship, the *Maine*, was sent to the
principal Cuban harbor to provide a refuge for United States
citizens who might be in danger, and, incidentally, to present a show
of force to the Spanish government. A few days after its arrival in
Habana the battleship was suddenly blown asunder by causes that
to this day have not been satisfactorily determined. In the heat of

the moment no one took time to investigate the matter seriously. The Spanish government denied responsibility, but the American press paid little heed to such protestations of innocence. Over 250 Americans had been killed, and forceful intervention in Cuba was demanded.

On April 11, President McKinley sent a message to congress offering that body the choice of decision as to whether the time for war had come. The response was a series of resolutions demanding the withdrawal of Spain from Cuba, empowering the president to use the armed forces to cause such a withdrawal, and disclaiming any desire on the part of the United States to control or exercise jurisdiction over Cuba. In spite of a last-minute offer of the Spanish government to suspend hostilities in the island, war was undertaken. Both Cuba and Puerto Rico were quickly occupied by United States armed forces, and in the distant Philippines the American navy met and defeated the Spanish Far Eastern fleet and occupied Manila. Quickly the Spanish government sued for peace, and by the end of the year a treaty had been signed terminating the war. Cuba, Puerto Rico, and the Philippine Islands were at the complete disposal of the United States. Promptly the attention of all Latin America was focused on the American government. Would Cuba be given her independence or would she become a United States possession?

The answer, when it finally came after over two years of military occupation of the island by United States forces, was not quite so simple. Cuba would be made independent under its own newly drafted constitution provided certain conditions were met. These conditions, commonly referred to as the Platt Amendment because they were first stated in a congressional amendment to a United States army appropriation bill, placed basic limitations on Cuba's sovereignty. They limited Cuba's freedom to enter into agreements with other foreign powers, they placed certain limitations on the borrowing power of the Cuban government, they reserved the right of the United States to construct a naval base on the island, and, most important, they gave to the United States authority to intervene in the island to preserve order and guarantee its independence.

As for Puerto Rico, it was annexed to the United States, as were the Philippine Islands.

Cuba became independent in 1902 and the island's first president, Tomás Estrada Palma, was inaugurated with great ceremony. He entered upon the administration of a country that had benefited materially by the brief period of United States occupation. Roads had been built, many steps had been taken to improve sanitary conditions, and a system of popular education had been established. During the course of occupation, American doctors had discovered that the mosquito was a carrier of yellow fever and that by eliminating the Anopheles variety the disease could be controlled and eventually stamped out. This discovery was to prove immensely beneficial to all of tropical Latin America where yellow fever and malaria were endemic.

The Spanish-American War had other and profoundly significant repercussions apart from securing the independence of Cuba and terminating Spain's last footholds in the Western Hemisphere. It demonstrated the growing military might of the United States and thereby discouraged further attempts of European powers to expand their influence in the Caribbean. It aroused new interest in construction of an isthmian canal owing to the difficulties of American naval movement during the war. Finally, it greatly stimulated American interest in Latin America and in the Caribbean area in particular.

Largely because of growing American commercial interest and investment in Latin America, a step toward closer relationships with the region was taken in 1889 by the then secretary of state, James G. Blaine, who succeeded in organizing a Pan American Conference, the first since one Bolívar had attempted to convene at Panamá in 1826. Bolívar's conference was not fully attended and little came of it, but Blaine was able to get started a series of gatherings, held generally at five-year intervals, which brought together representatives of all Latin American nations and the United States. As a device for cementing friendly relations among the participating powers, the early conferences achieved only minor successes. Latin American statesmen were far more influenced by the deeds of the

United States than by the friendly protestations of its diplomatic officials. Even the public statements of American government spokesmen were not always designed to inspire confidence. Within a few years after the first conference, President Benjamin Harrison rattled the sabre at Chile over an incident involving the behavior and treatment of American sailors in a Chilean port, and for a time the possibility of war was rumored. The incident left a legacy of ill-will and distrust. Then in 1895 Secretary of State Richard Olney issued an insult to all Latin Americans in terms and tone which were ominous. In writing of the Monroe Doctrine, he declared: 'Today the United States is practically sovereign on this continent, and its fiat is law upon the subjects to which it confines its interposition. . . .' Amid the echoes of portentous official declarations of this type, the words of friendship spoken in the conferences did not carry far.

The fact that after 1900 the United States moved rapidly into the ranks of capital exporting nations probably had less effect on American foreign policy than often asserted. Nevertheless, the rapid expansion of commercial and financial activities in Latin America coincided with the revival of Manifest Destiny, the concept that had been used earlier to justify expansion westward across the North American continent. A few vocal expansionists soon advocated turning the same slogan to useful purpose in the Caribbean area.

At the same time that the United States' interest in the Caribbean mounted as a consequence of the Spanish-American War, political and economic conditions of two island republics reached a crisis. In both the Dominican Republic and Haiti government was characterized by continuous chaos, wanton pilferage of the public treasury, and frequent revolution. Heavy loans had been negotiated abroad, and revenues were insufficient even to meet interest payments and carry on other government functions. Investors in the United States and Europe clamored for government intervention in their behalf. The United States became fearful that some European power, particularly Germany or France, might use local conditions as an excuse for intervention and perhaps more. At the same time, the Cuban adventure had demonstrated that much could be accom-

UNITED STATES PENETRATION
IN LATIN AMERICA 1899-1929

PENETRATION

MILITARY (Dates)

FINANCIAL *

MILITARY AND
FINANCIAL

* U.S. PRIVATE OR
PUBLIC CONTROL
OF CUSTOMS
COLLECTION

0 MILES 300

ALLEN K. PHILBRICK

plished through the imposition of honest collection of revenues. These factors pointed toward an arrangement similar to that provided through the Platt Amendment for Cuba. Within a few years President Theodore Roosevelt had installed American military government in the Dominican Republic and instituted a system whereby an American official was to act as receiver of customs until foreign indebtedness, at least, had been retired. In 1915 President Wilson took similar steps in Haiti, while armed intervention in Cuba had been repeated and prolonged. The conclusion was inescapable that all three island republics were little more than United States protectorates. Roosevelt made the point clear in his so-called corollary to the Monroe Doctrine, by which he asserted that if European powers were precluded from interfering in the Western Hemisphere to protect the financial and other interests of their nationals, then the United States, in whose behalf the Monroe Doctrine operated, was under obligation to protect their interests for them. Incidentally, of course, the private interests of American nationals were not overlooked. Indeed, charges were soon made by distressed nationals of the island republics that United States intervention was simply a method of exploiting the islands on behalf of foreigners. Improvements in sanitation and education were ineffective medications to apply to the wounds of injured pride and loss of national independence.

Throughout Latin America thoughtful people viewed the situation with growing alarm. Yankee Imperialism and fear of the Colossus of the North became the lingua franca of political utterances from the Río Grande to Patagonia. The theme was played particularly by social and political reformers who in country after country saw unscrupulous caudillos and politicians grow rich by accepting the apparent largesse of North American banks and private speculators. Would default signal the landing of American marines in Peru or Venezuela? Many fearfully thought that it would, and certainly the evidence they could marshal was impressive.

By far the gravest reactions stemmed from United States activities on the mainland. In 1903 Roosevelt 'took' the Panama Canal. In 1878 a French firm, the DeLesseps Company, secured from Colombia a concession to construct a canal at Panamá. The project failed owing to sanitary and engineering difficulties and poor financial management, but the arrangement had raised a storm of controversy in the United States and caused the American government to attempt to secure an alternate route through Nicaragua. The old British treaty, however, stood in the way of an American undertaking until finally, in 1901, a new agreement was ratified that terminated the Clayton-Bulwer Treaty. Promptly, a treaty was negotiated with Colombia by which the United States was to take over the rights and property of the defunct French company and obtain a perpetual lease of a six-mile strip across Panamá. Unfortunately, the Colombian senate refused to ratify the agreement. A sum of $40,000,000 was at stake, that being the amount to be paid to the stockholders of the New Panama Canal Company, successors to the bankrupt DeLesseps Company. The French concession was soon to expire, and upon expiration all rights to the property of the French company would revert to the Colombian government. It seemed worthwhile to delay the transaction. President Roosevelt thought otherwise. Conveniently, a small group of Panamanian conspirators staged a revolution on November 3, 1903, and conveniently American naval vessels were on hand to prevent the landing of Colombian troops to put down the rebellion. Washington immediately recognized the new government of the independent Republic of Panamá and proceeded to sign a canal treaty with its representative, a mystery-shrouded character by the name of Bunau-Varilla, who just happened to be in Washington. The fact that Bunau-Varilla was principal owner of the new canal company, formed to buy up large blocks of the defunct DeLesseps Company stock for a pittance in the Paris stock market, merely added spice to the whole affair. His interest in consummating sale of the French rights and properties before their reversion to the Colombian government was something more than Panamanian patriotism.

The Colombian government rightfully protested and demanded both an indemnity and an apology. For years all such requests were rejected, and anger against the United States burned deeply throughout Latin America. But the canal was built and opened to commerce in 1914. Its eventual construction fulfilled a dream as old as the Hapsburg kings of Spain who had made exploratory surveys of canal construction possibilities as early as the sixteenth century.

In 1913, United States marines entered Nicaragua, ostensibly to protect the lives and property of American citizens endangered by a bitterly fought revolution. Again an American receivership of the customs was established, and a British loan was refunded through New York bankers while new loans were extended for various Nicaraguan government purposes. A canal contract was negotiated, and the right of the United States to construct a naval base on the Gulf of Fonseca was included in the agreement, formalized in the Bryan-Chamorro Treaty of 1916. United States marines remained in Nicaragua, except for a few months in 1926, until finally withdrawn in 1933. So bitter was resentment against the United States for this intervention that in the later years of the occupation an unworthy bandit by the name of Sandino became an international hero by harassing the marines from his mountain 'hide-out' near Jinotega. His ability to escape capture became legendary, and news correspondents from afar sought to interview him. A Spanish correspondent even wrote a book in his praise. But throughout Latin America the good name of the United States was besmirched and blackened.

The long period of direct and forceful intervention by the United States in Latin American jurisdictions produced a reaction far more violent than is easily remembered today. It quickened the thinking of thousands of men, heightened the political urgencies of the epoch, and watered the seeds of an intense nationalism that soon enveloped the entire Western Hemisphere. Foreign investors, particularly those from the United States, appeared not as benefactors but as harbingers of political pressure and intervention, omens of the coming loss of sovereignty. Outward tokens of resistance to the anticipated or actual encroachments of the United States became an urgent necessity for governments of many Latin American nations. 'Yankeephobia' flowed from the pens of Latin America's most gifted writers, who warned their readers again and again to beware the 'Colossus of the North.'

Thus between the middle of the nineteenth century and the great world depression that began in 1930, Latin American civilization was deeply stirred by broad currents of change. Economically, great advances were made in agriculture and the extractive industries; socially, some regions experienced growing racial intermixture while others were transformed by the influx of new European stock; politically, liberalism finally achieved its day in court, while the increasingly aggressive activities of the United States aroused fear of intervention and fanned the flames of a growing nationalism. Crossing and mingling with all these currents was yet another which had a continuing impact — anti-clericalism. Its implications were intellectual, emotional, economic, and political, and at least some of its roots went far back into the eighteenth century. Those who attacked as well as those who defended were Catholics, and church doctrine was not the primary issue. The changes demanded, many of which had their advocates in the independence era and have already been noted, were in the realm of the church's temporal activities. Reformers protested the ownership of land by the church — land that was not used for religious purposes, but which, once it had passed into church hands, was never again available for private ownership and development. The least developed countries were least disturbed by the church issue, for continuous struggles among rival caudillos tended to preclude attention to social reform. By playing one military autocrat against another, the church was often able to retain its temporal power without serious challenge. Such was the case in Peru, Bolivia, Ecuador, and most of Central America. In Chile, Colombia, and Mexico, however, the church issue had already assumed momentous proportions and become a main feature of political controversy. Likewise in Argentina and Brazil the church problem was never very far below the surface and frequently emerged as a factor in partisan political strife.

Liberal parties throughout Latin America generally adopted platforms that included curtailing the authority and economic power of the church. Counter-movements frequently were begun in the name of religion and defense of the faith, but real motives were the maintenance of power by the clerical party and their usual allies, the landholding aristocracy. The most successful reactions against the general trend in favor of anti-clerical liberals were those led by García Moreno in Ecuador and Rafael Núñez in Colombia.

Brazil, a land generally free of sharp church-state antagonisms throughout most of its history, witnessed a clash over the emperor's asserted rights stemming from the colonial *padroado*, or patronage. The Brazilian liberal party saw the time ripe for separation of church and state, but the emperor did not choose to fly in the face of public opinion. The effects of the controversy that ensued were not far-reaching, but the popularity and prestige of Dom Pedro II were damaged, not only by his attitude toward clerical officials who resisted his authority, but because he turned back on the course the liberals had chosen for him.

In Argentina, where essential reforms were begun in the revolutionary aftermath, and in Chile, where both church and state exercised a fair degree of moderation, the position of the church was stabilized without resort to violence, but in Mexico and Colombia much blood was shed eventually over the clerical issue. In Paraguay and Uruguay, despotic governments were able to inflict their will upon the church with little opposition, for there was no large privileged group to whom the church could turn for support.

Before 1930 some of the principal currents of social, economic, and political change had begun to merge. Many of the nations developed distinct national characteristics that differentiated them from their sister republics. Argentina, vigorous, proud, and European in orientation, displayed an increasing tendency to regard herself as the champion of Latin American rights against encroachments by the United States. In this role she was occasionally supported by Chile, and the 'new' nations of South America gradually displayed the attributes of leadership on their continent — potential world powers of future eras. Despite generally harmonious economic relations with the United States, Brazil occasionally took a position alongside Argentina. The reasons for this course were not obscure. One needed only look to the Caribbean to discover that a large portion of the former Iberian empire of Spain had fallen into abject subordination to the United States.

World War I brought forcibly to the attention of many Latin Americans the full reality of their economic colonialism; and the economic, political, and social disorders of the post-war period were emphatic evidence to support their convictions. In a number of the smaller countries, the decade of the 1920's witnessed an unsurpassed orgy of foreign misinvestment. Popular reaction set in against a system that permitted such gross extravagance and dissipation of national wealth by the few who controlled. At the same time the 'liberal' trends which had appeared strong early in the twentieth century now gave evidence of having run their course, undermined and destroyed by the neglect of the many by the few. Too often, it appeared, programs of land reform, social welfare, and free elections were merely useful slogans employed to capture political office. Reforms were the subjects of debate, not the bases of action. The lofty optimism and impractical idealism of earlier times gave way to cynicism and pessimism. Pressing social and economic problems remained unsolved, too frequently for want of champions who could resist temptation. Those who remained loyal to their ideals, however, found their hopes frustrated and their efforts wasted in the labyrinth of anachronistic administrations.

The beginning of the world trade depression was soon to accentuate the economic disorders, bring discredit to governments unable to cope with the situation, and engender disillusionment with the apparently wasteful and fruitless activities of representative government. Together with the other currents of unrest, this widespread dissatisfaction stimulated a nationalism aimed at freeing Latin America from foreign economic and political domination and distributing natural resources for the benefit of the many at home rather than the few across the seas. Unfortunately no clear-cut programs were immediately forthcoming. Mexico had a vigorous program, but by 1930 it had failed to prove its merit. Sensing that the Latin Americans stood at a crisis in their history, European and even Asiatic powers entered upon an extensive courting program, to which the United States soon also became a party, each offering a solution in terms of ideology, economic assistance, and cultural transformation.

The various currents influencing men's thoughts during the long period from mid-nineteenth to early twentieth century produced dramatic changes in literature and the arts. At the opening of the era Latin American intellectuals were still strongly under the influence of European and particularly French romanticism, which stressed the symbolism of things and appealed to the emotions and the individualism of man. Picturesqueness and beauty of thought and idea were emphasized as opposed to realism and perfection of form. Latin American contributions in the arts and literature were essentially imitative and had no real basis in Latin American culture and society. After the turn of the century, the mood of Latin America began to reflect the long period of growth and change since independence. The clash of economic classes, the rise of mechanistic science, and the emergence of a spirit of skepticism combined to create a realism that challenged the concept of inevitable romantic progress. Strife and struggle were everywhere in evidence, and positivism was replacing the naturalistic philosophy that had conditioned the intellectual climate of the late eighteenth and early nineteenth centuries. Latin American writers picked up the new mood and made what is probably their first genuinely original contribution to world literature, modernism. The modernistic movements of Spanish America and Brazil were not at all the same, but both produced remarkable literary works that had deep roots in Latin American life as it was being lived. Latin American culture came increasingly to be valued for its own sake. Principal writers whose works reflected the awakening of interest in their own culture included Rubén Darío, the restless Nicaraguan poet, José Martí and Casal of Cuba, Amado Nervo and Gutiérrez Nájera of Mexico, Valencia and Silva of Colombia, and José Enrique Rodó of Uruguay.

Two of the works produced by the modernists were particularly outstanding. Darío's *Azul* was a collection of poems and short stories published in 1888, which had tremendous influence on writers in Spanish America and Spain. Rodó's *Ariel*, a small volume published in 1900, analyzed the nature of democracy and the pitfalls in the path of its development — mediocrity and materialism — which reminded him of Caliban, a brutish slave in Shakespeare's *Tempest*.

Rodó feared that the process of democratic development would push society toward the lowest common denominator, and that much that was good would be lost in the process. *Ariel* had a profound impact throughout Spanish America, for it pictured the United States as dominated by materialism and devoid of real culture, whereas Latin America was pictured as having a far greater appreciation for cultural values. The idea proved a soothing balm to the growing sense of economic inferiority of many Latin Americans, and to this day the impact of *Ariel* is still discernible in the thinking of multitudes who know as little about the United States as did Rodó.

Another innovation in modern Latin American literature was the appearance of women writers, principally poets. Worthy of mention were Delmira Agustini and Juana de Ibarbourou of Uruguay, Alfonsina Storni of Argentina, and particularly Gabriela Mistral of Chile.

Since 1900, the most significant literary achievements have been in realistic novels. Spanish American writers have shown an increasing interest in social conditions, and brutally realistic books have been written on the plight of the Indian, on the Mexican Revolution of 1911–19, and on the pathetic attempt of a mestizo or mulatto to rise above the level of the society into which he was born. The masterpiece on the revolutionary period of Mexico is Mariano Azuela's *Los de abajo*, completed in 1916.

Brazil's greatest literary figure of the nineteenth century was Joaquim Maria Machado de Assis, who was both poet and novelist. Among the romantic novelists, Alfredo D'Escragnolle, Viscount Taunay, won the most lasting fame. His most famous work, *Inocência*, published in 1872, concerned rural life in Mato Grosso, and was one of the forerunners of the realistic movement. The Brazilian work that has received the most widespread recognition, however, was *Os sertões*, by Euclides da Cunha, a book translated into English under the title of *Revolt in the Backlands*. It is a remarkable description of the Brazilian back country and its people, and centers around the rebellion of Antônio Conselheiro and his sertanejo disciples in the 1890's.

Growing out of the bitter social revolution that swept Mexico

from 1911 to 1919, the currents of which continued to flow strongly
on through the 1920's and into the present era, came outstanding literary and artistic endeavor. José Vasconcelos wrote incit-
ingly and bitterly against foreign economic domination and the
imperialism of the United States, while José Clemente Orozco and
Diego Rivera depicted the great social struggle of the Mexican lower
classes in murals that have become world famous.

Throughout all of Latin America, the strong currents of social,
economic, and political change were reflected in a larger awareness
of social and economic problems. Writers and aritsts were inspired
by awakened national pride, but they also reflected a growing feeling
of frustration and inferiority in those nations whose progress had not
been great and whose material advances were but tokens in comparison with those of the United States and Western European powers.
Evidence of maturity and less-confused thinking marked the close
of the epoch, when popular demands shifted from panaceas offered
by aliens to nativist solutions to the problems of the few and the
many. It was no longer easy for those in power to continue on the
reckless path which their predecessors had trod. The most insistent
demands were for a more equitable distribution of land and wealth
and the end of economic colonialism. The strong undercurrent running through these demands was that the natural resources of Latin
America should be enjoyed by Latin Americans.

XXXI

Southern South America: Rapid Growth and Political Experimentation

> Protect . . . private enterprises for the construction of rail-
> roads. Shower them with advantages, with privileges, with
> every favor imaginable, without hesitating at the means . . .
> Let treasure as well as men come from abroad to live among
> us. Surround it with immunities and privileges so that it will
> take out citizenship and stay.
>
> JUAN BAUTISTA ALBERDI *

I N 1860 Argentina, Uruguay, and Chile were still
relatively poor and sparsely populated regions, having been among the poorest parts of the Spanish empire in South
America. The wild Indians of the southern frontiers had yet to be
subdued, except in Uruguay; cattle ranges were open and unfenced,
and livestock was more remarkable for its fleetness and toughness
than for the production of meat or wool. The area of tilled land
was extremely small. A few thousand immigrants had come since independence to struggle for a living in the empty hinterland, or to
engage in commerce and industry in the cities. Trade and economic
activity were not greatly improved over their condition in the
colonial period. Short railroad lines penetrated the interior in a few
places in Argentina and Chile, but Uruguay had yet to build her
first line, and many fertile regions in all three countries were totally
without suitable means of communication. Oligarchies of the few

---

* *Bases y puntos de partida para la organización política de la República
Argentina*, Buenos Aires, n.d. (1853).

families of great landowners dominated economic and political life; the bulk of the populations was landless, illiterate, and poverty-stricken.

Argentina and Uruguay were yet to acquire the political stability and unity which had given Chile an initial advantage over her neighbors, and which made possible a gradual weakening of the power of the landed oligarchy through the rise of new economic forces in the major cities. The Liberal party had been regenerated by the rise of a middle class; this middle class demanded liberty in politics and thought as essential to social progress.

While Chilean liberals fought to curtail the power of the president and the church, in Argentina the main division was still between Buenos Aires and the other provinces. In 1861 General Bartolomé Mitre led the porteño troops against the confederation in an indecisive action at Pavón. His opponent, General Urquiza, regarded the result as a moral defeat, and retired to Entre Ríos. Following President Derqui's flight Mitre became not only governor of Buenos Aires but the provisional head of the confederation. Modern Argentina at last took shape, and provincial defections declined, to disappear altogether after the federalization of Buenos Aires in 1880. Settlement of the 'capital question' was the most important political achievement of nineteenth-century Argentina. In Uruguay, meanwhile, the blancos and colorados still fought desperate wars for control of the government.

Between 1860 and 1930 Chile and Argentina, and later Uruguay, underwent remarkable transformations and made striking advances in economic development, population growth, and social and political maturity. In all three countries powerful liberal movements developed whose aims included redressing the balance between the many and the few in the governments, and broadening the economic bases by the building of railroads and other means of transportation and by reviving or establishing livelihoods in addition to agriculture. In some of these economic designs all groups agreed in principle. One handicap common to all three countries was scarcity of population; encouragement of immigration was not new, but the period from 1860 to 1930 marked the high point in population growth by the introduction of foreigners. Intellectually, a resurgence of interest in Europe occurred, and French culture again rose to a preferred position.

In the years immediately following independence hopeful Europeans had come to the coastal towns as merchants and shopkeepers, and a few had acquired agricultural or pastoral lands. Disillusionment followed, and the stream of European immigration was diverted away from southern South America by social conditions, economic insecurity, and physical dangers arising from political chaos. Probably the most constant obstacle to attracting immigrants, however, was the system of latifundia, which restricted the prospect of acquiring land.

The problem of obtaining land was most acute in Uruguay, although much of the land made available for colonization in Chile was unattractive. In both of these countries European immigration played an influential role despite its smallness. Many of those who emigrated to Uruguay moved on to Argentina once their hopes of obtaining land had been dashed, or their lives and property imperiled by one of the numerous uprisings against the government. The Italians, most numerous of those who came to Uruguay, remained for the most part in Montevideo. In Chile the Germans were most numerous; they settled primarily in the south, and were especially influential in the growth of dairy farming and in the development of Valdivia.

It was in Argentina that immigration played its most striking role in Latin America. When the rift between Buenos Aires and the other provinces was healed, Argentina entered into an epoch of remarkable growth. Agricultural colonies of Swiss had been founded during the previous decade, and many others followed once their success had been assured. In most of the new Argentine agricultural settlements the colonists were able to obtain land, either as an outright gift or at a nominal price. Between 1869, when the first census was taken, and 1895, the population increased from less than two million to nearly four. By the latter date a fourth of the population was foreign born.

By 1900 the era of agricultural colonization was past, for the new uses made of the land in growing crops for export led to a rapid rise in land values. Thereafter it became extremely difficult for immigrants to obtain titles, and the colonization program necessarily was abandoned. Immigration continued, however, and reached its peak in the decade before the beginning of World War I. Immigrants who wanted to engage in agriculture either rented land as tenant farmers or became sharecroppers.

Most numerous of the immigrants to Argentina were the Italians and Spaniards, who supplied three-fourths of the total. Most influential in proportion to their numbers were the British, whose capital and commercial connections gave them enormous prestige, while English livestock rapidly replaced criollo stock on the ranges after the development of the refrigerated ship.

By the close of the century the immigrant Italians, Spaniards, French, Belgians, British, Germans, and Swiss had become firmly established and at home in Argentina, as landowners, merchants, shopkeepers, and operators of hotels and restaurants. In commerce and related occupations they were far more numerous than native Argentinians, who were forced to adapt themselves to changing methods of business or lose out. They gave Argentina a vigorous middle class, but a middle class that had, before 1912, little voice in the government.

Immigration to Uruguay and Chile continued to come in a small but fairly steady stream, until World War I caused a complete interruption. After the war immigration was resumed, but it had almost ceased before the hemisphere-wide movement to close the gates to Europeans and Asiatics occurred about 1930.

In both Chile and Argentina there were groups interested in improving the livestock industry and agriculture, but their first efforts aroused little enthusiasm. The Argentine *Sociedad Rural* was founded in 1866, but when its first livestock show was held, in 1875, the majority of the estancieros remained aloof. In the following year the first shipment of refrigerated beef to Europe was made, and the Sociedad Rural soon became a powerful force in improving the livestock industry. The first Chilean agricultural exposition was held in 1869, but in Chile, too, the lethargy of many of the great landowners was at first difficult to overcome.

Increasing revenues enabled the Chilean government to engage in various projects of physical improvement but many of those undertaken did not enhance the country's capacity to produce. Funds were allocated for forts and garrisons needed to defend the Indian frontier, for beautifying the capital, and for introducing streetcar lines and extending the railways. At the same time, however, private Chilean capital moved into the nitrate and guano fields of Bolivia and Peru. Over-expansion, the failure of revenues to reach expected proportions, and a costly Indian uprising in 1868 led to a severe depression in the 1870's. The crisis was heightened by the seizure of Chilean nitrate and guano properties in Peru and Bolivia, and by the War of the Pacific which followed.

Argentine economic development, too, was retarded by war, a costly and prolonged conflict with Paraguay, 1865–70. Although the country gained some war profits by the sale of supplies to the Allied forces, principally Brazilian, President Mitre's leadership was diverted from more appropriate domestic problems, and the lands taken from Paraguay were little compensation for the cost in effort, lives, and money, in comparison to the rich prizes that fell to Chile as spoils of the War of the Pacific.

Uruguayan landowners and merchants began in the 1870's to devote greater interest to their private affairs and less to politics, stimulated in part by the example of Argentinians. These individuals soon regarded the customary civil disturbances with strong disfavor, and they brought pressure on the government to preserve order. As a result of their pressure the governments became more authoritarian and took sterner measures against disturbers of the peace. But even the most strenuous efforts of soldier-presidents could not immediately stamp out the custom of decades, and Uruguay continued to be politically unstable. Economic advances were made in spite of political instability.

After the Paraguayan War had been concluded Argentina entered upon a period of economic growth unparalleled in South

America. Economic development became a national passion; foreign capital was welcomed, and surplus English wealth was poured into a multitude of enterprises such as municipal streetcar lines and gasworks. Promoters like William Wheelwright of Massachusetts won wealth and fame as railroad builders. The coming of immigrant and alien capital and the rapid expansion of agriculture and the live-stock industry soon made Argentina the most prosperous country in Latin America. The opening of vast lands to the south following the destruction of the plains Indians in 1880 and the final settlement of the capital question in the same year, combined to give added impetus to European home-seekers and speculators. At the same time the government followed a policy of encouraging foreign companies by granting overly generous concessions to those engaged in national projects such as the building of railroads.

In the 1880's commerce surpassed all previous records; railway lines were extended in many directions, and Argentine landowners enjoyed the pleasant sensation of suddenly acquired wealth. For much of the physical improvement Argentinians bestowed their gratitude indiscriminately on foreign promoters and companies. But because of the government's guarantees of minimum interest on investments for railroad construction and operation, in a distant day of calmer reflection many Argentinians realized that they rather than foreigners had, in the final analysis, supplied most of the money, and that their railroads and tramways had been dearly bought. At the moment, however, the broadening economic horizon which these improvements opened to Argentinians made them aspire to even grander projects.

The Chilean government, too, engaged in many government-financed public projects during the 1880's, while the rise of a native capital enabled the growth of private enterprises to keep pace. The speedy exploitation of the territories taken by conquest from Bolivia and Peru more than doubled governmental revenues in five years, and future prospects seemed even more promising. The government optimistically undertook new and more grandiose public projects, and strived to make Chile more attractive to aliens and their wealth. The construction of roads and bridges, and the technical skills provided by foreigners, greatly facilitated mining and agriculture, and, as in Argentina, the benefits of the physical improvements were widely appreciated.

Both governments, however, made the same crucial financial error. During earlier crises both had resorted to the printing press and the issuance of inconvertible paper money. This currency was still in circulation, and its value continually decreased, to the detriment of commerce. For a few years the Argentine government converted the paper pesos into stable gold notes, but abandoned the project in 1884. The paper peso began a more rapid decline in value, and threatened to carry the merchants to ruin. The cattlemen and wheat growers, however, approved of inflation. They sold their products abroad for stable European currencies; and they soon discovered that their pound notes and francs were more valuable as the peso declined. The government was still their instrument, and it did not jeopardize their pleasure by ending the inflation. It was, in fact, accused of secretly issuing additional paper pesos to encourage inflationary trends; this charge officials did not admit or deny.

In both countries inflation caused a marked increase in the cost of living, while wages rose too slowly to keep pace. The merchants were particularly troubled. Their desperation increased as they saw the governments blithely continue to pour vast sums into the building of railroads while making plans for future expenditures of a similar nature. No attempt was made to stabilize the currency. In Argentina the unfavorable balance of trade rose sharply, and in three years the public debt more than doubled. The government seemed unconcerned over its financial condition even while negotiating new loans to pay the interest due on old ones! In 1890 commerce virtually ceased, bringing ruin to the merchants and hardship to many others. The government fell, and because of the financial panic, immigration which might have benefited Argentina was diverted to southern Brazil for several years.

The crisis in Chile was heightened by the clash between president and congress. Inflation and high prices made the situation of the poorer classes critical, for their welfare had become increasingly associated with the demand for Chilean nitrates and copper. Much remained to be done in broadening the economic base, for poverty, drunkenness, and vagrancy were widespread. The growing tension caused by rising prices and the threat of a crash reacted against President Balmaceda's vast program of public works and the expenditures it involved, and in the civil war that broke out against his rule, his opponents fought with great bitterness.

Both Chile and Argentina made rapid recoveries from their economic and political crises of 1890, and by the end of the century foreign trade had risen to new highs, permitting the governments to turn once more to relatively unproductive but pleasing projects such as beautifying the capitals, laying out parks, and paving streets. The Avenida de Mayo in Buenos Aires began to have a Parisian flavor, reflecting the Europeanization of the Argentinian's outlook in the preceding two decades. The newly rich landowners of the 1880's had discovered the delights of Paris and the Riviera, where their liberality made Argentine wealth a legend. European, and particularly French, influences on Argentine life multiplied.

In the twentieth century Uruguay, having at last achieved political equilibrium, rose rapidly in the economic scale. She had not attracted alien capital to the same degree as had Argentina, and Uruguayan statesmen such as José Batlle y Ordóñez were determined to retain control of the country's natural resources and major industries. To provide Uruguayans with credit needed for business enterprises, the government expanded the activities of the Bank of the Republic and acquired control of the Mortgage Bank of Uruguay. Both institutions played an increasingly important part in the economic expansion of the country. Uruguayan economic development now followed an unusual course, for the government took an active role.

The Uruguayan government went into business itself, particularly in competition with foreign companies. It produced electricity, operated port facilities, and manufactured cement. Other industries were taken over in whole or in part. The Uruguayan program of governmental participation in economic activity is especially noteworthy, for it has been adopted in part by many Latin American governments since that time. Uruguay, despite her late start and her limited resources, marked out a path of moderate economic nationalism which attracted widespread emulation. The efforts of Uruguay were fairly successful in keeping her natural resources under the control of nationals, but as in Argentina and Chile, rural agricultural workers remained almost untouched by the forward sweep of commerce and industry.

In contrast to the political decline following the triumph of the advocates of parliamentary government in 1891, Chilean economic expansion continued. Foreign trade increased, and government revenues were ample despite waste and fraud. The apparent prosperity, however, did not permeate all classes, and labor unrest grew in proportion to the number of men engaged in mining and industry; the rural peasantry remained politically inarticulate.

The rise in demand for wheat and beef, copper and nitrates, during World War I, temporarily aided Argentina, Uruguay, and Chile. By the end of the war Argentina was no longer a debtor nation. All three suffered during the abrupt decline in demand in the readjustment of the 1920's, and Chile was particularly hard hit by the growth of the synthetic nitrate industry in Europe and a fall in the price of copper. One favorable step was taken to salvage the nation's currency after years of delay; the Central Bank was established, and the peso's more violent fluctuations were curtailed by backing it with gold.

Foreign investments continued to rise in Chile and Argentina, and at a slower pace in Uruguay. By 1929 the United States alone had 600 million dollars invested in Chile; the Chilean government continued borrowing money abroad until the world depression dried up the sources. The hostility toward foreign capital pervading all parts of Latin America was heightened by the depression, and the new economic nationalism reacted against the governments of Argentina and Chile, for they were blamed for the fact that many key industries and resources were the property of aliens.

Related to the problems of population growth, expansion of effective area, and attraction of foreign capital, was the continued existence of warlike Indians in the south of Argentina and Chile. These Indians were a centuries-old problem, for they had never been conquered nor effectively controlled, and they were not culturally adaptable to peaceful integration. Costly military establishments maintained a tenuous line of resistance. When, for any reason, the troops were needed elsewhere, the Indians overran the frontiers.

Both countries resolved to end the Indian problem. In Argentina the final destruction of the Ranqueles awaited General Julio A. Roca's war of extermination in 1879, while the Araucanians of southern Chile remained troublesome until the veterans of the War of the Pacific were sent against them in the 1880's. In both cases the Indian problem ended, and a vast new territory was opened for settlement. Uruguay faced no similar problem at this time, for her warlike Indians had been subdued and destroyed or absorbed before mid-century.

In the development of educational institutions and in national cultural activities, the period from 1860 to 1930 was particularly fruitful. Argentina and Chile, because of their earlier progress toward political stability, gained a vast lead over Uruguay. It must be remembered, in considering the expansion of public education, that public education was for the poor. The wealthy generally did not send their sons to public schools.

The promotion of public education was one of the ideals of the planners of independence. Bernardo O'Higgins of Chile, Bernardino Rivadavia of Argentina, and José Artigas of Uruguay were all strong proponents of the idea. Every Chilean government regarded the extension of public education in the nation's interest, despite the opposition of many members of the conservative oligarchy. Argentine education, and that of Uruguay, languished in the long era of political disorders. It was only in 1868, with the election of Domingo F. Sarmiento to the presidency, that rapid strides were made in Argentina.

Sarmiento, self-educated and of provincial background, was the greatest champion of education and civilization Latin America had produced. 'Mister Me,' as he was called because of his lack of modesty, vigorously set about educating and civilizing his countrymen. To him the enemy was ignorance, and the gaucho its epitome. Education would solve all problems once the gaucho and the caudillo had been cast into oblivion. One of his first acts as president was to order a census taken, the first of its kind in Argentina. He learned that the country had nearly two million inhabitants, a third of whom lived in the city and province of Buenos Aires. Only 12 per cent were foreign born. It did not take an official count to inform him that the vast majority of Argentinians lived in poverty and ignorance.

An admirer and friend of Horace Mann, Sarmiento sought to emulate him in reforming education in his country. He won noteworthy success in establishing a primary school system and in implanting his educational philosophy. With the aid of his minister of education, Nicolás Avellaneda, he doubled the number of public schools, and Argentina was able to boast the highest proportion of children attending schools of any South American country. In six years the number of students rose from 30,000 to 100,000. The literacy rate increased from 22 per cent in 1869 to 50 per cent in 1895. By 1930 it was above 80 per cent, the highest in Latin America.

Secondary education in Chile received a similar impetus under the lead of Diego Barros Arana, director of the National Institute and one of the greatest Latin American historians of the nineteenth century. For the first time instructors were required to specialize in certain fields of learning instead of attempting to teach all. Historical studies flourished, and the natural sciences were divided into separate courses. In the same period an agricultural school was founded. But even as late as 1920 only half of the children of school age were attending schools, and technical training was still inadequate for the country's needs.

Attempts to secularize education in Chile and to lay greater stress on the sciences were violently opposed by the pro-clerical wing of the Conservative party, who regarded the trend as anti-religious, and who also preferred to retain university positions in the form of political patronage. For a brief period in 1872 their views prevailed, and they were able to force through a law giving seminaries conducted by religious groups the right to grant certificates which must be accepted by the university. An auction of these certificates made the law an embarrassment, and it was repealed.

The first genuine accomplishments in furthering education in Uruguay came only in and after the era of professional soldier-presidents, beginning in 1875. In 1877 the average attendance in public schools was only about 12,000. In the next few years the number of schools and students was greatly increased, and the quality of instruction was improved. In 1900 there were less than 500 primary schools in Uruguay, and no secondary schools outside Montevideo. By 1930 the number of schools had tripled, but outside Montevideo educational facilities were available for only a third of the children. The late nineteenth century was, however, a time of marked upsurge in intellectual activity, and one in which interest in politics was gradually displaced by other pursuits.

In literature romanticism was giving way to realism, still under French influence. Argentina and Uruguay produced a number of noteworthy poets, particularly Estanislao del Campo, author of *Fausto*, and José Hernández, whose epic poem *Martín Fierro* glorified the vanishing gaucho, and was a reply to Sarmiento's earlier *Facundo*. Juan Zorrilla de San Martín was one of Uruguay's chief romantic poets, and also one of the early poets of the modernist school. Eduardo Acevedo Díaz and Carlos Reyles have been ranked among the best of Uruguay's novelists of the period. Alberto Blest Gana inaugurated the realistic novel in Chile. The Indianist theme inspired many writers, including the poet Pablo Neruda of Chile. After the rise of modernism in 1888, it, too, had many followers in all three countries.

Chilean historical writers of the period were outstanding, foremost among them Miguel Luis Amunátegui, Benjamin Vicuña Mackenna, and Diego Barros Arana. José Toribio Medina, historian and bibliographer, also made a monumental contribution to scholarship in his many volumes. Bartolomé Mitre, Juan B. Justo, and Joaquín V. González were among the best-known Argentinians concerned with improving the intellectual life of their country. Mitre, statesman, historian, and publicist, founded the eminent newspaper, *La Nación*, which shared with *La Prensa*, also of Buenos Aires, a reputation for excellence extending far beyond the limits of Argentina. Justo, a militant socialist, fought for the improvement of polit-

ical life and for the consolidation of democracy. González, statesman and educator, founded the National University of La Plata,
and wrote fifty volumes in the fields of politics, law, history, teaching, and literature.

One of the most influential of Latin American writers of the
period was José Enrique Rodó of Uruguay, whose small book called
Ariel was widely read by the youth of his generation. As already
indicated, Rodó gave his countrymen a comforting if inaccurate picture of their spiritual nobility, typified by Ariel, in sharp contrast
to the baser materialism of Caliban — the United States. *Ariel's*
following finally dwindled, but Rodó was still remembered for his
literary criticism and for his influence on style.

The establishment and improvement of newspapers was another
noteworthy feature of cultural development. *La Nación* and *La
Prensa* of Buenos Aires both appeared by 1870. There had been only
two noteworthy daily papers in Chile in 1860, but before the end of
the century the number had increased to thirty, for the desire to obtain news of the War of the Pacific greatly stimulated the habit of
reading daily papers. In 1872 freedom of the press was guaranteed by
law.

The conflict between church and state, characteristic of the
period, was present to some degree in each of the countries. The
colorados of Uruguay passed anti-clerical legislation, but the blancos
did not become a clerical party. The authority of the church
dwindled rapidly in the 1880's, when civil marriage was made compulsory and divorce legalized, and the registration of births and
deaths was taken over by the government. Financial support from
the government was drastically curtailed, leaving the church weak
and unable to participate effectively in political strife.

Differences between state and church in Argentina were settled
early by the government asserting and maintaining the right of
patronage formerly exercised by the king of Spain. The constitution
of 1853 specified Roman Catholicism as the official religion, but
conceded toleration to other faiths. Argentina has been relatively
free of church-state contention until very recent times.

The clash between church and state in Chile was more heated, for

the liberals soon began agitating for abolition of the ecclesiastical
courts, and of the church's right to register births and deaths, perform the marriage ceremony, and control education. One segment
of the Conservative party came to the support of the church. The
intensity of the struggle was caused by the conviction of the liberals
that the church was an obstacle in the way of change, and they were
determined to weaken its power. The first inroads into clerical
authority were the abolition of the clerical courts and the opening of
cemeteries to non-Catholics. Not satisfied with these measures, the
liberals renewed their efforts, and the partisans of the church resisted desperately. In the 1880's further laws were passed, largely
under the lead of José Manuel Balmaceda, which carried out most
of the anti-clerical program except for separation of church and
state. The constitution of 1925 added this last feature.

Foreign relations were marred during the epoch by two major
wars among Latin American nations, and a minor clash between
Spain, on the one hand, and Chile and Peru, on the other. The conflict with Spain, 1865-6, was caused by resentment over Spain's
brusque treatment of Peru. Chileans were indignant at Spain's seizure of the Chincha islands from Peru, and regarded the incident
as a threat to all of the Pacific Coast nations. A mob attacked the
Spanish legation in Santiago. The Chilean government offered an
explanation to the Spanish admiral, José Manuel Pareja Septién,
and considered the incident closed. In September, 1865, however,
while Chileans were celebrating the anniversary of their national
independence, the Spanish squadron appeared before Valparaiso
and Pareja demanded a twenty-one gun salute. The Chileans responded with expressions of patriotism and a declaration of war.

To carry on a naval campaign against the Spanish flotilla, Chile
had only one mediocre sloop, the *Esmeralda*, and the splendid traditions established under the aegis of Lord Cochrane during the
wars of independence. The *Esmeralda* left her refuge in Chiloé and
captured the Spanish schooner, *Covadonga*. On learning of this humiliation, Pareja committed suicide. His successor ordered a blockade of Chilean ports in an effort to recover the *Covadonga* and to

restore Spanish pride. Before retiring from the Pacific, the Spanish warships bombarded the undefended port of Valparaiso.

The conflict with Spain demonstrated once more to Latin American nations the need for collective defensive measures, and to Chileans the need for a naval force to defend their long coastline. The government ordered the purchase of two warships of most recent design, and built fortifications for Valparaiso. Chilean statesmen promoted the old idea of a Spanish American confederation. In 1865 this policy was implemented by offensive and defensive pacts with the governments of Peru, Bolivia, and Ecuador, but the project ended there. The new Chilean warships were soon to be used against Peru, for the foreign threat was quickly forgotten.

In the Plata region Uruguay, the much-chewed bone of contention between Argentina and Brazil, figured in the start of a major war. The blancos and the colorados, in their customary battles for the presidency, frequently sought help from Argentina or Brazil. In 1863, for example, the colorados under Colonel Venancio Flores, supported by aid from Buenos Aires, attacked the blanco regime of Bernardo P. Berro.

The disorders which had prevailed in Uruguay since her independence led to frequent violations of the Brazilian border. Separatist movements in nearby Rio Grande do Sul made the Brazilian government especially sensitive to Uruguayan political discord, but its many complaints were unavailing. In 1864 Brazil again presented strong demands to the Uruguayan government to restore and preserve peace along the frontier, a demand which the hard-pressed blancos could not meet. When they failed to control the raiders or to give satisfaction, the imperial government massed troops near the southern border.

President Mitre of Argentina attempted to prevent the outbreak of war, but Brazil's decision to make reprisals and the continued dissension in Uruguay made his effort fruitless. Francisco Solano López, dictator of Paraguay and commander of the largest army in South America, now perceived an opportunity to indulge his ambition to become arbiter of the continent. He protested the Brazilian action, promised support to the blancos, and demanded to know Brazil's intentions. His pretensions were slighted by Brazil, and his delusions ran rampant. He reacted by sending his troops into undefended Mato Grosso. Had he gone immediately to the aid of the blancos he might have died a hero. They resisted stubbornly, meanwhile vainly waiting for the aid he had loudly promised.

Argentine participation in the conflict was not long delayed. Solano López requested permission to cross Corrientes to reach Uruguay, but was refused by Mitre. He retaliated by secretly declaring war on Argentina; the declaration was not announced until a munitions ship en route from Argentina was thought to be safely in Paraguayan waters. By the exercise of discretion, Solano López might have won the support of Entre Ríos and other anti-porteño provinces; instead, he made an oblique contribution to Argentine unity by giving the contesting factions compelling reasons for uniting against him.

The Paraguayan War had little to commend it from any standpoint. The depraved character of Solano López, his stupid conduct of the war, and his brutality toward his countrymen, and even members of his own family, have made it easy to obscure the terrible responsibility which Argentina and Brazil shared for the devastating conflict. But the soon-published 'secret' treaty between them made it clear that Paraguay was fair game for partition. Knowledge of this treaty stiffened Paraguayan resistance and turned public opinion against the allies. Uruguay, too, joined the war against Paraguay, but her role was negligible, and she did not figure in plans for dismembering the country. All of the participants, however, suffered greatly as a result of the war; none made any gain.

The conquest of Paraguay proved far more costly and protracted than had been anticipated. The heroic and unexpected resistance of Paraguayans and misunderstanding among the allies prolonged the unequal conflict for five years. In 1868 Mitre, who had been forced to neglect domestic affairs to command the allied army, returned to Buenos Aires, and Argentina's active participation in the fighting declined. The Duke of Caxias, Brazil's ranking officer in the campaign, took charge of the war. The allied naval squadron, largely

Brazilian, played a significant role in the transport of troops and supplies, and in several decisive engagements, such as the reduction of the fort at Humaitá. Efforts to end the war by negotiation were negated by Emperor Dom Pedro's insistence on the removal of Solano López as a preliminary step, and the sanguinary conflict ended only with the death of the Paraguayan dictator at the hands of Brazilian troops. The cost of the war in human life was appalling, and it served no useful purpose.

Before the War of the Pacific began, in 1879, Chile and Argentina seemed on the verge of hostilities over their mutual boundaries at the southern extremity of the continent. Feelings rose high, as if the territory involved were of great value, and in 1878 both countries sent naval squadrons to the Strait of Magellan. In both nations there were many persons who regarded warfare between Chile and Argentina as unthinkable, and the governments agreed to negotiation. In 1881 they reached an agreement whereby Chile was left in possession of the strait. The dividing line agreed on was along the highest peaks of the Andes, erroneously believed also to be the continental watershed. The question arose again when it was discovered that the highest peaks did not divide the waters, and again there was a threat of war. Once more, however, the problem was amicably settled, as was a controversy over the boundary in the Puna of Atacama.

While the earlier issue with Argentina remained threatening, differences arose with Bolivia over exploitation of guano and nitrate deposits in the Bolivian province of Antofagasta. In 1866 Chile had acknowledged Bolivian sovereignty north of the 24th parallel, south latitude, and the two countries agreed to divide equally the revenues derived from taxes on minerals and guano taken from the area between the 23rd and 25th parallels. Chileans opened mines in Antofagasta, and their enterprise was responsible for a sudden increase in nitrate production in this zone. The first Bolivian railroad was a part of the same project, for it was needed to transport minerals from the mines to the port.

In 1874 the Bolivian government agreed not to assess any new taxes on Chileans in exchange for Chile's cession of all claims north of the 24th parallel. The Bolivian government was not long in the control of any group or party in this period, and the treaty was violated a few years later by the imposition of new taxes.

Relations between Chile and Peru were strained at the same time, also over nitrate exploitation, on this occasion in the Peruvian province of Tarapacá. Chilean companies refused to co-operate in a Peruvian plan to raise the price of nitrates. In 1873, fearing the consequences of taking action against Chile, Peru and Bolivia signed a defensive-offensive alliance. This treaty frequently has been called secret. There seems little doubt, however, that Chilean officials were aware of it, although the Chilean public did not take notice of it until it was employed in arousing a patriotic effort against the signers. Soon after the treaty had been made, Peru decreed the nitrate industry of Tarapacá a state monopoly, and set the price it would pay producers. Another law forced Chileans to sell their holdings to the government. In 1875 they surrendered their buildings and equipment on a promise of compensation, a promise which was not kept.

In 1878 a newly arisen Bolivian dictator, Hilarión Daza, decided to try similar action against the Chilean Nitrate Company of Antofagasta. His act of levying a heavy tax violated a treaty, while Peru had not been bound by any agreement. The Chileans refused to pay, and in February, 1879, the day the company's holdings were to be sold at auction, Chilean soldiers occupied Antofagasta.

Because of her treaty with Bolivia, Peru found herself suddenly involved in a war in which she had nothing to gain and much to lose. The Chilean government was asked to withdraw its troops and negotiate the dispute; on Chile's refusal Peru mobilized and Bolivia prepared for war. In April, denouncing the so-called secret treaty, Chile declared war on the allies.

If numbers alone were an important consideration, Chile's action appeared suicidal, for her army was outnumbered nearly four to one by the combined forces of the allies, and Peru's recently acquired ironclad cruisers were thought superior to those of Chile. Chilean progress since independence, however, was a factor to be considered. The contest proved unequal, as many expected, but the superiority lay with Chile. Antofagasta was easily held, and Bolivia could do little more than join forces with Peru.

On the sea the campaign was especially significant. Peru and Chile each boasted two formidable cruisers of recent design, in addition to outmoded sailing vessels. The Chilean cruisers were the *Cochrane* and *Blanco Encalada*, named after heroes of the wars of independence; the Peruvian cruisers were the *Huáscar* and the *Independencia*. Chile sent the old sailing ships *Esmeralda* and *Covadonga* to blockade the port of Iquique, where they were found by the Peruvian cruisers. In the actions that followed the *Huáscar* rammed and sank the *Esmeralda*, whose crew established a Chilean tradition by going down with guns manned and colors flying. The *Independencia*, in a similar attack on the *Covadonga*, struck a reef and was lost. For Peru the engagement was costly, for she lost her best warship; Chileans, on the other hand, were greatly stimulated by the heroism of their men and the destruction of the most powerful enemy vessel. Peru, nevertheless, carried the war to the coast of Chile with considerable success, until the *Huáscar* encountered the *Cochrane* and *Blanco Encalada* and was forced to surrender after a battle that made history as the first major clash of ironclads on the high seas. After this victory, Chile controlled the sea, and by October, 1879, the way was prepared for an invasion of Peru.

Chile immediately launched an attack against allied forces in Iquique. The province of Tarapacá fell in a single battle, the repercussions of which were felt in the allied capitals. General Mariano Prado resigned the presidency of Peru, and Daza was deposed. Tacna and Arica were taken, and the coast of Peru blockaded. An attempt to negotiate peace made on board a warship of the United States failed because the allies refused Chile's demand for cession of Antofagasta and Tarapacá. Warfare was resumed, with the Chileans determined on the conquest of Lima.

Late in 1880 a large Chilean force landed on the Peruvian coast south of Callao, and the march to Lima began. The Peruvians rallied to defend their capital with desperate but futile sacrifice. In January, 1881, their resistance was shattered, and Lima fell. The War of the Pacific was over, but for two more years guerrilla activity kept

Peru in a state of anarchy, and the problems engendered by the war endured for half a century. Not until 1883 could a peace treaty be signed. By this treaty, signed at Ancón, Peru ceded to Chile the province of Tarapacá and yielded possession of Tacna and Arica for ten years, after which a plebiscite was to be held to determine future ownership. A separate peace was made with Bolivia; title to Antofagasta became Chilean, leaving Bolivia completely landlocked.

The 'Question of the Pacific,' as the unsettled fate of Tacna and Arica was called, disturbed relations between Chile and Peru until 1929. Attempts to hold the proposed plebiscite failed, largely because the aggressive actions of Chileans in the provinces made Peruvians fear that a fair election would not be held. In 1911 Peru severed diplomatic relations with Chile. Numerous attempts to bring the two countries together failed. United States President Herbert Hoover took an active interest in the dispute, and he helped persuade the two countries to restore diplomatic relations and to reach a solution. In 1928 they exchanged envoys once more, and in the following year the issue was finally resolved. Arica remained a part of Chile, and Tacna was returned to Peru, along with an indemnity.

In 1891 Chile became embroiled in a dispute with the United States. Feeling against the North American power was strong, for the Congressionalist party, victors in the recent civil war, regarded the United States as having favored liberal José Manuel Balmaceda. During the war a congressionalist ship, the *Itata*, bringing munitions from the United States, had been intercepted by a United States warship. Patrick Egan, United States minister to Chile, incurred further disfavor by giving asylum to political refugees when the civil war ended.

Under these circumstances, with the unsettled conditions caused by the bitter civil war and the known hostility toward the United States, the captain of the *U.S.S. Baltimore* unwisely permitted a liberty party ashore at Valparaiso. The seamen apparently sought the entertainment customarily provided by port cities, and became embroiled in street fights with Chileans. The Valparaiso police either were reluctant or unable to disperse the mob, although Chilean army and navy officers acted quickly to escort some of the seamen to safety. Before all could be returned to the *Baltimore*, two had been killed and several injured.

The incident was unfortunate but not surprising, considering the state of tempers as a result of the civil war. The repercussions, however, were astonishing. Egan placed the blame entirely on Chilean officials, even before an investigation had been made to determine where the fault lay. His tactless demands were coolly received, and he heightened the tension by the irritation he displayed at what he regarded as procrastination on the part of the Chilean government. President Benjamin Harrison, who could have easily settled the dispute with little friction, chose instead to employ it for political ends in the approaching election in the United States, and the affair grew beyond reasonable proportions. A peremptory demand for an apology and reparations was sent Chile in January, 1892. Without waiting for a reply, Harrison delivered a war message to Congress. Chile offered an indemnity to be determined by the Supreme Court of the United States, and the incident was officially closed. It left Chileans with strong feelings about the United States which were neither flattering nor easy to dispel.

One of the strongest currents in the southern South American nations was the rising tide of liberalism. Liberal predominance was achieved first in Chile, for Argentina's political maturity was delayed by the provincial caudillos and the capital question. The nineteenth-century Uruguayan parties, the blancos or *nacionalistas*, as they began to call themselves, and the colorados, represented areas rather than principles. The blancos were the party of the rural landowners, and the colorados the party of Montevideo. Only after a spirit of compromise began to develop through agreements giving the colorados control of the national government and the blancos control of their own districts was it possible for Uruguay to free herself from the plague of revolts.

Already in 1861 the liberals had won initial triumphs in Chile, for President José Joaquín Pérez had been acceptable to them and he formed his cabinet from all political groups. The most extreme of the liberals now demanded immediate enactment of anti-clerical legislation and a weakening of the power of the president. They succeeded in 1871 in limiting the presidential term to prevent a president from succeeding himself, although he could be elected after an intervening term. In the same year Federico Errázuriz Zañartu, a liberal conservative, assumed the presidency. The enactment of anti-clerical legislation began.

Also during this administration the electoral system was reformed to remove elections from control of the municipalities, and indirectly, of the chief executive. They were placed under boards of leading citizens. The cumulative vote was introduced for election of members to the chamber of deputies in an effort to give minority parties representation corresponding to their strength. Each voter now had as many votes as there were deputies authorized for his district, and these votes could be cast for one or more candidates. The experiment proved less successful than its authors anticipated, for the proliferation of political parties that followed filled the chamber with many groups of nearly equal strength, none commanding a majority and none feeling deeply its responsibility to the nation.

Social legislation was not a part of the liberal programs of the nineteenth century. Instead liberals sought to extend the franchise where necessary to their rise to power, to reduce the church to political impotency, and to forward the physical improvements which were expected to enhance national prosperity. These movements were supported mainly by the middle class, and they were by no means radical. On many questions there was little difference of opinion between liberals and conservatives. The most critical issue between them was the role of the church. Some Chilean liberals supported measures intended to weaken executive control, such as making the president's cabinet responsible to the chamber of deputies. In the 1880's a Chilean law provided for over-riding a presidential veto by a two-thirds vote of both houses. In the same decade judicial and administrative officials were restricted in their authority to arrest individuals, a law intended to prevent arbitrary confinement of opponents of the government during political campaigns. The vote was extended to include all literate males twenty-five years of age, without property qualifications. Despite all these advances, the government's candidate for the presidency invariably won.

As the liberals accomplished their program step by step, the Chilean government became less and less effective. Able and energetic President José Manuel Balmaceda, 1886-91, faced a continuous succession of cabinet crises. There was no majority party in the congress, and his coalition cabinets changed with bewildering frequency. Relations between the president and congress became embittered, and government painfully difficult. Balmaceda tried to cooperate with the chamber of deputies by appointing ministers satisfactory to the volatile majority of its members, despite the fact that the constitution did not provide for ministerial responsibility to the congress. When this recourse failed, Balmaceda reverted to the former practice of choosing ministers from his own following.

When the time came to decide on a successor, Balmaceda attempted to follow precedent by appointing the man of his choice minister of the interior in order that he might be able to control the outcome of the election. His opponents in the chamber rebelled at this action and fought him through their control of taxation and the voting of appropriations. Even by yielding to their demands, however, Balmaceda could not resolve the quarrel, for congress adjourned without voting a new appropriation for the coming year. Irresponsibility in the legislature was shockingly great, and personal animosities loomed larger than legislative duties.

The opponents of the president had criticized him vociferously for his economic policies, even as Juárez Celmán of Argentina was being censured for supporting inflationary trends and for reckless government spending. In 1890 Juárez Celmán resigned in the face of revolt and financial chaos. Balmaceda did not succumb so readily. After congress adjourned, instead of calling a special session to provide an appropriation bill, he unconstitutionally declared the previous year's bill in force for the coming year. He did not stop there. Convinced that it was impossible to govern constitutionally, he assumed dictatorial powers.

The revolt of the Radical party against Juárez Celmán was easily put down, although the president's prestige was ruined. That which

arose against Balmaceda was far more effective. The Congressionalist party acted quickly to win the adherence of the navy, and sent
it north to seize control of the nitrate provinces acquired in the War
of the Pacific. By thus appropriating to itself the principal source of
governmental revenue, the Congressionalist party was well prepared
to finance the conflict. The war continued from January to August,
1891, when the congressionalist army captured Valparaiso and
Santiago. Balmaceda committed suicide in the vain hope of placating
his vengeful enemies and sparing his friends. When the destructive
war was ended Chile entered into an era of unsuccessful parliamentary government. The victory was an apparent triumph for liberalism, for domination by the president was replaced by that of the
legislature. In effect the change meant merely the triumph of governmental irresponsibility.

In the days of prosperity, speculation, and inflation of the 1880's,
the opponents of the Argentine administration gathered together to
form the Unión Cívica Radical, later the Radical party, composed of
middle-class merchants and politically conscious descendants of immigrants. It demanded the extension of suffrage and honest elections
in order that this group might wrest control of the government from
the estancieros. It was not, as its name implies, radical. It was
bitterly resisted because it represented landless 'foreign' elements,
and its abortive revolt against Juárez Celmán merely caused the
conservatives to tighten their grip on the government.

By 1900, freedom of suffrage and honest elections seemed to the
radicals no nearer than in 1890. It was not property qualifications
that prevented the immigrant and commercial classes from participating in the government, but fraud and force. Government en-
dorsement of a candidate, as in Chile, made his election certain,
for if control of the polls did not suffice, there was the added safeguard of counting the votes. As the desperation of the Radical
party grew, it turned increasingly to Hipólito Yrigoyen, an enigmatic
backroom politician of Basque descent, and a nephew of Leandro N.
Alem, one of the founders of the party. By 1900 Yrigoyen's influence was preponderant, for he carefully eliminated his rivals. When
the early leaders of the Radical party, such as Alem, Senator Aristó-

bulo del Valle, and Bernardo Irigoyen, fell from grace, he coldly ignored them.

To Yrigoyen it appeared that his party might never gain control of the government except by rebellion, but his tactics embraced that method only as a last resort. To emphasize that the country was ruled by a minority clique, the radicals abstained from voting.

What finally brought the radicals to power was not revolt, however, but a peaceful and astonishing transition. In 1910 Roque Sáenz Peña, son of a former president, won the presidency determined to reform electoral laws and end the boycotting of elections. In 1911 the 'Sáenz Peña law' was passed making voting secret and compulsory. Other changes allocated to the minority party a third of the seats in the chamber of deputies regardless of its voting strength. The Sáenz Peña law gave Yrigoyen an unparalleled opportunity.

The first elections under the new law were for deputies to congress, and the radicals won a clear victory. But the crucial test did not come until the presidential election of 1916. Yrigoyen's years of patient building up of a disciplined following were rewarded, for the first free and genuinely representative election in Argentine history gave him the presidency. When he took the oath of office he was surrounded by a delirious, optimistic mob. But throughout the demonstration the people's choice remained unsmiling.

Neither the parliamentary regime of Chile nor the radical administration of Yrigoyen made social and economic reform a major part of its activity. It was in Uruguay that a South American government first undertook to improve social and economic conditions by positive legislative action. The fact that Uruguay seized the initiative seems astonishing, for the internecine strife between blancos and colorados had barely been terminated when the country became one of the most advanced in the world in terms of social legislation.

Foremost in spearheading the drive was José Batlle y Ordóñez, a well-educated journalist with a passion for social reform. He had been in office only a year when Uruguay's last serious civil war broke out in 1904. The control over six departments consigned earlier to the nacionalistas made effective government difficult, and Batlle was determined to govern effectively. He suppressed the revolt, but only after much destruction of life and property. The rebels lost their previous position, but were granted amnesty and a promise of reform.

To eliminate the possibility of similarly destructive revolts in the future, Batlle improved army training and discipline, and had wireless installations placed in rural garrisons to prevent their isolation. More important as a step toward stabilizing the country was his effort to remove the cause of rebellions. The conduct of elections was made more satisfactory, and the nacionalistas received a greater share in the government, which helped to reconcile them and at the same time relieved their sense of frustration.

In 1911 Batlle began a second term as president, and it was at this time the major reforms were introduced. The government established the State Insurance Bank to compete with foreign companies, and certain types of insurance became state monopolies. In order that Uruguayans would not need to depend on alien capital to finance economic enterprises, the Bank of the Republic expanded its activities, and the government purchased control of the Mortgage Bank of Uruguay. At the same time the administration took other steps to prevent the domination of the Uruguayan economy by foreigners.

In the field of social reform Batlle's program made even more drastic changes. The abolition of capital punishment, the establishment of an eight hour day and a forty-eight hour week for laborers, old age pensions, compensation insurance for workingmen, and minimum wages for rural laborers were enacted into law despite strenuous opposition.

Batlle's influence left other lasting impressions. His toleration of his opponents made political persecutions unfashionable, and freedom of the press came to be regarded as a vital liberty. For the first time university education was placed within reach of all economic classes. A spirit of co-operation for national development replaced the venerable factionalism of earlier eras.

Batlle's prestige and purposes remained strong in the administration of Feliciano Viera, who followed him in 1915. Although Viera's term coincided with World War I, Uruguayan attention was not diverted from domestic affairs. Diplomatic relations with Germany were severed, and in other ways Uruguay expressed favor for the Allied cause; otherwise the war's effect was no more than that of any international crisis affecting world trade. More important for Uruguay was the promulgation of a new constitution.

The Uruguayan constitution of 1917 was the result of compromise between the nacionalistas, who favored a parliamentary regime, and the colorados, who were divided in their desires. Under the new constitution the president retained control over foreign affairs and national security, while a national council composed of members of both parties was charged with his former administrative duties. The president was to be chosen by direct vote rather than by congress, and proportional representation was introduced into local elections. The secret ballot and compulsory voting were also required.

After 1917 the honest management of elections and minority representation in the government removed most of the former grievances which had led to strife. The government continued to engage in business enterprises, most of which were successfully managed. In 1928 it opened a national meat-packing plant for the purpose of assuring better prices for producers. Preparations were made for a government corporation to manufacture and sell alcohol, and for another to compete with private companies selling petroleum.

In Argentina, meanwhile, the extravagant hopes of the reformers were dashed by the autocratic regime of Yrigoyen. He, who had long inveighed against undemocratic methods of government, surrounded himself by officials accustomed to accepting his complete domination without chafing. Yrigoyen's administration was more personal than any Argentina had seen for more than half a century. Those who had expected a regime of reform were mistaken in their man; Yrigoyen did not favor drastic changes. He made only mild reform gestures in comparison with Batlle. Retirement funds were provided for by law and labor unions were allowed greater freedom than before. Yrigoyen recommended the passage of laws providing for arbitration of labor disputes and collective bargaining, but he did not seem greatly concerned with getting them enacted.

Yrigoyen's political methods were those he had formerly fought so bitterly, and he directed his party's energies toward capturing control of provincial governments by questionable methods. To his credit was a noteworthy reorganization of the universities, which not only improved them but brought higher education within reach of students of the lower middle class. His promises had aroused far greater expectations, however, and there was profound disappointment on the part of many enlightened politicians. The conservatives loathed him for stirring up the hopes of 'foreigners' and laborers.

The nadir of Yrigoyen's first term was a labor massacre of January, 1919. Unrelated strikes broke out in a British metalworks and among maritime workers, and pickets skirmished with the police. One of these clashes caused a flare-up in feeling against the government, and mobs formed in the streets, bent on indiscriminate destruction. The police, apparently on instructions from the president, shot to kill, and they fired on anyone found in the streets. The Regional Argentine Workers' Federation ordered a general strike for twenty-four hours, and the city population became panic-stricken. Before the carnage and rioting subsided, hundreds had been killed, and destruction ran into thousands of dollars.

The Chilean counterpart of Yrigoyen and Batlle, as spokesmen for the opponents of the landed oligarchy and proponents of change, was Arturo Alessandri Palma, who won tremendous support by advocating laws favorable to labor. He campaigned for the presidency in 1920 as the candidate of the Liberal Alliance, and his appeal was directed not only at the middle class but at labor as well. In the bitterly contested election Alessandri won by a slender margin, while his party gained a majority only in the chamber of deputies. The conservative majority in the senate forced his cabinets to fall one after the other and effectively blocked his legislative program. The economic situation of Chile became critical, for European countries were protecting their new artificial nitrate industries. Chilean unemployment increased, and those in distress looked vainly to Alessandri for relief.

With economic ruin and governmental ineffectiveness the major problems facing Chile, the congress voted in 1924 to establish salaries for the members of both houses. The measure was necessary if governmental responsibility was to be shared by honest men without private wealth; previously congressmen had been unpaid, and the seats had been literally auctioned to members of the wealthy class. It was not the proposal itself but the precedence given it over more urgent business that caused interference by young army officers.

Possibly inspired by events in Spain and Italy, a committee of officers approached the president in September, 1924, and demanded a new cabinet composed of army officers. This thinly veiled threat of force intimidated the congress, and pending reform bills were quickly passed in profusion, and almost without consideration or dissent. Alessandri resigned and left the country, and a provisional government of high-ranking, conservative officers was installed. Their reactionary policies were no more pleasing to the young officers than those of former governments, and in January, 1925, the young officers seized the government and set up a junta composed of friends of Alessandri, whom they invited to return. The most powerful member of the cabinet was Colonel Carlos Ibáñez, Minister of War.

One of the first acts of the provisional government was the promulgation of a new constitution which restored presidential power to its former status, at the expense of the unworkable parliamentary system. Members of congress were not permitted to hold cabinet posts, nor was congressional approval needed for ministerial appointments by the president. Other changes were introduced, including separation of church and state.

The apparent ambitions of Ibáñez made the presidency uninviting to Alessandri after his return, and he resigned before the end of 1925. Emiliano Figueroa Larraín, a compromise candidate, replaced him, but Ibáñez retained his power. Governmental factionalism and class antagonism made many Chileans desire a dominant chief executive on whom they could rely to prevent social upheaval. In 1927 Figueroa Larraín resigned, and a month later Ibáñez was elected president.

As president, Ibáñez represented a return to the type of chief executive typical in Chile before 1860, but his program was one of social reform and labor legislation. Agrarian reform, however, was scarcely contemplated. Loans from Europe and the United States were used to promote an extensive program of public works which, together with the stabilization of the peso, made possible a modest improvement in the living conditions of urban laborers.

Foreign investments in Chile had risen enormously in the 1920's, and by 1930 the hostility to foreign capital which had appeared in all parts of Latin America reacted against Ibáñez, who was accused of permitting foreigners to influence the government through their financial power. Copper, nitrates, and other critical resources were owned primarily by aliens, and for this condition Ibáñez was blamed. As the impact of the world trade depression caused acute unemployment in Chile, agitation against the government became violent. In 1931 rioting by university students set off a wave of insurrections and strikes throughout the country; Ibáñez, unable to preserve order without resorting to greater violence, resigned.

Yrigoyen's second administration in Argentina coincided with the presidency of Ibáñez in Chile, and ended in the same manner. When he was elected for the second time in 1928, Yrigoyen was more than eighty years of age, and quite unable to govern. Unscrupulous members of his party soon discovered that Yrigoyen would sign any paper put before him, and they made haste to empty the treasury. Thus, at a time when the country urgently needed a government that could deal incisively with the complex economic problems of falling exports and fluctuating currency, it was under a senile president and a host of plundering politicians.

Protest from within the party and from without rose to such a crescendo that at last it reached the ears of the old caudillo himself. On September 5, 1930, Yrigoyen resigned in favor of his vice-president, but by this time matters had gone too far for the agitated country to accept anyone closely associated with the Radical party. The next day General José Félix Uriburu marched into Buenos Aires at the head of a column of troops, and the epoch of Yrigoyen and of pseudo-liberalism abruptly ended.

The period from 1860 to 1930 was one of population growth, economic development, and urbanization for Argentina, Uruguay, and

Chile. Their literacy rates rose impressively, and their cultural contributions achieved widespread recognition. It was also a time of political ferment, with a rising middle class, influenced by or composed of European immigrants, challenging the old order of the landholding conservatives. By 1920 the liberals had won control of the governments, but except in Uruguay their rule was disappointing to the lower middle class and labor. One of the most crucial problems, that of the landless, was scarcely discussed. In each of the countries two or three thousand families still owned up to 80 per cent of the agricultural land. By the end of the period the condition of labor was generally much improved, but the gulf between the few who owned the land and the many who worked on it was still immeasurable. Those who owned the land chafed at loss of control of the government; and the inadequacies of the liberal regimes, combined with a world-wide economic depression, prepared the way for a conservative return to power. Chilean and Uruguayan experiments with parliamentary government and with the dual executive proved visionary. Reaction to the discredited parliamentary regime in Chile led to the rise of an autocratic army officer who pushed through social legislation instead of endlessly debating about it. The failures of the Radical party in Argentina, on the other hand, caused a reaction which enabled the conservative minority, with the aid of the army, to return to power. In Uruguay it was not lack of social and economic reform that led to interference with the constitutional regime, but the difficulties engendered in a time of economic crisis by optimistic experimentation with divided executive authority.

XXXII

Indo-America: An Era of Stagnation and Retrogression

> In respect of civil rights, there is no legal distinction between the Indian and the white. Both enjoy the same citizenship for all private and public purposes, to both is granted the equal protection of the laws, equal suffrage, equal eligibility to office. This is to some extent a guarantee to the Indian against ill treatment, but it does not raise him in the social scale. He seldom casts a vote; not, indeed, that it makes much difference in these countries whether the citizen votes or not, for a paternal government takes charge of the elections . . . No one has yet preached to him the gospel of democracy; no one has told him that he has anything to gain from action as a citizen . . . There is, therefore, not yet any 'Indian question' in South America. There ought to be an Indian question; that is to say, there ought to be an effort to raise the Indians economically and educationally. But they have not yet begun to ask to be raised.

JAMES BRYCE *

P ERU, Bolivia, Ecuador, and Paraguay differed in many ways from Argentina, Uruguay, and Chile, and the differences were accentuated during the period from 1860 to 1930. Each of the former countries had a population basically Indian, and because of the presence of a large, servile class of laborers, because of the extreme concentration of land ownership, and because of the chronic political disorders, immigrants found little

---

* *South America, Observations and Impressions*, The Macmillan Company, New York, 1929, pp. 469–70.

to attract them in these regions. The 'Indian' countries, nevertheless, were not altogether untouched by the currents running through the rest of the continent. To a greater or lesser degree anti-clericalism, the rise of liberal movements, and the passion for physical improvements through the attraction of foreign capital infected them. The gulf between the few who owned the wealth and dominated the countries and the many who lived and toiled in poverty and ignorance was tremendous; and because the many were blighted additionally by the handicap of being the children of the conquered, their rise to an intermediate status was almost beyond hope. In these countries the heritage of the conquest and of the colonial era remained powerful and resistant to currents of social change.

The subordinate role of the Indians was a major obstacle to the achievement of national prosperity and cultural maturity, for unless all the population was allowed and encouraged to progress to the extent of its abilities, the economic and cultural productivity of these countries was limited to the accomplishments of a small group. Alien capital could acquire control of the natural resources with little competition from domestic capital. In addition to this enormous problem of raising the Indians to a status beneficial to themselves and to the countries at large — a problem that was not met frontally by any of the nations involved — Paraguay, Bolivia, and Peru suffered devastating setbacks by engaging in losing wars with their neighbors.

In 1860, Peru, Ecuador, Bolivia, and Paraguay were all in or on the verge of periods of political disorder, and political strife was one of the most consistent overtones of the epoch. Faction-torn Peru soon found herself facing serious difficulties with Spain over her refusal to receive a 'royal commissioner' sent, along with a naval squadron, to press claims for damages done to Spanish subjects. The title of the agent indicated that Spain still regarded Peru as a rebellious colony. Affronted by this insult to national honor, the Peruvians rejected the unwelcome visitor. The Spanish squadron retaliated by seizing the Chincha islands, source of guano and of more than half of all governmental revenue.

President Juan Antonio Pezet, who was willing to negotiate in order to avoid a war for which his country was unprepared, was overthrown in 1865 by those who favored a more aggressive attitude. Peru now declared war on Spain and joined an alliance composed of Chile, Ecuador, and Bolivia. Governments were short-lived for the next few years, but in 1868 Colonel José Balta emerged victorious from the many-sided struggle for power. By that time the Spanish fleet had made a damaging but fruitless assault upon Callao and left the Pacific. In 1871 Peru signed a truce with Spain, and in 1879 Spain belatedly acknowledged Peruvian independence. In the meantime the senseless conflict had heightened domestic confusion and retarded efforts at economic development.

Balta restored order and attempted to bring the Peruvian economy up to date by letting contracts for the construction of railroads, dock facilities, and similar improvements. His intentions were generally meritorious, but his accomplishments did not always deserve praise. He made foreign loans for which he pledged future deliveries of guano. The projects for which the money was spent were not in themselves productive of governmental revenue, and private industry did not expand at a rapid pace. Consequently, the outlay for interest on the loans grew while government income was shrinking.

The influx of foreign capital through official loans encouraged prodigal expenditures by the government, and much of the money was sidetracked from its intended use by corrupt officials. The country's financial future was made increasingly precarious by the continued practice of borrowing against future shipments of guano. This recourse had obvious attractions for the ephemeral governments; they received the cash and were able to dispose of it, while later administrations were left to face the day of reckoning.

To aid the expansion of agriculture and to speed the construction of railroads, the government admitted about 85,000 Chinese coolie laborers between 1861 and 1875; these Chinese were soon reduced to a condition little better than slavery on the coastal plantations, in violation of the contracts under which they had come. Henry Meiggs, fresh from his triumphs at railroad building in Chile, transferred his operations to Peru, where his success made him the social lion of Lima.

Before the end of his term, Balta was assassinated, and a new polit-ical epoch began. His successor was Manuel Pardo, the first civilian president of Peru and one of the few candidates ever to defeat the official choice. Pardo's victory reflected the triumph of the newly wealthy class of professional men and merchants and planters, who formed the *Civilista* party in opposition to the conservatives and the military. Balta's assassination was part of a desperate attempt to maintain military control, and he was punished for accepting the outcome of an election which went against the party in power! Such was the state of Peruvian politics at the time.

Financial chaos jeopardized the first essay at civilian government in Peru. The guano exports were no longer a source of governmental revenue, for the entire sales proceeds for years to come had been mortgaged to alien creditors. To make matters worse, artificial ferti-lizers were replacing guano in European markets. By 1876 it was necessary to suspend payment on the foreign debt, and Peru was mired in an economic morass from which it took several decades to extricate herself. Pardo attempted to reduce government spending. At the same time he sought to curtail the influence of the army in political life by disbanding certain troublesome units and by creating a national guard, and by stimulating greater interest in politics among civilians. He tried to raise educational standards by bringing in foreign educators, and he negotiated a treaty with China in an effort to humanize the Chinese coolie traffic.

The government was assailed for the financial chaos, and Pardo was hard pressed to discover methods for reviving the economy. The drop in the price of nitrates led him to formulate plans for a govern-ment monopoly of nitrate sales. Chilean companies operating in Tarapacá and the Bolivian province of Antofagasta, however, refused to co-operate in the plan to raise prices artificially. Peru and Bolivia signed a military alliance, aimed specifically at Chile, for both re-garded Chilean economic penetration as a common problem. In 1875 the Peruvian government created a monopoly of the nitrate industry and expropriated Chilean and other foreign holdings. The disastrous War of the Pacific began when Bolivia inaugurated similar policies.

Little advance in political life had been made in Bolivia since independence. Semi-military factions had battled for power, and none of them had accomplished more than a hasty reaping of the fruits of victory before being expelled in turn. The few attempts at social or political reform, such as that of José María Linares, a civilian president, were doomed to failure by the ephemeral nature of the administrations. Similarly, presidents who sought to reduce factionalism by conciliatory measures merely courted disaster, for tolerance of opponents was regarded as weakness and an invitation to revolt.

In 1864 Mariano Melgarejo, one of the most notorious examples of the violent caudillo, captured the government in a typical barracks revolt. An ignorant but shrewd soldier, Melgarejo had discovered that Bolivians would follow an audacious leader, and in time of battle he fortified his courage by generous applications of alcohol. His often-interrupted regime was one of lust, violence, and misgovernment. In 1866 he surrendered Bolivian rights to territory on the coast to Chile, and the following year ceded a large tract to Brazil. He debased the currency and despoiled the Indians of their tribal lands, greatly increasing the social and economic ills of the country. Melgarejo dominated the scene until 1871, when he was ousted by another barracks revolt.

The presidency continued to change hands frequently. In 1876 General Hilarión Daza seized power, and he soon found himself at war with Chile over his violation of the nitrate taxing agreement of 1874. The recklessness with which he precipitated the war indicated that Bolivians little appreciated the advances Chileans had made.

Bolivia's role in the War of the Pacific was insignificant and humiliating. Chilean troops easily overran the province of Antofagasta, and after their invasion of Tarapacá in 1879, Daza was overthrown. The Chilean victory at Tacna in the next year virtually ended Bolivian participation in the war. The loss of the coastal territory left Bolivia without access to the sea, and regaining an outlet has been the most consistent theme of her foreign policy since that time. A truce was made with Chile, but it was not until 1904 that a treaty was finally signed. Chile received title to Antofagasta, and Bolivia received an indemnity.

Peru suffered even more from the war than Bolivia, for her navy was destroyed, her land invaded, and thousands of her men killed, in addition to the loss of her richest nitrate province. Guerrilla opposition to Chile continued in the interior for several years, and it was not until General Miguel Iglesias assumed the presidency that Chileans could find a government willing and able to accede to their terms, formalized by the Treaty of Ancón in 1883.

The War of the Pacific was a grave setback to both Peru and Bolivia, for it greatly retarded economic development and political maturity. The injuries caused by the loss of the war were not always tangible, for the damage done to morale was manifested in many ways. In both countries attempts had been made to establish civilian administrations to replace the military despotisms, and statesmen had appeared who advocated economic and social change. The war upset both countries immeasurably, and made their financial plight even more precarious than before. The defeat and loss of territory, on the other hand, seemed to have a salutary effect on political life, for the dangers of dissension were driven home forcibly, and political factions accepted compromise more readily than before.

Ecuador, too, had been badly torn by revolt and counter-revolt since independence, and had no national government at all in 1860. The most powerful of the various caudillos was Guillermo Franco of Guayaquil. A contest for power ended with the triumphant emergence of the conservative lawyer Gabriel García Moreno. The country he undertook to govern was in deplorable condition. Roads were almost impassable, foreign commerce was negligible, and the majority of the people lived in poverty and oppression surpassing that of the colonial era. The Indians of the highlands eked out a miserable existence from an unfriendly soil whose products went largely for the sustenance of others while in the lowland port regions disease took a frightful toll. Property was everywhere insecure, and economic enterprise was conspicuous by its absence. To many Ecuadorians a despotic government that could restore and preserve order seemed far more attractive than chronic anarchy.

García Moreno, a religious zealot, assumed the disagreeable task of trying to form a government capable of maintaining order throughout the country. His methods were reminiscent of those of Rosas in Buenos Aires a few years before. Opposition was liquidated without such formality as trials. Revolts were furiously suppressed, and holders of liberal views were hunted out and executed or driven into exile. Gradually the entire nation took on the somber aspects of a monastery whose dreary, black tone bore little resemblance to the colorful era of colonial rule.

For fifteen years García Moreno remained the ruler of Ecuador. He permitted others to serve in the capacity of president between his own administrations, but he never relinquished control. The dictator might well have been a chief inquisitor himself, so complete was his fanatical devotion to the church. Experiences in France during an earlier period of exile — he had witnessed the revolutionary upheavals there in 1848 — had set his mind inexorably against all vestiges of liberal doctrine. He regarded anti-clericalism as a primary cause of disorder, for to him the church was the most vital institution in life. He brought back the Jesuits to Ecuador and gave them a prominent role in education. In fact, all education was placed in church hands, as was authority over all matters pertaining to literature and the arts. The church became the sole judge as to what books might be imported or published, and no literature was permitted to circulate without religious blessing. The theocratic dictator signed a concordat with the papacy giving the church a status even more powerful than it had possessed in the colonial era. García Moreno expected his support of the church to be reciprocated, and he endeavored to rid the clergy of many long-standing abuses and to purify its ranks to the end that priests and members of the orders would be at least as devoted to the holy cause as he. In 1873 he consecrated his tiny country to the 'Sacred Heart of Jesus.'

In spite of his efforts, García Moreno was never completely able to crush all opposition. Revolts were frequent, and to secure a firmer grip on the machinery of government, the dictator introduced a new constitution lengthening the president's term of office to six years and permitting immediate re-election. Even with this basic law he found it impossible to govern the country constitutionally. Opposition became more desperate, and the dictator's methods of suppression grew more and more severe.

The long period of García Moreno's rule, although far from peaceful, was more orderly than any previous era since independence. Some material progress was to be noted. A road was completed from Guayaquil to Quito. New schools were opened by the Jesuits and the French Christian Brothers. Political corruption was not tolerated, and the government's financial condition improved to the point that payments on the national debt were resumed. But animosity to the regime eventually became uncontrollable, and from neighboring countries plots to overthrow the theocratic state were continuously hatched. García Moreno's career was finally ended by assassination. Far away from the scene, Juan Montalvo, Ecuadorian journalist and one of Latin America's most gifted essayists, exclaimed on hearing of the dictator's death: 'My pen has killed him!'

For most of the twenty-year period after García Moreno's death the conservatives held the government, although sporadic uprisings, barracks revolts, and new constitutions disturbed the peace. Under Antonio Flores, 1888–92, Ecuador enjoyed an interlude of domestic peace and a fair measure of civil liberty. His successor became involved in a national scandal by permitting Chile ostensibly to transfer a warship to Ecuador while actually selling it to Japan for use against China. In the uproar that followed revelation of this act the liberals perceived an opportunity to drive the badly divided conservatives from power. Their victory brought in a new regime under General Eloy Alfaro.

Paraguay's political life since independence had been vastly different from that of her Andean neighbors, for she had known only two rulers in nearly half a century. In 1862 the second of these dictators, Carlos Antonio López, died, leaving the country in the control of his son, Francisco Solano López. While the father's methods may be classed as borderline benevolent despotism, the son's were far more despotic than benevolent. Despite the cultural influence of a visit to Europe, he apparently acquired little more on the trip than a mistress, a red-haired Irish adventuress named Elisa Lynch, and an overwhelming desire to emulate Napoleon Bonaparte.

Solano López began building up an army which would make him the arbiter of South America, and he had at his complete disposal the Guaranís, a courageous people thoroughly disciplined by centuries of rigid control. Where the depraved dictator ordered them, the Paraguayans obediently went, and that the nation survived his rule at all is astonishing.

The Paraguayan War began in 1864 with Paraguay's attack on Brazil. Because of the unsavory character of Solano López, he has generally been blamed unquestionably for the war. He had expected to receive aid from Urquiza, who also opposed Brazilian interference in Uruguay, but he alienated Urquiza by his ill-considered invasion of Corrientes, an attack upon Argentine territory made because Mitre refused him permission to cross.

The Paraguayan War was appallingly costly to all combatants, but especially to Paraguay, and in the final years her armies were manned by young boys or women. The allied casualties were also high, for the Paraguayans literally fought to the death. The population of Paraguay was reduced by more than half, and of the remainder only about one in ten was male. At the conclusion of the war, Paraguay escaped complete partition only because the victors could not agree. In 1870 a new constitution was drawn up for the purpose of preventing the rise of dictatorships in the future. As had been proven elsewhere, however, a basic law could not be effective if it ran counter to traditions and social conditions, and Paraguay did not change overnight into a democratic republic because of a new constitution.

Brazilian troops, who had borne the brunt of the fighting toward the end of the war, remained in Paraguay until 1876, partially to preserve order. Indemnities demanded by the victors could not be paid, nor were they ever seriously pressed. Misiones territory was ceded to Argentina, and a large section of the northern frontier passed to Brazil. Argentine claims to the Chaco were submitted to the arbitration of President Rutherford B. Hayes, whose award in

1878 was favorable to Paraguay. Grateful Paraguayans renamed a town Villa Hayes in his honor.

It was many years before Paraguay was to have a government nearly as effective as those of her first two dictators. Barracks revolts were frequent, and few presidents completed their constitutional terms of office. The uprisings fortunately were for the most part of local origin, and the country at large was little disturbed by them. Paraguay slowly and painfully began to recover from the devastation of war. Foreign immigrants and capital, although on a small scale, provided impetus for the development of commerce. Cattle raising and the exportation of yerba maté and quebracho extract became important, and by the end of the century Paraguay had made surprising strides toward recovery.

In Peru, also, the road to recovery was long and difficult. The civilista administration of Nicolás de Piérola, 1895–9, was a time of substantial economic advance. By diminishing the political influence of the army and by attempting to put an end to interference at the polls, Piérola attracted the growing liberal elements to his support, and with their aid he made a mild move against the church by legalizing civil marriage. Commerce was aided by stabilizing the currency and backing it with gold, and by various public construction projects. Election control was eased, and the power of the civilistas increased, for their great wealth enabled them to control the outcome by resort to bribery rather than force.

The civilistas remained in power until 1919, when Augusto B. Leguía deposed José Pardo shortly before the end of his term. Under the civilistas' twenty-five year regime, considerable progress had been made in reviving the national economy. One of their most significant accomplishments was the contract negotiated with the W. R. Grace Company for paying interest to holders of Peruvian bonds. The government's revenues had been barely sufficient for ordinary expenses, and payments on its tremendous foreign debt were long in arrears. Under the arrangement made with the Grace Company, the foreign bondholders were given control of the state railways for sixty-six years, the right to extract three million tons of guano, and the promise of 80,000 pounds sterling annually for thirty-three years. This was in exchange for assuming the payments on Peru's foreign debt.

In bettering social conditions the civilistas accomplished little, for social reform was not their primary interest. Guillermo Billing- hurst's mild attempt to improve the lot of Indian rubber-gatherers in the Amazon area helped to bring about his overthrow. Indians were still politically beyond the pale, but the lower middle class and urban laborers were becoming articulate and making demands. As in Chile and Argentina, they importuned the aristocratic government for benefits which were not granted. They became the bulwark of Leguía's Democratic party. Merchants and professional men, whose humble origins precluded a rise in the Civilista party, also rallied to the Democratic party, partly owing to conviction and partly be- cause of the greater opportunity it offered them.

These groups were mildly anti-clerical, and in 1915 they pushed through a Toleration Act permitting the exercise of other faiths than Roman Catholicism. It was these same middle and working classes who stood behind Leguía when he ran for a second term in 1919. Leguía had been elected as a civilista in 1908, but had broken with the party a year later. Like Alessandri of Chile, Leguía was de- termined to improve social conditions in his country. In the election of 1919 he received a majority of the votes cast, but his partisans feared that his opponents intended to prevent his taking office. They seized the government and deposed Pardo before his term expired. Peru was at last ready for a regime of social and economic experi- mentation backed by a strong and resolute government.

After the War of the Pacific the Conservative party of Bolivia remained in power until 1899 by carefully controlling elections, de- spite the increasing dissatisfaction of the liberals. The revival of silver mining aided economic recovery, and the extension of rail- roads began to end the degenerating influence of isolation and provin- cialism in many districts. The relative stability of the government aided economic development, for most of the liberal uprisings were localized, and the barracks revolts of former days did not recur.

In 1899 the liberals came into power by revolt over a matter of local concern, the location of the national capital. In the past Sucre, the Chuquisaca of colonial days, had been the official capital, but because of its isolated location many presidents had governed from more conveniently located cities. There had occasionally been proposals to transfer the capital, and the people of La Paz insisted on their city as the most appropriate choice. When the congress voted to make Sucre the permanent capital, the rival factions of La Paz forgot their differences and joined forces under Colonel José Manuel Pando to assert their claims forcibly. The La Paz contingent won the contest, and the capital was moved. Other groups then took advantage of the turmoil and seized the government.

In Ecuador, too, the Liberal party won control of the government by revolt. General Eloy Alfaro, who led the successful uprising in 1895, remained the dominant figure in his country's political life until his assassination in 1911. To Alfaro liberalism was more than the fetish it had been to his predecessors. Although his extreme anticlericalism was a reaction to García Moreno's policies, and made him anathema to the conservatives, his moderation and tact for a time prevented a 'religious' war from engulfing Ecuador. During his first term, however, a patronage law was passed giving the government greater control over clerical affairs.

In 1906 a new constitution, the twelfth since independence, was promulgated, and it aroused the conservatives to fury by omitting to make Roman Catholicism the state religion. Conspiracies and insurrections were frequent and Alfaro, again in the presidency, adopted severe measures to restore order. His problems were complicated by the threat of war with Peru over a boundary dispute. Despite the many difficulties, domestic and foreign, Alfaro energetically pushed to completion the project of building a railroad line from Quito to Guayaquil. This railroad was an important factor in subsequent political and economic progress, for it not only opened the interior to foreign trade but tended to lessen the regional strife between coastal and mountain factions.

The outbreak of World War I caused a temporary economic setback, but trade revived rapidly after 1916. The conflict between church and state subsided, and was no longer a source of civil disorder. One of the most significant accomplishments of the period was brought about during Alfredo Baquerizo Moreno's administration when, with the aid of the Rockefeller Foundation, sanitary improvements freed Guayaquil of yellow fever and bubonic plague. The port, once feared as a graveyard of foreign seamen and shunned by ship captains, became safe at last. Commercial expansion followed, and the country benefited by increased governmental revenues, part of which were used to build schools.

The issuance of unredeemable paper money in Ecuador led, as elsewhere, to depreciation and to hardship among the merchants and labor. In 1922 and the following year, riots were frequent owing to the rise of prices and the failure of wages to increase. The growing agitation of laboring groups and the fear of revolt induced the government to make concessions.

One of the concessions to the radical wing of the Liberal party was permitting the election of an extreme liberal, Dr. Gonzalo Córdoba, in 1924. The measure failed to mollify the opposition, owing in part to the illness and incapacity of Córdoba, and in 1925 the vice-president who succeeded him was driven from office. In the following year, after an interval of military rule, Dr. Isidro Ayora became provisional president. He attacked financial problems by adopting currency stabilization measures suggested by Professor Kemmerer of Princeton University. A short time later the world trade depression made further efforts futile.

As elsewhere in Latin America the depression produced intense political unrest in Ecuador. Hunger and privation increased alarmingly, and the government was held responsible for the nation's ills. The brief period of progress and promise came to an end in 1931, when Ayora resigned and the government once more became a bone of contention between political factions and the army.

In Peru, meanwhile, Leguía's second administration began with the promulgation of the first new constitution since 1860. The constitution of 1920 was designed to make effective the changes that Leguía and his supporters contemplated. A graduated income tax was introduced; compulsory arbitration of labor disputes and compensation for labor accidents were required. Freedom of religion was granted, but at the same time the government surrendered its claim to the right of ecclesiastical patronage, and the church was able to appoint its own officials.

Leguía's attempt to introduce sweeping social and economic changes met with strenuous resistance. His authority was upheld by military and police forces, and the wave of post-war prosperity aided his cause, for the government was able to spend vast sums on public projects. Copper mining and petroleum production contributed to national revenues. Transportation facilities were greatly extended and improved, and Lima was modernized. Education, which had occasionally been a matter of temporary interest to the government, was expanded under the guidance of commissions from the United States. In spite of the harsh aspects of Leguía's rule the country made rapid progress in economic expansion. Relations with the United States were especially cordial, and surplus American wealth flooded the country. Governmental extravagance was unfortunately encouraged by the availability of money, and unwise and dishonest financial practices made the situation explosive when the world depression ended the easy access to alien capital. As was the case elsewhere, the benefits of 'economic progress' were generally limited to the few in power, although the Indians were given some hope for the future. In foreign affairs the most notable event of Leguía's rule was the settlement of the ancient Tacna-Arica dispute, an event already described in connection with Chile.

The downfall of Leguía, like that of many of his contemporaries in Latin America, was caused largely by the government's inability to cope with an economic depression that was world-wide in scope. His government was undeniably censurable for some of its acts, for it had permitted the increase of the national debt to more than ten times its size when Leguía took office, and a shockingly large part of the borrowed funds had been sidetracked to reward the faithful or placate the hostile. When new loans became unavailable, bankruptcy followed. Political agitation became so great that Leguía resigned. He and his sons were tried and found guilty of misappropriating public funds, and he died in prison a year later. His successors faced growing political unrest and financial chaos.

In Bolivia the so-called liberal regime lasted from 1899 to 1920, and in political techniques differed little from its predecessors. Under Ismael Montes, El Gran Presidente, who served from 1904 to 1909 and 1913 to 1917, the most lasting improvements were made. This period was remarkable for the absence of civil disorders so characteristic in earlier times. The country's economic condition changed rapidly, and Bolivia's first foreign loans were negotiated for the purpose of building railroads. By means of revenue raised by a special tax and by using forced labor of Indians, the government pushed to completion a network of roads. Formerly isolated regions were brought into contact with the capital and the currents of world trade. A line between La Paz and Mollendo, on the coast of Peru, gave Bolivia access to the sea, as did another from La Paz to Arica, which Chileans built in accordance with the treaty ending the War of the Pacific.

The liberals introduced the usual reforms aimed at the clergy. Civil marriage was legalized, special courts abolished, and cemeteries were secularized. Opposition to these changes was fairly mild, and it did not lead to the violence which occurred in some other regions.

National revenues were greatly augmented by the development of tin and copper mining and a corresponding demand for these metals in Europe and the United States. The expansion of the Brazilian rubber-gathering industry in the Amazon basin led to a dispute over Bolivia's Acre territory. In 1903 Bolivia sold the region to Brazil for 200,000 pounds sterling and a railroad to be built around the cataracts of the Madeira river. Since the rubber market collapsed a few years later, the Bolivians may have come out of the dispute better than it first appeared. The money received from Brazil was especially important in the government's railroad building program.

In 1920 the Republican party, a newly formed opposition group composed of dissident liberals, overthrew the government. The republicans welcomed American capital, and the foreign debt grew rapidly. The uses to which the loans were put did not consistently promote economic improvement, and when the depression set in Bolivia had pledged nearly all her customary revenues in advance.

In 1930, service on the national debt was suspended, and in the wake of financial chaos president Hernando Siles was ousted in favor of a military junta.

Paraguayan liberals finally captured control of their government in 1904, and a succession of their presidents held office briefly during the next two decades. Only Dr. Eduardo Schaerer completed his full term during this period, and only his administration differed significantly from those of the conservatives. He brought relative order and stability to the turbulent country, and its commerce was aided by completion of the railroad from Asunción to Encarnación on the Paraná river. The government established the agricultural bank to aid farmers and passed laws to enable others to acquire farming lands.

In the 1920's Paraguay entered the same phase of national physical improvement which was to be found throughout the continent, and the country seemed at last to be well on the way toward subordinating its less fortunate customs when it was shocked by the world depression. President José Guggiari declared martial law in 1929 to prevent rioting, but the difficulties could not be overcome, and in 1931 he was forced to resign. Although he resumed office and finished his term, the liberal regime in Paraguay, too, was at an end.

By the close of the period Peru, Bolivia, Ecuador, and Paraguay had made hesitant advances similar to those which had occurred among their more prosperous neighbors, but they were still far behind Argentina, Uruguay, and Chile in this regard. The Andean countries had yet to make a genuine effort to improve national prosperity by raising the economic and social level of the Indians. Because of the racial issue attempts at social reform were little more than gestures, for the ruling cliques were apprehensive lest the Indian masses, once freed from ancient restraints, would overturn the social order. In some of these countries, however, writers and political leaders took up the cause of the Indians with a seriousness and determination rarely shown before.

The conditions which had retarded economic and cultural growth in the Indian countries also handicapped their literary output, and it was generally below that of Argentina, Uruguay, and Chile. There were, nevertheless, a number of noteworthy writers, such as the Peruvians Manuel González Prada, who campaigned vigorously for social justice, Ricardo Palma, the folklorist chronicler of Lima, the poets César Vallejo and José María Eguren, and the novelist Ciro Alegría. Ecuador produced the eminent essayist and polemic writer, Juan Montalvo, and the Indianist novelists Jorge Icaza, Fernando Chaves, and Enrique Gil Gilbert. In Bolivia, too, there were followers of the Indianist theme, most prominent of whom was Alcides Argüedas, author of *Raza de bronce*.

XXXIII

From Despotism to Social Revolution: The Caribbean Borderlands

> The majority of Latin American countries are agricultural. Over 75 per cent of the economically active population of Mexico are engaged in some kind of agricultural work . . . Before the 1910 Revolution . . . 2 per cent of the population owned 75 per cent of the land.
>
> LUIS QUINTANILLA *

THE countries of Latin America bordering or near the Caribbean sea had much in common in the decades between 1860 and 1930. These were the nations most seriously threatened with economic and political penetration by the Western European powers and the United States. These were the nations which, with one exception, lay athwart the narrow land mass that was the chief obstacle to inter-oceanic commerce between the Atlantic and the Pacific. Here the economic and social pressures of domestic life were heightened by the ever-present fear of foreign exploitation. No vast influx of new people swelled the population to alter the social balance and expand national productivity. All the old problems of the past were ever present while new ones were being added with alarming rapidity. Alien enterprise was everywhere in evidence, but its beneficiaries were far removed and its impact served more to embitter than to soothe the passions of those affected by its handiwork.

* A *Latin American Speaks*, The Macmillan Company, New York, 1943, pp. 76–8.

The seemingly universal conflicts between liberals and conservatives, between centralists and federalists, and between church and state were clearly in evidence. So, too, was the tendency to violence in achieving political change. As the era opened, liberal forces were in the ascendency from Mexico City to Caracas, but their achievements proved ephemeral, and either they collapsed violently or melted away before conservative counter-attacks. Racial animosities were also keen, for the process of amalgamating heterogeneous Indian groups and Spaniards was in evidence but far from complete. The multitude of caste and class lines based on the extent of European ancestry were sharply drawn, and the disunion that prevailed prevented government and economic development from becoming co-operative ventures supported by, and for the benefit of, all groups. Nevertheless, the almost total separation that characterized the racial structure of the Andean republics to the south had obviously gone far toward breaking down. Had not Mexico had a pure Indian as president? Was not the mestizo the dominant strain in much of Central America and considerable portions of Colombia and Venezuela? Clearly the countries of the Caribbean borderland were in process of rapid change, a change little less startling than that taking place on the vast pampas of the Argentine, on the grasslands of Uruguay, and in the central valley of Chile. But the direction of change was far less evident, and the era closed without sufficient evidence to indicate what form the developing nations would eventually assume.

Perhaps the most striking development peculiar to the Caribbean countries was the heavy and disturbing foreign pressure to which they were subjected. At first this pressure came from European nations in the form of old-style imperialism, as evidenced by the French misadventure in Mexico; but this mode of interference was rapidly replaced by the more subtle pressures following in the wake of foreign investments, pressures more often private than official, and for that reason more disconcerting. At times the interference was inspired by the strategic interests of the United States, as in the acquisition of the isthmian canal route and in the safeguarding of that route. Such interventions were likely to be blunt and forceful, neither subtly disguised nor considerate of Latin American sensibilities. After the Spanish-American War, when the United States undertook the political rehabilitation of Cuba and annexed Puerto Rico, pressure from the burgeoning North American power became intense, and astonished Latin Americans suddenly discovered that their ancient 'sea of destiny' had become an American lake. It was an era of resurgent Manifest Destiny when, as it appeared to Latin America, presidents of the United States such as Theodore Roosevelt and secretaries of state such as Richard Olney walked softly but talked loudly, carried big sticks, and went far, especially in their encroachments upon the sovereign rights of Caribbean governments. While strategic considerations seemed foremost to the United States government — and such considerations were not wholly misunderstood in Latin America — later cases of intervention seemed to stem from a quixotic determination to do good to others no matter how violently they resisted. To worried Latin Americans it appeared unmistakably clear that wherever Americans and their dollars were about to be separated as a consequence of chaotic political conditions United States marines were prompt to appear. When to the propensity to intervention was coupled a policy of refusing to recognize governments coming to power by other than constitutional means, there seemed little doubt that the 'Yankee Colossus' was setting itself up as the arbiter of the political destiny of Latin America. For financial and commercial reasons, the withholding of recognition was an extremely potent weapon that few governments in the Caribbean area could long withstand. Long before steamships began passing through the Panama Canal, numerous countries learned the shocking news that they had lost the venerable right to mismanage their own affairs.

The era was ushered in amid civil wars between liberals and conservatives in Mexico, Nicaragua, Costa Rica, Colombia, and Venezuela, while several Central American countries were involved in struggles against caudillo despotism, Cuba still sought vainly to achieve independence, and Santo Domingo was being readmitted to the Spanish empire. In Mexico, the War of the Reform ended with triumph for the Juárez liberals who were promptly ousted by the legions of Napoleon III. In Colombia, the liberal forces of Tomás Mosquera captured Bogotá in 1861, while to the east federalist liberals gained a partial victory in Venezuela where, in 1864, by pushing through a new constitution, they created a confederation known as the United States of Venezuela. Truly it was an inauspicious opening for an era of progress.

At opposite ends of the borderland region, events soon conspired to bring an end to the confusion of domestic strife and to inaugurate a long period of political tranquility. In Venezuela the weakness of the confederation soon became manifest, and the country remained strife-torn until 1872 when a resolute and able leader gained sufficient power over his rivals to establish a dictatorship. Antonio Guzmán Blanco was essentially of the 'liberal' stripe, which meant little more than that he took a firm anti-clerical stand and undertook important public works to bring railroads and telegraph lines to the country. He did nothing to stabilize the political institutions of his country or to further the practice of democratic government. Rather, he based his regime on popular appeals to the lower classes and a vigorous effort to befuddle his opposition. Although permitted only a two-year term of office by the constitution, the dictator was able to maintain control of the government even when out of office and get himself back in the presidential chair as soon as he was eligible again. Such an arrangement he managed to keep functioning for sixteen years. In the meantime, commercial activity increased rapidly, many men grew rich, and the country appeared to prosper. None prospered so much as did Antonio Guzmán Blanco, however. In fact, he was so proud of himself and his achievements that he had monuments erected to himself in conspicuous places throughout the country.

The Venezuelan dictator took many steps to break the power of the Roman Catholic Church. He legalized civil marriage, abolished monastic orders and confiscated their property, and even expelled a papal representative from the country. A Grand Master of the Masonic Order, Guzmán Blanco so opposed control of the church from Rome that he even considered establishing a national church independent of the Pope, a threat which he did not attempt to carry out, however. Instead, he was content to scandalize the clergy by encouraging Protestant missionaries to come to Venezuela. Naturally, opposition to the dictator became a religious issue that was fully exploited by his enemies.

By 1888 opposition to Guzmán Blanco had become intense. While he was absent from the country mobs gathered in the cities and began overturning the many statues of him and demolishing other reminders of his tyrannical rule. The dictator displayed his usual political sagacity in this crisis; he decided that it was time for him to retire from public life and enjoy his remaining years in Paris. Needless to say, he had prepared himself well for retirement by financial chicanery and plunder of the public treasury.

Guzmán Blanco's long rule was not without material benefit. Under the dictator's watchful eye a vast number of public works projects had been completed, including a railroad line, the paving of streets in the cities, and construction of many parks. At the same time government revenues mounted as international commerce increased, and a major portion of the national debt was retired. Over against such manifestations of progress was the fact that the country remained the patrimony of a few families who lived in ostentatious splendor while the great majority of the people — the lower classes — continued to serve in poverty and ignorance, without hope and without opportunity to improve their lot. The economic gulf between the few and the many widened appreciably. Also, in spite of material improvement, the country made little intellectual progress. Education was neglected generally, and few people even among the wealthy demonstrated more than a superficial acquaintanceship with literature, the arts, and the sciences. Social life was stodgy and represented little more than a feeble effort to seek relief from boredom through an occasional private party or dance. Religious observances provided some diversion for the poorer classes.

After the overthrow of Antonio Guzmán Blanco, Venezuela returned to a period of chaos and disorder while would-be wearers of the dictator's shoes struggled to get possession of them. Finally, one of Guzmán Blanco's old friends, Joaquín Crespo, succeeded in establishing order. With the aid of a new constitution he was able to maintain control of the country until his retirement in 1898. He was inclined to much the same course and policies as his more famous predecessor, and the outstanding event of his administration was a dispute with Great Britain over the boundary between British Guiana and Venezuela. The dispute dated back many years, and even in Guzmán Blanco's time had provoked a severance of diplomatic relations with England; but it came to a head in 1895 when some British officials were detained for trespassing on Venezuelan soil. Crespo appealed to the United States for support, and President Cleveland responded by invoking the Monroe Doctrine in a note which his secretary of state sent to Great Britain. For a brief period, relations between England and the United States became strained, but finally all parties agreed to abide by the decision of an international boundary commission which awarded most of the disputed territory to Britain. Strangely, once the United States had entered the controversy, the chief issue became that of British acceptance of United States doctrinal claims of paramount interest in the Western Hemisphere. All parties eventually compromised, but impending difficulties in South Africa no doubt influenced the British government toward a conciliatory attitude in the matter.

Far to the north and west another Caribbean borderland nation slipped quietly into the hands of a master dictator at about the same time Guzmán Blanco came to power in Venezuela. With the downfall of Maximilian, Juárez returned to Mexico City and in 1867 was elected president. In spite of prompt and substantial reductions in the armed forces, his popularity continued. Disgruntled ex-generals and would-be caudillos 'pronounced' from time to time, and the Indian tribes of the northwest engaged in continuous marauding expeditions, but gradually loyal juarista forces subdued the opposition and peace returned to the famine and misery-ridden country. Juárez set about making the doctrines of the 1857 constitution a reality. A program of free secular education was inaugurated, and town councils and owners of large haciendas were required to build schools. The program was entrusted largely to Gabino Barreda, an able educator imbued with positivist doctrines. By 1874 some 8000 schools were functioning and attendance reached almost 350,000, about one-fourth of those of school age. At the same time vigorous efforts were made to replenish the national treasury and to get back on the long road to national solvency through an honest administration of revenues.

Many approved of Juárez, but there were others who did not. Chief among the opposition was Porfirio Díaz, a general who had fought with Juárez against the French intervention. Díaz felt that his services — actually less than spectacular — had been insufficiently rewarded. He had no love for civilian government in accordance with the constitution and the law; he was an adherent of military dictatorship. In 1871, he came forth from his estate in Oaxaca to run against Juárez for the presidency. The vote was split by the candidacy of Sebastián Lerdo de Tejada, and no candidate received a majority. Congress had to decide, and it selected Juárez, who had received a plurality. Díaz pronounced, declaring the election illegal. He chose as his slogan, 'Effective Suffrage and No Re-election!' His brief rebellion was quickly suppressed, but a strong following remained led by army chieftains who wanted the spoils of public office. Then suddenly on July 18, 1872, Juárez died.

No one could take the Indian president's place. Lerdo de Tejada tried, and although he was an able man who had authored many of the juarista reforms, he failed. He lacked Juárez' popular following, his mystic grip upon the common people of Mexico and many in the upper classes as well. He remained honest, not turning the government over to anyone, even his own followers. He went ahead with Juárez' program, and while conditions in the country gradually improved his enemies organized against him. Díaz went abroad to plot, but in 1875 he returned and soon a new pronunciamiento was heard, the Plan of Tuxtepec. Civil war ensued, but Lerdo's position was hopeless. Late in 1876 he departed into exile and Porfirio Díaz took over the country.

Díaz was, of course, a liberal. He had been a supporter of Juárez. But Juárez had recognized him for the military opportunist that he was, an object of suspicion. All Juárez' suspicions were well justified, as Díaz soon proved. As a liberal, Don Porfirio became the answer to the prayers of all Mexican conservatives from Iturbide to the present. In contrast to Agustín I, he was shrewd and intelligent; unlike Santa Anna, he never became bored with his job; and in common with Lucas Alamán, he was a champion of orderly progress.

Díaz remained the master of Mexico for thirty-four years. True, he modestly stepped aside — not very far — to permit Manuel González to serve as president from 1880 to 1884; but otherwise the old refrain of effective suffrage and no re-election became a standing joke to which only a later generation could give any meaning. Díaz took care of his military friends by bringing them back to a share in the spoils, but he did not trust any of them. Shrewdly he played one against another while keeping them all amply supplied with pesos. He organized his private little band of paid assassins who proved quite capable of taking care of anyone who became 'dangerous' in a political sense. The country became a paragon of order, but the order was not that of law; it was the order of Don Porfirio solely.

As dictator, Don Porfirio turned his back on Mexico. His more outspoken opponents might say he held her while the foreigners raped her. The wealthy creole landholders found themselves in favor once more, and even the clergy soon discovered that Díaz looked the other way while the anti-clerical laws enacted under Juárez and during the period of the Reform were openly ignored. Once again the church acquired property, religious schools appeared, and the religious orders set up their establishments once more. Of far greater significance, however, was the welcome extended foreigners. Not only were foreign capitalists invited to invest in a pacified Mexico, but even the ranks of the priesthood were swelled with religious from Latin Europe. Mestizo and Indian elements found themselves cast aside or held in subservient status. Only that which displayed a European cast achieved social and cultural standing. All that smacked of nativist origin was disdained.

Díaz was a liberal in that he believed in progress and development. He would turn Mexico into a modern nation, a concept which he measured only in terms of physical improvements. In the social evolution that had been so fundamental an element in the program of Juárez, he had no interest. Indeed, it soon became evident that he opposed it. The Mexican lower classes would provide the labor, foreign investors would provide the funds, and Díaz would see that peace prevailed throughout the land. To this end he organized the terribly efficient *rurales*, a band of rural police composed of military stooges and ex-bandits. To keep them subservient to his personal control he paid them well, provided them with elaborate uniforms, and allowed them to plunder the property of his enemies. The rurales became a famous police force, feared by all Mexicans who dared express opposition to the government, who dared disturb the peace, or who happened to stray away from work projects or the fields of a wealthy hacendado. Banditry disappeared, foreigners were treated with courtesy and respect, property was secure, and those who could not see beneath the surface to the mass of suffering humanity looked on and approved.

At first Díaz' methods shocked the country and the world. In 1879 a *lerdista* plot was discovered in Veracruz, and some alleged plotters were seized by the governor. He asked Díaz for instructions and received the terse telegram: 'If they are caught in the act, kill them in cold blood.' Jails were soon filled to overflowing, but Díaz had no wish to construct new centers of incarceration. The *ley fuga* was everywhere invoked; that is, anyone trying to escape was promptly shot. Prisoners seemed particularly prone to make the attempt, it seems, for the guns of the rurales were seldom silent for long.

Díaz' harsh regime had the look of benign paternalism to many foreigners who themselves never encountered difficulty in Mexico but were greatly impressed with the pace of economic growth, the orderliness of the countryside, and the cleanliness of the cities. Thousands of miles of railroad track were laid, streets were paved, mineral production tripled, and plantation agriculture and new textile mills added to national exports. The capital city was beautified by improvements in parkways and boulevards, if not by the construction of the unlovely Palace of Fine Arts. A new water system was provided Mexico City, and sewerage and drainage works were undertaken — a major need in a city built upon a former lake bed. Strenuous efforts were made to hide all the ugliness and evil of Mexico's poverty. The rag-clad, barefoot lépero of the capital was driven from the streets or into forced service in the fields. At the same time luxurious and ornate homes were built by wealthy land-holders, foreign businessmen, and political favorites of Díaz.

Particularly disastrous for the rural peon was the passage of many estates into foreign ownership. Americans in particular, unused to the old-style paternalism of the Spanish hacendado, were prone to treat their employees as paid laborers and nothing more. They saw little cause to assume the paternalistic responsibilities that control of the destinies of many peon families had long implied. Laborers were expected to live on their miserable wages and look after them-selves, something to which most were wholly unaccustomed. This difficulty, coupled with absentee ownership, encroachment on com-munal lands, and the repressive efforts of the rurales caused great suffering and hardship. Debt slavery became general, and peons were slated to work forever to pay off the principal and interest of small loans advanced them.

In spite of great economic expansion, Díaz had difficulty keeping the Mexican treasury in a healthy condition. It was not until 1894 that the budget was first balanced, and all obligations were met on a current basis. The event was especially significant for the *porfiristas,* as the Díaz followers were known. Now they felt secure, for every man had his price.

Surrounding Díaz during the last fifteen years or more of his regime was a group of young intellectuals, the *científicos,* whose acknowledged leader was José Ives Limantour, son of an immigrant Frenchman, who became the financial genius of the porfirista re-gime. The científicos constituted the first genuinely bureaucratic class to emerge in Mexico after independence. Government employ-ment had become the refuge and the economic basis of the Mexican middle class, and Limantour and the small group around him were the cream of the crop. Their efforts made public administration more honest and efficient, but they abjured only the cruder methods of acquiring wealth through political power. Under the tutelage of the científicos the Díaz regime was harnessed more securely to the interests of alien investors. Their goal was government by a creole oligarchy, their methods were heartless efficiency in the collection and management of revenues, and their political philosophy was borrowed from the positivism of Auguste Comte.

As secretary of the treasury Limantour took a number of steps that were of economic benefit to the country, such as abolition of the alcabala, that ancient obstacle to commerce and relic of the colonial era. He also secured government control of the railroads by purchasing a majority of the stock with public funds, but in the transaction científicos made vast profits. The growing strength of the bureaucratic oligarchy caused unrest among many of Díaz' supporters, however, for in the years after the turn of the century the old dictator, seemingly secure in his position, allowed more and more power to slip into the hands of his chief officials. These men, cold and obsessed with their projects of financial manipulation, gave little thought to keeping Díaz' political fences mended. They seemed to think the regime could go on forever.

In the meantime the status of the lower classes grew steadily worse. The mining industry passed into the hands of American companies. Over 100,000,000 acres of the public domain were transferred to private ownership of foreign investors and land speculators, many of the latter group being Mexican friends of Díaz and his bureaucrats. Indian lands, traditionally protected as the property of the various Indian communities, were seized and opened to speculators and hacendados. As a consequence, concentration of land ownership reached a new peak. Just before Díaz' downfall in 1911, nearly half of Mexico was owned by fewer than 3000 families, and about 95 per cent of the ten million persons employed in agriculture owned no land at all. Industrial laborers were generally better off than the debt-enslaved peons, but their attempts to organize into unions were brutally suppressed. Since foreign interests owned the majority of the mines and oil fields as well as the textile mills, it was not surprising that Mexicans began to identify foreign capital with oppression. By 1900, American investments alone in Mexico were more than one billion dollars, and English, French, and Spanish capital had also found the country a fertile field. Díaz had succeeded in expanding the economy of Mexico, but the condition of the great majority of Mexicans had sunk below what it had been at any time during the colonial period.

Culturally, the Age of Don Porfirio was one of stagnation, although a few notable writers were produced, such as Justo Sierra and Francisco Bulnes, and the poets Gutiérrez Nájera and Amado Nervo were of first rank. Sierra's *Evolución política del pueblo mexicano* (*Political Evolution of the Mexican People*) was a thoughtful and interpretive history. In general, however, intellectualism languished and artistic endeavor consisted of unproductive attempts to imitate the tawdry extravagance of France during the Second Empire.

Díaz brought poverty and misery to his people during his long rule. Physical development and vast profits for a few were small compensation for the loss of human dignity and personal security by the Mexican citizen of humble status. But abroad Don Porfirio was a hero. He had brought peace and 'progress' to the land of Santa Anna, and that indeed was an accomplishment! His chest was covered with the medals bestowed upon him by his foreign admirers. He was the grand old man who had enabled thousands of aliens to grow rich and live in luxury with a retinue of docile servants in his beautified capital. The world would soon know the true extent of Mexico's progress.

South and east from Mexico the five republics of Central America weathered the long years from the collapse of the confederation till the world-wide economic crisis of 1930 with little internal change. Each of the countries went its own way and each was torn to a greater or lesser degree by the activities of caudillos and the interminable conflicts over the status of the church. Few notable figures emerged in political life, intellectual and artistic achievement was, with one notable exception, of minor significance, and economic advance consisted largely of the gradual entrance of American investors in the banana industry along the eastern coast of Guatemala, Honduras, and Costa Rica. Guatemala was for long years ruled by a military dictator, Manuel Estrada Cabrera, who held the country firmly in his iron grasp from 1898 to 1920. Honduras, thinly populated and isolated, remained as in colonial times the most backward and undeveloped region of Central America. El Salvador, fronting only on the Pacific ocean, escaped the pressures of European and American powers struggling for control of the Caribbean. Likewise, and for the same reason, this, the smallest of the Central American republics, escaped almost entirely foreign economic penetration. After the turn of the century the gradual development of native-owned coffee plantations along the volcanic slopes from Santa Ana to San Vicente added greatly to national economic productivity and foreshadowed the creation of an extremely rich class of coffee planters after the great depression of the 1930's. Other progress was marked by the building of railroads linking San Salvador, the capital, with Guatemala on the west and with the Honduran frontier on the east. British investors provided the capital and owned and operated the lines.

Costa Rica remained essentially isolated, with no direct means of communication by land with neighbors on either side. As such, she escaped the military aspects of the occasional conflicts that arose among the five countries when some strong man conceived the idea of reuniting Central America by force. Justo Rufino Barrios of Guatemala was the first to make such an attempt in 1885, and for his pains he met death on the battlefield. Costa Rica was involved in the coalition against him, but Nicaragua and El Salvador carried the burden of the conflict. Conflict arose again in 1906, and although Costa Rica sided with El Salvador and Honduras against Guatemala, the principal contestants were the northwestern republics. Costa Rica, largely devoid of Indian population, exhibited many European characteristics and gradually developed an agricultural economy based on rather extensive participation in land ownership by the rank and file. Principal crops were corn, as in almost all Latin American countries, and bananas and coffee. The country remained comparatively tranquil domestically, and self-government came gradually to exhibit as high a degree of free popular participation as in any of the Latin American nations. Strong men were held in check by the relative strength of the legislative body, a rare phenomenon in the region and one that still persists with considerable vigor.

As already indicated Nicaragua early became a principal recipient
of foreign pressure by reason of her geographic resources: a large
lake only thirteen miles from the Pacific ocean and a semi-navigable
river connecting the lake with the Atlantic. By reason of the attention focused on the area, Nicaraguan affairs attracted far greater attention outside of Latin America than did those events taking place
within neighboring countries. The William Walker filibustering expedition in the late 1850's struck fear to the hearts of men in every
Central American capital, and the struggle between Great Britain
and the United States for control of the Nicaraguan canal route
was watched closely throughout the region. In 1893, a tyrannical
liberal, José Santos Zelaya, seized the presidency, and his sword-
rattling for the next fifteen years disturbed the entire Central American area and even aroused fears in the United States that he would
sell canal rights to Japan to flaunt his dislike and contempt for the
North American power. The possibility of such a development can
hardly be said to have lessened America's willingness to intervene
on behalf of the Nicaraguan conservatives in 1913. Supported by
the United States marines, conservatives were able to dominate the
government until 1928 when a really free election was held under
American supervision. The liberals were promptly returned to power
with the election of José María Moncada.

By 1930, the Central American nations had taken on distinctive
characteristics and atmospheres that set each apart sharply from all
the others. In Nicaragua the age-old struggle between León and
Granada had provided a geographical twist to the party alignment,
but the emergence of Managua as the major city and capital of the
republic greatly reduced tension and provided some hope for a
more peaceful future. United States intervention and domination
branded the nation as an American satellite and earned for it the
contempt of its neighbors, particularly since strong factions had
encouraged and profited by the continued presence of the foreign
marines. Nicaraguans cherished their independence, and many were
willing to fight for it; but even after the last marine was withdrawn
early in 1933, ties with the United States remained close and Americans continued to be held in high regard by a substantial portion of

the population. This was a phenomenon that other Central Americans were never quite able to understand.

Guatemala's distinctiveness stemmed from her picturesque and mountainous landscape, her large and racially unique Indian population which remained unassimilated, and her pretensions of superiority and leadership. As the seat of the former captaincy-general, Guatemala never became fully reconciled to a status of no better than equality vis à vis her neighbors to the south and east. It was no accident that in the struggles which from time to time disturbed the peace of the isthmian region Guatemala frequently found herself aligned against a combination of her neighbors.

Chief rival to Guatemala for leadership in Central America was El Salvador, a situation carried over from the internal struggles of the confederation. Densely populated and with the process of racial amalgamation virtually complete, El Salvador was in position to play a potent role in Central American affairs should it be possible to raise the great bulk of her people out of their misery and poverty. In the early part of the century, however, after coffee became a major crop, land ownership became increasingly concentrated and the gulf between the few who owned and profited and the many who toiled and subsisted deepened appreciably.

Honduras remained essentially primitive with her largely mestizo population scattered over the mountainous countryside. As the United Fruit Company acquired large banana plantations along the northern coast social and economic life in the region acquired the characteristics of a large company settlement that set the region apart from the remainder of the republic. The company went its way and so did the small mountain town of Tegucigalpa, the Honduran capital and principal population center of the republic. Neither interfered in the affairs of the other and the country remained divided, exhibiting little evidence of national cohesion or unity.

Costa Rica, with her predominantly European population, had no real Indian problem. Her population, including an increasing number of immigrants from Germany and Austria, concentrated in the cool mountain valleys from Alajuela to Turrialba, worked hard to build their country and to enjoy the pleasant life which a tranquil region afforded. Popular education was emphasized and the literacy rate was pushed higher and higher. The small nation took on the aspects of a middle-class community that would not have seemed out of place if tucked in some mountain valley of Central Europe. Only the teeming and steaming port cities of Limón and Puntarenas belied the illusion.

Probably the most famous Central American of the era was Rubén Darío, the Nicaraguan poet whose verses captivated the entire Hispanic world. His influence was that of an oasis in an intellectual desert, however, for few other Central Americans interested themselves deeply in literature or the arts. There were no centers of higher education worthy of the name in the entire region.

In the Caribbean islands life was even less secure than in Central America. Social, economic, and political conditions in Haiti were deplorable, and education was completely neglected. Not until 1860 were relations restored with the papacy and regularized in a concordat which made possible the rehabilitation of the clergy. Educational institutions were founded by the Christian Brothers and other orders, but these could do little to dissipate the ignorance of generations. Not until the twentieth century, when American intervention occurred, were serious efforts made to improve health, education, and transportation. National finances were organized and taken out of the hands of covetous officials, and a police force was trained, in the hope that it could preserve order in lieu of an army.

The Dominican Republic, under constant threat of intervention from Haiti and by European powers as well, ended her precarious independence in 1861 by voluntarily returning to the Spanish empire. Spanish rule was no more satisfactory, and in 1865, after a destructive war, independence was restored. Like Haiti, the Dominican Republic remained politically and financially chaotic. For a short time the government hoped for annexation by the United States, but although President Ulysses S. Grant favored the move, the Senate opposed it. Under Theodore Roosevelt the United States assumed management of Dominican customs and the financial condition of the government improved. In 1916, a year after intervention in Haiti, American marines landed in the Dominican Republic.

Cuba and Puerto Rico, still colonies of Spain, were torn by various unsuccessful attempts to win independence, particularly the bloody Cuban Ten Years' War, beginning in 1868. Trade relations with the United States improved meanwhile, and American interest in Cuba remained strong. In 1895 Cubans rebelled once more, led by the eminent writer, José Marti, and Tomás Estrada Palma, later president. In 1898 the United States became a party to the conflict, after the unexplained sinking of the *Maine*. Cuba was granted independence, though the United States retained the right to intervene, and Puerto Rico was annexed.

As an independent nation Cuba's early political experiences were far from peaceful and gratifying to those who fought so bitterly for independence. The sugar industry became prosperous while high prices prevailed, but graft in government remained an insoluble problem. Political life continued to be unsettled, leading to intervention by the United States in 1906, and to the landing of marines on several occasions to protect lives and property of American citizens. In 1924 Gerardo Machado assumed the presidency, and he maintained himself in power by tyrannical means until his overthrow in 1933.

The other great region of the Caribbean borderland still languished in the throes of religious and sectional factionalism. The liberal-minded conservative president of Colombia, Mosquera, did not go far enough to please the truly liberal factions which were stimulated to action by the French revolution of 1848. In the election of 1849, no candidate received a majority, and as had happened so often before, final choice was thrown into the lap of congress. That body, under strong pressure from liberal supporters who swarmed into the building where the deputies were meeting, finally selected the liberal candidate, General José Hilario López. For the first time a new party took over control of the government. It embarked on a drastic and radical reform program aimed at converting Colombia into the image of the Second Republic in France.

Almost immediately after López took office, pressure was exerted to expel the Jesuits, who had been readmitted to the country only a few years before. Amid sharp religious antagonisms, the black-robed fathers were once again driven from the country, and the government quickly turned to other measures designed to reduce the authority and power of the church. In 1853 a new constitution abolished church exemptions and privileges, deprived it of state support, and declared complete freedom of religion throughout the nation. It also abolished slavery, decreed freedom of the press, established manhood suffrage, and provided for the secret ballot. It provided for the election of provincial governors, a step designed to provide a larger amount of 'home rule.' Truly, the constitution was an innovation.

Opposition to liberal rule was severe, and revolt flared quickly. Fortunately for the country, even the older factions preferred constitutional rule to military depotism and the barracks revolt. Revolution was suppressed, and soon the decentralizing steps of the 1853 constitution were carried even farther. Colombia became a confederation of virtually autonomous states over which the national government came to exercise less and less control. Disorders became widespread; and the Granadine Confederation, as the arrangement came to be called, seemed on the point of anarchy. Still the liberals were able to remain in power, and it was not until 1884 that the curtain was finally rung down on their chaotic rule.

The liberal regime took a variety of steps to improve the national economy. Roads and railroads were constructed and telegraph lines linked the principal regions, but commercial progress was minor. The regime, decentralized and ineffective, was unable to maintain order, banditry was everywhere a scourge, and military bands struggled for control of the provincial or state governments. Politics and strife struck the dominant note, and in such an atmosphere little economic and material progress was possible.

In 1880, a new figure emerged on the Colombian scene in the person of Rafael Núñez. One of the earlier extreme liberals who had become greatly interested in European socialist doctrines, he was rudely shaken from his former tendencies by his experiences in the presidency from 1880 to 1882. He watched the chronic turmoil of his country with growing distaste until he became convinced that it was his duty to bring an end to the confusion. He began organizing a party of his own dedicated to reconstruction of a strong central government that could re-establish law and order and make possible greater national development. In 1884 Núñez was re-elected and his new Nationalist party, composed of moderates from among the conservatives and liberals, dominated the council he assembled to prepare a new constitution. In addressing the group Núñez denounced the political changes of the liberal regime as entirely destructive. He called for a highly centralized government and a return to church control over education. The constitution was written in keeping with his wishes and was put into force in 1886. The president's power was greatly enlarged, his term of office was extended to six years, and he was authorized to appoint provincial governors and to issue decrees to supplement the laws passed by congress. Roman Catholicism was made once more the state religion, and education was to conform to the doctrines of the church.

Núñez remained in power until his death in 1894. In 1888 he negotiated a concordat with the papacy which restored to the church the privileges and authority it had enjoyed in the colonial period, except that the Inquisition was not reinstituted. The government agreed to compensate the church for the property it had confiscated earlier.

The liberals were no more willing to accept exclusion from the government than the conservatives had been, and revolts during Núñez' rule were frequent. The most serious uprising began after his death. It broke out in 1899 and lasted until 1903, completely disrupting the country and giving a watching world the impression of hopeless disorder. It was a struggle of wayward provinces against the capital, of Freemasons and liberals against the church and the conservatives, of would-be caudillos against the legitimate government. The revolt was finally suppressed, but the loss of life and the destruction of property had been great. Panamá had been the scene of a major disaffection, and the event lent credence to the views of Theodore Roosevelt that the region might easily be constituted a separate nation more favorable to his canal project. In 1903 he acted on this premise. As discussed in an earlier chapter, Colombia was unable to prevent the secessionist move, and she lost her province and all possible benefits of having a canal constructed across her territory. Panamá became independent and an American protectorate.

The loss of Panamá had a sobering effect upon political factions in Colombia. It made them more restrained when national stability was at stake. In 1906, during the administration of able, energetic, but impetuous Rafael Reyes, a law was passed providing for minority representation in the congress and the cabinet, and this helped to pacify the liberal opposition. In 1910 the constitution was amended to restrict the franchise by imposing literacy and property or income qualifications. The conservative regime was thereby strengthened, and the liberal and democratic tenets espoused by the opposition were dealt a serious blow.

During the years between 1910 and 1930, Colombia enjoyed relative peace under conservative administrations with which the liberals occasionally co-operated. It was under such conservative administrations, in fact, that most of Colombia's social legislation was passed. Measures were enacted in this period providing for pensions for school teachers, compensation for labor accidents, and improvement in public health conditions. Income taxes were also adopted in an effort to broaden the revenue base.

Once peace was re-established, a program was initiated to recall the worthless paper pesos in widespread circulation as a consequence of virtual financial collapse. Gold was auctioned off for bundles of the pesos, and enormous piles of them were burned. Much paper of dubious value remained in circulation, however, to the continued detriment of commerce. In 1922, after several unsuccessful attempts to reach a better understanding with the United States, a treaty was ratified whereby Colombia was to be paid twenty-five million dollars as compensation for the loss of Panamá. There was no expression of regret forthcoming, however, as to the manner in which the loss had occurred. In the following year the first installment was paid, and it greatly aided the government in introducing a new and more stable currency.

Economic progress in Colombia was slow. It was gradually discovered that the country was richly endowed with natural resources. The highland valleys of the south provide excellent agricultural lands, and the lower reaches of the mountains throughout the country are suitable for coffee growing. Indeed, coffee was planted widely and soon became the chief export commodity. The country is rich in minerals, including petroleum, gold, lead, mercury, manganese, iron, and various precious stones. It is the world's chief source of emeralds. The forests of Colombia abound in valuable woods. Geographic obstacles, however, have impeded large-scale development. The rugged terrain, with altitude varying from sea level to 18,000 feet, has made transportation difficult from the days of the Spanish conquest, and even though Bolívar was able to perform wondrous feats with troops of cavalry, the movement of goods has never fared so well. Steam navigation of the Magdalena river enabled limited areas to be served by ship, but the river has always been capricious and accidents have been frequent.

During the years from 1860 to 1930 Colombians remained generally poor. By the beginning of the great depression, Colombia had some eight million inhabitants, but the great majority of those engaged in productive activity worked in agriculture at a subsistence level. The country is a land of small towns and villages separated by high mountains. Only four cities — Bogotá, Medellín, Barranquilla, and Cali — developed into major population centers. Of these, only Medellín attracted industrial growth. Bogotá remained a political center, Barranquilla a port, and Cali became the chief distribution point for a large agricultural region. The unhappy experiences of other Latin American nations, plus antagonism against the United States after the Panamá incident, made Colombians suspicious of foreign capitalists and investors. Alien capital was not strongly encouraged in Colombia, and for the most part citizens of the country have shown an inclination to see their resources lie untouched rather than watch foreigners carry them away. In 1920, however, a

German aviation company, 'Scadta,' was given a concession to operate the first air line in Colombia and in South America.

In 1922 the liberals made a strong bid for the presidency after failing to enter candidates in some of the earlier elections. General Pedro Nel Ospina, the conservative candidate, won, nevertheless, and served until 1926 during a period of national prosperity. Coffee and petroleum produced considerable wealth, and loans from private investors in the United States were used for railroad construction and other public works. Inflation caused prices to rise, and when world trade collapsed the conservatives found themselves badly divided and disorganized. The liberals, who had at first been indifferent toward the election of 1930, perceived an opportunity to win, and their candidate, Dr. Enrique Olaya Herrera, was elected on a platform of social and political reform. Thus at a time when many other Latin American nations were ousting liberal regimes in favor of more incisive despotisms, Colombia peacefully made the transition from conservative to liberal rule.

Colombia produced many able men who were masters of the literary arts and whose greatest contributions were made during the second half of the nineteenth century. Probably the greatest poets of the era were Gregorio Gutiérrez González and José Asunción Silva, both widely known. José Joaquín Ortiz and Julio Arboleda deserve mention, as do also Diego Fallón and Rafael Pombo. In 1867 José María Vergara y Vergara published a work on national customs and folklore, a prose work that brought him fame and appointment to the Spanish Royal Academy. The Restrepo family, ever active in literary circles, continued to have illustrious representatives. Antonio Gómez Restrepo developed a notable work on Colombian literature which he published in 1926. In general, however, fewer men made significant contributions to Colombian literature after the turn of the century than in the preceding fifty years.

While Mexico was being exploited by the porfiristas and Colombia was torn by revolution and anarchy, Venezuela passed from the hands of one tryant into those of another. A revolt in 1899 enabled Cipriano Castro to establish himself as dictator. He attempted to

continue the road-building and other public works projects inaugurated by former rulers, but frequent revolts led to more destruction than construction. Castro ruled for nearly ten years, but by
1908 opposition to him was so bitter that he turned the government over to his vice-president, Juan Vicente Gómez. Castro departed for Europe for reasons of health, and indeed his health
would have suffered had he remained in Venezuela. He had gotten
his country into serious difficulties with several European powers
and the United States over failure to meet obligations and his
inability or unwillingness to protect the lives and property of
alien residents. England, Germany, and Italy had jointly blockaded
the seaports in an effort to force collection, and for a time it appeared that Germany might have somewhat broader objectives.
Even after the Hague Court had settled the claims of the major
powers, greatly reducing many of them, the Netherlands undertook
a new blockade. All that Castro did seemed to produce only trouble.

Juan Vicente Gómez proved himself a man of many talents, including the ability to maintain himself in power from 1908 till
1935, when he died in office from natural causes. He won support
from abroad by agreeing to meet all of the country's external obligations and keeping his word. Foreign capital was extended a ready
welcome, and within the period of his rule oil production, which
had amounted to a mere trickle when he first assumed office,
mounted to astronomical proportions. Value of foreign trade jumped
from less than 50 million dollars in 1910 to nearly 250 million in
1929. Proceeds from oil royalties and duties filled the government's
coffers and the pockets of Gómez and his friends and relatives. The
national debt was entirely liquidated, roads were built to link the
major portions of the country, and railroad mileage was extended
greatly. Obviously Gómez was a man who believed in progress.

Unlike Mexico under Díaz, however, Venezuela under Gómez
was not handed bodily over to aliens. Aliens were satisfied, however,
as long as they were permitted to tap the country's vast oil reserves
in the region of Lake Maracaibo. Gómez did not trouble the miserable back-country population or take away their land. He was content to confiscate and operate the business and commercial enter-

prises of the country, and he allowed oilfield workers to benefit by the high wages they received. In other ways his rule was utterly despotic. He destroyed every semblance of constitutional government, even though he did pause occasionally to tinker with the written charter. His enemies were ruthlessly imprisoned, tortured, and slaughtered. Gómez could spot a potential trouble-maker miles away, and his preventive measures were swift and entirely effective.

As the years passed Gómez became immensely rich. He built for himself a huge mansion, so elaborate indeed as to arouse almost as much laughter and ridicule as anger among those who feared and hated him. Gómez was an ignorant and crude man who lacked the sensitivities that might have prevented him from making such a tawdry display of his wealth. His vaste horde of relatives, including innumerable children, legitimate and 'natural,' were permitted to enrich themselves also at the country's expense; but with so many evidences of physical 'progress,' who should complain? The intellectual climate was stultifying, the press was rigidly controlled, and all opposition seemed hopeless. Nevertheless, when Gómez died in 1935, the news provoked one of the wildest celebrations ever witnessed in Venezuela. Between moments of rejoicing, mobs sought out Gómez' most obnoxious adherents and killed them.

In spite of harsh and oppressive dictatorship throughout most of the Hispanic nations bordering on the Caribbean, in spite of heavy foreign pressure, in spite of exploitation from within and without, the lower classes remained generally passive. The ignorant Indian or mestizo knew his place and kept to it. Not so in Mexico.

Class differentiation is an inevitable concomitant of human civilization, judging by all the lessons of history and anthropology, nonsensical communistic theories notwithstanding. Human differences — physical, intellectual, psychological, and accidental — account for the evolution of class structure. The great American ideal, so close to reality in the United States in the twentieth century, would place the whole concept of class on a purely rational basis. The individual would be free to move upward or downward in accordance with his abilities, supported in the process by relative equality of opportunity. Such social objectives have never been entirely alien to liberal Latin American thought, but the process of achieving them has been slow indeed. Occasionally, however, a violent effort has been made in Mexico. Such was the case in the revolutionary struggles of Hidalgo and Morelos, and in the long War of the Reform in the time of Juárez. A new effort was made beginning in 1911, and it toppled the porfirista regime to the ground.

Porfirio Díaz failed to provide for a successor; and as the 'Grand Old Man' grew increasingly senile, the question of presidential succession became an urgent issue. Bernardo Reyes, mestizo governor of Nuevo León, and Limantour, idol of the científicos, were potential candidates. In an interview with an American journalist named Creelman, Díaz announced that he planned to retire in 1910 and would welcome the formation of an opposition party. His words were undoubtedly meant for consumption in the United States, but they were received with enthusiasm by many elements in Mexico. The generation of young intellectuals now added its voice to the demand for free elections and reform. Díaz, old and out of touch with conditions, was unconcerned by the clamor. He sent Reyes off on a diplomatic mission, and no potential leader seemed left to oppose him. But so weakened had his position become that the old dictator was to be overthrown by a mild-mannered little vegetarian, Francisco I. Madero, who had written a book in which he gently suggested that Mexicans should be allowed to choose their vice-president!

Madero was virtually overwhelmed with supporters and launched bodily into a role for which he had none of the necessary qualifications. The first attempts at rebellion were fiascos, and Madero decided to abandon the affair. But his cause had been embraced by sterner men, the vaqueros and bandits of Chihuahua led by Pascual Orozco and by the local Robin Hood, Pancho Villa. They defeated the government troops sent against them, and soon uprisings broke out spontaneously throughout Mexico. The rotten timbers of the dictatorship crumpled in a manner astonishing to Díaz and Madero alike. On May 25, 1911, Díaz resigned and left the country to spend his remaining years in France. Hopeful Mexicans awaited Madero, who seemed from a distance to be the man needed to redress the wrongs of centuries. Instead they faced a decade of rapine and guerrilla warfare, fought by the contenders for the mantle Madero found to be ill-fitting.

Madero had no program but the overthrow of the Díaz regime. His understanding of Mexico's problems and aspirations was slight, to say the least, for he naïvely assumed that once Díaz was gone things would right themselves. The long-suffering Mexicans hungered for land as well as liberty from tyranny. A large proportion simply hungered. Most important to Madero was the establishment of immediate political democracy, a concept which not even he understood. While he remained impractically idealistic his brother Gustavo set about bossing Mexico in the established tradition. Soon disillusionment with the Madero regime surpassed the early enthusiasm for it. Emiliano Zapata, who epitomized the Indian's undying yearning for land, was the first to rebel. It was not long before revolts swept from one end of the country to the other.

Profoundly disturbed by the sudden changes in the Mexican administration, foreign businessmen and capitalists began to look for an official who could re-establish order and guarantee them the same protection they had enjoyed under Díaz. They considered a number of candidates before arriving at their choice, heavy-drinking, slow-thinking, sadistic General Victoriano Huerta.

Huerta's rise to power began when Madero sent him to quell revolts instigated by Bernardo Reyes and Pascual Orozco. After his success against the rebels, Huerta anticipated a handsome reward; instead he was retired. He became a bitter and unscrupulous foe of Madero. Other revolts broke out, but none was serious until the American ambassador, Henry Lane Wilson, began conniving with the opposition. Under his guidance the downfall of Madero was engineered.

Wilson's messages to the state department in Washington contained frequent and violent attacks on Madero and urged United States intervention. In the meantime, Madero's loathing of violence prevented his ordering the execution of rebels, and rebellion became safe. Soon his army was undermined, and when the final attack came in January of 1913, he made the fatal mistake of placing Huerta in command of his troops.

In February Huerta seized Madero and the vice-president, Pino Suárez. Francisco Madero's brother, Gustavo, was literally drawn and quartered while Huerta was significantly occupied elsewhere. Huerta, Félix Díaz, an ostensible rebel with whom Huerta had secretly been co-operating, and the American ambassador drew up a plan to save Mexico. A few nights later, Francisco Madero and his vice-president were shot, reportedly while 'attempting to escape.' Huerta took over the Mexican government and the American ambassador notified his government that a wicked despotism had fallen.

Before disposing of Madero, Huerta had required his resignation to maintain a semblance of legal form. To secure the resignation Huerta promised both Madero and Pino Suárez safe conduct from the country, but he made no pretense of keeping his pledge. Wives of the doomed men pleaded with the American ambassador to intercede to save their husbands, but Henry Lane Wilson dismissed them on the ground that he could not interfere in Mexico's internal affairs! After all, Madero had even harbored the thought of taxing idle lands.

Huerta's seventeen-month rule was one of the most sordid tyrannies that ever befell a Latin American country. His almost perpetual state of intoxication and his characteristic brutality made governing the country chiefly a process of plunder and extermination of enemies. His ministers, handpicked by the American ambassador, resigned or were shoved aside. Over a hundred members of congress were jailed. Murder became the chief public function. Huerta controlled the area around Mexico City, but in the south Zapata remained unconquered and was busily engaged in redistributing the land to his Indian followers. In the north new opponents arose.

Venustiano Carranza, governor of Coahuila, refused to recognize Huerta and called for his removal. He announced his *Plan de Guadalupe*, simply a restoration of the principles and constitution of 1857, and joined forces with Alvaro Obregón, governor of Sonora. Other allies were found in the persons of Pancho Villa and Pablo González in Chihuahua. A slow march on the capital began, and the real revolution got under way.

Carranza was a simple man and in no sense vicious. Obregón was able and astute and possessed a deep understanding of what was wrong with Mexico. His Yaqui Indian troops had been victims of Díaz' spoliation. Villa was a plundering bandit and nothing more. Both Carranza and Obregón distrusted him and he them. As the move on the capital progressed, a systematic pillage of town and hacienda began, and none of the leaders took serious steps to check it. Captured hacendados were promptly shot along with other members of their families after the women had been turned over to the soldiery. Death was dealt on every hand, and Villa and his lieutenants reveled in an orgy of blood. Carranza shuddered and Obregón frowned and would have no part of it, but the unpaid and ill-disciplined army had to be kept satisfied. The great estates continued to go up in smoke while their owners were left for the well-fed buzzards and their cattle were sold across the northern frontier for additional arms.

Mexico was offered a sorry collection of leaders. Carranza's greatest recommendations were his distinguished appearance and his basically gentle nature. In reality he was quite undistinguished, ignorant, and jealous of subordinates who demonstrated unusual ability. He did have enough respect for human misery to hold the vicious Villa back from entering Mexico City when finally the revolutionary armies approached the capital. For this 'betrayal,' Villa never forgave him. Obregón, by far the most promising of the northern rebels, lacked prestige, and the fact that he frowned on looting weakened his chances of becoming a popular hero to his troops.

In the south, the *zapatistas* proceeded with their crude but effective program of land distribution, that of killing off the hacendados and dividing their land. They were not concerned with more remote problems. In many ways, Zapata was the most attractive of the rebel chiefs, for he had a commendable goal in the rehabilitation of his people.

Foreign interest in Mexican problems increased dangerously.

British investors who had received favors from Huerta supported him enthusiastically, but American concessionaires and owners of mines and ranches called for intervention. President Woodrow Wilson of the United States reviewed the record of Huerta and found it loathsome. Belatedly he recalled his ambassador, Henry Lane Wilson, and urged Huerta not to be a candidate for the presidency. The American president was simply and not too politely ignored. Wilson took more drastic action. In 1914 he took advantage of the arrest and brief detention of a few American seamen at Tampico and ordered the navy to seize Veracruz. This ill-considered act aided Huerta more than it injured him, for it nearly united the Mexican factions in opposition to the Yankee invader. The error was quickly rectified, however, for President Wilson recognized the belligerency status of the forces of Carranza and Obregón and began selling them arms. This step quickly spelled doom for the besotted tyrant, Huerta. Heavily supplied with equipment for which they had traded the confiscated cattle of wealthy hacendados, Obregón and Villa raced with their troops down the Pacific coast and across the central valley, each hoping to reach the capital first and take over the government. Obregón's forces won, thanks to Carranza's interference with Villa. Huerta fled the country. Villa, however, considered himself betrayed, and turned his army against Carranza's, and for a time their struggle became the principal conflict.

By issuing a series of reform decrees in 1915, Carranza greatly strengthened his political position. Obregón, hoping to bring about some semblance of order, threw his support to Carranza whom he considered to be the lesser of two evils. This gave Carranza the ablest Mexican general. Both Carranza and Obregón, because they made political pronouncements and gave evidence of a desire to reform Mexico's social structure — however vague their objectives — were regarded as dangerous men. Conservatives and foreign capitalists gravitated toward Villa, who obviously was a type who could be bought. Their cause was lost. Obregón defeated Villa in a series of vicious and devastating battles, scattered his motley army, and returned him to his boyhood occupation of banditry in Chihuahua.

In October, 1915, President Wilson recognized Carranza as *de facto* head of the Mexican state. Villa was furious. He vented his anger and disappointment on all American citizens on whom he could lay his hands. He even raided the New Mexican town of Columbus across the border in the United States. This act prompted Wilson to send General Pershing into northern Mexico to capture Villa dead or alive. Such a measure greatly weakened Carranza's position for a time, for it faced him with a new American invasion of Mexico. He was, however, in no position to oppose, and Villa was as much his enemy as an enemy of the United States. Pershing's expedition was a ridiculous failure, for he had not the slightest chance of capturing the wily Villa.

In 1916 Carranza, who fancied himself the heir of Juárez, called for an assembly to revise the constitution. Although he contemplated nothing more striking than a provision to increase the authority of the president, a small group of radicals, led by General Francisco Múgica and Andrés Molina Enríquez and backed by Obregón, incorporated in the new constitution some of the basic ideas distilled from the revolutionary ferment. Article 27 was written as a masterful attempt to undo all the evils of the porfirista regime with respect to the alienation of Mexican lands and resources. National ownership of mineral and subsoil rights, recognized from the colonial period, was reaffirmed and declared to be inalienable. The ownership of surface land was limited exclusively to Mexicans and largely to individuals, except under very stringent conditions. The church was prohibited from holding property and corporate ownership of agricultural land was proscribed. The usurpation of Indian *ejidos*, or communal village lands, was to be reversed. Most of the land concessions granted since the days of Juárez were declared null and void.

Article 123 included most of the known guarantees for labor, and although no laws were passed immediately to make the principles operative, the article embodied the goals of the revolutionaries on behalf of the industrial worker.

The anti-clerical principles of the Juárez epoch were reaffirmed, and a number of more stringent restrictions were added. In addition to proscribing church ownership of property the constitution gave to state legislatures the authority to regulate the number of priests permitted within each state and required priests to register with the civil authorities. Because of the political activity of the church party on behalf of Díaz and Huerta, it now suffered once again the bitter consequences of defeat.

Even though Carranza had little sympathy with or understanding of the aspirations of the revolutionary leaders, and did not attempt to invoke any of the offending articles, opposition to the constitution of 1917 was enormous. It stemmed from the foreign interests, from the conservative landholders, from the church; but the Mexican middle and lower classes who understood applauded. Priests, hacendados, and foreign owners of mines and oil fields prepared to have the distasteful articles obliterated before any government should try to put them into effect. No fears were aroused by Carranza's actions, for he ignored the land problem except when his own followers wanted rewards, and he threatened striking workers with the firing squad.

Partisan forces in Chihuahua and Morelos still held out against government troops, but in 1919 Zapata was assassinated. This removed one of the most colorful and devoted of the revolutionary leaders, but his program of land reform was already accomplished and no one moved to interfere.

During 1919 the question of a successor to Carranza raised a furore, but Obregón was the only candidate with hope of success. He had the support of labor, and labor had suddenly become a powerful factor in Mexican politics. Labor unions were formed and consolidated into a national federation dominated by Luis Morones, an able figure dedicated to the revolutionary principles of the new constitution. The *Confederación Regional Obrera Mexicana,* or CROM, was controlled by an executive committee, the *Grupo Acción,* composed of trusted associates of Morones. Morones could throw the entire labor movement behind Obregón.

Carranza, despite his opposition to re-election in the past, was reluctant to surrender his power. Yet his term, which dated from 1917, was expiring. The Obregón faction found an occasion to revolt when Carranza threatened to use federal troops to break a strike in Sonora, in April, 1920. It immediately became apparent that Carranza was no match for Obregón, and the various regional chieftains quickly deserted the one and swore loyalty to the other. Carranza fled for Tampico, but his guide murdered him en route. By the time Obregón assumed the presidency in November of the same year, the country was more nearly pacified than it had been in the past decade. It was a peace of exhaustion, but a number of old wounds had been healed. The zapatistas were permitted to retain their lands in Morelos; Zapata's assassin had been shot; and Villa had been distracted from his normal trade by the gift of a cattle ranch in Durango.

Obregón began putting into effect some of the ideas of the revolution, although in most outward aspects his government was a replica of its predecessors. He had no intention of making immediately sweeping changes that might as easily be reversed. Mexico's first need after domestic peace, he believed, was a more efficient economy. He maintained control by skillfully balancing his supporters and opponents. Agrarian reform, which he regarded as dangerous to the economy, was permitted to continue at a slow pace as a safety valve, but it was not encouraged. The most noteworthy accomplishments of his administration were due to the heroic efforts of José Vasconcelos in the field of popular education.

The rural school system established by Vasconcelos and supported by Obregón was one of the most important factors in consolidating the ideas of the revolutionaries. The rural school teacher became the successor of the sixteenth-century missionary in spreading the new gospel of Mexico for the Mexicans. A tremendous task remained to be done, for more than a million Indians knew no Spanish at all, and most of them regarded anyone from outside the village with suspicion and hostility. These people had to be assimilated into the new Mexican nation.

Foreign capital presented the gravest problem to Obregón, for the revolution was pledged to recover Mexico for the Mexicans, and foreigners apprehensively awaited the first signs of danger in this direction. The taxes levied on the oil industry were violently denounced, but since the proceeds were used to resume payments to foreign bondholders, a significant element of foreign opposition was placated. Obregón finally declared that Article 27 of the constitution would not be applied retroactively, and in August, 1923, the United States recognized his regime, barely in time to prevent a serious civil war over the presidential succession.

The revolt of Adolfo de la Huerta was serious enough for three months, but in the end Obregón triumphed and was able to turn the presidency over to Plutarco Elías Calles, the president-elect, without incident. This was in 1924.

Calles, whose early career gave little promise of future greatness, at first devoted his remarkable energies to social reform. As president he ruled as personally as any of his predecessors, and although many of the revolutionary ideals were put in practice, political control became more and more concentrated in his hands. Educational improvement was continued, and the government organized and financed various projects to improve sanitation and to irrigate rural areas where rainfall was insufficient. Land redistribution, which had lagged under Obregón, received active support; progress still was made at a snail's pace, however. Labor organization proceeded rapidly, and Luis Morones became as powerful as any general and more wealthy than most.

The church was Calles' most determined opponent, and in 1926 its hostility became critical. Calles replied to clerical threats by deporting priests and closing churches and Catholic schools. Priests were forbidden to appear on the street in clerical garb, and they had to register with civil authorities as the constitution prescribed. A futile religious strike began which lasted for three years. Rebel bands of fanatical clerical supporters calling themselves *cristeros* sought to embarrass the government by acts of sabotage, such as the dynamiting of trains. Counter-measures of military chieftains were little more conducive to peace, and thousands of innocent persons suffered. Not a few priests paid the supreme penalty for their devotion.

Outside of Mexico, the world was shocked by this persecution of religion, and as such it was reported by church officials and the clerical party. Relations with the United States eased materially, however, when Dwight W. Morrow replaced Ambassador Sheffield in the Mexican capital. Morrow was probably the first American ambassador to Mexico who had a genuine appreciation for the efforts of the Mexican people to overcome their miserable heritage of a century of foreign and domestic exploitation. He also had a sincere respect for Mexican sovereignty and exercised a judicious restraint in interfering in the internal affairs of the country to which he was accredited.

In 1928, the question of presidential succession again threatened to precipitate a civil war, for many ambitious politicians saw their hopes dashed by the apparent plan of Calles and Obregón to alternate the presidency between them. Those who pronounced against the government were quickly disposed of, so that Obregón was left without serious competition and was overwhelmingly elected. Before he could take office, however, he was assassinated by a religious fanatic. Many thought that Calles had engineered the deed, but it was not proved. Actually, it was in the crisis following the assassination that Calles displayed his most statesmanlike qualities. He announced that thereafter Mexico should be governed by laws rather than ruled by men, and his words had a calming effect in spite of their patent insincerity. The congress selected Emilio Portes Gil, an *obregonista*, to serve as provisional president, and a return to anarchy was avoided.

By 1929 many of the old revolutionaries, including Calles, Morones, and scores of others, had become wealthy through the spoils of office. Little by little their revolutionary zeal deserted them until they came to regard reforms with displeasure. Calles, who had ostensibly retired from political life, began to interfere excessively in the administration of Portes Gil. The various political factions were welded into a single party, the National Revolutionary party, or PNR. It held its first convention in 1929 for the purpose of nominating a successor to Portes Gil. The choice was Pascual Ortiz Rubio, a man suggested by Calles. Despite a whirlwind campaign by Vasconcelos, Ortiz Rubio's opponent, the party candidate won by a tremendous majority, and Vasconcelos vanished into self-imposed exile to write his memoirs.

The control which Calles exercised over Ortiz Rubio brought the revolutionary reforms to a temporary end. From his palatial home in Cuernavaca, the *jefe máximo* ruled Mexico by means of a private telephone line into the National Palace. The administration of Ortiz Rubio came to a sudden if not surprising end in 1932. On the day after Ortiz Rubio had dismissed several *callistas* from his cabinet, the president read in the morning paper of his resignation, announced by Calles. Wealthy Abelardo Rodríguez was appointed to finish the term.

Many Mexicans felt that the revolution had been betrayed, that the still vital and necessary reforms had all been sidetracked. Calles was obviously running the country through his stooges and filling his pockets ever fuller in the process. The left wing of the PNR began determined agitation for change. Finally the callistas made a gesture toward placating them. The 1934 candidate for the presidency would have to satisfy the new generation and those demanding further progress toward the revolutionary ideals, but he would also have to be a man who would remain basically loyal to the one-time revolutionaries who had now 'retired.' In choosing Lázaro Cárdenas for this role, Calles grossly underestimated both the man and the power of the reform forces. With the election of Cárdenas a new era of the Mexican revolution opened. Soon Calles was living in exile in the United States and a new reform movement was sweeping all before it. The revolution had come of age.

XXXIV

Brazil: The Waning Empire and the Old Republic

Comparatively few show themselves sensible of the tremendous problems which the nation has to face, with its scattered centers of population to draw together, its means of communication to extend, its public credit to sustain, its revenues to be scrupulously husbanded and applied to useful purposes, above all, its mass of Negro and Indian population to be educated and civilized. Nowhere in the world is there a more urgent need for a wise constructive statesmanship.

JAMES BRYCE [*]

B Y mid-century Brazil appeared bound on a course quite different from those pursued by most of her Spanish American neighbors. The period of the regency had given the country an unhappy acquaintance with republicanism and federalism, and the experiences of near-by Argentina only fortified Brazilian faith in the monarchy. After his coronation young Dom Pedro II had gradually rejected attempts of court cliques to manage his affairs, and had established himself as the real ruler of Brazil. His remarkable character was to be one of the potent forces molding Brazilian life, and one of the reasons for an easy transition to republicanism in 1890. His chosen role was that of moderator between the political forces striving for power. During his long reign Brazilians enjoyed civil liberties unparalleled in the rest of the continent,

[*] South America, Observations and Impressions, The Macmillan Company, New York, 1929, p. 419.

and the men who held high offices displayed an enviable political morality. The emperor himself set the example by a life of sobriety, moderation, democracy, and intellectual curiosity which did little justice to some of his lusty forebears. But neither the emperor nor his statesmen were prepared to solve economic problems constructively, and Brazil's material progress remained shackled to slave-based agriculture.

Dom Pedro exercised his constitutional powers fully. Had it not been for his interference there would have been few changes in the complexion of the chamber of deputies, for the party controlling the ministry decided the outcome of elections. Dom Pedro transferred the ministry from the conservatives to the liberals, or the reverse, when he felt that a change was in the nation's interest, and elections were subsequently held which reflected this change in the assembly. The contending parties did not greatly appreciate the emperor's impartiality, for they felt that he could not be depended on for constant support. By 1862 a balance had been achieved between the conservatives and the revived Liberal party, and the empire politically was at high tide. From this point onward a strong democratic current developed, and the conservative flood began to recede. As it ebbed the fate of the empire was decided. Even in the 1860's some men voiced the belief that Dom Pedro would be the last emperor of Brazil.

As far as education was concerned, Brazilians continued to concentrate on law, and law colleges of necessity served a supplementary cultural purpose. All of those who studied law did not find employment in the legal profession; law became the basic training for politicians, diplomats, journalists, teachers, poets, and novelists. The ecclesiastical approach to education of colonial days was thus replaced by a secular, juridical spirit. Through the law schools the influence of French and English philosophers reached the ruling class. The law schools, and especially that of São Paulo, became deeply involved with politics, and most of the liberal movements of the epoch first found articulate expression there.

With the law colleges serving to prepare the cultural elite, technical studies were largely neglected. Two medical schools founded in the time of João VI had survived, but their days of most fruitful achievement were still in the future. The need for a school of mines was voiced early in the century. In 1832 a law was passed creating a course of mineralogical studies in Minas Gerais, but it was not put into effect until 1876, after the visit of Louis Agassiz and Charles Frederick Hartt from the United States. The lack of men with scientific training necessary for fully comprehending the material needs of the country was seriously felt. Although the empire and the Old Republic which succeeded it produced brilliant jurists, eloquent orators, impassioned poets, and extraordinary statesmen, they failed to provide men who could develop an effective program.

In literature romanticism was giving way to a Brazilian version of French naturalism by 1870. A realistic reaction had set in with the poems of Castro Alves, the 'poet of the slaves.' Castro Alves did not portray the slaves themselves in picturesque terms, but he gave telling poetical expression to their misery. His aid to the cause of abolition was tremendous, for he created a widespread sentiment against slavery. The first naturalistic novel to appear in Brazil was *O mulato,* by Aluísio de Azevedo, which concerned a young man's reactions to racial prejudices in society. The greatest Brazilian writer of the nineteenth century, however, was the mulatto Joaquim Maria Machado de Assis, novelist, poet, short story writer, and playwright.

Other Brazilians whose writings have won respect far beyond their country's borders are Joaquim Nabuco, abolitionist, historian, essayist, and literary critic; João Capistrano de Abreu, historian; and Rui Barbosa, who was not only an internationally renowned jurist but the greatest living authority on the Portuguese language. Shortly after 1900 there appeared two books which have had a profound impact on Brazilian literature of the twentieth century: the already mentioned *Os sertões,* by Euclides da Cunha, and *Canaan,* by José Pereira da Graça Aranha. Both of these works are characterized by a deep national consciousness.

During the lifetime of Dom Pedro the electoral process was under almost constant attack, and such reforms as were made failed to alter the situation appreciably. The most significant effort to make the chamber of deputies represent the will of the electorate rather than that of the ministry was the Saraiva Law of 1881. Among other changes the law established direct election of deputies, and extended the franchise. It provided for supervision of elections by committees representing both parties and for the removal of troops from the vicinity of the polls. The law was a worthy attempt at improvement, and it was fairly effective between its enactment and 1886. In that year former practices were revived by the conservatives in a desperate but futile effort to turn back the tide of abolitionist sentiment which threatened to engulf them.

The statesmen called by Dom Pedro to direct Brazilian affairs were usually men of high caliber. The monarchy was appreciated and effectively supported by a small group of men with keen insight, members of the aristocratic planter class which had dominated political life since independence. Republican sentiment never entirely died out, and it appeared sporadically in isolated insurrections. The overthrow of Napoleon III and the establishment of a republic in France had echoes in Brazil. In 1870, on the day after the birthday of Dom Pedro, the Republican party issued its manifesto. Its membership remained small for the next decade, but it soon boasted a number of capable men. In this same period the positivist philosophy of Auguste Comte gained adherents in Brazil, especially among the military.

The economic structure of the empire favored the continuance of domination by the landed class, for business was despised and generally left to immigrants and foreigners. It was not until the last days of the empire that many Brazilians cautiously entered industry, despite the spectacular and unique career of the Baron of Mauá in constructing railroads. The oligarchy of landholders dominated Brazilian political life until its ascendency was challenged by other classes less bound by ties to the monarchy. These began to appear by 1860, but they did not immediately make an effective bid for political power.

By 1860, through the activities of foreigners, modern business had come to Brazil. Banking houses had been established in the 1850's, and they provided credit for various enterprises such as railroad building. In 1854 railroads began connecting the coastal cities with the interior centers of population. Telegraph lines were extended to many parts of the country, and in 1874 a trans-oceanic cable began carrying messages between Brazil and Europe. Steamship navigation on the rivers opened the way for commercial development of previously isolated areas.

The greatest figure produced by the empire in the fields of industrialization, railroad building, and banking was Irineu Evangelista de Sousa, Baron and Viscount Mauá. Mauá, unfortunately, found the government unreceptive to his daring and multitudinous enterprises; and the government was apprehensive of his power, which was not based on the traditional ownership of land and slaves. Mauá frequently complained of the lack of imagination on the part of ministers of state, but the ultimate cause of his ruin in 1875 stemmed from the chaotic aftermath of the Paraguayan War, and the general decline of the slave-based economy.

Commerce based largely on the products of the fazendas of the north and the coffee plantations of the south grew immensely after 1866. The upsurge of commerce gave new life to the coastal cities, which were increasingly oriented toward Europe. The decay of the rural aristocracy was accelerated by the attraction of the cities for the young men from the fazendas, for after their educations had been completed few chose to return to the country. Instead, they stayed in the cities and followed careers of diplomacy, politics, journalism, and the liberal professions.

Immigration to southern Brazil began to modify society there even before the abolition of slavery. In the two decades after 1864 between twenty and thirty thousand immigrants came annually. By 1886 the number coming each year had more than doubled, and in the next ten years more than a million foreigners arrived in Brazil. Between 1864 and 1935 four million came. Half of these were Italians and Portuguese; half a million were Spaniards. Germans, Austrians, and Japanese came in smaller numbers. Because of the fact that a part of these immigrants congregated in frontier communities of their own making, their assimilation was sometimes slow. Most of the foreign frontier colonies remained isolated, for the line of dense settlement did not sweep past and engulf them. They usually had to provide their own schools, and naturally continued using the language of their ancestors. It was not the fault of these immigrants if they did not become Brazilianized quickly; this tardiness, however, did not become recognized as a problem for government attention until the major wars of the twentieth century.

Although foreign trade flourished the development of industries to meet domestic needs for manufactured articles did not make satisfactory progress until World War I. For as long as fazendeiros and lawyers dominated the government protectionism was not advocated with much enthusiasm. As new bases of wealth appeared, a new class began the struggle to wrest control from the powerful grasp of the fazendeiros. This class gradually became aware that it could not succeed without breaking the power of its opponents, and this power was traced to the ownership of slaves. Abolition became the most vital issue between the two forces, and other goals were momentarily forgotten while the crucial issue was settled. Through the efforts of Joaquim Nabuco, Rui Barbosa, and others, the Liberal party reluctantly embraced the cause of abolition, but its members saw in the crusade only the moral and human aspects.

After 1865 Brazil found herself almost alone among her hemispheric neighbors retaining the outmoded institution of slavery. Dom Pedro, who seems always to have favored abolition, was willing to proceed toward the goal in a cautious and moderate fashion so that it could be accomplished without bringing ruin to the slaveowners. For a time it appeared as if this policy would succeed, but progress was delayed by the Paraguayan War and the bitter resistance of the slaveowners.

The unfortunate conquest of Paraguay needs little further said of it in so far as military campaigns are concerned. Although it turned Brazilians forcefully away from ideas of armed intervention and imperialism, for the most part its effects were exceedingly detrimental. In addition to the loss of 50,000 men and severe damage to the nation's economy, the war postponed solution to many important domestic problems.

Because of the need for Uruguayan and Argentinian co-operation during the war Dom Pedro's government shunned agents sent by Maximilian to establish close and friendly relations between his ephemeral empire and Brazil. The statesmen of Uruguay and Argentina were outspoken against the intervention in Mexico, and some thought Dom Pedro had gone too far even in recognizing Maximilian, despite the fact that he refused to establish diplomatic relations with the French-supported imperial government.

The abolitionist sentiment in the meantime had built up considerable momentum. The Rio Branco 'law of free birth' of 1871 declared all children born of slave parents to be free after a term of service to their masters, and the eventual end of slavery was assured. But by the time the law was enacted the abolitionists were no longer satisfied with such a slow solution to the problem. In 1885 slaves over 65 years of age were granted their freedom, an act which merely aroused the abolitionists to fury. Several states with few slaves freed all within their borders, and voluntary manumission kept pace. Soon the demand for complete and unqualified emancipation became irresistible.

While the abolitionist campaign was striking at the vitals of the emperor's main support, a lost bout with the church damaged his prestige considerably. The strife between church and state in the 1870's was primarily political. The emperor claimed and exercised powers over clerical affairs granted to him by the constitution, and stemming from the royal patronage of the colonial period. Papal edicts were not to have force in Brazil except by his authorization, and he disagreed with the papal ban on masonic activities. In Brazil, liberal priests had previously regarded masonry as a bulwark of Christian liberalism, and some were members. On the matter of abolition the Masons and the church ultimately agreed. The masonic order had supported the cause from its inception.

In 1871 the Masons of Rio de Janeiro held a celebration in honor of the Rio Branco law. During the ceremony a priest delivered a sermon in terms which indicated his masonic affiliation. When challenged by the bishop of Rio de Janeiro, he refused to forsake his masonic sympathy, and was suspended. The masonic lodges resolved to attack the 'ultramontanism' of the church. The Grand

Master of one branch of the order was Baron Rio Branco, Prime Minister of the empire.

The masonic issue spread to other parts of Brazil despite the fact that Dom Pedro had not sanctioned the papal edict against the Masons. Other bishops took advantage of the quarrel to strike a blow at regalism. In the torrid outpourings on both sides, the colorful, symbolic language of the champions of the church, who spoke of 'shackles and crumbs' and the 'blood of Christ,' reached the masses more effectively than did the arguments of the regalists. The bishop of Olinda suspended one of the *irmandades*, semi-religious brother-hoods, which refused to expel its masonic members, and the bishop of Pará took similar action. The matter ultimately came before the Council of State, and the bishops were ordered to lift the interdicts. On refusing they were sentenced to four years at hard labor, which sentence was commuted to simple imprisonment. It was widely felt that the government had gone too far, and in 1875 Dom Pedro re-treated. The triumph of the church was a further step in the im-perial decline, for the clergy no longer supported the throne.

The aid of the church in the battle against slavery was enlisted by Nabuco on a visit to Rome, and in 1888 Pope Leo XIII an-nounced his support of the cause of the enslaved anywhere in the world. At the same time he canonized Father Pedro Claver, the 'apostle of the Negroes' in seventeenth-century Cartagena. Dom Pedro was in Europe, and his daughter Isabel was serving as regent when the chamber finally passed a law ending slavery without com-pensation to slaveowners. The suddenness of emancipation and the failure to compensate the fazendeiros seriously disrupted Brazilian economy and brought ruin to many planters. The traditional dom-ination of the northern landowners in the economic and political life of the nation had already been jeopardized by the growing prosperity of the coffee growers of São Paulo, and the emancipation of some 300 million dollars' worth of slaves was a serious blow. In the south immigrant labor helped the coffee planters to weather the storm with less injury.

Although Dom Pedro had supported the abolition movement with moderation, his failure to oppose it or to arrange for reimbursement of slaveowners cost him the loyalty of the fazendeiros. The rift with the church had already alienated most of the clergy. The army had long felt that he had not bestowed upon it the honors and rewards which its services merited. Thus while still popular with the rank and file of Brazilians, Dom Pedro was left with only indifferent support by organized groups.

One of the ironies of the abolitionist movement was that the laws of 1871 and 1885 were both passed by conservative governments. It was known in advance in both cases that the laws must be passed, and the decision as to which party would be in power was the emperor's. Both of the major parties were deeply offended, the conservatives at having to officiate at their own execution and the liberals at being robbed of the fruit of their labors. A few of the most ardent abolitionists such as Nabuco, Barbosa, the brilliant mulatto engineer, André Rebouças, and the freedman orator, José do Patrocínio, were unconcerned over the political results. The republicans cheered emancipation, for they correctly regarded it as the first step toward the establishment of a federal republic.

Immediately after abolition had opened the floodgates for reform, the idea of federalism swept the country, championed by Rui Barbosa. Nabuco remained a staunch monarchist, and vainly tried to save the throne by the only possible remedy — the establishment of a federal empire. His suggestions were considered too bizarre for serious attention, and he won no support for the idea. Barbosa was less concerned with the type of government than with its federalism, and although he did not call himself a republican his writings gave the party some of its most effective arguments. Dom Pedro was not oblivious to the danger to the throne, but he merely rejoiced that at last the slaves had been freed.

At the time of abolition the Republican party was still numerically small and had no seats in the chamber of deputies. Most of the republicans, it appeared, were content to permit Dom Pedro to serve out his lifetime as emperor. Many persons who did not embrace republicanism were apprehensive about the succession passing to the emperor's oldest daughter, Dona Isabel. She seemed bigoted in matters of religion, had been outspoken in behalf of abolition though warned it would cost her a crown, and was married to a French prince who appeared aloof and condescending because he was slightly deaf and extremely shy.

The overthrow of Dom Pedro came as the culmination to factional disputes between civilians and the military for supremacy. The plot which led to his banishment began simply as an effort to oust a ministry which had chastised several army officers. Marshal Deodoro da Fonseca, acknowledged leader of the military clique, hoped to force a change in the ministry favorable to the army. The republican spokesman among the military, Benjamim Constant, a professor of mathematics at the military school and a positivist, became one of the engineers of the plot, and the goal was raised to a higher level. What started as a mere barracks revolt to unseat a ministry bagged bigger game by merely raising its sights.

The downfall of the empire in the face of the universal acclaim for its ruler has the outward appearance of a paradox. On the surface it did not appear that Latin America's most stable and democratic regime was in any danger. But the gradual shifting of economic power from the old fazendeiro class to new business groups employing free labor had splintered the pillar on which the monarchy leaned. The quarrel with the church, the grievances of the military, imagined and real, the very neutrality of the emperor toward political change, and the prospect of his being succeeded by an overly religious woman and her foreign-born husband left the monarchy with few ardent supporters and created an atmosphere in which a few companies of disgruntled troops could topple the throne. The empire had become merely a hollow shell with a polished exterior. The overthrow of the empire was accomplished by a fraction of the army, without opposition; the majority of Brazilians had no conception of what took place before their eyes and remained merely as bystanders.

The downfall of the empire was engineered in a simple fashion. The uprising against the ministry had been planned for November 20, 1889, but rumors that the government might arrest Deodoro caused precipitous action on November 15. The cabinet was seized. Dom Pedro came leisurely to the capital from Petrópolis to name a new ministry. By the time Dom Pedro arrived the republic had already been proclaimed. The advice and guidance of Benjamim Constant was primarily responsible for Deodoro's change of plan.

The empire of Dom Pedro II, pushed so ignominiously into the discard in 1889, had served Brazil well and probably deserved at least to die before its funeral was held. In the political development of Brazil it represented a successful effort at unification. Its success enabled the republic to emerge secure from the rocks and shoals of fragmentation and caudillism. Dom Pedro gave Brazil half a century of domestic peace and pride, and he balanced as best he could the two main forces organized into political parties. Brazilians enjoyed a fruitful apprenticeship in self-government unhampered by tyranny or censorship. Because of the unifying power of the monarchy, the republic inherited intact all of the area that had been Brazil.

On November 17 the royal family was unceremoniously embarked on a ship for Europe; Deodoro was extremely apprehensive lest the emperor's plight should precipitate civil war. A provisional government was created, dominated by the army but including many prominent civilians such as Barbosa. A federal republic was proclaimed, and this act was followed by a multitude of decrees aimed at introducing the new order; the electorate was enlarged, church and state were separated, and titles of nobility were abolished.

Recognition of the new regime was soon forthcoming from Latin America. Uruguay, Argentina, and Chile acknowledged the republic during the remaining months of 1889, and other Latin American nations followed their lead. The United States took similar action in January, 1890. France delayed recognition until June, and in the interim tried to negotiate a favorable settlement of an old boundary dispute between Brazil and French Guiana. The boundary problem was not immediately solved, but the principle of arbitration was accepted by both nations. Most European nations withheld recognition until Brazilian elections had taken place.

The republic inherited a number of additional boundary questions. In 1889 Argentina and the imperial government had agreed to submit the ancient dispute over Misiones territory to arbitration. After Argentine recognition had been accorded the provisional government, however, it attempted to display its gratitude by an overly generous division of the territory regardless of claims. In January, 1890, a treaty was negotiated in Montevideo, but public disapproval in Brazil over abandonment of both Portuguese and Brazilian gains reminded the government that foreign policy was not the place to exhibit its philanthropy, and the treaty was not ratified.

The financial organization of the new government was undertaken by versatile and energetic Rui Barbosa, who inherited the chaos and confusion stemming from the last days of the empire. His opponents blamed him for all of the financial ills of the republic, but impartial investigations have revealed his measures to be wise if not miracle-working. He did not remain long at the post, and his successor sought to solve the currency problem by the common resort to paper, ink, and the printing press. Before long a whirlwind of feverish speculation swept the country; when the wind settled many paper fortunes and Brazil's foreign credit were no more.

Domestic peace was frequently disturbed during the infancy of the republic. Civilian politicians chafed under the unaccustomed restraints imposed by military rule, and they devised ways to embarrass and discredit the government. Deodoro, long used to commanding, was neither patient nor restrained in the exercise of his authority. Monarchists were usually blamed for all disturbances even where none was remotely involved.

One of the early acts of the provisional government was to begin drafting a constitution. Inspiration was drawn not only from the imperial constitution, but also from those of the United States, France, and Argentina. The power granted to the federal government to intervene in the affairs of states made the national regime potentially dictatorial, yet the same power had existed under the empire. When the delegates to the constituent assembly arrived to begin work, they were given a preliminary draft of the document. Attempts on the part of the assembly to make modest changes were coolly received by Deodoro. Church and state were separated, with the church retaining its property, and conflict between church and state disappeared.

Despite the many difficulties and the runaway emotions of the epoch, the constitution was promulgated in February, 1891. Its critics have pointed out various flaws and defects which they blame for its failure to function perfectly. The reasons, however, are to be found more in the ascendency of a small group of ambitious men than in the constitution itself. The hostility between the civil and military factions was an obvious obstacle to the success of any government. After 1930, however, the federalism of the republican constitution came to be regarded by many as an aberration.

When the constitution had been adopted a struggle for the presidency ensued between the strong-government group headed by Deodoro and the civilian faction supporting Dr. Prudente José de Morais Barros, a paulista republican. Deodoro won, for many Brazilians felt that the turbulent times required a firm hand at the helm of state. Marshal Floriano Peixoto was chosen vice-president. The choice was not that of the electorate, but of the constituent assembly.

The immediate tasks of the new government were concerned with pacifying the country and healing its economic ills. In neither of these labors did it win notable success. Unity was lacking; feeling between the civilian and military factions ran so high that the assembly spent eight months vainly trying to elect a presiding officer! Deodoro's martial impatience was not geared to accommodate such sloth, and he finally ended the bickering by abruptly dissolving both houses and assuming dictatorial powers. Although unconstitutional acts frequently did not cause even a slight murmur, on this occasion Deodoro faced a storm of protest so threatening that he resigned to avoid causing a civil war. He was succeeded by the enigmatic vice-president, Floriano Peixoto, who in the week preceding the overthrow of the empire had assured the ministry that it could count on the loyalty of the army.

Peixoto's political abilities proved considerably greater than those of his predecessor, and although his methods were no less drastic and often frankly unconstitutional, his regime gave the infant government the strength it needed for survival. The constitution called for a special election after Deodoro's resignation. Peixoto ignored it, declaring that the enemies of the republic were plotting to restore the monarchy. His most urgent problems, however, were raised not by monarchists but by vociferous military factions.

Within a few months a score of military revolts had broken out in Amazonas, Maranhão, Rio de Janeiro, Mato Grosso, São Paulo, and Rio Grande do Sul. Only a few of these insurrections were serious, for the opposition to the government remained scattered and disunited. The most formidable challenge to Peixoto's authority was the naval revolt of 1893; for the naval conspirators worked out plans for a joint campaign with the rebels of Rio Grande do Sul, and attempted to prevent munitions from reaching government forces from abroad. The standard of revolt was raised by Admiral Custódio José de Melo, whose main purpose was to depose the tyrannical Peixoto and end army domination of the government.

Peixoto met the naval revolt with unexpected courage and resourcefulness, coupled with deceit and subterfuge. To the chagrin of the navy the rebel army from the south failed to arrive. Greater disappointments were in store, for the foreign warships in Rio de Janeiro harbor, and particularly those of the United States, refused to recognize and permit the blockade since their governments had not accorded the rebels the status of belligerents. The navy was thus deprived of its only advantage, and its revolt was doomed to certain failure.

In the south the rebels of Rio Grande do Sul found the road to the capital effectively blocked at São Paulo. Advance turned into retreat, and retreat to rout. The collapse of the insurgents was followed by a period of terrorism in which suspected rebels and known enemies of the administration were hunted down and persecuted.

Relations with Portugal were strained to the breaking point because Portuguese warships granted asylum to some of the naval rebels who feared for their lives. On their way to Portugal the ships stopped at Buenos Aires, and some of their Brazilian refugees escaped. Peixoto was highly incensed, for he expected them to join his enemies in Rio Grande do Sul. He severed diplomatic relations with Portugal.

The terror continued until November 15, 1894, when Peixoto

astonished his countrymen by unhesitatingly surrendering the presidency to his recently elected successor, the civilian Prudente de Morais. Many writers have flayed Peixoto for his tyranny and severity, but his firmness had given pause to frivolous conspirators and had held the country together during a critical epoch. As a result, he left the republic on a more solid basis than it had been when he assumed its leadership.

During the interval of national calm, 1895–6, the dispute with Argentina was settled by the arbitral award of President Grover Cleveland, whose decision was favorable to Brazil. The boundary disagreement with France over French Guiana was submitted to the arbitration of the Swiss government. Soon national attention was again claimed by purely domestic issues.

In 1897 a serious rift between Prudente and his vice-president, Victorino Pereira, appeared over questions of policy. Opponents of the government were quick to perceive and exploit an opportunity to harass the president. The government became so shaky that it swayed dangerously in every current, and was pushed to the brink of ruin by a few hundred fanatic *sertanejos* in the backcountry of Bahia.

The people of the *sertão* were always little touched by the affairs of coastal Brazil. In their arid and forbidding land life was hard and somber at best, and the melancholy sertanejos were receptive to miracle-workers. A large following had become fanatically attached to a mysterious, bizarre old man whose life had been spent wandering through the sertão. Known as Antônio Conselheiro, Anthony the Counselor, he had finally settled with his nondescript horde of bandits and would-be saints at an abandoned ranch called Canudos.

Rumors that the monarchists were stirring up the sertanejos prompted the governor of Bahia to send a small force to disperse the miserable rabble. Before this apparently simple task had been concluded the national government had seen its troops twice defeated, and had finally undertaken a full-scale campaign. The fighting was bitter, for the followers of Antônio Conselheiro literally fought to the death. Probably the most far-reaching effect of the wretched affair was that it inspired Euclides da Cunha to immortalize the episode in Brazil's most famous book — *Os sertões* (*Rebellion in the Backlands*).

Elsewhere the government's enemies were more real and no less determined. Numerous plots continued to be hatched, and in parliament the opposition to the president almost equaled his support. In November, 1897, an attempt to assassinate Prudente reacted in his favor. The assassins failed, and public opinion rallied to the president, making his final year in office comparatively peaceful. Factionalism and militarism were not dead, however, but merely quiescent.

The civilian presidents of the next decade faced fewer insurrections, but the financial problems of the country were only slightly less vexatious and perplexing. Foreign credit had flown in the hectic years of speculation and fluctuation after the empire's fall, and it was no simple matter to lure the timid bird back to a secure roost. Manuel Ferraz de Campos Sales, Prudente's successor, personally negotiated with London bankers while president-elect. The result of his efforts was the funding loan of 1898, by which the house of Rothschild provided £8,500,000 to the Brazilian government in exchange for bonds bearing 5 per cent interest.

The success of Campos Sales and his minister of finance, Joaquim Murtinho, in restoring financial order had a salutary effect upon the nation's economy. Domestic and foreign commerce increased, and industry showed signs of expansion.

Francisco de Paula Rodrigues Alves, the next president, followed financial policies similar to those of his predecessor. In addition, he pursued two worthwhile objectives of somewhat local interest — the improvement of sanitary conditions in the capital and the modernization of its port facilities. The transformation of Rio de Janeiro from a pest-ridden provincial city to a modern capital world famous for its beauty was the work of Lauro Müller, Pereira Passos, and Dr. Oswaldo Cruz. Yellow fever vanished and the incidence of bubonic plague and smallpox was drastically reduced. The improvement of Rio de Janeiro was a major triumph for the administration, for it gradually aided the material growth of the country in general. The benefits were soon extended to other parts of the nation, although many regions were left unchanged. Railroad building was promoted by Müller, and the exploitation of the nation's natural resources was given added stimulus. On the other hand, very little was achieved to improve the condition of the landless or of the urban laborers. More than 70 per cent of the nation's agricultural land was concentrated in large holdings.

In the field of diplomacy the republic carried on in the successful tradition of the empire. One of the greatest figures in the conduct of foreign affairs was the Baron of Rio Branco, whose father had been a distinguished minister of Dom Pedro. In 1902 Rio Branco became minister of foreign affairs, which office he held until 1912. He had an active part in the peaceful settlement of several boundary disputes, and in 1903 persuaded Bolivia to sell Acre territory to Brazil. One of his first official acts was to raise the Brazilian legation in Washington to the rank of embassy, and Joaquim Nabuco was sent as first Brazilian ambassador to the United States. In 1907 Rui Barbosa was representative of Brazil at the Second International Peace Conference at The Hague. Barbosa, by a magnificent display of erudition and humanitarianism, became one of the outstanding delegates at the conference and the acknowledged spokesman of the smaller nations. When the sessions closed Barbosa had won for his country the esteem of the major powers of Europe.

In 1909 the mineiro president, Dr. Afonso Augusto Moreira Pena, died in office, leaving his vice-president, Nilo Peçanha, to complete the term. Moreira Pena had continued the program of national development, and had paid particular attention to stabilizing the currency. The army and navy had been made more effective by the purchase of improved weapons and warships. The naval program revived Argentine fears of Brazilian aggression.

The election of 1910 was one of the most bitterly contested in the brief history of the republic. The most powerful political figure of the era was Pinheiro Machado, the caudilho of Rio Grande do Sul, who literally dictated the election of Marshal Hermes da Fonseca, nephew of the late Deodoro. Hermes had displayed modest administrative ability as war minister under Moreira Pena, but his strength lay more in the thwarted aspirations of the military and the conserv-

atives who championed a return to military rule than in his political acumen.

The opposition joined in the formation of the *Civilista* party, and
held the first democratically elected nominating convention in
Brazilian political history. The choice for a presidential candidate
was Rui Barbosa, the learned and eloquent Bahian, who campaigned
in a vigorous and unprecedented manner. In his speeches he de-
plored the threat of militarism and the rule by cliques and factions.
The outgoing president, Nilo Peçanha, gave his support to Hermes
da Fonseca, and the government's intervention in the election was
decisive.

Hermes' promise of a regime of order and justice was soon shattered by an epidemic of revolts, for the men who had placed the
conservatives back in power were impatient for their rewards. Disaffection appeared once more in the navy, and for a time the government was unable to do more than yield to the demands made
upon it.

The economic problems of the era were too complex for easy
solution, for they were influenced by conditions and events beyond
the borders of Brazil. Immigration was encouraged by the government, however, and the greater availability of labor made possible a
rapid expansion of the railroads and some private enterprises. The
coffee planters were soon confronted by the problem of overproduction, while the rubber boom of the previous twenty years ended
in a dismal crash because of the competition from oriental rubber
plantations.

Subsidies to save the coffee planters and rubber producers failed.
They served merely to increase the national debt. A return to the
expedient of printing unconvertible paper money was no more successful, and once more it was necessary to seek a funding loan in
England. Dissatisfaction with the government's vacillating financial
policies became violent, and as the election of 1914 approached, resentment against the machinations of Pinheiro Machado rose.

Under ordinary circumstances Pinheiro Machado might easily
have succeeded to the presidency, for he was the choice of Hermes
and controlled a strong bloc of his own. But he was identified too

closely with the errors of the regime, and the paulistas and mineiros, who were accustomed to alternating the presidency between them, regarded him as an unscrupulous interloper. The conflict shaping up in Europe threatened to have a catastrophic effect on the Brazilian economy, especially if factionalism were intensified. Pinheiro was persuaded to withdraw from the race for the sake of domestic peace, and a compromise candidate was found in the vicepresident, Wenceslau Braz Pereira Gomes, a mineiro who was not held responsible for or closely associated with the misfortunes of the administration.

The outlook for the government of Wenceslau Braz was not encouraging, for the problems raised by World War I were added to the usual domestic issues. The Brazilian economy staggered under the impact of the blockade and counter-blockade of the warring powers. Foreign trade, which usually provided the principal source of government revenue, was drastically reduced, and distress was universal.

A reduction of government expenditures helped bring a solution to the financial problems nearer, but the search for new sources of revenue to replace export duties failed. Once again the government returned to the time-honored resort of printing unconvertible paper money. The economic dislocation caused by the outbreak of the war proved temporary, for the Allies began purchasing vast quantities of processed foods from Brazil in 1916, and the economy quickly recovered.

Political unrest added to the president's difficulties early in his regime, but the revolts were suppressed without undue excitement. Fears of sabotage and insurrection by the German settlements after Brazil entered the war on the side of the Allies led to an expansion of the president's wartime powers. Martial law was declared in supposed danger zones, and federal troops were stationed in strategic areas to maintain order. The anticipated uprisings did not materialize.

In the postwar election political compromises once more defeated the perennial candidate, Rui Barbosa, who was anathema to the army. In 1918 Rodrigues Alves was elected to a second term, but he died a few months after taking office. A special election was held, and the choice fell on Epitácio da Silva Pessoa of Paraíba, who had remained aloof from the partisan clashes between civilian and military factions, and who was distinguished as head of the Brazilian delegation to Versailles.

Pessoa irritated his military supporters by appointing civilian ministers of war and navy. Since the policies of these two men were not inspired by the military, they were criticized indiscriminately by the officer clique. Some militarists began to feel that the only way to secure what they regarded as their rightful place was through seizing the presidency by force.

Like many another Latin American nation in the early 1920's Brazil borrowed vast sums abroad, especially from the United States, for the purpose of promoting internal improvements. The administration was vigorously assailed by paulistas and mineiros for what seemed to them sheer extravagance. Discontent again became widespread, and the campaign for a successor to Pessoa found emotions high and tempers short.

The official candidate was Artur da Silva Bernardes, a mineiro. Nilo Peçanha, who was now associated with disgruntled army officers and desperate office-seekers, announced his candidacy. Hermes da Fonseca cast his line into troubled waters in behalf of Peçanha, but came away empty-handed. After the election of Bernardes, Hermes and the Military Club of Rio de Janeiro began interfering more forcefully in political battles, even to the extent of countenancing insubordination in the army. Domestic peace once more hung in the balance.

As far as internal affairs were concerned Bernardes' administration was virtually one long military campaign. Factional quarrels and strife in the states led to an abusive use of the state of siege and of federal interventors, for Bernardes was determined to keep his enemies in check at all costs. In July, 1924, there occurred the most critical challenge to his authority when a revolt broke out in São Paulo. A state of siege was declared, and federal troops dispersed the rebels in less than a month's time.

While Bernardes had concentrated upon containing his political and military rivals, the long-inarticulate, destitute laborers of plantation and city had acquired champions at last. Brazilian radicals of varying hues, including a young army officer named Luís Carlos Prestes, who had turned to Marxism, began to capture the attention of the illiterate, impoverished masses. When the government belatedly became aware of these activities, federal troops drove Prestes and others into exile. The seeds which had been planted had fallen into earth made the more fertile by the severity of economic conditions and the lack of promise on the part of the administration. Thereafter the government was obliged at least to make some pretense of improving the lot of urban and rural laborers, although the statesmen of the Old Republic did little more than discuss the problems. Concentration of land ownership was one of the most acute causes of distress, but this delicate matter was carefully skirted.

In 1926, when Bernardes' term drew to a close, he avoided political strife by naming his successor from among the paulistas. His choice, Dr. Wáshington Luís Pereira de Sousa, was elected with little opposition.

The major concern of Wáshington Luís was coping with the insoluble problems brought on by the world-wide economic depression. The drastic drop in international trade had especially severe repercussions in Brazil, so great was the dependence upon foreign markets. As the demands for Brazilian coffee and sugar decreased abruptly, privation and distress spread over the land. Loans from the United States failed to stem the tide and the government faced imminent bankruptcy. The undue dependence upon import and export duties left the administration with few resources, but it did not seek to save itself by introducing other forms of taxation which would have been unpopular with the ruling class.

As his hectic term approached its end Wáshington Luís crowned his career with a political blunder that cost him the last days of his rule. He felt that only another paulista would carry to a successful conclusion the economic program he had begun. Tradition, however, demanded that his successor be a mineiro. Casting caution aside he ignored the claims of the mineiro heir-apparent, Antônio Carlos, and declared in favor of Júlio Prestes, governor of São Paulo.

The outraged mineiros immediately sought to learn the temper of opposition groups elsewhere, and to find a rival candidate they could sponsor. Their choice was enigmatic Getúlio Dorneles Vargas, governor of Rio Grande do Sul, and an outspoken critic of the administration. The *Aliança Liberal* was formed by uniting the opponents of the government to promote Vargas' candidacy.

Enthusiasm for the Aliança Liberal surged high during the campaign and election, but when the votes had been counted the government announced Júlio Prestes the victor. Vargas and his supporters did not conceal their conviction that he had been defrauded of the presidency, and prepared for revolt. In October, 1930, they seized government installations in Rio Grande do Sul. The march to Rio de Janeiro was quick and eventful. On November 3 Vargas picked up the reins of government hastily dropped in flight by Wáshington Luís. The individualistic, generally liberal, but ineffectual career of the Old Republic was a part of history. Its social and political morality were soon to be scoffed at by men who stood for socio-economic changes, and who placed greater emphasis on efficiency than on liberty.

SUGGESTED READING

C. Beals, *Porfirio Díaz, Dictator of Mexico*, New York, 1933.

G. Blanksten, *Ecuador: Constitutions and Caudillos*, Berkeley, 1951.

P. H. Box, *The Origins of the Paraguayan War*, Urbana, 1930.

A. Brenner, *The Wind That Swept Mexico*, New York, 1943.

E. L. Bridges, *Uttermost Part of the Earth*, New York, 1949.

A. W. Bunkley, *The Life of Sarmiento*, Princeton, 1952.

W. H. Callcott, *Liberalism in Mexico, 1857–1929*, Palo Alto, 1931.

C. E. Chapman, *A History of the Cuban Republic*, New York, 1927.

E. Corti, *Maximilian and Charlotte of Mexico*, 2 vols., New York, 1898.

W. R. Crawford, *A Century of Latin American Thought*, Cambridge, Mass., 1944.

I. J. Cox, *Nicaragua and the United States, 1909–1927*, Boston, 1927.

E. da Cunha, *Rebellion in the Backlands*, Chicago, 1943.

W. J. Dennis, *Tacna and Arica*, New Haven, 1931.

H. Dunn, *The Crimson Jester, Zapata of Mexico*, New York, 1933.

R. B. C. Graham, *Portrait of a Dictator, Francisco Solano López*, London, 1933.

H. F. Guggenheim, *The United States and Cuba*, New York, 1934.

C. W. Hackett, *The Mexican Revolution and the United States, 1910–1926*, Boston, 1926.

L. F. Hill, *Diplomatic Relations between Brazil and the United States*, Durham, 1932.

W. H. Hudson, *The Purple Land*, Various editions.

H. M. Hyde, *Mexican Empire: The History of Maximilian and Carlota of Mexico*, London, 1946.

M. Jefferson, *Peopling the Argentine Pampas*, New York, 1926.

C. L. Jones, *The Caribbean Interests of the United States*, New York, 1916.

———— *Costa Rica and the Civilization in the Caribbean*, Madison, 1935.

F. A. Knapp, Jr., *Life of Sebastián Lerdo de Tejada, 1823–1889*, Austin, 1951.

G. M. McBride, *Chile, Land and Society*, New York, 1936.

———— *The Land Systems of Mexico*, New York, 1923.

P. F. Martin, *Salvador in the Twentieth Century*, New York, 1911.

C. Nabuco, *The Life of Joaquim Nabuco*, Stanford, 1950.

M. W. Nichols, *Sarmiento, A Chronicle of Inter-American Friendship*, Washington, 1940.

E. O'Shaughnessy, *A Diplomat's Wife in Mexico*, New York, 1916.

E. T. Parks, *Colombia and the United States, 1765–1934*, Durham, 1938.

E. Portes Gil, *The Conflict between the Civil Power and the Clergy*, Mexico, 1935.

T. Rourke, *Gómez, Tyrant of the Andes*, new ed., New York, 1948.

L. S. Rowe, *The Federal System of the Argentine Republic*, Washington, 1921.

D. F. Sarmiento, *Life in the Argentine Republic in the Days of the Tyrants*, New York, 1868.

W. Stewart, *Henry Meiggs, Yankee Pizarro*, Durham, 1946.

F. Tannenbaum, *The Mexican Agrarian Revolution*, New York, 1929.

M. C. Thornton, *The Church and Freemasonry in Brazil, 1872–1876*, Washington, 1948.

M. A. Watters, *A History of the Church in Venezuela, 1810–1930*, Chapel Hill, 1933.

S. Welles, *Naboth's Vineyard; The Dominican Republic, 1844–1924*, 2 vols., New York, 1928.

M. W. Williams, *Dom Pedro the Magnanimous, Second Emperor of Brazil*, Chapel Hill, 1937.

G. S. Wise, *Caudillo: A Portrait of Antonio Guzmán Blanco*, New York, 1951.

VII

THE CONTEST FOR HEGEMONY

AND THE RISE OF INDIGENOUS

NATIONALISM

XXXV

The Struggle for Economic Independence

In the United States domestic capital itself accumulated and sought outlets at home and abroad; in the management of foreign enterprises in the United States American citizens took a controlling part; and the effects of capital investment promoted rather than discouraged industrialization. In Latin America, on the other hand, the supply of native capital (traditionally invested in land) was always short; technical training and managerial experience were deficient; and foreign capital investments, rarely associated with domestic capital, had the effect of increasing rather than reducing the dependence of the Latin American countries for their trade and revenue on a few primary and staple commodities.

ROBIN A. HUMPHREYS [*]

T HE great economic depression crept like a dense fog all over the world in 1930. Its stifling dampness rapidly enveloped the countries of Latin America creating confusion and chaos. Old values were discredited and a deep unrest stirred among the population. Poverty and want, never strangers to most of the world's people, gnawed deeply into the vitals of society and stirred men to acts of desperation. In Europe vicious little men came forward with schemes to reshuffle the deck of social organization and thereby change the entire course of history. Seemingly the forces of liberal democracy had run their course and that course had ended in world economic collapse in which even the privileged

[*] *The Evolution of Modern Latin America*, Oxford University Press, New York, 1946, pp. 152–3.

few were to fare little better than the many who had waited in vain for the benefits of capitalist productivity to trickle down to them. The exponents of free enterprise and laissez-faire liberalism appeared baffled and helpless. They could only counsel patience until things righted themselves. But people would not wait.

The depression in Latin America brought extreme disillusionment, for it brought home to every nation the utter dependence of that region upon economic forces over which they exercised little or no control. The difficulty had been presented earlier during World War I when old trade lines were greatly disrupted by events in Europe, but readjustments were rendered relatively simple by tremendous expansion of the American market and by the orgy of reckless investment that characterized economic activity during the 1920's. Now no war could be blamed; the system itself seemed at fault. Now suddenly the value of Latin American exports declined nearly two-thirds. Agricultural and mineral surpluses piled up in the fields and warehouses, but almost no one wanted them. At the same time the sources of foreign capital dried up and money became desperately scarce. The fine paved boulevards and great stone buildings constructed with borrowed funds during the reckless years of the 1920's stood empty and silent; they produced nothing but mounting interest charges. The anachronistic reliance of governments upon import and export duties for revenue left them bankrupt as ships stood idle at the wharves and goods could not be moved. Foreign and domestic obligations could not be met, and at the very moment when government expenditures were needed to stimulate recovery there were no funds to be spent. The loss of earnings from unemployment further restricted the already feeble purchasing power for manufactured goods. At no point did it seem possible to lay an arresting hand upon the downward spiral.

The almost immediate reaction to all these difficulties was a change in government. Old-style liberal regimes were overthrown in Argentina and Brazil. Confusion reigned in Chile as no one seemed able to establish a stable regime. In Peru the long-standing dictatorship of Leguía was overthrown and that of Gómez in Venezuela was threatened. In Colombia the liberals won their first election in many years, and political unrest swept through Central America. In the years immediately following 1930 numerous political changes took place throughout Latin America, and on the whole the swing was toward the military dictators and away from both the conservative right and the liberal democratic left. Extreme left-wing groups were ominously active in Chile, Brazil, El Salvador, and Mexico, but generally they were kept in check by the firm rule of the military and the more palatable nationalistic socialism that gradually emerged to resolve the problems of economic colonialism.

In spite of the series of shifts from right to left and from left to right, certain fundamental changes in outlook soon became evident — changes indicating that the disturbances of the depression had been more than surface phenomena. They had roiled the waters deeply, and previously latent forces of nationalism now surged like a great wave across a continent and a half. In virtually every capital men turned with bitter indignation against all manifestations of foreign economic domination and sought some means of rebuilding a national economy less dependent on what transpired in the great manufacturing centers of Europe and the United States and in the financial marts of New York and London. In the same sweeping wave of change, the masses of the people came forward to assert their demands for a greater share in the national patrimony. Such demands, scarcely articulate in the sense of defined movements and programs, were none the less real as indicated by the increasing restlessness of urban labor, a rising interest in Indianist propaganda, and a growing fear that the seeds of Soviet communism were beginning to sprout in the fertile Latin American soil. Scholars throughout the hemisphere engaged in studies of the basic problems of their respective countries, and attention became increasingly focused on poor land distribution, idle land, illiteracy, inadequate production, outmoded methods, and particularly the almost total absence of nationally owned and operated industries. In those countries of sizable Indian population emphasis was given to the fact that many of these people still lived in the utmost ignorance amid filth, disease, and poverty, and that their tremendous contribution to the national entity had been neither appreciated nor permitted to attain its full potential. To act on these problems meant significant change in the role of government, for only by the exercise of governmental powers could significant change be brought about.

The trend toward greater governmental activity in fields previously reserved for private initiative was world wide. In the United States the Democratic party, under the leadership of Franklin Delano Roosevelt, gave birth to a tremendous program of governmental activities aimed at reviving the domestic economy and protecting the nation against future dangers of economic collapse. Major projects in the field of public works were coupled with large welfare outlays and the initiation of social security benefits to protect the working population from the economic disabilities of unemployment and old age. Business was subjected to a high degree of regulation in matters of financing, trade practices, hours of work, and wage rates. Such measures were intended to strengthen the private enterprise system by giving it better balance and protecting it from internal abuse. In Europe government had long been more active in economic matters than in the Western Hemisphere, but now that activity was intensified. Italy had long boasted a form of state socialism involving close co-ordination between government and private economic life. The system, known as fascism, attempted in theory to convert the state into a vast holding company in which industry, labor, and the consuming public were all represented. From this was derived the corporate state concept in which the fundamental distinction of public and private activity tended to disappear and the state became the supreme concentration point of all activity, all loyalty, and all national energy. The idea was ideally adapted to Hitler's scheme for revitalizing Germany and converting that nation into a tremendous military machine to serve his purposes of European and perhaps world conquest. Thus the National Socialist, or Nazi party, which came to power in 1933, placed the state above all other considerations and civil liberties and economic freedom quickly disappeared.

The statism of Soviet Russia had been in existence since the revolution in 1917, and in theory and practice it involved the almost total elimination of private rights and private property. The state became the only form of social organization. These systems, fascism, nazism, and communism, differed markedly from the program of increased government activities in the United States, England, and other democratic nations where the role of the state was viewed only as aiding and providing a suitable environment for individual citizens freely to choose and pursue their own destinies. Indeed, nations imbued with the democratic traditions and ideals tended to regard government as a necessary evil that posed a threat to individual liberty whenever it got too big or too active. Consequently, although there was a great deal of precedent for positive government controlling and regulating the economy, democratic countries moved in the direction of greater public authority reluctantly and with misgiving. Such issues were troubling the entire western world at the same time they were presented in Latin America.

The opposing political and economic ideologies of Europe were somehow viewed as exportable commodities. In reality the systems mattered little to Germany and Italy, or even to Russia. Rather, each of these powers was attempting with purely imperialistic objectives to bring other nations under its domination or into its system of political and military alliances. The alleged possession of a system or ideology to solve economic and social ills was merely a propaganda device to ensnare the unwary. Nevertheless, at the very moment when the Latin American nations were deeply engrossed with the problem of recasting their economic and political institutions, skilled salesmen from across the seas pressed upon them the apparent advantages of close political, economic, and ideological ties with the nazi, fascist, or communist powers. It would be naïve to state that such salesmen were without influence. Counter propaganda from the United States also had its effect. Despite the intensive competition for influence over the course of Latin American development, however, most Latin American social and political movements after 1930 were basically nativist in origin and their genesis could be traced to ideals and events stemming from the rich history of the region. Wisely, not a single republic, in spite of severe economic stress, saw much to be gained by placing minority groups in concentration camps, murdering the well-to-do, or hitching its wagon to the imperialistic star of a European power bent on world domination. Indeed, it was obvious to most thinking Latin American leaders that, apart from trade, all that any of the various isms had to offer them was a new and subservient colonial relationship to a European power. Part and parcel of the movement that swept Latin America during the third and fourth decades of the twentieth century was the rejection of colonialism in any guise, including that of economic domination. As a consequence, the economic power and aggressiveness of the United States, recently associated with the 'big stick,' a whole series of interventions in the Caribbean, and the financial manipulations of 'dollar diplomacy,' were viewed with much the same suspicion as were the economic and political machinations of Germany, Italy, Russia, and Spain. This phenomenon many elements in the United States have continued to find quite incomprehensible.

That governments should undertake a more positive role in determining the course of national economic and social development involved no significant departure from Latin American tradition. Republican governments, by and large, apart from a running struggle with the church over their respective domains, had been generally inclined to leave to private initiative the establishment of industries and the extension of agriculture, as well as numerous welfare and philanthropic activities to alleviate poverty and care for the indigent. Such limitation on the field of government action was in marked contrast with the almost extreme paternalism of the Spanish and Portuguese imperial systems. It marked a preoccupation with problems of government organization and political stability rather than serious convictions that the role of government should be minimized. Throughout the entire nineteenth century liberal groups in nearly all countries had advocated all sorts of reforms that only government action could bring about, but conservative landholders, the church, and the military interests had demonstrated general satisfaction with things as they were and drastic reform efforts had been blocked almost everywhere. Nevertheless, the empire precedent existed, and from time to time reform advocates, such as Juárez in Mexico, had attempted to utilize political power to remold the social structure.

One of the most immediate precedents available to the neo-nationalists of the depression era was embodied in the Mexican constitution of 1917 and the program of national regeneration espoused by the Revolutionary party. Mexico, during the long rule of Porfirio Díaz, had been as intensively and extensively subjected to foreign economic domination and exploitation as any country in the Western Hemisphere, and the social upheaval that followed Díaz' overthrow released the same passions and bitterness now brought to the surface fifteen years later all over the Latin American region by the great depression. The Mexican program itself had long roots reaching back to Juárez and Morelos in political aspiration, back to the colonial regime in reaffirmation of national ownership of subsoil rights and the social responsibilities attendant upon the ownership of property, and back to the pre-conquest era of both Spain and Mexico in regard to the communal landholding unit known as the ejido. On the other hand, the influence of European social philosophies was apparent in reforms designed to encourage, strengthen, and even coddle the labor movement and to take over and operate as government enterprises such key industries as railroads, financial institutions, and, eventually, petroleum production and distribution. At the same time, the old liberal anti-clericalism of Lerdo and Juárez was manifested by a tremendous assault upon the church and its control of the educational system. The impact of the socialistic aspects of the program was most drastically felt during the six-year administration of President Lázaro Cárdenas from 1934 to 1940. During Cárdenas' administration was achieved a high point in the realization of long-cherished objectives when oil properties of foreign concessionaries were expropriated by the government in 1938. This act, affecting primarily United States and English interests, represented an extreme manifestation of the nationalist goal — Mexico for the Mexicans. Fifteen years later the same fundamental issues and objectives were involved in Bolivia's expropriation of foreign owned tin mines.

Brazil's most striking changes came during the long administration of Getúlio D. Vargas, 1930–45. The *Estado Novo* or New State which he proclaimed in 1937 brought intensified nationalism and centralism to replace the easy-going, liberal regime of the federalistic Old Republic. Vargas himself remained undoctrinaire, but elements of corporatism appeared in the new political system and the government stepped forward firmly in the economic sphere. Industrial development proceeded rapidly, stimulated by World War II, the demands of the Allies, and the encouragement of the United States. The Vargas program, like that of Perón and his predecessors in Argentina, was greatly aided by the artificial prosperity stemming from wartime conditions and the rebuilding of Europe after 1945.

The Argentine solutions to the problems posed by world-wide depression and the evils of economic colonialism were slower to emerge than those of either Mexico or Brazil. For a time all that took place after the overthrow of Yrigoyen in 1930 was a return to the extreme conservatism of the military and landholding oligarchy. Some of the militarists, among whom Perón was a latecomer, found a degree of professional kinship with certain of the German Nazi clan; but this made them neither Nazis nor pro-German. Rather, it provided an opportunity for pulling Uncle Sam's beard as a gesture of defiance against the sheepherder proclivities evident in American foreign policy. The real 'revolution' in Argentine affairs took place after 1945 when Juan Domingo Perón was firmly in the presidential saddle and his wife, Evita, was holding the reins. A strong political following was built among the laboring classes, the *descamisados* or shirtless ones. Labor unions associated with the peronista movement were encouraged and patronized; independent unions were crushed. A vast amount of welfare and so-called social benefit legislation was enacted, all exacting a considerable toll from the businessman. Unofficial exactions were made on behalf of Evita's charities and 'cultural' projects, and penalties for non-compliance were often more severe than those applied in cases of tax-evasion. More significant than all the exactions of a corrupt political machine, however, was the monopolization by the government of virtually all foreign trade, particularly the export of staple commodities. The government purchased grain and beef from producers for prices fixed by itself and then sold at the highest obtainable price in an extremely favorable sellers' market abroad. Slowly but steadily important segments of the old landholding, cattle- and grain-raising aristocracy were brought to their knees. Proceeds of such practices were devoted to major works and development projects, expanded welfare activities, and military preparedness. At the same time, the government supported the creation of an Argentine merchant marine and forced British owners to sell rail and street transportation systems.

In one sense the peronista movement, belatedly termed justicialism and defined as a middle ground between capitalism and state socialism, represented the reassertion of porteño domination of the provinces; but the porteños in control were those who provided a circus for the masses. All this was not out of keeping with Argentine tradition, but it was the tradition of Rosas and not that of Mitre or Sarmiento. Like Rosas, Perón established a regime of regimentation in education, industry, and society. The press was subjected to rigid control and the defiant *La Prensa,* one of Latin America's great newspapers, was driven to the wall. As in the time of Rosas, the Eastern Republic of Uruguay soon became the home of thousands of Argentines in exile.

In Uruguay, swept by the same economic difficulties in the early 1930's, the government entered freely into business in competition with foreign companies, in large part to guarantee better marketing conditions for national producers. Banking and insurance became fields restricted to Uruguayan concerns, and while private enterprise was generally encouraged, the activities of aliens were closely supervised to prevent foreign domination. At the same time, a considerable array of welfare and social security legislation was passed to benefit the working classes and public employees.

Chile went through a series of shifts in governmental policy ending during the mid-thirties with a liberal government supported by a parliamentary coalition in which the so-called radical and the genuine left-wing elements had a major influence. To cope with the problem of extreme depression in the mining and nitrate industries, Chile experimented with government-owned development corporations, but more than new organizational devices were needed to operate successfully an industry whose product had been replaced by a cheaper synthetic one manufactured elsewhere. However, in 1939 under the administration of President Pedro Aguirre Cerda, there was created the *Corporación de Fomento* (CORFO), the Chilean Development Corporation, an institution endowed with sweeping powers and government funds for the industrialization of Chile. This institution, created with a much broader purpose than earlier public business-type institutions, produced a national development plan and then set about executing it. Soon the Chilean government, through the Corporación de Fomento, was deeply involved in all types of productive enterprises from the generation of electricity to the construction of steel mills. It joined private and government capital in a host of ventures all designed to industrialize the nation, develop its natural resources, and relieve its dependence on foreign industry for the manufactured goods it consumed. In many respects, the public business corporation was a great success, for through its efforts many new industries came into existence. The Chilean model has been studied and copied by other Latin American nations, but as yet none of them has been able to emulate it. It represents a striking experiment in state enterprise, but it has by no means solved Chile's major economic problems nor terminated the nation's dependence on world trade for its economic life.

During the 1920's Peru had given birth to a nationalist and socialistic movement that had far more of an intellectual and philosophic basis than any other major Latin American reform movement of the modern era. A forerunner was Manuel González Prada, a distinguished literary figure and journalist who died in 1918 at the age of seventy. A confirmed socialist, González Prada enjoyed a wide acquaintanceship beyond the borders of Peru and exerted considerable influence over a number of rather able young intellectuals. One of these, José Carlos Mariátegui, associated himself for a time with another young man, Víctor Raúl Haya de la Torre, in the organization of a movement known as the *Alianza Revolucionaria Popular Americana,* better known as APRA. These two men produced a body of doctrine and a program aimed at building in Latin America a new social system socialist in economic outlook and Indianist in its emphasis on ancient cultural values and the elevation of the Indian to a more significant position in national life. In part the movement was international and organizational activities were carried on in Brazil, Argentina, and other countries beyond the borders of Peru. The appeal to the Andean Indian groups was understandable, but in such predominantly European areas as Argentina the popularity of the movement rested largely upon its promise of improving the living conditions of the laboring classes and particularly upon its violent anti-imperialist and anti-foreign doctrines.

Mariátegui and Haya de la Torre soon broke over basic philosophic issues and the former drifted over into complete conformity with the Communist party line. Haya de la Torre became the outstanding leader and champion of *Aprismo* in the hemisphere. He traveled widely in Europe and established intellectual ties with British, German, and Russian socialists; but while he borrowed many concepts of social and economic organization from socialist and communist theorists, he did not become the tool or agent of European revolutionaries. Rather, he rejected many of the core points of socialist doctrine to view Indo-America as a unique and distinctive region requiring unique and distinctive solutions to its many problems. Haya de la Torre could identify no industrial proletariat in whom the powers of the state should be vested; industrialization was hardly yet begun in Latin America. Instead he saw the plight of the downtrodden rural Indian and a middle class struggling to come into existence. A class struggle within Latin America was meaningless when the true enemies of Indo-American development, as he saw them, were the foreign capitalists who wished to keep the region in a state of perpetual dependence as a source of raw materials while keeping to themselves the benefits of industrialization. Consequently, his program was one of stimulating industry through government action and promotion of better conditions for the Indians through land reform and co-operative agriculture. His political program, contrary to the monopolistic statism of Soviet communism, involved the preservation of intellectual freedom, individual liberties, and democratic institutions.

Aprismo attracted wide attention prior to 1930 even though numerically its supporters outside of Peru were few. In Peru, the organization's bid for political power came in 1931 when Haya de la Torre ran for the presidency. Although defeated, he continued his efforts to build a powerful organization by the cellular techniques and conspiratorial secrecy characteristic of socialist revolutionary activity. His efforts were bitterly opposed by Peruvian governments in power and the apristas were for years denied recognition as a genuine Peruvian political party. At the same time, Aprismo was under constant attack by the Soviet brand of communists as being deviationist and for refusing to acknowledge Russia as the source of true orthodoxy. As a consequence the two movements never united but instead drifted farther and farther apart. Indeed, during the critical years of the 1930's they largely canceled each other out as revolutionary forces in northern South America. Finally, in 1945, modified and tempered in doctrine and program by the long struggle for survival in Peru, apristas for a brief time shared power in a government that it had supported at the polls. In 1948 that government was overthrown by a military coup, Aprismo was driven underground, and Haya de la Torre was forced to seek asylum in the Colombian embassy. There he remained for almost five years while a Peruvian guard patrolled the exits to prevent his escape. His plight became a subject of international controversy until safe conduct was finally guaranteed him and he was permitted to depart for Mexico. Meanwhile, deprived of its leadership, the aprista movement slowly died. Outside of Peru it certainly has no following today. Attempts to link it to progressive nationalist movements and parties in other countries have little foundation.

The brief account of strong nationalist and quasi-socialistic movements that have stirred the currents of Latin American life during the past twenty-five years is far from complete. Individuals and parties have espoused such causes in every country from the Río Grande to Patagonia, but with widely varying degrees of success. During the war years and in the period just preceding, Nazi activities were a disturbing factor wherever large colonies of Germans were to be found. German agents were particularly active in southern Chile and in southern Brazil as well as in Argentina, but few took them seriously. Communism has been a far more dangerous and consistent threat because of its appeal to the ignorant and impoverished masses. Its agents are active in every country. It has been a particularly persistent force among the miners of Chile, and for a time it had a small but highly articulate following in Brazil. In recent years Soviet agents, financed through the Russian embassy in Mexico City, have plowed the fertile fields of Guatemalan ignorance and poverty. Latent hatreds of the United States and of American business concerns were exploited to the full, and communism spread openly and with official approval through the bureaucracy. However, the corrupt opportunists who went along with the movement, seemingly for personal advantage, were thrown from office by revolution in 1954 and the conspiracy was driven underground.

There is a genuine fear of communism in Latin America, but that fear has seldom fostered hysteria. Movements to overthrow governments by force are an old story, but one directed from outside the hemisphere runs counter to the whole trend of Latin American development. Sophisticated officials, far more accustomed to dealing with the advocates of European brands of radicalism and revolutionary socialism than their conservative, business-minded counterparts in the United States, have little fear of socialism, as such. Many have accepted a pragmatic mixture of private and state ownership in the economic sphere and do not see any incompatibility between the two. Consequently, they are better able to separate social revolutionary doctrine from unadulterated Russian imperialism. Equally important, perhaps, is a pronounced cynicism current throughout all of Latin America that creates the view that every man is seeking his own personal advantage. In this light the communist revolutionary is just as weak and just as corruptible as any one else. The Latin will die for glory and honor, and personal martyrdom is not excluded; but only a fool Russian or a crazy German will sacrifice his life for the personal advantage of a Stalin or a Hitler. Regimentation quickly breeds reaction and discipline is a scarce commodity. Individual freedom is highly prized. Much of the turbulence of Latin American political life stems from this philosophy. So does high absenteeism and indifferent application in mass production industry. But it provides an excellent insulation against a communist movement that requires strict discipline and self-abnegation from its adherents.

All the varied programs, reform movements, and assertions of economic nationalism occurring after 1930 had a pronounced effect on the climate of the Latin American economy. Foreign private capital was all but denied entry and existing investments forcibly liquidated. Country after country enacted legislation restricting the freedom of monetary exchange and limiting the profits that could be taken out of the country. Other laws required foreign corporations to employ high percentages of native personnel in every establishment; this was an effort to force the training of domestic technicians and to bring local talent into the management of important business activities. No such measures could immediately influence economic activity except in a negative and depressing way, for the conditions of investment were seemingly rendered less favorable and certainly less stable and certain. At the same time, efforts through diplomatic channels and at each international conference were made to secure adherence to the rule that foreign governments, particularly the United States, would have no right to intercede through exertion of political and diplomatic pressure on behalf of their nationals who became involved in business difficulties in Latin America. The only recourse of such people would thus be the same as that of local businessmen: resort to local courts in the respective country. In principle, at least, the rule was gradually accepted.

Virtually every Latin American nation was faced with the problem of trying to move in seemingly contradictory directions at the same time. Industrialization was sought while the necessary capital was discouraged from entering the region. Domestic as well as foreign business concerns were faced with a mass of social legislation that in some places fostered aggressive unionism and in others placed serious impediments in the path of traditional business operations. Progressive income taxation was tried to narrow the gap between extreme wealth and extreme poverty and to give the governments a more stable source of revenue than that provided by the traditional import and export duties, but such measures, if effectively enforced, would have had a depressing effect on private capital formation. In some countries the breaking up of large landed estates clearly disrupted agricultural enterprise at the very time that increased agricultural production was a major national goal. Behind many of these obvious contradictions, however, lay the firm conviction that old social and economic evils must be rooted out at whatever cost to make way for a more soundly based future development by which all elements in the nation would eventually benefit.

Economic independence for Latin America is only a relative possibility. As an absolute it would be neither attainable nor desirable. Individual countries are confronted with insurmountable geographic and material limitations. Some must always be hewers of wood and carriers of water. The real struggle is not for independence as such, although greater independence is most certainly sought, but for a greater and more diversified productivity capable of sustaining on a higher level the growing Latin American population. Such objectives call generally for an increased volume of exports under conditions that will permit the accumulation of public and private development capital in Latin America. Thus the proceeds of export sales must be spent in Latin America for domestically produced consumption goods and outside of Latin America for production goods to be installed in new Latin American industrial plants. Domestically, increased production in every line is necessary so as to reduce the volume of consumables that have to be imported, particularly foodstuffs. Thus as in every industrialization effort, the pleasures of immediate consumption must be sacrificed in expectation of greater consumption at some future date. This is a difficult pattern to force on any people, but particularly so when there is a scarcity of domestic savings available for investment, when there is a strong proclivity to invest savings and profits in land or secondarily in commerce rather than in the production of new commodities; when there is a strong tendency toward conspicuous consumption on the part of the wealthy classes; and when a large portion of the export profits is owned by foreigners who have not the slightest intention of investing or even spending their earnings locally. From difficulties such as these, rather than from a desire to exploit the foreign investor, have arisen such regulatory devices as capital export limitations, exchange control, import licensing, domestic personnel employment requirements, and similar measures. More drastic steps are those limiting the nature and scope of foreign-owned enterprise and outright forced sale and expropriation.

Faced with such difficulties, a sizable number of the foreign investors, particularly those in the transport, utility, and mining fields, have shown anything but enterprise and foresight. Many have been definitely unco-operative. Their chief objective has often been to derive the maximum possible return while providing the absolute minimum of service with obsolete and inefficient equipment. A vicious circle is fostered by the claim that, given the risk of expropriation and further restrictive legislation, outlays for capital improvement or expansion cannot be justified. No better path could be chosen to increase the very risks that are feared. On the other hand, some foreign corporations, particularly those in the petroleum and fruit export business, have been able to dispel much of the local antagonism toward them by energetic measures on behalf of their labor force, including such benefits as higher wages, housing projects, free medical service, and social security systems. Still others have joined confidently in the development program, investing capital in the production of manufactured goods for internal rather than external markets. Others have created new marketing facilities trading in domestic as well as imported goods. As foreign capital becomes increasingly interested in the Latin American domestic market, rather than in extracting products to be sold abroad, conditions favoring Latin American industrialization are created. Indeed, the key to the entire development effort is the creation of an effective domestic market based upon modern distribution and sales practices and a wider and greater distribution of purchasing power. New industries cannot long survive if their products cannot be sold in Latin America, for outside of the region they cannot compete at this time with the more advanced industries of Europe, North America, and Japan. Indeed, many require protection and even subsidy in the domestic market.

In countries where economic nationalism has flowered most luxuriantly and government has actively intervened to promote national development, few phases of national life have escaped attention. Industrialization is but one of many factors in the total development process. Labor groups have demanded recognition of rights equivalent to or even greater than those accorded them during the last twenty-five years in Western Europe and the United States. Collective bargaining has been fostered in Mexico, Chile, and Argentina, sometimes with such strong government support that it has gotten out of hand. Most of the countries make some attempt to protect the worker by wage and hour laws, severance pay rights, and job and pay protection for women before and immediately after childbirth. Generally, however, the administrative machinery is hopelessly inadequate. Growth of the labor movement, however, has not been free; it has been inextricably involved with politics. While some governments have promoted rapid labor organization, the majority have permitted unionism only under rigorous controls. Consequently, many so-called unions are nothing more than mutual benefit societies, and efforts to convert them into genuine trade union organizations are considered communistic and vigorously opposed by both management and government. As appendages of political organizations, unions have been torn with all the schisms and divisions of partisan activity, responsible leadership has been prevented from developing, and unions have been distracted from proper goals and their efforts dissipated. In extreme cases unions have been made completely subservient to the government, and labor's strength in such cases may be used for ends not at all in keeping with the desires of workingmen.

By and large, the most neglected group in Latin America has been the large body of agricultural workers. Many still live on a purely subsistence basis on plots of land belonging to great hacendados who utilize their services for two or three months during the year in harvest season. This is generally the case in the great coffee growing regions of Central America and in the coffee regions of Brazil and Colombia. Tenant farming has become increasingly prevalent in the northern pampas region of Argentina where the high cost of land has made individual farm ownership economically prohibitive except for the wealthy landholder whose fortune dates back to earlier days. Share cropping is common throughout all of Latin America. In no country do the various benefits available to industrial workers provide assistance to the small farmer or agricultural worker.

Land reform is a constant rallying point for political reformers, particularly those concerned with the status of the Indian. Only in a few countries has anything been done to bring it about. Mexico's program to break up the large estates and to foster communal agricultural colonies financed by government loans is by far the most outstanding. Everywhere land reform is fought by the large agriculturalists and great estate owners, even though much of their land may be idle. Co-operative agricultural improvement programs financed jointly by the various governments and the *servicios* of the Institute of Inter-American Affairs, an agency of the United States government, have in some areas introduced better farming techniques and improved crop strains. Emphasis, however, has generally been placed on experimentation to the exclusion of educational extension programs; and even in the few cases where extension has been emphasized the programs have scarcely scratched the surface of a tremendous need. More successful, perhaps, has been the work of the Rockefeller Foundation in its program to introduce highly productive hybrid corn types in Mexico and, more recently, in Colombia. Everywhere, however, the plight of the small farmer is desperate, his ignorance abysmal, and the effort to assist him inadequate. It is small wonder that agricultural productivity, except with certain specialized crops destined primarily for export, is very low.

Discussion of industrial possibilities and progress is significant, but it must not becloud the fact that all of Latin America remains predominantly agricultural with the great majority of its population living in small villages in the rural areas. It has been estimated that 65 per cent of South Americans are directly dependent upon agriculture for their livelihood, and the proportion can scarcely be lower in Central America, the Caribbean islands, and Mexico. Of those employed in agriculture only a small portion are concerned with the production of the great export crops: wheat, coffee, bananas, cacao, sugar, and beef. Even in Guatemala where coffee and bananas account for 90 per cent of the country's exports, three times as much acreage is devoted to growing corn and beans for local consumption than is used for production of the export crops. In Bolivia and Chile, where minerals are the principal exports, far more than half the populations derive their livings from agriculture rather than from mining and its subsidiary activities. Only in a few cases, such as Puerto Rico and Cuba, is the general population heavily dependent upon imports for basic dietary requirements. These facts lend emphasis to the importance of increasing the role that domestic agricultural production plays in providing benefits to the local population, large proportions of whom are undernourished.

Other basic problems are encountered in the fields of education and health. Illiteracy is an ever-present, pernicious condition in all of Latin America with the exception of two or three countries such as Uruguay and Costa Rica. Vigorous anti-illiteracy programs have been and are being conducted in nearly all countries, and tremendous strides have been made in extending elementary education even in rural areas. But these steps only begin to touch the real problem. The content of the educational program must be such as to develop not only the simple abilities of reading and writing, which are the mere tools of greater achievement, but it must also include the basic knowledge of commonplace phenomena that enable the individual to adapt himself to and utilize the tremendous achievements of a modern technological civilization. Industrialization requires this in order to develop a skilled labor force; it is essential in any large-scale improvement of agricultural practices. It is precisely for this reason that community education programs in Mexico and Puerto Rico have placed time-honored academic subjects lower on the scale of importance than such matters as personal hygiene, homemaking, agriculture, and rudimentary mechanics.

In the same sense, health is a tremendously important factor in national development, completely apart from the humanitarian factors involved. The Latin American loss in human productivity from undernourishment and disease is beyond measure. Again, only government action can alleviate the situation, for the medical and nursing professions are woefully understaffed and highly concentrated in the larger cities. A large-scale public health program is required in nearly every country to make a serious impression on the problem. Again, the Institute of Inter-American Affairs is active in this field, as is the World Health Organization of the United Nations, but funds are insufficient and other needs compete with equal force for the limited amounts that are available. The same countries that have been most energetic in effecting other social and economic reforms have given most attention to creation of government health and social welfare programs emphasizing medical care.

Inadequate housing is an obvious and contributory factor in health and educational deficiencies. Consequently, public housing on a mass scale has been a major platform in nationalist reform programs all over Latin America. The most significant progress has been made in relatively recent years in Mexico, Chile, El Salvador, and Venezuela, but other countries are also active in this field. Again, it is government that has taken the lead in every case, for private effort cannot begin to cope with a problem of such magnitude and in which there is so little prospect of profit.

Few measures taken by Latin American governments along the lines of progressive nationalism and moderate state socialism following the many revolutions of the early 1930's had much immediate effect in improving economic conditions. Nevertheless, economic conditions in Latin America gradually improved as a result of general world recovery, in some cases faster than in the United States. Influences from outside the hemisphere predominated, particularly the tremendous economic recovery of Western Europe under the stimulus of German war preparations. Raw materials again came into demand, and European purchasers turned to Latin America for them. The reviving German economy needed markets for its export industries, and goods were poured into Latin America under a whole series of barter agreements. Such measures, restrictive of free international commerce, were denounced by the United States; but they were clearly beneficial to the participating countries. Barter trade was better than no trade. Soon Germany had assumed a major role in the foreign commerce of Latin

America. By 1938 it was supplying 16 per cent of Latin America's imports and taking 11 per cent of its exports. In the same year Great Britain provided only 12 per cent of Latin America's imports, but it accounted for 19 per cent of its exports. The United States, taking 33 per cent of Latin American exports and providing the same percentage of imports, continued to dominate the total trade picture as it had for many years. Italy and Japan were also active in the Latin American market, but to a much smaller extent.

With the outbreak of World War II, trade boomed to tremendous proportions, even though the export market on the European continent was lost; for the Allied powers quickly absorbed the goods that could no longer be shipped to Germany, France, Italy, and the northern countries. Some goods continued to reach Germany through Spain, however. At the same time, a flight of capital from Europe poured funds into principal Latin American capitals, particularly Buenos Aires. A large part of such funds was held in idle cash, but substantial amounts became available for local investment. In Brazil, and to a lesser extent in certain other countries, mutual defense arrangements with the United States brought extensive development of military installations, large payrolls in affected locations, and numerous subsidiary benefits of a commercial nature. Soon nearly every Latin American nation had piled up a substantial dollar balance which for the time being could not be spent owing to the shortage of manufactured goods during the war years. Thus in Latin America, recovery merged quickly into a form of prosperity that encouraged the storing up of reserves to carry over into the readjustment period that was certain to follow once international peace was re-established.

Peace in 1945 did bring readjustment, but owing to continued prosperity in the United States and the tremendous effort to foster European recovery, the readjustment was not nearly as drastic as many had feared. It was a disappointing period for Latin America, however. Capital goods, with which many of the American republics had hoped to promote their own industrialization after the war, remained unobtainable or so high priced as to discourage their purchase. Gradually the pressure for consumer goods ate up the accumulated reserves while economic reconstruction as a concern of the United States government seemed to bear only a European tag. Opportunities slipped away, and growing disappointment and disillusionment burst forth in a wave of vehement protest at the 1948 Inter-American Conference in Bogotá. During the period of the New Deal and the war years that followed, the majority of the Latin American countries had been drawn rather close to the United States as a consequence of her 'Good Neighbor' policies. Although no firm commitments were made, many hopeful leaders in the American republics had come to expect that after the war the United States by granting governmental credit and trade priorities on production goods would make a significant contribution toward the industrial and social development of its southern neighbors. The seemingly more urgent demands for assistance in Europe and Asia, however, precluded all but a few token manifestations of American interest in Latin American economic development.

It might appear that the countries of Latin America had done an about-face with respect to their views on foreign investment and that once again the alien capitalist was welcome. On the contrary, what was sought after World War II was investment on an entirely different basis than that which characterized the activities of foreign companies prior to 1930. Inter-governmental loans were requested. That is, the modernization and industrialization effort was to be made primarily under governmental auspices in nearly every country, and the necessary funds were desired from government lending agencies in the United States such as the Export-Import Bank. After formation of the United Nations organization and creation of the International Bank for Reconstruction and Development, subsequently the World Bank, the latter agency became the chief source of developmental credit for Latin America. In most countries the private foreign investor continued to be viewed with suspicion and distrust. As the United States government felt its lending resources strained to the utmost, however, primary effort involving both loans and outright grants was channeled into those areas immediately menaced by communistic Soviet imperialism. Latin Americans were advised to review their thinking and their policies with respect to admitting and encouraging private capital. With the advent of a Republican administration to power in 1952, the possibility of the United States supporting financially government-owned industry or even major developmental public works projects declined appreciably. Republican policy, expressed repeatedly but subtly, when stripped of verbiage informed Latin Americans that they could either accept private capital for private development or do without.

In the meantime, all was not going well with the economies of the American republics. Growing consumer demands far outstripped official efforts to control imports and keep international payments in balance. For the past several years the currencies of Chile, Brazil, and Mexico have declined steadily on the international market. Other countries have seen their currencies fluctuate erratically. A few nations, such as Venezuela with its tremendous oil exports and El Salvador with its coffee crop, have continued to enjoy dollar surpluses while investing sizable amounts in national development programs through both private and governmental channels. Argentina, while short of dollars, has enjoyed a favorable sterling balance as a result of its exports of foodstuffs to Great Britain. It has even been able to extend credits to Paraguay and Bolivia.

In general, the major nations of Latin America have accomplished a great deal in their struggle to raise the levels of national productivity and achieve some degree of economic independence. They have been hampered seriously by the lack of adequate managerial skills, by obsolete and ineffective administrative practices in government and in public corporations, by much dreaming and little sound planning, and by social traditions that hamper the mobilization of domestic capital and that continue to discourage able young men from entering into business and commercial activity. Even the skilled trades are regarded as menial. Change is demanded on the one hand while on the other an undying effort is made to preserve the *status quo*. The result is often the form of change without its substance. Great pride is shown in national trade schools whose benefits are available to only a handful of students. New enterprises provided with the most modern equipment function at a level of efficiency that hardly justifies their existence; their products often cannot compete even in the domestic market with those of foreign manufacturers. Modern and beautiful cities hide from the casual observer the most wretched of urban and rural slums, and the glittering Cadillacs of the hacendados tell nothing of the miserable peonage of the agricultural worker.

In spite of the many contradictions and sharp contrasts — contrasts inevitable in a civilization boasting the gadgetry of the twentieth century and the social organization of the nineteenth — tremendous changes have taken place in all of Latin America in the past twenty-five years. Where a moderate degree of industrialization has come, as it has to Mexico, Brazil, Chile, Argentina, Venezuela, and Puerto Rico, it has brought into being new economic and political classes. These classes are a challenge to the ancient social order, and their gradually increasing purchasing power provides the great hope for a market that will enable the industrialization programs to succeed. Middle-class urban attitudes have begun to break down the powerful ties of the patriarchal family, and women increasingly step from the stultifying seclusion of the servant-operated home into useful employment in commerce, industry, and government. New and vigorous leadership has been injected into economic and political life, a leadership fired with an intensive nationalism that gradually transcends the stereotypes of the ancient caste-ridden social system.

Some of the most satisfying consequences of the great changes emerging in Latin America are to be found not in new factories, new highways, greater agricultural production, or in higher levels of consumer purchases; rather they are artistic, literary, and aesthetic in character. Few artists of the modern era have received such universal acclaim as José Clemente Orozco and Diego Rivera of Mexico, the former for his depth of feeling and portrayal of abstractions through vivid symbolism, and the latter for impressionism with a social revolutionary — even communistic — punch. Both men were products of the Mexican revolution and its nationalistic, reformist, and Indianist spirit. In architecture, extreme modernism in design has characterized the new spirit of progress. It is particularly to be noted in São Paulo, Brazil, and in Mexico City, where huge office buildings displayed story upon story of glass even as the United Nations building was being erected in New York City. Residential structures throughout the hemisphere, but particularly in the Caribbean area, reveal a remarkable appreciation for functional beauty ideally adapted to informal tropical living. Conventionalists are prone to criticize much of the modern Latin American architectural efforts as being garish and in poor taste, and certainly utility is often too little considered or sacrificed for effect. Nevertheless, much of it is truly indigenous, original, and a faithful expression of the modern nationalistic spirit, even to the flaws of poor planning and stark contradiction.

In the field of classical music, modern Latin America has displayed little originality. But to stop with such a statement would indeed be absurd. Perhaps no other area of the world has had such a tremendous impact in the realm of modern popular music as has Latin America. Mambos, rhumbas, tangos, boleros, and sambas from the American republics have captivated the dancing feet of millions from New York to Singapore. The plaintive *canción ranchera* of Mexico and the rhythmic calypso of the Caribbean islands are wonderful examples of a spontaneous folk music that the modern radio and phonograph have carried far beyond their locale of origin. It is through such media that the spirit of modern Latin America contacts and influences the average citizen in other parts of the world.

Today there can be no doubt that the American republics contain within their midst rising forces that are dynamic, virile, and potentially capable of solving the difficult problems with which they are faced. Latin America has been and remains one of the greatest areas of racial fusion known to the modern world. The process of amalgamation is necessarily slow and even painful at times, but the synthesis has begun to emerge. It reveals itself as a group of high-spirited and proud nations struggling to achieve a greater national unity based on a regional cultural, economic, and political self-sufficiency.

They are striving to escape the foils of anachronistic institutions and to resolve their problems through a pragmatic and rational approach that avoids the extremes of dogmatism and safeguards the freedom and dignity of the individual. The Latin Americans are in the process of building a culture which in every way they can call their own.

XXXVI

Mexico: A Study in Dynamics

Work is one of the foundations on which the Mexico of tomorrow must be built. The other is honesty.

PRESIDENT ADOLFO RUIZ CORTINES *

THE Mexico of today has advanced far beyond the chaotic land which spawned Iturbide and Santa Anna a century and a half ago. One need only to recall the agonizing trials of Morelos and Juárez, the selfish machinations of Santa Anna, and the suffocating hand of Porfirio Díaz to appreciate fully the remarkable changes since 1910, and particularly since 1930. It is against this somber background that modern Mexico must be viewed and judged.

For Americans beyond the Río Grande Mexico remains in many ways mysterious and fascinating, a land of sharp contrasts and inconsistencies, of hunger and privation, of violence and sudden death, of haunting folk music and brilliant artistry. The visitor to Monterrey, the northern industrial capital, is soon disabused of notions of Mexican lack of ingenuity and energy, for the multitude of enterprises and the tempo of activity is astonishing. He learns of the Technological Institute which the businessmen of Monterrey have sponsored, and which is playing an increasingly vital role in economic development. The transformation of this ancient colonial settlement into a thriving industrial center is typical of the changes

---

* *Christian Science Monitor*, September 6, 1955.

taking place in Mexico today. Monterrey leads the way in regional development.

The visitor to Mexico will be impressed in other ways. New highways have brought previously isolated hamlets and villages into the currents of Mexican life for the first time, and the propensity to travel of these villagers is immediately obvious. It appears that the intense regionalism of the past is finally on the wane. Those unacquainted with Mexico also will be impressed by the inherent artistic and musical qualities of the average Mexican. Even in the most remote villages the folk songs sung by barefoot and untrained children have an inspiring quality impossible to describe. Mexico's music, popular and classical, has reached a wide and appreciative audience throughout the Caribbean area and parts of South America as well as in the United States. Her composers and artists, particularly Agustín Lara, José Clemente Orozco, Diego Rivera, and David Alfaro Siqueiros, have won world-wide acclaim. Mexican writers, literary and historical, have also given Mexico a high position among Latin American nations. Her school of trained historians, which assembled at the First Congress of Mexican and United States Historians at Monterrey, in 1949, is second to none in Latin America.

Political life, too, has improved since 1930. In the interval between the assassination of Obregón and the election of Lázaro Cárdenas, Plutarco Elías Calles, who had now become wealthy and conservative, ruled the country through three presidents, Emilio Portes Gil, Pascual Ortiz Rubio, and Abelardo Rodríguez. To Mexicans who still believed in the aims of the Revolution, there was a feeling of betrayal, and the revolutionary sentiment grew too powerful to be safely ignored by Calles and his neighbors on the 'Street of the Forty Thieves.' * Counter activity to Calles became dangerously strong, and it was necessary for him to pick a candidate who would appear to satisfy demands for fulfilling the goals of the PNR, the National Revolutionary party, without actually having to surrender his control. While the PNR drew up its Six Year Plan to

---

* Name popularly applied to the street in Cuernavaca where Calles and many of his friends lived.

revive the movement for change, Calles chose General Lázaro Cárdenas to represent him in the presidency.

Two of the most powerful of the anti-callistas were Narciso Bassols and Vicente Lombardo Toledano, who prepared the way for Cárdenas by reorganizing education and labor. Bassols inaugurated a program of education aimed at instilling a new attitude toward government and property. He and his system were bitterly denounced as atheistic and socialistic, and the life of the rural schoolteacher became perilous.

Even during the presidential campaign it became clear that Calles had misjudged his man, and the idea that once the election was over revolutionary fervor would die out proved vain. Cárdenas campaigned as if it were possible that his opponents had a chance of defeating him. He visited regions never seen before by a presidential candidate. His travels gave him a feeling for long-standing regional problems, and what was equally important, enabled rural Mexicans to see and talk to their future president, and to become acquainted with a name other than Calles. His real opponent was Calles, and until the jefe máximo could be dislodged there was no prospect of reform. The campaign waged by Cárdenas was a part of his astute program for dethroning Calles.

In less than two years after his election, by skillfully drawing to himself the main clusters of power, Cárdenas was ready for the crucial test. This was an important step, for the callistas had been able to frustrate his efforts by various acts, including an attempt to stir up a clerical revolt by persecution of Catholics. In the struggle Cárdenas proved abler than his rival. He reorganized the PNR, renaming it PRM, Party of the Mexican Revolution, and brought it under his control. He increased the pay of the enlisted men in the army, so that they looked to the president for betterment, and he distributed more land to the landless than had been done in the entire period before 1934. Lombardo Toledano's new labor organization, the CTM, replaced the nearly defunct CROM of Morones, and gave Cárdenas powerful support.

By April, 1936, Cárdenas was ready to oust Calles and Morones, and the two were sent by airplane to Texas. After this event Cárdenas governed Mexico without a serious rival, his power resting firmly on labor, the agricultural peasantry, and the army, no one of which was permitted to prevail over the others. The method of divide and rule was traditional in Mexico, but the Cárdenas regime was unique in its diminished reliance on local chiefs and its efforts to create dependence upon the government and the party rather than on individual leaders.

Cárdenas carried out his reform program with astonishing rapidity, considering the intensity of opposition at home and abroad. By the beginning of 1938 he had distributed twenty-five million acres of land, which lessened but did not banish the problems of agricultural laborers. The venerable land problem was particularly acute, and Cárdenas sought a partial solution in the elimination of the hacienda.

To appreciate the determination of the followers of the Revolution party to eradicate the hacienda system from Mexico it is necessary to re-emphasize its role in the Mexican economy. The hacienda embraced more than half of the rural population. Three-fourths of all rural communities were located on haciendas. The semi-feudal system, which had been useful in extending the agricultural frontiers in times of insufficient population, was neither creative nor enterprising, and had long since outlived its usefulness.

Article 27 of the constitution contained the goal of the Revolution with regard to land: to recover that which had been granted in enormous tracts to companies and individuals, to break up the hacienda system, to free agricultural labor from peonage, and to promote the growth of agricultural communities. It was intended also as a weapon to give the state an advantage in its struggle with long-standing foes — the hacendados, the foreigners, and the church as a political force.

The agrarian reform movement gained ground slowly, and it was not until 1935 that the hacienda villagers received the right to apply for and obtain lands. This change reflected the determination of the Cárdenas administration to face the hacienda issue squarely. More than 20,000 communities have been granted lands; of these about 500 have been in the form of community units such as that of

Laguna, where 600,000 acres of rich land were organized into a co-operative project involving 30,000 families. Haciendas still exist in Mexico, but almost without legal status. The law recognizes only two types of property, small holdings and ejidos.

The problem of making small private holdings and large semi-communal ones compatible has not been solved, and much friction exists, friction which is customarily settled by violence. The ejido has the advantage of government protection and political power. Diversity in the land tenure pattern no doubt will continue to exist for many years, but the most obvious trend is toward communal and co-operative agricultural landholdings.

The agrarian reforms have created tremendous changes in Mexico, at least on the surface. The hacienda has lost its legal standing, as has the foreign-owned agricultural estate. Medium-sized holdings are still permitted on sufferance, but like small ones, which have legal status, they are under pressure wherever village populations are increasing.

Toward the goal of recovering Mexico for the Mexicans the most spectacular action was the expropriation of foreign oil properties. This occurred in March, 1938, following a two-year strike of oil workers and refusal on the part of the companies to accept the decision of arbitral boards upheld by the Mexican Supreme Court. The expropriation, which was hailed by Mexican labor as an act of liberation, was actually a triumph of Mexican nationalism backed by labor. The act created more immediate problems than it solved, for the government relied heavily on oil taxes and on the silver-buying policy of the Roosevelt administration. It assumed a tremendous debt to the oil companies while the United States ceased buying Mexican silver in retaliation for the seizure. *Pemex*, the state corporation organized to manage the oil industry, floundered for several years because of boycott by foreign nations, lack of a sufficient corps of competent technicians, and the necessity of making the transfer too rapidly.

After staggering for ten years the oil industry has been revived under the guidance of Antonio Bermúdez, who was appointed head of Pemex in 1948. New oil wells have been opened in the vicinity of Veracruz, and prospecting for oil is being carried on in widely scattered areas. By 1950 Pemex was annually paying into the treasury more than four times the amount realized before nationalization of the oil industry. Production of natural gas was also rising, and Mexico prepared to export $150,000 worth of gas daily to the United States.

Less noticeable was the policy of attrition by which foreign companies were gradually driven out and Mexican ownership of industries expanded. The government's support of unions against foreign-owned companies was one of the means of carrying out this program. Mexico became unattractive to foreign capital, and foreign investments dwindled rapidly, while foreign banks and insurance companies were eliminated completely.

Another activity of the Cárdenas administration which met with considerable unpopularity at home and abroad was its support of the Spanish Republic against Franco, and its offering refuge to Spanish loyalists. Many of them took advantage of the offer, and Mexico's economy and intellectual life were enriched by their coming.

Many other foreign pressures were felt in Mexico. A falangist movement patterned after that of Spain arose. Red Shirts and Gold Shirts fought for political power and to halt trends against their interest. In 1938 Cárdenas faced a rebellion led by General Saturnino Cedillo, the political boss of San Luis Potosí, who had risen from poverty and ignorance to wealth and influence through the means peculiar to Mexican generals. By 1938 Cedillo was the only local caudillo who still retained a private army.

Cedillo's abortive revolt resulted from the demand that he surrender his private army and leave San Luis Potosí. The uprising was easily put down by government troops, and the caudillo was slain. Particularly noteworthy aspects of the affair were that Cárdenas refrained from shooting the prisoners taken, thus breaking with tradition, and that the church supported him on the issue.

Education, efforts to integrate the Indian into national life, and promotion of a feeling of national consciousness were among the most important accomplishments of the Cárdenas regime. Mexico became acutely aware of her Indian heritage and of her unassimilated Indian millions. The educational program begun in 1920 under the tutelage of José Vasconcelos received a changed direction and a new impetus. Cárdenas favored acculturation rather than assimilation, acceptance of parts of Indian culture rather than rejection of it in its entirety. The rural and Indian schools and the cultural missions were the instruments of the drive to reach the long-neglected rural peoples, mestizos and Indians. The teacher and the missionary had to bring to the entire communities, not merely to children of school age, everything that was lacking.

The cultural missions served for a time as teacher-training schools, but they have since surrendered this function to the normal schools which have been organized. The agricultural schools have been associated with the normal schools, to prepare teachers more adequately for meeting the desperate needs of the impoverished communities. Much remains to be done, and Mexico's educational task must necessarily be long range. The system of rural education, however, is a noteworthy innovation. In recent years, under such appointees as Jaime Torres Bodet, the Ministry of Education has continued to receive the attention of some of the best minds in Mexico.

One of the strong drives in Mexico since 1930, and one which has grown in intensity down to the present, is toward industrialization. This drive is enhanced by the fact that Mexico is unusually well endowed with minerals. In the north the steel industry is well started at Monterrey and Monclova. The most important Mexican industry, however, is processing agricultural foodstuffs, and second in importance is textiles. By 1940 the textile industry was able to supply the domestic demand for low-priced cottons. About a third of the raw materials used in Mexican industry is imported, and most manufactures are protected by high tariff barriers.

In 1940 the *Nacional Financiera* was organized by the government to stabilize prices through purchases. It has gradually acquired vast economic powers, and has become the principal economic agency. Through its activities the government has become a partner in the expansion of industry. Because of the government's role, industry has remained unduly centralized around Mexico City.

As in most Latin American nations one of the principal obstacles to successful industrialization is the absence of an adequate domestic market. In Mexico this problem is acute, for while two-thirds of her population are engaged in agriculture, they have difficulty in producing enough food for her growing population, and agricultural workers have little to spend for even domestically manufactured goods.

Deforestation has increased soil destruction, and at the same time it has been necessary to expand cultivation to hillside areas with the result that soil erosion is a critical problem. Corn or Indian maize is the staple food crop, and nearly two-thirds of all land under cultivation is devoted to its production. The yield per acre, however, is extremely low; a single midwestern state in the United States produces five times as much as all of Mexico. Wheat is next in importance among crops, and its production is no more satisfactory. In recent years coffee production has grown rapidly in importance, so that Mexico has now replaced El Salvador as the third largest coffee producer in the world.

The problem of providing food for her people is one of the most crucial Mexico faces, for her birth rate is still high and her death rate declining. Many plans have been formulated for solving this dilemma, but thus far none has been even moderately successful. In recent years food has accounted for more than 20 per cent of Mexican imports.

The difficulties in the way of raising agricultural production to correspond to the needs of a growing population are enormous. They are not merely physical and financial, but include inherent resistance to change on the part of the rural peasantry. Ancient customs are difficult to uproot; the brightest hope for success in this direction lies with the understaffed and poorly financed rural and Indian schools. But it may take generations before a marked improvement is noticeable.

Another effort at stimulating agricultural production has been made by the Rockefeller Foundation together with a group of Mexican scientists, under the leadership of Dr. J. George Harrar. Experiments have been made with hybrid corns, and in some localities the corn yield has been doubled. Experimental stations are carrying on research with new varieties of rust-resistant wheat and other crops, and an intensive study is being made of plant disease and insect control. In 1947 the National Corn Commission was established to further the general program, and other governmental farm agencies have been organized to carry on similar research.

In 1953 the government began shifting farm populations from the arid north central region to the rainy tropical coast near Chiapas, Veracruz, and Tabasco. A vast area is being opened to cultivation in the Popaloapan river project on the gulf coast. More than 200,000 square miles of tropical jungle are being cleared, and homes are erected for the settlers by the government. The Alemán dam, largest in Latin America, is to provide water for irrigation as well as electricity for the project. A similar project is planned for Chiapas, along the Grijalva river. In the north the Falcón dam on the Río Grande and the Yaqui Alto canal opened fertile but arid regions to intensive cultivation through irrigation. By September, 1955, President Adolfo Ruiz Cortines was able to announce that for the first time Mexico was feeding her people without the need of basic food imports.

It has frequently been stated that Mexico benefited as a result of the war, that both shortages of imported manufactures and demands for Mexican products abroad greatly stimulated production, and helped put industry on its feet. Mining was revived, it is true, and the planting of certain crops such as guayule encouraged. For a time foreign capital in vast quantities sought safe investments in Mexico. But those who saw in the situation the fulfillment of the longed-for promise of economic independence ignored the fact that conditions were abnormal and demands artificial. The rising profits of the textile industry, for example, were caused mainly by the absence of foreign competition in the Caribbean area. They did not depend upon the domestic market to which the industry had to turn once the war ended. Mexican investors were well aware of the precarious situation, and preferred to risk their money in real estate.

The war also brought inflation, and prevented Mexico from reaching her usual sources of imports. It increased her economic dependence upon the United States, and the rising prices and other economic ills were soon blamed on the northern neighbor. But President Manuel Avila Camacho did not hesitate to cast Mexico's lot with the United States and the Allies, as Cárdenas had indicated earlier would be done.

The elections of 1946 and 1952 were relatively peaceful by Mexican standards. Miguel Alemán, the government's choice in 1946, was the first civilian elected to the presidency since Carranza; Ruiz Cortines, who followed him, is also a civilian. This indicates a change in Mexican political life, perhaps, but it is not to be taken as an indication that the army is no longer important. The army is still the chief support of the government, and no president could govern without its adherence.

Because of this situation the government is obliged to perpetuate itself in power by customary methods or invite insurrection. It conducts elections and permits free speech, for political democracy is one of the aspirations of the Revolution. No opposition candidate with a more attractive program has come forth to challenge the official candidates and none of them has been a serious threat. Most opposition candidates do not expect to win; their greatest hope is to create a moral justification for revolt, for none of them would be able to govern if by some miracle he defeated the official choice. If the army could be alienated and the government driven from power, an opposition candidate would be in a position to hold an election in which he and his followers would win control of the government. The military uprising is merely a means of transferring power from one group to another. The chief deterrent to rebellion in Mexico today is fear of United States aid to the government; without the sanction of the United States no rebellion could hope to succeed.

The reorganization of the PNR into the PRM by Cárdenas, and the later changes instituted by Avila Camacho in 1945, had no widespread effect on Mexican political conditions. Cárdenas relieved government employees of involuntary exactions for the support of the party treasury, and the government assumed the responsibility of financing the official party. The formation of a single official party made the country dependent upon the government for social change, and the later modifications merely emphasized the government's role. The president appoints the head of the party, and it serves as the electoral organization. This effective control makes it possible to permit other political organizations to exist and campaign without fear of their success.

The government has widened the base upon which its power rests by its role of leadership in social and economic reorganization, attracting to its support the benefitted groups in both urban and rural life. It has taken on the responsibility of directing the nation's economy, a burden made the more difficult by failure to inaugurate appropriate changes in administrative machinery and in political morality. Efficiency and integrity have not kept pace with the growth of government responsibilities. Neither have the processes of representative government. Congress remains largely a rubber stamp, while the president, as the most powerful figure in Mexico, implements his program by decrees. Congress simply empowers him to do so. The real political issues are thrashed out by personal negotiation with the political leaders representing the powerful factions that support the government party. In this environment, the sounds issuing from the legislative halls have a hollow ring.

The device of a government-sponsored party has been found effective for retaining control and avoiding rebellions. It does not mean, as might appear, that elections are less a reflection of popular expression than they would be if no official party existed. As compared with the era of Porfirio Díaz the change has made for greater stability and democratization in political life. The most obvious accomplishment in this direction is the principle of no re-election. The president can no longer succeed himself though his party remains in power. Legally he has the right to run for the presidency again after an intervening term, but since the assassination of Obregón no president has availed himself of the opportunity.

By creating a more stable civil service and by eliminating the worst aspects of the ancient spoils system, the government has acquired greater effectiveness and continuity in administrative departments. In the corps of civil servants it has also gained one of its most devoted groups of supporters.

The government's power has been strengthened through its support of organized labor, and it is partially because of this fact that the state has influenced the process of industrialization. The state is a party to every labor discussion or contract. When Article 123 was written into the constitution Mexico lacked a substantial industrial laboring class; most of the small group that might be so classed were in the employ of aliens. Governmental support of labor was in effect action against foreign capital, and no local interests were injured or threatened by the creation of organized labor. State concern for labor organization was two-fold: to improve the situation of the working man and to increase the authority of the state.

Every gain in power by the unions is reflected in a greater gain by the government. The unions, the collective labor contract, and the Boards of Conciliation and Arbitration have given the government great weight in the councils of industry. The Boards of Conciliation and Arbitration have become increasingly important since their creation. They have been granted additional powers from time to time, until today they possess judicial competency in the field of labor disputes.

The rise of organized labor has added a new force to Mexican political life, a force which may one day surpass the army in strength and influence. But as long as the threat of rebellion in the states remains alive, the government must continue to rely heavily on the loyalty of the army. Organized labor and the agricultural communities have rallied to the government's support in times of crisis, and the dependence upon the army has diminished. The unions and the ejidos give the president strong support among the masses of Mexicans, a support which previously was neither courted nor obtained.

The PRI, as the government party is now known, is a coalition of moderate elements of the left and the industrial right, labor, agrarian groups, the bureaucracy, and the army. Leadership of the country for a Mexican president depends upon his ability to hold this coalition together. His task is to harmonize the diverse interests of these groups sufficiently well to keep them united. The basic course of the government is determined by this method. For the president the task is not easy.

One of the means of controlling the states available to the central government is provided through the tax system. The bulk of taxes collected is claimed by the government; the states and municipalities must depend upon their good standing with the government to obtain financial favors. Within the states the political bosses, if they remain loyal to the regime, are all-powerful, and little can be done without their consent.

The amount of money in circulation increased considerably during the war, owing to the favorable balance of trade that resulted, the money spent by the United States to restore Mexican transport, the funds brought in by European refugees, and the money sent home by Mexican workers in the United States. Despite optimistic claims little new wealth was created. Industrial output did not increase after 1942, although its value doubled or tripled because of inflation. The result was merely harder times for the average Mexican working man and his family.

The government was able, however, to reduce its indebtedness and to spend vast sums for public works, and to settle the still-outstanding claims of the oil companies. In 1942 the minister of finance negotiated an adjustment of the external debt with the International Committee of Bankers for Mexico. The dollar debt was converted to a peso debt, at a peso to the dollar. Because of the later devaluation of the peso the obligation was thus reduced substantially. Pressure on Mexico's foreign exchange was drastically reduced by the measures to eradicate the external debt. The situation was temporarily, at least, favorable to Mexico. It would prove a tremendous obstacle, however, should she find it necessary to try to attract private foreign capital in the future. And in order to make possible the primary construction for a large manufacturing development, it has been estimated that more than ten billion pesos will be required.

Mexico's government-sponsored housing program has undertaken the construction of huge apartment houses, complete with schools, playgrounds, medical clinics, and fire departments. In 1949 the Centro Urbano Presidente Alemán was opened for occupancy, with facilities for more than one thousand families.

The conflict between church and state which embittered so much of the nineteenth century in Mexico has appeared occasionally since 1930, though without the extreme attitudes on both sides characteristic of earlier clashes. To the followers of the Revolution the church was identified with foreign interests instead of the social program found in the revolutionary doctrines. Once it assumed a role of opposition to the Revolution, the church found itself in a situation from which there was no dignified and graceful exit. The bitter strife which broke out in the era of Calles and the cristero rebellion continued until 1935, when Cárdenas quietly modified the government's policy toward the church without making any overt changes in law. Soon afterward he persuaded the state governors to follow his lead, and the tension died down. Relations between church and state have improved considerably since that time, although there have been few legislative changes except for modification of Article 3 of the constitution to remove the features most objectionable to the church.

One of the focal points of opposition to the PRI has been the *sinarquista* (with order) movement, a Christian Front organization motivated by various fanaticisms including religious, totalitarian, and anti-democratic. The shortage of food during the war gave the sinarquistas an opportunity to charge the government with shipping food to the United States while Mexicans starved. Even though the opposite was true, by careful nourishing of latent Yankeephobia and other hatreds, the sinarquistas created a large following. Their activities, like those of the cristeros before them, led to an outbreak of religious fanaticism which included persecution of Protestants. The sinarquistas have made bids for political power at the state and national level. They can not hope for victory at the polls, and such political activity is simply a means of preparing the way for revolt. The loyalty of the army to the PRI is the main safeguard against sinarquista insurrection.

Because of the integration and unity achieved through political stabilization since 1930, Mexico, less torn by domestic issues, began to play a more active role in international affairs. She rose rapidly in stature among Latin American nations, and has sought closer economic and cultural ties with the other republics, including Argentina. During the war she extended her markets for textiles and other products in Central America and the Caribbean.

Late in 1954 Mexican economic conditions improved considerably, in part because the drought ended and the need for importing food declined. Not all of Mexico's economic problems were solved, but her prospects were brighter. Dollar reserves had dwindled rapidly after the recent devaluation of the peso. The end of the drought was particularly important, for the abundant harvests curtailed the need of spending large sums on food imports, which in 1952–3 amounted to fifty-seven million dollars. Cotton and coffee exports, both of major importance to the Mexican economy, are expected to reach record highs. Natural gas and sulphur are soon to be available for export, and Mexico's newly developed sulphur deposits should enable her to become the world's second largest producer.

Mexico is still primarily a nation of small villages rather than scattered farms and ranches. More than 90 per cent of the inhabited places of Mexico have no more than 500 people living in them, and there are only twelve large cities. Of these, Mexico City is disproportionately favored in size, wealth, and industrial concentration. This situation makes it extremely difficult for the government to implement many of its programs outside the Federal District.

With a growing population of some twenty-four millions, Mexico has made remarkable progress toward achieving her various goals, although many of them are still far from reach and almost insuperable obstacles remain. The prospects for industrialization are not altogether bright; the situation of agriculture is still critical. Mexico remains a land of deeply rooted special interests, not all of which share the government's conviction that its direction is appropriate. The radicalism of the 1930's has given way to a moderate liberalism, and collectivism to a greater emphasis on middle class, individualistic values. There is no apparent effort to undo the agrarian and labor reforms which have been made, but the process has been slowed. Mexico has made great gains in national unity and has displayed an ability to achieve co-operation among the many divergent group interests.

XXXVII

The Restless Caribbean

> In all essential respects the defense of the vital Caribbean
> zone . . . , the cornerstone of hemispheric defense, is carried
> out unilaterally by the United States under such bilateral ar-
> rangements with individual Latin American governments as it
> deems desirable and is able to induce them to enter into.
>
> ARTHUR P. WHITAKER *

THE countries in and surrounding the Caribbean
Sea — Central America, the islands, Colombia,
and Venezuela — lie within the orbit of direct United States influence. Of greatest strategic importance in the area is the Panama
Canal. The international roles of the nations of the Caribbean
region are determined largely by the state of their relations with the
United States. In the years since 1930 defense of the area and of the
Panama Canal has figured more prominently in these relations
than any other single factor.

Before the pronouncement of the Good Neighbor Policy the
Caribbean was the region in which United States policy was stigmatized as 'Big Stick' and 'Dollar Diplomacy.' Since 1930 not only
has public policy with regard to the Caribbean nations changed for
the better with the abandonment of old-style intervention, but the
activities of American companies and individuals engaged in economic enterprises have also become more enlightened. Added to
this voluntary change is the determination on the part of most of

* The United States and South America: the Northern Republics, Harvard
University Press, Cambridge, 1948, pp. 246–7.

the governments of the region to extricate themselves from positions of economic subservience to foreign interests, a determination which ranges from fairly mild yet effective measures in Venezuela to the extremes reached in Guatemala, where expropriation of some foreign-owned property has already taken place.

The international problems of the Caribbean states are those of small nations lying in the shadow of a great power. It is not surprising that Colombia and her neighbors have shown a powerful predilection for hemispheric international organization on the basis of equality among the member states. To the Caribbean countries such international organization is for the purpose of protecting the small from the large; they have been particularly anxious, therefore, despite recent flare-ups among some of their number, to preserve unweakened the principle of non-intervention. Colombia and Venezuela have been especially active in promoting international cooperation, and have taken the lead in submitting proposals for strengthening the inter-American organization on many occasions.

At the Buenos Aires conference in 1936 Colombia proposed the creation of an Association of American States, a proposal which finally reached fruition at the Bogotá conference of 1948, when the Organization of American States was established. During the war and the years immediately preceding it, Colombia and Venezuela both strongly urged inter-American solidarity. At the Panamá meeting of 1939 Venezuela introduced two proposals which were accepted: the creation of the Inter-American Neutrality and the Inter-American Juridical committees. At Habana a year later Venezuela offered the Declaration of Reciprocal Assistance and Co-operation, which was adopted.

Frictions among the Caribbean nations seem to have been lessened slightly if at all by the advance of international organization. Venezuelans look askance at the economic activities of Colombians. Central America and the island countries have their own peculiar feuds in addition to sporadic resistance to the United States and the recurrent irritation between Guatemala and Great Britain over Belize, or British Honduras. Central American union is a long-standing desire on the part of some of the governments, but something that others wish to avoid at any cost. The discussions of 1934 and 1945 accomplished little toward making the goal a reality. In 1951 representatives of the Central American states met again in El Salvador and adopted the so-called Salvador Charter. Its object is to strengthen ties among the nations and to arrive at means of solving common problems. The idea of a customs union was brought up for further study, as was the possibility of establishing a Central American University. More recent relations among Central American states make it clear that they are far from ready to set aside their differences.

The Caribbean incidents occurring since 1947 have given the inter-American system most of its martial problems. The OAS has been appealed to on several occasions by the island republics and those of Central America. Most of the clashes would be classed as purely domestic affairs were it not for the exiles, refugees, and soldiers of fortune who drift from one fracas to another with the ubiquitous phalanx known as the 'Caribbean Legion.' Many charges have been made by the various governments that others have been harboring their exiles and aiding them in attempts to overthrow the existing governments, charges which frequently seem well founded. Thus Costa Rica charged Nicaragua with aiding revolutionary forces. Haiti charged intervention by the Dominican Republic. Venezuela leveled accusations against the Dominican Republic, which in turn issued blanket charges of its own against Costa Rica, Venezuela, and Cuba of organizing movements aimed at overthrowing the regime of Rafael Trujillo. An examination of these various charges and the findings of the Council of the OAS suggests that some of the Caribbean governments apply the principle of non-intervention only against the United States.

In January, 1950, the Council of the OAS decided to apply the Rio de Janeiro treaty to the persistent hostilities among the Caribbean nations, and a special fact-finding committee was created to make a study. Tension was heightened by the fact that Trujillo's compliant congress granted him authority to declare war, a gesture intended to intimidate countries harboring the numerous exiles and enemies of his regime. He was informed by the OAS that it possessed sufficient machinery for settling quarrels peacefully. The committee found evidence of misconduct on all sides, and called on Haiti and the Dominican Republic specifically to mend their ways and live up to their celebrated Joint Declaration of June 9, 1949, on mutual friendship. The OAS Council received assurances from Haiti, the Dominican Republic, Cuba, and Guatemala that they would abide by their commitments to the inter-American system. Trujillo's war powers were repealed, and it appeared that peace reigned once more.

After the special 'watchdog' committee considered its work done and disbanded, the Dominican Republic seized near its coast landing craft manned by Cubans, Guatemalans, and Dominican exiles, and the charges and counter-charges flourished once more. In 1951 the Dominican Republic freed five Cubans and three Guatemalans as a gesture toward peace. The underlying problem of the floating province of nationless political exiles and refugees, however, remained unsolved.

In 1950 Guatemala was accused of harboring the Caribbean Legion, which had its headquarters in Cuba. In various of the abortive invasions of the Dominican Republic the Legion was said to use Guatemalan rifles, planes, and other military equipment. The overthrow of Trujillo of the Dominican Republic and Anastasio Somoza of Nicaragua was the primary object of the Legion; these dictatorial gentlemen were also the main foes of President Juan José Arévalo of Guatemala, and of his Minister of Defense, Jacobo Arbenz, who succeeded to the presidency in 1951.

The fact that the Caribbean Legion has been able to keep the region in a state of turmoil for several years demonstrates what a slender reed peace depends on in the Caribbean. Its numbers have been estimated at between twenty-five and one hundred men, including communists, moderates, and rightists mainly from Nicaragua and the Dominican Republic. It has figured in three hapless attempts against the Dominican Republic, and it took part in the revolt which placed José Figueres in power in Costa Rica in 1948. The Central American states are not doctrinaire in their external relations; in the civil strife that occurred when José Figueres rebelled in an effort to secure the Costa Rican presidency for the legally elected moderate liberal, Otilio Ulate, the leftist forces were aided by Nicaragua and Honduras, while the moderates were helped by Guatemala.

Relations between Guatemala and the United States worsened steadily after 1945, when the regime of Arévalo came into power following the ousting of Jorge Ubico, who had ruled since 1930. Guatemala has undergone many reforms since Ubico's overthrow. Some of the reforms have been cautious and well-planned, and the need for them was apparent for years. Changing the land tenure system has long been an aspiration of Guatemalan reformers, and their demands became insistent after 1944. In 1952 the Agrarian Reform Law was finally passed; most of the holdings expropriated since then were those of Guatemalans, but more than 200,000 acres of United Fruit Company holdings were taken.

The Guatemalan–United States rift was complicated by the fact that the Arévalo and Arbenz regimes displayed favoritism to the small force of communists in the country. Anti-foreign demonstrations were encouraged, especially Yankee-baiting. All foreign holdings were imperiled, and the more intelligent policies of some foreign-owned companies in the past decade or two have not erased from the minds of Guatemalans the conviction that all foreign companies are in league with the forces of evil. Any unfavorable comment by officials of the State Department concerning communism in Guatemala was interpreted as action in behalf of the companies.

More alarming to Washington than land reform was the threat to the peace of Central America, and ultimately, to the Panama Canal, implied in the shipments of arms from communist areas in Europe. Many Latin Americans found it difficult to appreciate the concern of the United States or even of Guatemala's neighbors over the arms situation. They did not conceal their suspicion that the apprehension of the United States was based on the attacks on foreign-owned holdings.

The situation of Guatemala in January, 1954, was paradoxical. Economic and social reforms were being carried out in a democratic climate and with a view to economic development within capitalism and free enterprise, but political life was infiltrated and influenced by communists. The political power of the communists among the mass of people seemed weak, but it also appeared that President Arbenz was using the communists as a weapon against the United States. This situation was soon to produce his downfall.

In February, 1954, the American Federation of Labor took steps to persuade Guatemalans to abandon their pro-communist attitude. President George Meany, in a letter to President Arbenz, expressed his concern over the presence of communists in government and labor organizations, though he reiterated the A.F.L.'s support of the social reforms which were being made. He bluntly criticized the government for its continued support of communist control of labor unions. At the same time he praised the country's efforts to secure economic independence, to increase agricultural productivity, and to raise standards of living and of social justice. He agreed with the Guatemalan conviction that foreign corporations should not enjoy special privileges, and he defended the country's right to make its own decisions as to the use of its natural resources.

This type of persuasion, coming from a recognized labor organization, is far more likely to bear fruit than any statement by officials of the State Department. The views of the latter are automatically branded as 'imperialistic interference,' and treated to scorn in the press. Despite the apparent danger of doing more harm than good, in a radio address beamed to Latin America on May 31, 1954, Spruille Braden warned the Guatemalans and their neighbors of the threat inherent in the spread of communist activity.

The anti-communist issue was not the only one which split the Tenth Inter-American Conference, held in Caracas in March, 1954. Costa Rica, long hailed as one of the most democratic of Latin American nations, refused to send a representative. In a letter to the OAS, President Figueres made it clear that communism was not the only present danger to Latin America; dictatorship of any type was equally threatening, and a more persistent and widespread menace. Although he pledged that his country would adhere to any resolutions adopted for strengthening American solidarity and defense of the hemisphere, conditions in Venezuela convinced his government that it should not be represented at Caracas.

The conditions to which Figueres alluded have been of considerable concern to the friends of democracy and of civil liberties elsewhere. Following the death of the tyrant Juan Vicente Gómez, in 1935, Venezuela, considering her long and unhappy experiences with dictators in the past, made rapid strides toward creating a representative government. The constitution adopted in 1936, despite its maintenance of old forms, made gestures toward social reform. By 1941 the powerful *Acción Democrática* party had been organized, composed of labor and the intellectuals. Congress selected for president General Isaías Medina Angarita, who represented the alliance of the middle class and labor in opposition to the clique of great landowners and generals. Medina attempted to further the progress of democracy, but after breaking with Acción Democrática in 1945, he was overthrown.

The revolutionary junta, headed by Rómulo Betancourt, called for the election of a constitutional convention by direct vote, and women were permitted to participate for the first time. The regime of the junta was moderate rather than revolutionary; its goals were economic, social, and political reforms under representative government. In 1947 the new constitution, Venezuela's most democratic one, was adopted. In the presidential election which followed, Rómulo Gallegos, famed writer and candidate of Acción Democrática, received more than two-thirds of the total vote. His reforms were regarded as too radical by the army, and nine months after taking office he was ousted and exiled.

Since the overthrow of Gallegos Venezuela has been ruled by an army junta, and Acción Democrática was proscribed and driven underground. In 1950 Carlos Delgado Chalbaud, strong man of the junta, was assassinated. Desperate revolts against the junta in 1951 and the following year were suppressed. The military dictator against whom Figueres aimed his remarks was Marco Pérez Jiménez, who canceled election returns in 1952 when it became clear that he was on the way to certain defeat in the presidential contest. The leaders of Acción Democrática have been persecuted relentlessly and many slain or imprisoned.

In conclusion, Figueres wrote:

Costa Rica finds it beneficial to world democracy that, while other American states attend to the general needs of inter-Americanism and of western defense by their presence at Caracas, some country should express — by its absence under present circumstances — the anguish of the peoples sacrificed in the struggle against the totalitarianisms that are indigenous to the hemisphere. Thus we shall contribute to make the two struggles — the global and the internal — equally patent.

In making this responsible decision, my Cabinet was guided by the following reflections:

First — The American system tends to constitute a new world based on the respect for representative government, juridical order, and liberty.

Second — The Charter of the Organization of American States established the supranationality of human rights. No undue intervention can be found, therefore, in the disapproval expressed by one member of the violations of these rights by another member.

Third — The American republics are equally exposed to the dangers presented by the different forms of totalitarianism and tyranny, and not exclusively to communism. The grievous experience of Costa Rica which culminated in civil war in 1948, proved that the tyrannies called 'rightist' work hand in hand with the 'extreme left,' or international communism, to fight democracy and lawfulness.

The Costa Rican decision came at a time when the United States was already under criticism for its friendly attitude toward dictators, and when a new era of warmer relations with Argentina was being promoted. This situation made the United States' stand on communism and its views on Guatemala subject to more than passing scrutiny and wariness on the part of Latin American delegates at Caracas. Even before the meeting began the Guatemalan situation provided a crucial test for American foreign policy. The possibility of an embargo on Guatemalan coffee, of which the United States is the principal purchaser and which is the major source of income for Guatemala, was considered. The idea was rejected on the grounds that such an economic sanction would constitute a form of intervention. What to do about the communist activity in Guatemala faced the United States with a serious dilemma, for Guatemala lies within the perimeter of the Panama Canal defense zone as envisaged by American military leaders. No less concerned were Guatemala's neighbors, who saw in the importation of large quantities of arms direct and ominous threats to themselves.

In June, 1954, Colonel Castillo Armas raised a revolt against Arbenz, and in three weeks drove him into exile. Castillo Armas was elected president without opposition, and amity was quickly restored between Guatemala and the United States. Six months later Figueres, too, faced armed opposition, a rebellion of ex-president Picado, aided and abetted by Nicaragua and nurtured on Nicaraguan soil. The Costa Rican civil guard, for the country lacks a formal army, rose to the occasion, and the invaders were dispersed. Once more the Organization of American States was forced to deal with hostilities between Caribbean nations, and once more it could claim reasonable success, for its spokesman, Dr. Luis Quintanilla of Mexico, dissuaded Somoza from further aid to the rebels. But tensions remained alive in Central America, and the problem of establishing lasting peace was far from solved.

At the Caracas conference Secretary of State John Foster Dulles sponsored an anti-communist resolution warning international communism to keep hands off the Western Hemisphere. Only Guillermo Toriello, Guatemalan Foreign Minister, voted against the resolution, although Argentina and Mexico abstained from voting on it. The Guatemalan delegate refrained from voting on the Panamanian anti-discrimination resolution, since its preamble stated that racial discrimination not only was opposed to democratic doctrines, but promoted continuation of a climate favorable to communist propaganda.

Other Latin American delegates, less concerned than the United States about communism in Guatemala and the defense of the Panama Canal, enjoyed the spectacle of tiny Guatemala frustrating and irritating the powerful United States. Toriello won wide applause by attacking 'imperialism' and 'foreign monopolistic interests,' the favorite whipping boys of the governments intent on implementing economic nationalism by extending unwelcome governmental control over the national economies. The reception given Toriello's fulminations against the time-honored terms of 'big stick,' 'dollar diplomacy,' and 'monopoly' indicated that Latin America's conditioned response to these bugbears has not disappeared.

The anti-communist resolution which was passed condemns international communism as a threat to the peace of the Americas and provides for consultation among the American republics if one of them should come under the domination or control of the movement. The Guatemalan delegate countered by proposing prohibition of economic boycotts in the hemisphere, a proposal useful only for anti-United States propaganda.

Thus the role of the United States in the Caribbean is more difficult than ever. While ostensibly favoring democratic development, American spokesmen see the possibility of the spread of communism wherever dictatorial regimes are overthrown — the ensuing chaos would provide a favorable opportunity for a small, disciplined communist clique to gain a foothold in the government, as seems to have been the case in Guatemala. They often find the dictatorial regimes easy to deal with, and they have been charged with favoring these at the expense of democratic progress.

Economic assistance from the United States has been suggested by Latin Americans as the simplest and least involved means of bolstering the weak democratic regimes of the other republics, and at the same time providing an inducement to the dictators to make concessions to popular opinions. Economic assistance is badly needed by most of the countries of the Caribbean, and many American statesmen feel that it should be given on a basis of need and availability rather than for political purposes.

The economic nationalism which has swept the hemisphere since 1930 has made deep impressions on most of the Caribbean nations. Venezuela is striving to diversify her economy and end her heavy reliance on oil. The opening of iron mines promises an export commodity which may one day rival oil, but the basic problem of food production is still unsolved. The oil industry is controlled by foreign companies, and the production of iron ore has been undertaken by the major steel firms of the United States. The oil industry has not, as was once expected, promoted diversification, but has had the opposite effect. The agricultural interior has been abandoned by migrations of laborers to the oil fields. Dependence on foreign nations has greatly increased, for 95 per cent of the oil is exported, and its price is set by the world market. The growth of cities has meant a decline in agriculture and an increased dependence on imported foods.

Although her known oil reserves are extensive, Venezuela's overwhelming dependence on oil will leave the country in poor shape when they are exhausted. This future calamity lies in the background of the government's efforts at diversification and industrialization. During the war textiles, pharmaceuticals, chemicals, cement, and tires were produced in factories centered about the Federal District, but they are far from rivaling the oil industry as sources of national wealth.

Since the end of the war Venezuela has been the scene of an extensive project promoted by Nelson Rockefeller, one of the sponsors of the International Basic Economy Corporation. The main problem attacked was that of food production and distribution. The greatest successes were in the production and consumption of milk, which rose between 300 and 400 per cent, and in spreading the super-market idea. Most of the large-scale enterprises did not succeed.

In 1944 Venezuela established the Board of Development of National Production for the promotion of new economic enterprises. Its activities have been similar to the government agencies established elsewhere in Latin America for the same purpose.

Concentration of land ownership is still a vital problem for Venezuelan agriculture, and one which was attacked only half-heartedly by the government in 1938. It has been estimated that less than 1 per cent of the population owns more than half of the farm acreage. This condition in addition to the movement toward the coastal zone has heightened the problem of food production. In 1950 the junta finally reverted to the policy established earlier by Acción Democrática of opening the interior to foreign settlement. The junta has carried out its program under much closer supervision. It has organized agricultural colonies where immigrants can purchase land on liberal terms. Technicians and engineers are next to farmers in order of preference. One immigrant has already made a far-reaching contribution to the food problem. In 1948, Dr. Nacio Steinmetz, a Polish refugee, developed a black soybean far richer in protein than the ordinary black bean eaten by most Venezuelans, similar enough in flavor to be acceptable, and much cheaper to produce.

Colombia, too, has had serious political troubles since 1930, and her long enjoyment of peace and stability has been disrupted by bloody strife between liberals and conservatives. In 1930, unlike most of her neighbors, she established a liberal regime through electoral processes, and the liberals remained in power until 1946. During this period an extensive program of social legislation was passed in the interest of labor, and a vast extension of the educational system was achieved. The most articulate and implacable foe of the liberals throughout their ascendancy was Laureano Gómez, an arch-reactionary publisher who voiced the kind of Hispanicism and Catholicism which appealed to a segment of the population. Gómez lauded the Nazis and scourged the United States.

In 1946 the liberals split between the moderate, Gabriel Turbay, and the leftist, Jorge Eliécer Gaitán. The two liberal candidates polled a majority of the votes between them, but the conservative Mariano Ospina Pérez won a plurality. The liberals retained a majority in both houses, and Ospina gave them half of the cabinet posts.

During the inter-American conference at Bogotá in 1948 Gaitán was assassinated, and the city was badly damaged by several days of rioting. The liberals left the cabinet, and a period of uncontrollable violence followed in which thousands were killed. In 1949 Gómez won the presidency in an election which the liberals boycotted. Under Gómez the strife increased, and religious issues were fanned. Protestantism was associated in the minds of conservative Colombians with communism, and violent attacks were made on Protestant groups and their churches.

In June, 1953, army officers ousted Gómez, and General Rojas Pinilla was able to pacify the country by persuading the guerrilla bands to lay down their arms. This has been the major accomplishment of the military government. Late in 1953 the Rojas Pinilla regime startled the industrialists who had supported it by proposing to increase taxes sharply by raising the rate on incomes and on corporations, and by taxing formerly exempt dividends. At the same time *El Siglo*, the Gómez newspaper and most vociferous voice of arch-conservatism, was silenced. Even the liberals, who had suffered under the attacks of the Gómez paper for years, looked with misgivings on its suspension, for the movement toward press censorship, once started, would be difficult to check. In 1955 these fears were justified, for severe news censorship was decreed.

Traditionally Colombia has been a two-party country, with the military remaining largely aloof from political strife and factionalism. Now the army has become a political factor; officers hold high positions in the government and others are in training in public administration and economics. These activities have convinced many Colombians that the army is preparing for an extended stay in power. This prospect is not entirely unpleasant to some Colombians, who feel that the civil conflict between conservatives and liberals indicated that the two parties avoided the real issues and conducted their activities on a basis of tradition and emotion. An interval of military rule, they optimistically believe, will enable the political parties to produce sounder programs. They do not as yet see in the military government a genuine threat to Colombia's basic traditions of democracy.

Economic nationalism and its attendant urges have been strongly felt in Colombia despite the political upheavals. Thus far the textile industry has made the most noteworthy progress, and it supplies more than three-fourths of domestic requirements as well as providing exports to other Caribbean nations and Ecuador. An ample supply of coal is an important asset to the Colombian drive for industrialization. In 1946 Colombia, Venezuela, and Ecuador joined forces to organize the Grancolombian Merchant Fleet at the initiative of Colombia, and on her agreement to supply 60 per cent of the initial capital.

Diversification is less of a problem for Colombia than for any of the other countries within the Caribbean group, for her economy is already highly diversified. In addition to her textiles she produces oil, minerals, coffee, and sugar. Because of the configuration of the land, transportation is a critical problem. A vast network of airways makes passenger travel relatively easy, but freight must still rely on rivers and roads. Railroad and highway construction are still far behind actual needs.

Land ownership is less concentrated in Colombia than elsewhere in the Caribbean region, but the traditional independence of the small farmer is curtailed by dependence upon the coffee export market and by the government's efforts to stabilize the industry through national controls. These controls ordinarily favor the large planters at the expense of the small ones.

Like most of the Latin American nations Colombia organized a governmental agency for the promotion of industry, the Industrial Development Institute, which was created in 1940. It has since stimulated a variety of activities, including the manufacture of steel, iron, and tires, and the production of coal.

With a few minor exceptions Colombia's relations with her neighbors have been generally peaceful. In 1932 she neared hostilities with Peru over the seizure by Peruvians of the Amazon town of Leticia, which lay within the territory acknowledged as Colombian by Peru in 1922. The case was placed before the League of Nations; in 1934 Peru expressed regret and returned Leticia to Colombia. Another diplomatic controversy between the two countries occurred over Colombia's granting asylum to the aprista leader, Víctor Raúl Haya de la Torre, in her embassy in Lima. At the Caracas Conference of 1954 Peru finally agreed to grant him safe conduct from the country, and he departed for a refuge in Mexico.

Cuban political life since 1930 has been marked by progress toward representative democracy and social reform followed by retrenchment and re-establishment of strong man rule. In 1931 dictator Gerardo Machado y Morales suppressed a revolt against his tyranny, only to be expelled from the country two years later. Dr. Ramón Grau San Martín became provisional president, but the real power in Cuba lay with Fulgencio Batista, who favored labor and social legislation. Batista forced Grau out and installed Dr. Carlos Mendieta y Montúfur, who was no more successful in preserving order. In 1935 Mendieta resigned. In the election held the following year, Cuban women were allowed to vote for the first time.

Batista remained president-maker until 1939, when he was elected president. In 1944 he turned the presidency over to Grau San Martín, winner of the election, despite the fact that his own choice was Carlos Saladrigas. Grau's administration was beset by the problems of wartime dislocations and inflation. In 1948 his choice, Carlos Prío Socarrás, was elected.

In 1952 Batista toppled Prío from power and installed himself once more as Cuba's strong man. Although he was one of the candidates for the presidency in the election scheduled for June of that year, he learned that an army revolt would be staged whether or not he agreed to lead it. Batista accepted, and the revolt succeeded with little opposition. If the charges which have been made since against the regimes of his two predecessors are well founded, it appears that graft and corruption flourished almost unchecked.

Haiti and the Dominican Republic have had little cause for rejoicing in the years since 1930. American intervention in the former ended in 1934, and in the following year the government took over control of its finances once more. Sténio Vincent ruled the country from 1931 to 1941 by controlling the Haitian Guard, the constabulary trained by the American marines. Under Dumarsais Estimé, who was elected in 1946, Haiti made efforts at improving the shockingly poor living conditions of most of the people and at sweeping away economic and social privileges. Estimé pushed a road-building program, organized collective farms, and constructed model villages financed by the country's first income tax. In 1949 he was ousted by Colonel Paul Magloire because he sought re-election, and in the following year Magloire was elected president.

The Dominican Republic has been virtually the personal domain of Rafael Leonidas Trujillo Molina since 1930. By gaining control of the Dominican Guard he was able to achieve control of the country and to have himself re-elected at intervals except when he placed puppet presidents in office. His regime has not been entirely discreditable, for he has brought about improvements in agriculture, commerce, and education. Politically, however, his rule represents tyranny and severe repression. He and his personal friends, meanwhile, have become millionaires. Hundreds of Dominicans have taken refuge in exile, while others have simply disappeared. The exiles have been involved in the various attempts to invade the country since 1947.

Central America has not escaped the turmoil characteristic of the Caribbean region. Although all of the countries are small in area and population, there exist as many differences as similarities among them. Guatemala has the largest population and the highest percentage of Indians; El Salvador, smallest in area, is second in population. Nicaragua is greatest in territorial extent, followed by Honduras. Costa Rica is regarded as the most advanced, and Honduras as the most backward.

Political conditions in Central America have ever been turbulent, and the period since 1930 is no exception. In all but Panamá and Costa Rica strong men seized power in the 1930's and held it for years. In Guatemala, General Jorge Ubico ruled from 1930 until his overthrow in 1944. In 1931 Maximiliano Martínez established a virtual dictatorship in El Salvador which also endured until 1944, when a general strike defeated him. The year 1932 saw the rise of Honduran dictator General Tiburcio Carías Andino, who remained in power until he voluntarily stepped down in 1948. In 1937 General Anastasio Somoza became president of Nicaragua, and he has retained his control over the country ever since, although not always as president.

Costa Rica, 'the nation of school teachers,' has not been entirely free of domestic troubles during this period, but she has avoided the extremes to which her neighbors have gone. A powerful movement for reform began in 1940 under Dr. Rafael Calderón Guardia. In 1944 he was succeeded by Teodoro Picado Michalski, who encouraged communist control over labor organizations. In 1947 the moderates made a strenuous effort to recover control of the country, and nominated the well-known liberal publisher, Otilio Ulate, who won the election. Congress, however, declared the election void and arrested Ulate. It was then that Colonel José Figueres marched on the capital and overthrew the leftist Picado regime. In 1953 Figueres was elected to the presidency.

Panamá's independence and sovereignty were ostensibly enhanced in 1936 by treaties with the United States in which the guarantee of Panamanian independence was abandoned. At the outbreak of World War II President Arnulfo Arias was strongly anti-United States, but in 1941 he was ousted by pro-United States groups. The United States government was bitterly denounced for alleged complicity in the revolt, as undoubtedly will always be the case when regimes friendly to it come into power through rebellion. Since 1946 Police Chief José Remón has been the dominant figure in Panamá, and in 1952 he became president, only to fall by assassination in January, 1955.

Long a region of foreign economic penetration, particularly by capital from the United States, Central America today is in revolt against economic predominance of foreigners. While in the past there was much reason for complaint against the activities of some companies and individuals, in recent decades these concerns have displayed a more enlightened and co-operative attitude, and have made efforts to compensate for past errors. The anti-imperialist slogans retain their old force, however, and the legacy of ill-will remains alive. Foreign enterprises are under constant and increasing pressure, and the Central American governments are cheered to the attack by popular feeling elsewhere in Latin America.

In June, 1954, while the Guatemalan issue blazed, a Society of Friends of Guatemala was organized in Mexico. It charged that the communist issue was merely a smokescreen to cover up action in behalf of American companies. The right wing sinarquistas of Mexico accused the United States of sending arms to Guatemala's neighbors 'under the pretext of protecting a democracy that does not exist and a security that is not menaced and in reality for defending the illegitimate interests of North American monopolies that have robbed the riches of brother peoples.' Other Mexicans, however, stoutly defended the stand of the United States. In Chile, demonstrators burned the American flag, which drew a prompt apology from President Carlos Ibáñez. Few Latin Americans see or admit a genuine concern of the United States over the defense of the Panama Canal.

Guatemala's neighbors, El Salvador, Honduras, and Nicaragua, seem in no apparent danger of communism. Powerful oligarchic minorities exercise control without rivalry from the majority of the people in Honduras, and to some extent in Nicaragua, where Somoza has made the nation his personal and family patrimony to a marked degree. In El Salvador, a revolutionary movement overthrew the corrupt regime of Castañeda Castro in 1948, and a group of young and able leaders came to power bent on economic and social reform and national development. A new constitution was adopted in 1950, and Oscar Osorio was elected president under it in one of the most honest elections ever held in the country. Great efforts have been exerted to strengthen the economy and improve the status of the lower classes. Housing projects have been erected on a large scale and in widely separated sections of the country. Public water systems have been constructed in many communities, and a vast hydro-electric dam erected on the Río Lempa to double the power resources of the nation. At the same time, great attention has been focused on reorganizing and improving the administrative structure of the government.

The regime has been alert to the threat of communism and has chosen a course of social and economic action as the best means of safeguarding its people from the pernicious influences emanating from Moscow and, until recently, from Guatemala City. It remains to be seen whether the seemingly popular administration of Osorio can move fast enough and with sufficient self-assurance to satisfy the demands of both left and right and keep the small nation on an even political keel. The presidential election of 1956 will provide a real test, for Osorio cannot constitutionally succeed himself in office. Much depends on the manner in which power is transferred to his successor and who that successor is.

A peaceful and satisfactory solution to the political problems of the Caribbean region does not appear close at hand. Many subsidiary problems must be solved first, problems concerning public health, education, a more equitable distribution of land, and economic opportunity for all classes. Some of these problems are under consideration at present, and even in the case of Guatemala, the proposed solutions are primarily nativist in origin. Since a majority of the peoples of the Caribbean depend upon agriculture for a livelihood, increased agricultural productivity promises the most rapid and widespread benefits.

The effectiveness of the national markets of the Caribbean countries to provide for expanded manufacturing is closely related to the levels of living. Even a mild improvement brought about through increased agricultural productivity would make itself felt in increased demand for manufactures. But for most of the Caribbean nations the agrarian reforms necessary before such an increase can be achieved are yet to take place.

The most unique situation of any of the former Spanish colonies in the Caribbean is that of Puerto Rico. In July, 1952, the former American territory became a 'free' commonwealth associated with the United States. Despite the clamor raised against colonialism in other parts of the Caribbean, Puerto Rico chose to remain a close relative of the United States when granted the right to manage her own affairs. In Governor Luis Muñoz Marín the island commonwealth boasts one of the most astute administrators in the Caribbean. Under his regime Puerto Rico has industrialized rapidly, and the island's economic aspect has changed remarkably in the past decade.

When asked why Puerto Rico chose to remain associated with the United States Muñoz Marín replied: 'We would like to be the olive in the martini. In a martini . . . Puerto Rico cannot be the gin. There is too much. The United States is the gin. There is much less vermouth, but even this amount we cannot be. I like a drop of bitters in my martini, but we do not want to be the bitters. It is lost, swallowed up in the gin and the vermouth.

'We must be in this cocktail, however, if Puerto Rico is to survive and prosper. What is there left to be? In my martini, the olive. We want to be the olive — a sufficiently small ingredient in the martini, an ingredient improved by its presence there, but an ingredient that is of value because of its individuality, its own unique contribution.'

Puerto Rico is much changed from its days of dependence upon the production of sugar. The industry, ingenuity, and enthusiasm of its businessmen and statesmen is one of the astonishments of the modern Caribbean area. There is another aspect to the flowering of Puerto Rico, and one deserving of mention in connection with the Caribbean. The free associated state of Puerto Rico is the most striking example of the sincerity of United States' intentions in the Western Hemisphere concerning the free development of its peoples.

XXXVIII

Brazil: Destiny Not Quite Manifest

> Concession of amnesty, moral and physical health, rooting
> out . . . the agents of corruption . . . a systematic campaign
> of social welfare and health education, intensive diffusion of
> public education . . . , intensification of production by diversi-
> fication of agriculture and the adoption of a policy of inter-
> national economic cooperation, the creation of a Ministry of
> Labor charged with the supervision of social questions and
> the care of urban and rural workers, the promotion without
> violence of the progressive extinction of large landholdings . . .

GETÚLIO D. VARGAS, 1930 *

THE year 1930 marked a turning point in Brazilian history as the change from empire to republic. Politically, the easy-going liberalism and federalism of the Old Republic succumbed to a powerful trend toward central-ism and executive domination. Economically, the drive for diversi-fication and industrialization almost swept coffee from its lofty perch, as mining and manufacturing made tremendous gains. So-cially the long-neglected laboring classes at last had a champion to hand them much-needed and overdue favors which the parliamen-tarians of the earlier regime had never gotten around to granting. A drive to open the empty Brazilian West began, and the settle-ment of the Amazon valley became a government project.

The Brazilians themselves regard many of these changes with mixed feelings, for not all of the developments could clearly be

---

* *Brazil*, L. F. Hill, ed., University of California Press, Berkeley, 1947, p. 109.

marked as gains in the light of longstanding aspirations for truly democratic and representative government. Advances in certain directions meant retreat in others; the balance sheet does not appear the same to all Brazilians. Those who hold to the positivist motto of 'Order and Progress' can be delighted with the nation's orderly accomplishments. Those who hold human values above all others find some of the changes intolerable.

In 1930 Getúlio D. Vargas, governor of the southern pastoral state of Rio Grande do Sul, came into power by revolt during the world-wide economic crisis. As leader of the Liberal Alliance against the candidacy of Júlio Prestes of São Paulo, he saw the government of Wáshington Luís declare Prestes the winner of the election. His followers refused to accept the government's statement. Oswaldo Aranha, later to become a distinguished figure in international affairs, organized the rebellion. The entire affair took place within the month of October, and Wáshington Luís was easily swept from office.

Vargas immediately set about centralizing his authority by replacing state officials with interventors responsible only to himself. Without regularizing his regime or returning to constitutional rule, he began energetically to accomplish the objectives of the Liberal Alliance. He created a Ministry of Labor and reorganized that of Education and Health. Illiteracy was estimated as high as eighty per cent, and was obviously a matter in need of attention.

The Brazilians, long accustomed to constitutional rule, chafed under the provisional regime, and they became insistent in their demands that a constituent convention be called. In 1932 the paulistas, who had been deprived of the presidency, revolted. When the uprising had been quelled Vargas yielded to the pressure, and called for election of delegates to a constitutional convention in 1933. The product of the assembly's labors, a series of compromises between federalism and centralism, was adopted in the following year. The delegates were authorized to elect the president, and Vargas was their choice. He was dissatisfied with the constitution, and he prepared to replace it with one of his own creation.

His opportunity came in 1937, when the time arrived for the

presidential election. The constitution prohibited re-election, and Vargas systematically removed all of the candidates except Plínio Salgado, leader of the fascist Integralista organization. The fascists of Europe rejoiced too soon, for before the election was held Vargas abolished all political parties, canceled the election, and replaced the constitution of 1934 with one to his liking. The incubation period was over, and the *Estado Novo* or New State was abruptly hatched.

The new regime accentuated the trend toward executive domination by giving vast powers to the president and reducing those of the states. Federalism retreated before the principles of order, unity, and national defense imposed by the president. The new constitution, which was never officially promulgated, contained the ideals of the New State. Private property and private initiative were still recognized, but the government's right to interfere was greatly enlarged. A progressive labor policy was implied, but a policy which would be decided upon by the government without the aid of labor itself.

After 1937 Vargas ruled as a benevolent dictator and legislated by decree. The last article of the constitution declared that the document would enter into force after a national plebiscite, and such a plebiscite was never ordered. The preceding article stated that 'In the entire country the state of national emergency is declared.' During a state of emergency the constitution was suspended. Earlier articles dealt with such a condition. Since the declaration of a national emergency was part of the constitution, only an amendment could remove it. But a constitutional amendment required action by the legislative body envisaged by the constitution, and elections could not be held until after the plebiscite. The crucial article, and the actual constitution under which Vargas governed Brazil, was No. 180, which declared: 'Until the National Parliament meets, the President of the Republic shall be empowered to issue decrees on all matters of legislation for the Union.'

The socio-economic program outlined by other articles of the constitution, however, represented the goals of the administration, and the government lived up to its program. With the executive and legislative branches fused by Article 180 of the constitution Vargas was able to issue a multitude of decrees. One of his first efforts was to create a competent corps of civil servants.

The integralistas, bitterly disappointed at having the prize snatched from their outstretched hands, attempted to assassinate Vargas in 1938. The attempt failed, and Vargas learned that the German ambassador was implicated in the plot. The integralistas were crushed in accordance with his idea of a non-party state, and the German ambassador was handed his passport. Vargas emerged from the crisis more securely in power than before.

From this time until 1945 Vargas ruled Brazil without effective rivals though not without opposition. His regime worked smoothly, and the ever-present force was subtly veiled. Vargas was an astute and undoctrinaire politician, and a capable administrator. He kept opposition in check, and won the support of many Brazilians by his program for developing transportation, for wider education of the mass of people, for political unity on a national scale, and for his labor policies. In these goals he was favored even by those who loathed his scorn for democracy, civil liberties, and representative government.

The threat of war in Europe led Vargas to expand and modernize Brazilian military forces, particularly the air arm, which was placed under the new Ministry of Aëronautics. German and Italian commercial air lines were eventually expropriated by the government, and operated by Brazilian personnel. As Brazil's military strength grew, Argentina's envy and concern also mounted.

It was in industrial development, however, that the country made its most astonishing gains. Before the New State, industry provided only about thirty per cent of Brazilian production, but by the end of the Vargas administration the value of industrial products surpassed that of agriculture, and the country no longer relied on foreign sources for most of its consumer goods.

Most of the wartime industrial activity was centered in São Paulo and the Federal District. The São Paulo textile industry was particularly stimulated by the war, and Brazil emerged as one of the leading producers of cotton goods, with an export market in South America and South Africa. Her production of silk and other fabrics has also risen.

In São Paulo many other industries have been developed and most of them, like textile production, are favored by the availability of locally produced raw materials. All of these were not stimulated by the war, for many were actually retarded by the difficulty in acquiring machinery and by the shortage of shipping space. Unless the industries were essential to the war effort of the Allies they were unable to obtain allocations of equipment and raw materials necessary for rapid expansion. Much of the wartime development was limited to special projects such as the Volta Redonda steel plant, cement producing companies, and the national airplane-motor factory. By the end of the war nearly all Brazilian industries faced a critical problem of replacing outdated or worn-out machinery.

The development of steel production was one of the most noteworthy accomplishments during the period of wartime scarcity. Iron and steel were in great demand, and the metallurgical companies took on many new activities in the processing of crude metals. New blast furnaces and rolling mills were constructed, and by 1945 production approached domestic demands for certain types of crude and partly processed iron.

In 1941 the government inaugurated the *Companhia Siderúrgica Nacional*, the National Steel Company, which began constructing mills at Volta Redonda on the Paraíba river in the state of Rio de Janeiro, within three hundred miles of the fabulously rich iron deposits of Itabira in Minas Gerais. By 1946 the mills were producing.

The aircraft industry, too, was largely war-inspired. The production of copper, aluminum, cement, and glass was accelerated by wartime needs and shortages. The mining of strategic minerals such as manganese and chromite was also speeded up by the military requirements of the United States.

The government's role in planning the Brazilian economy was carried out through a co-ordinator of economic mobilization rather than by means of a governmental development corporation as was the practice in most of the other Latin American countries. A Ministry of Production was established to maintain control of industry and labor. Various nationalistic devices were employed to avoid the experiences of other nations which had encouraged foreign economic activities without regard to the promotion of domestic enterprise.

Measures restricting foreign participation in the Brazilian economy were introduced into the constitutions of 1934 and 1937. Foreigners were required to obtain specific authorization from the government to establish corporations or public utility companies unless a majority of the officials were Brazilian. Deposit banks and insurance companies could not be opened unless all of the shares were owned by Brazilians. Foreigners were excluded from newspaper and magazine publishing, and from liberal professions not guaranteed by treaty. Nor could foreigners constitute more than a third of the employees or receive more than a third of the wages in any of a number of specified enterprises unless the government acknowledged a shortage of suitable native labor.

The government went far in favoring industrialization, by granting exemption from customs duties for equipment and raw materials and by reducing tax rates. It also required the use of certain percentages of domestic products. A fairly high tariff has given protection to a number of activities. These restrictions have undoubtedly discouraged private capital from going to Brazil, but the government preferred to rely on more easily controlled official loans.

The lack of a domestic petroleum industry and the necessity of relying on imported oil have been one of the major obstacles to Brazilian industrialization. In 1938 Vargas set up the National Petroleum Council, and it began geological surveys, securing technical aid from American oil companies. The constitution provided that oil was national property. To obtain the oil needed from abroad until domestic production might fulfill the needs, the government negotiated a treaty with Bolivia, but it was necessary to construct a railroad connecting Santa Cruz de la Sierra in Bolivia with Corumbá in Brazil. In 1952 Brazil spent some $230,-

000,000 on oil imports, about a fifth of what was earned by coffee exports.

The development of hydroelectric power in various Brazilian rivers was encouraged by Vargas and carried on by his successor, General Eurico Dutra. The biggest project undertaken was at the Paulo Afonso falls on the Rio São Francisco, begun in 1949 and ready to produce power in 1953. It doubled the supply for the states of Pernambuco, Alagoas, Paraíba, Sergipe, and Bahia.

It is not necessary to catalog all of the industrial development achieved by Brazil in the fifteen years of the Vargas era. There can be no doubt that the development was phenomenally rapid. Coupled with it was a similar effort to bring about agricultural diversification and to reduce the dependence upon coffee. The government has undertaken the extension of cultivation in the hinterland along the entire coast, and in the Amazon valley. Since the end of the war a program of Japanese colonization in the Amazon has been inaugurated, with the idea of creating a small farming population which will produce rubber, jute, and other tropical products.

Vargas, the super-nationalist from the ultra-provincial state of Rio Grande do Sul, had virtually to learn about foreign affairs after driving Wáshington Luís from office. He displayed an interest and astuteness in promoting foreign friendship and respect for Brazil, and his efforts in this direction were ably conducted by Oswaldo Aranha. Aranha won wide acclaim in international circles, and supported Vargas' cause with unusual skill. In 1933 President Justo of Argentina paid an official visit to Brazil. In the following year Vargas returned the honor, at the same time calling on President Gabriel Terra of Uruguay.

In 1935 Vargas had sent Aranha as ambassador to the United States, and the friendly relations between the two countries were greatly strengthened by his presence. Aranha was able to dispel much of the suspicion current in the United States that Vargas leaned toward the Axis, and to convince American statesmen that Brazil was firmly devoted to the principle of American solidarity. The air was cleared further when Franklin D. Roosevelt visited

Vargas in Rio de Janeiro in 1936. After Vargas had decided to support the Allied cause he was able to point to his crushing of the integralistas as evidence of anti-fascist activity at a time when the major democracies were thinking in terms of appeasement.

As the war in Europe became imminent Vargas was in a dilemma as to which side might be expected to win. His attitude toward the contenders seems to have been based solely on this consideration, although he was suspected of inclining toward the Axis. After Italy attacked France in 1940 Vargas declared that the future belonged to 'vigorous young peoples,' and that only 'stubborn liberals' resisted the march away from 'decadent systems.' Friends of Brazil in the United States were shocked and dismayed, and it was not easy for his supporters to rationalize away the unfavorable impression he created. But the United States was determined to remain on friendly terms with Brazil, and the speech was forgotten.

After the war in Europe broke out there was never any doubt as to the sympathy of the majority of Brazilians for the Allies, though Vargas himself remained uncommitted and undecided. He did not lead his country into the war against the Axis; his decision happened to be in accord with public opinion. Once he had decided on the course to pursue, however, he followed it with his customary vigor and thoroughness. In almost all of his decisions with regard to foreign affairs and international commitments Vargas displayed far greater sagacity and vision than did his contemporaries in Buenos Aires. Thanks to Vargas or his advisers Brazil left Argentina far behind in the diplomatic race. She gained enormous prestige as well as crucial military and economic assistance by her course, while Argentina steadily lost ground. Brazil's position in Latin America and among the small nations of the world benefited tremendously because of her diplomatic course during and after the war.

This is one side of the Vargas ledger. The other side is far less favorable, especially from the standpoint of political progress and civil liberties. Freedom of the press, which had been slowly circumscribed after 1930, disappeared in 1937. The D.I.P., Department of Press and Propaganda, was created in 1939, and it was housed in the building formerly used by the then defunct Chamber of Deputies. Press censorship worked smoothly in Brazil, but behind the pleasant façade was the ugly threat of force. The D.I.P. controlled newsprint supplies, and censorship was imposed *ex post facto*. Newspapers were ostensibly free to print what the editors wished, but if their columns displeased government officials, their supplies were cut off. Foreign newsmen were given a champagne-and-dancing-girls treatment which generally succeeded in giving everything they saw a pleasant aspect. Those who could not see the situation as the government wished them to were soon on their way home.

Censorship of the press was generally handled with sufficient care and subtlety to avoid scandalizing Brazil's friends abroad. The threat of cutting off newsprint was much more effective and less noticeable than actually passing on each copy before it was printed. Perón of Argentina acknowledged the success of this practice by adopting it himself in 1946. But even in 1944, when Americans were greatly concerned over the attacks on Argentina's famous dailies, *La Prensa* and *La Nación*, no voice was raised in protest against the loss of freedom by the press of Brazil. This difference in attitude toward similar events in Brazil and Argentina caused Perón to comment: 'Every time we are called fascists by the American press, we look to the northern neighbor and smile.'

When the Brazilian government decided to enter the publishing field itself, the better to make its views appear in a favorable light, it confiscated O *Estado de São Paulo*, one of the most excellent papers of Latin America. The paper belonged to a family bitterly opposed to Vargas. The confiscation was justified on the grounds that an arms cache had been discovered in the building; apparently the arms were placed there by government agents for the police to find.

The use of secret police and of a Tribunal of National Security which served as a 'star chamber' and could be relied on to find political opponents guilty, was a method which many Brazilians found intolerable. But so skillfully did Vargas keep the opposition scattered and helpless that he had nothing to fear from it.

As a result the Brazilian bureaucracy became virtually a closed corporation, and there was no means of checking on the uses made of public funds. Lack of a healthy opposition encouraged graft and waste, though Vargas himself had no patience or sympathy with such activities. No Brazilian was permitted to rise to a position of power and popularity from which he might successfully challenge Vargas' rule. All potential rivals, including Oswaldo Aranha and João Alberto Lins de Barros, were kept in check.

The absence of elections and the excessive centralism of the Vargas regime stifled the embryonic democracy of the Old Republic. The only forms of democracy in which Vargas was purportedly interested were economic and social, but the constitution of 1937 nevertheless denied labor the right to strike. One of the unfortunate consequences of the suppression of opposition and the control of public opinion exercised by the government was that many highly qualified men became reluctant to take part in public service.

Toward the close of the war the pressure on Vargas to restore some semblance of representative government and democracy became strong, for a Brazilian expeditionary force was taking part in the European campaigns along with the Allied armies. In March, 1945, Vargas yielded; he restored freedom of the press and released political prisoners, including the communist leader, Luís Carlos Prestes. Plínio Salgado, exiled integralista champion, was permitted to return from Portugal. Political parties were allowed to organize once more, and a presidential election was scheduled.

Before the election was held doubts as to Vargas' willingness to surrender his power aroused fear and suspicion in the army. A delegation of high-ranking officers called on him and suggested that he return to his native Rio Grande do Sul. Vargas complied. Various explanations have been suggested as to the army's motives. One was that Vargas was planning to entrench himself with the aid of Prestes and the communists, and his ousting, therefore, was aimed primarily at the latter. There is another view which holds to the belief that the army was anxious to restore its influence in the government and Vargas' presence constituted a serious obstacle. At any rate he resigned in favor of Chief Justice of the

Supreme Court José Linhares, who conducted the government during the election.

General Eurico Dutra won the election, Brazil's first in more than a decade, and the first in which the extended suffrage incorporated in the constitution of 1934 was employed. Women voted for the first time. Dutra won a resounding triumph, and took office in January, 1946. Before the end of the year a new constitution had been promulgated. It preserved the social-democratic character of its predecessor of 1934, devoted much space to the rights of labor, and returned to the federalism of earlier days.

The communists, despite their long suppression, made a surprising recovery in the election, and Prestes won a seat in the senate. In 1948, however, the party was outlawed, and Prestes and others were expelled from the national legislature, to go into hiding once more.

In general President Dutra continued the policies of economic nationalism and promotion of industrialization that had been fundamental to the Vargas administration. The army's influence was restored, but the army did nothing to check the growth of industry and trade. New projects were undertaken or encouraged by the government, such as the vast flood control and hydroelectric program in the Rio São Francisco valley. In the last year of Vargas' rule the Ford Motor Company had turned over its holdings in the Amazon valley to the Brazilian government. In 1947 Brazil joined Peru, Colombia, Venezuela, Bolivia, and Ecuador in organizing the Hylean Institute for developing the resources of the enormous Amazon region.

In 1951 Vargas was returned to the presidency, as the candidate of the Labor party. His economic policies continued the trends he fostered earlier. In addition the government made a full-scale effort to integrate the Amazon region into the national economy. For nearly ten years a consitutional provision assigned 3 per cent of total federal, provincial, and municipal revenues to Amazonian development, but little had been done to put the provision into effect. The budget of 1954 included an appropriation of about twenty-five million dollars for use in the Amazon region. About a third of it was devoted to a program of agricultural, industrial, and transportation improvements. The first goal of the government was to stimulate food production to the point that the region would be self-sufficient in this respect. An intensive research program was also in progress. Japanese farmers already produced enough jute to supply the Brazilian market, and other families were brought from Japan for the purpose of developing rice cultivation on a similar scale.

Brazilian industrial output doubled in the decade after 1945, but the rapid and unequal growth raised many problems. In June, 1953, Oswaldo Aranha was named to the post of Minister of Finance, and a few months later he announced a program of economic reforms aimed at restoring economic stability and bringing about a better balance. His plans included tariff revision, a new national tax code, and consolidation of the public debt. Inflation was the key concern.

One of the Brazilian methods for improving the productivity and skill of laborers was a national program for training apprentices in free schools. By 1947 sixty different courses were available in the state of São Paulo, including textiles, woodworking, and masonry. The industrial Social Service, created in 1946, carried the program a step farther by educating workers socially with a view to improving their general well-being. By 1950 more than a million men were receiving the benefits of these programs.

In the spring of 1953 a vast, new improvement program for Brazil, financed in part by foreign loans, was under way. The aid was administered by the Joint United States–Brazil Economic Development Commission, which functioned as part of the United States' Point Four program of technical assistance. A five year plan for speeding up Brazil's economic maturity was laid down, and it was expected to require some four hundred million dollars' worth of foreign credits and a larger sum supplied by Brazil. Among the many projects approved were railway rehabilitation, installation of new power plants and expansion of others, purchases of agricultural machinery, and construction of port facilities. A subsidiary activity of the commission was arranging scholarships for

Brazilian students in American universities to provide training in transportation, economics, education, health, agriculture, and public administration.

The long-range aims of the program were to improve basic services such as transportation, electric power, and port facilities, to increase exports and to stimulate production to replace imports, and to encourage the production of capital goods.

In making the difficult transition from a basically agricultural nation to an industrial one Brazil has risen well to the front of other Latin American countries. Not all of her problems have been solved, for she is still troubled by the shortage of foreign exchange, by excess of imports over exports, and by a residue of commercial debts abroad. Inflation, too, is still a serious problem. The production of electrical power is far below needs, and the transportation system is inadequate. But the advances made since 1930, and especially since the end of the war, are extraordinary. Brazil created the greatest steel, textile, and rubber industries in South America. Although cement production was vastly expanded it still could not keep up with the heavy demands caused by the thriving construction business. Since the war the national income nearly doubled, as has the number of factories and of men employed by industry.

The Volta Redonda steel plant has steadily increased its capacity and its output, but the nation's demands also grew. It was organized on a mixed company basis typical of much of Brazilian industrial expansion. The government owns a majority of the common stock, with states, municipalities, and private investors owning the remainder. The company has been a financial success from the start, but only by reason of its operation in a protected market. A new loan from the Export-Import Bank permitted an expansion of facilities to double steel production, and a further expansion was planned which will bring production to the level of domestic needs. Coal is still one of the principal problems of the steel industry, for about half of that used must be imported. A recently discovered deposit of high-grade coal in Paraná raised hopes that all coal requirements may soon be met by domestic producers.

The assembly of motor vehicles from Europe and the United States has become an important activity in Brazil — more than 250 small firms produce automotive parts and accessories. The tire industry was greatly stimulated by the increase in the number of automobiles and trucks in use, and since 1950 Brazil has imported natural rubber. Although a million and a half tires were produced in 1951 they did not satisfy the demand. To meet the increased needs for rubber the government has encouraged rubber producers in the Amazon valley, and has established plantations in São Paulo and Bahia.

As the use of trucks in the transportation system and of passenger cars has become more widespread, the building of highways has taken on added significance. In 1946 Brazil began a large-scale road-building program; since then more miles of road have been laid than existed previously in the entire country. A national plan was followed in the laying out of thoroughfares, and a fund was created for the purpose by a single federal tax on fuel and lubricating oils. Despite the rapid progress made in road-building the program must go on for years before the country's needs can be met. In 1953 there were only some 45,000 miles of surfaced roads, and more than 70 per cent of these were concentrated in the eastern and southern coastal region, primarily in São Paulo and Rio de Janeiro. To assist Brazil in meeting the need for more and better roads in other parts of the country, the Joint Commission has drawn up plans for a tremendous road-building program that will require a large outlay.

The development of the petroleum industry has been placed under a mixed company, Petrobras, of which the government is the main shareholder, and which enjoys a monopoly in prospecting and drilling for oil. Foreign companies are still excluded, although some government officials fear that the cost of importing oil will become an overwhelming burden before Petrobras can discover and develop enough fields to meet the country's requirements.

The extraordinary progress of industrialization in Brazil has tended to obscure the fact that the country is still basically agricultural. More than sixty per cent of the population depends on farming for a livelihood, and coffee is still the most important cash crop. Brazil produces about one-half of the world's supply, and coffee constitutes nearly three-fourths of the value of Brazilian exports. Over half of the exported coffee goes to the United States.

The Brazilian government has followed a policy of establishing institutes for each of its principal agricultural commodities. Its purpose is to promote production and consumption, and to control prices and marketing policies with a view to lessening the harmful fluctuations which have occurred in the past.

Brazil's hopes for developing an atomic energy program are based on the huge cyclotron constructed at the new university city created on nine small islands in Guanabara Bay, Rio de Janeiro. While the cyclotron's completion was awaited Brazil trained a force of scientists in nuclear research.

Since the re-election of Vargas following Dutra's administration, organized labor has made new gains with the support and favor of the government. The number of unions and of union members has increased rapidly. Vargas, the candidate of the Labor party, stated his aim as the 'cordial and harmonious co-operation between capital and labor on a basis of equality.' The Ministry of Labor still exercises a powerful control over the unions, but this control appears to be in its last stages. However that may be, congress granted unions the right to affiliate with international labor organizations.

According to Brazilian law labor disputes must be taken to special labor courts, and these bodies have recently upheld claims for pay raises of 40 per cent over 1950 levels to meet the rise in cost of living. Labor laws also uphold the principle of job security, vacations with pay, social service benefits, medical and dental care, disability pay, and old age pensions. Minimum wages have been established for different regions, and the law requires pay for the seventh day after six days of work. The eight hour day is mandatory, and a code of safety regulations is in force in the factories.

The principal problem of labor in recent years has been the high cost of living caused by inflationary trends. Unemployment is not presently a problem, for there is still a greater demand for skilled labor than can be met, and there is a shortage of farm labor.

Railroad transportation remains a vital need, for most of the existing 23,000 miles of track were laid to bring raw materials to the ports, and consequently are concentrated in the coastal area. The first three projects begun by the Joint Commission were concerned with the railroad problem. The need of rehabilitating present lines was so great that the Commission placed that task ahead of construction of new ones. In addition to the repairs and purchases of new equipment, branch lines are being extended. The Northwest of Brazil Railroad was extended from Pôrto Esperança to Corumbá in western Mato Grosso, which gave Brazil a trunk line to the Bolivian border and a connection with the Brazil-Bolivia Railroad. This series of railroads links the Brazilian port of Santos with the Chilean port of Arica on the Pacific.

An oil refinery was built at Corumbá to refine crude oil from the Bolivian fields of Santa Cruz. The Corumbá plant was intended primarily to serve the undeveloped region of Mato Grosso, which figured prominently in plans for increasing food production. One of the encouraging signs of progress to Brazilians was the fact that their own industry was able to make important contributions toward providing the equipment and materials needed for railroad rehabilitation. The freight car building firms, for example, were able to turn out 500 cars a month and, with plate produced at Volta Redonda, to make tank cars, wheels, and other rolling stock.

Along with road and railroad construction Brazil developed an extensive system of domestic and international air lines that helped to link the widely scattered cities more closely, and gave Brazilians easy access to the major nations of the world. Since 1942, with the help of government subsidies, the air lines have increased by eight times the mileage served.

One of the most astonishing developments in Brazil since 1930 has been the growth of the city and state of São Paulo. The city is now the third largest in South America and the commercial center of Brazil. The state of São Paulo leads the nation in both industry and agriculture, produces about half of the national wealth, and is the source of about half of the exports. Paulistas also pay nearly half of the income taxes collected by the government. It is not surprising that they regard their accomplishments with considerable pride.

The construction business has grown enormously because of the large number of people moving into the industrial cities. Brazilian architects have won world-wide acclaim for their pioneering in architectural design, particularly with regard to office buildings and apartment houses. There has been a corresponding boom in real estate, for land is still regarded by many Brazilians as the safest investment, and real estate profits enjoy lower tax rates than those of industry. The annual investment in construction rose to more than twice the amount devoted to agriculture.

Agricultural expansion, nevertheless, continued. The planting of coffee trees in the frontier state of Paraná caused a spectacularly rapid filling up of that once empty state. Immigration from within Brazil and from foreign countries increased its population by more than seventy per cent in ten years. Its coffee production rose at a similar rate, from two per cent of Brazil's total crop in 1930 to one-quarter in 1955. With new coffee trees being planted at the rate of twenty-five million a year, Paraná was expected to surpass São Paulo in coffee production before 1960.

Mechanization in agriculture has lately been introduced on a small scale in Brazil, particularly in the coffee areas of São Paulo and Paraná. The program is under the Agricultural Mechanization Enterprise, E.M.A. Part of the task at present is clearing new lands for use by coffee planters. E.M.A. began as a joint Brazil–United States project, but today it is entirely Brazilian. Sementes Agroceres, S.A. or S.A.S.A., is a similar organization for producing better grades of seeds and livestock. Progress has been made especially in the development of hybrid corn for various regions, and in some cases production has been increased by as much as 50 per cent.

Financial troubles continued to plague the government, particularly inflation and declining value of the cruzeiro. In August,

1954, the currency was indirectly devaluated by a decree permitting exporters to exchange 20 per cent of their foreign currency earnings at the free market rate rather than surrendering them to the Bank of Brazil at the official buying rate. The policy of granting bonuses to exporters, instituted by Oswaldo Aranha in 1953, remained in effect. The decision to modify the system was caused by the sharp increase in the issuance of paper money, which lowered the gold reserve for each cruzeiro, and by the falling off of coffee sales at the minimum price fixed by the government.

A political crisis stirred up by the politically involved assassination of an Air Force major was another factor in the general unrest which enveloped Brazil in 1954. Early in August demands for the resignation of Vargas were followed by a drop in the value of the free market cruzeiro.

The events leading to the termination of the Vargas regime grew out of charges of corruption on the part of government officials, which were made in particular by Carlos Lacerda, editor of the *Tribuna da Imprensa* and Brazil's most articulate spokesman against dictatorship, corruption, censorship and manipulation of the press. On August 5, 1954, an attempt to assassinate him failed, but the Air Force major accompanying him was killed. The attack was quickly traced to the president's personal guard, although Vargas himself was not involved. He disbanded the guard while the Air Force spearheaded the capture of the main suspects. Rumors that Vargas planned to declare a state of siege heightened the tension, and mobs roamed the streets demanding his resignation.

Vargas categorically rejected demands for his resignation, while attempts were made to reach a solution to the impasse. Behind the opposition, which ultimately united the Army, Air Force, and Navy against him, were financial troubles, scandals among high officials, and the contention that the government did not provide sufficient money for the military. In June the Chamber of Deputies had made a token gesture toward impeaching the president, but the move was designed primarily to provide political propaganda for the forthcoming congressional elections.

On August 23 the opposition to Vargas reached a crescendo, and while crowds thronged the streets, overturning and burning automobiles, the final effort was made to satisfy the opposition. By this time, however, Army officers had been persuaded to join the Air Force in demanding the president's resignation, and this move left Vargas no recourse but to submit. After a stormy all night session he conceded defeat, and in the early morning of August 24, retired to his room in Catete Palace and took his own life.

Vice-President João Café Filho succeeded to the presidency in a day of widespread rioting and anti-United States demonstrations which caused damage to property amounting to millions of dollars. The outbursts against the United States were brought about because of the intensity of emotions aroused by the dramatic death of Vargas, his alleged suicide note, and quick action on the part of communist leaders to take advantage of the opportunity.

Not long after the death of Vargas two suicide notes appeared, one brief and in his own handwriting. The other, a long typewritten polemic denouncing 'international groups' as the cause of Brazil's troubles, was undoubtedly responsible for much of the rioting which followed. The authorship of this letter, however, was not at once satisfactorily established, and there was some evidence, such as grammatical errors, and the failure to excoriate domestic enemies, which suggested that the letter had been planted. There is no doubt that the letter served only the interests of those who would undermine Brazilian–United States relations; its effectiveness was demonstrated by the violent assaults on American consulates and private property.

João Café Filho began at once to form a coalition cabinet in hopes of quickly dissolving the political stresses and strains which had made the last days of Vargas so tumultuous. The towering economic problems remained to plague him, and their solution was made no easier by the bitter factional strife. Oswaldo Aranha, finance minister under Vargas, resigned, to be replaced by Eugenio Gudin. The post of finance minister was the most difficult to fill.

The Brazilian Labor party, which Vargas had led, soon abandoned the coalition with Café Filho's Social Progessive party which had won the presidency for Vargas. It declared its 'absolute independence' of the government, and restrained its members from accepting cabinet posts. With only his own party enthusiastically supporting him, Café Filho's following in the congress was not robust. At the same time another split raised the specter of continued strife and dissension, for military leaders became sharply divided in their stand, some voicing strong dissatisfaction over the action taken against Vargas. The legacy of bitterness and recrimination made Café Filho's undertaking unpromising. He was soon incapacitated by ill health. In the election of October, 1955, the mineiro, Juscelino Kubitschek de Oliveira, won. Despite talk of a coup to prevent his taking office, he was inaugurated on January 31, 1956.

In spite of the recent financial and political difficulties, Brazil today is at the forefront of Latin American nations, not only in industry and commerce, but in international standing and in cultural activities. The trends exemplified by the economic nationalism of Latin America since 1930 have come nearer to reaching fruition in Brazil than in any other country.

XXXIX

Argentina, Uruguay, and Chile

> This was the Argentina of June, 1943; disunited, deeply cynical, without purpose or direction. Its spiritual bankruptcy was as patent as its physical prosperity in the war boom, and at the helm of the government was a class that no longer had the power to change its direction, or to prevent outside influences from bringing a change of direction. A nation, a society with all its values, was adrift on a wide ocean, with no one to set the course and no one even to point a destination. Argentina had reached the end of an era.
>
> YSABEL FISK RENNIE *

ARGENTINA, Uruguay, and Chile are largely beyond the sphere of United States' influence and, in matters of trade and cultural interests, are more closely tied to European currents than to the affairs of the United States. That they should be especially sensitive to European happenings is understandable, for Europe has long been their chief market and France their cultural ideal. Added to this natural tendency to face toward Europe has been the Argentine effort to create a southern bloc, dominated by herself, to offset the economic and military preponderance of the United States.

All three countries were severely shaken by the world depression, for they relied heavily on exports to Europe. Political agitation and resentment engendered by economic ruin caused forceful changes

* *The Argentine Republic*, The Macmillan Company, New York, 1945, p. 342.

in the governments and fostered a powerful spirit of uncompromising hostility toward foreign capital. The inept radicals of Yrigoyen gave way to a temporary regime of army officers and to restoration of conservative domination in Argentina. Uruguayan president Gabriel Terra found the divided executive powers unsatisfactory in time of crisis, and he restored presidential powers at the expense of the administrative council. Chilean strong man Carlos Ibáñez, on the other hand, despite his social and economic reforms, was opposed violently for tyranny and financial extravagance, and forced to resign.

Economic recovery was the immediate problem, and although the governments made modest headway in strengthening their economies, they were powerless to accomplish much. Recovery depended upon the revival of industry and trade beyond their borders. General Agustín Justo, who won the Argentine presidency in 1931, rescued the cattle industry at the expense of other parts of the economy by means of the Roca-Runciman Agreement with England in 1933. In the following year an income tax was introduced, and other measures provided for greater control of exchange to limit the free flow of international payments, and the establishment of national boards to give the government a measure of control over grain and cotton. These acts signaled the end of the historic policy of free trade in Argentina, the policy which had favored the cattlemen and grain producers.

Across the Río de la Plata in Uruguay Gabriel Terra dissolved the congress and the council and assumed dictatorial powers. In 1934 a new constitution restored executive power and replaced the administrative council by a vice-president. The government had entered the grain business earlier in an effort to assure satisfactory returns to farmers by establishing minimum prices at which it would purchase grain. The program proved costly, and public works had to be curtailed. Unemployment rose; the government placed restrictions on immigration and pared down its budget. Many additional recovery measures were tried, such as exchange controls, restrictions on imports, and heavier taxes, but without appreciable effect. The problems were world-wide, not domestic.

The downward trend continued until 1934, when exports began to rise and tensions to decline.

In 1934 the government created the Import and Export Exchange Committee to control imports more effectively by means of a quota system based on available exchange arising from purchases by each of the countries involved. A further reduction in the budget enabled the government to produce a treasury surplus by the end of 1935.

Terra's social program was fairly well completed before his term expired. Homes for workingmen were built and sold on easy terms; minimum wage laws, old age pensions, and health insurance were extended. His successor attempted to strengthen national finances by increasing trade through a barter agreement with Germany, but the European war began before the plan had been in operation a year.

For Chile, too, the problems of the world depression were insoluble. The outlay required to service the foreign debt necessitated a critical reduction of the budget and of public works. Ibáñez sought to stimulate recovery through government controls over foreign exchange and trade, and he made a futile effort to sustain the price of nitrates through granting a monopoly of foreign sales to the Nitrate Company of Chile, COSACH. The government temporarily abandoned its export tax on nitrates, but the price continued to fall until it was below the cost of production.

After the failure of Ibáñez and his overthrow, the Radical party began demanding more than temporary relief measures. President Juan Esteban Montero was reluctant to engage in state intervention in the economy, for he was more concerned with restoring constitutional government. His support of civil liberties and his neglect of reforms stimulated action by organized labor and by the socialists and communists. Law and order were no longer all that the government was expected to provide, and Montero was forced to turn more and more to the establishment of controls over the economy in seeking a way out of the chaos. Socialism and state capitalism were stressed increasingly by critics of the government as solutions to Chilean troubles. Labor demanded heavier taxes on wealth and government control of essential items such as food and oil.

The socialist, Carlos Dávila, who succeeded Montero by revolt, and whose power was equally short-lived, favored extension of the COSACH idea of state-dominated companies in all essential industries. His program of social reforms appealed to Chilean workingmen, and they developed a firm conviction that the government should regulate matters concerning their welfare. But some of the reforms promised, such as heavier taxes on the large estates, nationalization of credit facilities and the Central Bank, and unemployment relief aroused the conservatives to action. Others, who held to the old-style liberalism and its stress upon orderly governmental activity, were concerned at the startling prospect of state intervention on a grand scale. The army turned against Dávila and removed him from power, but the ideas he fostered left a deep impression.

In the election that followed former president Arturo Alessandri won a majority and assumed office in December, 1932. The radicalism for which he was noted in the 1920's was now subordinated to a determination to see Chile's customary constitutional processes restored. While astutely if severely checking the opposition, he nevertheless did not try to stem the growing tide in favor of economic and social reforms. For a few critical years his power was strengthened by the Republican Militia, an independent force committed to defending the existing order and constitutional government. The militia was assailed from all sides and resented by the army. In 1935 it peacefully disbanded.

Because of Alessandri's moderation in promoting social legislation the Radical party and labor abandoned him, ultimately to create the Popular Front. Only by publicizing anti-foreign measures, such as expropriation of foreign holdings, was Alessandri able to distract the attention of labor and keep a part of it behind him. By the end of his term he could point to Chilean economic recovery, but the powerful demand for major social reforms was still unsatisfied. Additional credit had been provided for agriculture, industry, and mining, but little had been done in the cause of labor. The group most neglected was the agricultural peasantry.

The Chilean Radical party, unlike its counterpart in Argentina, embraced a program of major reforms, and its abandonment of Alessandri changed the balance of Chilean political parties. The rift was widened in 1936 by Alessandri's severity in suppressing a strike of railway workers. His zeal for maintaining internal security raised fears that he intended to establish a dictatorship and drove the opposition to seek victory through co-operation. Alessandri apparently had no such intention, but the Popular Front was the result.

The Chilean Popular Front, through a coalition of moderate and left wing groups, broke the long domination of the middle and the right, the domination of land and wealth. None of Chile's many parties enjoyed a majority, but the combination, while it lasted, provided control of the presidency and the congress for the radicals. The Front was aided indirectly in its efforts to capture the presidency in 1938 when youths of the Chilean Nazi party rebelled and were shot without trial. The anger of the Nazis helped the Front candidate, Radical party leader Pedro Aguirre Cerda, to win by a slight margin over Gustavo Ross, able finance minister of Alessandri and arch-enemy of the radicals.

In the second half of the decade of the 1930's Chile moved to the left under the aegis of the Popular Front, Argentina swung in the opposite direction, toward an authoritarian regime in the tradition of Rosas, while Uruguay weathered the storm and returned to constitutional rule in keeping with her twentieth-century ideals.

For a time after the election of Roberto M. Ortiz in 1937 it appeared that the Argentine radicals would soon return to power. Ortiz, to the chagrin of his conservative supporters, seemed determined to restore honest elections and government by majority. He intervened in provincial elections to insure honesty and to uphold secrecy of the ballot. Radical hopes rose, and the conservative minority grew desperate.

The hopes of the radicals were violently dashed in 1940, for

Ortiz became seriously ill, and was forced to turn over the government to his vice-president, conservative Ramón S. Castillo, who quickly undid all that Ortiz had accomplished. He intervened in the provinces wherever it was necessary to return his party to power. The radicals retained a slender majority in the chamber of deputies while the conservatives dominated the senate, and little could be accomplished. The Radical party did not enlarge its program in the direction of social and economic reforms, and its failure to do so was partly responsible for the successful intervention of the army a few years later.

Castillo ran the government from 1940 to 1943 with an iron hand. After the Japanese attack on Pearl Harbor in December, 1941, he used the extension of the war to the Western Hemisphere as an excuse to impose a state of siege. He explained his action as necessary to preserve moral unity, to prevent inconvenient modes of expression, by which he meant pro-Ally declarations, and to safeguard neutrality and continental defense. The Argentine press, which had not yet been stifled, commented acidly on the suppression of individual guarantees as a means of defending democracy.

Castillo and his foreign minister, Enrique Ruiz Guiñazú, did not conceal their antipathy for the United States, and when Chile called for a meeting of foreign ministers at Rio de Janeiro in January, 1942, Castillo used the opportunity to advance his country's plan for an Argentine-dominated southern bloc. Ruiz Guiñazú's overtures to other Latin American delegates were not welcomed; even Chileans, who had special reasons for fearing a rupture of relations with the Axis at that unpromising stage of the war, did not take their neutral stand in support of Argentina. By steadily resisting pressure from other nations to agree to severance of relations with the Axis, however, Ruiz Guiñazú finally won his point, and the conference ended by merely recommending such action. Argentina won a diplomatic victory, but one which was to cost her the respect and friendship of a large part of Latin America as well as the largesse which the United States bestowed on her friends in the form of economic and military assistance.

The rising cost of living and the wartime shortages increased the unpopularity of Castillo. As the time for the election of 1943 approached the radicals and socialists discussed the possibility of a coalition, though with little enthusiasm, for a majority of votes would not insure them a victory. Revolution seemed the only hope, but it could not succeed without help from the army. The radicals still did not generate the policies and leadership which might have won them a large and enthusiastic following, and their apathy increased the general cynicism.

Castillo's choice of a successor was Robustiano Patrón Costas, the sugar baron of Salta. He had no following even among the conservatives, but his election seemed certain because of Castillo's determination to force it on the country. The opposition desperately tried to subordinate its factional differences to form a democratic union, but the attempt only widened the rifts. The election, however, was never held.

Early in the morning of June 4, 1943, the old era came to an abrupt but scarcely violent end. Except for brief and bloody resistance by the personnel of the Naval Mechanics' School, an army coup succeeded smoothly and with little trouble. Motives for the barracks revolt varied, but the rumor that the radicals planned to nominate General Pedro P. Ramírez precipitated the action. General Arturo Rawson, who led the troops, desired primarily to repair Argentine prestige abroad and to join the Allied effort to the extent necessary to qualify Argentina to receive military aid from the United States as Brazil was doing. The radicals among the military looked upon the end of conservative rule as a proper goal. The clique of super-nationalists known as the Group of United Officers, the G.O.U., the military wing of Argentine nationalism led by Colonel Juan Domingo Perón, had deep-laid plans for establishing an authoritarian state. The only basis of agreement among these groups was that Castillo must go.

During the war Uruguay was troubled by the threat of Nazi activity, high-lighted by the discovery of a plot to make the country a German colony. The anti-Nazi policy of the government and its close co-operation with the United States did not please all factions, and the nationalist-isolationist followers of Luis Herrera were particularly offended. After 1942 Juan José Amézaga continued the policy of co-operating with the United States, while Argentine irritation mounted. The sheltering of Argentine exiles by Uruguay was another cause for animosity, and Perón encouraged the political maneuvers of Herrera in hope that he could establish a pro-Argentine administration. Perón tried to influence the outcome of the election of 1946 by withholding Argentine wheat from Uruguay until a bread shortage occurred. The Colorado candidates, Tomás Berreta and Luis Batlle, were elected despite his aid to Herrera.

In Chile, meanwhile, the Popular Front had run its course. Aguirre Cerda, soon after taking office, had an opportunity to begin carrying out his plans for economic and social rehabilitation as a result of the devastating earthquake of January, 1939. The emergency relief program created to restore the destroyed cities grew in a short time into an instrument of state capitalism, the *Corporación de Fomento* or Development Corporation. It represented the radicals' program for promoting industry and conservation, and it was given wide latitude in conducting economic studies, making loans, and encouraging the expansion of old and the creation of new industries. It succeeded in speeding up industrialization, and eventually set up the iron and steel industry in the south.

Once the radicals and socialists smoothed out their internal differences the greatest disturbances were caused by the communists and the fascist-type groups which opposed them. After the Russo-German non-aggression pact was signed, the communists became violent in their attacks on the government which they ostensibly supported. The sharpest thrusts were reserved for the socialist ministers, whom they regarded as rivals for control of labor rather than as partners in government.

In 1940, while Aguirre Cerda was calling for a temporary suspension of strikes, the communists intensified their agitation for labor disorders. When the Habana conference brought up the inevitable question of Chile's attitude toward the war, the communists bitterly denounced the United States and stigmatized the socialists as pawns of imperialism.

From the Nazi party came similarly vehement attacks on the government. Gustavo Ross and Ibáñez were known to be in Buenos Aires, and they were believed to be plotting the downfall of the Front, a suspicion which raised the hopes of the rightist groups. At the same time the Spanish government of Francisco Franco offered indirect encouragement to them by severing diplomatic relations with Chile. In 1941 the socialists withdrew from the Front, and the Front dissolved a few weeks later. Differences of opinion on evolutionary methods as opposed to revolution and on hemispheric solidarity as opposed to resistance to 'Yankee imperialism,' the fall of popular front regimes in France and Spain, together with the Russo-German pact were the main factors contributing to the break-up of the unharmonious coalition.

After the Front fell apart the radicals joined with the democratic and radical socialists for the approaching election, and the communists threw their weight behind this union. The main body of socialists, led by Marmaduke Grove and Oscar Schnake, refused to associate themselves with the communists. When Germany attacked Russia the communist tactics changed quickly, and for a time it appeared that the Popular Front would arise from the ashes stronger than before. At this juncture Aguirre Cerda died suddenly, and the trend toward reviving the Front was checked.

Rivalry for leadership of the Radical party became intense between Juan Antonio Ríos, outspoken enemy of the communists, and Gabriel González Videla, who was regarded as more cordial to the extreme left. Ríos won the radical nomination, and he called for a coalition of democratic and progressive forces, carefully excluding the communists. The socialists nominated Schnake, and the conservatives backed Ibáñez. Schnake withdrew his name and gave his support to Ríos.

Foreign affairs played a powerful role in the campaign, and the range of opinion regarding international commitments was so wide that the candidates could not express themselves freely without offending lukewarm supporters. In the campaign Ríos was portrayed as pro-democratic and anti-Nazi, while Ibáñez was branded with the opposite label. The campaign managers of

Ibáñez hastily countered with claims of his friendship for the United States. Both men were careful to obscure their views as far as possible, but it was well known that the Chilean Nazis were ardent supporters of Ibáñez, and the triumph of Ríos was in part a victory for the cause of hemispheric solidarity. At the same time it indicated a swing toward the center and away from the left in domestic politics.

The most striking success of the Popular Front was in the stimulation of industry and raising the level of production. The Development Corporation's effectiveness was generally acknowledged even by those who loathed state interference. Provided with capital by the government and by the Export-Import Bank of the United States, it devoted attention equally to expanding and modernizing old industries and to creating new ones. In many cases the Corporation retained more than half of the stock in the plants it subsidized, thus maintaining a continuing control over their policies.

In the field of health and social security the most significant action of the Front was providing free breakfasts and lunches for thousands of school children who otherwise would have gone without them. Malnutrition was a main health concern of the country, and the root of much of the prevalent illness. This problem was closely tied to that of agricultural production.

Agriculture received some mild benefits from the Corporation's efforts to expand mechanization and to improve breeds of livestock and varieties of crops, although the results were far less impressive than those in industry. The land tenure and peonage systems remained as bulwarks against change in agriculture, and the political power retained by the great landowners prevented any government from making a frontal attack on the problem. Rises in wages and other benefits received by urban labor and government employees were not reflected in similar advances for agricultural laborers.

Numerous proposals were made for stimulating agricultural production, such as breaking up the large estates into small farms, collectivizing them, and introducing up-to-date methods and machinery. In 1935 a law was passed providing for distribution of uncultivated lands among the landless, but in the face of uncompromising hostility of the landowners no effort was made to disturb the ancient system and the extreme concentration of ownership.

The war, with its international overtones, aggravated all of the problems of the Chilean government, for the delicate balance among the many parties necessary to create an effective majority was barely possible without having to adjust external ideological differences. Had the radicals constituted a majority party at the outset of the war it seems likely that Chile would not have delayed for a year after the Rio de Janeiro conference to break relations with the Axis. She had compelling reasons for hesitating to take the action — the acute cleavages of her multi-party system, her long coastline exposed to Japanese attack while the United States fleet was incapacitated after the Pearl Harbor disaster, and fear of trouble in the south among Chileans of German descent. Chile's reasons for delay were appreciated by officials of the U.S. State Department; what caused a strain in relations was the fact that the government did not make a serious effort to prevent Axis espionage agents from operating until after January, 1943, when the rupture in relations finally came.

During the wartime presidency of Ríos the idea of government intervention in the economy flourished, for as the expansion of industry progressed, Chileans raised their sights to objectives undreamed of a few years earlier. The industrialist class rose rapidly in wealth and power under government protection, and the Radical party under Ríos swung away from its close alliance with labor to one with the industrialists. The temporary measures of economic nationalism begun during the depression were strengthened and extended.

In the election held after the untimely death of Ríos, Gabriel González Videla won the presidency. His administration was complicated by the post-war economic crisis which he inherited and by the activities of the communists. He began by giving communists ministerial posts, but because he found it impossible to co-operate with them, he persuaded the congress to outlaw the party, and his government severed diplomatic relations with Russia.

Among the features of the González Videla administration was a reawakening of interest in the far south. In strengthening her historic interest in the area Chile developed the oil resources of Punta Arenas, and in 1947 sent an expedition to the Antarctic to establish a base in her polar region known as O'Higgins Land. The trans-Andean railway from Antofagasta to Salta was completed in 1948. Two years later the government celebrated one of its major triumphs when the Huachipato steel works began operations.

By the close of the González Videla administration Chile had come a long way since 1930. Politically she remained true to her traditions of constitutional government. Economic development had raised new classes to wealth and political power, and though the gains had been costly in governmental outlays, Chileans were determined to base their hopes on further industrialization. Only in agriculture did colonial anachronisms still persist. In two decades the radicals were able to force through the changes they sought in urban areas, but the countryside remained unaffected. The powerful landowners of the south were traditionally members of the Radical party, and they acted as a brake against any movement toward change in the land system.

Since the war Chile has enjoyed friendly relations with the United States, and by 1949 González Videla's government had received more than one hundred million dollars in loans for his program of economic development. Inflation remained the most threatening problem of post-war Chile, and crisis followed crisis. After devaluating the peso late in 1949 González Videla was threatened with a general strike over the wage-hour freeze he proposed in February, 1950. His cabinet resigned, and he was forced to withdraw the bill. The copper price conflict with the United States ended temporarily in 1952 when the United States raised its ceiling price for Chilean copper. The contract was hailed by Chileans as strengthening their position for future negotiations, but copper sales remained a critical problem.

Politically the key issue of 1952 was the presidential election, and inflation the primary point of argument. The main contenders were Pedro Enrique Alfonso, backed by the government, Carlos Ibáñez, perennial candidate, and the conservative, Arturo Matte. The Ibáñez campaign was strongly nationalistic, and he attacked the radicals as being subservient to the traditional whipping-boy, 'Wall Street.' He made the greatest possible use of the chronic inflation by asking Chileans to compare the price of bread during his first administration with the price in 1952. He promised a strong executive who could take effective action without having to placate various political groups or foreign countries. His most enthusiastic supporter was Perón of Argentina; one Argentine consul was expelled from Chile for meddling in the election.

The resounding victory of Ibáñez at the polls indicated disillusionment with the radicals and their failure to check inflation, and the strength of Chilean nationalism. Fears that Ibáñez would revert to dictatorship were reflected in a sharp drop in the stock market. It was not so much Ibáñez himself who caused apprehension as his advisers, who were reputedly ex-members of the Chilean Nazi party. The communists, too, cheered loudly for Ibáñez, for he had promised to annul the law for 'permanent defense of democracy' which proscribed the party. But those who expected immediate nationalization of the American-owned copper industry were disappointed, for Chile's dollar-short economy could not stand so violent a shock.

In February, 1953, Perón crossed the Andes for an official visit with Ibáñez, while Chileans watched fearfully for signs that their country had been brought into the Argentine fold. Argentine ambitions for hegemony were well known, and the strong Chilean nationalism made subordination to Argentina an unattractive prospect. It was necessary for Ibáñez to adjourn congress before the visit in order to prevent an embarrassing debate. After the visit, during which bilateral barter agreements were signed, Ibáñez was forced to yield more and more to firm opposition to anything approaching economic union with Argentina as visualized by the peronistas.

By 1954 Chileans who had expected Ibáñez to perform a miracle and check inflation single-handed were beginning to display their disillusionment. Inflation, far from being stopped, continued at a faster pace than before. The ultra-nationalists, who longed for expropriation of foreign holdings, were also disappointed, and political tensions rose until martial law was declared.

Having no majority party of his own to rely on, Ibáñez had increasing difficulty in satisfying the miscellaneous and unharmonious following which placed him in power. As a result he was forced to appeal for co-operation of all parties, including the Radical, whom he had lately blasted with devastating charges of fraud and incompetence. He learned that it was easier to capitalize on popular discontent than to eradicate its causes. By 1954 it was clear that he came to power with a negative program, with good intentions rather than constructive ideas. He had no plan for checking inflation, and it has been as great as under any previous administration. Devaluation of the peso continued, and in 1954 it reached its lowest point.

The government's neglect of agriculture in favor of industry has also had repercussions, for the deficit of 400,000 tons of wheat in 1954 was as large as any that had occurred, and shortages of other foodstuffs were also serious. A program of increasing agricultural production began in 1951, with technical and financial aid from the United States, but its progress was hampered by inflation. By the middle of 1954 the cost of living had risen 60 per cent since Ibáñez came to power, and members of the administration feared that an explosion was imminent. Ibáñez dismissed his entire cabinet and replaced them with financial and economic experts. Inflation continued through 1955, in spite of all efforts to check it.

In Argentina the changes which followed the ousting of Castillo were rapid and far-reaching. Within six months after the army coup of 1943 Argentina's historic liberalism was dead. In the prolific output of decrees by the Ramírez government it became increasingly clear that the army had no attachment to democratic processes or civil liberties. Those who had rejoiced at Castillo's fall in the belief that any change would be an improvement found themselves saddled with a nationalistic, state-centered regime determined to replace the old individualistic values dear to Argentinians with new ones such as order and duty.

The ultra-nationalistic wing of the army, led by Colonel Perón, gradually rose to a predominant position, and men like General Rawson, who favored a break with the Axis to qualify Argentina for American aid, were shunted aside and silenced. The ill-advised and poorly timed Storni note to the State Department and Cordell Hull's icy reply made pro-Allied sentiments seem almost unpatriotic. The ascendancy of the nationalists turned what had begun as a middle-class movement to seize power from the landed oligarchy into something far different.

The military government at first sought to solve labor problems by resort to repression, but when Perón was named head of the newly created National Department of Labor, the policy changed to one of wooing labor. Little by little Perón strengthened the position of labor by decrees in its favor, and at the same time he gained control over it. Control of the labor movement became one of the most important rungs in Perón's ladder to power.

During the war Argentina's isolation cut her off from her usual sources of supply. Although some industries were aided by the absence of foreign competition, lack of replacement parts caused the transport system to grind slowly to a halt. Faced with increasing pressure, and seeing no other way out of the dilemma, Ramírez reluctantly announced in January, 1944, that Argentina had severed diplomatic relations with the Axis. The fanatic nationalists were outraged by the act, and within a few weeks Ramírez was ousted in favor of Vice-President Edelmiro Farrell, leaving the nationalist clique firmly in control. At the same time Argentina's prestige in the Western Hemisphere sank toward its nadir.

Perón's fame grew rapidly meanwhile, for as minister of labor he introduced long overdue reforms such as minimum wage laws for agricultural laborers. He won general favor by forcing the British-owned railroads to grant wage increases, and by introducing tenure, retirement pay, and disability insurance into the civil service. These reforms came at the expense of labor's independence, but only the socialists protested. The nationalists silenced the traditional parties and began the task of breaking the predominance of the great landowners. Industry was favored and encouraged, not only to gain the support of the industrialists against the landed class, but because industry was essential to what the nationalists considered the needs of national defense. By shrewdly stressing objectives neglected by the old political parties, such as nationalization of foreign enterprises, development of national resources on a wide scale, and a vast program of social legislation, the nationalists won a large measure of popular support.

In 1944 and 1945 the government proceeded slowly with its economic and social changes while solidifying its control. The goal of the G.O.U. was a corporate state in the Hispanic tradition. Overtures were made to the church, and the government won the adherence of the clerical hierarchy by reversing the law and decreeing compulsory religious instruction in the schools.

The economic program of the government was directed toward achieving independence of English industry, nationalizing the public utilities, developing mining in the Andes, building a vast industrial organization, and achieving an economic balance between wealthy Buenos Aires and the impoverished provinces. Underlying these aims was the primary goal — economic self-sufficiency and predominance in South America. Military preparedness on an unprecedented scale was an important part of the program, and by 1948 the appropriation for the armed services absorbed about one-third of the total budget. The great stress on expanding the armed forces and arms production, and the creation of many new garrisons on Argentina's borders gave all of her neighbors cause for concern.

Toward the close of the war the government displayed greater astuteness than its predecessors by returning to the inter-American system and winning an invitation to the Chapúltepec conference and admission to the United Nations. War was declared on Germany and Japan a few weeks before Nazi resistance collapsed completely.

Feeling itself firmly entrenched, the government relaxed its controls slightly and called for presidential and congressional elections in February, 1946. By this time Perón was no longer the man behind the scene, but in the open as the man of destiny. During the campaign he skillfully increased his advantages by forcing employers to grant bonuses to employees, and by sending men to break up the meetings of his opponent, Dr. José Tamborini. United States Ambassador Spruille Braden, in an ill-fated effort to encourage Argentine liberals, spoke out strongly against Perón, while the State Department published an account of the pro-Nazi activities and dictatorial methods of the military regime. The net result of these actions was to strengthen the hold of the ultra-nationalists, for voices raised against them were stigmatized as favoring outside interference in domestic affairs. Perón won a popular majority and an overwhelming victory in electoral votes.

As president, supported by a strong majority in congress, Perón moved swiftly to fulfill his economic and social objectives. A Five Year Plan for industrialization was drawn up, unions were brought under closer regulation, the Banco Central was nationalized, and a government trade agency, I.A.P.I., was created. The press was brought under strict control by the use of quotas of newsprint and by intimidation. Educational institutions were forced into line by wholesale dismissals of teachers. In 1947 women were granted the right to vote, and they became enthusiastic supporters of Perón and Evita, his wife and astute political partner.

In 1949 a new constitution replaced that of 1853. Among its features was the authorization of two successive six year terms for the president, a prohibition against forming coalitions by political parties, and a provision for severe punishment for anyone showing disrespect for the president or other public officials.

Perón was fortunate that his grandiose program was introduced at a time of unusual prosperity caused by heavy demands for Argentine products in European recovery. In 1946 he authorized the creation of the National Economic Council which was granted wide powers in organizing and subsidizing industries, particularly the mixed companies in which the government and private interests shared ownership. Air transportation and the national merchant marine were developed rapidly by the Council, for these were as essential as industry to furthering Argentina's aim to become the commercial center of Latin America. The trade agency ended the era of free competition in grain and beef by monopolizing foreign sales. It purchased commodities at prices which guaranteed a minor profit to the producers, and sold them abroad at high profits for the government. The funds made available through this recourse were used to purchase and nationalize foreign-owned public utilities, such as the British railways and the American telephone system. During her post-war prosperity Argentina became a creditor nation.

Perón named his program of economic nationalism and social integration 'Justicialism,' and called it a 'third position' between capitalism and communism. Despite the frequent charges that it was fascism pure and simple, it was not a copy of the regime Perón admired while living in Mussolini's Italy. It has been called a blend of Rosas and Mussolini with something new added, Perón's own original touches.

Under Justicialism regimentation flourished. Argentinians, long committed to an individualistic, liberal way of life, chafed under the stifling cult of Perón, with its strict censorship and thought control. The world-famous free press of Argentina ceased to exist; in 1951 *La Prensa* was closed down and turned over to the General Confederation of Labor.

As time for the presidential election of 1951 approached it was clear to all that no one had a chance of defeating Perón. Suggestions of army opposition appeared in the withdrawal of Señora Perón's candidacy for vice-president, and in the abortive, easily crushed revolt of September 28. Early rumors that Perón had planned the revolt himself for the purpose of scattering his opponents were later believed to be erroneous, for the uprising apparently was a genuine if feeble bid of a military clique to seize power.

In the election of 1951 women voted for president and campaigned for national offices for the first time. By encouraging women to participate in political affairs Perón showed again far greater astuteness than the leaders of the traditional parties, and he won enthusiastic support. The Radical party candidates could only make an oblique appeal to the army for aid, but to no effect.

Perón began his second term with far less reason for optimism over the country's economy, for gold and foreign credit reserves were low, and the huge profits provided by meat and wheat sales in 1946 had dwindled. Argentinians, once celebrated for the prodigious amounts of meat they consumed daily, now endured meatless days, and in 1952 Argentina was forced to import wheat because of a two year drought. Many businesses went bankrupt during the year, and persistent rumors of plots against the government kept political tension high. A second five year plan to make Argentina self-sufficient in raw materials and to speed up industrial production, was announced, for the first one had been partially frustrated by economic decline and the drought. As economic conditions worsened Perón tightened his control, and Argentine exiles repeatedly accused the police of terrorism and torture.

The General Confederation of Labor became one of Perón's most powerful political and economic supports. The C.G.T. controlled nearly all organized labor and enjoyed a privileged position with the government. It was a vital aid in holding the wage and price line. The five million members were organized as a civilian militia, ready for action against his foes. The army watched its growth with displeasure, and the prominence given in the official press to stories of popular triumphs over the army in Iran and Bolivia suggested that Perón was moving toward a gradual elimination of the army as a political factor. C.G.T. members were granted a privileged position equal to that of members of congress.

In 1954 Perón seemed still secure in his power and less dependent upon labor. A new wage policy announced during the year indicated that the days of favoritism toward labor were over. New wage increases, the president declared, would be granted only in case of increased output. At the same time the C.G.E. or Employers' Confederation was built up to rival the C.G.T.

In the congressional elections of 1954 the Peronista party held its strength, although opposition candidates as usual had no opportunity to bring their names before the voters. After the election Radical party leaders were arrested, ostensibly for violating the law against showing 'disrespect' to the president. A month later, however, Perón admitted that there were two main sectors of Argentine opinion, the peronistas and the radicals. He also announced the time had come for 'depersonalization' of the revolution begun in 1943. Before the end of the year he became aware of a third group, the Roman Catholic Church.

In June, 1955, after an eight-month battle with the church, Perón initiated legislation for separating church and state. Church authorities, despite acts of violence by peronistas, continued to defy presidential bans on certain religious activities. The Vatican excommunicated the president and his aides, and on June 16 naval air units rose in brief but violent rebellion. The army soon restored order, but it was clear to all that Perón's touch had lost its magic.

The church quickly regained its prestige, and the government offered to rebuild churches destroyed in the rioting. In July Perón offered an 'open hand' to his political opponents, and soon after resigned as head of the Peronista party. The opposition refused to grasp the open hand until constitutional guarantees were restored, the state of internal war lifted, and general amnesty granted to political prisoners and exiles. Perón made a gesture at resignation before his most devoted followers, and allowed himself to be persuaded to continue in office. Reassured, he announced a fight to the finish against his opponents. All indications pointed to a resumption of his anti-Catholic, anti-church campaign, though a congressional committee authorized him to postpone the constitutional assembly for the purpose of separating church and state.

On August 31, Perón withdrew an offer to resign and promised to crush the opposition, meeting violence with 'greater violence.' On September 2 he sought to tighten his grip on the country by means of a congress-approved state of siege, which actually gave him no greater special powers than he exercised under an earlier declaration of a 'state of internal war.' On September 16, new uprisings broke out in the army and navy and swept all before them despite repeated announcements of government victories. Three days later Perón took refuge on a Paraguayan gunboat, and an army junta took charge and submitted to rebel demands. General Eduardo Lonardi declared himself provisional president September 20, and Argentina began the tremendous task of liquidating the effects of a decade of peronismo, secret police brutality, and legislative and judicial subservience. The task did not appear easy.

On November 13, Lonardi was ousted by General Pedro Eugenio Aramburu. The new regime accelerated the return to democratic procedures and promised to hold free elections 'in the future.'

It is in Uruguay, not Argentina, that the most remarkable political experiment is found. In December, 1951, Uruguayans voted to abolish the presidency in favor of a nine man executive council, superficially resembling the Swiss system. President Martínez Trueba, elected in 1950, was the chief exponent of the plan, despite the fact that it would cost him his position as president. The council represents the nation in all matters of internal and external relations, and is composed of members of both the major parties. By this change Uruguay returned to the political course she was following in 1930. Her action is unique in Latin America.

XL

Paraguay, Bolivia, Peru, and Ecuador

> One cannot say what the future holds, but dark days must be expected for Peru; a country cannot always remain the property of a feudal minority which blocks all progress.
>
> PEDRO HERNÁNDEZ ZELAYA *

THE so-called Indian countries of South America contrast sharply in many ways with most of their neighbors. Here the most distinct class and race cleavages are to be found, the most flagrant examples of rule by clique, the greatest concentration of ownership of land and wealth, and the most corroding examples of acute poverty among the mass of people. In all of them political instability and military intervention are chronic, despite occasional tyrants who are able to suppress opposition for a decade or longer. Most of the social, economic, and political ills generally ascribed to Latin America are found in these countries to an advanced degree. Their history since 1930 has been one of repeated violence and frequent governmental change, and there is no obvious reason for believing that this phase has ended.

Their main problems are similar, and their efforts at solving them so far have proved equally futile. In each country a large and neglected or maltreated Indian mass is the most numerous element of the population, and the condition of the Indians has not improved significantly since the close of the colonial era. A basic need is to rehabilitate the Indians, to integrate them into

* 'Peru Moves Backward,' *The Nation*, Vol. 168, January 1, 1949, p. 11.

national economic life, and to give them incentive to raise themselves above the subsistence level at which most exist. The economic potentialities of the countries cannot be approached while so large a part of their populations produce no more than for their barest daily needs.

In Ecuador and Peru the economic depression added to the chronic political unrest and precipitated the overthrow of the governments. In 1930 Colonel Luis M. Sánchez Cerro ended the Peruvian dictatorship of Augusto Leguía, and in the following year Dr. Isidro Ayora was forced out of the Ecuadorian presidency. Sánchez Cerro was assassinated in 1933, while no one was able to remain long in power in Ecuador until the army established a dictatorship in 1935.

International disputes among the four countries and with their neighbors led to further disharmony and chaos in the 1930's, in particular the senseless Chaco war between Paraguay and Bolivia. The vast, almost empty Chaco area had long been a subject of dispute, and fruitless negotiations had been carried on for years. Both governments upheld their claims with uncompromising attitudes, although except for rumored oil deposits there was nothing at stake but national pride.

Paraguayan troops provoked the conflict by a surprise attack on Fortín Vanguardia in December, 1928. Bolivians quickly retaliated by capturing the Paraguayan posts of Mariscal López and Boquerón. Diplomatic relations between the two countries were severed, but the war did not break out in full fury until 1932.

Most Latin American nations sympathized at first with Paraguay, because the presence of a Standard Oil Company concession in Bolivia enabled jingoists to raise the irresistible cry of foreign imperialism. Standard Oil, with only a small operation in Bolivia, was accused of arming powerful Bolivia for aggressions against weak and poverty-stricken Paraguay. No evidence has been presented to indicate that Standard Oil was in any way involved, and Bolivian military preparedness was vastly overrated by Paraguayan sympathizers, for the Bolivian army had been trained for the parade ground rather than the battlefield. When they left the altiplano for the unaccustomed rigors of the tropical lowlands, Bolivian troops suffered severe hardships.

In 1932, when the fighting began in earnest, Argentine Foreign Minister Carlos Saavedra Lamas, reflecting the general delusion regarding the comparative strength of the contenders, obtained unanimous approval of the American republics of a declaration that no territorial conquest would be recognized. Thus would Bolivia be shorn of the spoils of war should she persist in conquering Paraguay, as was believed likely. The declaration made the fighting fruitless, yet neither side would compromise. In the end it was Paraguay which gained disputed territory by conquest, and the declaration was forgotten.

The events of the wasteful and useless conflict are not significant, but its effect on the participants was demoralizing. An estimated 100,000 men were lost, and the financial condition of both countries became chaotic. By the end of 1934 the Paraguayan army was within striking distance of Bolivian oil fields, but was held off by a desperate effort. Both sides were exhausted, and in June, 1935, a truce was signed, a truce negotiated by a mediation commission composed of representatives of Argentina, Chile, Uruguay, Brazil, and the United States. Three years later the two warring nations signed a treaty, and agreed to arbitrate the boundary under conditions which would leave Paraguay most of her conquests. Bolivia received token compensation in the form of access to the upper Paraguayan river and free use of Puerto Casado in the Chaco.

The Chaco war badly disrupted the economies of the contestants and furnished both with a rich supply of ambitious army officers who have made intermittent bids for power ever since. In 1937 Bolivia expropriated the Standard Oil holdings, but was unable to make any headway in developing a domestic oil industry.

Peru came dangerously near to war with Colombia over seizure of the Amazonian town of Leticia, which lay within the formerly disputed area conceded to Colombia by treaty in 1922. Peruvians resented the treaty, and in 1932 a group of adventurers seized

Leticia and expelled Colombian officials. Sánchez Cerro disavowed the act, but made it clear that Peru would resist any effort of Colombia to restore her authority. Both countries allocated large sums for the purchase of arms, but the death of Sánchez Cerro brought General Oscar Benavides to power. He accepted the findings of the League of Nations and permitted the return of Leticia to Colombia.

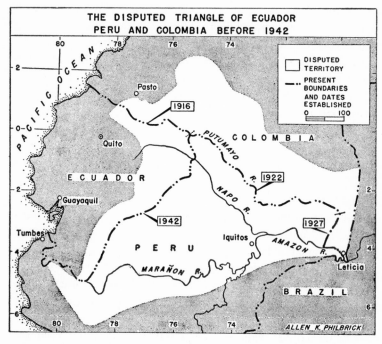

In 1941 Peru sought compensation for her loss of territory to Colombia by fighting an undeclared war with Ecuador over disputed lands also in the Amazon region. At the 1942 conference in Rio de Janeiro Ecuador and Peru were persuaded to settle the boundary question by negotiation. As a result of the settlement Ecuador lost to Peru most of the area she had claimed in the upper Amazon.

These disputes and wars greatly hampered efforts to bring about economic advances in keeping with the current trends in Latin

America. The conflicts were by no means the sole causes of the inferior position of the four countries in comparison to their neighbors, however, for the colonial legacy is basic to most of their ills.

Political life, which in Latin America is frequently an accurate mirror of the general state of affairs, has remained in these countries turbulent and irresponsible, subject to frequent and violent changes. Nativist reform movements have arisen, but they have had no lasting effect, although it is too early to assess the M.N.R. administration of Paz Estenssoro in Bolivia. There seems to be no likelihood, however, that any of the reform governments which may arise will be able to bring about major changes peacefully. Revolution and dictatorship is the course prescribed by custom and precedent, and necessitated by the presence of powerful and unyielding oligarchies. Where reform leaders such as Víctor Raúl Haya de la Torre of Peru have declined to employ violence in place of constitutional methods, they have been easily prevented from accomplishing their goals by opponents less susceptible to legalistic means.

The Aprista party which Haya helped create was constantly harassed by the Peruvian government. In 1931 APRA nominated Haya for the presidency, on his return from exile. The government declared Sánchez Cerro the winner, although there was a general belief that Haya had been defrauded. His followers were ready to sweep him into office by force, but he declined to take that recourse.

In 1933 a revolt against Sánchez Cerro was used as the justification for exiling Haya once more, and in 1936 APRA was not permitted to name a candidate on the grounds that it was an international organization rather than a political party. While the charge was technically true, APRA was essentially a Peruvian reform party. Denied a candidate of their own, the apristas supported the socialist, Luis Antonio Eguiguren. Once more victory was snatched from their hands. The constituent assembly, fearful of the outcome, canceled the election and extended Benavides' term until 1939.

In 1939 Benavides was able to secure the election of his candidate, Manuel Prado y Ugarteche, by prohibiting the apristas from participating. After Peru broke relations with the Axis, in January, 1942, the apristas offered to co-operate with the government, but their aid was not accepted. At the conclusion of the war, however, democratic sentiments were so powerful that the government was induced to hold one of the freest elections in Peruvian history. The apristas, now known officially as the People's party, were permitted to participate.

The campaign of 1945 enabled the apristas at last to enter the government, as one of the members of the 'national democratic front' which elected José Luis Bustamante y Rivero. The apristas were the largest group in the coalition, but at first chose to remain outside the cabinet. All that they advocated in the way of social and economic change was bitterly resisted by their opponents in the cabinet and the congress, and the government was torn by antagonisms. There was no middle ground between those determined to preserve the *status quo* and those pledged to a platform of social legislation and rehabilitation of the Indians. All that the apristas prescribed was a threat to the old order.

One of the most astonishing actions of the apristas was their forcing through congress a press censorship law to silence the vociferous conservative newspapers of Lima. Bustamante refused to sign the bill, and defended freedom of the press in convincing terms. To save the apristas from embarrassment he signed their bill after another had been passed rendering it ineffective. This episode, together with the furor over aprista activities in the municipalities, weakened APRA's position.

In the process of restoring municipal government to the elective councils which Leguía had abolished in 1920, the apristas had an opportunity to engage in practical foundation-building for the future. They were accused of general misuse of funds, a charge which they stoutly denied, and which may have been merely an indication of their success. Bustamante apparently was convinced that there was justification for the accusations, for he ordered congress to omit subsidies to the municipalities from future budgets. The rift between the president and the apristas widened.

If the apristas were to remain in the government in the face of bitter opposition from the conservatives, they needed to have at least a part of the army behind them. In order to work aprista officers into key positions they proposed lowering the retirement age and increasing army pay. The plan to retire a large group of officers aroused strong resistance; the pay increase passed but lowering the retirement age did not, and the resentment of the army toward the apristas was greatly aggravated.

In January, 1947, the publisher of anti-aprista *La Prensa* of Lima was assassinated, and suspicion fell heavily on the party. Aprista cabinet members resigned, and a wave of labor unrest swept the country. Bustamante selected a new cabinet composed largely of army and navy officers, for his most urgent task was restoring order. The democratic front was in complete collapse, and the conservatives seized the opportunity to break down the government by absenting themselves from the senate so that a quorum was unattainable. The anti-apristas in the chamber of deputies imitated the action, and legislative sessions became meaningless.

This situation continued into 1948, leaving Bustamante in a position of having to govern without help from congress. In October a part of the navy rebelled in Callao, and the apristas were accused of connivance in the plot. The uprising was quelled, and Bustamante retaliated by outlawing the party and arresting its leaders.

The conservatives were far from satisfied with Bustamante's moderate reprisals, and a few weeks after the naval revolt they persuaded army officers to oust the president and destroy APRA. A junta of conservative officers headed by General Manuel Odría seized the government. Severe measures against the apristas now followed, and by 1950 the party had been scattered and silenced so effectively that Odría was able to stage a presidential election in which he was named for a six-year term without opposition. His supporters seeking election to congress, however, found enemies of the regime fairly numerous and courageous.

Today Aprismo seems to have been almost completely destroyed as an organized party by the relentless attacks of the conservative-military regime. The socio-economic problems for which the apristas offered solutions remain largely unsolved, however, and it is impossible to estimate the size of the residue of the party still existing.

Ecuador's political history since 1930 has been even more chaotic than that of Peru. After Ayora was forced out in 1931 and his successor impeached two years later, José María Velasco Ibarra was elected. Velasco Ibarra struggled with insoluble economic problems, quarreled with congress and with his supporters, and lost his influence with the army. In 1935 he tried to assume dictatorial powers, and was forced to resign.

The military dictatorship of Federico Páez lasted two years, while unrest and military revolts continued. He finally withdrew in favor of his minister of war, Alberto Enríquez, who dissolved congress and issued a series of reform decrees including a minimum wage law and authorization for expropriating foreign holdings. Enríquez lasted only one year, and three more men held the presidential office briefly before 1940, when the liberal Carlos Arroyo del Río was elected.

Arroyo del Río's difficulties were heightened by wartime inflation and by the Peruvian seizure of Ecuador's Amazon territory in 1941. His government granted the United States the right to build bases on the Galápagos islands and the mainland as part of the defenses of the Panama Canal, and Ecuador in turn received a loan from the Export-Import Bank to be used for highway construction, the purchase of railroad equipment, and the eradication of tropical diseases. The government established a development corporation to carry out the program.

Political strife continued unabated, and in 1944 Arroyo del Río went the way of his predecessors. A loose alliance of opposition parties selected Velasco Ibarra once more, but he was soon at odds with many of those who had supported him. By 1946 his unpredictable acts had cost him most of his popularity, and in the following year the army sent him once more into exile. During his rule Ecuador's newspapermen had instituted a program for eradicating illiteracy, in the hope that political and economic life would both benefit. The project, which was conducted by volunteers, provided daily instruction, and quickly spread over most of the country.

The victor of the presidential election of 1948 was Galo Plaza Lasso, candidate of the Independent Citizens party and son of former president Leonidas Plaza Gutiérrez. Plaza, who had been born and educated in the United States and who had served as his country's ambassador to Washington, announced his goal as raising Ecuador's standard of living through improvement of agricultural production.

Plaza's hopes for material progress were set back in 1949 by the worst earthquake in the country's history. Thousands were killed, towns were completely destroyed, and roads were blocked by landslides. The president inaugurated a reconstruction program to provide the ravaged towns with quakeproof buildings. His most outstanding achievement, however, was unique only because of its rarity — he served out his entire term. By a policy of moderation and of minimizing outbursts of opposition, he gave Ecuador her first taste of political stability in a quarter of a century. In 1952 he was followed by the perennial contender and admirer of Perón, Velasco Ibarra.

Although Velasco Ibarra soon broke with some of his most powerful supporters, thus raising doubts as to his ability to duplicate Plaza's feat, he helped stabilize Ecuador's finances by an agreement to settle the country's dollar debt which had been in default since before the war. The move cleared the way for Ecuador to receive loans from abroad, and gave a belated boost to economic development. He also launched a major road-building program to link the isolated Andean region more closely with the coast.

The Bolivian and Paraguayan political patterns differed little from those of Peru and Ecuador. Both countries suffered setbacks as a result of the Chaco war, and military uprisings became even more frequent than usual. Governmental stability and reforms were badly needed, but neither could be achieved. Champions of change arose among the military heroes of the war, who were determined to restore order and introduce radical programs. Paraguayan Colonel Rafael Franco and Bolivian Colonel David Toro seized power in 1936 and attempted to establish socialistic regimes along authoritarian lines in their respective countries. One year later both proponents of the new era were ousted by *cuartelazos* or barracks revolts. Franco's precipitous downfall was caused by opposition to his program on the one hand, and by impatience at his inability to carry it out quickly on the other. A law of 1936 authorized the government to expropriate land not under cultivation for distribution among the landless, but Franco did not dare move against foreign-owned holdings, most of which belonged to Argentinians.

Toro's efforts to introduce a brand of national socialism to Bolivia were equally fruitless, and he was replaced by Colonel Germán Busch. As was the case with Paraguay, Bolivia's economic condition went from bad to worse, and none of her military dictators was able to check the trend. Busch attempted to force the tin companies to invest their profits in Bolivian enterprises, but he was stopped by their threat to suspend mining operations. He considered seizing the mines, but was dissuaded by the knowledge that the tin interests also owned the only available smelters, which were located in England. In 1939 Busch died a violent death officially reported as suicide.

In Paraguay Franco was followed at first by a provisional government, and in 1939 by General José Félix Estigarribia, the chief military hero of the war. Estigarribia's efforts to return to the new Paraguay envisioned by Franco were defeated by the discordant elements among his supporters. In February, 1940, he issued a proclamation declaring that he had tried to restore political freedom and promote public works, but that the country was bitterly divided and on the verge of anarchy. Because of the chaos he assumed total power. He saw his mission as one of starting the country on the road to prosperity. While waiting for a new constitution to be written he reopened the university, inaugurated public works, and resumed division of land among the landless. He had other plans for the country, including a new highway system, railway connections with Brazil, acquisition of a fleet of merchant vessels, and creation of a sounder currency. The new constitution of 1940 gave the president the power to interfere in the economy of the country. The senate was replaced by a state council composed of representatives of the army, the church, agriculture, industry, and government employees. Estigarribia did not live to enjoy the new constitutional order, for he was killed in an airplane accident in September, 1940.

Higinio Morínigo, minister of war under Estigarribia, and General Enrique Peñaranda, Bolivian commander during the Chaco war, became chief executives of their countries in 1940, and both lasted somewhat longer than usual because the outbreak of the war in Europe made the opposition hesitant. Peñaranda, facing growing hostility and branded as the tool of tin magnates and Yankee imperialists, was ejected in the coup of 1943, but Morínigo remained in office throughout the war.

Peñaranda's fall was engineered by a group of young officers led by Major Gualberto Villaroel and the National Revolutionary Party or MNR under Víctor Paz Estenssoro. The junta professed itself the champion of the people against exploitation by the tin barons, Patiño, Hochschild, and Aramayo, and promised to fulfill the country's inter-American obligations faithfully. Because of the well-known pro-Argentine and pro-Nazi leanings of junta members, the sincerity of its promises was doubted by other Latin American states. Recognition of the regime was delayed for six months; by that time Paz Estenssoro and others regarded as objectionable because of real or supposed fascist connections had been removed from office.

After its recognition the junta called for elections, and brought Paz and the others removed with him earlier back into the government. Terroristic methods were used to destroy political opposition, and the government was soon notorious for its savagery. An attempted revolt was suppressed with unusual severity, but in August, 1946, another occurred in which a vengeful and bloodthirsty mob hunted down Villaroel, flung him from a balcony of the national palace, and hanged him from a lamppost in the plaza. Paz Estenssoro escaped, but other officials suffered a fate similar to the president's. The debacle proved to Paz that he had based his power too heavily on the tin miners to the neglect of other and more powerful groups.

In 1942 Bolivia, like Peru and Ecuador, organized a development corporation to promote exploitation of natural resources and to expand the inadequate transportation system. Within a few years it had commenced projects in mining, oil production, and road-building. By 1945 its attention was concentrated on agriculture and on the highway from Cochabamba to Santa Cruz.

Bolivia has attempted to raise rural living standards by means of the *Servicio Cooperativo Interamericano de Educación*, which has undertaken community projects analogous to those carried out in Mexico. Despite some suspicion and even hostility in the beginning, many communities have embraced the program with enthusiasm, and they are slowly making headway in increasing food production, constructing more comfortable houses, and removing sources of epidemics. The communities themselves provide almost everything that is used.

Peru has an agricultural program underway also, conducted by the *Servicio Cooperativo Interamericano de Producción de Alimentos* and directed toward a goal of lessened demand for imported foods. Machinery pools have been established and irrigation projects inaugurated in the coastal area. The cost of the program originally was shared by the United States and Peru, but the Peruvian government gradually assumed both the financial and administrative responsibility for the undertaking. Peru also has a housing program under the National Housing Corporation, which developed a vast settlement project in the Lima-Callao area.

In the development of industries Peru took the lead among the four countries. In 1943 the *Corporación Peruana del Santa* was created to administer a program for industrial development of the Santa river valley. Because of her rich mineral and coal resources Peru has the potential for producing special steels, and a steel industry is one of the nation's industrial goals. The Santa Corporation has also devoted attention to transforming the outmoded transportation system by extending highways and railroads.

After the downfall of Villaroel, political chaos continued in

Bolivia. Enrique Hertzog, who succeeded to the presidency in 1947, declared a state of siege six times before he retired in 1949. The MNR, urged on by Paz from exile in Buenos Aires, was the principal instigator of revolts, and it kept constant pressure on the government. When Vice-President Mamerto Urriolagoitia replaced Hertzog, a sharp drop in the price of tin intensified hostility toward the government. Mines were closed down and unemployment among miners became critical. Tensions rose and rioting increased. In May, 1950, demands by La Paz teachers for pay increases led to mob violence, for enemies of the government seized the opportunity to demonstrate against it.

As the tin crisis mounted the government began encouraging oil production as a means of providing foreign exchange. Attention was now focused more intently on the eastern tropical lowlands, which comprise more than half of the national territory, to develop both their oil and agricultural resources. Refineries were planned for Cochabamba and Sucre to process crude oil piped from the lowlands. Lack of transportation facilities was one of the greatest handicaps to developing the eastern area, and the government negotiated a loan from the Export-Import Bank for building a highway from Cochabamba to Santa Cruz. Meanwhile Brazil pushed through completion of the extension of the São Paulo railroad to link it with Santa Cruz and ultimately with Cochabamba, and Argentina also worked on a spur line to Santa Cruz.

Competition for Bolivian oil became strong between Argentina and Brazil, for both countries had critical oil shortages. Argentina, fearful of being excluded by Brazil, offered Bolivia financial assistance, and charged that United Nations' and Point Four aid was merely a cloak for American penetration.

In the election of 1951 Paz Estenssoro campaigned from exile and won forty per cent of the votes cast, the remainder being so divided as to give him a plurality. It was the duty of congress to choose a president from among the three leading candidates, but Urriolagoitia and military leaders who had been severely treated under the Villaroel regime established a military junta under General Ovido Quiroga and refused to permit Paz to enter the country. In April, 1952, however, the junta was overthrown by an MNR rebellion, and Paz returned in triumph. Nationalization of the tin mines immediately became the key issue.

Soon after his inauguration Paz created a government mining corporation to operate the tin mines once nationalization was accomplished. The new corporation was an adjunct of the Ministry of Mines and Petroleum, headed by labor leader Juan Lechín. The government commission established to make a study and to recommend a procedure to be followed in taking over the mines, advocated reimbursing the companies for their investments and equipment, but not for the value of tin still underground, which presumably belonged to the nation. Toward the close of 1952 the nationalization decree was enacted.

Bolivia's long-standing problem of an outlet to the Pacific was heightened by fears of Chilean reprisals for expropriation of Chilean tin holdings. The election of Ibáñez diminished the danger, for he, like Perón, had applauded the contemplated nationalization as a measure against 'foreign imperialism.' Perón offered the land-locked country an outlet for its tin through the Argentine port of Rosario, though access to Rosario from the altiplano was more difficult than reaching the Pacific coast.

The most powerful figure in the Paz administration was Juan Lechín, Minister of Mines and Petroleum, whose strength was derived from his position as executive secretary of the national confederation of labor. Lechín rose to the top of the labor movement by gaining control of the tin miners' union during the Villaroel interlude, and his power grew enormously thereafter.

By the end of 1953 Bolivia and the United States had negotiated a technical assistance agreement for the purpose of increasing food production and expanding the network of roads. The action followed the working out of a satisfactory formula for compensating the dispossessed mine owners. Indian riots have been frequent because of impatience with the government's slowness in effecting its heralded land program, and Cochabamba was besieged by Indian hordes. The government finally passed an agrarian reform decree. In May, 1955, soldiers were sent to clear land in the Santa Cruz area in the first major effort to settle empty eastern Bolivia with people from the altiplano.

The Paz government made a special effort to establish friendly relations with all of Bolivia's neighbors, and to avoid being drawn into a position of economic subservience to Argentina. In December, 1953, Paz and Getúlio Vargas met at Santa Cruz and Corumbá to celebrate the opening of the railroad line which gives Santa Cruz access to the Brazilian port of Santos.

Early in 1954 Bolivia, like Argentina, assumed a less hostile attitude toward foreign oil interests when she granted a concession in the Yacuiba region to an American oil man. The agreement marks a return of foreign capital to the Bolivian oil industry, following the expropriation of Standard Oil holdings in 1937, and emphasizes the tremendous difficulties and expense involved in developing and maintaining oil production.

The state oil corporation remained in existence despite its failure to advance production substantially, and the government exercised care in obtaining technical and financial aid to avoid involvement with the most famous names among the foreign oil companies. The powerful current of nationalism made this precaution necessary, for the administration was obliged to avoid the devastating charge of selling out to foreign interests. In this regard, Mexico's loan of oil experts to Bolivia was particularly helpful.

The Paz administration did not escape the usual outbursts of opposition. The nationalization of the tin mines and the threats of some of the labor groups in the MNR alarmed conservative factions into action to slow up or bring a halt to the program. In January, 1953, right wing elements of MNR and an army clique struck a blow against the government but failed to unseat it. The rebels were decisively defeated by the 'workers militia' which had overthrown the junta in 1952, and by loyal elements of the army. The military had chafed at its exclusion from the government, and was aroused by the building up of a potential rival in the militia. One of the chief aims of the rebels was to remove Juan Lechín from the ministry of mines, for he was held responsible for many of the administration's policies which the conservatives found most objectionable. The rebellion apparently upset the delicate balance between the extreme groups composing the MNR by crushing the right and leaving Paz supported largely by the left.

Since the overthrow of Bustamante Peru has been ruled by Odría and the army. With the exception of the Arequipa revolt in 1950, he has not been seriously challenged. The revolt was inspired by the action of the National Electoral Board in nullifying the candidacy of General Ernesto Montagne, leaving Odría unopposed for the presidency. The Arequipa uprising was blamed on *Acción Cívica*, the communists, the apristas, the Democratic League, in short, on any supposed enemies of the junta. In this way it was possible to eliminate or stigmatize all opponents.

Odría justified his suppression of opposition on the grounds of necessity if governmental stability was to be achieved and his program of housing development, education, and social welfare put into effect. This program was organized for the purpose of capitalizing on sentiments favoring reforms already publicized by the outlawed apristas, but without seriously disrupting the *status quo*.

Peru's hope for industrialization and commercial expansion was enhanced by Argentina's efforts to create an economic union in the south and the development of the Colombia-Venezuela-Ecuador bloc in the north, for both groups hoped to include Peru. Ecuador's position became precarious, for she was in grave danger of being crowded out of the northern bloc by Peru. In August, 1955, Peru offered Bolivia unrestricted use of all her transportation facilities and ports, and the two countries laid plans for building additional railroads.

Paraguay, too, could not avoid being affected by the outcome of negotiations to create economic unions, for the arrangements made for the benefit of the larger nations were certain to have far-reaching consequences for the small ones. This situation was responsible for Paraguayan and Bolivian efforts to foster commercial relations with Brazil as a means of countering Argentine economic pressure. In both countries there were powerful pro-Argentine forces which placed obstacles in the way of closer relations with Brazil.

After the downfall of Morínigo in 1948 Juan Natalicio González, one of Paraguay's greatest writers, was elected to the presidency. He was opposed by conservatives and by pro-Argentine members of his own party, who resented his enthusiasm for the construction of a railroad to link the country with Santos in Brazil and his resistance to Argentine overtures. Natalicio González survived this opposition only half a year before he was ousted.

After a short interval Federico Chaves, foreign minister under Morínigo and an admirer of Perón, assumed the presidency. In 1953 he was elected for a five-year term. His supporters, like those of Odría in Peru, upheld the use of severe methods in restraining the opposition in the name of political stability and economic progress, despite the fact that he took office committed to permitting the return of the traditional parties. His first efforts were dedicated to raising the production of cotton, beef, and quebracho extract, but his program also included plans for social legislation and for an extension of the highway system.

Paraguay began making a determined effort to achieve the degree of prosperity which her resources permit. The government welcomed immigrants and provided loans and other assistance to farmers who wished to settle in Paraguay. Among the immigrant groups brought to Paraguay were 700 Kalmucks, European descendants of the legions of Genghis Khan, who were given 9000 acres of fertile land and a supply of livestock.

Chaves showed himself an ardent supporter of peronism during his rule, and Paraguay was the first country to adhere to the type of economic union proposed by Argentina with respect to Chile. Paraguay is, in fact, at the mercy of Argentina in economic affairs, for Argentinians have heavy investments in Paraguayan agriculture and Buenos Aires controls the country's main access to the sea. But nationalism grew stronger in Paraguay, and with it a powerful undercurrent of resistance to Argentina.

Partly as a result of nationalistic resentment Chaves was ousted by the army in March, 1954, shortly before Perón was to visit Asunción. General Alfredo Stroessner, leader of the uprising, was elected to complete the unfinished term. Paraguayan prospects for achieving representative government, however, seemed as remote as ever.

Defection of Paraguay from the southern bloc proved a serious setback to peronista dreams of Argentine hegemony in the south. The overthrow of Chaves came at an awkward time for Perón, for the Argentine congress had ordered the return of all war trophies captured from Paraguay nearly a century earlier and had granted Perón a leave of absence from his presidential duties for a trip to Asunción. His return visit had been expected to consolidate Paraguay's position within the economic bloc.

The Indian countries of South America have fallen far behind the continental leaders, and none of them is in a condition which gives grounds for optimism for the near future. The root of their many difficulties is the colonial heritage of racial and class cleavages, failure to integrate the numerous Indian elements into national life, concentration of ownership of land and other forms of wealth, lack of economic opportunity, illiteracy, malnutrition, militarism, and inertia born of oppression. Each of the countries has made some gestures toward solving its basic problems, but only halfway measures have been tried. While it is still too early to know how far the Paz regime may go, it does not seem likely that any fundamental changes can be made on a permanent basis in any of the four countries without producing a new resort to violence and dictatorship.

SUGGESTED READING

R. J. Alexander, *The Perón Era*, New York, 1951.

G. Arciniegas, *The State of Latin America*, New York, 1952.

G. I. Blanksten, *Perón's Argentina*, Chicago, 1953.

P. Blanshard, *Democracy and Empire in the Caribbean*, New York, 1947.

S. E. Bradford, *The Battle for Buenos Aires*, New York, 1943.

H. E. Davis, *Social Science Trends in Latin America*, Washington, 1950.

P. Ellsworth, *Chile, an Economy in Transition*, New York, 1945.

R. H. Fitzgibbon, *Uruguay, Portrait of a Democracy*, New Brunswick, 1954.

G. Freyre, *Brazil, an Interpretation*, New York, 1945.

T. Gill, *Land Hunger in Mexico*, Washington, 1951.

R. and L. Greenup, *Revolution before Breakfast*, Chapel Hill, 1947.

S. Hanson, *Utopia in Uruguay*, New York, 1938.

A. C. Hicks, *Blood in the Streets; the Life and Rule of Trujillo*, New York, 1946.

L. F. Hill, ed., *Brazil*, Berkeley, 1947.

R. Josephs, *Argentine Diary*, New York, 1944.

H. Kantor, *The Ideology and Program of the Peruvian Aprista Movement*, Berkeley, 1953.

J. L. Kuntz, *The Mexican Expropriations*, New York, 1940.

K. Loewenstein, *Brazil under Vargas*, New York, 1942.

S. Macy, *et al, Costa Rica: A Study in Economic Development*, New York, 1952.

S. Mosk, *The Industrial Revolution in Mexico*, Berkeley, 1950.

F. Ortiz, *Cuban Counterpoint: Tobacco and Sugar*, New York, 1947.

H. Osborne, *Bolivia, a Land Divided*, London, 1954.

G. Pendle, *Paraguay, a Riverside Nation*, London, 1954.

—— *Uruguay, South America's First Welfare State*, London, 1954.

D. Perkins, *The United States and the Caribbean*, Cambridge, Mass., 1947.

L. Quintanilla, *A Latin American Speaks*, New York, 1943.

J. F. Rippy, *Latin America and the Industrial Age*, New York, 1944.

—— *Latin America in World Politics*, 3rd ed., New York, 1938.

G. I. Sanchez, *Mexico: A Revolution by Education*, New York, 1936.

E. N. Simpson, *The Ejido: Mexico's Way Out*, Chapel Hill, 1937.

J. R. Stevenson, *The Chilean Popular Front*, Philadelphia, 1942.

W. S. Stokes, *Honduras: An Area Study in Government*, Madison, 1950.

C. C. Taylor, *Rural Life in Argentina*, Baton Rouge, 1948.

W. C. Townsend, *Lázaro Cárdenas: Mexican Democrat*, Ann Arbor, 1952.

C. Wagley, *Amazon Town: A Study of Man in the Tropics*, New York, 1953.

F. Weil, *Argentine Riddle*, New York, 1944.

N. Whetten, *Rural Mexico*, Chicago, 1948.

A. C. Wilgus, ed., *The Caribbean at Mid-Century*, Gainesville, Fla., 1951.

——, ed., *The Caribbean: Contemporary Trends*, Gainesville, Fla., 1953.

G. Wythe, *Industry in Latin America*, 2nd ed., New York, 1949.

Index

Abascal, José Fernando, Viceroy of Peru, 441
Abolitionist movement, Brazil, 777, 778, 780
Abreu, João Capistrano, Brazilian historian, 774
Academies, in Spanish American colonies, 57
Academy of Fine Arts (Brazil), 520
Acapulco (New Spain), western terminus of Manila galleons, 104, 205, 232, 313
Acción Democrática party (Venezuela), 844, 845
Acevedo Díaz, Eduardo, 700
Acosta, Pedro de, 70
Acuña, Juan de (Marquis of Casafuerte), Viceroy of New Spain, 302
Additional Act (Brazil), 571
Adelantado, administrative officer, 53, 58
Administrator of Southern Mines, Brazil, 255
Afonso de Sousa, Martim, 130, 132
Africa, interest in coast of, 9, 10, 12, 14; Negro slaves from, 29, 182–3; contributions to Brazilian economic and cultural development, 142–3
Agassiz, Louis, 774
Agrarian reform, 826–7
Agrarian Reform Law (Guatemala), 842
Agricultural colonization, southern South America, 691–3
Agricultural Mechanization Enterprise, EMA (Brazil), 874

Agricultural population, predominance of, 813–15
Agricultural workers, most neglected group, 813
Agriculture, American Indian practices, 22; in Brazilian settlements, 131; Latin American colonies, 177; in New Spain during 17th century, 209; improvement programs, 814
Aguilar, Jerónimo de, interpreter for Cortés, 84
Agustini, Delmira, Uruguayan writer, 687
Aimorés, Brazilian Indians, 137, 255
Alamán, Lucas, Mexican political leader, 538, 627, 628, 633, 646, 647
Alamo, Mexican attack, 633, 634
Alarcón, Juan Ruíz de. See Ruíz de Alarcón y Mendoza, Juan
Alberdi, Juan Bautista, Argentine statesman and political theorist, 584, 665, 689; Political Organization of Argentine Republic, 592
Albuquerque, Duke of. See Fernández de la Cueva, Francisco
Alcabala, sales tax, 43, 747
Alcaldes mayores, administrative officials, 53
Alcaldes ordinarios, 55
Aldama, Josefa María, 482
Aldama, Juan, Mexican patriot, 482
Aldéias, Indian villages, 58
Alegría, Ciro, Peruvian novelist, 736
Alem, Leandro N., leader of Argentine radical party, 712

924

Miranda, Sebastián Francisco de, 414, 417, 429, 459, 460, 461; ardent revolutionist, 455–7
Missionaries, among Latin American Indians, 57–8, 93, 98–9, 101, 170–72, 185, 193, 196, 247; role of, 170–72, 185, 196; essential concomitant of frontier life, 203, 246; successes among conquered tribes, 211. See also Jesuits
Missions, in Spanish American colonies, 57–8; secularization, 99; a frontier institution, 171–2
Mistral, Gabriela, Chilean writer, 687
Mita, Inca government institution, 25, 31, 233–4, 245
Mitre, Bartolomé, 584, 700; a centralist porteño of Buenos Aires, 591; conducted war against Paraguay, 703–4
Mixton War, 95, 96
MNR (National Revolutionary Party, Bolivia), 909, 911
Mobile, French post at, 160, 222
Moderados, supporters of constitutional monarchy and regency, 570
Modernism, 686, 700
Molina Enríquez, Andrés, Mexican radical, 766
Mompó, Fernando, leader of Paraguayan comuneros, 366
Monagas, José Tadeo, President of Venezuela, 598, 599
Monarchical system, deeply rooted in civilized world, 533–4, 538
Moncada, José María, President of Nicaragua, 750
Monclova, Count of. See Portocarrero, Melchor
Money, coining of, 179
Monroe, James, 514
Monroe Doctrine, President Monroe's message to Congress, 421–2; Roosevelt's corollary to, 680; invoked, 742
Monserrat, Joaquín, Marquis of Cruillas, Viceroy of New Spain, 303
Montalvo, Francisco, Viceroy of New Granada, 463
Montalvo, Juan, Ecuadorian journalist, 727, 736

Monte Caseros. Rosas' defeat at, 590
Monteagudo, Bernardo de, Argentine political leader, 449
Montero, Juan Esteban, President of Chile, 880
Monterrey, Count of, Viceroy of New Spain, 103, 104, 241
Montes, Ismael, President of Bolivia, 734
Monteverde, Juan Domingo, loyalist political leader of New Granada, 460
Montevideo, 364, 431, 436, 438, 440, 443, 506, 512, 517, 584, 588
Montezuma, Aztec emperor, 24, 85; meeting with Cortés, 88–90
Montezuma, Count of, Viceroy of New Spain, 222
Montt, Manuel, President of Chile, 563, 564
Morais Barros, Prudente José de, 784; President of Brazil, 786
Morazán, Francisco, Honduran liberal party leader, 544, 638; President of Central American Confederation, 636
Morelos, José Mariá, Mexican revolutionary leader, 486–8
Moreno, Alfredo Baquerizo, President of Ecuador, 732
Moreno, Mariano, 433
Morgan, Henry, English pirate, 195
Morillo, Pablo, Spanish general in South America, 463
Morínigo, Higinio, President of Paraguay, 909
Morison, Samuel Eliot, *Admiral of the Ocean Sea*, 3fn
Morones, Luis, Mexican labor federation leader, 767, 769
Morrow, Dwight W., United States Ambassador to Mexico, 770
Mortgage Bank of Uruguay, 714
Moscoso, Luis de, in conquest of Florida, 80
Moslems, in Iberian peninsula, 5; occupation and influence in Spain, 7–9; Spain's campaign against in West, 37
Mosquera, Joaquín, 595; President of Colombia, 476, 753

New Mexico (*continued*)
to, 160; province of New Spain, 202, 305; silver mining, 203; Mexico's claim to, 641

New Panama Canal Company, successors to bankrupt De Lesseps Company, 681

New St. Andrew, Scottish fort at, 162

New Spain, administration over Indians, 30–33, 103–4; viceroyalty, 50–51; administrative difficulties, 94–8; economic, social and religious life, 97–100; society stratified, 99–103; trade with Orient, 104–5; at close of 16th century, 105–6; 16th-century viceroys, 143; growth and expansion in 17th century, 159–60; political divisions, 202; warfare with frontier tribes, 203; cities of, 205–7; Mexico, 205–7; Nueva Galicia, 207; administration 17th century, civil and ecclesiastical officials' strife, 207–20; political and social development, 211–15; territorial extent, population and preeminence, 296–300; Bourbon reforms and reinvigoration, 300–307; surface accomplishments of the viceroyalty, 302–16; 18th-century life, commerce, and industry, 308–14; economic self-suffering, 311–15; maltreatment of Indians, 315–16; viceroys (1700–1790), 318–19; reaction to Spain's fall from power, 416; independence movement, 418–21; effect of events on peninsula, 479–80; viceroyalty during first Mexican revolution, 480–95; clandestine clubs and societies, 482; constitution 1812 proclaimed and reaction, 496. See *also* Mexico

New World, features, 19–20; contribution to European awakening, 282

Newspapers, in Southern South America, 701

Nicaragua, 853, 855; Indians of, 196; 17th-century activity, 200; close ties with U.S., 682, 750

Nichols, Madaline W., *The Gaucho*, 359

Nicuesa, Diego de, attempt to colonize mainland, 66, 67–8

Nitrate industry, 608, 705, 805–6

Nóbrega, Manuel da, Portuguese Jesuit missionary in Brazil, 134, 136, 138

Noche Triste, Cortés' retreat, 90–91

Nombre de Dios, 66, 123, 189; founding of, 69

Noronha, Fernão de, exploitation in Brazil, 128, 129

Nueva Andalucia, 70, 71

Nueva Galicia (West New Spain), 202, 207

Nuevo Toledo, town founded by Ocampo, 70

Núñez, Rafael, President of Colombia, 684, 754

Núñez Cabeza de Vaca, Alvar, Spanish explorer, 80, 105

Núñez de Balboa, Vasco, Spanish explorer, 67–9

Núñez de Cáceres, José, Santo Domingo revolutionist leader, 494

Núñez de Vela, Blasco, first Viceroy of Peru, 116–17

Nuño de Guzmán, Gonzalo, first audiencia of Mexico presided over by, 65, 94, 95

O

Obligado, Pastor, in Buenos Aires province, 592

Obrajes, textile workshops, 19, 98, 178, 246

Obregón, Alvaro, 763, 764; President of Mexico, 768–70

Ocampo, Gonzalo de, Spanish mariner, 16, 63, 70

Ocampo, Melchor, Mexican liberal political leader, 646–52

O'Donojú, Juan, Spanish viceroy to New Spain, 497, 620

Odría, Manuel, President of Peru, 905, 914

O'Higgins, Bernardo, organizer of Chilean independence movement, 417, 434, 441; dictator of Chile, 450, 555–7

Torres, Camilo, author of United Provinces of New Granada pact, 458; patriot leader in New Granada, 463

Torres Bodet, Jaime, Mexican educator, 829

Totonac Indians, Cortes' meeting with, 86

Toussaint L'Ouverture, Pierre Dominique, Haitian Negro general, 479

Town-building, Caribbean area 17th century, 197

Towns, on frontier in Spain, 8; in Spanish America, 54–5; founding in Caribbean area, 197

Trade, Spain and colonies, 44–7; oriental, 104–5; 18th-century activity, 290–91; 1930's and World War II, 816–17

Trade fairs, 313

Trade routes, 9

Trading companies, 333–5

Trafalgar, 480; Spanish defeat off, 429, 480

Transportation, 178

Trapiches, textile shops, 308

Travis, William Barrett, commander of Texans at Alamo, 633–4

Treaty of Ancón, 708, 725

Treaty of Guadalupe-Hidalgo, 647

Treaty of Tordesillas, 13, 161

Tribuna da Imprensa (Brazil), 875

Tribunal de Minería, miner's guild, 315

Trigarante army (New Spain), 497

Trinidad, Columbus discovered, 60; attempt at settlement, 71; British capture, 408; ceded to England, 409

Trist, Nicholas P., U.S. agent to Mexico, 644

Tromp, Maarten von, destroyed Spanish fleet, 153

Trujillo, Torcuato, loyalist leader in Mexican Revolution, 485

Trujillo Molina, Rafael Leonidas, President of Dominican Republic, 852; war powers, 840–41

Tucumán, Congress of, United Provinces of Río de la Plata declared independent, 442–3

Tucumán (United Provinces of Río de la Plata), 123, 236, 237, 362, 376, 444

Túmbez, Inca town, 110–11, 231

Tumultos, 170

Tupac Amaru, Inca Indian chief, 122

Tupac Amaru II. See Condorcanqui José Gabriel

Tupí-Guaraní, linguistic family, 129

Turbay, Gabriel, Colombian liberal political leader, 849

Turks, attacks on Western Christendom, 37

Typhoid fever, 198

U

Ubico, Jorge, Guatemalan President, 853

Ulate, Otilio, Costa Rican President, 842, 853

Ulloa, Antonio de, Spanish scientist report on conditions in colonies, 346–7

Ulloa, Osores de, Governor of Chile, 242

Ultramontanism, Masonic lodges' attack on, 778–9

Unánue, José Hipólito, Peruvian scholar, 357

Union Civica Radical (Argentina) reform party, 712

Unionism, under rigorous control, 813

Unitarists, 580–81, 582, 583, 591

United Fruit Company, interests in Caribbean area, 751, 842

United Nations, 818

United Provinces of Central America, 622, 636–9

United Provinces of New Granada, federation of, 458–9

United Provinces of Río de la Plata, Congress of Tucumán declared independence, 442–3; internal disunity, 443; congress of, 451; war with Brazil, 516–18; Uruguay, 586. See also La Plata, Viceroyalty of and Plata region

United States, Monroe Doctrine, 421–2; recognition of independence of Spanish American countries, 422;

CARIBBEAN
AND
SOUTH AMERICA

0   MILES   500

A.K.P.